NUMBER.

THE

RIO DE JANEIRO
TRAMWAY
LIGHT & POWER

COMPANY
LIMITED

SHARE WARRANT
TO BEARER
FOR
1 SHARE
OF
$100 IN GOLD

TITRE
AU PORTEUR
DE
1 ACTION
OR DE
$100

TITULO
AO PORTADOR
DE
1 ACÇÃO
DE
$100
EM OURO

Burrup, Mathieson & Sprague, L.ᵈ London.

The Light

The Light

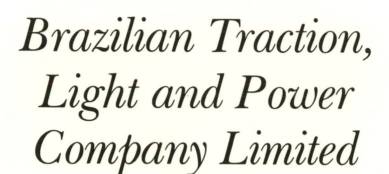

Brazilian Traction, Light and Power Company Limited

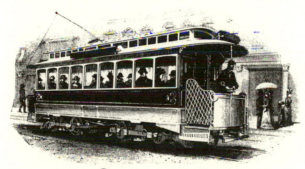

1899-1945

DUNCAN McDOWALL

UNIVERSITY OF TORONTO PRESS

Toronto Buffalo London

© University of Toronto Press 1988
Toronto Buffalo London
Printed in Canada
ISBN 0-8020-5783-7

Printed on acid-free paper

Canadian Cataloguing in Publication Data

McDowall, Duncan, 1949–
The light : Brazilian Traction, Light and Power
Company Limited, 1899–1945

Includes index.
ISBN 0-8020-5783-7

1. Brazilian Traction, Light and Power Company.
2. Public utilities – Brazil – History.
3. Brazil – Economic conditions. I. Title.

HD9685.B74B73   1988   338.7′6213′0981   c88-093665-7

All photographs come from the Brascan Archives except
for the following, which come from the Eletropaulo Archives:
the first eight photographs and 'A "second class" tram
for workers, São Paulo, 1916' and 'Local sourcing:
making concrete poles, São Paulo, 1930.'

This book has been published with the help of
a grant from the Social Science Federation of Canada,
using funds provided by the Social Sciences and
Humanities Research Council of Canada.

*For my mother
and in memory
of my father*

Contents

ACKNOWLEDGMENTS ix

Introduction 3

1 North America in South America / 11

2 In Pursuit of a 'Rich Return':
Toronto Capitalists Look Abroad / 48

3 First Light:
The São Paulo
Tramway, Light and Power Company Limited,
1899–1908 / 80

4 New Growth:
The Rio de Janeiro Tramway, Light and Power Company Limited,
1903–1908 / 123

5 The Creation of the
Brazilian Traction, Light and Power Company Limited, 1908–1915 / 165

6 The Survival of the Fittest:
Brazilian Traction and the First World War / 208

7 Drought, Expansion, and the End of the Old Republic:
The 1920s / 242

8 The Belgian Croesus / 283

9 Nationalism and Depression:
Brazilian Traction in the 1930s / 300

10 The Second World War and the Changing of the Guard / 343

Epilogue: 'Run Like the Light' / 382

APPENDICES
A Summary Interpretation of the Water Code and
Related Legislation in Brazil / 401

B Operating Statistics of the Principal Subsidiary Companies
of the Brazilian Traction, Light and Power Company, 1912–1978 / 405

NOTES / 409

GLOSSARY / 447

INDEX / 451

MAPS

General Outline of Brazil / 26

The Serra do Cubatão Hydroelectric Development, 1928 / 257

Acknowledgments

Research for this book, much like the company it chronicles, spanned three continents. Corporate archives in Toronto, Rio de Janeiro, and São Paulo furnished a solid foundation for the structure of the book. Other corporate, university, provincial, and national archives supplied the finishing materials. Much of the effort in mining these sources was undertaken in locations that were strikingly different from the spotless, orderly world of North American archives. Take, for instance, the dusty, dark, and humid labour of working through long-stored corporate files found in an old car barn on Rio's Rua Larga. Locational difficulties were compounded by linguistic difficulties. While most of the documentation was in English, there were strong veins of Portuguese, French, and, at times, German material in the archives. Finding and interpreting documentation for *The Light* thus made intriguing and formidable demands, demands that required new skills and a willingness to move beyond the traditional research boundaries of Canadian history. That this book should therefore ever have come to fruition is testament to the generous support I have received in the course of my research and writing from people in Canada, Brazil, and England.

In Canada, my foremost debt is to the management and staff of Brascan Limited. No writer could have wished for a more open, supportive, and non-interventionist liaison with his subject. In particular, I wish to extend my sincere thanks to Peter Bronfman and Trevor Eyton for their abiding faith and interest in this research. This interest was shared and reinforced by Dr Roberto Cezar de Andrade in Rio. In the course of my work, I was privileged to have the continuing support and frank views of two pillars of

Brazilian Traction's post-Second World War management: the late Dr Antônio Gallotti of Rio and Henry Borden, Brazilian Traction's president from 1946 to 1963. Similarly, I shared many lively and informative hours with the late Frank Schulman.

In recent years there has been much theorizing about the contribution of a vigorous corporate culture to corporate performance. From this historian's perspective, the willingness of past and present Brascan employees not just to tolerate but to encourage the endless queries and requests that constitute historical research bespeaks a very positive corporate culture. I owe all such participants in my research sincere thanks for their time and interest. In particular, Wendy Cecil-Cockwell, Ross Sutherland, Jim A'Court, Ted Freeman-Attwood, Duncan McAlpine, Laurie Blachford, Carla Gorka, and Pat Melley deserve special mention.

Without question, my greatest vote of thanks is owed to F.W. Orde Morton, my unfailing helmsman whenever I ventured into Brazilian waters. A scholar, former diplomat, and associate secretary at Brascan, Orde never stinted in sharing his encyclopedic knowledge of Brazil. From Orde, I learned to appreciate not just Brazilian history but Brazil itself.

In Brazil, the work of gathering illustrations was greatly facilitated by Allan Minz, a commercial counsellor at the wonderfully efficient Canadian consulate in São Paulo, and Roberto Maranhão of Eletropaulo. I am indebted to Dr Mircea Buescu and Dr Américo Jacobina Lacombe for their reading of and expert commentary on the manuscript. The late Charles J. Dunlop of Rio generously shared his knowledge of his native city. Sra Lidia Diaz of Rio made innumerable arrangements for me, all of which made my work more efficient. To Eduardo de Brasil Vivacqua for evenings in Ipanema and Annette Baughan and Heikki Maattanen for weekends on their farm away from the heat of Rio, I send my love and thanks. Thanks are also due to Stephen Bell for research in the Public Record Office in London, and to Michael Bliss, Viv Nelles, and Ian Drummond in Toronto for their comments on the manuscript.

The typing of the manuscript was undertaken with the assistance of the Conference Board of Canada, my former employer, and Carleton University, my present employer. This generous support allowed Margaret Shane to complete an arduous task in a magnificent manner. Dorothy Wallace typed the much longer first draft of the book, and Patricia Nagy helped in the home stretch. Ruth Kirkpatrick did the maps. Michael Grant read chapters, went running, and played squash whenever the need arose. Jim Taylor nobly undertook to proofread the galley proofs. Gerry Hallowell of the University of Toronto Press and Margaret Allen oversaw the editorial arrangements for this book with masterful competence. Thanks to Gerry, I never, I hope, became a 'grumpy author.'

Authors frequently acknowledge the role of long-suffering spouses. One of the joys of this work for me has been the way my wife, Sandy Campbell, became a willing and enthusiastic partner in the venture. From Kincardine and Toronto to Rio and Manaus, she shared this business historian's hopes and frustrations. Together with Phaedra, she made the work worthwhile and doubly pleasant.

Festooned with British, American, and Brazilian flags,
a São Paulo tram inaugurates the São Bento service, 7 May 1900

Laying track, São Paulo, 1900

Hauling penstock plates to Parnaíba, September 1900

Power for the people: electric lamps in Jardim Público, São Paulo, 1908

Building up the traffic: a freight car in São Paulo, *c.* 1905

São Paulo car shops, 1912

Made in Brazil: a tram built in the São Paulo shops, 1910

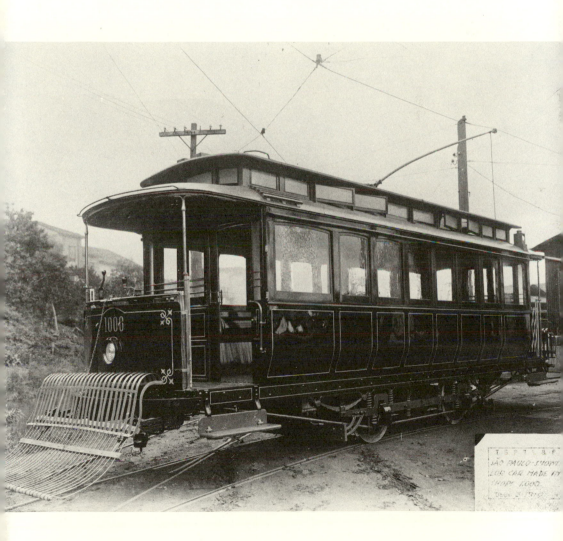

Power to the politicians: a triumphal arch
for Brazilian president Afonso Pena, São Paulo, *c.* 1906

Fred Stark Pearson: electrical engineer to the world and
Brazilian Traction's first president, 1912–15

In pursuit of a 'rich return': E.R. Wood, F.S. Pearson, Sir William Mackenzie, and
Z.A. Lash (left to right) stroll on Bay Street, July 1912

Sir Alexander Mackenzie:
Brazilian Traction's second president, 1915–28

Rio's Copacabana beach, *c.* 1906. The first trams appear

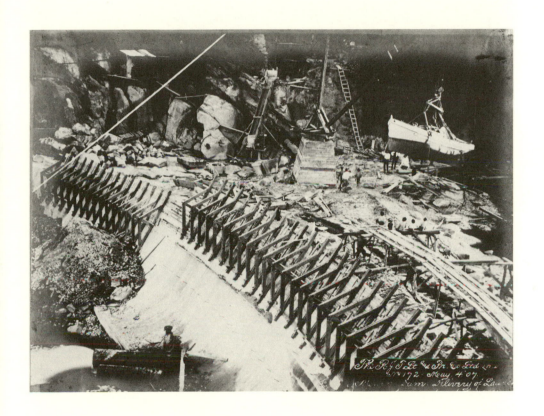

The Lajes power plant: hauling a steam launch over the incomplete dam, May 1907

North America in South America: Canadian and American engineers relax
while constructing the Lajes power plant. Electricity, but not baseball,
has become a central facet of Brazilian life

The R. J. T. Ld P. Co. Ltd.
No. 225 – Nov 18·07
Main Power Hou
Rio das Lages, Brazil

The Lajes powerhouse and penstocks outside Rio, 1907

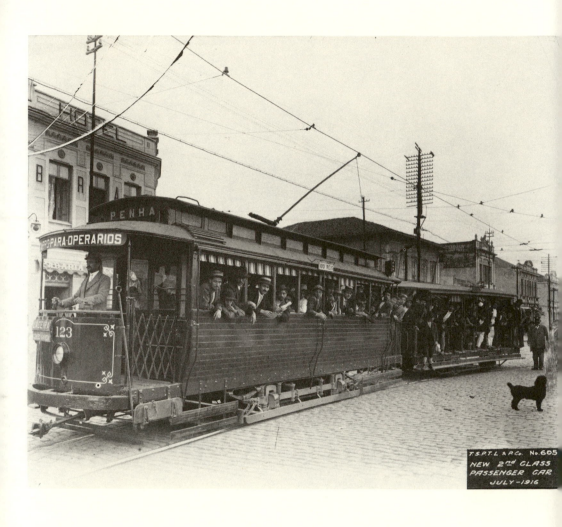

A 'second class' tram for workers, São Paulo, 1916

The 1924 São Paulo Revolution: looters at work

Local sourcing: making concrete poles, São Paulo, 1930

The Belgian Croesus: Alfred Loewenstein

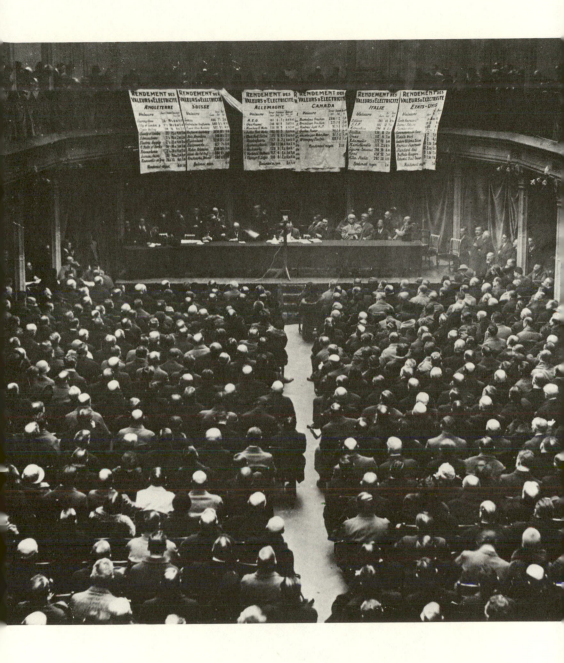

Alfred Loewenstein (blurred, on stage) addresses Belgian investors
in Brussels, 1926

Machine gun damage to a power pole: the São Paulo Revolution of 1932

Phone pole damaged by street fighting: São Paulo, 1932

The Cubatão power plant and penstocks outside São Paulo, 1927

A Brazilian naval bomber attacks the Cubatão power plant.
A bomb plume rises above the powerhouse, July 1932

Damage to the powerhouse control room, Cubatão, July 1932

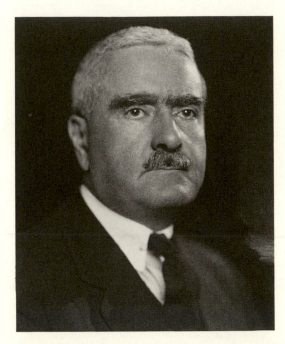

Miller Lash: Brazilian Traction's third president, 1928–41

Sir Herbert Couzens: Brazilian Traction's fourth president, 1941–4

Asa W.K. Billings: Brazilian Traction's fifth president, 1944–6

Brazilian Traction president Henry Borden (centre) and
COBAST executive vice-president Antônio Gallotti
announce plans to incorporate the São Paulo Company in Brazil, 1956

Rose and cigar in hand, Brazilian president Getúlio Vargas
tours a company construction project outside Rio accompanied by
COBAST executive vice-president J.R. Nicholson, March 1952

The Light

Introduction

In the late 1920s, the tramcars that served the citizens of the Brazilian city of São Paulo bore the proud message '*São Paulo é o Maior Centro Industrial da América do Sul*' painted in gold letters along their sides: 'São Paulo is the major industrial centre of South America.' It is a status that the city has never relinquished. Today, with a sprawling population of nearly fifteen million, São Paulo is indisputably the locomotive of the Brazilian economy and, together with its sister city of Rio de Janeiro, has provided a model of economic advancement, with all its perfections and imperfections, for what has come to be known as the developing world.

When, in 1979, São Paulo's *prefeito*, or mayor, Olavo Egydio Setúbal, retired as Brazil's most prominent municipal politician, he used his valediction to assess the foundation of his city's strength. 'There are three factors,' he noted, 'which account for the greatness of São Paulo. Coffee, the Light and the immigrants produced the wealth, the energy and the culture which formed São Paulo.' Among *paulistanos*, the citizens of São Paulo, there could be little mistaking Setúbal's meaning. The coffee staple had furnished their city with a steady, if at times fluctuating, source of export earnings, which had provided much of the capital used to build the infrastructure of its economy. The immigrants, mostly Italians, Germans, and Japanese who had flooded into south-eastern Brazil at the turn of the century, had supplied the entrepreneurial drive that allowed the local economy to thrive and diversify. It was the third factor, electric power from a Canadian-owned company universally known to Brazilians as 'the Light,' that had been the catalyst by which capital and entrepreneurship were transformed into economic growth.

The Light had come to Brazil in 1899 as the São Paulo Railway (later Tramway), Light and Power Company, a venture that combined Canadian entrepreneurship, American engineering prowess, and European capital and applied them to the inviting, untapped Brazilian market for electricity. Joined in 1904 by the Rio de Janeiro Tramway, Light and Power Company, the São Paulo Light expanded to supply a broad and rewarding range of power, transit, gas, and telephone services to its Brazilian customers. In 1912, the Rio and São Paulo companies were amalgamated under the auspices of a Toronto-based holding company, the Brazilian Traction, Light and Power Company Limited. Few Brazilians ever fully understood the corporate affiliations that underlay the Brazilian Traction family of companies. For most Brazilians, whether *cariocas* in Rio or *paulistanos* in São Paulo, the company that provided all their daily utility needs was simply known as 'the Light.' So pervasive was the presence of the Canadian company in Brazilian lives that the term 'light' eventually became synonymous with electricity in the Portuguese vocabulary of its customers. At other times, Brazilians likened their largest utility company to an octopus – *o polvo canadense*; but even so, few Brazilians could deny the Light's contribution to the economic development of the industrial heartland of south-eastern Brazil. In a country then lacking even meagre supplies of coal or oil, electricity from the Light and the public-utility services that it made possible helped to prepare the urban infrastructure of Rio and São Paulo for the spectacular growth they were to experience in the twentieth century. 'These two cities were but miserable colonial towns,' wrote Assis Chateaubriand, Brazil's great press baron and most renowned journalist, in a 1962 *O jornal* editorial, 'infested with yellow fever and malaria, when the Canadians came in. They brought not only a business, but a mission.'

Ironically, the Canadian company, which employed more than 50,000 Brazilians at the height of its operations in the late 1940s, has remained virtually unknown in the land of its origin. Beyond the immediate circle of its shareholders and management, the company with the peculiar name – Brazilian Traction, Light and Power (later Brascan) – has been only vaguely familiar to most Canadians. It was, for instance, with considerable amazement that two young Canadian journalists reported their 'discovery' of the Light in a *Maclean's* article of 1947. 'You have to go to Brazil to find Canada's biggest public utility,' wrote Pierre Berton and Charles Lynch. 'It is, in short, a sort of Brazilian version of Bell Telephone, Ontario Hydro and the Toronto Transportation Commission rolled into one.' The Light was, however, more than an enormous utilities monopoly; it was also an economic partnership that bonded the needs of the developing Brazilian economy with the capital and technical expertise of Europe and North America. In many important respects, the history of the Light provides a mirror for Latin America's most dynamic economy, reflecting its fundamental strengths and weaknesses.

The constructive nature of this relationship was recognized by Pierre Trudeau when he became the first Canadian prime minister to visit Brazil. 'Almost a century ago,' he told a São Paulo audience in 1981, 'Canadian and Brazilian entrepreneurs and engineers worked together to provide São Paulo with electric power, to build the street railways, the city gas companies, the telephone system – enterprises integral to much of the impressive industrial developments for which the city and state of São Paulo are famous.'

Brazilian Traction and its associated companies operated in Brazil for more than eighty years. Brascan, the present-day descendant of the original São Paulo company, still maintains extensive holdings in Brazil, although it severed its final tie with that country's utility industry early in 1979. From its modern, twenty-sixth-floor offices overlooking Rio's Botafogo Bay and Sugar Loaf mountain, Brascan Brazil continues the tradition of Canadian direct investment in Brazil with holdings – now, in one instance, shared with Brazilian investors in real estate, mineral exploration, manufacturing, and consumer products. A Brazilian now sits on the Brascan board in Toronto. Unlike other Canadian corporations holding investments in Brazil – such as Alcan and Noranda – Brascan (and Brazilian Traction before it) was never really a multinational corporation. Although Brazilian Traction has often been mistakenly described as a multinational corporation, it was in reality a *bi*national corporation that confined its activities to two countries, Canada and Brazil. Until the late 1960s, in fact, the group was operationally active only in Brazil: its Toronto head office served to co-ordinate corporate decision making, financing, procurement, and shareholder relations. Unlike the modern multinationals, which shift their manufacturing and extractive activities around the face of the globe in search of the most lucrative comparative advantage, Brazilian Traction was wedded to Brazil and its political and economic fortunes. Once built, a hydroelectric dam or power-distribution grid could not be closed down, crated, and shipped to another, more amenable entrepreneurial climate.

If the Canadian octopus survived in Brazil, it was because it learned to adapt to its surroundings. In this sense, Brazilian Traction's history as a company in Brazil is best explained by the pull of two often-contradictory forces in twentieth-century Brazilian life – the drive for material improvement and the quest for national economic self-determination. At first, the Canadian company gratified the former desire, providing Brazilians with power, urban transportation, and telephones – the sinews of modern life. In return for this contribution, Brazilian politicians imposed few restrictions on the foreign entrepreneurs who introduced North American and European capital and technology to their urban landscape.

As the century progressed, Brazilian Traction increasingly had to contend with Brazilians' awakening desire to take control of their economic destiny; as in many developing countries, electricity became a symbol and then a tool of the nation's will to economic betterment. This manifested itself, especially after the Revolution of 1930, in demands for national control over the 'water' powers of Brazil. While Brazilian Traction fought against the most extreme implications of this desire – the nationalization of all foreign power companies – it also learned to accommodate this basic national aspiration by 'Brazilianizing' its management and eventually by admitting Brazilians to its ownership. With the impulse for economic self-determination came the impulse for regulation. The halcyon days in which the Canadians had negotiated their first Brazilian concessions were displaced after the fall of the Old Republic in 1930 by the spectre of regulation, which soon overtook every aspect of the hydroelectric industry. In the end, it was the implications of regulation, not the direct challenge of nationalization, that brought about the sale of the Light to the Brazilian government in 1979.

In many ways, Brazilian Traction was a unique Canadian company. During the first two decades of the century, it shared this status with a 'family' of Canadian-based utility companies operating as far afield as Spain, Mexico, and throughout the Caribbean. 'Travel the six continents or the seven seas,' journalist Beverley Owen wrote enthusiastically to the readers of the *Canadian Magazine* in 1927. 'You can't escape Canada. At every turn – contact! Explore Mexico; at Vera Cruz throw a lever – the roar of the dynamo is the pulse of Canadian daring, enterprise and vision.' The companies that together constituted what has been called Canada's utilities imperialism were all marked by similar methods of promotion and drew upon the same tight circle of entrepreneurs, most notably the brilliant American engineer Fred Stark Pearson and the flamboyant Canadian railway promoter Sir William Mackenzie. Various light, power, and traction ventures within Canada, including the Toronto Street Railway, boasted a similar corporate paternity.

As the century progressed, revolution in Mexico, civil war in Spain, and the inexorable spread of municipal and provincial ownership in Canada reduced this 'utilities empire' to, by the outbreak of the Second World War, a single survivor – Brazilian Traction. Unlike its sister enterprises in Spain and Mexico, the Light mastered the delicate art of successfully balancing the interests of its shareholders, its customers, and its host government. To a degree, history was also on its side – Brazil never succumbed to the traumatic political and social upheavals that engulfed Mexico and Spain. Brazilian Traction learned to exercise what Brazil's Assis Chateaubriand dubbed 'Canada's healthy imperialism,' an imperialism that transferred technology and managerial expertise to a Latin American economy that lagged well behind the developed economies of Europe and North America. In its way, Brazilian Traction thus helped to close the economic gap between the continents. It showed, as the *Globe and Mail* pointed out in 1967, that 'Canadian private capital can provide the nuts and bolts of economic growth in developing nations.' In doing so the company became the largest privately owned business corporation in South America, until it was surpassed in the 1950s by several of the leading companies in Venezuela's burgeoning oil industry.

Despite the fact that it was a company 'with a mission,' Brazilian Traction never lost sight of the fact that it had come to Brazil in search of business profits. While the Light had its share of lean times – brought on by the vicissitudes of Brazil's staple-oriented economy, a volatile inflation rate, and its periodic exchange crises – it was a company that rewarded its shareholders well over time. In some instances, especially in the case of the original Bay Street promoters of the São Paulo and Rio companies, it rewarded its backers extremely well. This, then, is the story of the Light and of the men and times that made it what it was for eighty years. It is a story that today, as Pierre Trudeau has pointed out, 'provides us with an experience which is unique in the context of current north-south problems.'

The history of the Light could be written in many ways. This analysis has chosen to interpret the evolution of what was, until the late 1960s, Canada's largest overseas investment in terms of corporate decision making, finance, and external relations. As a monopolistic enterprise in a capital-intensive industry, operating in what was in many ways an alien business environment, this Canadian company's existence was profoundly dependent on these three factors.

Other interpretive windows could be opened on the history of the Light. These are hinted at in this broad rendering of Brazilian Traction's history, but must await fuller treatment at the hands of other historians. As Brazil's largest private employer for more than six decades, the Light is of formative importance in Brazilian labour history. It acted as a school for the inculcation of workplace discipline, technical skills, and, one assumes, some sense of identity among a labour force that was clearly in the aristocracy of Brazilian labour. Similarly, the Light's history could be written in terms of organizational development. How did the 'visible hand' of management, as Harvard's Alfred Chandler has labelled it, mould the organizational response of an enterprise that eventually served millions of customers in five Brazilian states? What was the departmental structure of an organization engaged in services as varied as power generation and telephone servicing?

Economists will undoubtedly seek to test theories of economic development against the Light's prominent role in what has become a leading member of the developing world. While this analysis does not directly attempt to measure the Light's achievement in terms of dependency theory or technology transfer, it provides strong circumstantial evidence that over the decades Brazilian Traction survived because it *did* transfer technology, both by training Brazilians in its shops and by meeting ever larger amounts of its needs through Brazilian suppliers. The relatively smooth emergence of a national hydroelectric industry in Brazil in the 1950s and 1960s, a development unopposed by the Light, suggests that Brazilians were never locked in hydroelectric dependency. Economic theorists will also seek to use the Light as a testbed for theories of the relationship of abundant hydroelectricity and economic growth. This book attempts to test none of the foregoing theories nor to impose specialized perspectives on the Light's evolution. Such analysis must await the findings of future visitors to the Light archives. Instead, *The Light* attempts to open one big window on the history of Brazilian Traction, fashioning a frame into which later, more specialized studies may be placed.

The genesis of this book requires some explanation. It was originally commissioned and financed by the board of directors of Brascan Limited.

From 1978 to 1980, the author worked as an employee of Brascan as its 'corporate historian.' The company adopted a completely open and non-interventionist attitude to the author and his task, allowing him access to the obscurest reaches of the company's archives, both in Toronto and in Brazil. No doors were closed to the author, and Brascan's staff, particularly its accountants, engineers, and lawyers, willingly lent their professional knowledge in explaining many of the intricacies of the company's operations, ranging from the arcane principles of penstock construction to the minute legalities of utilities concessions in Brazil. An editorial committee, formed by the company, provided advice, read the manuscript with a discerning eye, and pointed out errors of a factual or technical nature. No company could have co-operated more fully in the writing of its own history without demanding that its imprimatur be stamped upon the finished product. In 1987, Brascan legally released the manuscript of the history (for the years 1899 to 1945) to the author, free of any editorial constraint.

This is not, therefore, an official history. The opinions herein represent the interpretation of the author alone, and it is to him that all criticism should be addressed. The author at this time can only express the hope that more Canadian, and possibly Brazilian, corporations will emulate the example of Brascan and open their archives to the inquiring mind of the historian. It has become almost *de rigueur* for historiographers to note that business history is still very much in its infancy in Canada. The situation is similar to that encountered by English business historian Charles Wilson in the early 1950s when he began work on his magisterial history of Unilever. 'For business history has as yet been but little studied in Britain,' Wilson wrote in 1954, 'and the inquiring reader still has to choose between what are virtually two sorts of propaganda: an heroic mythology on the one hand and a kind of economic crime club on the other.' What was lacking was 'a balanced view of the evolution of a large-scale business.'[1]

One further word of introduction is needed. In covering the years down to 1945, this volume might well be subtitled 'the making of a binational corporation.' The conclusion of the Second World War provides a natural watershed in the history of both the Light and Brazil. Internally, it marked the end of the period when Brazilian Traction's management was dominated by the ideas and policies of the 'old guard' who dated from its founding years. A new president, recruited from outside the company 'establishment,' new methods of management, and an accentuated emphasis on Brazilianization all set the corporation on a new course. More importantly, the war removed the last vestiges of the company's pioneering phase in Brazil. By 1945, the Light had reached full stature in Brazil; its concessions, services, and assets had spread over the industrial heartland of Brazil. This expansion had in many respects taken place in an unfettered way, unimpeded by regulation or the interventionist state.

After 1945, the company was left to wrestle with the problems of maturity, both its own and Brazil's. These materialized in many guises – nationalism, political upheaval, the pressurized economic growth of Brazil's 'economic miracle,' and the inexorable movement of Brazil toward national control over its 'water powers.' It was not an easy fight; what made it remarkable was that the Light managed to stay in the ring so long. 'But,' Canadian ambassador Jean Chapdelaine reported from inflation-ravaged Rio in 1963, 'it is an ever more gaunt Brazilian Traction which comes out of every squeeze.'

The history of Brazilian Traction's involved and at times masterful response to these intense post-war pressures remains to be told. Ample resources – both in terms of personalities and documentation – exist to support such an endeavour. In its stead, an epilogue has been added to this volume to furnish the reader with a sketch of the Light's evolution down to its eventual sale to the Brazilian government in 1979. A fuller picture of these years is central to an understanding of the interaction of foreign capital, management, and technology with the evolving priorities of the world's foremost newly industrializing nation.

CHAPTER ONE

North America in South America

In the early morning hours of 7 May 1900, the narrow streets of São Paulo reverberated to an unfamiliar sound. Down the Rua Barão de Limeira and onto the Largo São Bento, a small square in the centre of Brazil's second-largest city, came a clattering, open-sided electric tramcar, its front lamp piercing the darkness as curious citizens, roused from sleep, peered down at the passing spectacle. At the throttle of the tram stood Robert Calthrop Brown, a thirty-five-year-old American engineer who, just over a year earlier, had been manager of the tramway company in far-off Halifax, Nova Scotia. Brown had ventured out at 1:00 a.m. to make a clandestine last-minute inspection of the just-completed line, which was to be officially inaugurated later that day. The American-built electric tram on which he rode (a nine-bench Brill Car chassis and body powered by a General Electric motor) was the first in service in the prosperous and expanding Brazilian city of 240,000 people. After an uneventful run, Brown reversed the tram and brought it back to the car barn on Rua Barão de Limeira, assured that all was ready for the impending festivities. Above the car-barn doors, a sign gave notice of the proprietorship of this new enterprise. The São Paulo Tramway, Light and Power Company Limited, incorporated under Ontario law, with its head office in Toronto, had come to do business in Brazil.[1]

Around noon, the inauguration began in earnest. The official party, composed of civic, state, and federal politicians, assembled at the company's Rua São Caetano power plant and prepared to initiate electric service from its coal-fired boilers and steam generators. The plant was only a temporary facility, acquired through the purchase of a local gas and water company. The new company hoped shortly to supersede this inefficient facility with a large, new hydroelectric-power installation of its own design that was feverishly being constructed by more than 1,200 workmen at a site on the Tietê River, thirty-six kilometres outside the city. Following a precise timetable, the dignitaries were directed by T.W. Bevan, the American superintendent of the powerhouse, to set the machinery in motion. Dr Domingos de Morais, vice-president of the state of São Paulo, first closed the field switch; Dr Antônio Prado, the prefect (or mayor) of the city, then closed the circuit breaker, and, finally, Dr Rodrigues Alves, the president of the state, opened the throttle on the generator. Throughout these proceedings, Dr Prudente de Morais, president of Brazil from 1894–8, looked on benevolently. Bevan, hovering in the background, anxiously watched his political guests, fearful that one of them might errantly contact some piece of the machinery and bring both himself and the festivities to an untimely end. At 1:28 p.m., the power was on, ready to propel the waiting trams, and the party adjourned to the nearby car barn.

Awaiting the politicians at the car barn were R.C. Brown, general manager of the new utility company, and Alexander Mackenzie, the tall, rather solemn Canadian lawyer who for nearly a year had been overseeing the complicated legal affairs of the fledgling enterprise in the Brazilian city. Inside, six new tramcars stood ready for the official party, outside, a throng of expectant *paulistanos* awaited the moment that would open a new era in their civic history. At 2:10 p.m., the car-barn doors swung open and the first car, with R.C. Brown as motorman, eased its way into the crowd. As it did so, the São Paulo Police Brigade band struck up the Brazilian national anthem, followed by 'God Save the Queen' and 'The Stars and Stripes Forever.' Brown's illustrious passengers included Rodrigues Alves and Antônio Prado, the state and municipal politicians whose governments had supplied the concessionary rights the Canadian company needed to operate in the city and to generate power on its outskirts. For Prado, this maiden tram ride was a somewhat humbling experience. He had at first decried the promoters of the new power company as the perpetrators of an 'American bluff,' an elaborate speculative gambit that would produce quick profits for the foreign entrepreneurs and no trams for São Paulo. Now, looking out over the immense crowd that lined the route, there could be little doubt that he had not been the victim of a bluff. To underscore the point, Brown took the tram to the very end of the São Bento line, from where *Conselheiro* Prado could view his own *chácara*, or small farm, on the edge of the city.[2]

When the cars returned to the barns on Rua Barão de Limeira, the two hundred official guests were treated by the company to a 'profuse and liberal lunch,' served to the music of the Police Brigade band. From the rafters of the building hung the flags of England, the United States, and Brazil. In response to Antônio Prado's toast of welcome to the company on behalf of the city, General Manager Brown drank to 'the prosperity of the State of São Paulo and the aggrandizement of the Brazilian economy.' When the banquet concluded, Brown ordered the tramcars back onto the streets, where free rides were offered to all who could clamber aboard. 'All along the route,' *O estado de São Paulo* reported the next day, 'an enormous crowd gathered acclaiming the Company with "vivas" and applause as the heavily laden vehicles passed by.' *Correio paulistano* attempted to place the inauguration in a broader perspective by noting that it was 'an event of the highest importance and one which marks the beginning of a series of great improvements, which the powerful Company is to introduce among us. It assumed the proportions of a great event, which in an extraordinary way, stirred the life of the capital; its population anxiously crowding to those places from where it could appreciate this further element of progress so long desired.'[3] By 6:40 the cars had inched their way back to the barns and the power supply was shut down. The next day the trams, stripped of flags and bunting, began scheduled service, collecting a fare of 200 réis (about four cents in Canadian funds) per zone traversed. The atmosphere of euphoria and hyperbole began to evaporate as São Paulo residents became accustomed to the new electric-streetcar service. On 13 May, a second route, to Bom Retiro, was initiated, followed on 27 May by a third line to Vila Buarque. By the end of 1901, the Canadian company had thirty-three electric trams operating over fifty-six kilometres of track. Soon, riding on the cars of the São Paulo company, *a companhia canadense*, was to become an accepted and necessary fact of life in São Paulo, proud evidence of the city's aspiration to become the commercial and industrial centre of the Brazilian nation.

It was at first sight most peculiar that a Canadian company should have established itself in such an alien and remote environment. Historically, Canada and Brazil had had few contacts and were, consequently, little acquainted with each other's cultural and political conditions. North Americans as a whole in the nineteenth century tended to display their ignorance of South America by blithely referring to the whole continent as 'the Brazils,' oblivious of the many ways in which Portuguese-speaking Brazil differed from the Spanish-speaking remainder of the continent. As one American visitor to Brazil in the 1860s complained, the 'popular notion' of Brazil revolved around visions of snakes, humidity, and a distinct lack of civilization. 'Mighty rivers and virgin forests, palm trees and jaguars, anacondas and alligators, howling monkeys and screaming parrots, diamond-mining, revolutions and earthquakes, are the component parts of the picture formed in the mind's eye. It is probably hazarding nothing to say that a very large majority of general readers are better acquainted with China and India than with Brazil. How few seem to be aware that in the distant Southern Hemisphere is a stable constitutional monarchy, and a growing nation.'[4]

Only the prospect of direct trade between the two countries worked against the lamentable lack of understanding. Canadians in the middle decades of the nineteenth century harboured a desire to expand their lucrative export trade in the timber and fish staples to areas beyond the traditional markets of England, the American Republic, and the Caribbean. This urge was accentuated when it became apparent in the early 1860s that the United States would not renew the Reciprocity Treaty of 1854. Aware that the Catholic nations of Latin America offered alluring prospects for trade, especially in fish, Canadian merchants and politicians began to look southward past the United States and the Caribbean in search of new markets.

In 1864, representatives from the as-yet-unconfederated Canadian colonies met in Quebec to request that the British government take steps to place trade between the Canadian colonies and the West Indies, Spain, Brazil, and Mexico 'on a more advantageous footing.'[5] In December 1865, this initiative was followed by the dispatch of a trade delegation of politicians. After making its hopes known in London, the delegation divided into two groups and toured Latin America and the Caribbean. One group paid visits to the Brazilian coastal cities of Belém, Recife, and Salvador before arriving in Rio in February 1866.[6]

The delegation was quick to identify two major impediments to the development of Canadian-Brazilian trade: the lack of direct sea communication and the absence of favourable trade treaties. Such Canadian trade as existed between the two countries was almost invariably forced to pass through the port of New York, where regular steamer service was available. In their subsequent report, the commissioners concluded that, with better communications and the reduction of the duties that prevailed in Latin American countries on Canadian flour, fish, lumber, pork, butter, and other staples, Canadian merchants could hope to break into Latin American markets. Such goals could, however, be pursued only with the aid of 'prudent legislation' and a 'sound fiscal policy.' Unfortunately, Canadian politicians were by this time too much occupied with the intricacies of confederating their colonies into the nation that was to emerge in 1867 to devote much energy to opening up to trade areas that had so far been of only peripheral importance.

More than a decade later, in May 1879, Prime Minister John A. Macdonald informed the Commons that his government was ready to provide a $37,500 subsidy to the Roche Line of steamers to establish, on a trial basis, a monthly service from Canada to the West Indies and Brazil. This initiative, Sir John stated, was the result of prodding by a Brazilian government official who had visited Canada and who had assured the government that the Brazilian government would match Ottawa's subsidy.[7] Although a mutually advantageous exchange of the staple products, especially Brazil's coffee for Canada's fish, offered great potential for trade, little seems to have come of this temporary link. In the meantime, direct Canadian exports to all of South America remained a trickle, amounting to only $381,414 in 1878.[8] Of Brazil's export trade, estimated at an equivalent value of £36 million in 1878, only the merest fraction, most of it coffee, went to Canada. What continued to be especially dismaying was the tendency of Canadian trade with South America to be routed through intermediaries, principally New York and London.

So underdeveloped were ties between Canada and Brazil that in 1880 one trade advocate complained that 'so little was known in Brazil of North America' and 'its products and manufacturers' that he himself had been forced to supply the *Jornal do comércio* in Rio with basic statistics on Canada's size, population, and products.[9] 'To sum up,' he lamented, 'here are two countries each requiring what the other produces, and yet they have been receiving these products through the medium of others instead of making a direct interchange.'[10] Little occurred in the last two decades of the century to remove this lassitude. No move was made towards diplomatic representation, Canada being content to have the British watch over its interests in Rio. Canadian-Brazilian trade continued to register only barely in each country's statistical report on trade. In 1902, for instance, Brazilian exports to Canada equalled only 0.5 per cent of total Brazilian exports.[11]

Throughout these years, the Canadian government continued its sporadic efforts to broaden commercial relations with Brazil. The efforts of trade commissioners dispatched to Rio in 1887 and 1912 by the Department of Trade and Commerce were largely nullified by Brazil's increasing resort to tariff protection against foreign manufactured goods, as well as the ability of American and German producers to penetrate the Brazilian market.[12] Canadians simply could not compete for the Brazilian market against large, export-oriented American producers, especially after 1891, when the United States and Brazil signed a reciprocal trade agreement. Furthermore, the British, who had long dominated Brazil's foreign trade, controlled many of the mechanisms (such as the warehousing and shipping services) that governed Brazilian exports and imports. The British were also responsible for conducting Canada's diplomatic affairs in Brazil. It was somewhat ironic when, as late as 1916, Arthur Peel, the British minister in Rio, inquired of Sir Edward Grey in London 'whether it would not be as well that some intimation should be conveyed to the Brazilian Government that the Government of Canada do not in future wish to be overlooked when important discussions are taking place affecting the general commercial relations between North and South America.'[13] Despite this prompting, it was not until 1919 that Canada established a permanent trade commission in Brazil. Even then, and well into the 1920s, trade officials continued to air the same time-worn excuses for Canada's failure to penetrate the Brazilian market, most notably the absence of regular steamer service. 'There is no magic formula to American success here,' the Canadian trade commissioner grudgingly admitted from Rio in 1927. 'It is the result of enterprise, and the necessary capital outlay.'[14]

If Canadian trade with Brazil languished, Canadian investment in certain areas of the Brazilian economy began to flourish with the dawn of the new century. The São Paulo Tramway, Light and Power Company's uniqueness as a Canadian firm that had penetrated the Brazilian economy was chiefly due to its ability to muster sufficient 'enterprise' and 'capital.' Its ability to prosper in Brazil was not unique, but was merely another example of the long-standing involvement of foreign investors in the Brazilian economy. That other Canadian investors did not, or could not, follow suit reflected the immaturity of the Canadian economy and its own need to rely on foreign capital and expertise more than it did any lack of Brazilian receptivity to foreign enterprise.

Apart from obvious cultural differences, late-nineteenth-century Brazil bore a striking resemblance to Canada. Both were young nations: Brazil had taken its independence from Portugal in 1822 and Canada its from England in 1867. After Brazil replaced its monarchy with a republic in 1889, both nations operated under a federal system of government, though Brazil's was more decentralized than the strongly centralized Canadian federation. Economically, Canada and Brazil both prospered and stagnated according to the commercial fortunes of their staple products. 'As a kind of huge plantation for tropical products, Brazil was closely integrated with European economies, on which the colony was dependent,' one of Brazil's leading economists has written. 'The country was not an autonomous system, rather a mere appendage of other major systems.'[15] As Canada had relied on its staple exports of fish, fur, timber, and wheat, so Brazil had staked its livelihood on the international demand for sugar, gold, cocoa, and, by the late nineteenth century, rubber and coffee. Each staple had a distinct regional base in Brazil – and it was coffee that gave São Paulo its economic hegemony within the country. Thus, as world commerce revived in the late 1890s after two decades of depression and falling commodity prices, both Brazil and Canada responded with vigorous economic activity. The thriving staple trades of each provided impetus for the expansion and diversification of the national economic base, especially for the emergence of secondary manufacturing and for widespread railway construction. Throughout the same years, both countries benefited from large-scale European emigration. For emigrants of German, Italian, and many other extractions, both Canada and Brazil represented beckoning lands of opportunity.

Few visitors to Brazil in these years failed to sense that Brazil was a nation in motion, coming alive in response to international economic stimulus. Symptoms of the change abounded everywhere. Slavery had been abolished in 1888, and the next year saw the departure of Emperor Dom Pedro II and the proclamation of the republic. Brazil began to play an independent part on the world stage, joining the Pan American Union in 1891 and, under the forceful leadership of foreign ministers such as the Baron of Rio Branco, became a power to be reckoned with in Latin America. Internally, Brazil bustled with activity. It became, as one historian has stressed, 'obsessed with the idea of material progress.'[16]

Despite this metamorphosis, serious structural problems jeopardized Brazil's economic prospects. By 1900, in this nation of just over seventeen million, economic development was still dangerously dependent upon the cyclical demands of the country's monocultural export sector. Blessed with abundant land and a salubrious climate, Brazil excelled in the production of its staples; but a lack of capital, entrepreneurial expertise, and manpower impeded its efforts to diversify its economy into manufacturing and the processing of its primary products. Furthermore, since it continued to rely on exports to cover the heavy cost of its imports of finished goods, Brazil became subject to periodic exchange crises brought on by any slackening of world demand for its coffee and rubber or by disruptions, like wars, which severed the arteries of international trade. For much of the nineteenth century, Brazil was held back from the threshold of industrial self-development by this pattern of export dependency. As Brazilian economist Celso Furtado has noted: 'Development based on the internal market becomes possible only when the economic system attains a certain degree of complexity with relative technological autonomy.'[17] A policy of tariff protection for such fledgling Brazilian industries as textile manufacturing in São Paulo was pursued by early republican finance ministers eager to promote the displacement of costly imports that consumed precious exchange funds.[18] Where local industry failed to emerge, Brazil learned to rely on foreign capital and expertise as a lever for diversified economic growth.

Other factors impeded Brazil's path to economic maturity. Industrial progress was afflicted by the country's lack of energy resources and by the narrowness of its entrepreneurial base. With no oil and only low-quality coal, Brazilian industry and the vital railway network were fuelled with costly English coal, the price of which fluctuated with every exchange crisis. Although the advent of practicable hydroelectric-power generation, as developed in North America and Europe in the late nineteenth century, offered a ready salvation for Brazilian industrialists, few sought it.

From the Brazilian perspective, the heavy price of importing generating equipment to power a mill, factory, or municipal utility was outweighed by the cost of further reliance on expensive imported coal. By the 1890s, small hydro-power installations were being erected to feed individual consumers in the more populated and prosperous areas of the country. In November 1899, a small 125 kw hydro plant was inaugurated at Marmelos-Zero to power fabric mills in the state of Minas Gerais to the north of Rio.[19] Such plants contributed to Brazil's first surge, albeit a small one, of electric-energy development. Whereas in 1883 the country had only 52 kw of installed thermal-electric generating capacity, by 1890 it had 5,030 kw of thermaland hydro-power capacity, and by 1900 it could boast of 12,085 kw. None the less, by 1907 steam still furnished 73 per cent of Brazil's industrial power output, while electricity contributed a mere 5 per cent.[20]

This initial spurt of electric development by no means solved Brazil's energy problems, but it did at least point the way to a satisfactory solution of one of the country's most conspicuous industrial deficiencies. Most of the plants erected in the 1890s were small and technologically primitive, incapable of effecting a wholesale conversion of Brazilian energy production. If such a transition were to be accomplished, Brazilians would need access to several crucial ingredients of the 'electric revolution' as it had developed in North America. Since electric energy was a capital-intensive industry, an ample supply of capital was imperative, as was the requisite expertise for developing and distributing electricity. None of these essential preconditions was present in Brazil. Even the Marmelos-Zero plant, while promoted by Brazilian textile manufacturer Bernardo Mascarenhas, was built with the technical assistance of the American firm of Max Notham and Co.

It was hardly surprising that Brazilians were unprepared to furnish their inchoate hydroelectric industry with sufficient capital. In the south-eastern areas of the country, where industrial enterprise was most concentrated, the hydroelectric industry had stiff competition for capital investment. At a time when the coffee economy of São Paulo placed immense pressure on the use of land, few Brazilian investors felt inclined to place large sums in intricate electric-power projects that promised to return their outlay at a low rate over a long period when real-estate speculation offered lucrative, short-term rewards. The coffee staple was still unchallenged in its domination of the São Paulo regional economy. 'The coffee trade not only generated a demand for industrial production,' economist Warren Dean has observed, 'it also paid for much of the economic and social overhead necessary to make domestic manufacturing profitable.' Thus the coffee-planting commercial oligarchy tended to set the economic priorities, especially since São Paulo's *latifundios*, or large estates, possessed a disproportionate influence over the politics of the Old Republic. For these reasons, development of electric generating capacity in Brazil's infant industrial heartland was allotted a low priority in the economic planning of the coffee-dominated entrepreneurial class. The electric-power advances that were undertaken were intended to 'adorn' the coffee planters' 'inland towns with modern devices,' rather than build up the industrial infrastructure of the economy.[21]

A less-tangible impediment to the development of electricity may be found in the psychological composition of the Brazilian entrepreneur. As the American and Canadian experience would illustrate, the electric industry was one of the most dynamic sectors of a national economy. Technologically, it was an industry that devoured innovation.[22] It epitomized the 'bigger and better' mentality that pervaded the thinking of North American promoters. These factors, coupled with the industry's substantial capitalization, placed a premium on the talents of the men who would promote electric power. The successful power entrepreneur had to combine an eye for the potential market with a comprehension of technological complexities and a capacity for large-scale financial management. Although North American and Brazilian entrepreneurs can by no means be confined to tight sociological compartments, there is evidence to suggest that many a São Paulo entrepreneur in the late nineteenth century was either unable or unwilling to make the entrepreneurial effort necessary to ensure the initiation of a power industry in Brazil.

The Brazilian businessman was, and to some degree remains, motivated by different goals from his North American counterpart. 'I do not pretend to know the character of the Latin American, but have conversed with men who have studied him,' a visiting Canadian trade official somewhat ethnocentrically noted in 1912; 'one gathered that in his business transactions he is not always guided by sound principles, but is sometimes led away by his feelings, or his desire to make a display, and might be inclined to seize a hollow victory if put his way.'[23] As late as the 1960s, it has been remarked that the Latin entrepreneur tends 'to consider business not as an impersonal activity of "economic man" directed at maximization of profit but as an extension of his family's drive for social status. The family supplies his financial contacts, perhaps his initial job, and the links to influential politicians and bureaucrats without which it is impossible to get business transactions done.' Such social motivation in business must perforce impose a certain rigidity upon entrepreneurial activity, an unwillingness to venture into unfamiliar business territory, especially when it means sacrificing the social prestige of an established commercial occupation. Not only does this tend to preclude innovation in business, but it also means that business has come to have an 'orientation toward immediate results, mostly to the neglect of long-range considerations.'[24]

Given these factors, Brazilian businessmen, with the possible exception of those in the coffee trade and various immigrant communities in south-eastern Brazil, evolved a different attitude to the whole process of 'risk taking.' Competition, market limitations, productivity trends, and the supply of capital and credit all came to be viewed 'at best with moderate optimism and at worst with fatalistic inertia.'[25] None of these tendencies, even if only generally present, augured well for the autonomous development of hydro power by Brazilians for Brazilians. By 1900, as with many other spheres of economic activity in their country, Brazilians had little choice but to look abroad for the capital and expertise to generate power for their industries and cities. Brazilians for their part preferred, quite rationally, to devote their energies and capital to the coffee trade and certain ancillary industries that, when world markets permitted, furnished a respectable return on their investment.[26]

By 1900 the foreign investor was therefore not an unfamiliar factor in Brazilian economic life. In the century of the *Pax Britannica*, it was hardly surprising that British goods and capital should have held a predominant role in Brazilian commerce and industry. 'Until 1914,' one historian of Anglo-Brazilian relations has emphasized, 'British capital, British enterprise, British shipping, and British goods predominated in the economic life of Brazil.'[27] This relationship extended back to the Cromwellian era, when England had secured preferential access to the trade of Portugal's overseas colonies. Although by the late nineteenth century this dominance was beginning to be challenged by the United States and Germany, Britain remained Brazil's principal foreign trader and investor until the 1920s. Britons invested more heavily in Brazil than in any other Latin American country, principally because Brazil was politically more stable than the rest of the fractious continent. Investments in Brazilian government bonds, mining ventures, railways, and public utilities had consistently provided a steady return on investment, estimated by one economist as being about 6 per cent in the 1880s and 1890s.[28] Despite an occasional default and the menace of fluctuating exchange, investment in Brazil provided the English investor with a better return than most investments in his home country. Only in the 1890s did Argentina surpass Brazil as a favoured destination for British overseas investment.

British investment touched almost every sphere and every region of Brazil. In 1886, for instance, British capital established the Rio de Janeiro Flour Mills and Granaries Company Ltd, and in 1869 the San Paulo Gas Company[29] began business in São Paulo. The latter paid a then-astonishing average dividend of 12 per cent over the period 1882–1912.[30] Regionally, British investment was concentrated in the most densely populated and economically thriving south-eastern section of Brazil, where English capital was applied to building up the infrastructure and ancillary services for the all-important staple trade in coffee. Railways, banks, port facilities, and granaries all served to expedite the shipment of coffee, sugar, cocoa, and grain to world markets. By 1888, one estimate placed British investment in São Paulo state at over six million pounds sterling, while consular reports placed this figure at over twelve million pounds by 1890.[31]

British investment in Brazil represented more than a simple transference of capital from the developed European world to the better-paying, if riskier, opportunities of the underdeveloped economy of Brazil. Such investments also signified a response to Brazil's need for expertise and innovation. Thus Britain and to a lesser extent the United States and Germany were in a position to export not only capital but also the entrepreneurial and technical competence necessary to ensure that their investments flourished.

One of the best examples of this pattern was the British-owned San Paulo Railway. By the mid-nineteenth century it had become evident that if São Paulo were to prosper it would have to overcome the disadvantage imposed on it by the unbroken coastal escarpment, the Serra do Mar, that separated it from its port city of Santos. Without efficient transport over the nine-hundred-metre-high Serra, São Paulo would be unable to develop its coffee trade and would be prevented from importing the necessities of urban and industrial life. This predicament was recognized by Brazilian entrepreneur Irineu Evangelista de Souza, later Baron Mauá,[32] who in the late 1850s obtained a concession to construct a rail link between São Paulo and the coast. Despite the attractiveness of the concession, Mauá was unable to find Brazilian backing for his scheme and in 1860 sold his rights to an English syndicate. Mauá's inability to exploit the opportunity was directly attributable to a scarcity of capital and labour for railway ventures in Brazil as well as to the unwillingness of São Paulo's coffee growers to back the scheme. 'For these reasons,' the historian of the San Paulo Railway has remarked, '*paulistas* were themselves not ready to build a railroad in the 1850s. While they had the incentive – the need for improved transport – and while they had examples – the successful railroads in England and the United States – they lacked capital, labour, technology, and, most importantly, the entrepreneurial vision to locate and combine these scarce resources.'[33] Once the English supplied these, the scheme prospered. Not only did the San Paulo Railway yield a handsome average dividend of 10 per cent a year throughout 1880–1920, but it also brought forth 'new financial and business strategies and structures' within the Brazilian economy.[34]

The conspicuous success of the San Paulo Railway provided Brazilians with an object lesson in the role of foreign investment and also served to underscore their own lack of entrepreneurial development in some fields of modern economic activity. Exposure to this and other external influences bred a receptivity to foreign ideas and methods amongst various prominent Brazilians. Throughout the late nineteenth century, this loose circle of 'modernizers,' men who had imbibed European notions of material progress and institutional reform, sought to emulate the commercial and industrial affluence of Europe and America within their own country. These modernist ideas were a manifestation of a developing sense of nationalism in republican Brazil – a nationalism that was not essentially xenophobic or autarchic but was instead built on a sense of Brazil's growing self-assurance as a nation and its need to join the mainstream of modern Europe and American progress. This willingness to throw over or alter traditional ways, largely articulated by the liberal middle class, made itself widely felt in turn-of-the-century Brazil. The establishment of the republic in 1889 and the subsequent framing of the 1891 Constitution were formatively influenced by the spirit of European Positivism and the example of the American federal constitution. The adoption of the national motto *Ordem e Progresso* – order and progress – (today emblazoned on Brazil's flag), bore testimony to the strength of this spirit. The same desire made itself felt in demands for the abolition of slavery and for a separation of church and state. Having turned their critical attention on the traditional institutions of church, monarchy, and slavery, Brazil's 'modernizers' soon found fault with the economic status quo in their country.

The vanguard of the modernization movement was provided by the small but influential urban middle class, among men whose education, social standing, and liberalism had nurtured a restless desire for change. 'Brazilian liberals in the nineteenth century,' historian Richard Graham has noted, 'were elaborating the bases of a modern society ... They were searching for intellectual tools with which to file down the fetters of tradition and pry open the manacles of ancient custom. The instruments they chose had been forged in Britain but the result was a growing awareness of man's potential freedom in Brazil.'[35] While Baron Mauá may be taken as an energetic early apostle of modernization, three later examples furnish a fuller understanding of this crucial development. Rui Barbosa (1849–1923), Brazil's most revered liberal intellectual and constitutional theorist, ranked high among the modernizers. As a member of the committee charged with drafting the new republican constitution, Barbosa was responsible for imparting a strong flavour of American federalism to the new Brazil. Barbosa subsequently used his tenure as the first finance minister of the republic to promote reforms designed to encourage capital formation, credit facilitation, and the issuing of paper money. Barbosa's reforms and the policies of his successors, Tristão de Alençar Araripe and Henrique Pereira de Lucena, triggered a speculative boom, the *Encilhamento*, which ultimately collapsed in the mid-1890s, with dire consequences for Brazilian exchange and credit. Despite this setback, Barbosa remained a staunch advocate of economic self-interest and individual freedom, liberties he saw as fundamental to the material advancement of Brazil. During a stay in England in 1894–5, Barbosa formed an abiding admiration for the social and political values espoused by the English middle class. The emergence of a similar class in his own country became Barbosa's abiding goal. As Brazil's great sociologist Gilberto Freyre has remarked, 'intellectual *éminences grises*' have had a formative influence in the evolution of modern Brazil. 'Some of these men,' Freyre has stressed, 'were noted for initiatives that mere politicians would never have taken unless inspired by intellectual *éminences grises* ... But the outstanding fact is that in few other modern countries have intellectuals played such an important role as in Brazil.'[36]

Francisco Pereira Passos (1836–1913), and Antônio Prado (1830–

1928), while they lacked the sweeping national vision and influence of Barbosa, also applied their minds both as entrepreneurs and municipal politicians to the promotion of modernity in Brazil. The son of a wealthy São Paulo coffee planter, Prado had been trained as a lawyer, but it was not until he toured Europe in the early 1860s that his eyes were fully opened to the progressive power of technology combined with enlightened entrepreneurship. Deeply impressed by the British industrial economy, Prado returned to his native São Paulo to promote a succession of industrial ventures ranging from glass factories to the Companhia Estrada de Ferro Paulista. He soon developed close ties with several foreign companies operating in Brazil, most notably the Brazilian Warrant Company, a British-owned coffee-exporting firm. Prado applied much the same zeal to his duties as prefect of the city of São Paulo from 1899 to 1911. It was, therefore, natural that Antônio Prado should have taken his place beside R.C. Brown on the front platform of the first electric tram to wind its way through the streets of São Paulo in May 1900.

The career of Francisco Pereira Passos, Rio's most renowned prefect, closely paralleled that of his São Paulo counterpart. The scion of a Rio de Janeiro coffee planter, Passos studied engineering in Brazil. In 1871, he visited England, where he acquired an unshakable belief in the economic power of railways and a passion for the *laissez-faire* ideals of Adam Smith and Herbert Spencer. In Brazil, Passos managed the Estrada de Ferro Dom Pedro II and in the 1880s promoted an ingenious inclined-plane railway, which ran up the side of Corcovado mountain in Rio. Not, however, until Passos became prefect of the city of Rio in 1902 did the full scope of his modernizing vision emerge. Under the aegis of Passos, Rio was transformed from a grimy, constricted colonial town into a more spacious and better-planned city, worthy of its stature as the nation's capital.[37]

Nothing aroused the fervour of these reformers as much as the prospect of modernizing Brazil's cities. The cities were 'the beachheads of the modern world' in Brazil. Since the leadership of the modernizing élite was largely drawn from the urban middle class, it was only natural that their attention should have fixed at an early date on the sorry and neglected state of the nation's two largest cities, Rio (population 926,000 in 1900) and São Paulo (population 239,000 in the same year). Both cities contended with topography that hampered their ability to furnish their inhabitants with a satisfactory urban environment. Rio de Janeiro was a

General outline of present-day Brazil

community hemmed in along a narrow coastal strip by a chain of steep *morros*, or barren volcanic plugs. As a result, *cariocas* (as the citizens of Rio are known) found themselves confined to the congested and densely populated old colonial city of Rio, prevented from spreading inland or along the coast by the *morros* and the lack of any suitable form of collective transport.[38] São Paulo faced different problems. Perched on an inland plateau at the confluence of the Tietê and Pinheiros rivers, São Paulo had to contend with a hilly, broken territory as it expanded and took shape. Hindered by this terrain from servicing its hinterland, São Paulo was furthermore subject to severe annual flooding whenever the swollen Tietê overflowed its banks in the rainy season. But by far the most pressing problem for São Paulo in the late nineteenth century was coping with the unprecedented growth brought by the spectacular expansion of the coffee trade. As the service centre for the lucrative coffee trade, São Paulo had exploded from a mere 23,243 souls in 1872 to 129,409 in 1893, then to nearly a quarter of a million at the turn of the century. This 'tumultuous will-to-power'[39] imposed an unmanageable strain upon the civic government of the burgeoning city. 'With the pressure of growth,' a historian of the city's evolution has noted, 'the authorities were ill-adapted to cope. Public utilities could not be expanded fast enough. Street cleaning and paving, garbage and sewage disposal, and drainage of the lowlands were all inadequate.'[40]

Early attempts were made to tackle the urban problems of the two cities. In 1862, the London-financed Rio de Janeiro City Improvements Co. Ltd began installing a modern water system, a task that was largely complete by the mid-1890s. British engineers also provided São Paulo with potable water. Throughout the 1870s and 1880s both cities witnessed the first attempts to provide crude forms of gas and kerosene street lighting. Small and poorly financed traction companies endeavoured to give the urban populace greater mobility. Rio recorded a major stride forward in this respect, when, in 1892, the 'Tunel Velho' (now called the Alaor Prata Tunnel) was punched through to Copacabana, a beach district along the city's Atlantic seaboard, thus allowing mule-drawn tramcars access to this area and neighbouring Ipanema, both of which were to offer *cariocas* some much-needed new residential space. None the less, all these civic improvements took place in a piecemeal fashion, unguided by any central co-ordinating force and generally having only a palliative effect. The grave urban predicament of Rio and São Paulo thus engendered an acute sense of exasperation in Brazilian urban middle-class citizens, a sense that was sharpened by exposure to the remarkable urban progress of other nations.

In the late nineteenth century, cities were the pre-eminent symbols of modernity. When Brazilians like Barbosa, Passos, and Prado made their way to Europe it was to cities like Paris, where the great Baron Haussmann, the city's prefect, had transformed the urban landscape with *grandes allées*, striking new forms of architecture, and bold schemes of urban planning. Closer to home, Brazilians jealously watched the emergence of Buenos Aires as the 'Paris of South America.' Under the guidance of Torcuato de Alvear, Buenos Aires's renowned *Intendente* from 1880 to 1887, the *gente decente*, the Argentinian middle class, had initiated an impressive array of civic improvements, including better sewage facilities, new hospitals, broad paved avenues, parks, and the spacious Plaza de Mayo.[41] The sights of Paris and Buenos Aires deeply impressed travelling Brazilians and predictably gave rise to 'an anxiety to look like Europe.' 'Water systems, sewage facilities, urban transport companies, gas works, and electric plants were all necessary if urban Brazilians were to hold up their heads.'[42]

Equally striking, if perhaps less grandiose, were the changes that Brazilians observed in urban North America. Electricity was making possible advances in urban life that had seemed scarcely conceivable, let alone practical, a generation earlier. Efficient and cheap surface transportation, powered by electricity, allowed American cities like New York and Boston to extend their boundaries, opening up large, previously inaccessible areas of land for suburban residency. Electric traction did what animal traction had never been able to do: it moved vast numbers of city dwellers at reasonable cost and with minimum inconvenience beyond the traditional core areas of the city.[43] Across Europe and America, city dwellers became accustomed to 'the riding habit.' The expansion of the American streetcar network was phenomenal. In 1890, 2,900 electric trams rode on 2,092 kilometres of electrified track in America. By 1902, 51,000 cars circulated on 35,404 kilometres of track.[44]

The streetcar triumph was, moreover, the triumph of private enterprise. In an era in which national and municipal governments felt no compulsion to initiate more than the barest minimum of civic services, both the development of streetcar technology and its application to the urban needs of American cities were left in private hands. While cities made some effort to regulate streetcar entrepreneurs through the concessions they awarded, the streetcar industry moved along the tracks of profit maximization. The concept of 'service at cost' was largely unknown to nineteenth-century politicians. The streetcar revolution was essentially the product of 'privatism,' that great secular tradition of American life that 'assumed that there would be no major conflict between private interest, honestly and liberally viewed, and the public welfare.'[45]

The efficacious touch of the streetcar had also been felt in Toronto. Since 1861 the horse-drawn trams of the Toronto Street Railway Company had moved through the city streets, opening a network of 108 kilometres of track by 1890. When this concession lapsed in 1891, Toronto's city fathers briefly toyed with the contentious idea of municipal ownership but, recoiling from the prospect, sold a new concession to a syndicate headed by William Mackenzie, a successful local railway contractor. For $1,453,788, Mackenzie's Toronto Street Railway Company obtained a thirty-year exclusive franchise to provide Toronto with electrified streetcar service, at five cents a ride. On 15 August 1892, Toronto's first regular electric-car service was initiated along Church Street, and by August 1894 the last cumbersome horse-drawn car was retired.[46] In a very significant way, the streetcar changed the daily habits of Torontonians and directly contributed to the awakening of a new sense of secular freedom in their previously dour and puritanical city.[47] For this, Torontonians were generally grateful. Mackenzie and his associates had brought 'health, comfort and convenience' to Torontonians and therefore, *Toronto Illustrated* concluded in 1893, must be 'regarded as purely and simply public benefactors, and, as such, are fully entitled to every financial benefit that may accrue from their enterprise.'[48]

By contrast, in the early 1890s the citizens of Rio or São Paulo could derive little civic pride from the motley collection of traction companies on their streets. Indeed, the streetcar was widely regarded as more of a nuisance than a convenience. Even the Brazilian word '*bonde*,' popularly used to describe the mule-drawn streetcars, found its origins in the streetcar's nuisance value. When passengers complained that they were unable to tender the standard 200 réis fare because of a chronic shortage of coinage, streetcar companies resorted to strips of five tickets, similar in appearance to a bond or coupon, that could be purchased for one milréis, a paper note.[49] Hence the label '*bonde*' developed. Others disparaged the trams by simply calling them *vacas de leite*, or milch cows. The mule-drawn streetcar possessed many drawbacks and few advantages. The animals could generate only minimal uphill traction, an important factor in hilly São Paulo; they were subject to contagions and, of course, did little to beautify the city streets. Consequently, São Paulo's mule trams offered irregular, relatively expensive, and uncoordinated service. The Companhia Viação Paulista, the result of an 1889 consolidation of several smaller tramway companies, maintained the city's largest stable of mules and the most extensive network of routes.[50] Despite its size, the Viação Paulista's service left much to be desired, as one American engineer, who came to the city in 1899, was later to recall: 'That "Companhia Viação" was a good deal of a "go as you please concern," no schedule.'[51] On one occasion, a driver halted his *bonde* for twenty-three minutes to enable a potential woman rider to complete her toilette before boarding the tram.

Brazilians shared the American's opinion of the dismal service of the Viação Paulista. Complaints were frequently aired in the São Paulo municipal council, or *câmara*, concerning irregular service and the company's inability to honour its contractual agreements. Of particular annoyance to *paulistanos* was the company's failure to keep the cobblestones around its tracks in good repair. In a city where horse-drawn traffic abounded, a displaced paving stone could often have lethal results.

The plodding mules and delinquent drivers of the Viação Paulista offered little hope that São Paulo, a city that had grown in population by 664 per cent between 1872 and 1900, would ever be able to offer its citizens an efficient and cheap means of transportation. The civic government, lacking both an adequate tax base and administrative competence, had no illusions about its ability to initiate a publicly owned service. Brazilian private capital, as has already been stressed, displayed a similar reluctance to invest in utility ventures, preferring to place funds in the faster-yielding real-estate market. Electric traction required not only sizeable outlays on track and equipment, but also a source of inexpensive electric power. In coal and oil-starved Brazil, this meant a hydro facility within transmission distance of the city. The challenge of efficient public transportation in São Paulo was thus destined to be taken up by foreign interests, probably aided and abetted by local speculators. As with most business ventures, a middleman was needed to marry business opportunity to an appropriate form of risk-taking entrepreneurship. In São Paulo's case, the middlemen were drawn from Brazil's urban class, a group eager to profit both themselves and their nation through the introduction of electricity, and the ultimate promoters were members of a Canadian-based syndicate, heavily flavoured with international finance and American technology.

The story of the São Paulo Tramway, Light and Power Company's concession has complicated and peripatetic beginnings. It began not in São Paulo but in Montreal, where an Italian-born engineer, Francisco Antônio Gualco,[52] had enjoyed moderate success as a railway contractor during the building of the Canadian Pacific. Gualco was somewhat of a schemer and a business adventurer; when railway work dwindled in the early 1890s, he turned to new means of business advancement. Mindful that the coffee planters of São Paulo were eager to replace their freed slaves with industrious immigrants and that his own Italian government had taken measures to prevent Brazil from siphoning off Italy's rural peasantry, Gualco concluded that the hardy French Canadian farmer, who had already displayed a willingness to migrate to the United States, might be induced to forsake Canada for Brazil. Gualco's initial approach to the São Paulo government was interrupted by the outbreak of civil war in 1893–4. Undeterred, Gualco re-established contact with Bernardino de Campos, the president of São Paulo state, in 1895. Intrigued by the prospect of having *habitants* settle on the coffee *fazendas* of São Paulo, Campos dispatched one of his six sons, Américo, to Canada to meet with Gualco.

That Gualco and Américo de Campos found ample ground for agreement was evidenced in September 1896 by the arrival in Montreal of the ss *Moravia* of the Brazilian Line. Gualco, now an official agent of the São Paulo government, was rumoured to be active in the Montreal district canvassing for as many as ten thousand French Canadian immigrants. In a province that viewed emigration as a direct threat to its prospects for racial survival, Gualco's efforts raised an immediate storm of protest. When questioned in the Commons by a backbench Quebec MP about what his government intended to do about the Brazilian scheme, Prime Minister Laurier stated that there was little the federal government could do to prevent its citizens from exercising their right to emigrate. He added, however, that Canadians 'would make a great mistake to go to Brazil to settle' since Canada was 'a far better country for them than Brazil.'[53] Laurier did promise to investigate 'the truthfulness of any inducement' held out to any prospective emigrants. Within a month it became apparent that Quebec fears were groundless. Only a handful of adventurous *habitants* took up Gualco's offer and sailed on the *Moravia*, and of these only a few permanently remained on the *fazendas* of São Paulo. In 1897, the Canadian government spent $3,778 repatriating some of the now-disconsolate French Canadians who had been lured away from their homeland by Antônio Gualco.[54]

Although the emigration scheme was a failure, the friendship of Antônio Gualco and Américo de Campos eventually bore fruit in Brazil. During his stay in Montreal, Campos developed a warm affection for Gualco and his charming young wife, Josephine, and extended an invitation to visit his native land. When Gualco arrived in São Paulo in late 1896 he already had *entrée* to the highest levels of society and politics through Campos, whose father had just retired as president of the state and was soon to be called to the finance portfolio of the federal government. Gualco was particularly fortunate in that São Paulo state exercised a disproportionate influence in the federal politics of the Old Republic (1889–1930) in Brazil. The political life of Brazil was dominated and guided by what have been described as the politics of *café com leite*, that is a political power base built on the coffee wealth of São Paulo and the cattle wealth of Minas Gerais.[55] This dominance was reinforced by an élitist tendency in Brazilian political life, a tendency towards *clientelismo*, which bound, through patronage and kinship, leader and led into a political block that tightly governed the dispensing of political and economic favours.[56] Almost without exception, the São Paulo–Minas Gerais political axis groomed and selected the incumbents of the federal presidency down to 1930. The first three civilian presidents of Brazil – Prudente de Morais, Manuel Ferraz de Campos Sales, and Francisco de Paulo Rodrigues Alves – were all drawn from *paulista* politics. Although Rio de Janeiro occasionally shared in this hegemony, not until 1930 did the usually resilient political machine fuelled by São Paulo's industrial and agricultural wealth malfunction and break apart, allowing hitherto excluded regions a share in national politics. Until then, it would rule supreme. Into this very privileged and influential world Antônio Gualco stepped.[57]

At the bidding of Bernardino de Campos, Gualco undertook a tour of the state. Under the guidance of Dr Alípio de Borba, a Brazilian engineer, and Carlos de Campos, Bernardino's eldest son and a lawyer, Gualco toured the coffee-rich region and was struck by the contrast between the wealth of the *fazendas* and the disorder of the city, especially its lack of adequate public services. Alípio de Borba was quick to encourage the Italian's interest and showed him a site on the Tietê River at Cachoeira do Inferno, or the Rapids of Hell, that offered excellent potential for a hydroelectric installation. His appetite whetted, Gualco made discreet inquiries about obtaining a concession to exploit the water power and to apply its power to a street railway. When Borba, who was somewhat distrustful of the Italian's flamboyance, turned down Gualco's proposal to form a partnership, Carlos de Campos suggested that the Italian contact his father-in-law, Antônio de Souza. Gualco could not have found a better partner. Antônio de Souza had gained experience in the tribulations of promoting traction companies as an original partner in the Companhia Viação Paulista.[58] By 1897 he had, however, become completely exasperated by that company's failure to flourish and was ready to join forces with Gualco as Gualco e de Souza, Incorporadores.

Armed with no more than a promise to secure adequate capital, the new partners approached the municipal government with a request for legislation to facilitate the establishment of an electric traction company. On 15 June 1897, the municipal *câmara* obliged by passing law No. 304, by which Souza and Gualco were given the 'privilege for forty years to construct, use and enjoy the benefit of street cars, by electric traction, running to different points of this city and its suburbs.'[59] What was of crucial significance was the fact that Gualco and Souza had convinced the *câmara* that the concession must be an exclusive one. Electric traction, they argued, could only be exploited on a monopolistic basis, since only a monopoly allowed sufficient economies of scale to permit inexpensive service and some surety for long-term investment. A monopoly was also a means of precluding any repetition of the chaotic competition of unregulated mule-drawn trams.

Gualco and Souza proceeded to draw up a detailed contract, which was completed on 8 July 1897. The contract, signed with the municipal intendant of police and hygiene, stipulated that construction must begin within one year and conceded to the concessionaires the important right of intersection with the Viação Paulista lines. The concessionaires were given the exclusive right to exploit their routes for forty years. The intendant of police was given extensive powers to set fares, govern routes, inspect company equipment, and impose fines, albeit small ones, for any failure to honour the contract. Fares were set at 200 réis per section. The concession provided Gualco and Souza with a potentially lucrative hold on a public service for which there was a clear demand, and for which the necessary technical expertise and equipment were readily available in Europe or America. For this potent privilege they had expended the barest minimum of capital; nothing more than their legal fees, in fact. What remained unclear were the astute promoters' intentions. Had they acquired the concession as a speculative gamble, trusting that its right of exclusivity would attract outside investors who would eagerly relieve them of their duties for a handsome consideration? Or had the two partners hopes of promoting the enterprise themselves, relying upon Souza's past experience with the Viação Paulista and Gualco's skills as a railway contractor?

Regardless of their intentions, Souza and Gualco met with little success in their search for capital, either domestic or foreign, throughout the next year. Gualco travelled to New York and Europe, both obvious sources of capital for foreign investment, but his efforts were unavailing. In one sense, the spurning of the concession by American and European capital was peculiar and out of pattern. By 1900, for instance, British investors had placed £6.8 million in public-utilities ventures in Latin America. This sum represented investments in fifty public-utility enterprises, of which fourteen were electric utilities.[60] Similarly, by the turn of the century, investors in the United States had begun to take an interest in Latin American utilities. All of the major American electrical-equipment producers were showing a keen interest in 'internationalizing' their sales.[61] Edison General Electric and Thomson-Houston Electric, for instance, were eager to tap the expanding Latin American market for generating and distributing equipment. In 1892, the first electric trolley to operate in Rio did so using Thomson-Houston equipment. The next year General Electric placed an agent, James Mitchell, in Rio to spearhead its sales drive into Brazil. Mitchell had little difficulty in marketing apparatus for street lighting and power generating.

The failure of Souza and Gualco to secure sufficient backing to establish their concession on an operational basis must therefore be attributed to their lack of credibility in the eyes of foreign investors and to certain flaws in their original concession. Without an *entrée* to the financial houses in London or New York and without ties to one of the large electrical manufacturers, Gualco and Souza possessed little to differentiate them from what must have been a small army of would-be promoters, eagerly peddling foreign concessions around the financial districts of Europe and America. Furthermore, it would have been readily apparent that Gualco and Souza had obtained only a concession to operate an electric-traction company and did not yet have the right to generate power or to distribute it for lighting purposes, both highly lucrative functions in North America and Europe. The initiators of electric traction service in São Paulo would also have to contend with competition from the welter of animal-traction companies, all of which would have to be conquered in competition. In this light, the Gualco and Souza concession must have appeared a risky proposition. Faced with these problems, the two promoters bided their time. They were able to convince the intendant of police and hygiene to extend the deadline for starting construction of their tramway system by six months, from July 1898 to December of the same year. This alteration notwithstanding, the prospects of Gualco and Souza were distinctly unpromising by mid-1898.

The decisive breakthrough came in September 1898, when Gualco, desperate to obtain financial backing, returned to Montreal. In Montreal he contacted James Ross, one of the premier contractors for the Canadian Pacific Railway, and tabled his São Paulo concession for Ross's consideration. In Ross, Gualco had found a potential backer who not only was well connected with a small group of highly successful promoters of Canadian railways and utilities but also had ample ties with the London money market and leading practitioners of applied electrical science. Ross took the concession to William Mackenzie, the Ontario-born promoter of western Canadian railways and the prime mover behind the Toronto Street Railway Company. Convinced by his success in Toronto and Montreal that a well-framed, monopolistic streetcar concession was a sure way to steady profits, Mackenzie was always on the lookout for further enticing prospects in the utilities world. In 1896, Ross and Mackenzie had set their sights on the potentially lucrative market for electric traction in Birmingham, England. They formed the Birmingham Tramway Company, bought out existing traction concerns, and sought to consolidate all of Birmingham's tramway services under one, all-encompassing concession. These hopeful beginnings were soon superseded by bitter controversy as city officials demanded that power lines be placed in underground conduits, a costly stipulation that the company would not meet. Faced with a stalemate (which was eventually to end with the sale of the Birmingham Tramway Company assets in 1902 and municipalization in

1904), Mackenzie and Ross turned their promotional energies to new utilities schemes, schemes with less danger of municipal interference and the same prospects of profit.[62] In 1897, they won an electric-traction concession from the Jamaican government. A year later Gualco arrived on their doorstep offering another Latin American concession, a concession they imagined would be free of the constraints with which English municipal politicians had been keen to yoke them.

Ross was by no means immediately converted by Gualco's tales of São Paulo's tremendous potential for electric power. Like most Canadian businessmen of the day, he knew little of Brazil, except the unflattering fact that it had recently emerged from civil war. Furthermore, he was immediately aware that Gualco's concession did not furnish an iron-clad monopoly for the São Paulo market. None the less, he was intrigued by the prospect of duplicating his Canadian tramway successes in Brazil and awaited William Mackenzie's opinion. Mackenzie in turn called in Fred Stark Pearson, a forty-year-old American engineer who had a thorough grasp of the intricacies of the electric industry and a proven record of establishing power and traction services in some of America's largest cities. The most that Ross, Mackenzie, and Pearson could agree upon was that Gaulco's concession deserved closer examination. Since none of them had the time to undertake the lengthy journey to São Paulo, it was decided that Pearson would seek a competent technical expert who could be dispatched to São Paulo to investigate both the concession and the potential market. The choice fell upon Robert Calthrop Brown, a close friend of Pearson and the general manager of the Halifax Tramway Company. F.S. Pearson approached Benjamin Franklin Pearson, a principal backer of the Halifax Tramway and (although no relation to the American engineer) an associate of the Mackenzie-Ross coterie of business promoters, and requested that Brown be released to undertake the mission. Anxious to obtain an initial stake in what might evolve into a profitable investment, B.F. Pearson complied, and in November 1898 R.C. Brown departed by steamer from New York en route to Santos, the port city of São Paulo. These hurried, informal arrangements, prompted by the prospect of profits on a distant continent, represented what may be described as the first loose syndicate of promoters prepared to underwrite Canadian investment in São Paulo.

Brown's report to his North American backers in March 1899 provided a speedy solvent for any doubts they may have held about São Paulo. 'Such a city as São Paulo,' Brown concluded after his three-week stay, 'should give excellent returns to a street railway, especially one operated by electricity and one that is managed with the view to giving its patrons convenient, quick and cheap service.'[63] Brown's observations were the product of the trained mind of an engineer and the inquiring mind of a foreigner, groping to make sense of the strange complexities of the Brazilian urban world. Above all else he was struck by the vitality of the city. At the centre of a state-wide railway network drawing in the produce of the coffee *fazendas*, São Paulo was alive with commerce. The city's population, he reported, was growing at the astounding rate of 12½ per cent per annum. 'I think a stranger would notice that the people of São Paulo and the surrounding country are very much more energetic than one would expect to find after having visited the sea coast cities.' This, he speculated, was partially due to the absence of yellow fever, a disease dreaded by northerners. More significant in explaining São Paulo's prosperity was the presence of large numbers of European immigrants who tended to make the city 'cosmopolitan' and diminish the opposition to 'foreign customs and enterprises,' a tendency he believed was 'natural to the people of the Portuguese and Spanish races.'

Having ventured his opinions on the city's cultural and climatic conditions, Brown turned his attention to the surer ground of analysing its potential as a market for electric power. Many areas of the city were densely enough populated to warrant electric tramway service. 'Even now,' he emphasized, 'with circuitous routes of the mule trams, the traffic is excellent, notwithstanding that the slack methods of operation, the poor track connections, the necessary round-about routes to avoid grades and the consequently long time consumed in making trips have rendered the tram service very unsatisfactory.' So bad was the prevailing mule-tram service that one could often 'save time by walking.' Brown was quick to point out that the routes secured by Gualco and Souza would, once in operation, have little difficulty in drawing off a large part of the mule trams' traffic. Furthermore, the city offered an inviting market for electric lighting and power. An existing small company, supplying electric power from an uneconomic coal-fired plant, was completely over-whelmed by the size of the market, with the result that streets, public buildings, and factories were all 'inferiorly lighted.' 'The electric light service,' Brown commented, echoing local complaints, 'begins at sun-down, and barring a few large customers, extends only until ten o'clock in the evening.' Such indifferent service could easily be supplanted if an efficient source of hydroelectric power could be harnessed. In fact, Brown recommended, a hydro-power facility was the key to the whole power situation in São Paulo. 'No other company using any other source of power other than water, will be in a position to compete for the railway, light and power business of São Paulo.' Brown felt sure that at a 'conservative estimate' 10,000 horsepower could be consumed in the city. To underscore this, he enumerated 140 São Paulo industries currently consuming 4,994 horsepower of costly steam or gas energy.

The most reassuring aspect of Brown's report for his northern sponsors was his discussion of the attitude of the people and government towards any prospective foreign utility company. São Paulo exuded eagerness for civic improvement. Sewage projects, the paving of streets, and the appearance of an impressive urban architecture were all 'indicative of the policy of the City Government and of the people, to make a first class city of São Paulo.' Haunted by memories of their treatment at the hands of Birmingham politicians, Ross and Mackenzie must have been heartened to learn that São Paulo's municipal politicians were 'anxious to aid the company which undertakes to go ahead with the work, which for several years has been talked of by various visiting foreigners representing foreign syndicates.' Furthermore, the rights ceded in the concession were described by Brown as being 'very liberal,' a condition that promised welcome relief from the fractious relations that often prevailed between the Toronto Street Railway and that city's politicians.

Brown presented his report to F.S. Pearson in January 1899 on board Pearson's schooner yacht, the *Coronet*, as it lay at anchor in Kingston, Jamaica. Pearson had ventured into the Caribbean partly in an attempt to gain a respite from his exhausting round of business commitments, but also, and more importantly, to investigate a proposal to electrify the street railways of Havana and to oversee the affairs of the Jamaica Electric Railway Company. In the wake of the Spanish-American War, American entrepreneurs had embarked on a headlong rush for spoils in newly 'liberated' Cuba, where opportunities for electrification and railway development abounded. Canadians were also quick to pick up the scent of profit in the Caribbean, and such promoters as Sir William Van Horne, the renowned builder of the Canadian Pacific, vied to secure liberally framed concessions.[64] With similar aplomb, Pearson now moved speedily to bring Brown's positive assessment of the São Paulo situation to the attention of prospective investors back in Canada. Time was now at a premium, since some concrete evidence of a beginning to construction had to be given to São Paulo politicians as proof of the good faith of the concession holders and to minimize the danger that another foreign syndicate would appear on the scene and outbid the Canadians for the concession. Gualco and Souza, for their part, were now proceeding under the tacit assumption that their concession would shortly be bought outright by Ross and Mackenzie and their associates. To this end, they managed to cajole the intendant of police and hygiene into yet another extension of the construction deadline, which was now set at 7 July 1899.

Convinced that the São Paulo concession was well worth exploiting, James Ross and William Mackenzie resolved to give the loose, informal syndicate that had backed Brown's southern trip some legal and financial substance. Ross had extensive connections with the railway-building fraternity in Canada, and William Mackenzie had forged strong links with the corporate legal profession in Toronto. In any railway or tramway promotion, a competent legal assessment of the concession and other relevant documents was just as important as an engineer's feasibility report. William Mackenzie had relied in these matters on the highly respected Toronto legal firm of Blake, Lash and Cassels, and it was to Zebulon A. Lash, a senior partner at the Blake firm and probably Canada's best corporate legal mind, that Mackenzie turned with the São Paulo concession.[65]

Through Lash, William Mackenzie arranged for the incorporation by letters patent from the province of Ontario of the São Paulo Railway (later Tramway), Light and Power Company Limited on 7 April 1899. Since the company was to operate entirely outside the borders of Canada and since its head office was to be in Toronto, there was little reason to seek a federal charter. The provincial charter empowered the São Paulo company 'to lay out, construct, complete, maintain and operate works for the production, utilization and sale of and to produce and sell steam, gas and electricity, and steam, gas, electrical, pneumatic, mechanical, hydraulic and other power for all purposes.' The company was also enfranchised to operate tramway, lighting, telegraph, and telephone services wherever it might successfully negotiate concessions for such services. To initiate these services, the company was to have a capitalization of six million dollars, divided into sixty thousand shares of one hundred dollars each. The officers of the new traction company were endowed with wide powers 'to enter into contracts and agreements with any or all legislative, governmental, municipal or other authorities, councils, corporations or bodies, and private individuals respecting the exercise by the Company of all, or any, of its rights, concessions, privileges, franchises and powers, and respecting the acquisition by the Company of rights, concessions, privileges, franchises and powers in connection therewith.'[66] The way was therefore left open for the company to accumulate and consolidate whatever other concessions it could possibly acquire, either through negotiation or outright purchase, in the São Paulo area. Lash had thus provided the Mackenzie syndicate with what might be described as the kernel of a monopoly, a nucleus around which might be assembled the structure of a municipal public utility offering the broadest possible range of services.

In many respects the São Paulo company charter was not unlike that given to innumerable Canadian utility concerns of the period. The men named to the company's first board of directors were most notable for their obscurity. James Gunn, John Maitland Smith, Herbert Evelyn Harcourt Vernon, Archibald James Sinclair, Richard Selby Gosset, Alexander William Mackenzie, and Ernest William McNeill, the company's first directors, were not captains of industry, but stenographers, legal clerks, junior lawyers, and accountants from the legal office of Z.A. Lash and the head office of Mackenzie and Mann. It was in every respect a pro tem board of directors, created simply as a matter of legal convenience. In April 1899, the São Paulo Railway, Light and Power Company was still very much a speculative venture. Mackenzie and his associates had yet to secure the Gualco concession and had as yet made no financial commitment to the venture. The São Paulo company was therefore no more than a legal shell, powerless until put in possession of the crucial operating concession still in the hands of Gualco and Souza.[67] Only two of the temporary directors were to have any subsequent standing in the group of companies promoted by William Mackenzie. James Gunn served as a director and as the superintendent of the Toronto Street Railway, while John Maitland Smith, whom Mackenzie had transferred from the offices of the Canadian Northern Railway, was to become the long-serving secretary of the São Paulo company.

Behind the façade of provisional directorships, the first steps were being taken to give the São Paulo company sufficient financial substance to establish itself. On 26 May 1899, in an agreement drawn up by Lash, William Mackenzie defined his rights and obligations in relation to the newly incorporated firm. Although the document acknowledged that Mackenzie 'owns or controls the properties, concessions, franchises, rights and privileges' acquired by Gualco and Souza, there was in fact little evidence to suggest that he had anything more than a tacit understanding to purchase these rights from the Brazilian promoters. None the less, the 26 May agreement declared that the São Paulo company had been created to acquire these 'properties' from Mackenzie and operate them. For his part, Mackenzie contracted to sell to the company all 'properties' he had or might acquire in São Paulo and to purchase or find purchasers for specified amounts of the five million dollars of 'First Mortgage' bonds that the São Paulo company now planned to issue. Mackenzie was also obliged to secure the services of F.S. Pearson as a 'consulting engineer' for the years 1899 and 1900 'without expense to the Company.'

In return for these services, Mackenzie was to receive $6,150,000, of which $150,000 was to be in cash and the remainder in the company's stock. He was also given the right to purchase up to $3,000,000 of the yet-to-be issued bonds at a rate of ninety cents on the dollar. The $2,000,000 in bonds not underwritten by 'Mackenzie and his associates' were not to be issued 'until the same are required for capital expenditure by the company connected with enlargements, extensions and better-ments of its railways and works or of other railways and works acquired by the Company.' The agreement was signed by Mackenzie on his own behalf and by James Gunn, as chairman of the São Paulo company board, and J.M. Smith, as its secretary. The ubiquitous Z.A. Lash witnessed the agreement.[68]

The agreement placed William Mackenzie in an unassailable position of control over the São Paulo company. It gave him ownership of all the voting stock of the young company. Moreover, it placed him in a position to reap a handsome, if not spectacular, return on his investment, which up to this point had been limited to certain legal and promotional expenses. The combined proceeds from common-stock dividends and sale of the discounted bonds would be immense, but only if the Gualco concession could be successfully placed on an operational basis.

It now remained only to finalize arrangements with Gualco and Souza for the transfer of the concession and to initiate construction work before the tolerance of the municipal government was tried beyond repair.

Despite the need for urgency, Mackenzie himself could not spare the time from his hectic railway-promotion activities in Canada to undertake the time-consuming journey from Toronto to New York and on to São Paulo. Accordingly, on 29 May 1899, he assigned powers of attorney to F.S. Pearson and Alexander Mackenzie, a thirty-eight-year-old bachelor lawyer in Lash's office, 'to sign, seal and deliver all such writings, deeds and documents as may be necessary or as they or he may think proper, relating to or in any way connected with, the undertakings and business of the São Paulo Railway, Light and Power Company, Limited,' including the transfer of any concessionary rights.[69] Armed with this authority, Pearson and Mackenzie sailed from New York on the ss *Hevelius* bound for Rio de Janeiro. Accompanying them were Pearson's wife, Mabel, and the three Pearson children; Hugh L. Cooper, a bright young American hydraulic engineer with a quick eye for the generating potential of any stream; and the redoubtable R.C. Brown.

Three pressing tasks awaited this North American mission when it arrived in São Paulo. Most urgently, some start had to be made on construction of the tramway line. This R.C. Brown undertook, working in the nominal employ of Gualco e de Souza, Incorporadores. On 4 July, a fitting day for the American engineer, the first track gangs set to work on the streets of São Paulo, although their progress was severely hampered by the almost complete lack of equipment and material, most of which had only just been ordered from American and European producers by F.S. Pearson's New York office.

Upon the shoulders of Pearson and Mackenzie fell the second task, that of tailoring the Gualco concession to the exact needs of the northern promoters. This was best done, Mackenzie shrewdly concluded, by Gualco and Souza, who had an established rapport with civic officials, rather than by two inexperienced foreigners, neither of whom had yet mastered the Portuguese language. Mackenzie also recognized the necessity of securing competent and well-connected Brazilian legal assistance. In this respect, he was exceptionally fortunate to enlist the services of Gualco's ally, Carlos de Campos, a former secretary of justice in São Paulo, and Dr A.J. Pinto Ferraz, a prominent law professor and legal adviser to the London and Brazil Bank. In December 1898, Gualco and Souza had successfully petitioned the municipal council for permission to erect poles for the distribution of electric power and light in the city. Now, under the guiding influence of Carlos de Campos and Mackenzie, a municipal law was obtained, on 8 July 1899, regulating the distribution of electricity in São Paulo. This in turn opened the way for the authorization, on 30 September, of a contract between the city and Gualco and Souza for the provision of electricity to certain specified areas of São Paulo.[70]

With assured rights for the distribution of electricity within the city, it was now imperative to obtain legislative sanction for the harnessing of a ready source of hydro power. Antônio Gualco had finally managed to purchase suitable lands adjacent to the Cachoeira do Inferno site on the Tietê River, some thirty-six kilometres outside the city. Obtaining legislative sanction to generate and transmit electricity to São Paulo was to prove an involved task, since the site fell under the jurisdiction of another municipality, the town of Parnaíba, and the right to transmit power rested with the state. After Pearson and Cooper had hurriedly surveyed the Parnaíba site, Mackenzie and Campos again applied their legal talents to the question of obtaining appropriate authorization to harness the water power. On 3 August 1899, Gualco, Souza, and, for the first time, Pearson of the São Paulo company, successfully petitioned the State Legislative Congress of São Paulo for the right to expropriate riverside lands necessary for the construction of the Parnaíba dam and the right to erect transmission poles. This was soon followed by a petition in the name of Gualco, Souza, and Pearson to the municipal *câmara* of the town of Parnaíba requesting power to expropriate any lands needed to construct the generating station. The petitioners were quick to emphasize that the power development would bring the town 'extraordinary benefits,' especially since much of the capital employed in the construction would remain in the area 'to facilitate new and profitable undertakings for the progress of the place.' The *câmara* accepted the petition and permitted the North Americans an exemption from local taxes in exchange for a power contract by which the company would illuminate the town streets, the city hall, and the jail.[71]

In the space of just over two months, Pearson and Mackenzie thus transformed the original Gualco concession into an all-embracing privilege to generate and distribute electric power to domestic and industrial users, as well as to apply it to a tramway. The rapidity with which these rights were confirmed was in large measure due to the favourable political *entrée* given the North American promoters by Carlos de Campos and Antônio Gualco. To a lesser degree, it was attributable to the acuity of Pearson and Mackenzie, who mastered the legal and engineering intricacies of the situation in a minimum of time. The remarkable success of Mackenzie and Pearson in acculturating themselves to an alien economic environment greatly helped their efforts to achieve the third objective of their mission to São Paulo, that of obtaining legislative permission for their fledgling company to operate within Brazil's borders. A major step in this direction was accomplished when the President of Brazil, Manuel Ferraz de Campos Sales, acceded to a request by Alexander Mackenzie that the company be given 'the necessary authority to carry on their business in the Republic of Brazil.' The decree stipulated that the company was 'obliged to have a representative in Brazil with full and unlimited powers to act and definitely resolve any questions which may arise either with the Government or with private individuals.' Furthermore, the Canadian company was to abide by Brazilian laws and regulations and to submit any alteration of its by-laws to scrutiny by the federal government. Failure to do so would annul the company's right to operate in Brazil.[72] Alexander Mackenzie announced that the company would offer a 'moral guarantee' that it would abide by the conditions of its charter and by-laws. Alexander Mackenzie, it was also announced, would represent the company in Brazil.

Federal approval was just the first step. If the Canadian-controlled enterprise was to exploit the Gualco concession to best advantage, it would have to obtain the co-operation of the municipal politicians with whom it would have the closest relations. Antônio Prado, the prefect of São Paulo, shared the widespread local belief that Pearson and Mackenzie were no more than 'American bluffers,' eager to turn a quick speculative profit at the expense of São Paulo's untutored municipal politicians. Above all else, the young company could not afford to excite xenophobic hostility to its presence. The Companhia Viação Paulista, whose chances of survival stood to be immeasurably enhanced by the speedy demise of the Canadian company, did much to propagate such sentiment. With the assistance of José Custôdio Alves de Lima, a former Brazilian consul in Canada, Mackenzie cleverly countered this popular scepticism by arranging to take Dr Prado to the São Paulo branch of the London and Brazilian Bank, where bank officials explained to the doubting prefect that William Mackenzie had deposited sufficient funds in London to cover the initial construction costs of the tramway.[73] This had the immediate effect of converting São Paulo's leading civic politician into a staunch proponent of the Canadian enterprise. To reinforce this public-relations *coup*, F.S.

Pearson made several carefully selected public appearances in São Paulo parks and halls throughout July and August. Using Carlos de Campos as an interpreter (the Campos family name alone lent credibility to the new company), Pearson expounded the very tangible benefits that the citizens of São Paulo could expect from electric traction and cheap industrial and domestic electric power. Before their eyes, Pearson waved 'the wand of applied science'[74] and aroused that desire, so close to the hearts of Brazil's urban middle class, to place São Paulo on an equal footing with Paris, New York, and its Argentinian rival, Buenos Aires.

By late September, a mood of hopeful expectancy surrounded every item of news concerning the company and its affairs. More and more the São Paulo Railway, Light and Power Company and the names of its Canadian backers were publicly associated with the Gualco concession. Both Pearson and Mackenzie appeared before the municipal *câmara* and the state congress to explain the company's intentions. Assured of a sympathetic public reception, Mackenzie and Pearson concluded that the time had come to assure outright control of the São Paulo concessions. Their decision was prompted by two further considerations. William Mackenzie was anxiously waiting in Toronto for news of the closing of the deal. Until this vital transaction was performed, Mackenzie would be unable to assure his own financial backers that the deal was clinched and the way open to profits in Latin America. In São Paulo, the Canadian negotiators found further reason for expediting the transfer of control when it was discovered that Gualco was seriously and, most believed, fatally ill.[75] If Gualco should die before the act of transfer was consummated, Mackenzie feared that the whole arrangement might be thrown into legal doubt. Thus, on 28 September 1899, Alexander Mackenzie and F.S. Pearson made their way to Gualco's home at 18 Rua Piratininga in the São Paulo suburb of Liberdade and, before a public notary, took possession of the assorted concessions that the local entrepreneur and his partner had assembled over the preceding two years. Under the terms of the agreement, Francisco Antônio Gualco, 'Italian, married capitalist, a resident of Montreal,' and Antônio Augusto de Souza, 'Brazilian, married capitalist,' ceded to William Mackenzie all their rights to the concessions for power generation and distribution in return for which they received 248 contos in Brazilian funds.[76] Based on the prevailing exchange rate of approximately 7½d. per milréis in 1899, Gualco and Souza received about £7,750 (or at an exchange rate of $4.85 to the pound, $37,587 Canadian) for their concession.[77] Considering that neither Gualco nor Souza had invested any capital in their venture, £7,750 represented a fair return on what amounted to just over two years of intensive legal preparations, lobbying, and promotion of the São Paulo concessions. It also seems very probable that Gualco at least took delivery of a large block of São Paulo company common stock, stock that could have been carved out of William Mackenzie's large personal holdings.[78]

On 9 October Alexander Mackenzie appeared in the office of the secretary of the prefecture of São Paulo and there filed the transfer documents. After paying a small fee, he met with Antônio Prado, who ratified the company's provisional plans for its first tramway lines to Penha de Franca, Barra Funda, Avenida Paulista, and Bom Retiro. Prado's imprimatur erased the last rumours of an 'American bluff.'

Within a month of signing away his rights to the São Paulo concession, Francisco Antônio Gualco died, at the age of fifty-nine; the result, in all probability, of a heart attack.[79] 'It is too bad that Gualco,' a saddened F.S. Pearson wrote to R.C. Brown, 'after all his efforts to promote this enterprise and, just at the time when he could see success, should have been taken away. It is difficult for us to imagine that he is gone.'[80] Gualco was thus deprived of the chance of seeing São Paulo's first electric tram move through the crowds along Rua Barão de Limeira on that day in May 1900. The most that Gualco may have witnessed was the steadily increasing flow of imported electrical and engineering equipment that was arriving in São Paulo from the port of Santos throughout the last months of the nineteenth century.

The crates of generating equipment, disassembled penstocks, and knocked-down Brill cars signified that São Paulo was about to enter the twentieth century in more ways than one. As the local citizenry observed the work of Hugh Cooper at the Parnaíba power site and the track crews of R.C. Brown on their streets, they were confronted with tangible evidence of the presence of North America in South America. In late 1901, when the directors of the young company issued their first promotional booklet, it was to this same image that they turned to describe their enterprise in South America. The intention of *North America in South America*, a large-folio volume copiously illustrated with scenes of trolleys, dams, and American generating equipment, was to convey the impression to investors that in São Paulo they had found a solid and remunerative investment. 'Of São Paulo a great deal might be written, much good, little bad,' the text stressed. 'The language is bad (Portuguese), that is to say, there were only a few of us who ever really did master it. But the City itself is beautifully built, and is located upon a plateau, 2,500 feet above the sea and about 45 miles from its seaport, Santos, Brazil ... São Paulo is a remarkably healthy City, and has a death rate less than New York City. The City is finely laid out, has well paved streets, splendid buildings, both [sic] commercial, public and domestic. A modern gravity water system, sewage system, sanitary commission and hospitals are all to be found and in a state of development that challenges your admiration, and gives you a feeling of comfortable assurance about your surroundings. The State of São Paulo was the birth place of the Republic of Brazil and the *Paulistas* run the Government, furnish the Presidents and in a general way are omnipresent. The *Paulistas* are often called the South American Yankees.'[81]

CHAPTER TWO

In Pursuit of a 'Rich Return':
Toronto Capitalists Look Abroad

Torontonians must have been puzzled that a public-utilities company operating in a distant, Latin American city chose to establish its head office in their city's financial district. Only a few would have had the vaguest notion of the location of São Paulo, while most would have been intrigued by what had drawn Canadian capitalists to so foreign a locale. There was one simple explanation for this. The São Paulo Railway, Light and Power Co. Ltd had gone to Brazil in search of profits. In return, it offered cheap, efficient electric power, one of the most constructive forces in urban industrial life.

While climatic and cultural differences made Toronto and São Paulo very dissimilar at first sight, Toronto capitalists had been quick to realize that skills acquired during Toronto's emergence as a modern urban centre could readily be applied to similar problems in São Paulo. In Brazil there was, of course, added risk engendered by the lingering political instability of the early 1890s and by the economic precariousness of a country with a staple-based economy. None the less, Brazil offered an inviting prospect for foreign capital, especially when one considered the absence of the 'progressive' forces that had begun to limit and oversee the capitalist process in North America, most notably the incipient distrust of privately owned utilities and the suspicion of 'money power.'

The inclination of Toronto capitalists to risk money in Brazil was explained by William Hume Blake, a prominent Toronto lawyer and a close friend of the promoters of the São Paulo venture. Blake visited Brazil nearly a decade after the initial investment of 1899. 'To the writer, at least,' Blake reflected in a memoir, 'it seems that present conditions make for permanence, that causes of disturbance and upheaval are quite remarkably absent, and that there may be found in Brazil as stable a foundation upon which to erect the superstructure of commercial enterprise as can be discovered elsewhere.' Brazilians, Blake reported, were 'sensible of the desirability of developing their resources, and to that end of attracting foreign capital and are well aware that in order to do so the rights of foreign capital must be strictly preserved.' Secondly, Brazilians had 'a great respect for the accomplished physical fact, and would never be likely to interfere with the legitimate operation of an established business.' If the city fathers of Birmingham were prepared to usurp the role of private capital in the utilities business and if Ontario politicians were willing to entertain notions of 'people's power,' the promoters of the São Paulo venture need have no worries about the security of their investment. 'The series of tendencies grouped under the broad and somewhat misleading name of "socialism,"' Blake concluded, 'are scarcely apparent in the country.'[1]

Judged from a broader perspective, certain similarities emerged between São Paulo and Toronto. Both were growing commercial and industrial centres vying to assert their new-found economic prowess over the older commercial centres of their respective countries. Although founded in the 1530s, São Paulo had not flourished commercially through the next three centuries, principally because of the rugged barrier of the Serra do Mar, the mountain range between it and the coast. With the expansion of its railway connections by the late 1890s, however, the state of São Paulo was finally able to establish a remunerative trade in coffee and attract a steady flow of industrious European immigrants. As a consequence, the city of São Paulo, with its population of a quarter of a million, found itself in a position to challenge the long-established commercial dominance of Rio de Janeiro, with its magnificent harbour, its banks, and its extensive network of foreign commercial ties.[2]

Similarly, Toronto, with a population of 208,000 in 1901, was beginning to challenge the commercial pre-eminence of Montreal. Blessed by geography, Montreal had been well placed to take advantage of Canada's developing staple trades, and in doing so had established itself at the centre of the Canadian banking and transportation systems. Montreal exercised a great magnetic force on the Canadian economy: not only did railways and shipping converge on its harbour, but the financial under-pinnings of Canadian commerce were governed from that city's boardrooms. St James Street became synonymous with Montreal's financial supremacy. It was, after all, to James Ross and his Canadian Pacific Railway associates that Antônio Gualco had first brought the São Paulo tramway concession in 1898. Toronto had always held Montreal's sway over the country's commerce in jealous regard, and during the latter half of the nineteenth century mounted a challenge to its supremacy. Aided by geographic and economic trends that favoured its central location, Toronto began to accumulate the attributes of metropolitan power. Banking, manufacturing, and transportation facilities all prospered as the city came to fill a service function not only for its own Ontario hinterland but also for the Canadian West.

By the turn of the century, Toronto could even boast its own, albeit incipient, transcontinental railway, a railway that would offer a competitive threat to the Montreal-based Canadian Pacific. Cleverly assembled out of an assortment of western branch-line railways by William Mackenzie and Donald Mann, the Canadian Northern Railway epitomized Toronto's new-found commercial stature in Canada. Although it would not be completed until 1915, the Canadian Northern prospered, on the one hand because it offered westerners an alternative to the much-begrudged monopoly of the Canadian Pacific, and on the other hand because it drew upon the commercial prowess of Toronto.[3] It was this same commercial prowess that would ultimately find an outlet in the utilities industry of south-eastern Brazil.

It was in large degree the emergence of a new breed of Canadian capitalist that enabled Toronto to extend its commercial sway to the western plains of Canada and the emerging industrial heartland of Brazil. Toronto's success was rooted in its ability to assemble the business talent and connections necessary to partake in the global development of what has been called the golden era of 'finance capitalism.' Finance capitalism denoted an ability to deploy large amounts of capital whenever and wherever promising opportunities for its investment arose. It also entailed a fundamental change in the nature of capitalist 'risk taking' and a significant alteration of the relation between the investor and the manager in capitalist enterprise. These changes were drawn forth by the huge capital demands generated by new technology-based industries and the turn-of-the-century trend towards industrial consolidation. Given impetus by the desire of Europe and America to emulate England's early advances in industry and railways, the search for capital became a prime ingredient in modern large-scale business.

London, the traditional centre of world finance, saw itself joined and partially challenged by the emergence of new financial centres, notably New York, Brussels, and Paris, all of which were now scrambling to purvey capital to the promoters of schemes on every continent of the globe. This function had traditionally been performed by the investment or merchant banker, a financial intermediary who had first honed his talents on the capital demands thrown up by the Napoleonic wars. By the late nineteenth century, the merchant banker found himself in a position of immense power as the indispensable link between promoter and investor, a channel through which savings were directed to long-term investment. 'Investment bankers, operating in a virtual regulatory vacuum,' as one historian of American finance capitalism has remarked, 'were largely free to respond as they saw fit to the changing market forces of the times.'[4] This development saw the investment banker move away from the traditional, essentially passive role in which he simply provided capital, to a more active role, which saw him venture into the realms of actual promotion and management of enterprises. Wall Street and the City now both demanded that their men be admitted to the inner sanctums of industry, either to promote new undertakings or to watch over established investments.

Finance capitalism called forth new financial methods. The demands of new industry had strained the traditional arteries of finance with an unprecedented flow of capital, thereby placing the established norms of raising capital under severe stress. To cope with this, financiers devised new means of handling large investments and, above all, of diminishing the often enormous risk involved. Fearful of the consequences that the collapse of a single railway or industrial promotion might have upon the whole investment community, investment bankers resorted to syndicate financing, by which they were able not only to draw on more varied sources for their capital requirements but also to minimize their risk and at the same time centralize control of their invested capital. Organized and directed by one financier or financial house, usually called the 'manager,' the syndicate offered an ideal means of apportioning the investment underwriters' responsibilities, risks, and rewards. Furthermore, by virtue of the near-dictatorial control of the 'manager,' it placed tremendous power at the disposal of the syndicate to impose its will on the course of any stock promotion or industrial merger it undertook.

Not surprisingly, the ability not only of government but of the financial community itself to regulate this new form of financial management lagged far behind the actual progress of syndicate financing. While the syndicate did facilitate the expeditious capitalization of both North American and European industry, it also opened the way to new forms of financial abuse. By virtue of its tight, secretive discipline, the syndicate was able to dictate the market conditions under which any one of its offerings eventually found its way into the hands of the small investors who constituted the bedrock investing public. Furthermore, the syndicate could both minimize its own risk and maximize its own profit by generously providing its participants with stock bonuses as a gratuitous accompaniment to any bond-underwriting agreement. The syndicate had such sway over the capital-hungry promoters of any venture that it was also in a position to 'overcapitalize' or 'water' the capitalization of any undertaking. Such control was frequently guaranteed by the placing of financial representatives on the boards of the very companies the syndicates had promoted, a process now known as 'interlocking.' Abuses like these were not, of course, pervasive, but in the United States they were prevalent enough to arouse widespread criticism before the First World War of the so-called money power, culminating in the famous Pujo Committee hearings of the House Banking and Currency Committee. Although financial capitalism's repute in the public's eyes down to the fateful 'crash' of 1929 was to become increasingly tarnished, its methods and practitioners were undeniably at the heart of the unbounded industrial growth of much of America and Europe in the first decades of the twentieth century.[5] This pattern was duplicated, as usual on a less grand scale, in Canada.

Like Brazil, Canada at the turn of the century was a nation incapable of meeting its own capital needs. A young country that needed immense amounts of capital to build up its economic infrastructure but whose small population had little ability to save and invest, Canada was forced to rely upon the willingness of foreign investors to underwrite its development. While institutional investors, especially the insurance companies, were making significant progress by 1900 in cultivating investment by Canadians in Canada, the successful promotion of Canada's railways and industries remained very much governed by the disposition of English and, to a lesser degree, American investors to place their funds in Canadian ventures.[6] By the end of the nineteenth century, Canadian railways like the Grand Trunk and the Canadian Pacific, together with Canadian municipalities, had an established financial credibility in the

English financial markets. It was through similar channels of investment that William Mackenzie moved to underwrite the enormous capital demands of his Canadian Northern Railway network. 'The final reliance of Canadian railway expansion,' wrote D.B. Hanna, Mackenzie's financial lieutenant, 'was, of course, on the comparatively small British investor. But with so many opportunities to place money all over the world, this multitudinous host could not be depended on to produce, at a day or two's notice, all the money that was required to build a thousand miles of track from Pembroke to Port Arthur.'[7] The market had to be 'made.' Faced with this task, Mackenzie was obliged to forge links with English merchant bankers skilled both at tapping the savings of Britain's 'multitudinous host' and at building powerful syndicates that would erase the risk and ensure the smooth transfer of railway securities from promoter to investor. 'To the windward of the small investor,' Hanna picturesquely noted, 'there must, therefore, be anchorages in the deeps of underwriting.'[8]

The spectacular success of William Mackenzie in charting his way to 'the deeps of underwriting' was due to his reputation as a wily and profit-minded railway contractor and to his ability to forge links with influential members of Canada's legal and financial community. 'I consider him one of the great creative men we have produced in Canada,' Joseph Flavelle, long-time president of the National Trust Company and successful meat packer, noted respectfully in 1906. 'His courage, capacity, astuteness and resourcefulness command my admiration ... [as do] his remarkable talent and capacity for planning and carrying out big things.'[9] Mackenzie's rise to this stature was the product of his irrepressible urge to succeed, an urge moulded by the combination of his humble Ontario backwoods origins and his canny Scottish Presbyterian ancestry.

Mackenzie was born in a log house on the outskirts of the small town of Kirkfield, just east of Lake Simcoe, in 1849. After an inauspicious attempt at a teaching career in Toronto, he returned to Kirkfield in the early 1870s to join his older brother, Alexander, in the lumber trade. A contract to provide railway ties for the expanding railway network in Toronto's hinterland gave young Mackenzie his first taste of railway construction and led, in 1872, to a small contract for the Victoria Railway, a line running between Lindsay and Haliburton. A later contract on the Credit Valley Railway brought Mackenzie into contact with James Ross, the line's construction manager, and Herbert S. Holt, Ross's hard-driving young

Irish assistant. Ross was impressed by Mackenzie's ability to meet deadlines and by the frugality with which he performed his tasks. Throughout this period, Mackenzie supplemented his lumber and railroading activities by supplying local flour and saw mills with steam engines, which allowed the mills to operate despite the winter freezing of their mill-ponds. By 1880, the young Scottish Canadian had built a prosperous, diversified business career in his home district, an achievement he reinforced by serving as reeve of Eldon township in 1880–1.[10]

Mackenzie's transformation from successful local entrepreneur to the doer of 'big things' came in 1884 when, through James Ross (now superintendent of construction for the prairie stretches of the CPR), he obtained a contract to construct bridges through the Kicking Horse Pass section of Canada's first transcontinental railway. Once again, Mackenzie met his deadlines, despite the fact that he operated on the slenderest of budgets and employed construction methods and materials at which other contractors scoffed. It was as a CPR contractor that Mackenzie met Donald Mann, the man who was eventually to share his greatest endeavours as a railway builder. Another Ontario-born Scot, Mann was slightly Mackenzie's junior; however, in terms of ability and drive, he was his future partner's equal. Like Mackenzie, he realized that once a contractor had perfected his method and assembled a competent crew, he stood to reap large profits from railway work. It was on account of the relentless – if well-rewarded – efforts of men like Mackenzie, Mann, Ross, and Holt that the Canadian Pacific was completed in record time in late 1885. When the contract that had been their main source of work ended, Mackenzie and Mann, in partnership with Ross and Holt, spent the next six years earning handsome profits building railways in Manitoba, Alberta, Saskatchewan, and Maine (where the CPR found its oceanic outlet). By 1892, however, the lucrative tide of railway construction had turned, and the four partners decided to go their separate ways. Ironically, three of the four returned to eastern Canada, where they capitalized on a new wave of Canadian development fever, this time in the cities. Ross and Holt soon established themselves in the tramway and utilities business in Montreal, while Mackenzie, in a feat of considerable financial legerdemain, wrested control of the Toronto Street Railway from the city's municipal politicians and placed it on an extremely profitable basis of private operation. Donald Mann, for his part, went abroad in search of railway contracts in lands as disparate as Chile and China.

By the mid-1890s, Mackenzie had acquired a reputation as the first person to knock on opportunity's door wherever it might be found in Canada. Some may have been critical of his sharp bargaining practices; but all marvelled at his financial success. Mackenzie was, as one historian has stressed, 'a product of the Ontario backwoods' who had 'remained essentially a frontier entrepreneur with a recklessly expansionist backwoods development strategy.'[11] Although his recklessness, especially in financial matters, was eventually to bring about his ignominious downfall, his urge to exploit the entrepreneurial opportunities thrown up at the frontiers of new regions and technologies placed Mackenzie at the centre not only of the building of Canada's second transcontinental railway but also of the development of public utilities in cities as scattered as Winnipeg, Toronto, and São Paulo.

It was a measure of Mackenzie's indefatigable energy and entrepreneurial dexterity that he could simultaneously manage not only the promotional but also the operational and financial affairs of railway and utilities ventures spread across three continents. Beginning with the Toronto Street Railway in the early 1890s, Mackenzie steadily expanded his activities as the decade progressed. Traction companies were promoted in São Paulo, Winnipeg, Saint John, Cuba, Jamaica, and Birmingham. With the exception of Birmingham, Mackenzie was able to apply his experience in negotiating railway contracts to the intricate business of drawing up utility concessions that both ensured the promoters substantial returns on their investment and closed the door on potential competitors. It was, ironically, with the object of creating competition that Mackenzie, once again allied with Donald Mann, embarked upon his greatest project, the Canadian Northern Railway. Mindful that the Canadian Pacific's monopoly irked western Canadian sensibilities, Mackenzie and Mann devised a strategy to build a second railway across the prairies, one that would provide farmers with another outlet to the sea and a chance to undercut the much-maligned rates of the CPR. In return, the shrewd contractors would collect largesse in the form of land grants and bond guarantees from grateful provincial governments and, eventually, the federal government as well.

Beginning with the Lake Manitoba Railway and Canal Company and the Winnipeg and Great North Railway and Steamship Company, Mackenzie and Mann managed to assemble enough branch lines to enable them, in December 1898, to announce their intention of transforming their regional system into a national line. Although the subsequent history of the Canadian Northern's trials and tribulations, ending in its nationalization during the First World War, is of only passing importance to the development of the São Paulo enterprise, this railway venture gave William Mackenzie tremendous prestige in the eyes of Canadian businessmen and investors and provided him with a wealth of experience in dealing with the financiers and politicians whose support was so essential to bold development schemes, whether in Canada or, as it was to turn out, in Brazil. In the years down to the First World War, there was no hint that the Canadian Northern's tangled financial affairs would eventually overtake it. Instead, Mackenzie was universally portrayed as Canada's boldest and most successful promoter on the ever-expanding frontier of railway and utilities development. As T.D. Regehr, the historian of the Canadian Northern, has opined: 'Both William Mackenzie and Donald Mann were Protestant Ontario pioneers. The Protestant work ethic and the challenge of developing and utilizing a continental treasurehouse of natural resources provided both the purpose and the method of their undertakings. The satisfaction of building something permanent and worthwhile was of far greater importance to them than the mere accumulation of wealth.'[12]

The hub of the Mackenzie, Mann and Company empire lay in the Toronto Railway Chambers at the corner of Toronto and King Streets in Toronto. From these offices the construction and operations of varied tramway and railroad enterprises were planned and directed. Through its portals walked the engineers, bankers, lawyers, and financiers upon whom Mackenzie relied to assemble the capital and material for his far-flung endeavours. Within blocks of the Toronto Railway Chambers stood the banks, trust companies, brokerage houses, and legal firms that serviced the daily needs of Mackenzie's companies. Despite the city's economic growth at the turn of the century, the business leaders of Toronto remained an exclusive community, closely intertwined and capable of prodigious collective effort in pursuit of shared goals. In an era when there were few legal prohibitions governing the financial community's activities, lawyers, bankers, and promoters snugly ensconced themselves on the boards of both the companies they had created and the firms that serviced the financial and legal needs of their creations. They showed no qualms at participating in a company's originating syndicate and then taking a seat on its board, while at the same time acting as an officer of a prominent bank to which the same company was applying for a capital loan. The lines that defined possible conflicts of interest in turn-of-the-century Canadian business were very faintly drawn. Such cohesiveness had the distinct benefit of providing promoters who held the respect of those within this omniscient business circle with a greatly enhanced chance of survival for their various enterprises. Once admitted to the circle, a new promotion was assured of the full benefit of the best legal and financial corporate support available in Canada, while the purveyors of these services were given an opportunity of participating in these ventures and thereby reaping handsome rewards for their co-operation and loyalty.

Besides Mackenzie himself, only one other person occupied a truly indispensable position in the Mackenzie syndicates. Zebulon Aiton Lash, a senior partner in the Toronto legal firm of Blake, Lash and Cassels, was not only present at the inception of nearly all Mackenzie's creations but played an invaluable part in nursing innumerable railways, power companies, and public utilities to a prosperous maturity. The decision to establish the head office of the São Paulo Railway, Light and Power Company in Toronto was primarily occasioned by the desire of its initial promoters to avail themselves of the incisive legal mind of Z.A. Lash. The legal talents of Lash and his associates constitute the one uniquely Canadian ingredient in the early history of the São Paulo enterprise. If not for its principals' desire to avail themselves of the services of Blake, Lash and Cassels, the São Paulo company could easily have been domiciled in any other location that offered a suitable framework of company law to accommodate the promoters' intentions.

Lash was born in Newfoundland in 1846, but spent his childhood in Dundas, Ontario, before attending the University of Toronto and Osgoode Hall Law School. He was called to the bar in 1868 and practised in Toronto until he was appointed deputy minister of justice in the federal Liberal government of Alexander Mackenzie in 1874. During his tenure in Ottawa, he had a formative influence on the implementation of Canada's first federal bank act. A prominent Liberal, Lash returned to private practice in Toronto when the Macdonald Tories recaptured power in Ottawa in 1878. Lash was then invited to join the well-established firm of influential Liberals Edward and Samuel Blake. He brought to the firm a special competence in commercial and financial legal matters and in this capacity was soon drawing clients from the Toronto business community, including the Canadian Bank of Commerce and, later, the embryonic Canadian Northern Railway. Lash possessed an infallible talent for providing promoters with superbly framed charters and a keen eye for the legal worthiness of trust deeds, bond guarantees, and concession documents. 'It is considered,' noted *Saturday Night* on his death in 1920, 'that he had few peers anywhere in drafting a business agreement, penetrating an obscurity in existing laws, or framing a statute of a clear and binding character.' Lash was never a 'gum-shoe worker,' but was instead 'a man of the most scrupulous personal honor,' whose 'keen dark eyes could see through a problem in shorter time than those of any contemporary Canadian.'[13] D.B. Hanna, who worked closely with Lash in many boardrooms, later commented that 'though others might embody an intention in a series of paragraphs apparently beyond criticism, his mastery of precision and shade was such that he could clothe it in language which had the exactitude of a multiplication table and the clarity of a mirror.'[14]

Mackenzie's ability to command reliable legal advice in Canada was matched by his ability to establish his reputation in the capital markets of England and to attract the savings of English investors. With the metamorphosis of the Canadian Northern from a regional to a national railway, it had become apparent that the restricted Canadian capital market could not underwrite the full extent of Mackenzie's ambitions. Although Canadian railways were no strangers to the British investing public, neither Mackenzie nor Mann had the time to devote to the involved business of cultivating the British market for the stocks and bonds of a largely unknown Canadian railway. They were therefore singularly fortunate to make the acquaintance of Robert Montgomery ('Monty') Horne-Payne. The scion of a prominent English legal family, Horne-Payne had made an early and impressive start to his financial career. As a member of the prestigious City brokerage firm of Sperling and Co., he had, at the age of twenty-two, skilfully orchestrated the acquisition in 1894 of the Victoria Electric Railway and Lighting Company in British Columbia. Within a few years, he had solidly established himself as the principal influence in the affairs of the British Columbia Electric Railway, a British-controlled public utility providing traction, light, and heat services to the residents of Vancouver Island and New Westminster. Exercising tight control over the BCER from London, Horne-Payne acted as chairman of the profitable utility from 1897 to 1928.

The secret of Horne-Payne's success lay in his deft manipulation of the English money market. He had an unerring sense of financial timing and an encyclopaedic grasp of the habits of English investors. He frequently boasted of the accuracy with which he could predict how many bonds or stocks any English town or village could be expected to take in a Canadian venture. Horne-Payne was alleged to have placed half a billion dollars' worth of Canadian securities on the British market before he died in 1929.[15]

By the time William Mackenzie approached Horne-Payne in 1900 or 1901 with a request to handle the financial needs of the Canadian Northern, the English financier had important and extensive ties with the Canadian economy. He had severed his connection with the Sperling firm and had established himself as chairman of the British Empire Trust Company in the City. Confined to a wheelchair by a spinal disorder, Horne-Payne seldom ventured into the capital, choosing instead to direct his affairs from 'Merry Mead,' his country estate in Essex.[16] For visiting Canadian capitalists like Horne-Payne's close friend Sir William Van Horne, 'Merry Mead' was an obligatory stop on any tour of England.[17] Millions of dollars of securities bearing the name of the Canadian Northern Railway and its various allied companies passed through the offices of the British Empire Trust Company. Horne-Payne was thus able to provide Mackenzie with two invaluable services. In the first place, he could co-ordinate the syndicates of English financiers necessary to underwrite Mackenzie's Canadian enterprises; and secondly, he could generate favourable press comment on these same enterprises so as to ensure that the all-important small English investors would be predisposed to take up the Canadian securities offered them. As D.B. Hanna somewhat grandiloquently put it, Horne-Payne was 'a man of extraordinary mentality and financial genius. His services to Canada are really registered in the creation of vast agricultural regions out of solitude, and in the firm establishing of communities from quiet hamlets to rushing cities, where the highest amenities of civilization have succeeded the wandering buffalo, and have substituted the saw mill for the towering pine.'[18]

Even with Lash to guide the legal fortunes of his enterprises and Horne-Payne to harness the power of English investors, the entrepreneurial framework of Mackenzie's São Paulo venture was still lacking in one respect. William Mackenzie was by experience a railroad engineer.

His reputation rested on his ability to lay track across the prairies at minimum expense and maximum speed. For his forays into the urban tramway business in Toronto and Montreal he could rely to some extent upon this expertise. None the less, he lacked the technical competence needed to exploit fully the lucrative possibilities of the electric-utilities revolution. It was possible for him to graft Jamaican or Brazilian public-utilities ventures onto the legal and financial structure of his railroading ventures, but it was not possible, especially since the Canadian Northern increasingly monopolized his time and talents, to lend his technical competence to their development. What was needed, Mackenzie quickly realized, was an engineer whose skills had been developed in the age of electricity rather than the age of railroads. Once again, Mackenzie was singularly lucky to locate an associate who was without parallel in his field.

In the summer of 1892, William Mackenzie was introduced by B.F. Pearson, the Halifax lawyer and promoter, to a young New England engineer, Fred Stark Pearson, who by the age of thirty-two was already being hailed as America's most innovative electrical engineer. 'Dr. Pearson was first and foremost an engineer in the fullest and best sense of the word,' the *General Electric Review* later observed; 'he was a builder, a constructor, a man who carried through great schemes to a successful conclusion; he was one who met many different kinds of difficulties and obstacles, both technical and financial, and overcame them all. His whole life was spent in converting the forces of nature to the useful service of man.'[19] In a career that was to span just three decades, Pearson made a significant contribution to the public-utility industries of his native United States, Canada, Mexico, Spain, the Caribbean, and Brazil. 'It is said,' an early colleague commented, referring to Pearson's Spanish power projects, 'that Caesar dammed the rivers of Spain for the purpose of war to enable him to destroy his enemies; Pearson dammed the same rivers for the purpose of peace to save life and to make it better worth living.'[20] Pearson was a technological missionary, carrying the message and the means of electricity into urban America and then abroad to lands eager to emulate the prosperity of North America. If he was also the servant of business profits, he never lost sight of 'the vision of the more perfect future' for his fellow man.[21]

Pearson was born in 1861 in Lowell, Massachusetts, the son of a railway engineer. The death of the senior Pearson in 1876 left the family in financial straits and forced young Fred to take a job as a station assistant on the Boston and Lowell Railway. This did not prevent Pearson from pursuing his fascination with physics and chemistry to the campus of Tufts College, where he enrolled in 1879. After a year-long interlude at the Massachusetts Institute of Technology, Pearson was back at Tufts adding to his reputation as a hard-working, quick-witted student. Constantly short of money, the young engineer financed his education by continuing to work as a station master. Exposure to the railway allowed Pearson to marry his theoretical knowledge of physics to the practical demands of applied engineering. It was said that in order to minimize his time at the station, Pearson devised a solenoid tripping mechanism that warned him, as he studied, of the approach of each train and allowed him to arrive punctually on the platform as it arrived.[22]

Pearson exhibited his keenest interest in mathematics and, upon graduation in 1883, he eagerly accepted an instructorship in the subject at Tufts. At this time, he made the acquaintance of Robert Calthrop Brown, a fellow student and son of Professor Benjamin Brown, who had taught physics to the undergraduate Pearson. By 1884, Pearson had rounded out his academic career with a Master of Mechanical Arts degree from Tufts, just in time to take an interest in electrical engineering. Responding to the demand for trained engineers produced by the nation's booming electrical industry,[23] Tufts had established a department of electrical engineering. Pearson was immediately captivated by the possibilities of electricity, partly because it demanded a thorough knowledge of physics and mathematics, but more importantly because, as a new, evolving science, it engaged his inventiveness and his penchant for applying the theoretical to the realm of the practical.

Even in his mid-twenties, Pearson was plagued by a frail constitution, a condition made all the more pronounced by the unflagging energy he poured into his teaching and engineering activities. It was in search of a respite from this trying routine that Pearson first visited Brazil in 1887. Invited by a former college chum to investigate some gold properties in the state of São Paulo, Pearson, who had recently married, decided to combine the pleasures of a southern honeymoon with the exploration of a prospective investment. A sea voyage of twenty-eight days brought the couple to Rio, where the two were treated to a memorable ride up the steep sides of Corcovado on the inclined-plane railway recently put into operation by the Brazilian engineer Pereira Passos. The search for gold in

São Paulo, however, proved fruitless, although it was later said that Pearson gained an indelible impression of the formidable topography of the Serra do Mar on his overland journey from Rio to São Paulo. The Brazilian trip none the less provided only a pleasant diversion from Pearson's determination to plunge into the promising world of electrical development in his native United States.

In 1888, Pearson forsook the academic world and entered his first business venture. He helped organize two electric-light companies in the Boston suburbs of Somerville and Woburn and, at a salary of $2,500 a year, took up the duties of manager and treasurer for both concerns. The Woburn and Somerville Electric Light companies were immediate successes, in large measure as a result of Pearson's skill in designing boilers and generators capable of producing sufficient power to serve large urban areas. Herein lay the key to Pearson's ultimate renown as an electrical engineer. He defied prevailing notions and theories about the limits of practicable electrical-power generation and, at the same time, devised new methods of boosting the productivity of generators and lengthening the distance of efficient power transmission. 'He was always leading his profession,' one of Pearson's colleagues from these early years recalled, 'in the demands which he made upon the manufacturers for increase in size of engine, dynamo or transformer, for the highest practical efficiency, for the highest operating pressure; in fact, he was always pushing everything and everybody to the limit ... His work was permanent and reliable, and eminently practical and successful.'[24]

The success of the Somerville and Woburn electrifications brought Pearson to the attention of Henry Melville Whitney, a steamship operator and real-estate speculator who had adeptly bought up a series of horse-tram companies in Boston and was eager to solidify his grip on the city's transit system through electrification.[25] Whitney lured Pearson away from his Somerville post and appointed him chief engineer of the West End Street Railway. By 1892, Pearson had directed the electrification of nearly all of Boston's tram lines and had thereby brought about the early retirement of 9,000 horses.[26] The key to the electrified system was a large, central generating station on Albany Street in Boston, equipped with 500-kilowatt generating machines that surpassed the capacity of all previous dynamos. Drawing an ever-larger salary and widespread acclaim, Pearson moved on in 1894 to a position as chief engineer of the Metropolitan Street Railway in New York, another Whitney promotion.

The enormous 96th Street power station, generating 52,000 kilowatts of power from a battery of 1,500 kilowatt machines, brought new accolades for Pearson. Pearson's greatest challenge in New York came from the problems of distributing power. In response to civic politicians' exasperation with the growing tangle of overhead wires, Pearson devised a costly but practical system of supplying power through underground conduits implanted in the streets along the tramway routes.[27]

Pearson's remarkable capacity for innovation in electrical engineering was the product of the ease with which he could move between the testing laboratories of the large electrical manufacturers and the operating utilities that relied upon their *matériel*. New England was the seedbed of the young American electrical industry: by keeping in constant touch with the developing giants of the field, such as the Thomson-Houston Company at Lynn, Pearson could follow each new piece of electrical apparatus from design to application. Success in the utilities industry went to the man who stayed at the forefront of the industry's rapidly advancing technology. Pearson put himself in the vanguard of this movement, tackling and solving problems of polyphase direct-current power generation, transmission-line insulation, track construction and bonding, and switchboard control.

Individually these technical advances were not of outstanding significance, but cumulatively they were to have a revolutionary impact. The West End and the 96th Street power stations, like the massive hydro-generating project at Niagara Falls, caught the nation's attention and accelerated the pace of nation-wide electrification. In everyday parlance, electricity was soon 'white coal' to the American public. 'In these cases of pioneer innovation,' the historian of the early years of the electric industry has remarked, 'the size of the investment and the publicity the installation received were the prime factors which distinguish it from the earlier cases which cannot be labeled acts of pioneer innovation. Underlying these factors of investment size and favourable publicity were the technical characteristics which permitted reliable and economical operation. These technical characteristics resulted from the vision of the pioneer innovator, who saw the place that innovation could occupy in the economy and had the technical ability to develop those characteristics.'[28]

Throughout the early 1890s, as his reputation grew, Pearson gathered about him a close group of associates, men who served as apostles for his innovative ideas and who often relieved the strain imposed by each project. Since it was not uncommon for Pearson to be engaged at any one time in several electrical developments along the American Atlantic seaboard, he had to be able to call upon a capable group of subordinates. Given his reputation as an innovator and his extensive connections with the academic and electrical manufacturing world, Pearson had little difficulty in attracting talented followers. From Tufts, for instance, he enlisted R.C. Brown, his former student and friend, who oversaw the installation of the generating equipment at Somerville and in the West End power station. Elihu Thomson and E.W. Rice at the Thomson-Houston Company (which, in 1892, merged with Edison General Electric to become General Electric) in Lynn, Massachusetts, provided advice on the practicality of Pearson's schemes. For operating personnel, F.A. Huntress of the Worcester Consolidated Street Railway and T.W. Bevan of the United Electric Light Company in Springfield, Massachusetts, were recruited to superintend the daily operations of the generating plants and tramway systems in New York and Boston. Louis J. Hirt was hired away from the Cleveland Clutch Company to serve as Pearson's master mechanic. The linchpin of the whole organization was W.P. Plummer, who, as Pearson's personal secretary, valiantly tried to co-ordinate his peripatetic employer's frantic round of business obligations.

In later years, when members of this small circle of electrical engineers reminisced about the formative years of the Pearson enterprises, they all recalled the tremendous feeling of camaraderie that pervaded their working relationships. Men like Brown, Bevan, and Huntress held Pearson in deep esteem (their letters frequently referred to him as a 'wizard' and 'genius'), and they maintained a fierce, lifelong loyalty to him. Fred Huntress, dying of cancer in 1926, refused to leave his work at the Brazilian Traction offices in Toronto and insisted even on his deathbed that he would return to his desk the next day.[29] Exposure to the dazzling brilliance of F.S. Pearson marked a man for life.

With his team of loyal engineers, Pearson had a pool of talent upon which he could draw whenever a new promotional opportunity presented itself. As engineers, they were undoubtedly drawing salaries well in excess of what was the norm for electrical engineers – Pearson himself was reputed to be earning $75,000 a year by the time he reached New York in 1894. None the less, there was a large measure of devotion in their motivation. Brown, who could have commanded a handsome salary anywhere in North America by the late 1890s, chose instead to oblige

Pearson by taking up an arduous and demanding assignment in distant São Paulo. The only deficiency in the expertise of the Pearson team was in the area of hydraulic engineering. In New England, with its lack of large, fast-flowing rivers, electricity was thermally generated. Pearson rectified this shortcoming when he made the acquaintance of Hugh L. Cooper, a bumptious but clever young hydraulic engineer from Minnesota. Cooper was to prove an invaluable addition to the Pearson circle, especially when work was undertaken in countries like Canada and Brazil, where rivers abounded.

Engineers were not the only colleagues that Pearson's brilliance attracted. Projects of the magnitude of the West End power station would have been condemned to a blueprint existence without the transforming power of such promoters as H.M. Whitney, who could muster the efficient capital backing and concessionary rights needed to place Pearson's technical advances at the disposal of investors. As his interests expanded, Pearson found himself inexorably drawn into the world of finance capital. To syndicates aspiring to undertake traction and utility projects, the association of Pearson as a consulting engineer lent an immediate credibility to their prospectuses. Pearson's competence ensured that their project would benefit from the best available engineering expertise, while his prestige tended to diminish the difficulties of overcoming the hesitancy of politicians and investors confronted with any number of dubious utilities promotions. Pearson's name and expertise lifted any scheme out of the ranks of the obscure and set it on its way to successful prominence. 'The Company,' as an early piece of promotional literature by the São Paulo company emphasized, 'had the great advantage of having its entire system laid out by Mr. F.S. Pearson, well known as the Consulting Engineer of the Metropolitan Railway Company, and identified with other great engineering works.'[30]

Pearson's first contact with Canadian capitalists came in the summer of 1892 when, in order to restore his health, he took a yachting holiday in Nova Scotian waters. An apparent mistake by the post office sent F.S. Pearson's mail to the legal offices of B.F. Pearson, who held the franchise for horse-drawn tramway service in that city. The resultant accidental meeting led directly to the American's decision to assist in the electrification of the Halifax tramway. Pearson was soon joined in his interest in the Nova Scotian economy by H.M. Whitney, and by 1900 the two men had a financial stake not only in the Halifax Electric Tramway Co. Ltd but also in the Cape Breton-based Dominion Iron and Steel Co. Ltd and the Dominion Coal Company. These were the first ventures in which Pearson crossed the line that divided salaried engineering from actual promotion. In Cape Breton, Pearson not only assisted the coal and steel companies with designs for coal wharves and power facilities, but also sat as a director, together with Whitney, the other Pearson, and a triumvirate of prominent central Canadian businessmen: George A. Cox,[31] Sir William Van Horne,[32] and James Ross. Through Ross, Pearson came to know William Mackenzie better and was drawn into the world of utilities promotion in Montreal, Toronto, and Winnipeg. In 1903, for instance, when Mackenzie and two Toronto associates incorporated the Electrical Development Company to exploit the energy of Niagara Falls, they turned to Pearson for engineering advice.[33] The Canadian business environment provided an opportunity for Pearson's own developing talents as a promoter. Realizing that Nova Scotian coal could find a large and steady market among the thermal-electric plants of New England, he established the New England Gas and Coke Company and the Massachusetts Pipe Line Company to purvey coal to the American east-coast market. As was his pattern in the United States, Pearson left behind various associates to manage and assist the Canadian promotions to which he had been attached. R.C. Brown assumed the post of general manager at the Halifax Tramway Company and, when he was transferred to São Paulo, was succeeded in Halifax by F.A. Huntress.

Pearson's appearance on the Canadian scene in the 1890s provided William Mackenzie with the last of the preconditions that would, throughout the last two years of the old century, mould his decision to investigate and then exploit the Brazilian concession offered him by Antônio Gualco. Lash, Horne-Payne, and Pearson were the one indispensable – and distinctly international – ingredient in the response of the Toronto business community to the prospect of doing business in São Paulo. With ready access to the myriad investors of England through Horne-Payne's financial connections and the stellar legal abilities of Zebulon Lash at his beck and call, William Mackenzie could also now rely on the engineering skills of Fred Stark Pearson and his crew of New England engineers.

The one autonomous act performed by Mackenzie was the creation of the original São Paulo syndicate, a syndicate he was able to assemble out of his varied contacts in the world of Canadian railway, industrial, and utilities promotion. Gualco's arrival in Montreal had initiated this process in the summer of 1898. Once R.C. Brown had presented his positive assessment of the potential Brazilian market for public utilities, the process accelerated, culminating in the incorporation of the São Paulo Railway, Light and Power Company Limited, in April 1899, with a capitalization of $6 million. Mackenzie appointed a board of interim directors and turned his attention to the important matter of honouring the conditions of the contract he had signed, on 26 May 1899, with the fledgling corporation. If the São Paulo company was ever to move beyond its status as a legal shell, Mackenzie had to obtain additional underwriters who could relieve him of some of the responsibility of acquiring and marketing up to $3 million worth of the incipient company's first-mortgage bonds. As 'manager' of the syndicate, Mackenzie had two factors working in his favour. In the first place, he was obtaining his bonds at the advantageous price of ninety cents on the dollar. Secondly, he was in a position to reward each partner in the syndicate with a generous stock bonus, drawn from the $6 million worth of stock he had been awarded in return for the surrender of the rights he had obtained from Gualco and Souza. Mackenzie was thus offering his prospective partners an opportunity to buy discounted bonds and to receive a stock bonus. When the São Paulo venture became operational and profitable, the syndicate would be in a position to direct its substantial holdings of São Paulo stock onto the market and take a handsome profit. Mackenzie's ability to construct such a syndicate was a reflection of the 'virtual regulatory vacuum,' as Vincent Carosso has pointed out, in which syndicate financing had evolved.

Not surprisingly, William Mackenzie had little difficulty in attracting participants to his São Paulo syndicate. On 26 May 1899, he placed the names of George A. Cox and Benjamin F. Pearson before the provisional directors of the São Paulo company as sub-underwriters for a portion of his own large block of bonds. The directors accordingly approved this arrangement as 'satisfactory' and when, on 6 July, Mackenzie disclosed that Frederic Nicholls,[34] a Toronto electrical promoter, had purchased $100,000 worth of the bonds, the board once again acquiesced. Five months later, on 6 December, the board approved the sale of another $100,000 worth of the bonds to Pat Burns, a wealthy Calgary meat packer and life-long friend of Mackenzie.[35] Mackenzie's success in securing syndicate allies was attributable to the very positive profit outlook for the São Paulo company, especially after the Gualco concession had been secured from its original owners. It was also due to the fact that, under his agreement of 26 May 1899, Mackenzie was obliged to put down by 20 June a deposit of only 10 per cent on the bonds he had taken. Further instalments of equal proportions were to be spread out over the next year and a half. Mackenzie and his 'associates' had therefore obtained, for marketing purposes, control of $3 million worth of São Paulo bonds for a 10 per cent down payment and relatively generous long-term payment conditions. On at least one occasion, the company deferred payment of an instalment from the underwriting syndicate, excusing them from their obligation because 'funds in hand would be sufficient to meet the requirements of the Company for about two months.'[36] To expedite underwriting the bonds, Mackenzie arranged, at the board meeting of 30 May 1899, for the $6 million worth of stock to which he was entitled under the terms of his agreement of 26 May to be passed into the hands of the provisional directors, from whence they were passed to the control of Mackenzie's underwriting syndicate. In the space of six months, Mackenzie provided a classic illustration of the ability of Canadian financiers at the turn of the century to employ the syndicate as a tightly controlled vehicle for transforming a business opportunity into a business reality.

With his financial backing solidified, Mackenzie soon removed the interim board of directors and replaced it with the actual promoters. At a directors' meeting on the second day of the new century, three of the interim São Paulo directors resigned, making way for William Mackenzie, Frederic Nicholls, and George A. Cox. A month later, B.F. Pearson and E.R. Wood (a financial associate of Senator Cox) displaced two further directors, and William Mackenzie was elevated to the presidency of the São Paulo company with Frederic Nicholls serving as vice-president. Of the original directors of the concern, only James Gunn, of the Toronto Street Railway, remained.[37] The only subsequent addition to the board in 1900 was Alexander William Mackenzie, the president's second son, whose position seems to have been a sinecure.[38]

William Mackenzie had formed additional financial alliances that would stand the fledgling company in good stead. Mackenzie's greatest *coup* in this respect was soliciting the interest of George A. Cox in the São Paulo project. By 1900, Cox was undeniably the kingpin of Toronto business. Since his arrival in the city in the 1880s, Cox had worked assiduously to place himself at the centre of a network of thriving insurance, banking, brokerage, and trust companies, so that by the height of his business career in the middle of the first decade of the new century, he was in a position to influence, if not monopolize, much of Toronto's financial activity. Beginning with his own Central Canada Loan and Savings Company, Cox had expanded and diversified his influence, forging links with the Canada Life insurance firm and the Canadian Bank of Commerce. He also took a leading role in the inception of new financial and business ventures, notably the National Trust Company, Dominion Securities, Canadian General Electric, Dominion Iron and Steel, and, of course, Mackenzie, Mann and Company.

Faced with the growing prosperity and increasing complexity of the Canadian economy in the 1890s, Cox participated in the creation of new forms of financial institutions that would perform the banking and fiduciary functions that facilitated the emergence of modern big business.[39] The National Trust Company, founded in August 1898 by Cox and several associates, was closely held by other Cox-controlled companies, notably the Central Canada Loan and Savings and Canada Life. Similarly, Dominion Securities grew out of the bond department of Central Canada Loan and Savings. Clustered around the corner of King and Victoria Streets, the Cox family of companies stood, literally and metaphorically, at the centre of Toronto business. While these new forms of business services, so necessary to the operation of a modern business corporation, would have been available to the young São Paulo company for its needs under any circumstances, Mackenzie's success in inducing Cox to participate in his Latin American venture ensured the active support, for this newest Mackenzie promotion, of the National Trust, the Bank of Commerce (of which Cox became president in 1890), and various institutional investors.

Cox was not only at the centre of an institutional framework supporting large sections of Toronto business; he was also intimately connected with the men who formed the oligarchy binding these institutions together.[40] From his earliest days in Peterborough, Cox had had an uncanny ability to select and groom promising associates. Most prominent in this respect were Edward Rogers Wood and Joseph Wesley Flavelle, both of whom were eventually to serve the São Paulo company and profit from it. Flavelle, like Cox a steadfast Peterborough Methodist, progressed under Cox's auspices and rose from his first job as a telegram messenger to the presidency of the National Trust Company in 1898. Wood, who also began his career by delivering telegrams for Cox in Peterborough, followed his first employer to Bay Street and, by the turn of the century, held senior positions in Central Canada Loan and Savings, the National Trust, and Dominion Securities. It was at Dominion Securities that Wood discovered his real *métier* as a bond salesman. Until his death in 1941, Wood honed his talent for placing bonds not only on the Canadian market but also on the all-important markets of Europe. In retrospect, he 'must be considered the pre-eminent person in the development of the high-grade bond business, and particularly with reference to the underwriting and mass distribution of such securities.'[41]

Other prominent figures in the Cox business firmament included Byron Edmund Walker, general manager of the Canadian Bank of Commerce, and J.H. Plummer, his assistant. Z.A. Lash freely circulated among all the Cox concerns, serving as legal counsel to both the National Trust and the Canadian Bank of Commerce. When Alfred Ernest Ames married Cox's only daughter in 1889, Cox gained not only a son-in-law but also a ready connection with the Toronto brokerage firm of A.E. Ames and Co. and through it ties with other Toronto brokerage houses, like that of Henry Pellatt and his son, Henry Mill Pellatt. This truly remarkable conjunction of Toronto business talent and organization, all brought together by the rising fortunes of George A. Cox, was in one sense the natural product of the smallness of turn-of-the-century Canadian business. 'Financial institutions survive,' one economist has noted, 'if they guess the future more or less correctly ... Naturally they will feel more certain about their guesses, and will lend more easily, if they know the persons to whom they are lending. In a relatively new and inexperienced financial community this need for security may be especially strong.'[42]

Mackenzie's São Paulo syndicate also reflected the general absence of regulations governing financial transactions in the years preceding the First World War. Both federal and provincial company laws provided businessmen with the loosest possible framework within which to structure and promote their enterprises. The success of a syndicate therefore depended upon each member's willingness to abide by the dictates of its manager and to honour an unwritten code that placed loyalty to the syndicate and its goals before all else. Since the financial community had as yet no mechanism to police its own activities, Mackenzie's main guarantee of the loyalty of his syndicate partners was his knowledge that their desire to profit through the syndicate's operation would bind them solidly around him. Any participant who broke ranks and dumped his bonds and shares on the market to reap a short-term gain could be effectively ostracized from further flotations by Mackenzie's extensive financial influence – in Toronto through E.R. Wood, and in England through Horne-Payne. The syndicate was thus, in essence, a gentleman's agreement among financiers cemented by a desire for profit, the legal vigilance of Z.A. Lash, and the reputation of William Mackenzie as a successful promoter.

With the original syndicate in place, the São Paulo company was quickly drawn into the web of Cox-related companies. Zebulon Lash was appointed legal counsel and was present at most board meetings as an invited guest and eventually as a director and vice-president. On 27 June 1899 the Canadian Bank of Commerce was appointed as company banker and was represented on the board by George Cox, as well as by J.W. Flavelle and B.E. Walker, who came as frequent invited guests. The circle of ancillary services was made complete by the designation in February 1900 of the National Trust Company as the trustee of the São Paulo bonds.[43] The National Trust had by 1899 already acquired considerable experience in ministering to other utilities ventures as far afield as the Demerara Electric Company and as close to home as the Ottawa Electric Company.[44] Affiliation with the National Trust once again brought the São Paulo company into contact with the multifaceted talents of J.W. Flavelle, its president, and E.R. Wood, who had briefly served as general manager of the trust company before yielding the post to William Thomas White,[45] a skilful young property lawyer recruited to National Trust from the assessment office of the City of Toronto. Flavelle, Wood, and White had all participated in the underwriting of the company's bonds. In February 1900, Wood was elected to the board, thereby providing, together with George Cox, a direct link with the Toronto investment community, most notably with Central Canada Loan and Savings, Dominion Securities, A.E. Ames and Co., and the brokerage firm of Henry Mill Pellatt,[46] all of which had lent support to the underwriters of the first São Paulo bonds. Mackenzie put in place the capstone of his São Paulo company framework in November 1901 when F.S. Pearson was brought onto the board to provide an engineer's perspective on corporate affairs and to represent his own sizeable holding of São Paulo bonds and stock.

The tight, interwoven nature of the entrepreneurial framework supporting the São Paulo company was amply illustrated in November 1900, when, in order to expedite construction in São Paulo, the board approached National Trust with a request for a million-dollar loan. On 17 November, Cox, Nicholls, and Mackenzie were delegated to negotiate the loan with the trust company and to offer as surety for the loan two million dollars in company bonds. The negotiations proceeded quickly and, on 28 November, agreement was reached with the National Trust for a loan of one million dollars secured by two million dollars in bonds and subject to 6 per cent interest.

The most remarkable aspect of the loan was the fact that it was guaranteed on behalf of the company by the same men who had ratified it for the trust company.[47] J.W. Flavelle, president of the National Trust, as one of the six guarantors, put up a personal guarantee of $166,666 to secure the loan. George Cox, a director of the National Trust, underwrote another $166,666 of the loan, while William Mackenzie and Frederic Nicholls, also both directors, put up $300,000 and $33,333 respectively. B.F. Pearson covered the remainder of the guarantee. In return for their services, the six guarantors were given an option to purchase $1,125,000 worth of the bonds pledged as surety on the loan and were allowed to exercise this option as late as 1 March 1902 at the discounted price of eighty cents on the dollar. A commission of 4 per cent of all expenses incurred in negotiating the loan was to be paid to the National Trust Company.[48] The ease with which the company could procure capital assistance from the Toronto financial community was reaffirmed in April 1901, when a $500,000 loan was procured from the Canadian Bank of Commerce, which was to receive 6 per cent interest and a $20,000 commission for its services.[49] As with the National Trust loan, the agreement was drawn up by Z.A. Lash, who was also a vice-president of the bank, and guaranteed by the same six guarantors,[50] this time under the direction of Cox, who was president of the bank, and Flavelle, who was a director. When, in September 1901, the Bank of Commerce complained that the company had over-extended its credit under the loan, negotiations were begun to expand and extend the terms of the loan.[51]

By the end of 1900 the financial foundations of the São Paulo company had been unshakably laid in Toronto. William Mackenzie had dextrously redirected the considerable prowess he had acquired in railway and tramway promotion in Canada and had focused it upon a business opportunity in a strange and unknown land where such skills were distinctly lacking. The initial success of the São Paulo company was founded in what one Canadian historian has perceptively labelled 'this flowering of Canadian capitalism.'[52] It was a phenomenon that contemporaries did not fail to notice. 'The flotation in London of a company to exploit a Brazilian enterprise would be taken as a matter of course, a mere everyday affair,' noted the Toronto *Globe* in early 1902. 'Here, where we still look for outside capital to build our railways and to work our mines, the formation of a local company to operate electric railways and supply electric light and power in São Paulo is decidedly a novelty. We should not, however, fail to appreciate the enterprise of our fellow-Canadians who take the risk of such a venture, nor to congratulate them if they bring home (as they bid fair to do in this case) a "rich return."'[53]

The 'rich return' that Mackenzie and his associates would reap from their São Paulo investment over the next years was, of course, partially the result of their boldness in facing 'the risk of such a venture' in Brazil. Operating a tramway company in São Paulo involved many more imponderables and uncertainties than pioneering a similar venture in Montreal or Toronto. In this sense, the investors were taking the classic capitalist risk. But as classic capitalists they also acted to reduce that risk as much as possible. The syndicate and its allies, for instance, possessed the crucial power to influence the market value of São Paulo securities; at the same time, they were able to finance their venture on generous lines through the assistance of closely affiliated banks and trust companies. The real risk of the venture thus lay less in Toronto than in São Paulo, where the ultimate success or failure of the company in furnishing Brazilians with cheap and efficient electric services would govern the ability of Monty Horne-Payne to work his magic on the English investing public, thereby removing vast quantities of São Paulo securities from the vaults of the promoters and depositing them in the hands of the small, permanent investor.

An essential step in this process was to establish a head office from which the affairs of the São Paulo company would be co-ordinated and directed. To achieve this, Mackenzie simply grafted the administration of the new Latin American utility onto the administrative structure of the Canadian Northern Railway and the Toronto Street Railway. The Toronto Railway Chambers on Toronto Street thus became the locus of Mackenzie's far-flung business empire. None of these three companies had a staff exclusively dedicated to its own affairs. Instead managers, accountants, and secretaries held dual and sometimes triple appointments, apportioning their time among Mackenzie's various enterprises. In later years, as the business of managing the various companies became more complex, the clerical staff adopted a system by which the correspondence of each concern was colour coded so that, for instance, the intricate process of negotiating for a concession in São Paulo would not become accidentally muddled with the involved financial affairs of the Canadian Northern or a stock subscription inadvertently misdirected.

The Toronto Street location also placed the officers and directors of Mackenzie's varied enterprises within easy reach of the legal and financial services requisite to their profitable existence. A few minutes' walk would bring Mackenzie to the offices of the Blake law firm, where he could avail himself of the best corporate legal advice in the country, or to the National Trust or the Canadian Bank of Commerce, where loans and trust documents could be expeditiously arranged. The head office of the São Paulo company was indeed little more than a collection of desks in Mackenzie's Toronto Railway Chambers, manned by clerks and accountants who kept track of correspondence and tallied corporate expenditures and income. The real direction of the company's affairs emanated from the nearby Bay and King Street offices of men like E.R. Wood, Frederic Nicholls, Z.A. Lash, and George Cox. Whenever the peripatetic F.S. Pearson or William Mackenzie appeared in Toronto, the officers and directors of the São Paulo company informally assembled in one of their offices to discuss policy and lay out the company's direction. These decisions were formalized in short and infrequent directors' meetings, which were often attended by no more than two or three directors and which were usually chaired by Nicholls, in the Toronto Railway Chambers. The São Paulo company's initial annual general meeting followed this pattern. These brief, sparsely attended meetings allowed the shareholders, who were of course largely representing the same interests as the directors themselves, to set their seal of approval on the policies adopted and pursued by their officers.

The frequent absence of William Mackenzie from Toronto and the increasing tendency of the Canadian Northern to monopolize his time ensured that those to whom he delegated his responsibility for overseeing the operation of head office played a crucial role. While Frederic Nicholls shouldered responsibility on matters of policy, the onerous task of managing the day-to-day affairs of the company fell to John Maitland

Smith, a young legal clerk who had begun his career in Mackenzie's Toronto streetcar venture.

In many ways Smith, as company secretary, was the administrative hub of the whole São Paulo operation. Across his desk passed all the company's correspondence. Only he had a complete grasp of every aspect of its corporate affairs. Contending not only with a small, untried staff, but also with the mysteries of overseeing a business in a country he had never seen, Smith excelled at his work. The vast distances involved were perhaps the most trying aspect of Smith's duties. The Toronto office stood at the centre of a network that linked the actual site of operations in São Paulo with the legal and financial ancillary services in Canada, with Pearson's offices at 621 Broadway in New York (from which all the company's technical work was handled), and with the offices of the British Empire Trust Company in London (from which Horne-Payne marshalled the financial resources necessary to ensure the company's survival).

To a remarkable degree, therefore, the São Paulo company's early existence was characterized by an unending stream of telegrams (usually coded in Lieber's commercial code) connecting São Paulo, Toronto, New York, London, and the scattered outposts of business promotion that Mackenzie and his associates so tirelessly frequented. Wherever F.S. Pearson or William Mackenzie travelled – from the steel works of Cape Breton to the construction camps of the Canadian Northern – each man always found time to ponder the peculiar problems of the São Paulo enterprise and to dispatch a trail of telegraphic instructions, through Smith, for appropriate action.

Smith performed another crucial task at head office. As the São Paulo operation gained momentum and permanence, it became important to procure competent administrators who could be posted to Brazil to oversee the company's affairs. In this respect, Pearson undertook to furnish the engineering staff, drawing upon his extensive connections in the American engineering fraternity to secure the services of engineers with broad experience in American tramway and power-plant construction and operation. As with most spheres of the company's operations, suitably qualified Brazilians simply did not exist to fill the senior engineering positions in the company. While Brazilians were given every opportunity to learn the skills necessary to operate trams and power stations, there was a strong feeling that overall management of the system should remain in the hands of 'experienced men from the north,' at least during the initial phase of the company's operation. 'I agree with you,' Pearson wrote to Brown in March 1900, 'that all of the employees who are to have charge of the machinery should be from the United States and I think it would be very unwise for us to attempt to get men for this purpose from Brazil; at least for the first few years ... it is of the utmost importance to have all of our work run with smoothness and with perfect satisfaction to the public and I should advise you to have enough competent men to accomplish this proceeding on the theory that after the first year's operation, some of these men could be sent home.'[54] In this fashion, T.W. Bevan, the first superintendent of the São Caetano steam plant in São Paulo, was recruited. Bevan had been employed by Pearson in both Boston and New York and now, through Brown, was brought to São Paulo. As Bevan later admitted, when he received the offer to migrate to Brazil he had at first been reluctant, 'but it was like a command to receive a letter from R.C.B. to follow him.'[55]

Similarly, Smith in the Toronto office selected and groomed suitable candidates for administrative posts in São Paulo. From the beginning it had been decided that the Brazilian company would duplicate the administrative framework of the Toronto Street Railway as closely as possible. Thus when the directors decided to have the accounts in São Paulo 'kept substantially the same as the Toronto Street Railway company,'[56] Smith selected Daniel Mulqueen from his staff in the Toronto Railway Chambers. In April 1900, Mulqueen was dispatched from Toronto to São Paulo, where he was placed in charge of the company's office on Rua Direita. Mulqueen's was to be an especially difficult assignment, primarily because he was faced with the nearly impossible task of converting and balancing the company's expenditures and income from the always fluctuating Brazilian milréis into the relatively stable Canadian dollar, often through the intermediary of the British pound or American dollar. From its very first days, the São Paulo company was to be an accountant's nightmare. 'Also I would suggest,' Pearson brusquely instructed Mulqueen, 'that you state each month on these [expenditure] statements the average exchange at which you have figured any money received from Canada during the month, in order that we may check your milréis with our estimate in dollars.'[57] It would never be easy.

Under the auspices of J.M. Smith, who was to hold his position as secretary until 1929, the corporate structure in São Paulo slowly began to evolve. With the initial work of securing the concession and forming the syndicate complete, Mackenzie increasingly retired from the daily affairs of the company, preferring to let Smith, Nicholls, and Lash consult him on urgent matters and to leave the more routine work of building up the São Paulo concession in the competent hands of Brown and Alexander Mackenzie. For matters that required technical expertise, F.S. Pearson was always available, ready to divert his attention from his latest promotional scheme to the problems of tramways and power generation in Brazil. What William Mackenzie had essentially done was to lay out a blueprint for introducing foreign capital and expertise to an economically less-developed area of the world. He had assembled the financial backing and the technical staff that would enable him to acquire and exploit utilities concessions in countries that, while at first sight very different from his native land, were capable of producing rates of return comparable to those of his Canadian railway and streetcar ventures. The most important element in Mackenzie's foreign-investment formula was the ability to adapt local conditions to the needs of foreign capital while ensuring benefit and progress for the foreign users of his utility enterprises. In this respect, the presence of an adroit local manager, Alexander Mackenzie, and the availability of unparalleled technical advice, in this and many other cases from Pearson, gave Mackenzie and the companies he founded a truly unique advantage over competitors, whether local or foreign. It was a formula that Mackenzie and his associates were to reapply, with some variation, over the next decade and a half to utilities investment opportunities in Rio de Janeiro, Mexico, and Spain.[58] The resultant group of traction companies, sometimes referred to as the 'Pearson empire,' bore all the marks of Mackenzie's style of promotion and Pearson's style of engineering. All were nominally controlled from the same offices in Toronto, and all were largely financed and directed by the same group of promoters. All that kept them separate was that, in legal terms, they were autonomous entities and, of course, that the secretaries in Toronto meticulously coded their correspondence with different colours.

The essence of William Mackenzie's entrepreneurship was his ability to identify a promising business opportunity, seize it, monopolize it, and turn it to his advantage. In the words of a contemporary journalist, Mackenzie was 'a wizard of a species of applied finance.'[59] Yet in all that Mackenzie tackled, there was a large element of national benefit.

Ironically, it was to preserve and protect the public's interests in these ventures that municipal, provincial, and federal governments eventually moved to divorce Mackenzie from his extensive network of Canadian railway, power, and traction enterprises. Mackenzie, the magnificent creator, was never equal to the task of carrying his ventures through to their culmination. Beset by the sometimes recklessly over-extended finances of the Canadian Northern and by the increasingly insistent demand in Canada for public ownership of utilities, Mackenzie was to discover by the time of the First World War that he was no longer able to mesmerize the Canadian people with his financial wizardry. Until then, however, he reigned supreme not only as the creator of Canada's newest transcontinental railway but also as a prominent sponsor of national prosperity. 'Without a doubt,' journalist Augustus Bridle reflected in 1921, 'William Mackenzie had a mandate from the country to do a great work – and he overdid it. Bankers and other financiers agreed that he had found new ways of investing creative money. Scarcely a teacher of geography but admitted that Mackenzie was changing the map of this country so fast that a new one became necessary every three years. New towns sprang up at the rate of a mile a day of new railway built by Mackenzie. Every new town became a monument to this man's faith in the future of Canada.'[60]

For Mackenzie and his associates, nation building went hand in hand with profit making. In the case of his Latin American utilities ventures, he turned his opportunities into profitable enterprises, which, while they undeniably brought him rewards that were handsome in the extreme, would ultimately also contribute to the economic advancement of south-eastern Brazil. In eulogizing Mackenzie's contribution to the company after his death, the board of directors underscored their late chairman's role as 'a pioneer in demonstrating that in the initiation of enterprises this country had reached an international status.'[61] In Brazil Mackenzie had sensed a different and in some ways more inviting environment for the business of profit making and nation building. In the early years of the century, the São Paulo venture simply appeared as one facet of Mackenzie's great entrepreneurial crusade. 'The more he borrowed in England on Government-guaranteed bonds, and the more he invested in Mexico and South America, and the greater [the] number of street railways, power plants, transmission lines, ore mountains, new towns, smelters, docks, ships, whale fisheries, coal mines and land companies that he and his able partner Mann were able to octopize, the greater the country thought both these men were — especially Mackenzie.'[62] Significantly, when he died in 1923, it was only the Latin American utilities ventures that remained under Mackenzie's direct control, untouched by the hand of public ownership, which by then had taken hold of the Canadian Northern, the Toronto Street Railway, and the Electrical Development Company. Unlike Toronto and the western prairies of Canada, the city of São Paulo provided a different and ultimately more salubrious social, political, and economic environment for William Mackenzie's 'octopizing' ambitions.

CHAPTER THREE

First Light: The São Paulo Tramway, Light and Power Company Limited, 1899-1908

Above all, the engineers, accountants, and lawyers sent from Toronto to establish the São Paulo company had to contend with a pervading sense of isolation – a sense that they were alone, pioneering a new form of enterprise in an alien environment. 'I can only repeat,' Alexander Mackenzie stressed in a letter from São Paulo to Z.A. Lash, 'that they cannot send too good a man [here] – remember that he will be almost alone ... The manager must be in constant communication with the state and city governments and be in good relations with the officials and a man of great tact is needed for this.'[1]

With only telegrams and a painfully slow postal service for communication, and with thousands of miles of sea and land between the company's offices on Rua Direita and the head office in Toronto, the men working under Alexander Mackenzie and R.C. Brown felt a profound sense of separation. The journey home took twenty days by sea and rail, schedules permitting. From an early date, the São Paulo staff came to refer to their homeland, be it the United States or Canada, as 'the North.' 'There will always be difficulty in keeping men here from the North unless the salary is made such that will make it worth the while to put up with the conditions,' warned Daniel Mulqueen, the assistant treasurer in São Paulo. The cost of living in Brazil was, for instance, more than twice that of Toronto. The greatest irritant, Mulqueen concluded, was that 'most of these men are married' and 'find it hard to be separated from their families and could not bring them here at their present salaries.'[2]

In addition to the emotional deprivation, there were the frustrations of doing one's job in unfamiliar surroundings. São Paulo was unlike

Toronto, Halifax, New York, or any other place to which these engineers had been sent to install the sinews of the electrical age. The work may have been the same – the universal applicability of electricity was, after all, its greatest attribute – but the cultural, economic, and political setting in which they exercised their talents was distinctly different. From the first day of operations, the engineers and managers sent south to São Paulo found themselves engaged in a constant process of adaptation to conditions for which their North American experience had not wholly prepared them.

The first and most pressing goal was to establish the power-generation and tramway services. Without plentiful electricity, the company would be unable to exploit its concessionary rights and would be incapable of overcoming its remaining competitors. Similarly, if the remaining mule-drawn trams were to be forced out of business, the company would have to provide, as quickly as possible, an efficient and inexpensive electric tramway service. These two achievements, coupled with the aggressive marketing of electrical power to local industry, were to set the São Paulo company well on its way to a complete monopoly over the power and traction services of Brazil's fastest-growing city.

The key to the company's plans was the rapid development of the Parnaíba water power site, some thirty-six kilometres outside São Paulo on the Tietê River. The Cachoeira do Inferno, or Rapids of Hell, had been visited by R.C. Brown, who enthusiastically reported that they were 'capable of furnishing constantly a probable minimum supply equal to about 11,000 horse power.' Brown predicted that the relatively flat and unwooded terrain between the dam site and the city would make 'it a simple matter to build a transmission line between Parnahyba [sic]³ and São Paulo which would be perfectly safe and free from difficulties incidental to a transmission line built through forest or localities where rapid growing vines are likely to weight down the poles and wires.' The Parnaíba site was doubly attractive because Gualco, on F.S. Pearson's instructions, had bought up enough of the adjacent river banks to preclude any rival concern from infringing upon a concessionaire's riparian rights. If demand warranted further power development, Brown had already laid claim to another site, at Itú, about thirty-five kilometres further west on the Tietê.

The task of translating Brown's prophecy into reality fell to Hugh Lincoln Cooper, a thirty-five-year-old American hydroelectric engineer, whom Pearson had recruited and brought south with him in 1899. Unlike Pearson, Cooper had no formal training as an engineer, but had begun his career as a railway apprentice and attained considerable renown as a hydroelectric engineer. Like Pearson, Hugh Cooper was on the verge of establishing an international reputation. Parnaíba was to be followed by hydroelectric projects on the Nile, Tennessee, and Dnieper rivers. 'Long after this civilization has passed or merged into another,' the *New York Times* noted when Cooper died in 1937, 'his magnificent dams will testify to the daring, imagination and energy of an epoch dominated by the scientist and the engineer.'[4] After surveying the Parnaíba site, Cooper devised a scheme whereby the Tietê would be dammed and diverted through a huge iron penstock to a reservoir. The granite dam that Cooper proposed to contain the reservoir would not only have the effect of producing a 'head'[5] of 11.8 metres for the powerhouse but also serve to minimize the seasonal fluctuations in the flow of the Tietê and thereby provide sufficient water to generate 20,000 horsepower from four 2,000-horsepower generators even in the driest season.

While Cooper's conception of the Parnaíba power station was remarkably straightforward, its implementation was to tax the young engineer's powers of perseverance. The first impediment to progress was the site's total isolation; an isolation that forced Cooper to create a network of more than thirty kilometres of roads. By means of ox-carts on these dirt roads or by means of a flimsy light railway, more than 450 tons of generating equipment and 8,000 tons of construction materials were painstakingly hauled into the Parnaíba site. On one occasion in April 1901, it took seven days to move 25 tons of electrical apparatus along eleven kilometres of the makeshift rail line from the railhead at Barueri to Parnaíba. Cooper's crews were only able to manage this by re-laying sections of track over which the freight cars had already passed.

Accessibility was far from the most trying problem facing Cooper at Parnaíba. The surrounding terrain was covered with steep hills and low swamps, drenched in the hot summer months by almost continuous torrential downpours. Cooper's initial attempts to probe the riverbed for a solid foundation for the dam were hampered by the complete absence of proper tools, so that his surveyors and navvies were forced to claw away at the boulder-strewn riverbed with their bare hands. On the positive side, he was able to report that there was an 'abundant' supply of Portuguese and Italian immigrant labourers who were prepared to work hard for reasonable wages. By February 1900, there were 1,200 of these labourers. None the less, the labour situation became a cause of unending concern. There was the constant fear that some dreadful contagion like yellow fever or malaria might strike, thus bringing construction to a halt. Cooper, for instance, reported that the local water produced 'violent diarrhea' in his workers and that the company had been obliged to provide mineral water and beer. 'The quality of native labour,' Cooper reported, 'improves as the men are enabled to feed regularly and the general health of the Camp is good.' But good health and good pay had the unfortunate tendency to bring to the surface racial antagonism between the Italians and Portuguese. By January 1900, Cooper reported that after several outbreaks of violence the Italians, far and away the largest immigrant group in the state, had 'succeeded in driving away the Portuguese as there are now only about 40 Portuguese on our rolls.' The Parnaíba site had overnight become the largest construction project in the São Paulo area, and Cooper proudly confessed that 'we continue to be overwhelmed by men seeking work.'[6]

By early February 1900, Cooper's diligence began to pay a return. 'All of Mr. Cooper's ideas as to the development of the water power seem to have been correct,' R.C. Brown confided to B.F. Pearson in Halifax. 'He has found a solid ledge for the edge of the dam in the banks of the river and a solid ledge across the river so that there cannot be the least concern as to its stability.'[7] Cooper was doubly blessed in that he located 'in the immediate vicinity an inexhaustible supply of the finest granite, sand and other materials.' Drawing on this reserve, he supervised the erection of almost 30,000 cubic metres of masonry at the dam site. Work of this magnitude required the training of the largely unskilled labour force in such skills as blasting, forging, and carpentry. Within months of its arrival in São Paulo, the Canadian company had thus initiated one of its most beneficial activities in Brazil, the familiarization of large numbers of largely unskilled local workers with the knowledge and discipline needed to build and maintain a modern, electric utility system.

With construction of the dam underway, Cooper began to order the feeder pipes and electrical equipment that would provide the generating capacity of the plant. From the Escher-Wyss Company in Switzerland came the enormous three-metre-wide penstock, which would carry the water from the primary reservoir to the secondary reservoir above the powerhouse. Each section of the pipe had to be shipped into the site by ox-cart and reassembled to exacting engineering specifications. Fred Pearson used his extensive contacts in the American electrical-machinery industry to obtain priority booking at General Electric for the production of four 1,400-kilowatt generators.[8] All this equipment had to pass through the port of Santos, which was notorious for its inept handling of cargo, and then had to come by train up across the Serra do Mar to be delivered at Barueri for the final journey by ox-cart, or 'by blood power' as Cooper called it, to the site. The process of filing orders for broken or missing parts was tedious and time-consuming, since it took a whole day for a message to be passed by messenger from the site to the company offices in São Paulo. The whole operation at Parnaíba was an exercise of North American engineering ingenuity under the most inauspicious conditions. Aside from abundant labour, there was understandably little that Brazil could contribute to the project. Brazilian industry as yet lacked the capacity to provide electrical apparatus, copper wire, insulators, and even proper cement. Everything had to be imported and installed under the supervision of foreign technicians. In return for this foreign usurpation of their power industry, Brazilians were to receive the direct benefit of Latin America's largest power installation, a power plant that was to vault São Paulo into the electrical leadership of the continent.

Over the years, the relationship between the São Paulo company and the social and economic environment in which it operated was destined to change slowly but inexorably. From a time when foreign managers and imported materials were indispensable, the Canadian company would become increasingly dependent on Brazilian skills and materials. These were the skills and products of the urban, industrial age. Brazil's previous experience with large-scale enterprise had been confined to pre-industrial sugar and coffee plantations or gold-mining enterprises that were often based on slave labour and rudimentary technology. The São Paulo company appeared in Brazil at a time when such local business families as the Matarazzos of São Paulo were pioneering urban industrialism in the country. Canadian investment in Brazilian utilities thus provided Brazilian entrepreneurs with both an efficient source of power and a model of modern management. What was of crucial significance in this changing relationship was the fact that the company played a dynamic role. The company thus exposed Brazilians to the art of managing a large-scale business enterprise and, at the same time, created stimuli that gave Brazilian entrepreneurs the incentive to undertake the production of products as disparate as tramcars and cement. These stimuli, which economists describe as 'linkages,' were to form one of the Canadian company's most positive contributions to Brazilian society and its economy.

Work at Parnaíba was largely complete by September 1901. Cooper had accomplished his task in just over twenty months. 'This work,' F.S. Pearson wrote, 'is of first class character, equal to anything that can be found in this country [the United States], and there is no reason why it should not give perfect satisfaction in service.'[9] By the time Parnaíba was inaugurated in September, the actual cost of construction was remarkably close to the $426,738 that Cooper had estimated. Furthermore, the plant was soon found to have 'exceedingly low' operating costs and a very high 'load factor,' or ratio of average output to plant capacity. The Parnaíba plant thus provided the company with a steady and relatively cheap power base, which enabled it to relieve the pressure on the small São Caetano thermal-electric plant. At the same time, Parnaíba gave the foreign utility a reservoir of electricity that completely dwarfed the now-meagre generating capabilities of its nearest competitors. 'It is very important for us to build up our business as fast as possible,' Fred Pearson instructed the São Paulo staff, 'in order to get a large gross and net income to aid us in raising the additional money required. Our people here (in the North) have already invested a very large amount of money, and naturally want to see some result before going in still deeper. It is perhaps wholly unnecessary for me to request you to spare no pains nor expense in keeping this plant in continuous operation during the first few months of its history, and until a good reputation is well established for us.'[10] The Parnaíba plant was ready to play a formative role in the industrialization of São Paulo.

Plentiful power would be an advantage only if it could be expeditiously applied to the streetcar service, which from the start was intended to be the heart of the company's operations. The first adjustment the company had to make to pursue this objective was to change its name. By December 1899, Alexander Mackenzie reported that the title 'São Paulo Railway, Light and Power Company' was creating confusion in the minds of local citizens and foreign investors, both of whom were confusing the company with the English-owned San Paulo Railway Company. Accordingly, an Ontario order-in-council was obtained to allow the company to alter its name to the São Paulo Tramway, Light and Power Co. Ltd.[11] Clearly established in the public's mind as a tramway operation, the company set out to make good its promise of cheap and efficient public traction service. Above all else, the São Paulo company had to provide better service than the mule-drawn teams of the Companhia Viação Paulista. The Viação Paulista was determined to fight its efficient new competitor by any means possible. Realizing that friction would invariably result, R.C. Brown appointed Alípio de Borba, a Brazilian engineer who had advised the concessionaires since Gualco's first visit in 1897, as traffic superintendent. 'I have thought it advisable,' Brown confided to William Mackenzie, 'that a man who deals with the public as much as the Superintendent is obliged to, should be a Brazilian.'[12] This first appointment of a Brazilian to an executive position in the company soon paid dividends.

The Gualco concessions gave the company the right to lay track along specified city streets. It was, however, unavoidable that at certain points these lines would intersect with those of the Companhia Viação Paulista. Anticipating this difficulty the municipal government had empowered the new Canadian company to 'intersect in one or more places those [lines] of the present Companhia Viação Paulista.' If this provision was clear on the actual concession document, its implementation was none too straightforward on the streets of São Paulo. Whenever R.C. Brown's track-laying crews made any move to intersect a Viação Paulista line, they were blocked by angry officials of the rival company. In an attempt to circumvent such encounters, Brown instructed his crews to do their work under cover of night. This tactic had the effect of intensifying the friction and resulted in violent confrontations between the pick-wielding work gangs of the respective companies. Only the intervention of a squad of cavalry, called out at the request of Alípio de Borba, curtailed these nocturnal donnybrooks.[13]

The São Paulo company's victory over the Viação Paulista on the question of track laying was but a tactical triumph. As the crews continued to set their 'girder' and 'T' rails into the streets, the company began devising a strategy that would give it complete control of its faltering competitor. As early as December 1899, Pearson had visited Toronto to discuss with Senator Cox and William Mackenzie the possibility of gaining financial control of the Viação Paulista. The company committed itself without much hesitation 'to get these properties as cheaply as possible.'[14] Control of the CVP would give the company a near monopoly on streetcar service and would also allow it to approach the municipal government with a request for a 'consolidated' concession that would make it extremely difficult for new competitors to enter the field.

Pearson's plan to buy out the Viação Paulista was complicated by the appearance of a syndicate, backed by French banking interests, that had managed to establish itself as the predominant shareholder and creditor of the company. Backed by the Paris-based Comptoir d'Escompte, the rival syndicate took refuge in the argument that the Gualco concession of 1897 had infringed on the earlier concession of the CVP and was therefore invalid. In April 1900, Pearson candidly admitted to Frederic Nicholls in Toronto that he did not know if the French syndicate was acting 'either as a bluff or in good faith.' 'I have no doubt,' he assured Nicholls, 'we shall come out ahead before we get through and get the Viação on reasonable terms, as there are so many ways in which the French Bank people can be attacked and their work hindered in São Paulo, that ultimately we ought to succeed.'[15] Accordingly, Pearson arranged for pressure to be brought to bear on the Comptoir through the General Electric Company and through James Ross, the Montreal railroad contractor who had a joint interest in the Central London Railway in England with the same French financiers. Pearson's campaign was strengthened a month later when the São Paulo company inaugurated its electric tram service, thereby throwing into stark relief the uncompetitiveness of the Viação's decrepit mule trams.

Throughout 1900, intermittent negotiations were conducted for the purchase of the CVP, with Pearson travelling to Paris to deal directly with the French syndicate and Alexander Mackenzie handling the jurisdictional battle over the concession in São Paulo. By December, a frustrated Mackenzie admitted that he had 'no idea' what the local interests in the rival syndicate would take in settlement of their claim. 'I have had experience enough of the Viação gang and Judges [sic] and our own lawyers to know that when we have anything in apparent order the unexpected happens – and I can't make any more prognostications.'[16] A breakthrough in the negotiations was not, however, far off. With the São Paulo company's electric trams steadily eating into the ridership of its mule trams, the Viação was forced into liquidation, and in April 1901 its assets and concessions were bought at auction by the São Paulo company. This did not end the legal and financial turmoil surrounding the company. Although Pearson and William Mackenzie paid at least £77,000 to the French syndicate to clear their claims, the liquidators of the CVP held out for their rights until 1906, when a Brazilian court finally decided in the São Paulo company's favour.[17]

The Viação Paulista was a significant acquisition. As soon as the sale had been consummated, Pearson came to São Paulo and, with Alexander Mackenzie, arranged with the prefect, Antônio Prado, to consolidate the Gualco concession with that of the Viação. The proposed unified contract ensured the company an ironclad monopoly on electric traction and, because the proponents of competition realized this, the ratification of the new concession by the *câmara* was accompanied by what Mackenzie described as a 'rather hot fight.' None the less, with the backing of Prado and the intensive lobbying of the council by the company's legal counsel, Carlos de Campos, the unification contract was approved and duly registered.[18] 'The terms of the new contract are very favourable,' Alexander Mackenzie informed Lash in Toronto. 'The provisions relating to taxes and payments are particularly valuable and we have got rid of a number of very obnoxious provisions in the Viação contract, including the obligations to provide second class cars, construction and maintenance of pavements, etc., which many were very anxious to retain. The new contract must be considered as adding immensely to the value of the old concessions.'[19]

In anticipation of the Viação Paulista acquisition, the company had moved to take over the Companhia Carris de Ferro de São Paulo e Santo Amaro, a short-line steam railway established in 1880 that ran from the city centre to the small town of Santo Amaro. Although only nineteen kilometres long, the railway ran through the city's rapidly expanding suburbs and, as such, represented the only other potential competitor in the immediate vicinity of São Paulo. The Santo Amaro's value to its new Canadian proprietors was greatly enhanced in July 1901 when the state government extended the railway's concession to match the forty-year concession of the São Paulo company and empowered the new owners to convert it to electric power.[20]

As the legal and financial intricacies of solidifying the concessions were worked out, R.C. Brown and Harry Hartwell, yet another American engineer, pushed ahead with laying tracks. Their work was complicated by the narrowness of the São Paulo streets and the unevenness of its granite-block pavements.[21] On Pearson's express orders, only 'first class' materials were used, despite the fact that practically everything except the hard-wearing peroba wood ties had to be imported. Throughout this initial phase, Pearson exercised a remarkable supervision over even the smallest detail of the construction work. Drawing on memories of his visit to São Paulo in 1899, Pearson was able to dispatch long, detailed letters of instruction to Brown and Hartwell. The precision of Pearson's memory and the accuracy of his suggestions were uncanny. Dictating a letter from his Paris hotel room or from his office at the Cape Breton steelworks, Pearson could recall a gradient of a São Paulo hill and its unsuitability for a tramway route or advise that without a coating of rust inhibitor a certain component of a car chassis would soon deteriorate. It was this gift for supervising the largest and the smallest details of an engineering endeavour that enabled Pearson to spread his talents across the face of the globe.

By May 1900, sufficient track had been laid and electrified to permit the operation of the first eight cars. The cars, designed by the J.G. Brill Company of Philadelphia, were shipped to Brazil in component form and assembled in one of the company's two new car barns. By early 1902, the company had sixty-five of these nine-bench cars operating over fifty-six kilometres of electrified track and, as a result of the Viação purchase, was also operating forty-four mule trams over thirty-five kilometres of unelectrified track. There was little choice for the company on the question of animal traction, since, if the Viação Paulista concession was to be honoured, some form of service had to be offered along its routes. The mules were none the less a constant annoyance. Not only did they make strict scheduling virtually impossible, they were dirty, smelly, and unpopular with passengers. Furthermore, there was the constant fear of contagious disease, which might devastate the mule stables overnight. To combat this danger, Pearson had sheep placed intermittently throughout the stables on the theory that the sheep, which reacted to disease more quickly than mules, would provide some warning of an incipient epidemic. Above all, the mules were not good money-makers. Whereas an electric tram produced earnings of $44 per day, a mule tram brought only $17. All of these factors, coupled with Pearson's dislike, as an electrical engineer, of coping with the problems of providing fodder and harness gear, inevitably led to a policy of what was harshly called 'mule suppression.' On 6 June 1903, the last mule was retired from the service of the São Paulo Tramway, Light and Power Company.

Equal in importance to the construction of a well-engineered streetcar system was the need to build up a steady and profitable ridership. At first this presented little difficulty, since the company's routes were still relatively restricted and the very novelty of the electric *bondes* was in itself sufficient inducement for *paulistanos* to clamber aboard. During the first two months of operation, R.C. Brown reported that 'people were fairly crazy to ride upon them.'[22] To William Mackenzie, Brown reported by late May 1900 that the streetcar operation was 'very satisfactory ... We have no difficulty in obtaining men who are competent to handle cars on the street, and our superintendent, Mr. Alípio de Borba, a Brazilian, is showing himself well-fitted for the position.'[23]

As the network of streetcar routes grew, problems began. By January 1904, routes criss-crossed the city, from Vila Clementino in the southern suburbs to the banks of the Tietê River in the north sector, along Avenida da Intendência to the eastern suburbs, and along Avenida 9 de Outubro to the western suburb of Agua Branca. Cars working these routes could pass through three fare zones, each of which cost the passenger 200 réis, or the equivalent of three to four cents in Canadian currency.[24] Despite some willingness to construct 'pioneer' lines into the suburbs, the company preferred to concentrate on the high-density, central areas of the city, where it was assured of the highest return per car kilometre. This desire brought the company into conflict with the municipal government, which looked to electric traction to alleviate the problems of the urban core by shifting population to the periphery of the city. William Mackenzie had faced much the same problem in Toronto, where the Toronto Street Railway adamantly refused to extend its service beyond the central urban zone created by its 1891 franchise, thereby forcing Toronto commuters to transfer (and pay an additional fare) to smaller radial streetcar companies operating into the suburbs. In São Paulo, Mackenzie and Pearson insisted that the fledgling company's first objective must be to build up a solid, profitable base of ridership in the central portions of the city, before venturing into the as yet thinly populated suburbs. 'Pioneer' lines designed to make headway into the suburbs would be developed when such areas would bear the traffic. 'So far as my observation goes in São Paulo,' Pearson candidly admitted in September 1901,

this city is not of a character to warrant very frequent headway on any of the lines as there is no other method of transportation and the people would be more inclined to wait than walk. In our Northern cities where everyone is in a hurry, it very often happens that a company will make the mistake of operating too few cars thus diminishing riding and educating people to walk, but in Brazil I do not think there is much danger of this as the people are more indolent and not in any such great hurry, and with reasonably frequent service we would probably get all the business there is.[25]

Despite Pearson's reservations, the company endeavoured to expand its service as rapidly as possible. The growth in ridership was phenomenal. By 1905, the trams were carrying just under twenty million passengers a year. Such ridership exerted a tremendous strain on the company's ability to keep pace, especially in the area of acquiring new cars, and also on the quality of its service. 'With nearly every car in service for 18 to 20 hours per day,' Alexander Mackenzie complained to Toronto in March 1903, 'it has been impossible to keep them in proper condition.'[26] To relieve this pressure, the company placed an order for twenty cars with a Rio firm and began experimenting with new car designs in its own shops. These Brazilian-built trolleys, the first major purchase by the company in Brazil, were adapted to the exigencies of tramway operation in the tropics. The bodies were, for instance, constructed of native woods, because the wood used in American-built cars rotted with alarming rapidity. Like any new service, the São Paulo company experienced its share of teething problems, but as R.C. Brown, reflecting on his North American experience, admitted: 'It is impossible to start a new road and put it into operation on a basis that is to be the final one. I think that no close criticism should be made until the road has been operated long enough to work down to a basis.' Despite the unavoidable problems, the response of the São Paulo citizenry to the Canadian *bondes* was so great that by 1905 even Pearson had abandoned his initial caution about expanding the service. 'Inasmuch as we have a monopoly in the city for tramway lines,' he advised the board, 'we are bound to provide all reasonable facilities and make such extensions as are required. As these extensions will all be profitable, and probably earn as much per track miles as the lines we now have, I should advise that they be constructed immediately.'[27]

Passengers were not the only profitable business. The company endeavoured to build a freight service, for which it constructed a small fleet of trams especially designed to carry meat, freight, mail, gravel, and water. Traffic in freight would serve to provide off-peak business for the system and would allow the company to share in the city's tremendous industrial expansion. The freight trams met with considerable consumer resistance in a city that was already well served by an abundance of cheap, if slow, ox-carts. As in other aspects of its operations, the North American managers had to adapt to the cultural traits of their clientele. An exasperated Robert Brown, for instance, reported in 1901 on his inability to extract any freighting business from the suburbs, where ox-carters abounded. 'It is very difficult to argue with people who do not value their own time any more than these people do,' he ethnocentrically complained. 'You have no idea what an independent lot they are ... It is hard work to worm business out of people of this temperament.'[28] Slowly customer resistance was eroded and, by 1903, the freight department had become a thriving concern. Similarly, enormous success was enjoyed when a 'special' car, especially fitted out to cater to wedding parties, civic festivities, and even funerals, was introduced. In a city that had yet to experience the coming of the automobile, the 'special' car set a new standard for prestigious transportation in São Paulo. 'The directors must not deal with this,' Alexander Mackenzie said of the 'special' car, 'having regard to conditions in Toronto. There are no similar conditions there. While such a car might be a "white elephant" in Toronto, here I am satisfied it would be a sure earner.'[29]

The passenger service remained the backbone of the system and, as such, was faced with the thorny question of rate structure. The original concession had granted a flat 200 réis fare per zone that, despite its apparent cheapness when judged by North American standards, had placed tramway service within the reach of only the middle and upper classes, leaving all but the most affluent of the working class to walk to work or dwell in close proximity to their places of work. On his initial visit to São Paulo, Fred Pearson had informally promised Antônio Prado that the company would introduce a system of second-class fares as soon as the tram service had been solidly established. Naturally, the company's promoters were eager to preserve the lucrative benefit of the full-fare system. In 1901 Pearson himself instructed James Mitchell, the new general manager in São Paulo, 'to be very careful in any negotiations that you have with the City Authorities not to yield more than is absolutely necessary in any of these matters.'[30] When Prado inquired when cheap fares for workers and school children were to be introduced, Pearson weakened in his resolve. 'I think it is far better,' he instructed Mitchell, 'for a corporation to carry out everything to the letter that it agrees to do and then be very careful about promising anything. This is better than half promising and evading the promise.' Mitchell was to visit Prado and tell him that cheap fares would be introduced because 'we consider this necessary in order to comply with the concession.'[31] Only after prolonged negotiations, however, was a new concession framed and approved by the municipal *câmara* in 1909. The company agreed to provide 'cars suitable for workmen, or any class of labourers, even though bare-footed, with 100 réis fare, they being permitted to carry with them small packages and tools.' Many of the old Viação Paulista horse cars were refurbished and attached to the rear of the electric cars during the peak hours. These 'trailers,' or *carros para operários*, served to bring the tramway revolution to São Paulo's working class and, although the policy was not fully implemented until 1909, greatly increased ridership.[32] Similarly, reduced fares of 100 réis for school children introduced the youth of the city to the age of electric traction.

Problems with second-class fares did little to diminish the enormous overall success of the tramway system. 'I may say that the outlook for business is most promising,' Alexander Mackenzie had noted just after the inauguration of service in May 1900, '... and there is no doubt of the immense success of the enterprise.'[33] Between 1901 and 1905, the annual gross earnings of the trams more than doubled from \$630,282 to \$1,357,926. The net income jumped even more spectacularly, primarily because costs steadily declined after the first few years of intensive construction.[34] For William Mackenzie in Toronto, these returns must have been very gratifying, especially in comparison to the returns of the Toronto Street Railway. In almost every respect, the São Paulo trams were better profit makers than their Toronto counterparts. The São Paulo fleet, running over 75 miles of track produced gross earnings of 37.50 cents per car mile in 1906, whereas the Toronto fleet, operating over 105 miles of track, generated only 22.60 cents per car mile. While operating expenses per mile were slightly higher in São Paulo (13.43 cents vs 11.97 cents), operating expenses as a percentage of gross income were considerably in the Brazilian system's favour (35.74 per cent vs 52.9 per cent). It was in the area of cost of labour and municipal taxation that the São Paulo company really excelled. The highest rate paid per hour to a trainman was only 19.85 cents in São Paulo, whereas in Toronto it was 23.50 cents. Taxes as a percentage of gross earnings were only 3.39

per cent in São Paulo, while in Toronto they equalled 11.22 per cent.[35]

When Fred Pearson returned from an inspection of the São Paulo tramway system in 1906, he reported that these splendid financial results were the product of 'exceptional local traffic conditions.' *Paulistanos*, he claimed, had taken to the trams with such avidity because of the hilly terrain of their city and its hot, humid climate. Furthermore, because of the relatively high population density, there tended to be a high ridership over short distances, thereby giving the company the best possible return for the least outlay in construction and maintenance. Lastly, the trams benefited from the availability of abundant Parnaíba power.[36] William Mackenzie and Fred Pearson, it seems, had chosen the right city at the right time.

While the tramway service had been designed to consume the base load of the power system, it was hoped that demand for lighting and industrial uses would soon consume the residual electricity. Here the company had a much tougher fight. It was to take more than a decade before the São Paulo Tramway, Light and Power Company was able to dislodge its competitors for the lucrative public-lighting business of the city and thereby consolidate its grasp on the full spectrum of power and traction services in São Paulo. Delays in reaching this goal were the result of the municipal government's insistence that some modicum of competition be maintained in the public-lighting field.

There was no doubt that a sizeable market for electric lighting existed in São Paulo. After Brown had surveyed the city in 1899, he had confidently reported that the 'City and State Governments both desire the introduction of arc lighting for the streets, and I feel sure ... they will be glad to make a contract as soon as the certainty of the Light is assured.' The inadequacy of São Paulo's public lighting in the 1890s was painfully apparent to anyone who dared to venture onto its streets for an evening stroll. For a semi-tropical city, where nightfall came with little variation every evening at six o'clock, São Paulo had only an inadequate system of gas lights, which at intermittent distances cast a murky, flickering light. This universally decried service was provided by the British-owned San Paulo Gas Company, which had inaugurated gas lighting in the city in 1872 under the terms of an 1863 concession granted to a mixed British-Brazilian syndicate by the state, under whose jurisdiction the operation of gas companies fell. In 1869, a purely British syndicate bought the concession. The British company registered some success in erecting a gas works, but the service subsequently became the focus of much public criticism.[37] This was attributable to several factors. The 1863 concession was ill suited to the exigencies of a rapidly growing city, a situation that was exacerbated after 1869 by the split in jurisdiction over the gas industry between the state and municipal governments. More importantly, the producers of coal gas were obliged to import all of their coal and consequently found themselves at the mercy of Brazil's fluctuating exchange rate. To counteract this financial uncertainty, the San Paulo Gas Company demanded a 'gold clause' in its concession, guaranteeing a certain proportion of its earnings in gold. This request predictably bedevilled relations with Brazilian politicians and led to a complete stalemate in 1888, when the original concession lapsed. Not until 1897 was a new contract signed, giving the San Paulo Gas Company a thirty-year franchise and a gold-clause privilege, but denying it an absolute monopoly on city lighting.[38] After two decades of indifferent service, the state government left the door open to potential competitors who, they trusted, would induce the English company to provide a higher standard of service.

It was this possibility of competition that Gualco and Souza sensed when they approached the municipal government of São Paulo with a request for a contract for public illumination. Under the cautious guidance of Antônio Prado, the city had just passed a detailed act regulating the 'distribution of power and light by electricity.' The principal feature of this legislation – a feature designed to ensure competition – was the division of the city into four sectors for lighting purposes.[39] Prospective concessionaires might apply for rights in any or all of the sectors, although other promoters were not barred from applying for similar rights. In September 1899, Gualco and Souza secured a contract from the municipality giving them privileges 'for the transmission, exploitation or sale of light and power' in all four sectors of the city.[40] The gas company therefore retired to its established trade in gas lighting and prepared to contend with its would-be competitors. Prado, for his part, could draw satisfaction from the fact that, with these companies vying to serve the city's lighting needs, a decent measure of competition had been preserved.

Prado's satisfaction was short-lived. Instead of dealing with Gualco and Souza, two local entrepreneurs, the city soon found itself confronted by

the São Paulo Tramway, *Light* and Power Company, which had inherited
the lighting concession when it bought out its Brazilian progenitors.
Prado was now confronted with two well-capitalized foreign firms, one
dealing in gas, the other in electricity, and only one small, indigenous
firm, the Companhia Água e Luz, dealing in electricity. Even this situation
did not remain for long. From the beginning, the São Paulo Tramway,
Light and Power Company was determined to live up to its name and
install itself as *the* light and power company of São Paulo. The first step
was to gain control of the Água e Luz firm and thereby clear the field of
any potential competition for electric lighting. Founded in 1886, the
Companhia Água e Luz was, by any standard, a puny competitor. It
produced a mere 500 kilowatts of power from its steam generating plant
on Rua São Caetano. The Água e Luz, like so many indigenous São Paulo
enterprises, was starved for capital and thereby prevented from expanding to meet the growing market.

Realizing the vulnerability of the Água e Luz, the São Paulo company
acted quickly. In February 1900, the directors empowered Pearson 'to see
what could be done in the way of procuring the franchise of the Electric
Light Company [sic] in the City of São Paulo, for about $250,000.'[41]
Throughout the early months of 1900, Alexander Mackenzie quietly
purchased stock in the Água e Luz company. By June, he reported to the
board that he had obtained 86 per cent of the Água e Luz stock and 60 per
cent of its debentures 'for about $250,000.' Financial cover for this
transaction had been provided by a £50,000 advance from the Canadian
Bank of Commerce in Toronto.[42] The acquisition immediately provided
the São Paulo company with a temporary source of thermal-electric
power with which it could inaugurate its streetcar service. It also dealt a
blow to the plans of Prefect Antônio Prado to preserve an element of
competition in the city's electric lighting.

Fred Pearson was determined to use this victory to fashion a complete
monopoly over the city's lighting needs by routing the gas company. In
anticipation of this campaign, he ordered 25,000 incandescent lamps
from the General Electric Company in March 1900. Pearson realized that
if the company was to achieve its goal, the first victory would have to be a
psychological one, gained by showing *paulistanos* that electric lighting was
in every respect better than gas lighting. 'I would suggest if you have not
made a contract with city authorities for street lighting,' he instructed
Brown, 'that it would be a good plan to illuminate Largo São Bento, and

perhaps some street in the central part of the city where it would attract attention ... [and] ... demonstrate to them the great advantage of electricity over gas illumination for street purposes.' By securing a firm grasp on public lighting, the company could then hope to build up its electricity sales to private consumers, once again displacing the gas company.[43]

Pearson's hope of a complete monopoly of both domestic and public electric lighting was, at least for the time being, stymied by his opponent. The gas company countered by lowering its prices for domestic gas consumers and by clinging to its 1897 public-illumination contract with the state. The municipal government, with which the São Paulo company would have to negotiate, steadfastly refused the Canadian company's demand that it be allowed to illuminate densely populated areas of the city's central core, the so-called Triângulo, as well as the suburbs. The impasse resulted from the city's eagerness to have the sprawling, largely unilluminated suburbs efficiently lit and the company's determination not to undertake suburban lighting without some access to the more lucrative market in the urban core.[44] The company's position was doubly complicated by the fact that jurisdiction over São Paulo utilities was divided between the municipal and state governments. While the company had to petition the municipal politicians for a city lighting contract, it was to the state legislators that it had to turn for redress against the San Paulo Gas Company's 1897 contract. Operating in this jurisdictional maze required incredible tact.

Political intransigence and competitive jealousies held the company's public-lighting ambitions in check throughout the first decade of its existence. During this period, the managers were keenly aware of the need to fend off the 'growing competition' from gas, which still supplied a large amount of street lighting and was favoured by *paulistanos* for cooking. As one manager noted in 1907: 'As the Gas Company here is going after business, making installations free, and giving rates that are reasonable, we cannot take any chances of giving dissatisfaction to our customers and must moreover be ready to quickly satisfy the desires of prospective customers.'[45] Such competitive vigilance opened the way to two tactical gains. In 1906, the company signed a street-lighting contract with a group of private businessmen in the central business district. The following year a combined group of merchants and bankers from the city petitioned the state governor to provide electric lights for the urban core.[46] These two developments underscored the fact that large areas of the city were receiving inadequate lighting service and consequently opened a chink in the San Paulo Gas Company's monopoly on public illumination.

The other significant gain for the São Paulo company came in 1909 when it managed to defeat a challenge to its right to generate and distribute electricity. In 1908, the municipal *câmara* had granted a power-distribution concession to a powerful Rio firm, Guinle and Company. It was a potent challenge since, if successful, it would once again have thrown the electricity industry in São Paulo wide open. 'I hope you will find some way of preventing the Guinles getting a foothold in São Paulo,' Pearson cabled from Paris, 'and that Mr. Mackenzie will be able to arrange with Dr. Prado for some kind of quasi-monopoly for Light and Power. I appreciate, however, that this will be a very difficult matter to accomplish on account of the great objection to monopolies, which is general throughout the world.'[47] In the ensuing, vigorously contested lawsuit, company lawyers successfully maintained that the Guinle contract infringed on the company's rights as laid out in the 1899 municipal code governing electricity distribution. The court sustained this point of view, arguing that any area in which the company provided service was in fact *lugares occupados*, or occupied territories, and therefore closed to further competition. As Pearson had feared, the legal decision in the company's favour was an unpopular one with those who sought to induce competition in the city's utilities. None the less it opened the way for the company to secure, in 1911, its first contract to provide lighting in those areas of the suburbs as yet unlit by gas or electricity.[48] It was not until 1916, however, that the São Paulo company was able to sign its first unified lighting concession with the state government. The company's seventeen-year wait for this contract was primarily caused by the dogged persistence of the San Paulo Gas Company and the civic politicians in their opposition to the Canadian company.

While São Paulo politicians seemed reluctant to illuminate their streets with electricity, the local citizenry displayed little resistance to electric lighting in their homes. Despite the fact that rates for domestic electric lighting were high and only within reach of the more affluent, the company enjoyed a steady growth in its private lighting business. From 11,000 connected incandescent lamps in 1901, the number of lamps increased to 51,320 by 1908. By 1908, however, there were only 1,458 arc lamps in the company's circuit, indicating that its campaign for the broad use of arc lighting in São Paulo's streets had been a modest success at best.[49]

São Paulo industrialists embraced the electric age with astonishing alacrity. It was in the field of furnishing power to São Paulo's burgeoning industrial economy that the Canadian company had its most dramatic impact. R.C. Brown had sensed the tremendous potential for industrial electric power when he first visited the city in 1899. Several manufacturers had already installed small thermal-electric plants in their factories. The rest maintained their reliance on steam engines, fuelled by costly imported coal. The prospect of obtaining this market made it imperative that the Parnaíba water power be developed as expeditiously as possible. Industrial consumers could not be courted until the company had a large surplus of power. The four 1,400-kilowatt generating machines at Parnaíba gave just such a surplus. With coal selling at the equivalent of $13 to $16 a ton, Parnaíba power offered an immediately competitive alternative.

One of the chief explanations of the company's ultimate success in São Paulo was the constant availability of power for growth. Except during the occasional drought, such as that in the early 1920s, the São Paulo company's generating capacity was always one step ahead of demand. It was not until the hectic years of post-war urban and industrial growth in the late 1940s that this pattern was broken. The original Parnaíba plant had, for instance, an initial generating capacity of 5,600 kilowatts, well above the demand projected by Brown in his 1899 survey of the market. Without waiting for demand to exceed supply, the company added an additional four generating machines at Parnaíba by 1910 and instigated an intensive search for new water-power sites. After investigating several sites, Pearson strongly advised William Mackenzie to have the company acquire a promising site at Pau d'Alho, near the town of Pirapora on the Tietê River. For Pearson this was 'the most valuable water power in the vicinity of São Paulo and it is greatly in the interests of the company to control this rather than to have it fall into the hands of parties antagonistic to us.'[50]

The rapidity and thoroughness of electricity's conquest of São Paulo's industry was astounding. By July 1904, the company had 169 large power consumers, whose 231 electric motors had a capacity of 2,060 kilowatts. Power users ranged from the flour mills of Francisco Matarazzo (with

28.7 per cent of the company's industrial power load) and the cotton mills of the Companhia Industrial de São Paulo and Rodolfo Crespi Cia to a broad range of small users including machine shops, food processors, sugar mills, and coffee-cleaning mills. In March 1907, the company could report that it was providing 3,767 kilowatts to 257 large consumers with 418 motors. One indicator of the growth of large-scale, factory operations was the expansion of Francisco Matarazzo's flour mills to take 39.9 per cent of the company's industrial power business.[51]

Not surprisingly, the pervasiveness of the company's control of industrial electricity prompted a persistent debate over the reasonableness of its rates. The Gualco concession stipulated a flat rate of 700 réis (about eighteen cents) per kilowatt hour for power to motors of a capacity of five horsepower or more. While this rate was adhered to in many contracts, it was lowered when a consumer was prepared to sign a long-term contract. Indeed the company was more eager to find buyers for its surplus of Parnaíba power than to impose high rates on a restricted clientele. Low rates had the further advantage of dissuading potential competitors from entering the power-generating market.

The appearance of prospective competitors on the scene in 1908 in the form of Guinle and Company, to whom the *câmara* had awarded a concession, was sufficient to make the São Paulo company reconsider its rates. 'Personally,' Pearson confided to E.R. Wood, 'I do not have much fear from any competition with the Guinles as we have the tramways which yield a great part of our income and while they might reduce the price of power and light somewhat by competition, I do not think it possible for them to take very much of our business and as soon as we get ample power, I am strongly in favour of reducing our price for light very materially ...'[52] In 1909, with the expansion of Parnaíba to eight units nearly completed, the company reached agreement with the municipality for the downward revision of its rates. The maximum rate for electric power was, for instance, cut from 700 to 300 réis. As Pearson had predicted, power sales surged.

Electricity was thus at the very heart of São Paulo's remarkable industrial expansion in the opening decade and a half of the twentieth century. Symptoms of this tremendous growth abounded. The population of São Paulo state increased from 2,282,279 at the turn of the century to 3,256,610 in 1914, while that of the city swelled from 239,820 to 375,439. More significantly, the industries of the city, principally its textile, milling, and light manufacturing sectors, grew to assume a dominance in the national economy that was out of all proportion to the state's population. By 1914, São Paulo state contributed 30.7 per cent of all Brazilian industrial production.[53] Brazilians have often jokingly, and to some degree jealously, compared São Paulo 'with its powerful coffee interests and its precocious industrial progress' to a locomotive 'pulling the twenty more or less empty boxcars representing the other Brazilian states.'[54] If this is so, then surely the locomotive was an electric model.

While scholars have differed over many facets of modern Brazil's economic development, an unprecedented consensus has emerged concerning the crucial significance of electricity in São Paulo's industrial evolution. Richard Morse, in his study of São Paulo's urban development, has emphasized that in a city where solid fuels were scarce, the presence of hydro power was of central importance and that, without it, subsequent economic growth 'would have been far milder.'[55] Stanley Stein has attributed the 'golden years' of the Brazilian cotton industry – from the 1890s to the 1930s – to four factors: tariff protection, the great coffee boom, the abundance of cheap labour, and 'the establishment of hydroelectric plants by foreign corporations,' which permitted cotton mills 'to abandon dependence upon direct water and costly coal-burning steam installations for cheap and more reliable hydroelectric power.'[56] Warren Dean and Werner Baer, two of the leading theorists of Brazilian economic history, have also isolated electricity as a formative factor in São Paulo's accelerated economic growth.[57] Above all else, electricity was providing São Paulo, and indirectly all of Brazil, with a means of diversifying its economy away from what had often proved to be its dangerous reliance upon commodity exports and finished imports. The price that Brazilians would ultimately have to pay for this more balanced, less externally reliant economy was a continued disproportionate concentration of economic power in São Paulo. Recognition of this regional imbalance was already apparent by 1902, when Alexander Mackenzie reported to Toronto on the city's steady advance. 'I think we can fairly look forward to São Paulo in the near future being a city very much larger in population and wealth than it is today ... The manager of the German Bank in Rio ... told me the other day that notwithstanding that São Paulo was only a city of something like 300,000 and Rio about 700,000, there was really more legitimate business done here [in São Paulo] by the banks than in Rio.'[58]

The operational success of the São Paulo company was firmly rooted in its financial management. While the power and tramway operations in São Paulo quickly proved to be steady profit earners, they required large inflows of capital to keep pace with the ever-expanding market for utility services. When it was incorporated in 1899, the São Paulo company had a capital stock of $6 million, which was divided into 60,000 shares of $100 each. It was also authorized to issue up to $6 million in thirty-year gold bonds, bearing 5 per cent interest. Under the terms of the original agreement of May 1899 between William Mackenzie and the company, the entire capital stock was issued to William Mackenzie, who in turn disposed of it to his immediate circle of friends and financial associates in the Toronto and Montreal investment community. Not only was this arrangement lucrative for Mackenzie; it also allowed him to maintain a tight rein on the company's affairs. At a shareholders' meeting on 30 April 1902, for instance, Mackenzie was able to muster either proxies or representatives for 43,249 of the company's 60,000 shares. William Mackenzie's control of the common stock gave him not only complete control over corporate policy but also tremendous power over the market value of the stock.

Since his close friends and financial allies felt honour bound not to dispose of their stock without prior permission, Mackenzie was virtually assured that São Paulo stock would remain protected from market fluctuations. During the 1903 stock market 'panic,' for instance, São Paulo stock rode out the storm while other stocks foundered. 'The reason that it did not fall more,' Fred Pearson boastfully reported, 'is due to the fact that the stock is owned by a few people who did not care to sell it, and that very little of it is held on margin.'[59] From the beginning, therefore, São Paulo stock won a reputation as a steady, reliable investment and, as the first decade of the century wore on, the circle of ownership slowly widened to include small, independent buyers in Toronto and Montreal and, gradually, in the United States and Europe, who eagerly bought up modest lots of the stock, confident of a good return on their investment. When it came time for the annual meeting, however, it was William Mackenzie who invariably tabled a thick envelope of proxies and assumed control of the proceedings.

Similarly, the São Paulo company's board of directors remained fully within William Mackenzie's pale of influence. While by 1906, the board had been expanded to ten members, it still contained a hard core of the president's financial associates. George Cox, Frederic Nicholls, Henry Mill Pellatt, E.R. Wood, and J.H. Plummer all represented the tight Toronto community that had supported the company from its inception. Alexander Mackenzie sat on the board and voiced the operational concerns of the enterprise. F.S. Pearson provided an engineer's view, while R.M. Horne-Payne, who joined the board in 1906, represented English financial interests. The premature death of Alexander William Mackenzie, the president's second son, made room on the board for Z.A. Lash, the distinguished legal counsel. The full board seldom met. Instead, meetings were sparsely attended and usually did little more than set the official seal of corporate approval on decisions already taken by William Mackenzie and F.S. Pearson.

The early shareholders of the São Paulo company had much to be satisfied with during the first years of its operations. By January 1902, William Mackenzie was able to report to the shareholders that, even though its installations were still under construction, the company was showing 'a gratifying earning power.' On 1 July of the same year the first of what was to become a steady stream of dividends was paid out to the shareholders. Between July 1902 and December 1910, quarterly dividends ranging from 1¼ to 2¼ per cent were paid out to São Paulo shareholders to a total of $6,869,676.83.[60] 'The Company's earnings are splendid,' Byron Walker of the Canadian Bank of Commerce wrote to his assistant general manager in 1903, 'and would doubtless warrant a larger dividend if the Treasury bonds were but sold.'[61] From São Paulo, Alexander Mackenzie reported in the same year to his good friend W.H. Blake, a Toronto lawyer and a shareholder in the São Paulo company, that he foresaw 'nothing but a steady increase in our earnings.'[62] Fred Pearson, in a moment of financial euphoria in late 1905, confidently predicted that 'the net earnings of our company will be from 15 to 18% on the stock and I should not be surprised if the company was showing 20 per cent before the end of five years.'[63]

If the rewards of risking capital in São Paulo were gratifying, the costs of building and maintaining public-utilities services in São Paulo were immense. Between 1902 and 1910, the company's capital expenditures in the city totalled $7,779,883. Operating costs totalled $6,361,714 for the same years. At times, particularly during the financial 'panics' of 1903 and 1907 when European and North-American capital became scarce, the company had difficulty finding sufficient capital to meet the obligations stipulated in its concession. On occasion, the board was forced to finance capital expenditures on the basis of a generous line of credit from the Canadian Bank of Commerce, and even this was sometimes exceeded. 'While the directors appreciate the conditions in São Paulo,' Pearson complained to J.M. Smith in 1906, 'I do not imagine the Bank of Commerce have any appreciation of the amount of work we have done since the original bonds were sold, and I think it would be well for you to explain to them how much money has been expended in extensions and developments of the property since the original financial plan was completed.'[64] The periodic cash crises were to some degree brought on by Pearson's impetuous spending habits, which often overcommitted the company. In 1907, for instance, when the world money market was plunged into confusion by a brief recession, the company was caught overextended and was forced to institute a regime of severe financial austerity in its construction program.[65]

The financial management of the São Paulo company placed a heavy burden on the shoulders of its promoters. On the one hand, there was the need to satisfy the expectations of the original underwriters by maintaining a high dividend return, usually about 8 per cent, on their investment. On the other hand, there was the insatiable demand for capital in São Paulo, where the company was caught up in an expensive process of forced growth. Expenditures such as the electrification of the Viação Paulista system and the installation of additional units at Parnaíba were unavoidable if the concession was to be consolidated. The cost of such expansion was onerous and, as Pearson complained in 1908, other aspects of the company's financial affairs, such as maintaining its surplus account, suffered on account of the devotion to capital expenditure.

Incessant pressure of capital expenditure was alleviated by the gradual expansion of the company's capital stock from the original $6 million to $10 million by October 1907. As William Mackenzie assured the shareholders in April 1902, when the first of these increases was approved, the enlarged capital stock was 'advisable and necessary because of the most satisfactory growth of the company's business, and the gratifying results of its operations in São Paulo.'[66] As with the original flotations, these increases were taken up and sold to the investing public by the directors and their friends.[67] Eventually, the shares found their way into the hands of scattered independent investors, usually through the medium of such Toronto brokerage houses as Pellatt and Pellatt and A.E. Ames and Co., which were under the influence of São Paulo directors Henry Pellatt and George Cox, respectively.

The funded debt experienced similar expansionary pressures through-out the first decade of operations. Although an issue of $6 million worth of 5 per cent thirty-year gold bonds was originally created, only $4,125,000 worth were initially sold.[68] By early 1900, however, the bonds were being offered to Canadian investors through the local press and, in February 1900, a 'pooling' agreement was made with the National Trust, the trustee, to facilitate the movement of the bonds onto the open investment market.[69] In November of the same year, the board issued the remaining authorized first-mortgage bonds, thereby placing in the public's hands the entire funded debt of the company.

From an early date, however, it became apparent that the restricted Canadian capital market was incapable of absorbing all the securities offered to it by the expanding Brazilian utility. The São Paulo company was forced to turn to the English and European capital markets for its capital requirements. By 1900, São Paulo bonds were being offered to English investors in sterling denominations. In 1906 arrangements were made for R.M. Horne-Payne and the British Empire Trust Company to act as the São Paulo company's transfer agent and registrar in London.[70] In the same month, Horne-Payne was elected to the São Paulo board, thereby giving would-be European investors representation in the direction of corporate policies. Through the British Empire Trust, Pearson was able to make contact with some of the most prestigious and successful English financial houses. By 1908, the company's securities were handled by some of the most aggressive and successful financial houses of the City, notably Sperling and Co., Kitcat and Aitken, and Dunn, Fischer and Co. Mackenzie and Horne-Payne employed this same chain of financial connections to harness the savings of investors scattered throughout the British Isles to the capital needs of the Canadian Northern Railway and, later, the other Latin American utilities in which Mackenzie took an interest.

From London it was but a short jump to the centres of European investment in Brussels and Paris. Once again, Pearson and Wood reconnoitred the potential market and reported back to Toronto that if the small European investor was to be attracted to the São Paulo company, he would have to be offered a highly portable form of security in small denominations. 'In my talk with brokers in London and on the continent,'

Pearson reported, 'it is evident that the São Paulo stock at its present price, and it will probably go higher, is too large a share to find a ready market in England and on the continent.'[71] A partial solution to this problem was found in 1908, when bearer share warrants were introduced, thereby providing European investors with a highly portable security and one that enabled its holders to preserve their anonymity in such countries as Belgium, where taxes weighed heavily upon investors. As a consequence, Pearson was able to negotiate an option covering as many as 10,000 shares with the Brussels brokerage firm of Stallaerts and Loewenstein in March 1908. Alfred Loewenstein, an aggressive young Belgian broker, assured Pearson shortly thereafter that he believed 'a very large and free market [in Europe] can be created which would cause a great appreciation in the price of the São Paulo stock' and that 'there would be a constant transfer of shares from Canada and England to the Belgian and Swiss investors.'[72] To expedite the process of creating the European market, the company contributed about £3,000 to a newspaper 'campaign' launched by Loewenstein to publicize the São Paulo enterprise to Belgian investors.[73]

The creation of an international market for the bonds and shares of the São Paulo company did not extend to Europe alone. While it was financially advantageous to offer shares to Europeans, it was politically expedient to offer shares to the citizens of the country in which the company generated its profits. As early as April 1902, William Mackenzie had advised the shareholders that the directors had decided to offer 4,000 shares 'for subscription by prominent citizens of São Paulo, as it is felt the company's interests will be well served by increasing the amount of our capital owned locally in Brazil.'[74] As a result of his decision, small numbers of São Paulo bonds and shares found their way into the hands of such influential Brazilians as Carlos de Campos, the company's leading legal counsel, and Henry Schulman, a Scottish-born engineer who, as a successful local merchant, had assisted the Canadian company in its first years in the city. The capital garnered from such subscriptions was relatively unimportant, but the political insurance provided by having Brazilians hold even the smallest amount of stock was immense. It was the same instinct of self-preservation that had prompted Pearson to appoint Alípio de Borba as traffic manager for the São Paulo trams. In 1909, Dr Alfredo Maia, a former federal minister of railways and public works, was appointed to the board, thereby becoming the first Brazilian to be admitted. The necessity of taking such precautionary measures was indicative of a series of nagging political and financial problems, which, no matter how successful the company was at making profits in São Paulo or winning the support of European investors, were never far from the minds of its promoters in Toronto. The problems of fluctuating exchange rates and Brazilian politics were central to this anxiety.

Nothing affected the company's overall welfare as much as the mercurial behaviour of Brazilian exchange. The rate of exchange directly governed the company's ability to convert its earnings in milréis into 'hard' currency. From the first day of its operations in São Paulo, the ever-present problem of exchange introduced a dangerously unpredictable aspect into the company's calculations. A low rate of exchange could, for instance, substantially reduce the foreign-currency equivalent of milréis earnings. 'It is pure guessing what the rate is likely to be for any given period,' Alexander Mackenzie rather dejectedly reported to E.R. Wood in 1902. 'When we are remitting please remember this and pray that we may guess right.'[75]

Fluctuating exchange rates were endemic to Brazil's economic situation. With its heavy reliance on finished imports, staple exports, and capital inflows, Brazil was always in delicate financial health. Any appreciable slide in the value of its coffee exports or any advance in the costs of American or British goods could push down the value of the milréis. On the other hand, a good coffee crop and a buoyant world market could inflate the value of the milréis. Fluctuating exchange therefore elicited differing responses from various interests within the economic community. Importers feared a falling milréis because it made the goods they imported more expensive and forced them to boost prices, thereby constricting their market. On the other hand, Brazilians interested in stimulating economic diversification looked for a lower milréis value to choke off the flow of imported, finished goods and to deflect demand to domestic producers. Exchange was thus a crucial mechanism in the Brazilian economy and one over which, to a large degree, Brazilians had no control.

In the 1890s, Brazilian exchange had slipped inexorably downward. The confidence instilled by the declaration of the republic in 1889 had triggered a speculative boom, the so-called *Encilhamento*, in Brazilian investment that had pushed the milréis to a record equivalent of 27½d. in British funds by November 1889. The ensuing collapse of this speculation initiated a steady decline in the value of the milréis. By 1897, the milréis had shrunk to a meagre 5½d.[76] This decline had a disastrous impact on Brazil's ability to clear its foreign debts. Loans contracted when exchange was high came due when it took double the number of milréis to honour the original obligation in foreign currency. The imminent danger of a massive default was only averted by the timely intervention of H.M. Rothschild and Sons, who in 1898 were able to arrange a funding loan that consolidated and postponed the amortization of the Brazilian national debt. Brazilian exchange was thus a matter of transoceanic concern and stood, in the eyes of Brazilian coffee growers and London bankers alike, as the prime indicator of the country's at times precarious economic health.

The São Paulo company established itself in Brazil at a time of low, but gradually recovering, exchange. Initially, this had a beneficial effect because it allowed the company to maximize the purchasing power of the dollars it was bringing into the country. 'We have a magnificent property in São Paulo,' William Mackenzie boasted in 1908, 'and are to be congratulated upon the fact that the greater part of our money went in there when exchange was low so that the dollar purchased a greater number of milréis, and thus accomplished a greater amount of work than now, and as a result, we at present obtain an excellent return upon the investment.'[77] It did not, however, take long for the company to change its tune on the question of exchange. Once the tramway and power departments began generating profits in São Paulo, the company developed a vested interest in maximizing the foreign-currency equivalent of its milréis earnings.

Throughout its first decade the São Paulo company benefited from the efforts of the Brazilian federal government to push exchange rates upwards. An average rate of about 12d. prevailed throughout the first five years of the new century, and peaks as high as 18d. were achieved in 1907. The procurement of exchange for remittance was still fraught with difficulties. In September 1907, J.M. Smith in Toronto reported to Horne-Payne that earnings for the preceding month had shown 'a most gratifying increase in Brazilian currency' but that 'on account of the depreciation in exchange the same relative increase is not exhibited in Sterling or Canadian currency.'[78] Fluctuating exchange had the further effect of enormously complicating the company's accounting. It also made the process of reporting earnings to Canadian and British investors, who did not understand the vagaries of Brazilian exchange, an almost impossible task. When Alexander Mackenzie submitted his draft comments for the 1905 annual report, he complained that 'with exchange it is always the unexpected that happens.'[79]

Exchange fluctuations also had a direct bearing upon the company's rates in São Paulo. A tram fare of 200 réis, while an adequate return on investment at the time a concession was signed, might become grossly inadequate as a falling rate of exchange eroded the foreign value of the milréis. The company's fixed tariff schedules came with a built-in vulnerability to Brazilian inflation and exchange. Some companies, such as the San Paulo Gas, were afforded a measure of protection from this phenomenon by the inclusion in their concessions of a 'gold clause,' which guaranteed that a set portion (usually half) of each billing would be calculated at the prevailing gold rate. The São Paulo company had the right only to renegotiate its fare structure on a periodic basis. In response to the problem of exchange fluctuations, the Brazilian government moved in 1906 through the Convention of Taubaté to implement a policy of 'coffee valorization' aimed at preventing a glut of the coffee market through overproduction. If coffee prices slipped below a specified level, the federal and state governments would intervene in the market, buying up surpluses that would be fed back onto the market when prices improved. This bold precedent had the effect of moderating exchange fluctuations and of keeping exchange high and stable at around 15d.[80] Even with this support and the buoyant pre-war Brazilian economy, the exchange problem became a perennial *bête noire* for the São Paulo company for the all-important reason that it threatened the lifeblood of the whole enterprise – the flow of remittances from Brazil to the investors and creditors of North America and Europe.

The precariousness of exchange was the most visible example of a broad spectrum of economic and political variables. On the very broadest plane, there was the problem of political instability in Brazil. The political upheavals of the early 1890s, when Brazil had succumbed to civil war, had implanted a lasting impression in the minds of foreign investors that Brazil was a political volcano. As an English bank official nervously confided to Byron Walker of the Canadian Bank of Commerce in 1901: 'Everything in the future, however, depends upon the government keeping straight.'[81] Few who visited Brazil, however, came away with nagging doubts about political security. After a period of initial turmoil, republican Brazil functioned smoothly under the guidance of a succession of presidents who exercised power in the interests of the prosperous states of São Paulo and Minas Gerais. This suzerainty was embodied in the federal presidencies of Prudente de Morais (1894–8), Campos Sales (1898–1902) and Rodrigues Alves (1902–6), all of whom were *paulistas.*[82] 'I have not the slightest fear of serious trouble arising from revolts,' Alexander Mackenzie reported in 1906.

The result of the last futile attempt in Rio (a barracks' mutiny), 14 months ago, to turn out the Government must have persuaded the few discontented spirits left in the army that the people will not submit to military domination ... It must be borne in mind that any such reports are almost certain to reach the outside world in a greatly exaggerated form. I cannot too often repeat that it is my firm conviction that property and life are just as safe here as in any large American or European city, and that foreign enterprises can always count on the sympathy and protection of the Government.[83]

The beneficence of the federal government did not ensure that the Canadian enterprise would enjoy universal popularity in Brazil. Like utility companies everywhere, the São Paulo company's trams and electricity touched the lives of practically every *paulistano.* It consequently soon attracted considerable attention and, at times, animosity. The focus of this hostility was the company's bid to consolidate its concessions into a thoroughgoing power and traction monopoly. Creation of such an unchallenged sway over São Paulo's power and traction needs was central to the company's plans. Such integration of services, they argued, benefited both promoter and citizen alike because it provided the greatest economies of scale and ensured the best co-ordination of power and traction services. Critics thought otherwise. Opponents of the business plans of William Mackenzie complained that monopoly in the electric-utilities industry left the door open to rate structures that were un-governed by competition and to arbitrary decisions affecting the nature of the services offered. Already by the turn of the century there were outspoken proponents of public control of utilities in Ontario, and their crusade for 'people's power' was to triumph ultimately with the creation of Ontario Hydro in 1906 and the 'clean-up' of Toronto's private utilities in 1921. In São Paulo, both the tenor of the criticism and the outcome of the contest between private and public control of utilities was to be otherwise.

The crucial difference in São Paulo was the nature of the competition the company faced. Judged by any standard, the Viação Paulista, Água e Luz, and San Paulo Gas companies had failed to rise to the challenge of the city's demand for efficient utilities. This conspicuous failure of entrepreneurs already established in São Paulo to meet the city's needs in part explained the willingness of civic politicians to embrace the Canadian promoters who appeared in their city in 1899. Company prospectuses emphasized the 'very liberal' nature of the concession it had purchased. Company officials, like Alexander Mackenzie, were always quick to praise Antônio Prado, the chief architect of this liberality. 'A more capable and intelligent administrator of the city's affairs,' Mackenzie noted in 1906, 'it would be difficult to find.'[84]

The São Paulo company was keenly aware that it would have to provide more than gratitude in return for its concession. Pearson constantly reiterated the need to provide 'good service' to the public, because it would fend off competitors and preserve the friendly disposition of civic politicians. The *bondes* of the Canadian company quickly established themselves as symbols of a swelling tide of civic pride. 'They are very proud of our street-car system,' Alexander Mackenzie commented in 1903, 'and are never tired of comparing it with Rio and Buenos Aires, and indeed the rest of the world.'[85] For most *paulistanos*, the Canadian company soon became known simply as 'The Light.' The calibre of service provided by the Canadian company therefore never really provided a focus for opposition. Instead, early opposition to the company's presence in São Paulo adopted a nationalistic, almost xenophobic bent that emphasized its foreign origins.

'It is fortunate,' Fred Pearson confided to the board in 1905, 'that we can legitimately expend a large amount of improvements on our property during the next two years, as otherwise, there would be certain to arise a feeling of jealousy against the company as a foreign corporation, which sooner or later, would affect us in some prejudicial manner.'[86] Despite such initiatives, attacks on the company became a fact of life for its managers. In some cases, they amounted to little more than verbal assaults, often instigated by such competitors as the San Paulo Gas, or the Guinle family in Rio, who were interested in breaking into the São Paulo market. On other occasions, the assaults became violent, as in June 1906 when striking workers on the Paulista Railway attempted to induce the tramway workers to follow their lead. 'Our men have held fast,' General

Manager Walmsley reported, 'and I believe are satisfied with their positions, and do not favour this movement at all. However, yesterday, crowds collected in the centre of the city, and becoming unruly smashed the windows on 10 or 12 of our cars.'[87] To protect company property, Prefect Prado supplied policemen to ride on the front platforms of the tram cars.

At times, the company's very success engendered hostility amongst its critics. The Guinle campaign to obtain access to the São Paulo market for electricity was justified by its promoters on the grounds that their Canadian competitors were making lavish profits. Yet, as Alexander Mackenzie was quick to point out, the rates these would-be competitors offered to the city in return for a concession were 'so absurd' that few could believe that they were designed for any other purpose than to sabotage the São Paulo concession and to force 'excessive and unwarranted reductions in our prices.'[88] None the less, the Guinles attracted considerable support. William Hume Blake, the Toronto lawyer, visited São Paulo in 1908 and provided a vivid description of the reaction of some *paulistanos* to the judicial defeat of the Guinle pretensions for a share of the São Paulo market. 'The students of the Law School,' he arrogantly reported

welcomed this as an opportunity to cultivate their oratory, and for a night or two there was a great deal of declamation at the street corners on the theme of 'monopolies' and 'the people's rights.' The riff-raff took a hand in it and stones got flying. Some car windows were broken and some heads were cut; but when the disturbance got past a joke and police interfered, and their work in quietly and peaceably establishing order was beyond all praise ... the whole thing resembled a Hallowe'en gathering in its acute states.[89]

There was, in reality, nothing comical about such outbursts, for, as company officials recognized at an early date, they were indicative of the most fundamental problem confronting a business enterprise operating in a foreign land: maintaining the delicate balance between profits and the interests of the community. The company's ability to provide efficient public services and thereby meet a long-neglected need in the São Paulo community enabled it to preserve this balance largely unmolested throughout the first decades of the century. Internally, the Light paid its workers well, generally in excess of prevailing norms, and thereby ensured that it presented a united and efficient front to the public at large. The critics of the Light were thereby relegated to a minority position and often acted as agents for its competitors. Nevertheless, the appearance of widespread hostility was always a distinct possibility that might be brought to life by any number of factors, ranging from slackening in service to an alteration in the Brazilians' attitude towards the role of foreign enterprise within their borders. In this respect, the São Paulo company was still in its honeymoon stage, protected from the ultimate implications of its presence in Brazil by the highly visible contribution it was making to the as-yet-undeveloped country.

It would be a mistake to assume that the company functioned in a regulatory vacuum. At the federal level even at the turn of the century, foreign capitalists were obliged to abide by a myriad of state regulations, ranging from the necessity of obtaining permission to operate in Brazil to regulations governing the number of Brazilian employees on staff. Still, there was a remarkable lack of statutory control over the activities of electricity producers using the 'water power' of Brazil. This was attributable to the inevitable lag between the march of technological innovation and awareness of the need for statutory regulation. Not until 1903 did the Brazilian federal state make its first attempt to regulate the electric industry on a national basis. When this legislation proved ineffectual, a proposal for a national 'water code' was placed before the Congress in 1907, but Congress again failed to act. The situation was quite different at the state and municipal levels.[90] The same concessions that Brown had described as being 'very liberal' also contained the seeds of what was to become a pervasive system of municipal and state supervision of the company's activities. The tramway and power concessions contained elaborate stipulations for the authorization and inspection of the concessionaires' properties and activities. In the power contracts, the municipality reserved the right to veto the placement of any pole or to insist that wires be 'canalized' underground in order to diminish the clutter of overhead wires.

While such rights of intervention were easily acceded to on paper, they soon became a source of unending exasperation in practice. 'We have people in the *Câmara* here to fight all the time,' Assistant Treasurer Mulqueen complained as early as 1901. 'You cannot do anything without first getting sanction ... You cannot imagine the difficulties in the way of getting approval to do anything.'[91] When, for instance, Prado insisted that the company erect iron power poles instead of wooden poles, Pearson replied that while he shared the prefect's concern for the 'beautification' of the city, he questioned the wisdom of having neophyte linemen string electric wires on iron poles. Without the 'scientific supervision and inspection from the State and City authorities,' which Pearson deemed as yet unavailable in São Paulo, the use of iron poles could prove 'a dangerous practice.'[92] Despite such occasional irritations, the company generally adopted a policy of acquiescence. 'As a matter of policy,' Pearson wisely concluded in 1905, 'I feel that this Company should co-operate as far as they can with the Authorities in beautifying the City.'[93] Sometimes compliance with municipal demands unexpectedly enhanced the company's competitive prospects. 'If we put our wires underground in the principal streets,' Pearson commented on a *câmara* request, 'there is practically no possibility of any other company asking for the right to compete with us, and very little possibility of the City Authorities granting the right to tear up the streets again for the installation of underground conduits so long as we serve the public at reasonable rates.'[94]

Coping with regulation was just one aspect of the more pervasive problem of protecting the company's interests in Brazil. The very nature of the concessions that governed the São Paulo company's activities ensured that it would be drawn into Brazilian politics. The tramway, light, and power services that the company offered to *paulistanos* fell within the jurisdictional purview of all three levels of Brazilian government. Within this jurisdictional area, there was a skein of municipal, state, and federal powers. Furthermore, the generation of hydroelectric power was a form of new technology that did not conform neatly to the existing notions of jurisdictional competence. At times, for instance, the authority of state and federal legislators seemed to overlap, especially over the touchy question of riparian rights.

This welter of jurisdictions worked both to the Light's advantage and to its detriment. The existence of contending and sometimes overlapping authorities opened the way for a utilities concessionaire to exploit areas of disputed jurisdiction, playing one sphere of government off against another. Under the 1891 constitution, with its strong tendency to favour states' rights, the promoters of the Canadian enterprise looked to the strong São Paulo state government of Rodrigues Alves (1900–2) and Bernardino de Campos (1902–4) for constitutional protection. Good relations with the state usually paved the way for the establishment of a co-operative understanding with the federal government in Rio, especially after Alves assumed the federal presidency in 1902. However, just as the São Paulo company might exploit the constitutional and legal system to its advantage, so too could its competitors. From 1899 onwards the company's existence in Brazil was characterized by an unending series of legal disputes in which it was repeatedly forced to seek clarification of its concessionary rights and to contest the alleged rights of its competitors. Given the pace at which the Brazilian legal system meted out justice, this process was frequently an irritating and expensive experience. When, for instance, a manufacturer named Penteado claimed that the Parnaíba power development had damaged the value of the water-power rights he held farther downstream, the company called out its lawyers. 'The case will go along merrily doubtless for a long time to come,' Alexander Mackenzie stoically reported in 1903, 'but I think we shall win out.'[95] The case was eventually won in 1911.

The complexities of concession rights and legal disputes drew the São Paulo company farther into the realm of Brazilian politics. The erection of barriers of political defence around the Light entailed the exercise of extreme tact and a subtle understanding of Brazilian ways. As Alexander Mackenzie told Lash in 1901, 'a man of great tact' was needed to direct the company's affairs in São Paulo. For the manager of the Canadian company to have engaged overtly in Brazilian politics would have excited local hostility and would inevitably have brought disaster upon the enterprise. From the beginning, therefore, all direct participation in Brazilian politics was strictly avoided. 'You should have it thoroughly understood,' Pearson categorically stated in 1901, 'that we are there [in São Paulo] solely for business and that we do not wish to interfere in politics in any way. I wish you would have it generally understood that while the company does not intend to advise its employees in any way how they shall vote in politics, that the company will insist that none of its employees shall take an active part in politics.'[96]

Having shunned direct political action, the company chose to defend its interests through a system of subtle alliances and precautionary measures. The success of this strategy revolved around the existence in Brazil of prominent and influential citizens who were favourably predisposed to the participation of foreign capital in the building of São Paulo's economic infrastructure. Such allies were drawn from the ranks of Brazilian politics and the law, men who not only saw a place for foreign entrepreneurs in

Brazil but also possessed the skills and influence to protect foreigners' interests. It was to men like Bernardino de Campos, twice president of the state and once federal minister of finance, and Antônio Prado, São Paulo's prefect, that the company turned to represent and preserve its place in Brazil. While Prado later frequently found himself at odds with the company over such issues as civic beautification, he never abandoned his belief that there was a place for foreign enterprise in São Paulo. 'If you can tell Bernardino and Prado and one or two other prominent people that this is our position,' Pearson not infrequently instructed the general manager in São Paulo, 'I think they will do the rest and do all that can be done.'[97]

The most important participants in the front line of defence were the lawyers. Whenever a contentious issue threatened to check the company's progress, Pearson invariably advised his manager in São Paulo to 'get some first class lawyer who is a fighter and has political influence and would defend our interests to good advantage.'[98] The two most effective legal counsels thus retained were Carlos de Campos, son of former state president Bernardino de Campos, and Dr A.J. Pinto Ferraz, a prominent law professor and legal consultant to the London and Brazilian Bank. In innumerable disputes it was Campos and Pinto Ferraz who, in Alexander Mackenzie's words, had 'always borne the brunt of the battle.'[99] For a company whose existence in Brazil was to prove relentlessly litigious, such men were doubly important because they also acted as unofficial representatives before the country's political authorities. This was a role that no foreigner could have undertaken successfully. Lacking fluency in Portuguese and untutored in the intricacies of Brazilian law, many of the company's managers would have appeared awkward and conspicuously alien in a courtroom or the office of a cabinet minister. In later years, the company was to have singular success in preserving its ties with the local élite and was able, at varying times, to rely upon the minds of such illustrious Brazilians as Rui Barbosa and the great Baron of Rio Branco.

Indigenous legal talent by no means precluded the necessity of assimilating the company's managers to the realities of Brazilian life. Neither William Mackenzie nor Fred Pearson was prepared to make this crucial transition from a North American cultural environment to a Brazilian milieu. William Mackenzie's commitment to the São Paulo enterprise was essentially financial. He had little interest in routine operational details and, in fact, never even visited Brazil. Pearson's interest in the project was that of an engineer and, although his letters reveal a remarkable grasp of the nuances of the Brazilian situation,[100] his focus was largely on technical and financial affairs. Furthermore, Pearson's peripatetic career permitted only infrequent visits to São Paulo. What the company needed was a man 'on the spot,' ready to respond to the exigencies of local politics, exchange, operational difficulties, and personnel management. Neither Robert Brown nor Hugh Cooper could fulfill these qualifications. Their commitment to the enterprise had been temporary, and both had returned north by the end of 1901 to take up assignments with Mackenzie's Niagara power development. Brown's replacement as general manager, an American engineer named James Mitchell, had been active in Brazil since the early 1890s as the sales representative of various American and British electrical-equipment manufacturers. Although Pearson had expressed a hope that the new general manager would be of 'great service' on account of his 'thorough knowledge of Brazilian affairs,' Mitchell quickly revealed a propensity for exciting jealousies and intrigue in the São Paulo office and was replaced in 1906 by Walter N. Walmsley, another American-trained engineer.

It was a matter of deep satisfaction to the promoters of the São Paulo enterprise to make the discovery that Alexander Mackenzie, the bachelor lawyer seconded from the Blake legal firm in 1899 to vet the Gualco concession, possessed an uncanny knack for adapting to Brazil and functioning in it like a Brazilian. No man, Canadian, American, or Brazilian, contributed as vitally and constructively to the ultimate success of the São Paulo venture as Alexander Mackenzie, whose tenure as resident vice-president in São Paulo and later as company president stretched from 1899 until 1928 (with one break between 1911 and 1915). Throughout his long career, Mackenzie drew unstinting praise from all those with whom he came into contact. From his desk at the Canadian Bank of Commerce, B.E. Walker, a participant in the original São Paulo syndicate, praised Mackenzie's opinions on matters of Brazilian law as being 'so clear, and so evidently right' that they could be unquestioningly relied upon by the Toronto directors.[101]

Alexander Mackenzie was at first sight unlikely material for a business career in a tropical foreign country. Born in the small Ontario town of Kincardine, on the shores of Lake Huron, Mackenzie came from staunch Scots Presbyterian stock. His father, Donald, was a farmer, blacksmith, and carriage maker who had come to Canada in 1851 from Sutherlandshire. Young Alexander spent his youth on the 90 hectare family farm outside Kincardine. It was perhaps the fact that his older brother, Kenneth, stood to inherit the Mackenzie farmstead that prompted seventeen-year-old Alexander, as soon as his schooling was complete, to leave Kincardine for Toronto to launch a professional career. This transition to the bustle of Toronto was aided by his father. As a loyal Liberal, the elder Mackenzie had befriended Edward Blake, the eminent Toronto lawyer who represented South Bruce in both the federal and provincial parliaments. Through Blake, Donald Mackenzie was able to secure his son an articling position in the prestigious Toronto legal firm of Blake, Kerr and Boyd. Under such expert tutelage, Alexander progressed smartly and was called to the Ontario Bar in 1883, at which time he was invited to continue with the firm. For the next nineteen years, Mackenzie remained with the Blake firm, eventually becoming a partner. During these years, he was exposed to some of the outstanding legal minds in Canada, including Edward and Samuel Blake, Walter Cassels, and Z.A. Lash. Above all else, he gained an intimacy with the intricacies of Canadian corporate law, a field of law that was acquiring a rapidly expanding clientele in turn-of-the-century Canada.

The decision of the Blake firm's senior partners to ask Mackenzie to accompany R.C. Brown to São Paulo in June 1899 was moulded by their confidence in their junior partner's obvious legal talents and by the fact that he had resisted the temptation of marriage. Although he was later to marry Mabel Blake, the daughter of Samuel Blake and sister of his close friend W.H. Blake, Mackenzie was single in 1899 and therefore eminently suited to undertake the long and arduous journey to Brazil. Mackenzie accepted the Brazilian challenge, no doubt thinking that it would provide an interesting diversion from his prosperous and staid existence in Anglo-Saxon Toronto. Despite his initial declarations to the contrary, Mackenzie had embarked on an assignment that was to keep him in the Latin surroundings of São Paulo and Rio for almost three decades.

Certainly Mackenzie never looked the part he came to play so adeptly. In photographs, he appeared the sombre Anglo-Saxon; tall, rigidly erect, and invariably clad in a three-piece worsted suit. The only concession he ever seemed to make to the tropical climate was a straw boater to ward off the rays of the broiling summer sun. Yet beneath this façade, Mackenzie learned to think and act like a Brazilian. He quickly mastered the Portuguese language, and this in turn made possible the most remarkable of Mackenzie's early feats in Brazil: his comprehension of the Brazilian legal system and its ramifications for the company.

The legal system that Mackenzie encountered in São Paulo was markedly different from that to which he had grown accustomed in Ontario. Unlike the English legal system, with its strong emphasis on judicial precedent and common law, Brazil was a civil-law jurisdiction that relied on codes. Law in Brazil has tended to be more an administrative than an interpretive process, with a strong emphasis on the framing of broad codes from which legal specifics can be delineated. To the present day, this inversion of the legal system as North Americans know it has baffled the foreign businessman in Brazil.[102] The rapidity with which Mackenzie acquired a grasp of Brazilian law placed him in the advantageous position of being able to work alongside such corporate counsels as Carlos de Campos. His expertise also put him in a unique position to explain the often-bewildering complexities of the company's concessionary situation to its Toronto promoters.

Despite his astonishing adaptation to Brazilian conditions, Mackenzie initially had little desire to make the affairs of the São Paulo company his life's work. He looked on his assignment in São Paulo as a temporary sojourn, which he felt obligated to see through to its successful completion out of a sense of duty to the senior partners. In July 1901, just after the consolidated tramway concession had been won from the *câmara* in São Paulo, Mackenzie wrote to Lash in Toronto to express his desire to return home: 'Mr. Pearson once suggested that I should remain here permanently in some capacity. If the directors have any such notion,' he categorically stated, 'please disabuse their minds as no salary would induce me to remain. I feel that I have done my duty in remaining so long. Now all I want is to get home.' It was to this same sense of duty, so ingrained in Mackenzie's Presbyterian character, that the directors appealed when Mackenzie returned to Toronto in late 1901. As Mackenzie himself had admitted to Lash, 'there is really no one here who can be depended upon to do much in the class of work I have been doing.'[103] In mid-1902, Mackenzie relented. At the board meeting of 12 June 1902, he was elected vice-president, resident in São Paulo, and given power of attorney 'to exercise and execute all powers and authorities exercisable by the Company in Brazil.' This arrangement was consistent with a *de facto* demarcation whereby the Toronto directors retained ultimate authority over all the company's affairs, while supervision of all operations and defence of corporate interests was delegated to the vice-president resident in Brazil. This arrangement persisted for many years and contributed in a crucial way to the São Paulo company's longevity in Brazil. 'The job here is a pretty big one,' Mackenzie wrote to W.H. Blake in 1905 from Rio, 'and needs constant and daily attention from someone other than the man directly concerned with the daily operations of the Company. São Paulo pretty well runs itself in this respect, but even there, after having been away from it so much during the past year, I am beginning to appreciate better, the necessity of being on the spot oftener.'[104] When Mackenzie eventually assumed the presidency of the parent Brazilian Traction, Light and Power Company in 1915, he perpetuated this policy, knowing that only by remaining in Brazil could he adequately understand and cope with the vicissitudes of business in Brazil.

Mackenzie's decision to remain in Brazil marked a coming of age for the São Paulo company. It signified the solidification of its management strategy for Brazil. Under Mackenzie's diligent direction, the company was soon able to extend both its services and its concessions and, despite the presence of the San Paulo Gas Company, to create the kind of integrated power and traction system that had been envisaged by its promoters. Furthermore it created a pattern of management and a pool of personnel that would soon be reapplied to the inviting market for traction and power services in nearby Rio de Janeiro. It was an achievement that had not been easily won. Company managers had quickly learned that establishing a public utility in Brazil was not as straightforward a matter as R.C. Brown had initially suggested in 1899. Where Brown had predicted smooth sailing, the Light had encountered vexing problems, brought on by the uncertainty of exchange, technical complications, cultural adjustment, and an unknown and at times puzzling political environment. Meeting these challenges took a heavy toll on employees. By April 1907, General Manager Walmsley complained that his staff was 'fagged out' from their exertions in São Paulo. Even the indefatigable Alexander Mackenzie felt the strain. 'I wonder if I shall ever have any play again,' he wrote to his friend William Hume Blake in 1908; 'I certainly have had none since I was last on the St. Lawrence – I am afraid to say how many years ago.'[105]

Occasional complaints from managers could not obscure the obvious success of the São Paulo company. When he returned from his São Paulo visit in 1908, W.H. Blake expressed 'the very sincere opinion that among the tangible and intangible assets the chiefest [sic] are the men who, more or less expatriating themselves, have devoted and are devoting their ability, tact and unwearying labour to the affairs of the companies. But for their skills and resource, and but for the confidence engendered in the minds of the Brazilians by punctual and honourable fulfillment of engagements, success would never have been attained.'[106] This success was a matter of great satisfaction for the board of directors in Toronto. While they had been forced to modify the tactics they had learned in Canada and had watched their original estimates of capital expenditure being greatly exceeded, the Toronto promoters had also seen their expectations generously fulfilled. With the inauguration of the Parnaíba power plant and tram service, William Mackenzie and his associates found themselves in possession of a secure and rewarding investment. In return for this, the citizens of São Paulo could take pride in the fact that their city boasted one of the best and most extensive tramway and power systems on the South American continent. The company's contribution had more profound ramifications than civic pride. The trams, for instance, were playing a formative role in the creation of an urban industrial work force, while the city's ready access to plentiful Parnaíba power was an undeniably crucial factor in placing São Paulo in the vanguard of South America's industrial revolution. In later years, *paulistanos* would point with satisfaction to the slogan painted on the side of each São Paulo Tramway, Light and Power Co. Ltd. *bonde*: '*São Paulo é o Maior Centro Industrial da América do Sul.*'

Such success had not gone unnoticed. William Haggard, the British ambassador in Brazil, had closely watched the progress of the Canadian company from his chancellery in Rio and was duly impressed. 'You may have observed,' he wrote to Under-Secretary of State for Foreign Affairs Sir Edward Grey, at the Foreign Office, in July 1907,

my notice in previous despatches of the activity of Canadian enterprise in this Country of late ... Brazil is emphatically – if I may use the term – virgin soil, and Canadian vigour has already – and that during the span of a very few years – made a deep impression on it. The first great project was the 'S. Paulo Light and Power Company' which has been successfully established mainly by the efforts of Mr. A. Mackenzie, in the teeth of the most vigorous opposition and detraction, not to mention that he had to conquer great physical obstacles. He may indeed both metaphorically and actually be said to have overcome — if not to have removed — mountains ... It is true that in these schemes the Canadian group have been supported by capital from England and other countries, largely from the United States, but it is to Canadian enterprise, ability and fore-sight that these qualities have come to life.[107]

New Growth: The Rio De Janeiro Tramway, Light and Power Company Limited, 1903-1908

No city in the world creates so startling and lasting an impression on the newcomer as Rio de Janeiro. The dramatic effect of the Pão de Açúcar, Sugar Loaf mountain, with its steep, barren sides, rising beside the broad bay of Guanabara leaves an indelible image on the minds of travellers, especially those who arrive by ship. Nestled between the brooding mist-enshrouded *morros* against a backdrop of the distant Serra do Mar, Rio de Janeiro confronts the stranger with its uniqueness. 'Nothing can be more striking,' Charles Darwin noted when he arrived in Rio on the *Beagle* in April 1832, 'than the effect of these huge rounded masses of naked rock rising out of the most luxuriant vegetation.'[1] Others were more expansive in their comments. An American clergyman reported in 1866 that he had 'seen the most rude and ignorant Russian sailor, the immoral and unreflecting Australian adventurer, as well as the cultivated and refined European gentleman, stand silent upon the deck, mutually admiring the gigantic avenue of mountains and palm-covered isles, which, like the granite pillars before the Temple of Luxor, form a colonnade to the portal of the finest bay in the world.'[2]

Once ashore, the nineteenth-century visitor's impression of the city usually changed abruptly. The Portuguese had first settled on the shores of Guanabara Bay in 1565 because the magnificent, sheltered harbour afforded a safe, defensible location for the imperial colonizers of Brazil. As a site for permanent habitation, Rio had much less to offer. From its earliest days, the city had struggled to survive on the hilly, heavily wooded terrain that surrounded it and restricted its growth to the lowlands adjacent to the bay. The city's expansion was governed by its ability to push through the valleys between the *morros*. Thus small pockets of settlement, such as Botafogo, where Darwin sojourned during his 1832 visit, sprang up inland, somewhat isolated from the original settlement on the bay. Many years later, a Canadian engineer, sent south to investigate Rio's topography, reported that 'Rio is not one, but several cities.' The Federal District, which Rio de Janeiro became under the constitution of 1891, was 'a sea of mountains and isolated hills, particularly at its westerly end, where the city of Rio is situated upon the comparatively narrow beach bordering the shore, and in the valleys between the peaks. To connect the various strips available for building, cuts have been made through the lower ridges, and tunnels driven through the higher ones; to make more available land for development, hills have been levelled, and large areas reclaimed from the bay, yet in principle Rio remains today as when it was founded, a straggling community spread along the level ground between the mountains and the sea ... Totally unlike São Paulo, which is pre-eminently a single community, Rio is a group of quasi-self-contained communities.'[3]

Denied sufficient space to expand, Rio became a distinctly unpleasant place to live. The scarcity of land gave the city an abnormally high density of population and forced its citizens to pass along streets that were often so narrow that both the sun and the cooling ocean breezes were unable to penetrate to the heart of the city. As the city grew in commercial and financial stature, its hard-pressed municipal government proved incapable of furnishing even the most rudimentary public services. By the mid-nineteenth century, the lack of a proper sewage system forced the local citizenry to deposit offal on the beaches every night, so that the morning tide would carry it out to sea. The near-total absence of adequate street lighting led to the practice, by those who could afford it, of having a torch-bearing slave precede them when venturing out in the night. Such urban conditions proved conducive to the spread of disease, and in the early 1850s Rio experienced its first visitation of the deadly yellow fever. The presence of low, swampy ground to the north, excessive heat and humidity, and high population density turned Rio into a perfect incubator of disease. In a desperate effort to combat such devastating epidemics, the municipal government constructed the Mangue Canal in 1853 to drain stagnant waters in the central part of the city. Even so, British diplomats complained as late as the 1890s that the city 'swarmed with yellow fever.'[4] Those who could afford the journey sensibly removed themselves from Rio during the oppressive summer months and retired to Petrópolis, a small city in the hills behind the capital.

With the coming of the republic in 1889 and the spurt of economic growth that followed, there came a growing realization among civic-minded *cariocas* (as Rio's inhabitants are known) that their city was in dire need of improvement. Without thorough urban reform, Rio's political and commercial dominance in Brazil might be eclipsed. Under the 1891 constitution, Rio had been made the nation's capital. Its selection as capital did little to disguise the fact that Rio de Janeiro was still a 'colonial' city that compared poorly with its rival, Buenos Aires, with its broad boulevards and modern port. 'Everyone believed that, without a healthy environment in Rio,' one Brazilian historian has noted, 'the country would not develop, nor would it become civilized, and everyone knew that only through the alliance of science and administration could Brazil break free of such a humiliating obstacle to its progress.'[5]

Not until the federal presidency of Rodrigues Alves (1902–6)[6] did these pressures coalesce into a concerted urban-reform movement. Alves, with his impressive credentials as a lawyer, past president of the state of São Paulo, and former federal minister of finance, assumed the office of federal president in the firm belief that Brazil had passed the stage of political experimentation and must now modernize its economy. Without efficient port facilities, expeditious transportation, and a salubrious urban environment, Brazil would never be able to transform itself into a modern industrial nation. Rio, the unhealthy and congested national capital with a population of 750,000 in 1903, epitomized all that was wrong with the Brazilian economy from Alves's perspective. Alves's desire to revivify the national capital was immensely facilitated by the power of the federal president to appoint the prefect of the federal district. In an attempt to preclude possible friction between the federal government and the municipal government, the 1891 constitution had made the government of the federal district the creature of the national government. This federal power opened the way for a most remarkable and productive conjunction of talent and ambition, a combination that would dramatically change Rio from a crowded colonial city to a bustling urban centre of international stature.

In December 1902, President Alves appointed Francisco Pereira Passos to the prefecture of Rio de Janeiro. Passos's work over the next four years has been portrayed as a wholesale assault on the city's decrepitude, a crusade that permanently altered Rio's urban character and national function. Passos was a typical example of the late-nineteenth-century liberal 'modernizers' who sought to reshape Brazil's national energies. An engineer by training, Passos had combined his early exposure to French and English ideas of progress and entrepreneurship with his own experience as a railway engineer on the San Paulo Railway to create a blueprint for Brazil's economic future. In the 1880s, Passos had displayed entrepreneurial verve by constructing and operating, very profitably, an inclined-plane railway up the side of Rio's precipitous Corcovado mountain. Now, in the first decade of the new century, he dedicated himself to urban reform with the same enthusiasm.

Passos's goal was more than simply to give Rio a *belle époque* veneer. Instead, he wanted to remake the city and to allow it to function and expand without impediment. Structural deficiencies necessitated structural renovation. For instance, the city's maze of narrow and airless streets had to be superseded by major arteries, which would facilitate the movement of traffic and allow ocean breezes to ventilate the urban core. In this respect, the outstanding achievement of Passos's administration was the completion of the Avenida Central, a broad boulevard that cleanly bisected the heart of the cramped older quarter of the city. To expedite the movement of traffic along the harbourfront, the Avenida Beira Mar was constructed. Similarly, Passos's reforming touch was felt in almost every aspect of Rio's public administration, from the provision of sewage facilities to the establishment of new codes governing buildings, streets, and industry. He was, as one Brazilian historian has put it, 'the magical creator of the Brazilian metropolis.'[7] Years later, the great French architect Le Corbusier exclaimed after a visit to Rio: 'of a colonial city, charming and hidden in the trees, this other Haussmann had made the most dazzling township in the world.'[8]

Passos's ability to remake Rio de Janeiro hinged on two factors: his wide powers as federal prefect and the assistance he received from like-minded reformers. When he took office, Passos was endowed with plenary powers over all aspects of municipal government. He began by postponing elections for the municipal *câmara*, thereby stifling any possible opposition to his bold plans. In response to those who labelled his powers draconian, Passos resorted to the justification that reform on the scale that he envisaged necessitated the type of decisive action that a democratically elected *câmara* would not countenance.[9] The construction of the Avenida Central, for instance, was vehemently opposed by the entrenched Portuguese mercantile community, which fought any move to expropriate its extensive holdings in the old central core. Passos's ability to overcome such opponents was attributable to the staunch backing he received from Rodrigues Alves and to the fact that his actions were part of a broader reform movement. At the same time as Passos had assumed office in Rio, Alves had delegated his minister of transportation, industry, and public works to tackle the problem of Rio's chronically inefficient dock system. Under the energetic direction of Lauro Müller (1863–1936), a German-Brazilian engineer, a technical commission supervised a major renovation of port facilities by English contractors. It was to one of the members of Müller's technical commission, an engineer named André Gustavo Paulo de Frontin (1860–1933), that Passos turned for much of the technical guidance needed to plan and construct the Avenida Central.[10] In the press and the public mind, the triumvirate of Passos, Frontin, and Müller was commonly seen as the chief force behind Rio de Janeiro's new-found grandeur and self-confidence. When, on 15 November 1905, Rodrigues Alves cut the ribbon opening the Avenida Central, it was as if Rio had entered a new era. 'This transition from a meanly built and unhealthy, although large and picturesque Portuguese colonial city,' an English visitor noted some years later, 'to a modern Rio de Janeiro has had perhaps no equal anywhere in point of rapidity of execution.'[11]

Less tangible than the engineering triumphs of Frontin and Passos, but equally momentous, was the work of Dr Oswaldo Cruz in eradicating yellow fever from the Rio district. Alves realized that no amount of remodelling of the urban core and harbourfront would improve the prospects of the city without comparable attempts to cleanse Rio's far-from-healthy environment. In 1903, J.J. Seabra, Alves's minister of the interior, appointed Cruz, a young Brazilian doctor trained at the Pasteur Institute in Paris, to launch a wholesale assault on the yellow-fever scourge that had plagued the city for more than half a century. Drawing on medical theories newly developed by the Americans in Cuba and Panama, Cruz vigorously attacked the disease and registered a victory over it that was both thorough and astoundingly quick. In 1903, when he began his campaign, there were 584 recorded deaths in Rio from yellow fever. By 1906, not a single *carioca* succumbed to the disease.[12]

Cruz's application of the advances of American medical science to the exigencies of the Brazilian situation was symptomatic of a much broader reliance on foreign ideas, capital, and expertise. Without exception, all of the prime movers in the urban reform movement had been profoundly impressed by the example of European and American economic prosperity.[13] However, the inculcation of foreign ideas and patterns of progress was not sufficient in itself to ensure Rio's transformation. It was quickly recognized that foreign expertise and capital were 'indispensable'[14] if the schemes of Alves and Passos were ever to become reality. Given the scale of Passos's projects and the rapidity with which it was hoped they could be accomplished, resort to foreign capital and expertise was unavoidable. In May 1903, Rodrigues Alves negotiated a loan with the Rothschilds in London that provided £8.5 million for the work of Passos, Frontin, and Müller.[15] By the time the major construction projects were completed, a total of £12 million, by one estimate, had been expended.[16]

Foreign bankers were followed by foreign contractors and engineers. The paving of the broad Avenida Central was, for instance, entrusted to the Hastings Pavements Company of New York, while the main contract for the docks was let to C.H. Walker and Company of London. Another English firm provided Rio with a modern sewage system. Because Passos was the appointee of the federal president, and because he faced no organized opposition, there was little to impede the participation of foreign entrepreneurs in the economy of the Federal District. This welcoming environment was enhanced in 1903 when Nilo Peçanha assumed the presidency of Rio de Janeiro state, which surrounded the small federal district and had a powerful influence over its economic life. It was Peçanha who, for instance, in July 1910, officially inaugurated the new port of Rio de Janeiro.

It was this favourable political alignment of federal, state, and municipal politicians so amenable to foreign business that the promoters of the São Paulo Tramway, Light and Power Company Limited encountered when they turned their attention to Brazil's largest city in early 1903. When Alexander Mackenzie and F.S. Pearson first received news that there was an attractive but as yet unexploited concession for power distribution available in Rio, their initial reaction, as it had been in São Paulo, was to investigate the political mood of the national capital. If the political powers governing the city could be won over, as Antônio Prado had been in São Paulo, then an element of political certainty could be guaranteed for a new Canadian public-utility operation in southern Brazil. 'For your information,' Mackenzie later recounted for a Brazilian newspaper editor, 'I may say that before taking any steps towards the purchase of any concessions or property in Rio, I consulted the President, Dr. Rodrigues Alves, Dr. Lauro Müller and Dr. Passos, to whom we exposed in a general way the scheme of acquisition and unification of the various concessions and services. The President was enthusiastic: Dr. Lauro Müller offered not the least objection and neither did the *Prefeito*.'[17]

The enthusiasm with which Rio politicians received Alexander Mackenzie was moulded by the knowledge that the Canadian promoters had already shown their mettle in São Paulo and that, secondly, this entrepreneurial prowess, if applied to Rio, offered a solution to one of the city's most debilitating deficiencies, the inadequacy of its power-generating and transportation services. The importance of a supply of cheap and plentiful electric power was a central tenet of the creed of modernization espoused by Pereira Passos and his fellow reformers. Renovated port facilities, arterial thoroughfares, and seafront boulevards were of only limited utility if inadequate public illumination and lack of an integrated transportation system prevented *cariocas* from extracting a full measure of private and public benefit from these amenities. Similarly, the industries and commercial firms that made the port so necessary would require an abundant source of power if the city was to break its reliance on imported coal.

Efficient and cheap transportation was the key. Many of the problems that Passos had endeavoured to correct were the product of Rio's unusually high density of population, a density brought on by the city's inability to break through the encircling *morros* and create for itself some *lebensraum* to its north and along the Atlantic littoral to its south. Without some means of piercing or circumventing the *morros*, Rio de Janeiro would be condemned to the cramped confines of its original colonial setting. The electric tramway system and the hydro-power facility that Mackenzie and Pearson laid before Pereira Passos offered the obvious solution to the city's long-unsolved problem of power and transportation. 'The *bonde*,' the great Brazilian liberal Rui Barbosa was later to reflect, 'was, up to a certain point, the salvation of the city. It was the grand instrument and incomparable agent of its material progress. It expanded the urban boundaries, allowed the city to spread its population and made the suburbs possible. The *bonde* – one must say – was a providential institution. Had it not existed, we would have had to invent it.'[18]

The abysmal state of Rio's public services was not the product of any want of effort on the part of Brazilians. It was instead the result of a myriad of uncoordinated attempts to service the city's needs. Some of these attempts lacked sufficient capital; others the proper technical expertise. As early as 1837, mule-drawn omnibuses had appeared on the Rio streets and were employed to carry those who could afford the fares to the nascent suburbs of the city at Botafogo, Laranjeiras, and São Cristovão. In 1856 a mule-drawn tramway was inaugurated to Alto da Bôa Vista in the Tijuca forest above the city. Organized by an English doctor, the Tijuca line was granted a government franchise and subsidy but failed to prosper and collapsed in 1866. More successful was the Brazilian-controlled Companhia Ferro-Carril do Jardim Botânico, a tramway company that catered more to the movement of *cariocas* within the city. Founded in 1856 with the financial assistance of Baron Mauá, the company prospered by providing service between downtown Rio and the growing suburb of Botafogo, on a bay at the foot of Sugar Loaf. Through Mauá, American capital was attracted and the line rechristened as the Botanical Gardens Railway Company. The expanded line soon became 'one of the most profitable investments in Brazil and the first in which United States capital formed a large part.'[19] It was the thirty-passenger tramcars of the Jardim Botânico company that local citizens first began to refer to affectionately as *bondes*.

The success of the Jardim Botânico venture induced other entrepreneurs, both Brazilian and foreign, to enter the field. In 1869, American capitalists established the Rio de Janeiro Street Railway Company, which inaugurated service to the developing suburb of São Cristovão. The company transferred its headquarters from New York to Rio in 1873, rechristening itself the Companhia de São Cristovão and had by the 1890s built up sixty kilometres of lines. A Brazilian-controlled tram service, the Companhia Ferro-Carril da Vila Isabel, was formed in 1872 under the direction of João Batista Viana Drumond (later Baron Drumond) to serve the areas to Rio's north as far as Engenho Novo. Another Brazilian enterprise, the Emprêsa Ferro-Carril Vila Guarani, was founded in 1886 but shortly thereafter fell under British control. When the English managers were forced into liquidation, control once again changed hands, and the German-controlled Brazilianische Elektricitäts Gesellschaft, which already operated a rudimentary telephone service in Rio, acquired the tramway company, combined it with the Vila Isabel company, and in 1899 negotiated a unified concession with the municipal government. Another company formed by the fusion of smaller companies was the Companhia de Carris Urbanos, which in 1878 brought together a motley collection of small freight and passenger-tram companies.

This profusion of tram companies, while impressive in numbers, did not collectively provide the city with an adequate transportation system. Although ridership on the combined companies grew from 62,030 in 1870 to 729,000 in 1896, it was readily apparent by the early 1890s that the system could not cope with the growing pressure exerted by *cariocas* eager to escape the crowded city and relocate in the suburbs.[20] Furthermore, mule-drawn trams were both expensive and ill-suited to Rio's hilly terrain. The Rio tram network was thus in no sense a system, but was instead an uncoordinated hodge-podge of competing companies that frequently relied on different gauges and mismatched equipment. As such, the trams were conspicuously failing to ease the problem of high density in the urban core. In 1890, for instance, 44 per cent of the Federal District's population was crammed into the 8.18 square kilometres of Rio's seven central districts, Candelaria, Santa Rita, Sacramento, São José, Santo Antônio, Sant'Anna, and Gambôa.[21]

In 1892, *cariocas* had a glimpse of the ultimate solution to their transportation problems. The Jardim Botânico company in that year electrified its route to Flamengo beach. The power for this service, the first electric traction operation in South America, was supplied by a thermal-electric plant (burning precious coal) in downtown Rio. In the same year the Tunel Novo was punched through the rocky spine joining Sugar Loaf to the mainland, thereby allowing the *bondes* to circulate into Leme, and from there along the as yet relatively unpopulated coastal districts of Copacabana, Ipanema, and Leblon. For the first time, those Brazilians who could afford it were able to establish residences along Rio's South Atlantic beaches and still be within easy access of the commercial districts of Rio beyond the *morros*. While the Jardim Botânico company capitalized on this breakthrough by electrifying its entire system by September 1904, its competitors were slow to follow suit, most likely because they never had to compete directly with the electric *bondes*. Rio de Janeiro therefore entered the twentieth century with a municipal transport system that was more dependent on alfalfa than kilowatts for its motive power.

The development of efficient public illumination in Rio during the nineteenth century was hampered by similar circumstances. The lack of indigenous capital, expertise, and power stood in the way of those who wished to illuminate Rio. After several sporadic attempts to initiate lighting service had failed, Irineu Evangelista de Souza (Baron Mauá) won the right to illuminate the central city with gas in 1854. Soon afterwards, foreign visitors to the city reported that the Passeio Público, Rio's oldest and most frequented park, was 'brilliantly illuminated' and was attracting scores of evening promenaders.[22] Mauá was, however, an atypical Brazilian entrepreneur who was both willing and able to exploit such opportunities because his extensive banking connections provided him with capital that other Brazilians were unable to procure. After Mauá sold his interest in the gas company to English interests in 1866, the challenge of lighting Rio was left entirely to foreign entrepreneurs, the most successful of whom were the Belgian promoters of the Société Anonyme du Gaz de Rio de Janeiro (SAG). Under the terms of the concession given to SAG in 1886, its owners won the exclusive right to furnish the city with gas for public illumination and any other uses.

The idea of illuminating the city with electric lamps had been prevalent in Rio since 1879, when Emperor Dom Pedro II inaugurated an experimental system of arc lights erected by the Estrada de Ferro Central do Brasil, the railway that had served Rio since 1858. Not until the last decade of the century did the practical advantages of electric lighting become widely understood. Arc lamps not only provided a steadier, brighter light than the murky gas lamps, but required less maintenance and did not have to be tended at night. In 1899, when the Société Anonyme du Gaz renegotiated its concession with the federal government (under whose authority Rio's illumination fell), it won the right to furnish the city with electric lighting for public illumination.[23] A small thermal-electric station was brought into service in September 1899 to provide electric illumination for some of Rio's prominent places, most notably the popular promenade around Botafogo Bay. Progress was not swift, however, and in most cases electric lighting was used merely to supplement rather than supplant existing gas lighting. When Alexander Mackenzie surveyed Rio's public utilities in the early years of the new century, he reported that the Belgian company had been prevented from exploiting the market for electric lighting more fully 'on account of poor management during the last few years,' which had put the company 'in a very bad financial condition.'[24] By this time, the SAG's ownership rested in the hands of a widely scattered group of Belgian shareholders who, Mackenzie speculated, would be only too willing to part with their investment if offered an attractive proposition.

Rio was, therefore, being held back from the age of electricity by its inability to develop a large source of electricity that was not dependent on expensive imported coal. Until a site for hydroelectric-power generation could be found and developed in the hills behind the city, Rio would have to content itself with the relative trickle of power from the small Jardim Botânico and sag thermal plants. However, the challenge of hydro power had not gone untried. In December 1899, the municipal council of the city awarded an English engineer, William Reid, the privilege of generating and distributing electric power.[25] Reid's concession for power distribution was exclusive for fifteen years and provided the kind of security needed for anyone to undertake the heavy expenditure required to produce hydro power. Reid discovered a suitable location on the Lajes River, about sixty kilometres outside Rio, but got little further than clearing the site and beginning engineering studies. Although the Jardim Botânico company agreed to purchase much of the power produced at Lajes, the Reid venture stalled – probably for lack of sufficient capital – and eventually, in January 1904, transferred its concessionary rights to the Banco Nacional Brasileiro. Like Reid, the bank was quick to sense the lucrative potential for hydro power in Rio and organized the Companhia Nacional de Eletricidade to exploit the Lajes water power. Impatient for results, the municipal government stipulated that the new proprietors of the site be ready to furnish Rio with electricity not later than the end of January 1906.

It was the Reid concession that drew the promoters of the São Paulo Tramway, Light and Power Company to Rio. The concession was the key to the whole electricity market in the city and, like the Gualco concession in São Paulo, offered foreign promoters a ready-made *entrée* into an expanding metropolitan market. More than anyone else, it was F.S. Pearson, aided by Alexander Mackenzie, who recognized this opportunity in Rio and seized it, often in the face of stiff opposition from the Canadian colleagues who had accompanied him so willingly into São Paulo. In this sense, the Rio project had a distinctly American flavour in its early stages and, had it not been for Pearson's persistence in wearing down his Canadian associates' resistance, might easily have been a New Jersey-based corporation rather than a sister for the Toronto-based São Paulo company.

When Pearson first fixed his attention on Rio, his intention had been to duplicate the strategy that had been so successfully employed to secure a virtual monopoly in São Paulo. The key was to obtain sure control of one sector of the utilities business in the city, preferably the crucial power sector, and to use it as a nucleus around which additional services could be built. Once the company's range of traction services had been sufficiently broadened, its promoters could approach the municipal government with a request for the unification of its concessions into one all-encompassing concession. Pearson was initially dubious that the Reid concession in Rio could be used to work this magic. 'As regards the Reed [sic] concessions,' Pearson instructed Alexander Mackenzie in April 1903, 'I would say the best way would be to say to the Prefeito [Passos] that you would like to get a concession for power but the Reid concession stands in the way of your negotiations with the municipality, and if they could revoke the Reid concession, which they would be amply justified in doing in view of the long time Reed has had, that you would be in a position to discuss a new concession with them.'[26] This advice was prompted by the knowledge that the Reid concession was exclusive only until 1915, and then non-exclusive (i.e., other companies could enter the field) until 1950. If the exclusivity could be extended to provide an airtight monopoly beyond 1915, then the power business in Rio could be made to be extremely enticing for prospective concessionaires. With such a concession in hand, the promoters could begin to absorb the gas and tramway companies of the city 'in several instalments,' thereby avoiding having to amass the 'enormous amount of money' that would be required to consolidate these services in one initial, vast take-over gambit.

By early May, Pearson had changed his mind. Having made discreet inquiries in London, Brussels, and Berlin, he had discovered that plans were afoot to supply both the SAG and the Vila Isabel tramway with new capital to accelerate their electrification. Fearful that the electricity market might pass beyond his reach, Pearson suggested that Mackenzie might go to Rio 'to see just what could be done with the Reid people. If we could get this cheap enough it might pay us to take it rather than to make a long fight to get a new charter.' With clear title to the concession, they could then request some 'radical modification' to their privileges. 'I wouldn't advise paying much cash [to Reid],' Pearson cautioned, 'but [we] might give some stock.'[27] Confident that Mackenzie would be able to acquire the Reid concession, Pearson undertook the task of marshalling the requisite financial support in the north to capitalize on the concession. This proved an onerous task.

Pearson's enthusiasm for the Rio proposition coincided with a sudden business slump that severely affected the financial well-being of many of the Toronto capitalists who had so avidly backed the São Paulo project. 'For various reasons,' Pearson dejectedly reported to Mackenzie in mid-1904, 'this Rio proposition does not appeal to any of our friends in Canada, chiefly on account of the great losses that have been incurred by prominent men of wealth in the last two years, and it has been exceedingly difficult to get Mr. [William] Mackenzie or any of the other São Paulo stockholders to take a real and enthusiastic interest in the proposition.'[28] The only Canadian interest in Rio de Janeiro as a business opportunity came from Montreal, not Toronto. A young broker there, E. Mackay Edgar, who had extensive ties with the moguls of Montreal promotion, expressed a willingness to undertake part of the initial underwriting of the project. Elsewhere in Canada, Pearson complained, it was like 'making water run up a hill to get these men to undertake the enterprise at all.' The bankers, who kept a tight rein on their closest customers in the wake of the 1903 recession, were especially vehement in their opposition to the scheme. Byron Walker at the Bank of Commerce was 'absolutely opposed to any scheme outside of Canada, and has done everything possible to kill this scheme.' Similarly, E.S. Clouston of the Bank of Montreal had reacted coolly to Pearson's glowing reports of the Rio market. Without the support of the banks, Pearson reported, it was 'practically impossible to borrow any money in anticipation of the payment of the underwriting,' and consequently William Mackenzie had made only a minimal commitment to the whole project.

Pearson himself continued 'to have great faith in the enterprise' and simply redirected his attempts to interest other parties in the venture. His first instinct was to enlist the support of some of the few prominent Brazilian businessmen who could furnish much-needed financial support and provide the nascent enterprise with valuable connections within the Brazilian economy. Remembering how fruitful his relationship with Francisco Gualco had been, Pearson was delighted to discover that the powerful and wealthy Guinle family of Rio was interested in participating in his plans to electrify the city's lighting and traction services. The Guinle family fortune was rooted in the famous partnership of Eduardo Guinle and Cândido Gafrée, a partnership that, by the end of the nineteenth century, had complete control of the harbour facilities of Santos, the port city of São Paulo.[29] By the turn of the century, the Gafrée-Guinle firm was eager to expand its activities and had already made a tentative attempt to secure the right to distribute General Electric equipment in Brazil.

From distribution of machinery to its actual operation was a short step and a step the Guinles were more than willing to take. The Santos Docks Company had already erected a small generating plant to serve the needs of the industries and warehouses in its immediate vicinity. Some time early in 1904, Eduardo Guinle, Junior, approached Pearson on behalf of his father to discuss 'the possibility of his people coming into the enterprise.' Pearson speculated that if the Guinle family could be induced to join him, perhaps by means of allowing them to handle all General Electric purchases, the Rio project would have won an immeasurable advantage. With the backing of the Guinles, 'there will be absolutely no probability of anything ever being refused us; or of there ever being any native opposition to anything that we may undertake to do.'[30] Satisfied that the Guinles held the key to the situation, Pearson authorized Mackenzie to make a 'provisional offer to Mr. Guinle that we would let him join us to any amount up to $5,000,000 par value of bonds of underwriting on the basis of 60% stock bonus.'[31] It was a unique offer that would have married Pearson's considerable technical and managerial skills with the prestige and capital of one of Brazil's leading entre-preneurs.

The seeming willingness of Brazilians to back the American engineer's aspirations was matched by support from other Americans, among them David E. Thompson, the American chargé d'affaires in Rio. Times were propitious for American investment in Brazil. In view of the Baron of Rio Branco's campaign to extract diplomatic recognition of Brazil's borders, especially in the Amazon Basin, from its South American neighbours, the Brazilian government was, wrote the American chargé, 'exceedingly anxious to do anything to propitiate the American government, because of prospective boundary difficulties with other South American countries ... and that as the United States might be in a position to intervene in the case of Brazil bringing pressure to bear upon some of her weaker neighbours, the government officials are anxious to do everything they possibly can to stand in the good graces of the Americans.'[32] Pearson could therefore be 'absolutely certain' that Brazil would provide a workable concession. It was not, however, to the diplomatic corps that Pearson turned for direct support, but to a brash young American promoter named Percival Farquhar, who had already displayed prowess in organizing railways in Cuba and Guatemala and possessed extensive financial connections in New York and Montreal.[33] Farquhar had close working ties with the great Montreal promoter William Van Horne through endeavours in Cuba and Guatemala, and with W. Lanman Bull, an influential New York financier. The combination of a conducive political environment and Farquhar's eagerness to support the project led Pearson to obtain a charter in May 1904 under the lax corporate laws of New Jersey for the Rio de Janeiro Light and Power Co. Ltd.[34]

Just as it seemed that the Reid concession would become the kernel of an American public utility in Rio, events in Brazil and Canada conspired to pull the enterprise back into Canadian hands. First, William Reid dropped all pretence of exploiting his concession and, in late 1903, passed control of it to the Banco Nacional, represented by Luís Rocha Miranda, a Brazilian businessman, who quickly expressed 'a willingness to sell out on a reasonable basis, and to have the payment extended over a reasonable period of time, if necessary.'[35] Seeing an opening, Pearson instructed Mackenzie to open negotiations with Miranda, but cautioned him to 'bluff a good deal' until he could convince the capitalists of New York or Toronto that the proposition was a sure money-maker. The breakthrough came in June 1904, when William Mackenzie and his allies committed themselves to the venture. As the caution instilled in Toronto financiers by the 1903 'panic' was slowly dispelled by better times, the São Paulo-company syndicate had begun to take a keener interest in the Rio venture. Toronto's scepticism was also allayed by the encouraging reports from Alexander Mackenzie, whose calm and positive appraisal of the Rio project contrasted sharply with Pearson's ebullient, almost reckless predictions. On 11 June 1904, a federal charter was obtained in Ottawa for the Rio de Janeiro Light and Power Co. Ltd.[36] Acting on Pearson's advice, Zebulon A. Lash deliberately excluded any mention of 'traction' or 'tramways' in the company name, so as not to draw attention to the fact that the company's ultimate goal was to seize control of Rio's still-scattered tramway companies. Like most incorporations meticulously put together by Lash, young lawyers and legal clerks were used to constitute the Rio company's first board of directors.[37] In November the actual promoters of the Rio company emerged, at which time William Mackenzie, William Van Horne, F.S. Pearson, W.L. Bull, Z.A. Lash, E.R. Wood, and Frederic

Nicholls all took places on the board. Both Bull and Van Horne concurred with Mackenzie's plan to domicile the company in Toronto, and the New Jersey company was wound up. William Mackenzie, who was elected president of the Rio company, had thus brought another Brazilian utility company under the roof of his Toronto Railway Chambers.

The experience of organizing and financing the São Paulo venture allowed Mackenzie to act with speed and self-assurance in the Rio enterprise. The promoters' syndicate, so crucial in financing and controlling the young company, was this time given a formal legal existence with the creation of the Brazilian Securities Company Limited, incorporated just two weeks after the Rio company's incorporation. Brazilian Securities was to obtain control of certain 'properties, concessions or rights in Brazil' on behalf of the Rio company, under whose control the concessions and any other properties acquired in the Brazilian city would eventually be placed.[38] This role was formalized in an agreement of 10 August 1904. Brazilian Securities was obliged to enlist the services of F.S. Pearson as 'engineer negotiator' for the next three years and to procure purchasers for at least $5,000,000 of the Rio company's $25,000,000 bond issue. In return for these services, the Rio company made a cash payment of $30,000 to Brazilian Securities and promised 'to issue and deliver to the Securities Company' the $25,000,000 par value of the company's shares. The first $5,000,000 worth of bonds placed by Brazilian Securities would be sold to it at 90 per cent of face value with terms of payment spread out over the period up to June 1906.[39]

The August 1904 agreement achieved the two principal conditions that Pearson deemed essential to the successful realization of the Rio project. It provided tangible evidence that Toronto capitalists were ready to match his faith in the venture and thus allowed Alexander Mackenzie, who had been patiently biding his time in Rio 'bluffing' his opponents, to commence his bid for the Reid concession in earnest. Secondly, the agreement ensured that the Rio enterprise would be both well financed and tightly controlled. With William Mackenzie as president, there was now little worry that the company's stocks and bonds would fail to be placed in the hands of North American and European investors. Rio securities would join those of the São Paulo company, the Canadian Northern, and Mackenzie's various Canadian utilities under the watchful eye of Monty Horne-Payne in London.

The agreement also succeeded in assuring members of 'the syndicate' of a generous return for their promotional backing. At the Brazilian Securities board meeting of 18 November 1904, Mackenzie and his fellow directors received portions of Rio shares. As president of the Rio company, Mackenzie was issued $600,000 par value of Rio stock; Van Horne, Pearson, and Bull $394,700 each; Nicholls $189,400; Wood and Cox $197,300 each; Lash $131,900, and the National Trust Company $1,500,000, for a total of $4,000,000.[40] This transaction marked the culmination of almost two years of dogged persistence on the part of Fred Pearson. His eventual success in orchestrating the incorporation of the Rio venture as a Canadian company testified to his transformation from a consulting engineer to what the August agreement aptly labelled an 'engineer negotiator.' 'I have led a very strenuous life for the last two years,' Pearson complained to Alexander Mackenzie in 1906, 'and have had a great deal of worry due to interference of others who have hindered work without helping, which has made the work doubly hard.' The 'responsibility of this business and keeping matters in line at Rio, London and at home,' Pearson concluded, was 'no sinecure.'[41] A Canadian company was thus born of American paternity.

With the financial and organizational framework established in Toronto, the onus now fell on Alexander Mackenzie to procure the Reid concession, wrest modifications to it from the municipal council and use it as a nucleus for an integrated utilities system in Rio. Obtaining the concession presented small difficulty. With both Reid and the Banco Nacional having failed to develop the Lajes 'water power,' Mackenzie had little trouble purchasing the concession on 7 January 1905. Although the deed of transfer does not record the price, it is probable that Mackenzie paid about '$105,000 or thereabouts' plus about 4,500 Rio common shares for the concession.[42]

Although the concession was in many ways still unsatisfactory to the Toronto promoters, it at least afforded them a position of dominance. 'This concession gives exclusive right to sell power in Rio for twelve years with non-exclusive right for thirty-five years longer,' company secretary J.M. Smith reported. 'Inasmuch as we have secured control of all the water power available in the neighbourhood of Rio, the non-exclusive part of this concession gives us very little concern.'[43] On 16 October 1906, Alexander Mackenzie transferred ownership of the Reid concession from himself to the Rio company. What remained for Mackenzie to do was to gain control of some, if not all, of the lighting and tramway companies in the city and then, once the company had a *de facto* monopoly, approach the municipal government with a request for a 'unification' of all its concessions. Unification would tighten the Canadian company's hold on the Rio market and would ensure a base load for the power of the Lajes power plant.

Buying control of a motley collection of public-utilities companies already operating in Rio required considerable financial legerdemain on three continents. In the case of some of the companies, such as the Société Anonyme du Gaz and the Vila Isabel tramway, which were controlled by non-Brazilians, negotiations to purchase control were initiated by the Rio company's financial allies in Toronto and London. Brazilian-owned and -managed concessions were tackled directly by Alexander Mackenzie in Rio. What made this broad campaign to secure control of diverse enterprises in the same city so delicate was the need for haste. The 'unification' contract had to be drawn up as quickly as possible. The urgency placed the company's negotiators in a poor bargaining position. By moving too openly the company would arouse suspicion that it was seeking to build a monopoly and thereby allow the owners of the remaining companies to hike their price. With this in mind, Pearson and Alexander Mackenzie decided to place the Jardim Botânico tramway operation, the most successful and most electrified of Rio's tramways, at the bottom of the purchasing list and hope that, by purchasing all the rest of the city's traction enterprises, they could isolate the Jardim Botânico, deny it any chance of expansion, depress its value, and thereby open the way to its eventual acquisition.

The first acquisition was the Belgian-controlled Société Anonyme du Gaz de Rio de Janeiro, with its promising concession for electric lighting. Discreet inquiries made at the Banque Internationale de Bruxelles revealed that the SAG was widely held and that its shareholders were disgruntled over their company's failure to pay dividends. From this intelligence, Pearson and Mackenzie concluded that proper management and adequate financing could turn the gas company into a profitable concern. It was therefore decided to try to purchase a controlling interest in the company on the open market in Brussels. In a series of agreements signed in mid-1905, Brazilian Securities made arrangements for SAG stocks and bonds to be bought up by a syndicate of European brokers. Headed by Alfred Loewenstein, the Brussels broker who had placed the first São Paulo securities in European hands, Rod A. Demmé, a Paris broker, and James H. Dunn, an aggressive young Montreal financier, the syndicate worked with lightning precision and, by April 1907, had secured 94 per cent of the gas company's securities, which they exchanged for Rio common stock.[44] The $12 million in bonds and shares bought in Belgium on behalf of Brazilian Securities were in turn vested in a Maine holding company, the Rio de Janeiro Gas Company, which had been specially set up by Lash to disguise the Toronto company's intentions. The Maine holding company also served to place some of the Rio enterprises nominally under American control and would thus provide the parent company with the possibility of American diplomatic assistance should the Brazilian government ever move against foreign investors. Such assistance was never sought, and it was unlikely that it would ever have been proffered.

Much the same procedure was used to gain control of the Vila Isabel tramway and the small Rio telephone company, both of which were owned by the Brazilianische Elektricitäts Gesellschaft of Berlin. The Companhia Ferro-Carril de Vila Isabel was purchased outright by E.R. Wood and Walter Gow, a young lawyer from the Blake, Lash and Cassels firm, who travelled to Berlin in July 1905. The crucial ingredient in the deal was a million-dollar loan that Wood negotiated with the Deutsche Bank. The transaction was typical of the kind of financial errands and favours performed so skilfully by Wood, who had already acquired a peerless reputation as Canada's leading technician of international finance. Having acquired the entire Vila Isabel stock on behalf of the Brazilian Securities syndicate, Wood then sold it for $12 million to another Maine corporation, the Vila Isabel Tramway Company.

The same transaction brought control of Rio's fledgling telephone system, which had also been owned by the Berlin company. Once again, Wood and Gow arranged the deal for Brazilian Securities, which, in return for $2 million, vested the securities in yet another Maine corporation, the Rio de Janeiro Telephone Company. As with the Belgian gas company and the Vila Isabel tramway, the head office of the holding company was maintained in the country of incorporation. Thus William Mackenzie assumed the rather unlikely position of president of a German-domiciled telephone company. Although the telephone company's concession extended only until 1930, there was great potential for expansion, especially since the system had won a complete exemption from municipal taxation in return for a direct payment of 10 per cent of annual net profits. The telephone company therefore had special significance because it opened the way for the Rio company to seek control over the broadest possible range of public services, from telephones to trams. There was to be nothing partial about the company's presence in Rio.

The purchase of the four Brazilian-controlled traction companies proved more straightforward. By buying on the open market or by dealing directly with holders of large blocks of stock, Alexander Mackenzie was able to acquire control of the São Cristovão and Carris Urbanos companies (two animal-traction tram operations in the centre of the city), the Tijuca electric railway, and the Corcovado Railway, a steam-powered cog-railway catering to the tourist trade. By April 1907, acquisitions in Europe and Brazil had thus given the Rio company control over a motley collection of five traction companies, with a total of 212 kilometres of routes, of which only 64 kilometres had been electrified. With the routes came more than 330 tram cars and 4,779 mules. Only the prosperous Jardim Botânico company and the Carioca Company, a short-line electric tram service in a wealthy residential area, remained outside the pale of the Rio company. In 1905, Pearson had rejected any move to acquire the Carioca Company because of 'the exorbitant price demanded by minority shareholders.' None the less, Mackenzie persisted in buying whatever Carioca shares he could find at reasonable prices and, by March 1906, had at least 10,616 of the company's 25,000 shares.[45] Similarly, Mackenzie quietly bought securities of the Jardim Botânico under an arrangement with the Banco Nacional Brasileiro, so that by 1908 the Rio company had control of about 75 per cent of its last remaining competitor.[46]

While the rapid acquisition of so many Rio tramway companies was a cause of great satisfaction in Toronto, the ensuing tangle of concessionary rights had a distinctly dismaying effect. Each of the five new subsidiaries had a different expiry date for its concession, ranging from 1930 for the Carris Urbanos to 1950 for the São Cristovão. The gas-company concession for private lighting ran until 1915 and for public lighting until 1945, while the telephone concession extended until 1930. Unification of the tramway concessions was imperative, partially for reasons of operating efficiency – tramway service had to be co-ordinated on a city-wide basis according to standard practices – and partially because European and North American investors would not risk their capital on the venture unless they obtained an ironclad guarantee that the Rio company had an exclusive privilege for an extended period of time. 'There is a general feeling in Europe,' Pearson informed Alexander Mackenzie shortly before the unification concession was eventually signed in late 1907, 'that our concessions are valueless and that it is impossible for us to get the new concessions and this, of course, makes it very hard to get additional funds.'[47]

That it took Alexander Mackenzie almost two years of concerted effort to erase the impression that the company's concessions were 'valueless' was largely the result of a changed political atmosphere in Rio. As the Canadian promoters of the Rio company progressively gained control of the city's independent public-utility operations, the initial receptivity among local politicians to the Canadian enterprise began to wear off and be replaced by a sense of apprehension. While public opinion remained largely sympathetic to the company, an outspoken minority emerged to criticize its growing control in the most vehement fashion.

Two factors contributed to the emergence of hostile sentiment. There was, in the first place, genuine concern about the wisdom of placing the city's tramway services at the mercy of a foreign corporation. While few denied that the *laissez-faire* competition of the nineteenth century had brought the city only mediocre utility service, there was a general scepticism about conceding the field to one enormous producer and supplier of electricity. Foremost among those who took exception to monopoly was the great Brazilian liberal Rui Barbosa, who, as early as 1899, had criticized the terms of the SAG gas concession and the Reid electricity concession on the grounds of their exclusivity. 'The conquests of civilization,' Barbosa said of modern electric and gas technology, 'are the property of no one, they are the common property of the civilized world, except those rights, created and protected by law, for the benefit of "inventors, perfecters and initiators."' To allow any company the sole right to exploit such inventions over an extended period would 'jeopardize industrial development' and deal constitutional liberty a 'most arbitrary blow.'[48]

A more violent source of opposition to the Canadian company's aspirations came from its would-be competitors, headed by its erstwhile allies, the powerful Gafrée-Guinle family. It is not clear what exactly soured relations between Alexander Mackenzie and the Guinle family after each had displayed an initial willingness to co-operate in exploiting the Rio power market, but it is clear that by early 1905 the Guinle family, with its franchise to market General Electric equipment, had designs of its own and had launched a vitriolic assault on the Canadian company's claims. The key to the Guinles' strategy was to undermine the supposed privileges of the Reid and Société Anonyme du Gaz concessions and thereby open the way for their own entry into Rio utilities. The Guinles were to prove the company's most persistent and resourceful opponents. Not only could they draw on large financial and political resources, which included the Rio newspaper *Jornal do comércio*, but they could easily capitalize upon anti-foreign and anti-monopoly sentiments. 'The Gafrée people have now settled their plan of campaign, which is to be violent, persistent and a determined opposition all along the line to anything and everything we propose in the City,' Mackenzie woefully informed Pearson in November 1906. 'They make no pretence of secrecy ... There is no doubt that they have succeeded in creating considerable antipathy, and it is going to take a lot of education of the public to enable them to appreciate not only what we are asking but what we now have.'[49]

The first hurdle that the company had to clear was to obtain simple permission from the federal government to operate in Brazil. Such a decree had been readily forthcoming for the São Paulo company, but in Rio, with the forces of opposition now alerted, progress was much slower. The constant bombardment of the company in the editorial columns of the *Jornal do comércio* had the effect of unsettling the political climate. Lauro Müller, the federal minister of public works on whose advice the necessary decree would be issued, was reluctant to comply with the company's request without imposing some restriction on the rights pertaining to Lajes so as to placate the critics of the incipient foreign monopoly. By April 1905, Alexander Mackenzie reported to Toronto that he was having 'a pretty stiff fight' with Müller, and it was not until late May that Mackenzie's persistent lobbying convinced the minister to issue the decree permitting the company to operate in Brazil.[50]

Having won the initial victory, Mackenzie turned his attention to the municipal government of Rio de Janeiro, with which he hoped to renegotiate the gas concession and to consolidate the tramway concessions into one unified concession. In his more optimistic moments, Mackenzie believed that he could win a ninety-year extension for the consolidated concession. 'Once this concession is obtained,' he told Company Secretary Smith, 'I feel sure that we shall enjoy much the same freedom from interference on the part of the public authorities as we have had in São Paulo for the last 5 years, where everything continues to go to our entire satisfaction.'[51] Unfortunately for Mackenzie, little in the tumultuous world of Rio politics was to be to his 'entire satisfaction' for the next two years.

The Rio company now encountered resistance on all fronts. In the first ranks of its opponents stood the Guinle family, which by 1907 had created the Companhia Brasileira de Energia Elétrica (CBEE) to promote its ambitions. Although Mackenzie privately doubted that the Guinles could muster sufficient capital and expertise, the CBEE began work in 1907 on a generating station on the outskirts of the city. Eager to enlist nationalist sympathies, the Guinles christened their hydro project after Alberto Torres, a former state governor and outspoken proponent of Brazilian economic nationalism. Within the city, the Guinles kept up their constant harassment of the company in several 'captive' newspapers and by means of their extensive political connections. So virulent was the Guinle onslaught that the British ambassador felt moved to report on it to his superiors at the Foreign Office. 'This Company,' Ambassador Haggard commented upon the newly established Canadian enterprise,

has inveterate enemies here in various directions, most of them professing the purest motives of hatred, for instance, of the immorality of monopolies, all of them probably not unwilling to share in its profits: the champion of these malcontents is a native firm named 'Gafrée and Guinle' who, having failed so far by consistent and unscrupulous methods of opposition to blackmail the 'Light,' as it is called for brevity, still hopes, if not to secure a direct influence in it, at least to injure and discredit it and then themselves to build up a successful competition on its ruins.[52]

The Guinle threat was exacerbated by the pervasive instability of Rio municipal politics. The year 1906 was a particularly inauspicious one for the company to launch its bid for renegotiation of its concessions. Not only was the federal presidency slated to change hands but so too was the presidency of Rio de Janeiro state and the prefecture of the Federal District.

Even before the final year of his administration, relations between the company and Pereira Passos had become frayed over the interpretation of the company's existing rights. Pearson, the bullish American who had less exposure to the Brazilian temperament than the patient Mackenzie, frequently grew exasperated by the slow pace of events in Brazil. 'I shall not be surprised if I find matters in exactly the same condition as when I left last December,' he complained in mid-1906. 'I think this Rio crowd is about the worst I have ever had anything to do with so far as getting anything settled in a business-like way.'[53]

Only with the swearing-in of the new Rio prefect, General Souza Aguiar, in November 1906 did the chances of expediting the unification contract appreciably alter. Aguiar, who had been Brazil's representative at the 1893 Chicago Exposition, was described by the company's general manager as being 'fully cognizant of American ideas of progress.' The final stages of the fight to secure the new concession were played out during the early months of 1907 in the offices of prominent politicians and lawyers. As soon as the new president of Brazil, Afonso Pena, was elected in early 1906, Pearson began urging Mackenzie to 'commence a campaign with a view of securing the influence of those who will be prominent in the next administration.' This was doubly necessary because Pearson had 'no doubt' that 'Gafrée will be pulling strings in order to gain these same people on his side.'[54] The electrically illuminated triumphal arch to President Pena, illustrated in this book, provides an example of Mackenzie's subsequent campaign to win federal favour. It was the art of building local alliances that Alexander Mackenzie mastered so superbly during these tension-filled months. Mackenzie had an unerring knack for cultivating precisely the right type of prominent Brazilian lawyers and politicians to assist in the protection of the company's interests in Rio. The successful conduct of a business enterprise in Brazil demanded that any company, Brazilian or foreign, take great pains to erect a line of political defence behind which it could prosper. To the gimlet eye of the British ambassador, who watched the activities of local politicians and foreign businessmen, it was all illustrative of 'an element of conditions in Brazil which does not appear on the surface and is not discussed in the newspapers. Everything hinges on politics, and law and order, particularly in the [Brazilian] States, are liable to disruption for purely party motives.'[55]

Changing political conditions augured well for Mackenzie in late 1906 and the first half of 1907. With Aguiar replacing the 'arbitrary' Pereira Passos and Pena superseding Rodrigues Alves, the federal president whom Mackenzie had found 'weak,' the company began to make progress on the unification concession. In December 1906, Mackenzie informed Lash in Toronto that President Pena was a 'stronger man' than Alves and that 'among his advisers are powerful friends of ours, whose wishes will I have no doubt be treated with every consideration.' Furthermore, the municipal council had 'recently authorized the Prefect to enter into an agreement with us unifying and extending all the existing concessions and we are now in negotiation with him.'[56] The news of Mackenzie's progress through the maze of Brazilian politics brought great relief in Toronto, where it had become increasingly difficult to arrange financing so long as the new concession remained unsigned. 'My great fear,' Pearson confided to Mackenzie, 'is that with the procrastination we shall suddenly find ourselves without money and be obliged to stop all work in Brazil.'[57]

Any explanation of why a Canadian company was able to survive in the fiercely contested fight for the public-utility services of Rio de Janeiro must, therefore, focus on Mackenzie's talent for playing the Brazilian game in the Brazilian way. 'Mr. Mackenzie,' another admiring British ambassador noted some years later, 'has lived for many a year at Rio and I may say that there is no British subject in this city who knows Brazil better than he does or has greater influence.'[58] Mackenzie's Rio home, a cool haven perched high on the side of Corcovado mountain, soon became a gathering place of foreign diplomats and influential Brazilians alike.[59] As in São Paulo, Mackenzie excelled in attracting the best legal talent and well-placed political friends. He was able to do this partly because the company could afford to hire the most prestigious Brazilian lawyers, partly because, in the case of politicians, he could form strong bonds of sympathy with those Brazilians who believed that foreign capital and technology had a beneficial role to play within their borders.

'I think that the greatest danger will be that Guinle will attempt to break into the city ...' Pearson warned Mackenzie in 1907, 'and unless you have some strong lawyer who is aggressive, to secure injunctions and make a fight in these attacks, we are liable to be seriously compromised.'[60] Mackenzie did not just recruit a 'strong' lawyer, he obtained the services of Rui Barbosa, a man who was probably Brazil's greatest lawyer. Despite his earlier denunciations of monopoly, Barbosa was by 1906 providing the Canadian company with legal briefs upholding the opinion that utility monopolies were a 'natural' phenomenon. As a legal scholar, federal politician, diplomat, and outspoken proponent of liberalism in Brazil, Barbosa had immense influence among his countrymen. Once convinced that the company's concessions were legally airtight, Barbosa became a dogged proponent of its right to operate in Brazil. It was Barbosa, Mackenzie reported to Pearson in late 1907, who had assured him that the Guinles 'had no right whatever to bring power to Rio.'[61] Not only did Barbosa supply legal advice, but through his good offices the company was able to lay its case before the highest political authorities. Mackenzie frequently concluded his reports from Rio with the codicil: 'I am now mainly relying upon our relations with Rui Barbosa.'[62]

Barbosa's attachment to the company's cause was undoubtedly due in part to the handsome stipend it was able to pay him, but a more profound influence also lay behind his conversion. Barbosa's liberalism had bred in him a strong affinity for the ideals underlying the English and American economies. Mindful of the astonishing success of the São Paulo company, Barbosa saw in Mackenzie the embodiment of these ideals. 'Our group,' Mackenzie reminded Barbosa in 1905, 'is one of the first which, on a large scale, has succeeded in interesting American capital in this country, and has done something towards making Brazil better known in the United States.'[63]

A similar bond of friendship emerged between Mackenzie and the Baron of Rio Branco, Brazil's great foreign minister during the presidency of Rodrigues Alves (1902–6). Rio Branco, who had 'always shown himself friendly enough towards us,' frequently provided Mackenzie with informal advice during the long negotiation for the 1907 concession. The Rio company seldom sought to enlist the assistance of foreign diplomats to fight its battles. For Mackenzie such interventions were 'a sort of two-edged sword.'[64] While a little pressure from an ambassador might win short-term results, it could also provide a focus for nationalistic hostility. Mackenzie preferred to fight his battles in the arena of Brazilian politics. Most foreign diplomats were, in any case, wary of entering the Brazilian fray. 'I would venture with great deference to suggest that in view of the character of the contest going on between the "Light" and various forces,' the British ambassador informed the Foreign Office in 1910 '... that this struggle has almost, if not quite, assumed the character of very bitter local politics, each party with its press champions ... it would not be advisable for His Majesty's Legation to enter into the fray, save in the case of real and imminent necessity, in support of the "Light," which is generally very well capable of taking care of itself ...'[65]

In early November 1907 the unification contract was finally signed. The infuriating delay was occasioned by what Mackenzie described as 'the strong animosity' between Aguiar, the prefect, and 'the political chief for the Federal District, Senator Vasconcellos,' who was under heavy pressure from the Guinle interests.[66] On 7 November 1907, Pearson discovered that the infuriating delay had been more than worth the wait. Under the terms of the agreement with the municipal council, the existing concessions governing the São Cristovão, Carris Urbanos, and Vila Isabel tramway companies were integrated and greatly modified. The unified contract gave the companies permission to operate until 1970 and assured them of exclusive privileges to operate within their respective zones until 1940. The new tramway concession established a 200 réis per zone first-class fare and required the company to offer second-class fares of 100 réis to working-class passengers. The company was also accorded the right to acquire other tramway lines in the Rio area.

The combined terms of the Reid and unification concessions gave the young company solid assurance of a prosperous and secure future. Although the monopoly on the city's power supply lapsed in 1915, there was little likelihood, Mackenzie assured his Toronto superiors, that newcomers, including the Guinles, would attempt to break into the Rio market once the company had a ten-year head start on providing service. From the city's point of view, the Canadian company's possession of the Reid and unification concessions had profound implications. It brought to an end the chaos created by a handful of uncoordinated traction and power companies vying for the city's fare-paying customers. Except for the Jardim Botânico and Carioca tramway operations (which would soon fall under the sway of the Rio company), the entire city had now come under the control of an integrated power and transportation system. On the other hand, the comprehensiveness of the concession portended poorly for the aspirations of local power entrepreneurs like the Guinles, who now had little realistic hope of breaking into the expanding Rio market. When in 1909 the Société Anonyme du Gaz concession was successfully renegotiated by Mackenzie and extended to cover the period up to 1945,[67] the Canadian company found itself in virtual sole possession of the traction, light, and power services of a city of 882,000 inhabitants.

While Mackenzie was struggling with the politicians and would-be competitors in Rio, another equally vital struggle was unfolding in the foothills of the Serra do Mar. From the beginning it was evident that the Rio market would be worth exploiting only as long as the company was able to develop a relatively low-cost source of electricity. William Reid had located a promising site for hydro generation on the Lajes River, some sixty-four kilometres from Rio. Like Parnaíba outside São Paulo, Lajes was isolated and set in hilly, densely vegetated terrain, accessible only on horseback. The first engineer to reconnoitre the site on behalf of the Canadians was James Mitchell, the general manager of the São Paulo company, who reported in late 1903 that the site was 'capable of developing 100,000 h.p. (or 75,000 kw) in the driest season.' With Welsh coal selling in Rio for the equivalent of $9 per ton and a potential market of 15,000 kw, Mitchell was quick to assure his Canadian sponsors that the estimated $4,445,000 it would take to develop the generating and transmission facilities[68] could be quickly recouped.

As had been the case in most of Mackenzie's utility ventures, F.S. Pearson was appointed 'consulting engineer' to the Lajes project, but since his talents were so much in demand elsewhere, a young American engineer, C.H. Kearny, was hired to oversee the actual construction. By December 1904, Kearny and a survey crew had hacked their way through the dense *mato* and begun to probe for a suitable dam site. It was gruelling and dangerous work. Not only were there heat and humidity, but deadly snakes and malarial mosquitoes were ever present. 'Unfortunately,' a dispirited Kearny reported to Alexander Mackenzie, 'the difficulties we have had to contend with on all sides have worried me to such an extent that I feel I cannot stand it much longer.' Kearny persevered and by May 1905 had formulated a general plan of attack. A curved, concrete dam, 35 metres high and solidly anchored in granite, would block the flow of the Rio das Lajes as it moved around the end of a steep hillock, thereby creating a reservoir with a capacity of 204 million cubic metres. A tunnel would then be driven through the escarpment to take water from the reservoir and deliver it by means of two 1,800-metre-long penstocks to a powerhouse in the next valley. The effective 'head' would be 312 metres. The actual production of power would be handled by six Westinghouse Electric generators, each with a capacity of 4,400 kw. With one unit always in reserve, the remaining five units would furnish 22,300 kw for transmission. F.S. Pearson believed that this would provide sufficient power for the market for at least five years. When that ceiling was reached, Kearny advised, a tunnel could be built to divert water from the nearby Piraí River into the Lajes reservoir, thereby providing enough water for an additional 37,300 kw.[69]

While the plan for the Lajes development was enticingly straightforward, its implementation was to try the ingenuity and, at times, the sanity of the company's best engineers. Throughout 1905, Kearny pushed ahead with survey work. An access railway, twenty-two kilometres long, had to be built from Antas, a small town on the Central Railway, to the site. It was a tough initiation for Kearny, who complained in March 1906 that there had been 'an awful lot of rain here the past few months' and that the crude roadbed over which his small locomotives were running was constantly being washed away.[70] At Lajes, a temporary dam and power plant were erected to supply the construction crews with sufficient power.

In the meantime, Alexander Mackenzie was encountering problems of his own. 'In the vicinity of the water power,' he lamented to Pearson, 'every man, woman and child is trying to make a fortune out of the Company, and when he has not a piece of land to sell, he buys something with the view of blackmailing us.'[71] Land speculation was accompanied by other problems, ranging from the shortage of such basic construction materials as cement to the unavoidable unruliness of the work camp. In one particularly unpleasant incident, a drunken tunnel worker shot two of his fellows, killing one. The worst menace by far, and the one that could easily frighten the work force into wholesale panic, was the malaria mosquito. In 1908, malaria struck the nearby municipalities of Piraí and São João Marcos. 'It is no exaggeration,' the company doctor reported, 'to affirm that about 95% of the population, principally in the municipality of São João Marcos, was attacked by malaria.'[72] Although the company and government spent large amounts to combat the outbreak, F.A. Huntress, the general manager, reported that work at Lajes had been 'very much delayed on account of the excessive fever which reigned throughout the entire district in 1908–9.'[73]

Despite the difficulties, progress at Lajes was astonishing. On 19 May 1906, state president Nilo Peçanha inaugurated the railway line. A shorter second railway line was built to carry men and equipment up and over the escarpment to the dam site. In one particularly remarkable feat, a large steam launch (to be used to ferry sand across the reservoir) was transported from Rio to the construction site. By December 1906 the plant was ready, and, once the transmission lines were completed, power was first delivered to Rio in May 1907. One year later Alfredo Backer, the new state president, presided at the official inauguration. The whole construction project had been a race against time. Kearny had had to have his power 'on line' before the rival Alberto Torres plant was ready and thereby beat the Guinles to the Rio market. Furthermore, state and municipal politicians had had to be given tangible evidence that the company could fulfil its promises. To help accomplish this, a guest house was built at Lajes to which Brazilian politicians like Peçanha and Backer were brought to be entertained and to inspect the power plant. Kearny was also striving to satisfy the demands of the company's European investors, who were anxious to see the Reid concession profitably exploited. Like the Parnaíba power station, Lajes was a monument to the prowess of American engineers. All those who viewed the project commented on 'the grandeur of the work' and the dedication of the staff. 'They make me feel that life is worth living,' a visiting engineer remarked of the Lajes staff, 'after all the fatigue of a 30 kilometer horseback ride, even though it be in the wilds of a tropical Brazilian forest.'[74]

Lajes power and the ratification of the 'unification' contract placed the Rio company in a highly advantageous position to exploit the market for electricity in Rio. While it could have imposed the maximum rates permissible under its concession, the company chose to protect its long-term prospects by offering reasonable rates and efficient service. 'I am very strongly of the opinion,' Pearson instructed Mackenzie,

that we should fix a scale of rates in Rio which will be fair and as low as they would be if we did not have a monopoly. I do not think it is for the interest of the Rio Company to impose high rates for power on the public, merely because they have a monopoly as I think the indirect benefit from building up a large industrial community will very much offset the loss in profits through reducing our prices to low rates. Furthermore, I think it is a mistaken policy for any company holding a monopoly to endeavour to get the last pound of flesh out of the public. My feeling is that we should make about the same rates in Rio as we are making in Mexico, where they are very low and where we have built up an enormous business through the low rates.[75]

In keeping with this crucial policy, the company agreed in 1907 to lower its power rate for street lighting from 800 réis per kilowatt hour to 500 réis. 'The Government had a right to object to this high price,' Pearson conceded, 'and I think that you did well in meeting their view.'[76] In 1910 the rate per kilowatt hour was again cut from 500 to 285 réis. But even attractive rates, Pearson argued, were not enough to woo power customers. He urged General Manager Huntress to appoint a 'very active general agent' who would despatch an army of 'canvassers' to stimulate the market. 'You will find that you are ready to deliver power at short notice.'[77] To attract industrial power consumers, the company stockpiled a large number of electric motors, which it offered to install at cost for those undertaking to purchase power. An attempt to draw further customers was made by placing a large, illuminated sign reading 'Buy Lajes Power' on the roof of the company's downtown office. Cumulatively, these early decisions to structure rates in such a way as to build a broad customer base were of immense importance to the future success of both the company and Brazilian industrialization. Electricity was consequently disseminated through Rio quickly and efficiently.

The key to developing the Rio market lay in what Alexander Mackenzie called 'educating' the public to the obvious advantages of electricity. As soon as Mackenzie gained control of the gas and power concessions, he instructed his engineers to devote the entire output of the small thermal generating plant erected by the gas company to illumination of the city's important streets and shops. In October 1905, Avenida Central, the showpiece of the city's reconstruction, was illuminated for the first time by electric light, followed shortly thereafter by Botafogo Park, a popular shorefront promenade for *cariocas*. 'Although our apparatus for lighting at Botafogo is somewhat crude,' General Manager Huntress reported, 'the results we have obtained have been very satisfactory to the Government and they are very much pleased.'[78] When Rio hosted the Third Pan-American Conference in 1906, the company installed 4,600 incandescent lamps in the St Louis Pavilion and the Itamaraty (Brazil's Ministry of Foreign Affairs) where the conference sessions were held. Special arrangements were made to light the lodge in which American Secretary of State Elihu Root was accommodated. The dark and gloomy streets that had characterized Rio in the nineteenth century quickly became a thing of the past. 'In consequence of this lavish use of light,' Huntress boasted in 1910, 'the city of Rio is the best lighted city in the world, there being at least double the amount of illumination on its principal streets and avenues to that in the best lighted streets of the other large cities of the world.'[79]

While gas and electric lighting had a startling effect upon Rio's appearance and civic pride, it was a relatively small segment of the company's overall business. As in São Paulo, power consumed by the tramway system and industry loomed largest in the managers' minds. The company's success in converting Rio industry from steam power to electricity was astonishing. Aided by the high cost of imported coal, power salesmen had little difficulty in convincing local industrialists to adopt electricity. Contracts were offered on a long-term basis at low rates and often with the added inducement of the installation of electric motors at cost. By the end of 1907, 2,070 kw had been contracted by local consumers and this increased to 6,924 kw by the end of 1908. By 1909, the more than six hundred consumers of the company's power included practically all the city's major industrial concerns, most notably the Bangu cotton mills, the Rio de Janeiro Flour Mills and Granaries, and the machine shops of the Brazil Central Railway. With the signing of a contract with the Confiança Mills in 1910, the entire cotton-spinning and flour-milling industries had been electrified, with the exception of several mills controlled by the Guinles.[80] Although São Paulo was well on its way to outstripping Rio as the nation's leading industrial centre, electricity enabled Rio to modernize its industry and to expand. Between 1905 and 1915, Rio's industrial power supply, which was now overwhelmingly electric, grew by 207 per cent, while that of São Paulo increased 294 per cent.[81] In each city, electricity was both the harbinger and facilitator of a new economic order.

The Light facilitated Brazilian economic growth in other ways. The high cost of importation created a strong incentive for the company to buy local goods whenever possible. A major saving was effected by the decision to construct all tramcars for the two systems in the Rio Light shops. In 1910, for instance, the shops turned out sixty-eight thirteen-bench electric tramcars, together with an assortment of specialty cars for freight and street cleaning. In future, only the most complex pieces of electrical equipment were to be imported, such as the funicular railway locomotives bought in Switzerland for the Corcovado Railway.

The creation of an integrated, electrified tramway service profoundly affected the daily lives of *cariocas*. Electrified track increased from 55.5 kilometres at the end of 1907 to 219.8 kilometres by the end of 1909. Animal traction's share of the routes slipped from 143.5 kilometres in 1907 to a meagre 6.4 kilometres in 1910. In 1909, 213 electric trams and 300 mules transported 93.6 million passengers' whereas in 1907 it had required sixty-eight electric trams and 5,082 mules to haul 90.1 million passengers.[82] The trams enabled *cariocas* to escape the congestion of the old 'colonial' city and to move into less densely populated suburban areas. This was especially true in the coastal districts of Leme, Copacabana, Ipanema, and Leblon. The trams, in conjunction with the suburban lines of the Central and Leopoldina railways, speeded development, to the north-west of the old city, of such districts as Engenho Novo and Méier and, to the west, Maracanã.[83] Striking evidence of the tramway's transforming effect on the city was provided by the small São José district in downtown Rio, which had a population of 42,980 in 1906 but, with the trams siphoning away its inhabitants into the suburbs, had decreased to 27,714 by 1920. Whereas the seven districts of the 'old city' had contained 44 per cent of Rio's population in 1890, they contained only 19 per cent by 1925. The growth of suburban habitation was also indicated by the fact that the six districts of Santa Teresa, Copacabana, Gambôa, Andarai, Tijuca, and Méier, all of which registered little population in the 1906 census, had by 1920 a combined population of 234,693, out of a total Rio population of 1,170,660.[84] Such statistics provided ample proof of Rui Barbosa's contention that the *bonde* was 'a providential institution' in the history of modern Rio.

The earning power of the Rio trams was also providential. When James Mitchell first surveyed the market in 1903, he reported that as independent entities the gas and various traction companies generated net earnings of $695,000 annually, but that with electrification and unification net earnings could be boosted to $4,102,500 a year.[85] By September 1905, Pearson happily informed William Mackenzie that the fledgling company was already meeting its fixed charges and producing an annual surplus of $130,000, 'even with the poor condition of the Gas Company, and the fact that we have had the control of the [tramway] properties only about two months, and consequently have not been able to effect much economy.'[86] With Lajes power and the unification contract clinched, Pearson optimistically reported that 'the gross earnings of our tramway will greatly exceed those first anticipated and the profits from power and light will also be much greater than at first expected.'[87] As if to fulfil Pearson's prophecy, the net earnings rose steadily from $2,120,321 in 1907 to $3,068,306 in 1909 and finally to $5,393,092 in 1910. The Rio company's annual reports invariably conveyed the message that during the year 'most satisfactory progress had been made in all departments of the Company's undertaking.'

The Rio company's early financial performance was none the less governed by a delicate balance of heavy expenditure on plant and steady earnings, both driven by the constant expansion of services. If either capital inflow for expansion or earnings faltered, the company risked a serious financial squeeze. The financial 'panic' of 1907, which gripped both North America and Europe, had exactly this effect. The ensuing crisis was exacerbated by a lack of financial co-ordination and controls between head office and Brazil. As early as 1905 the company secretary, J.M. Smith, demanded that the general manager in Rio supply him with 'monthly reports' on progress in that city. In the same year, Toronto directors of the company complained that the 'whole Rio business' so far had been 'run in an unbusinesslike manner' and was capable of swallowing 'large amounts of money' without a trace.[88] Under great pressure to finish the Lajes plant and electrify the tram system, the company had only minimal control over capital expenditures. By mid-1907, the Rio company had overspent its approved budget in practically every area of its operations. This coincided disastrously with what the Canadian Bank of Commerce described to Smith as 'the extreme money stringency' in Canada. Suddenly the company was thrown into a desperate financial predicament, deeply indebted to the bank, committed to costly construction projects and unable to extend its line of credit. The Rio company even owed $300,000 to the São Paulo company.[89] The time had arrived for a financial reckoning.

Toronto's response to the crisis was to dispatch Robert J. Clark, a hard-nosed Toronto accountant, to restore a measure of financial order in Rio. After a vigorous investigation, Clark concluded that the Rio enterprise was basically 'well-organized.' So thorough had been Clark's financial probe that a storekeeper at Lajes had been caught pilfering company property. Clark's principal recommendation was the imposition of rigorous financial restraint, designed to instil in the employees 'a spirit of retrenchment, retrenchment and again retrenchment.' Kearny was instructed to order only material that was 'absolutely essential' for the completion of the Lajes installation. The climate of austerity prevailed until, in early 1908, F.S. Pearson and E.R. Wood were able to place a second issue of Rio-company bonds on the European market, a stroke of good fortune largely made possible by the aggressive Belgian financier Alfred Loewenstein.[90] The successful flotation of the second-mortgage bonds did much to restore optimism in the company's finances. 'All the companies are showing handsome earnings,' Alexander Mackenzie confided to his close friend W.H. Blake in Toronto in January 1908, 'and the prospects are considerably better than we ever expected. It is true that we are also spending more money than we ever expected, but any possible increased expenditure will be taken care of by the earnings.' Never again would the company be 'caught napping.'[90]

The financial stringency of 1907 underlined the large and constant capital needs of the Rio enterprise. When incorporated, the Rio de Janeiro Tramway, Light and Power Co. Ltd had a capitalization of $50 million, evenly divided into $25 million in common shares and $25 million in 'First Mortgage Gold Bonds.' The entire capital stock of the young company was issued to William Mackenzie's 'syndicate.' While Mackenzie, Lash, Wood, and their colleagues in the syndicate were careful to retain enough stock to give themselves voting control, the rest of the stock was placed in what E.R. Wood called the Brazilian Securities 'treasury,' from where it could be drawn on for 'stock bonuses' to be given to the underwriters of the company's bond issue. In the three 'campaigns' or 'issues' undertaken up to December 1905, $16,680,000 of Rio first-mortgage bonds were placed in predominantly Canadian hands. Up to mid-October 1905, the 'syndicate' had issued a total of $21,959,400 par value of common stock, almost all of it as stock bonuses. A proportion of the remaining stock was employed to pay for Pearson's services as a consulting engineer, for Alexander Mackenzie's services in Rio, and for the acquisition of the Reid concession.[91]

The list of purchasers of the Rio first-mortgage bonds read like a short list of Canada's financial establishment. In the first place, there were those intimately connected with the company. William Mackenzie led the list of 'insiders' with a commitment for $396,000 par value of bonds. He was joined by close associates of the Mackenzie enterprises, including Z.A. Lash, D.B. Hanna, Henry Pellatt, the Blake family, Sir William Van Horne, and even Mackenzie, Mann and Company. The second echelon of bondholders was made up of institutional investors, among them Central Canada Loan and Savings in Toronto, the Sun Life Assurance Company in Montreal, and the occasional English house, such as Sperling and Company in London. The third group encompassed a wider range of 'outside' or independent investors, who felt sufficiently confident to purchase Rio bonds. This amorphous group included bankers like B.E. Walker (of the Canadian Bank of Commerce) and E.S. Clouston (of the Bank of Montreal), independent financiers like W.M. Aitken (later

Lord Beaverbrook) and Herbert Holt, and a few wealthy independent investors like Sir William Mulock (a prominent Liberal politician) and Samuel Nordheimer (a successful Toronto piano maker). The eagerness with which these men placed their money in the Rio venture provided sterling testimony of the esteem in which the Canadian investment community held William Mackenzie in the early years of the new century.

There was never any doubt that some resort would have to be made to the European bond market, either as a means of reselling some of the bonds taken up by Canadian underwriters or simply as a means of disposing of the unsold bonds. Once again William Mackenzie provided the necessary connection. With alacrity, Monty Horne-Payne now took up Mackenzie's offer of introducing Rio stocks and bonds to English investors. Horne-Payne was joined in his effort by two eager young Montreal brokers, James H. Dunn and E. Mackay Edgar, who were in the process of breaking into the lucrative transatlantic securities trade. Horne-Payne, Dunn, and Mackay Edgar moved large quantities of Rio first-mortgage bonds across the Atlantic and created a market for them almost overnight. 'We have sold a great many of your bonds in Europe,' Dunn reported to Company Secretary Smith late in 1905. 'These certificates have been passed around from one person to another to such an extent that the majority of certificates in my name for instance are not in the hands of my clients or parties to whom I sold them.'[93] Through Dunn, Rio securities were fed to continental investors, initially as part of the exchange of securities that had allowed the company to gain control of the Société Anonyme du Gaz in Belgium.

The ease with which the Rio company established itself in the minds of English investors was the result of Monty Horne-Payne's assiduous cultivation of that market. It was said that Horne-Payne's mastery of the mores of the English investing public was so great that 'he could conjure cash out of the very cobblestones of cathedral towns.'[94] Horne-Payne's secret was the subtle art of creating an atmosphere of confidence among prospective purchasers. In carefully planned newspaper 'campaigns,' he inundated the English press with flattering accounts of the progress of the Canadian West or, in this case, the beneficent impact of electricity upon distant Rio. Thus the *Daily Express* proclaimed the message: 'A City Beautiful – Rio de Janeiro, where Canadian Enterprise is at work.'[95] Similarly, the Belfast *Northern Whig* featured a description of 'Brazilian progress: Rio de Janeiro's wonderful development, British Canadian enterprise provides electric tramway, light and power.'[96] Newspaper readers in Cardiff, Nottingham, Liverpool, and Plymouth received like tidings, all within a week of each other. Once he had gained the investor's attention, Horne-Payne knew how to retain it. In January 1906, he requested J.M. Smith's 'energetic assistance' to ensure that he received, promptly each month, a statistical synopsis of the São Paulo, Rio, and Winnipeg tramway operations. 'We shall train,' he boasted to Smith, 'the public throughout England to look for our traffic on the 25th day of every month, and great harm will result if they do not find them there, as it will give the impression that they are being held back for speculative purposes.'[97] The object of Horne-Payne's exertions was to banish any thought of political instability or financial risk from the minds of investors. Observing these tactics from the perspective of the embassy in Rio, a British diplomat warned the Foreign Office that many of the glowing reports about Brazil appearing in English newspapers were 'often full of inaccuracies and misrepresentations calculated to mislead persons who, with little knowledge of business methods seek to add to small incomes by investment.'[98]

In return for his services, Monty Horne-Payne exacted his price. He demanded a prominent voice in the administration of company affairs. As chairman of the board of the British Columbia Electric Railway, Horne-Payne had kept a tight rein on that company's Canadian operations from his English country estate.[99] Now, as a Rio director, he expected to exert the same kind of influence, an influence that was predicated on financial, not operational, interests. Above all else, in Horne-Payne's eyes, the stability of the investment as perceived by English investors must be preserved. 'You will note,' he crisply informed Fred Pearson in 1906, 'that I am issuing the Rio traffic simply as gross working expenses ... This is the result of a good many years' experience. I find that the public only care for grand totals, and on the other hand, I have before now been seriously embarrassed in the market by some sudden falling off of one branch.'[100]

On another occasion, Horne-Payne instructed Alexander Mackenzie to cable him immediately if he heard of 'any prejudicial news leaking out through London' adversely affecting operations in Brazil 'and give me rough particulars of it so that I may at once trace it to its source.'[101]

It was inevitable that conflict should have arisen between Horne-Payne's financial conservatism and the exigencies of operating a Brazilian public utility. Alexander Mackenzie, for instance, was repeatedly annoyed by Horne-Payne's habit of publishing glowing reports of earnings in the English press. As J.M. Smith warned Horne-Payne in 1906, 'whatever is published in *The Times* or other London papers with reference to this Company will be seen in Rio very soon after and republished there,' adding that such information greatly undermined Alexander Mackenzie's position at the bargaining table in Rio.[102] Horne-Payne's response was that such reports were all so much 'harmless newspaper gas.' The financial 'panic' of 1907 exacerbated the situation. In the face of Pearson's demands that the company must proceed at Lajes and thereby be in a position to clinch the market for power in Rio, Horne-Payne called for a vigorous tightening of the purse strings. 'I am not a croaker and I am not a rat,' Horne-Payne complained to William Mackenzie, 'and I will fight under your orders to the last, but I do not want any aspect of the market to escape your attention, and I do want you, no matter what Pearson or Alexander Mackenzie may think or say, to shut down tight before it is too late.'[103] This stance precipitated a confrontation long in the making. An infuriated Pearson told Alexander Mackenzie that he found Horne-Payne's attitude 'perfectly childish' because it was 'simply impossible to shut down construction and stop all expenditures at this end and in Brazil without putting the company in a receiver's hands.'[104] Matters came to a complete impasse when Pearson declared that Horne-Payne was 'a sick man and I do not believe is absolutely right in his mind.'[105]

Pearson's resolve to continue the work in Brazil made it imperative that new bridges to European investors be built to circumvent Horne-Payne's intransigence and to ease the financial stringency brought on by the 'panic' of 1907. When Pearson announced in March 1908 that a further $7 million would be required to complete work in hand and to pay off several bank advances, the board had little option but to increase the company's funded debt. At a London meeting the directors agreed that an issue of £3.5 million worth of 'Five Percent Gold Second Mortgage Bonds' would be offered to English and European investors. To facilitate the sale of the bonds to Belgian and French investors, the company established an office in Paris and brought three European financiers, two French and one Belgian, onto its board.[106] The drive to place the bonds was headed by William Mackenzie, who worked tirelessly in London and on the continent to secure syndicate support. Aided by Walter Gow, the

Toronto lawyer, and Percival Farquhar, the New York promoter, Mackenzie registered his first success in April 1908 when a syndicate headed by Stallaerts and Loewenstein in Brussels took 20,000 bonds. By July, most of the remaining bonds had been taken up by Robert Fleming and Co. and Dunn, Fischer and Co. in London. William Mackenzie had thus succeeded in broadening the Rio company's investment base in Europe, especially by attracting such aggressive bond salesmen as Alfred Loewenstein in Brussels and 'Jimmy' Dunn, who had by now established himself in the booming securities trade of the City. Monty Horne-Payne was no longer indispensable.

The financial crisis of 1907–8 was indicative of a much more deeply rooted problem confronting the Rio company: where was its ultimate seat of authority? The company's head office in Toronto was little more than a legal shell. The corporate secretary, J.M. Smith, frequently complained that he had 'been placed in a rather embarrassing position' owing to 'lack of information which I was supposed to have had on hand.'[107] His task was made the more trying by the 'frequent absences' of the company president, William Mackenzie. In most respects, Toronto was an awkward location from which to oversee the company's affairs. Forced to communicate with Rio by cumbersome commercial codes, the Canadian head-office staff operated at a distinct disadvantage in discharging its duties. 'Unless you have someone in charge of Rio affairs [in Toronto] who supersedes me and who had been to Brazil and has had at least a year or more experience,' Pearson bluntly informed William Mackenzie in 1907, 'it will be impossible for Toronto to answer questions promptly or satisfactorily as there is no one there who has much of any information concerning the company.'[108] The only possible alternative would have been Pearson's New York offices, from where most of the company's orders for machinery were placed. Here too there were problems of distance, codes, and Pearson's own busy schedule, which often placed him out of communication's reach while he busied himself building dams in Mexico or supervising irrigation schemes in Texas. London, the only other possibility, suffered from many of the same deficiencies, although Pearson did maintain a residence there.

As in the case of the São Paulo company, real authority over the affairs of the Rio enterprise devolved to the man on the spot, Alexander Mackenzie. Only Mackenzie could combine a subtle knowledge of local conditions with a keen sense of what was in the company's best interests and an ability to take prompt action to promote those interests. Mackenzie displayed an amazing ability to cope with the exigencies of business in Brazil. When Lash wrote to inform Mackenzie in 1906 that he had been made resident vice-president, he praised his former legal partner's dextrous performance and marvelled at how he had been 'kept on the go by the indefatigable F.S. Pearson.'[109] Mackenzie's appointment set the seal on what was to be the company's pattern of command for many years to come: nominal control in the hands of the board and head office in Toronto with effective command left at the discretion of Alexander Mackenzie in Brazil. Even Fred Pearson welcomed Mackenzie's ascendancy. By 1908, Pearson's unique talent for pioneering utility enterprises in foreign lands was no longer in as much demand by the two Brazilian enterprises he had fostered since inception. The companies were attaining maturity, and Pearson was eager to shed his personal responsibility over what were now established enterprises with problems of a largely routine or administrative nature. 'There is no reason,' he testily complained to Alexander Mackenzie in November 1907, 'why I should be personally responsible for this company's affairs in this way but there is apparently no one else who pays any attention to them except at rare intervals and I suppose I shall have to continue to look after the company.'[110] This was, of course, unfair criticism, brought on, no doubt, by Pearson's always frail health and his feud with Monty Horne-Payne. Alexander Mackenzie had already by 1907 assumed many of Pearson's functions in the Brazilian enterprises. Although he would continue to serve as president of the Rio company, Pearson now wanted to conserve his overtaxed health and to devote his energies elsewhere, 'as I have so many other interests of great importance.'

That the 'indefatigable' Fred Pearson should have been eager to shed his responsibilities in Brazil was hardly surprising. By that year, Pearson had become a global entrepreneur, whose engineering talents were constantly in demand by the promoters of railway and public-utilities ventures on two continents. 'We are not in favour of any new enterprises in Brazil which depend for their technical management on Dr. Pearson until the Rio de Janeiro Tramway, Light and Power Company is a completed proposition and paying dividends on its shares,' James Dunn, Pearson's close friend in the London merchant-banking fraternity, told the renowned German banker Martin Schiff. 'Dr. Pearson is pretty much the connecting link between the properties which are controlled by

Mackenzie and the other propositions which I mention.'[111] The letterhead on the stationery used at Pearson's Broadway offices in New York listed, in two columns, the companies the American engineer had advised and created. In Canada, there were, for instance, the Electrical Development Company of Ontario, for which Pearson had acted as 'consulting engineer' during the construction of the Niagara power plant, and the Winnipeg Electric Railway Company, for which Pearson had supervised the construction of the Lac du Bonnet power project. In the interim, Pearson had provided advice on mining schemes to American promoters and joined Percival Farquhar in an ill-starred and recklessly financed venture to turn the lowly Chicago-based Rock Island Railway into an American transcontinental railway. Pearson, in the words of his only biographer, had become 'a juggler on a cosmic scale.'[112]

The enterprises built around Pearson's technical genius and the financial manoeuvrings of men like William Mackenzie, George Cox, and Percival Farquhar by no means constituted a formal 'empire.' Instead, they simply shared common methods and goals as well as common legal and financial channels centred in Toronto, Montreal, New York, and London. What these men were doing in essence was transferring the capital, technical expertise, and entrepreneurial verve they had acquired in building up the infrastructure of the North American economy to the less developed areas of the world. In the unindustrialized countries of Latin America they found a receptive and unregulated environment for their activities. As such, they were contributing to the first wave of modern international business. As Mira Wilkins, the historian of American multinational enterprise, has commented:

The U.S. triumph abroad was one of ingenuity: new products, new methods of manufacturing, and new sales and advertising techniques. Americans who made overseas commitments had something distinctive to offer foreign customers. They sought not only to cater to, but to create foreign demand. From sewing machines to drugs to oil to insurance, aggressive and imaginative marketing gave Americans an advantage. Americans went abroad when they discovered their advantage.[113]

The same might be said for turn-of-the-century Canadians like William Mackenzie. While Pearson was an American, many of the companies he fathered were Canadian. This was perhaps best illustrated in Mexico where, during the first decade of the new century, Pearson joined various

Toronto and Montreal financiers to establish a series of electric-power, traction, and light enterprises. The Mexican Light and Power and Mexico Tramways companies were developed to serve Mexico City by drawing power from Pearson's power development on the Necaxa River and applying it to the urban needs of Mexico's largest city. For this, the Montreal-based companies secured concessions that extended as far into the future as 2012. Elsewhere in Mexico, Mackenzie secured control of the Monterrey Tramway, Light and Power Co. Ltd and proceeded to administer its affairs from the same Toronto office as the Rio and São Paulo enterprises. In 1909, the same promotional forces were mustered to develop the Mexican North Western Railway Co. Ltd, a railway system tapping the timber resources of northern Chihuahua state. This spurt of Canadian investment in Mexico took place under the complaisant regime of President Porfirio Díaz. Whenever Alexander Mackenzie reported that he was encountering opposition among Brazil's politicians in his concession negotiations, it was the spirit of Díaz, so amenable to the needs of foreign business, that Pearson yearningly invoked.

The subsequent histories of the Rio and São Paulo companies were to be markedly different from those of the Mexican enterprises, but there was an element of commonality in their origins. In supplying the sinews of the electric age to the cities of both countries, Canadians had found their 'advantage.' Motivated by the quest for profit, Pearson and Mackenzie saw their opportunities in Mexico and Brazil and seized them. In doing so, they not only made themselves immensely wealthy but also helped to equip Brazil's largest cities for the challenge of modern, industrial society. It was said, perhaps apocryphally, that when Pearson first visited Rio de Janeiro in the late nineteenth century, he stood one evening atop the towering Corcovado mountain and described how electricity would one day transform the darkened city below. If this was so, he would undoubtedly have taken great pleasure from the 1913 report of the British Ambassador in Rio to his superiors in London. 'It is hardly too much to say,' Ambassador Haggard commented, 'that at this moment Rio de Janeiro and São Paulo are as well lighted and served by tramways as any other cities in the world.'[114]

The Creation of the Brazilian Traction, Light and Power Company Limited, 1908-1915

By 1910, the Canadian utility companies in Rio and São Paulo had acquired an appearance of maturity. About both companies' affairs there was an expectant mood of optimism, nurtured by the belief that most of the obstacles to the companies' progress had been surmounted and that a profitable future lay ahead. With the Rio 'unification' contract of 1907 and the Guinle family seemingly held in check, the managers of the two enterprises exuded confidence. Propelled by buoyant world demand for Brazil's staple exports, Rio and São Paulo continued their phenomenal growth, thereby providing a sure foundation for the services of the two companies. By 1915, Rio was a city with slightly in excess of one million inhabitants; São Paulo, although growing at a faster pace, trailed with 469,748. 'The Rio Company is of course a very much more important one than the São Paulo,' Alexander Mackenzie confided to an English friend in early 1909, 'because its field of action is so much larger. You must remember that for some time yet we will be engaged in construction and that the real earnings of the Rio Company will not be known, until the work is finished.' The British ambassador was quick to endorse Mackenzie's prophecy. 'The members of the "Light and Tramways Company,"' he reported from Rio in late 1907, 'have control of many great enterprises throughout the Country; its first great venture was the São Paulo Light and Tramway Company, which is considered a brilliant success, and the same brilliant result is awaited here.'[1]

Optimism about the companies' future not only pervaded the thinking of observers in Brazil, but extended to the capitalists of Toronto and London. In the eyes of financiers like Monty Horne-Payne and Jimmy

Dunn, the two Brazilian ventures still offered tremendous scope for further offerings to the investing public. Out of this mercenary desire and the ambition of the local managers to unify the overall direction of the two companies, the Brazilian Traction, Light and Power Company would eventually emerge. The creation of Brazilian Traction as a Toronto-based holding company retaining absolute control of both the Rio and São Paulo enterprises was a complex affair, involving businessmen, lawyers, and financiers on three continents. In one clear sense, it was a product of the age of 'finance capitalism,' a period when the dictates of financiers governed the development of modern, large-scale enterprise. In another sense, however, Brazilian Traction satisfied the very practical needs of the managers who oversaw the day-to-day administration of a foreign-owned public utility in Brazil.

The groundwork for the Brazilian Traction consolidation had to be laid in Brazil. Despite the well-being of the two companies in 1908, much remained to be done before the Canadian promoters could be assured of a lasting hold on the market for utility services in south-eastern Brazil. Before foreign investors could be invited to participate in a holding company designed to amalgamate the two independent companies, it was imperative for the managers on the spot to tighten the concessions governing operations in each city, expand services to keep pace with demand, and continue to hold would-be competitors at bay. Having painstakingly pioneered the two Brazilian power companies, Alexander Mackenzie and his subordinates would now initiate the battle of consolidation and expansion.

The brunt of this consolidation campaign was borne by company managers in the field. Only when the managers had achieved their goals would northern promoters like Fred Pearson and William Mackenzie, with their high profiles in the world of investment, consummate the Brazilian Traction amalgamation. 'I am desirous of relieving myself of the responsibility of the management of the São Paulo enterprise,' F.S. Pearson declared to the São Paulo general manager, Walter Walmsley, in April 1908, 'and I am arranging for the Toronto office to take charge of the work so that I may gradually drop out of the São Paulo Company's affairs entirely.'[2] Even with his retirement from routine administration, the spirit of Pearson's genius lingered on. Frederick Huntress, the general manager of the Rio company was an old protégé of the company president. Huntress was familiar with Pearson's bold style of operation and displayed a similar penchant for quick-witted response to the myriad problems thrown up by local conditions. Much the same talent was exhibited by Walter Walmsley. Formerly the managing director of a Chicago electric-contracting firm, Walmsley, who was hired by William Mackenzie, had shown a tremendous capacity for adapting to the exigencies of public-utilities work in the alien urban environment of São Paulo. As Pearson lessened his grip on both companies' affairs, the responsibility for managing the São Paulo and Rio operations increasingly passed into the capable hands of Walmsley and Huntress.

The crucial task of co-ordinating the work of the general managers and plotting the legal and political course best suited to the companies' ambitions devolved on Alexander Mackenzie. Company officials in the 'North,' like J.M. Smith in Toronto and J.M. Plummer, Pearson's secretary in New York, simply tendered advice on the availability of funds for supplies and demanded to be kept informed of events. Only when Mackenzie, Huntress, and Walmsley had guided the two companies to a position of steady earnings and secure concessions could the principal promoters in Toronto, New York, and London again intervene to capitalize on their managers' success by unifying control of both enterprises in the Brazilian Traction holding company.

Neither company by 1908 was assured of complete control over the public-utilities market of its respective city. Conspicuous gaps remained in the concessionary armour of both companies. In São Paulo, the British-controlled San Paulo Gas Company continued to enjoy a substantial share of the city's lighting business, while in Rio the Companhia Ferro-Carril do Jardim Botânico plied a profitable trade with its electric trams right in the heart of the Canadians' concession area. Outside these two metropolitan areas, the Canadian companies were confronted by the Companhia Brasileira de Energia Elétrica, the home-grown power company controlled by the Guinle family. The Guinles had managed not only to construct the Alberto Torres power plant outside Rio, but also to secure concessionary rights to supply power to parts of Rio state, including the nearby cities of Petrópolis and Niterói. Since Niterói was directly across Guanabara Bay from Rio, there was no doubt that the Guinles would eventually try to penetrate the Rio market and, having achieved that goal, might even turn to the São Paulo market. By 1908, therefore, it was clear that the Canadian companies would have to wage a two-front campaign to maintain their hold on the local market for electricity. On the one hand, the Guinle pretensions would have to be held in check by constant legal and political vigilance, while on the other hand, some means would have to be devised to enable the Rio and São Paulo companies to dislodge their last remaining competitors. It promised to be a tough struggle.

The Guinles were politically well-connected foes who had already provided ample evidence of their aggressive tactics as challengers for the lighting and tramway business of Brazil's two largest cities. The Jardim Botânico and San Paulo Gas were well entrenched (the Jardim Botânico tramway concession, for instance, did not expire until 1960) and were determined to cling to their franchises. Any attempt to dislodge them, the managers of the two Canadian companies knew, would be vehemently opposed and, even if successful, would cost dearly. In both cases, the key to success would be stealth and financial dexterity rather than the overt tactics of a straightforward take-over attempt.

The first target was the Jardim Botânico company with its electrified tramcars. Rather than make a direct offer to all the shareholders of the largely Brazilian-owned Jardim Botânico, Pearson instructed the Rio staff to acquire control in a piecemeal fashion through the Banco Nacional Brasileiro, which acquired any Jardim Botânico stock that drifted onto the market in return for a commission. 'There were reasons which you can understand,' the Rio company's treasurer informed head office, 'why this [the Rio] Company should not appear as purchaser.'[3] Employing this method, by 1905 the Rio company had obtained control of about 75 per cent of Jardim Botânico shares. Continued buying put the Rio company in a position to take control of the Jardim Botânico system in 1910 and thereby integrate that company's operations with those of its own tram system. Such control allowed the Rio company to make the Jardim Botânico a formal subsidiary and, as of 1911, enter its earnings on the monthly earnings card that Monty Horne-Payne distributed to the company's English investors. To secure the new subsidiary, the Rio company issued £1.2 million of 5 per cent bonds on the English market, the proceeds of which were used to retire the Jardim Botânico's outstanding bonds. The Jardim Botânico acquisition improved the company's competitive position in the national capital, contributed (with earnings of $958,108 in 1909) to the overall earnings of its parent, and pushed the value of Rio shares up on the Toronto market.[4]

Closing the gaps in the São Paulo concession proved more arduous and called for even greater dexterity. With its long-term concession, a guarantee that linked part of its earnings to gold, and the desire of municipal politicians to preserve some modicum of competition in public utilities, the San Paulo Gas Company was in an excellent position to fend off the advances of its Canadian rival. Although the São Paulo company had made sizeable inroads into the gas company's lighting business, all its attempts to acquire actual control had been spurned by the management of the London-based enterprise.[5] In May 1911, an offer to purchase the entire capital stock of San Paulo Gas was made in London by the Guarantee Insurance and Investment Company. Sensing that this was a disguised bid for control from the Pearson group (which indeed it was), the San Paulo board summarily refused the offer.[6] This failure brought Fred Pearson to the realization that more indirect means of seizing the São Paulo company's chief competitor must be devised.

In March 1910, the São Paulo company's Toronto lawyers created a small, Canadian-chartered company with the unlikely name of the Brazilian Electro Steel and Smelting Co. Ltd. While this new addition to the Pearson group seems initially to have been designed with the purpose of 'creating a large and profitable customer for the Rio company and thereby increasing the industrial importance of Rio,' it was soon metamorphosed into a decoy company through which the São Paulo company could obtain additional concessions and assets. In May 1911, Brazilian Electro Steel and Smelting changed its name to the São Paulo Electric Company. Behind the usual board of interim directors, a syndicate known as the 'Southern Securities Limited' held real control and, under an agreement of August 1911, promised to secure 'certain properties and assets' for São Paulo Electric. At the centre of Southern Securities were William Mackenzie and F.S. Pearson. Through the syndicate and the newly created São Paulo Electric, Pearson formulated his attack on the San Paulo Gas Company.

The linchpin of Pearson's strategy was the Scottish engineer Henry Schulman, a long-time friend, who had recently returned to the British Isles after years of commercial activity in São Paulo. When Pearson was pioneering the São Paulo enterprise in the late 1890s, Schulman had made his extensive experience of Brazilian business practices available to the promoters of the Canadian enterprise. Now, in 1911, Pearson again looked for Schulman's assistance. Using monies advanced by the Canadian Bank of Commerce, Schulman established the General Gas Securities and Trust Co. Ltd and began to buy San Paulo Gas stock on the London market. Schulman's steady purchasing was deliberately shrouded in mystery. 'It is just as well to leave the shares in the name of Mr. Schulman for the moment,' Pearson directed the company secretary, 'in order that the Gas Company will not know that they have been transferred.'[7] By January 1913, Schulman had acquired sufficient stock to oust the dumbfounded English management of the San Paulo Gas and install himself as its new interim chairman. The cost of this take-over was, by November 1913, $785,000, which the São Paulo Electric duly paid over to the General Gas Securities and Trust Company.[8] To set the seal on the new relationship, an agreement was made in December 1913 whereby the São Paulo Electric would provide all the capital requirements of the gas company in return for its operating revenues. Having so admirably acquitted himself, Schulman returned to his own business activities and delivered control of the newest subsidiary of the 'Pearson group' into the hands of the parent company's trusted London officials. It was a crucial victory. It removed the company's final rival, leaving it with an unchallenged sway over all the gas and electric-lighting concessions in São Paulo. The Schulman façade spoke volumes about Pearson's wiliness as a financial schemer. Backed by the Canadian Bank of Commerce and supported by influential English financial interests, Pearson had at his command incomparable resources that few of his rivals for the utilities business of Brazil, Mexico, and Spain could match.

In the years following the absorption of the San Paulo Gas, other smaller additions were made to the two companies. In 1911, for instance, the Jacarepagua Railway, a short-line suburban railway in Rio, was acquired. During these same years, Alexander Mackenzie scouted out and purchased promising water-power concessions in the Rio–São Paulo region, so as to provide the companies with ample room for the expansion of their power-generating facilities. The conquest of rivals was now replaced by a pervasive concern for fending off the advances of the Guinle family, whose Companhia Brasileira de Energia Elétrica hovered threateningly on the edge of the Rio and São Paulo concession areas. The struggle to vanquish the Guinles became the longest and bitterest episode in the early history of Canadian investment in Brazil. 'Messrs. Guinle and Company are people with great wealth and look with very unfriendly eye on foreign capital,' Alexander Mackenzie complained to the Foreign Office in 1910, 'and with true Boxer spirit contend that all Brazilian industries should be owned, financed and managed by Brazilians only.'[9] While the Guinles framed their ambitions – such as the desire to exploit their franchise to import General Electric equipment into Brazil – in nationalistic terms, the Canadian companies' battle with the Brazilian family was essentially one of foreign capital, with its superior technological resources, contending with indigenous entrepreneurs less tutored in the ways of international finance and technology.

The Guinles mounted a two-pronged attack on the Canadian companies. First, they attempted to enter the Rio market both by challenging the 1907 'unification' contract and by actively opposing the Rio company's plans to expand its generating capacity at Lajes. Once the battle was raging in the national capital, they launched a new attack on the São Paulo market, using their well-established dock operations in Santos as a platform for their assault. Before the battle was done, each side would resort to an assortment of tactics, ranging from the employment of lawyers and ambassadors to the unscrupulous use of newspaper harassment and political influence. As Alexander Mackenzie confided to the British chargé d'affaires in 1911, the whole Guinle episode constituted an 'ugly feature' in the companies' early existence in Brazil.[10]

The first skirmish between the Guinles and their Canadian competitors took place in the hills behind Rio. Despite the initial success of the Lajes power plant, it became apparent at an early date that some means of supplementing the flow of the Rio das Lajes would have to be found to boost the capacity of the plant. As early as 1904, engineers had suggested that a tunnel, driven nine kilometres through the surrounding hills, would enable the company to draw additional water (enough to add another 37,300 kilowatts of capacity) from the nearby Piraí River. 'This is a matter of the utmost importance to us,' Pearson informed Alexander Mackenzie; 'every cubic foot of water that we can obtain from the Piraí will be worth an enormous amount to us.'[11] Once again, Mackenzie began the process of securing new concessionary rights. Since the Piraí was a non-navigable river, jurisdiction over its flow fell to the Rio state government, from which Mackenzie was able to obtain permission to divert Piraí water into the Lajes.[12] The speedy ratification of the company's plans was attributable to the co-operation of state president Alfredo Backer, who was, like his predecessor, Nilo Peçanha, an avowed admirer of the company's operations. Then, just as the company seemed poised on the verge of this bold expansion, fate intervened.

Throughout 1908 and 1909 a devastating outbreak of malaria moved through the Lajes area, bringing severe suffering to the small nearby towns of Piraí and São João Marcos. The Lajes reservoir, the Guinle newspaper allies alleged, had provided a breeding ground for the deadly mosquitoes, and the planned new reservoir on the Piraí would simply expand the area of contagion. Although the charges were later disproved by government-appointed medical experts, the Guinles had found an excellent issue to excite local passions. Bombarded by newspaper criticism and petitions from local citizens, both orchestrated by the Guinles, the state government retreated into inaction, demanding further investigations. 'The situation therefore is plain,' Mackenzie dejectedly reported in 1911. 'The *Secretária* of the Government will continue to study our plans and send them from one department to another or to other engineers or medical men specially called in for the purpose of finding or inventing objections.' This impasse was aggravated by the election in 1910 of a new state president, Oliveira Botelho, who had less sympathy for the Canadian company's problems. Botelho's private secretary, Dr Osorio de Almeida, Junior, the son of one of the partners in Gafrée, Guinle and Company, proceeded to poison his superior's attitude towards the exasperated Alexander Mackenzie. Botelho began demanding compensation for the malaria epidemic, even though government doctors had shown it was not of the company's making. 'I have used all the influence we possess with the President of the State and so far without inducing him to take any action,' Mackenzie told Pearson in 1911. Without the Piraí power, the company would be forced to rely on costly coal-fired steam plants to supply Rio's growing appetite for power. In desperation, Mackenzie protested to his old friend, the Baron of Rio Branco, the federal minister of foreign affairs, that 'no justice could be had from the Rio State Government.' Acting on Rio Branco's suggestion, Mackenzie cabled the British Foreign Office in London and requested that the British chargé in Rio be instructed to lodge a complaint.[13] What infuriated Mackenzie most, a British diplomat reported, were the incessant 'demands for money made to him by various members and officials of the State Government.' Such behaviour, the same diplomat stoutly concluded, warranted 'a friendly official representation' by the British chargé and the exertion of some pressure on the Brazilian minister in London.[14]

In the midst of the Piraí imbroglio, the Guinles launched an assault on the Rio power market from another angle. In April 1910, the Companhia

Brasileiro de Energia Elétrica obtained a concession from Rio prefect Inocêncio Serzedelo Correia empowering it to supply the city with electricity from its Alberto Torres plant for ninety years. The concession, as the British ambassador was quick to detect, was 'absolutely illegal,' principally because it infringed on the Rio company's monopoly, a privilege that was guaranteed as exclusive until 1915 under the terms of the Reid concession.[15] The success of the Guinles in obtaining this dramatic breakthrough was due in large measure to their political influence, but also to their practice of making what Mackenzie described as 'absurdly' unrealistic quotations on the price of electricity. 'Our difficulty,' Mackenzie later said of the business of negotiating concessions, 'is that neither the government nor the municipality much cares whether the person who applies for the concession can carry it out or not. Concessions are given, not according to the standing of the applicants, but on account of the influence they possess.'[16]

The Guinles' effective cultivation of influence continued, much to Mackenzie's consternation, in São Paulo. In 1909, the municipal *câmara* had denied the Companhia Brasileira entry to the São Paulo utilities market and upheld the Canadian company's exclusivity until 1919. This decision was largely due to the influence of Antônio Prado, the city's prefect, who had long been favourably disposed to the São Paulo company's ambitions. In 1911, however, Prado was replaced by the less-sympathetic administration of Raimundo da Silva Duprat, and the Guinles were able to secure an injunction against the Canadian company's 1909 contract with the city and to begin work on a transmission line from Santos to São Paulo. Mackenzie attributed this political volte-face to the ever-changing pattern of influence in Brazilian public life. 'Moreover,' he explained to Pearson,

the present Câmara is not like that of 1909, subject to the direction of the dominant political party. It is composed of a good many independent units and it is therefore more difficult for us to use to advantage such influence as we can obtain through the political chiefs. The present Prefect is a weak man and, in the Câmara of 1909, was one of the three who voted in favour of Guinle and Co.'s pretensions, and probably is inclined to do the same today ... the Guinles will be prepared to take a concession, even if limited to one street. All they want is to get a foothold, trusting to the future to extend themselves everywhere.[17]

The Companhia Brasileira improved its competitive position by obtaining federal permission to construct a hydro-power station at Itapanhau near Santos. The Guinles, it seemed by 1911, had completed their encircle-ment of their Canadian rivals.

Pearson and Alexander Mackenzie were not unduly disturbed by the Guinle challenge. The Canadian companies were incontestably in the legal right. Secondly, both Pearson and Mackenzie doubted the ability of their Brazilian competitors to fulfil the terms of their contracts. As early as 1905, Alexander Mackenzie had received reports from his engineers indicating that, while the Guinles had access to General Electric equip-ment, they lacked competent personnel to install it. Although the Alberto Torres generating station was eventually completed, it had only three 3,700 kw generators. With concessionary obligations to supply Niterói, the Companhia Brasileira, Mackenzie estimated, would have little more than 3,500 kw left to satisfy its would-be market across the bay in Rio. 'It is well to bear in mind that not a post has been erected or a meter of wire strung by Guinle & Co. in the Federal District,' Mackenzie reminded Pearson, 'nor has one brick been laid for the construction of stations or other work done by them in the Federal District whatever they may say or insinuate to the contrary.'[18]

If the Guinle interests were not feared as bona fide contenders for the Rio power market, their ability to generate popular opposition to the Canadian company was deeply respected. With the influential newspaper *Jornal do comércio* under their control, the Gafrée-Guinle partnership had considerable sway over public opinion in Rio and used this to rail against the 'foreign' power company. In 1908, for instance, it was insinuated that the Rio company had violated its charter by failing to submit changes in its by-laws to the authorities. 'Of course it was all moonshine,' Alexander Mackenzie reported to Toronto, 'as we can show that the Company acted with more than usual expedition in sending the new by-laws for approval within such a short space of time after their approval.'[19] Later, the Guinle newspapers directed their attention to the Rio company's allegedly 'tortuous' finances. Once again, Mackenzie dismissed such 'poisonous' articles, arguing that 'most of the public here understand them and are not influenced by them.'[20]

Mackenzie's dismissive attitude was not always borne out by events. Erroneous reports of the Rio and São Paulo companies' finances, planted in the English press by the Guinles, did adversely affect Horne-Payne's campaign to establish the companies in the eyes of English investors. As late as 1914, for instance, London financier James Dunn complained that misrepresentation of the true earnings of the Brazilian companies had provided 'ammunition' for 'bears' on the London market and had consequently pushed down the value of their stocks.[21]

Far more dangerously, Guinle hostility to the companies' ambitions capitalized on popular, if sporadic, reaction to foreign capitalists in Brazil. Like public services elsewhere, the companies' activities had begun to touch the daily lives of almost every *carioca* and *paulistano*, thereby providing critics both of the Canadian enterprise and of many other unrelated aspects of urban Brazilian life with a common denominator and focus for their discontent. From an early date, the company trams served as convenient targets for dissidents who had taken to the streets, whether their wrath had been provoked by the company or not. Toppling a tramcar off its tracks became a popular act of social protest.

As the *companhia canadense* expanded its electric services and diversified into gas and telephones, it became an increasingly inviting target for such adverse attention. A favourite portrayal of the companies, employed by their critics from an early date, was that of 'the Canadian octopus,' wrapping its tentacles around the whole range of Brazilian public-utility services. The combination of this image with what a British diplomat described as the 'consistent and unscrupulous methods' of the opposition posed a deadly threat to the Canadian companies and to their ability to serve these markets efficiently.[22]

Early in 1909, the Rio company received a brief but disturbing lesson along these lines. In both Rio and São Paulo, the Light had since its inception enjoyed peaceable relations with its Brazilian workers. Like most turn-of-the-century Canadian employers, it sought to treat its workers in a paternalistic fashion, barring unionization but providing benefits and wages designed to keep its employees better remunerated than their peers. Light workers were in fact in the aristocracy of Brazilian labour. The uniforms they proudly wore seemed to symbolize their place in the vanguard of modern industry. Labour-management relations were, none the less, rooted in paternalism and a total rejection of any form of collective bargaining by management. In June 1908, however, the company encountered its first labour unrest when employees of the gas company left their jobs in a dispute with management. Not all the employees joined the strike and, when the company attempted to maintain operations, events turned violent. The strike was settled in the company's favour, allowing it, as the 1909 annual report noted, to shed its 'disloyal employees,' but the friction continued as disgruntled former employees rallied support to their cause by attacking the company on nationalistic grounds. In January, popular demonstrations in the streets against the Rio company led to violence. Several tramcars were burned, and armed police were called to quell the rioters. The 'ostensible object' of this outburst, the British consul reported, was 'changes of service' in the streetcar service. In reality, the British diplomat believed, the riots were the work of 'several well-known agitators.'[23] Genuine or not, such hostility became an ever-present danger for the Canadian enterprise in Brazil.

In the years 1908 to 1915, the Canadians managed to contain and eventually counter the Guinle threat. A series of legal victories checked the Guinle pretensions to the companies' concessions. In 1909, the courts upheld the validity of the original Reid concession in Rio and barred the Companhia Brasileira de Energia Elétrica from entering the Rio market until 1915, by which time the Canadian company would have a firm grip on the local power market. Similarly, an injunction was obtained in 1909 preventing the Santos Docks Company from entering São Paulo, on the grounds that the new company would infringe on the established company's 'occupied' area of service. In 1912, the courts upheld the Rio gas concession, absolved the Rio company of any blame in the Lajes malaria epidemic of 1908–9 and disallowed the Guinle claim to the Itapanhau power site near São Paulo. In September 1912, the São Paulo company's lawyer, Carlos de Campos, proudly reported to Alexander Mackenzie that the Guinle cause had been 'entirely lost in São Paulo' and that it only remained for the company to stay 'cautiously vigilant' in future.[24]

The thoroughness of the victory over the Guinles was attributable to the solidity of the company's legal position. Its concessions, meticulously framed when negotiated, allowed little if any room for infringement. Secondly, the concessions were defended by the best lawyers available in Brazil. Carlos de Campos in São Paulo and Rui Barbosa in Rio not only possessed superb legal minds, but also were well placed politically and therefore able to present the companies' case to Brazil's most prominent politicians. The disposition of politicians to favour the Canadian utility company was ensured by the solid progress exhibited by the Rio and São Paulo companies in bringing power to Brazil's leading cities.

By 1915, the Guinles had become so discouraged by their failure to break into the Rio and São Paulo markets that they intimated that they would be willing to sell their concessionary rights. This inviting prospect was closely examined by Huntress and Mackenzie, who concluded that such a purchase offered the possibility of ending years of friction, but only if the purchase could be accompanied by a wholesale extension of the Canadian companies' concessions. 'There will be nothing gained by purchasing the Guinle properties,' Huntress reluctantly concluded, 'unless we can be assured of the extensions of our monopolies, for others might apply and obtain competing concessions.'[25] The economic upheavals shortly brought on by war in Europe made renegotiation of concessions an unlikely proposition. The Guinle family in turn resigned themselves to maintaining a secondary presence in Brazil's electric industry, a presence they kept until the late 1920s, when they sold out to the American-controlled Electric Bond and Share Company.

For the two Canadian utilities companies operating in Rio and São Paulo, the lesson of the Guinle struggle was clear. While company lawyers were able to hold would-be competitors at bay within the concession areas, other power companies would continue to hover on the periphery of the Canadian companies' operations. Mackenzie and his managers could never afford to be complacent. With others eager to usurp the Canadians' rights, the two companies had always to be 'cautiously vigilant,' as Carlos de Campos had warned. Yet, with the defeat of the Guinle pretensions in 1912, the companies' managers understandably displayed a triumphant mood and a certain degree of complacency. 'Should the proper authorities decide to grant further concessions for these services,' Alexander Mackenzie confidently noted in 1916, 'we are quite prepared to meet any competition that may ensue. The granting of concessions will not constitute competition.'[26]

The idea of bringing the Rio and São Paulo companies under the ownership of a holding company originated in Canada, not in Brazil. The emergence of the Brazilian Traction, Light and Power Company Limited in 1912 was only indirectly the product of the exigencies of the Brazilian situation. It was, more accurately, the product of the Rio and São Paulo companies' promoters' anxiety to find a means of extracting the full financial benefit from their South American promotions and, at the same time, to take out a long-term insurance policy on their investment. Above all, William Mackenzie and his associates in the electric-utilities business of Ontario wanted to protect their Brazilian utilities from the spectre of public ownership that by 1910 had come to haunt their Canadian operations. Subsuming control of the São Paulo and Rio investments under one central offshore authority offered a means of welding all the utilities operations built up since 1899 into one entity, which, it was hoped, would prove invulnerable to future onslaughts from those who wished to compete with the Light.

From the operational point of view, the creation of Brazilian Traction could be seen as only a precautionary move, calculated to provide protection in the long term rather than to furnish any immediate benefit. After all, Brazil in 1912 was in many respects an Elysium for the private utilities promoter. Not only had the two Canadian companies effectively countered the challenge of would-be competitors, but the power business in Brazil existed in a virtual regulatory vacuum. The notion that any level of Brazilian government could have a role in the generation of electric power had as yet little popular support in Brazil. Concessions governing the generation and distribution of hydro power were awarded by all three levels of Brazilian government and guided by *ad hoc* considerations rather than by a national regulatory code. When, as late as 1921, the Brazilian National Congress made another ill-fated attempt to legislate a national 'water code,' Alexander Mackenzie reacted with alarm. 'It is a monstrous piece of work and, if passed, will put an end to power development here for many years to come, as it limits concessions to 25 years and regulates so many different things, including prices, that we would never think of developing a [water] power under its provisions.'[27] The bill became mired in the legislative process and was never passed. It was not until the early 1930s that the Brazilian state would establish an interventionist presence in the electric industry. In the interim, what opposition the two Canadian companies did face was not of a regulatory bent but, more simply, a reflection of pure nationalism. While the creation of Brazilian Traction may have been motivated by a far-sighted premonition of a Brazilian interventionist state, it is far more plausible to regard the holding company as a reflection of its promoters' Canadian experience.

It was in Ontario that the promoters of the two Brazilian enterprises first encountered the crusade for 'people's power.' In the early years of the new century, an anti-corporate, anti-monopoly critique of the private power industry had emerged in the province. Led by the dynamic Adam Beck, a cigar-box manufacturer and local politician from London, the 'people's power' movement pushed the power question to the forefront of provincial politics. In 1906 the movement registered its first victory with the creation of the Hydro-Electric Power Commission of Ontario by the Conservative government of James Whitney. Ontario Hydro was at first empowered only to distribute power. By the time it acquired the right to generate power in 1914, the contest between public and private power had been sharply defined. Was Ontario to have hydroelectric power on the basis of 'service at cost,' as supplied by a public corporation, or would it continue to rely on power provided by private capitalists where and when the profit motive allowed?[28]

At the very centre of this fractious debate were the public-utility enterprises in which William Mackenzie had taken so prominent a role. The Toronto Street Railway Company and the Niagara power companies were held up to meticulous examination by Beck and his followers and found wanting. The favourite target was the Toronto Street Railway, whose healthy profits and refusal to extend its services to the city's suburbs rankled proponents of public power. Mackenzie doggedly faced his critics with the argument that he was not prepared to undertake 'service-at-cost' operations and that he would cling to his lucrative franchise until it expired in 1921.[29] Mackenzie's attitude only served to exacerbate the tension. Even some of Mackenzie's closest associates began to cast a critical eye on the service offered by the Toronto Street Railway. Joseph Flavelle, who had taken large amounts of Rio and São Paulo stock, complained in 1906 that he found the 'character' of Mackenzie's administration 'meant inefficiency in the service of the Street Railway Company, and would lead to the continuance of the unsatisfactory condition of affairs, which in my judgment had become scandalous,' especially because the poor service imposed 'a grievous burden upon thousands of working people daily.' 'I will only say,' Flavelle concluded, 'that it seems too bad that a gentleman with the commanding interests of Mr. Mackenzie, should continue to hold a position which neither by temperament nor by reason of the overwhelming claim upon his time it is possible for him to fill efficiently.'[30]

Criticism, even that of erstwhile friends, did not diminish Mackenzie's resolve to exploit the profit potential of the Toronto streetcar franchise. Under attack, on the one hand, by advocates of public power who wished to divest him of his Niagara generating plants and, on the other hand, by politicians now eager to establish municipally owned public services, Mackenzie concluded that it was imperative to build a strong line of defence. Aided by the legal advice of Zebulon Lash and the dexterity of such Toronto financiers as Henry Pellatt, Mackenzie adopted the strategy of consolidating his scattered holdings in Ontario under one unified ownership. This process was initiated in 1908 when the Toronto Street Railway assumed ownership, by means of a share transfer, of the Electrical Development Company of Ontario. In justifying the transaction, Henry Pellatt, the president of the EDC, said that it had been made necessary by continual harassment of the company by the public-power lobby, a tactic that had severely injured the company's ability to raise sufficient capital for expansion.[31] The consolidation of Toronto's electric utilities continued in 1911 when Mackenzie outbid the city government for control of the Toronto Electric Light Co. Ltd, another Pellatt creation. By late 1911, therefore, Mackenzie had forged a group of companies that controlled the generation, distribution, and application of electrical energy in Ontario's largest urban market. Although Mackenzie's public-utility companies continued to attract the ire of Toronto politicians, the amalgamation implemented between 1908 and 1911 put the companies in a good position to weather the storms of protest. Only on the eve of the expiry of the streetcar franchise in 1921 did Mackenzie and the municipal government finally strike a deal bringing about the withdrawal of private capital from the city's public services and the transfer of generating facilities to the Hydro-Electric Power Commission of Ontario. The 'Clean-Up Deal' of 1921 signified the triumph of 'people's power' in Ontario and, with the exception of a few scattered power companies, removed the electricity industry from the realm of private entrepreneurship.

The spectacle of William Mackenzie's rearguard action against the politicians of Ontario had a bracing effect on the managers of the two Canadian companies operating in Brazil. While no political support for the 'people's power' movement materialized in Rio or São Paulo at this time, the two Canadian companies were acutely aware of their vulnerability to a broad range of nationalistic, political, and economic forces and therefore sought to shore up their defences against any possible onslaught. The example of 'people's power' in Ontario and the possible appearance of a Brazilian-style Adam Beck became a recurrent theme in the correspondence of the directors and managers of the São Paulo and Rio companies. 'The general law of Brazil relating to water power,' Alexander Mackenzie once reported to Toronto, 'is much the same as that in force in Ontario before the Hydro people got to work.'[32] The phobia bred by the prospect that 'Hydro people' would appear in Brazil gave rise to intensive theorizing about how the two companies could entrench themselves in the Brazilian economy. The Toronto Street Railway consolidation of 1908–11 offered a model that could readily be adapted to the Brazilian situation.

Further inspiration for the prospective Brazilian merger was provided by the extension of Fred Pearson's utilities imperialism to the Iberian Peninsula. Having mastered the art of establishing profitable companies wherever powerful rivers could be matched with willing governments and large urban markets, Pearson was by 1910 much sought after by the would-be promoters of utility ventures all around the world. In 1911, he had visited Spain on the invitation of a Spanish engineer and, when shown the mighty Ebro River near Barcelona, marvelled at its tremendous hydroelectric potential. Pearson's rapture with Spain was reciprocated by the rapture of Spaniards for Pearson as the prospective initiator of a propitious electric revolution in their country. Pearson was even fêted in the court of King Alfonso XIII. This mutual enthusiasm opened the way for the creation of the Barcelona Traction, Light and Power Company Limited (with capital stock of $42.5 million and £8 million in bonds) under a Canadian federal charter in September 1911. Just as the Parnaíba plant had provided the hub of the young São Paulo company and the Necaxa dam had epitomized the plans of the Mexican Light and Power Company, Pearson's bold plans for the development of the Ebro mesmerized the citizens of Barcelona with visions of a prosperous and electrified future.

What was unique about the Barcelona company from the point of view of its Toronto promoters was its style of operation. The work of Barcelona Traction was carried on in Spain by the Ebro Irrigation and Power Company, a small subsidiary of the Toronto parent. Through the Ebro company, concessions and small Spanish power companies along the Ebro River were bought up and unified under royal decree. Once sufficient water rights were secured, construction work was initiated on the Seros power project, and planning was begun on two further dam and powerhouse complexes at Talarn and Fayen. The unification of existing concessions by a newly created, foreign-controlled company was, of course, reminiscent of the manner in which the Rio de Janeiro Tramway company had established itself, but the overall amalgamation of all the Spanish concessions under the control of one immense, 'offshore' holding company was a new innovation. By December 1913, the Barcelona company had unified ten Spanish power companies under its control, thereby providing a model for the Toronto directors of the two Brazilian enterprises.

The consolidation of the Rio and São Paulo companies under the control of a holding company offered many advantages. It would allow all the assets and concessions of both companies to be grouped under common financial management and thereby provide a measure of efficiency for the whole range of services in which the companies were engaged. Such integration would increase the ability of management to defend or renegotiate any one of the myriad concessions held by the Toronto-based companies and, at the same time, diminish the power of Brazilian authorities to tamper with any one concession without disturbing a broad range of foreign-financed services. This quest for inviolability was echoed by Pearson in a 1908 letter to Alexander Mackenzie: 'The Rio securities are so widely owned and distributed throughout Europe, that anything which tends to injure these securities hurts the pockets of thousands of investors, and you can understand, an investor who becomes disgusted with one Brazilian security, naturally classes all Brazilian securities under the same category, and declines to invest in enterprises of that country.'[33] A consolidated corporate structure had the further practical advantage of assuring the capital needs of the Brazilian subsidiaries and the discharge of their financial obligations. A series of 'operating agreements' could cement this arrangement and effectively join parent and subsidiary in an umbilical relationship. Transborder financial transactions would thus become internal matters.

The desire for inviolability, the need to provide blanket protection for assets and concessions in Brazil, and the prospect of 'internalizing' corporate finances all combined to favour the creation of Brazilian Traction, Light and Power. In later years, London financier James Dunn claimed that he and Fred Pearson had concocted the whole Brazilian Traction scheme some time in 1911 or early 1912, mapping out their ideas on the tablecloth of a Parisian restaurant.[34] While Dunn and the European financiers who had provided support for the Rio and São Paulo ventures would undoubtedly have been consulted, the real spark of genius behind the creation of Brazilian Traction was supplied by William Mackenzie's brilliant legal counsel, Z.A. Lash, and by his principal financial adviser, E.R. Wood. Nobody was more familiar with the legal anatomy of Mackenzie's scattered enterprises than Zebulon Lash. He had supervised the incorporation of railways, public utilities, and even land companies for Mackenzie. Lash had overseen the complex arrangements for the Toronto Street Railway–Electrical Development Company amalgamation of 1908, and now it was to Lash that Mackenzie looked for guidance in charting the course for the new Brazilian holding company.

Lash's able handling of the legal problems of the two Canadian companies operating in Brazil was crucially influenced by the wishes of the powerful interests who had a stake in the financial affairs of the two companies. While the establishment of a holding company promised great practical advantages to those who managed the Rio and São Paulo companies, it offered even greater opportunities to those who had a speculative financial interest in the Brazilian investment. Since the early days of the São Paulo enterprise, financiers had played the vital role of purveying the capital necessary to exploit the Brazilian concessions. At times, especially under the demanding regime of Monty Horne-Payne, they had actively participated in the administration of the companies to ensure the paramountcy of the financiers' interest, often to the detriment of what the managers in Brazil had deemed to be in the companies' best interests.

The members of William Mackenzie's original Toronto syndicate had over time been joined by brokers operating in London, most notably former Canadians James Dunn and Mackay Edgar, Scottish merchant banker Robert Fleming, and European brokers, such as the aggressive Alfred Loewenstein of Brussels. All of these men were united by a common desire to realize the tremendous speculative potential afforded by the concessions secured by Mackenzie and Pearson in Brazil. From 1899 to the formation of Brazilian Traction in 1912, the brokers of Toronto, Montreal, New York, London, Brussels, and Paris had thrived on the trade in securities generated by the two Canadian companies. An astute broker stood to profit not only from commissions paid for the initial placement of Rio and São Paulo stock but also from subsequent market transactions of the same securities. Given the close control exercised over São Paulo and Rio stock by Mackenzie and his friends, there was also ample opportunity for those well connected with the promoters to govern the market price of the stock and thereby induce investors to enter the market.[35] Others seized on the opportunity of profiting from arbitrage, that is, from trading stock between various markets in order to capitalize on slight international variations in price. Finally, brokers who had loyally served the promoters stood to reap windfall profits from 'bonus' stock that was liberally distributed as an inducement for brokers to underwrite blocks of newly issued bonds. Such practices pervaded turn-of-the-century financial capitalism and stood diametrically opposed to the free play of the securities market. As the new century unfolded and as the operational success of the two Latin American utility enterprises became a well-publicized fact for North American and European investors, financiers came to look on William Mackenzie's two Brazilian creations as the geese that laid the golden eggs.

The years 1904 to 1911 had already witnessed a steady expansion of the capitalization of both the Rio and São Paulo companies. From its initial capitalization of $6,000,000 in 1899, the São Paulo company had increased its capital stock to $8,500,000 by 1906 and, by December 1907, to $10,000,000, where it remained until the 1912 merger. In 1911, £600,000 – equivalent to $2,920,000 – worth of 5 per cent 'Perpetual Consolidated Debenture Stock' was also issued. Such periodic increases in capitalization were justified as necessary to finance growth. Similarly, the capitalization of the newer Rio company underwent a dramatic increase between 1904 and 1911. From a capital stock of $25,000,000 at its outset, the Rio company swelled to a total capitalization of $45,000,000 by December 1911. Including debenture stock and all bonds, the two Brazilian utilities had a joint capitalization of $118,920,000 by December 1911.

It would be impossible to recreate an accurate financial history of the São Paulo and Rio companies and thereby attempt to match the face value of the stocks and bonds issued by the two enterprises with the underlying value of the assets, but, given the proclivity of Mackenzie and his associates to resort to such practices as 'bonus' and 'watered' stock in their other promotions, it can be ventured with a good deal of certainty that the face value of the securities exceeded that of the assets. This was ultimately recognized in December 1942 when write-offs of intangible assets totalling US $102 million were recorded by Brazilian Traction and certain of its subsidiaries.[36]

The acquisition of the São Paulo and Rio companies by the Brazilian Traction, Light and Power Company unfolded in two stages during the middle months of 1912. First, the legal groundwork had to be done by the company directors and lawyers, and then the actual exchange of securities had to be executed through brokers on both sides of the Atlantic. The initial stages of this process took place quietly, while the second stage was heralded by a sudden fanfare of financial publicity followed by an intense campaign to convince Rio and São Paulo shareholders to exchange their old securities for shares in Brazilian Traction. Little written record of the initial discussions surrounding the transaction exists. The idea of a holding company was undoubtedly hatched during informal discussion, perhaps (as James Dunn suggested) at luncheon and dinner meetings when Mackenzie and his associates gathered to formulate company policy. Discussion could not have progressed much beyond the theoretical stage without some consultation with Fred S. Pearson, whose name and reputation as the engineering *éminence grise* behind the Mexican, Brazilian, and Spanish enterprises was indispensable if the new project was to gain credibility in investors' eyes. With Pearson's blessing secured, the proposal could be taken to the offices of Blake, Lash, Anglin and Cassels. The minutes of the Rio and São Paulo company boards give no indication that such a process was under way during the early months of 1912, and there are only a few cryptic telegrams, passed across the Atlantic between William Mackenzie, Pearson, and various English brokers, to give any indication that a new holding company was in gestation.

Not until early July was there an indication that the scheme was about to come to fruition. On 12 July 1912, letters patent were issued under the federal Companies Act incorporating the Brazilian Traction, Light and Power Company Limited. The purpose of the new corporation was only generally stated. Brazilian Traction was empowered 'to underwrite, subscribe for, purchase or otherwise acquire and hold ... the bonds or debentures, stocks, shares or other securities of any Government or municipal or school corporation or-of any bank or of any other duly incorporated company or companies or corporation or corporations.' After laying out a broad range of hydroelectric activities in which the new corporation was entitled to participate, the letters patent empowered Brazilian Traction 'to amalgamate with any other company having objects similar to those of this company.' Nothing in the act of incorporation, except the actual name of the company, gave any indication of the precise intention of its promoters. The word 'amalgamate' was of crucial significance. An authorized capital stock of $120 million did however provide an indication that the intentions of the promoters were indeed large. As with previous incorporations orchestrated by Z.A. Lash, the identities of the real promoters of the concern were masked by a set of provisional directors drawn from Lash's office. When the board met for the first time on 15 July, it was in the offices of their employer that its members convened, under the eye of Z.A. Lash.[37]

Three days after the charter was obtained a letter was mailed from Toronto to the shareholders of the Rio company, the São Paulo company, and the São Paulo Electric Company. Writing 'on behalf of the Boards of the respective Companies,' F.S. Pearson unveiled the details of the share exchange that would breathe life into Brazilian Traction. Pearson's letter had a tone of *fait accompli* about it. 'Your respective Boards have decided,' he haughtily informed the shareholders, 'that it is advisable in the interests of the shareholders to bring your three companies together through an exchange of shares of these companies for the shares of the Brazilian Traction, Light and Power Company Limited ... which has been organized for that purpose, as by so doing the rights and privileges of the three companies can be better safeguarded and the properties more economically developed and operated.' Without elaborating on how the arrangement would better 'safeguard' their interests, Pearson simply added that the directors of the three companies were 'of the opinion that the basis of exchange is equitable and advantageous.'[38]

Pearson's terseness was rooted in his confidence that few shareholders would reject the share exchange. In the first place, the shareholders would be strongly impressed by the names of the prospective directors of Brazilian Traction. Heading the list were William Mackenzie and Pearson himself, who were designated respectively to fill the positions of chairman of the board and president of the new company. In 1912, there were few figures in the realm of Canadian business whose names were more synonymous with solid and profitable investment than those of Mackenzie and Pearson. Mackenzie, in 1911, had been knighted for his services as the promoter of the Canadian Northern Railway. Pearson, as his Barcelona triumph had illustrated, had acquired a shining reputation as a consistently successful initiator of electric services on three continents. The repute of the new chairman and president was reinforced by the addition of Alexander Mackenzie's name to the board. Mackenzie's talent as the resident representative of the Rio and São Paulo companies in Brazil was already well known to shareholders. The proposed election of Dr Alfredo Maia of Rio to the board held out the prospect of some indigenous Brazilian representation. Maia, who had sat on the Rio company board since 1907, had strong ties with many influential Brazilian politicians. The inclusion of the dynamic, if somewhat impetuous, American promoter Percival Farquhar rounded out the element of the board with experience in Brazilian business. The remaining places at the table were filled by familiar representatives of the Canadian and English financial world. R.M. Horne-Payne and one of his junior associates, H. Malcolm Hubbard, were to sit on behalf of English shareholders; while Henry Pellatt, William Van Horne, E.R. Wood, and D.B. Hanna (from the Canadian Northern) sat for Canadian investors. Finally, Z.A. Lash, joined by his lawyer son, Miller, accepted seats on the board to signify the close ties of the new holding company with the Toronto legal fraternity. Viewed from the shareholders' perspective, it was a slate of sterling directors, carefully designed to inspire confidence.

Much more alluring to any hesitant shareholder were the actual terms of the transfer. Brazilian Traction's authorized capital stock was set at $120 million, divided into 1,200,000 shares of $100 each, to be distributed to shareholders of the three existing companies on the basis of two and three-quarter shares of Traction stock for each São Paulo share; one and three-fifths shares of Traction stock for each Rio share, and a straight exchange of Traction stock for the São Paulo Electric shares (all of which were held by the São Paulo company). On this basis, $72 million worth of the Traction company's capitalization would go to former Rio stockholders; $27.5 million to former São Paulo shareholders, and $5 million to former São Paulo Electric shareholders. A reserve of $15.5 million worth of unissued stock was to be established. Pearson proffered no explanation of why the combined $60 million capitalization of the Rio and São Paulo companies had been transformed into $99.5 million on the books of the new holding corporation. Obviously the offer of exchange had to be made at a premium. Both the Rio and São Paulo companies were in a strong financial position just before the exchange. They had respectively reported 'most satisfactory progress' and 'most gratifying results.' Both had paid out handsome dividends in 1911. The São Paulo company alone had a net surplus of $1.7 million. None the less there was no indication of how Brazilian Traction had arrived at an exchange ratio of 1.6 for the Rio shares and 2.75 for those of the São Paulo company.

In a further bid to entice stockholders to exchange their shares, Pearson disclosed that the 'estimated revenue from the combined undertakings' would be sufficient to justify the immediate payment of dividends by the Traction company at an annual rate of 6 per cent. He prophesied that 'the expected increase' in the future revenues of Brazilian Traction would enable it 'without doubt' to undertake larger dividends in the near future. With bait such as this, there was little doubt that the Rio and São Paulo shareholders would hurry, if not scramble, to take up the exchange offer. Pearson's confidence that Brazilian Traction's offer would meet with avid acceptance was revealed by the relatively short period of time provided for the deposit of shares. 'Should the necessary majority not be deposited by the 1st September, 1912,' shareholders were warned, 'the proposed exchange will be abandoned.' To facilitate the collection of shares, banks in Toronto, London, Brussels, Liège, Antwerp, Basel, Geneva, and Rio were designated as places of deposit. The disclosure of the terms of the exchange, the setting of a deadline, and the designation of agents for the exchange thus brought to a close the public unveiling of the new holding corporation. In almost every respect, Pearson's offer was a *tour de force*; an attractive business proposition that few could resist.

The details of the public offer were straightforward enough. It was behind the scenes that matters became complex. Given the immense sums at stake, Pearson, Mackenzie, and the financial interests most intimately associated with the new company could not allow the exchange to run its natural course and thereby run the risk, no matter how small, that the offer might be rejected.

Months before the Brazilian Traction charter was obtained, quiet preparations were underway to ensure the smooth execution of the exchange. The key participants in this bid to prod the shareholders into action were the brokers: they were most closely in contact with the scattered shareholders, and their co-operation was indispensable if the shareholders were to accept Brazilian Traction's offer. After years of relying on the brokers to disseminate his shares, William Mackenzie now called on them to collect all the shares that had been painstakingly placed in the hands of investors in Belgian hamlets, English cathedral towns, and the backwoods of Ontario. In return for their services, brokers were to be awarded a ¼ per cent commission on the face value of every Rio or São Paulo share deposited with the banks. J.M. Smith (who would soon be appointed secretary and treasurer to the new company) reported to Pearson that he had asked the Toronto and Montreal stock exchanges to post notices advising members of the ¼ per cent commission. Arrangements were made with many of the large, influential brokerage firms of Toronto, Montreal, London, and Brussels to spearhead the share-exchange drive. In Toronto, Henry Pellatt, senior partner of Pellatt and Pellatt and a prospective Brazilian Traction director, was quick to urge Pearson to make 'every effort' to get in all shares possible and thereby avoid the problems attendant on exchange offers that were only partially accepted.[39] The fact that Pellatt, like many of his financial associates, held a substantial amount of Rio and São Paulo stock provided a further incentive for the brokerage community to co-operate. By the time Pearson dispatched his proposal to the shareholders on 15 July, the active co-operation of such prominent Canadian brokerages as Aemilius Jarvis and Co. in Toronto and McDougall and Cowans in Montreal had been assured.

On the other side of the Atlantic, European brokers headed by James Dunn in London and Alfred Loewenstein in Brussels had been making similar plans. Dunn conducted a series of intensive negotiations with Pearson and E.R. Wood to finalize the details of the share exchange. A hard-driving, pragmatic broker from the backwoods of New Brunswick, Dunn was ideally qualified to divine what shareholders would accept. With Wood, Dunn established the ratio of exchange î:2.75 for São Paulo shares and 1:1.60 for Rio shares. Dunn and Wood then turned their attention to the important questions of 'commissions to brokers, bankers, etc., and press funds for the Continent.' Once these details were settled, Dunn provided his assurance that he would muster sufficient support for the share exchange among fellow English brokers. Finally, Dunn spelled out his quid pro quo. In return for his willingness to organize a syndicate of European brokers 'for facilitating exchange and keeping prices of new shares above relative prices of old shares,' Dunn would be entitled to underwrite the $15.5 million of unissued stock in the new company.[40] Throughout these discussions, Dunn kept Loewenstein in Brussels well posted, since the full backing of the Belgian financial community was imperative. Although Loewenstein at first expressed 'strong objections to [the] Brazilian project' and protested that he had not been kept fully informed of the mooted exchange, his attitude became co-operative when the possibilities for profit were explained to him. In particular, Loewenstein was offered a generous share of the underwriting of a new issue of £1 million worth of São Paulo Electric bonds.[41] Dunn's timing in all these matters was extremely tight. Just days before Pearson's proposal was made public, he frantically cabled Loewenstein that he was 'arranging the Syndicate we discussed of which you wished to take 25%. It is very important that you be here on Monday to conclude the matter as market in Traction stock should be made immediately circular is issued and I have many matters of detail to settle.'[42]

Although Dunn complained that 'every minute of my time has been taken to get the Brazilian merger settled,' his efforts to ensure broker support and to 'make' the market for the new shares paid off handsomely. Shareholders in Europe and North America appeared at their local banks in droves, eager to surrender their old Rio and São Paulo shares. By 27 August 1912, the company secretary, J.M. Smith, reported that, of a total of 450,000 outstanding Rio Company shares, 322,427 had been deposited. Similarly, 71,135 of the 100,000 São Paulo shares were on deposit with the banks, as were all but 1 per cent of São Paulo Electric shares. In light of this very positive response, the share exchange was declared 'effective' at the directors' meeting of 27 August 1912. To ensure that all remaining shares were deposited, the last date for deposit was extended to September 13. Constant chivvying of hesitant shareholders by Pellatt, Dunn, and Loewenstein dissolved the fears of those who had still to deposit their shares. By March 1913, J.M. Smith was able to inform inquiring shareholders that more than 98 per cent of Rio and São Paulo shares were on deposit and that the National Trust, as the new company's transfer agent and registrar, was in the throes of issuing new Traction shares to those who qualified.[43] With their shares now vested in Brazilian Traction, the Rio and São Paulo companies became virtually wholly owned subsidiaries of the new Toronto holding company.

The consummation of the share exchange was followed by a period of careful vigilance when the financial friends of the new traction company nurtured the market for the new shares to ensure that they maintained a respectable value and were not subjected to attacks from 'bears' intent on forcing the value downwards. William Mackenzie and Fred Pearson were eager to start feeding some of the $15.5 million of unissued stock onto the market, and for them to do this a stable and high price for Traction stock had to be maintained. Like Monty Horne-Payne in the early days of the Rio company, Jimmy Dunn took charge of managing the all-important English market for Brazilian Traction shares. By March 1913, he had made arrangements for the distribution of the company's earnings card to jobbers in the City. 'I think this is very important,' he told Pearson, 'considering that we are anxious to raise the price of the stock.'[44] The market soon began to respond to Dunn's blandishments. 'Brazilian Traction have certainly proved during the past period of depression,' he reported to Canadian broker A.E. Dyment during the commercial slump of 1913, 'that they are well regarded by a large circle of shareholders and under anything like normal market conditions I believe they will continue to advance in price. The earnings of the company are showing most satisfactory increases and the outlook ahead is for this to continue.'[45]

The ultimate aim of Dunn and the other promoters of the new traction company was to induce what they called 'independent buying' by the myriad small investors of England and the Continent. Once the cautious Belgian *bourgeoisie* and the English middle class took a liking to Brazilian Traction shares, the promoters could rest assured that they had tapped into the bedrock foundation of the investment community. 'Stock is going every day into the hands of small investors,' Dunn proudly informed Dyment in April 1913, 'and the market position in it is certainly becoming stronger. I do not think there is any stock today more popular.'[46] Under Dunn's scrupulous overlordship, Brazilian Traction took its place beside the other Mexican, Spanish, and Canadian utility promotions of William Mackenzie. When the Brussels market became 'bearish' on Brazilian Traction, Dunn was quick to remind Loewenstein of 'the uselessness of maintaining other Pearson stocks if this one is left to such attacks.' By June 1914, 'the small public,' as Dunn labelled them, had become habituated to Brazilian Traction stock and were buying the shares, as Dunn boasted to American tycoon Henry Clay Frick, 'as high as 104' in London.[47]

From the promoters' perspective, the launching of Brazilian Traction was an astonishing success. In two months, Pearson, Mackenzie, and their allies had welded control of their two, hitherto separate, utility operations in Brazil into one unified corporation. The share exchange formalized many of the financial and operational practices that had previously bound the two companies together on an *ad hoc* basis. The thoroughness and speed with which it was executed testified to the ability of financiers like James Dunn, Henry Pellatt, and Alfred Loewenstein to mobilize the investing public.

The ability of brokers to 'make' a market, to feed the European press on a prepared diet of material concerning the stability of investment in Brazil, and to reap handsome profits from 'bonus' share deals was by no means restricted to the Brazilian Traction syndicates. In an age when the financial community found itself untrammelled by either the watchful eye of government regulators or the constraint of self-imposed regulation, men like James Dunn thrived on practices that, judged by later standards, were unethical and undercut the free play of the securities market. If promoters like Pearson and Mackenzie were prepared to capitalize on the devious ways of men like Dunn, it was partially because they stood to benefit personally from the successful launching of Brazilian Traction, but also, and more importantly, because the financial interests of London and Toronto alone could furnish the capital necessary for the pursuit of their entrepreneurial ambitions in South America.

The primacy of financial interests was once again revealed in early 1913. Under an agreement of 17 July 1912, Dunn, Fischer and Co. was given an option to dispose of the $15,500,000 worth of unissued stock in the new corporation. After consulting with his fellow London brokers in March 1913, Dunn assured Pearson that 'if we can wait a little while we can sell without hurting the market a further $10,000,000 Brazil Traction stock.'[48] Within two months, Dunn was able to convince the board that, instead of common shares, preference shares would have a much greater appeal to the investing public, and so, in May 1913, $10,000,000 worth of 6 per cent convertible preference shares were issued under Dunn's auspices. The shareholders were told that the issue was required to provide funds 'for the extensions of the plant and other capital developments and outlay of the subsidiary Companies.' In return for his services as 'manager' of the syndicate, Dunn received a commission of 3 per cent and the privilege of subcontracting blocks of stock to his friends. When the preference shares were eagerly taken by investors, Dunn rejoiced that it was 'a strong bull point' that the company was 'now [well] financed instead of remaining largely over-borrowed at [the] banks which was its former condition.'[49]

The financial security brought about by the adept, if incestuous, handling of the investing public by men like Pellatt and Dunn enabled the Toronto promoters of Brazilian Traction to finalize their exchange. In October 1912, the provisional directors declared a 6 per cent dividend on the common stock. On 30 April 1913, the permanent board took office. The new board signified the putting in place of the keystone in the new organizational structure. With Pearson occupying the president's chair not only of Brazilian Traction but also of the Rio company, the São Paulo company, and, by 1914, the São Paulo Electric Company, the management of the whole Canadian investment in Brazil was closely interlocked. This relationship of parent and subsidiary was cemented by the signing of the 'operating agreements' of 2 October 1912. The operating agreements owed their inception to the fertile mind of Zebulon Lash. The wording of all three agreements with the São Paulo, Rio, and São Paulo Electric companies was virtually identical. In light of 'the rapid growth and development of the territory served by the São Paulo Company,' the agreements read, 'a large amount of expenditure is immediately necessary for the purposes of making extensions and additions to its plants and installations.' Furthermore, the São Paulo company would 'from time to time hereafter during the period of its concessions' require 'further large expenditures.' Brazilian Traction undertook to provide sufficient funds to effect these objectives. Such advances would constitute a loan account that would stand as a liability of each of the subsidiaries to the parent company. Brazilian Traction's advances were to cover the capital expenditures of each of the three Brazilian subsidiaries and certain other costs, such as debt service. For their part the São Paulo company, the Rio company, and the São Paulo Electric Company surrendered to their Toronto parent 'the right to receive for its own use all the net earnings' of their operations after all operating costs, interest charges, and local taxation costs had been met.[50]

The operating agreements were remarkably simple and remarkably important. They were designed to establish loan accounts between the subsidiaries and Brazilian Traction and to ensure that the operating companies retained no revenue. The balance of their net revenue would automatically pass to the parent company and not into retained earnings. The annual report of the Toronto corporation simply reported the 'advances to subsidiary companies under the management agreements' on the debit side of its accounts and, on the credit side, the 'revenue from securities owned and under contracts with subsidiary companies.' Once, when the company secretary, J.M. Smith, was asked to elaborate on this agreement by an American financier, he neatly replied: 'I beg to advise that both of these companies are operating under an agreement with this Company, whereby the net earnings are paid over to it, and no statement of the detailed earnings of said companies has been published for circulation. I will say, however, that the earnings of said companies are very largely in excess of all charges for bond or debenture interest, sinking funds, bank loans, etc.'[51] Above all else, the operating agreements 'internalized' the finances of the Brazilian Traction empire, screening the companies, costs and profits from Brazilian and Canadian eyes alike.

The share exchange and the operating agreements did not escape criticism. Some shareholders voiced resentment over the manner in which they had been stampeded into the exchange by their brokers. In July 1913, one English shareholder wrote to complain that no sooner had he exchanged his old shares for new Brazilian Traction than the company had unloaded an additional $10 million in Brazilian Traction preference shares on the market. This new issue, aided by the general recession in the value of stocks brought on by the 1913 slump, had resulted in 'a serious shrinkage in the value of my shares, about 15% in two months ... It really appears that some who have inside knowledge must be pressing the shares continually for sale,' the disgruntled shareholder correctly guessed, 'and none of the financial papers here have ever had a good word to say for any of the utility shares of the Pearson group.'[52] On the Continent, the Parisian newspaper *Le comptant* complained of the 'North American financial methods' that underlay the Brazilian Traction 'labyrinth.' 'How is the small investor to understand,' the attack continued, 'that the Brazilian Traction is only a kind of superstructure that has no original foundation, and that in reality it consists of a kind of general office that directs the three distinct enterprises? ... From that combination of combinations there has come for the small capitalist an inextricable and inevitable confusion.'[53] Despite the fact that hostile attacks were often financed by those eager to create a 'bear' market in Brazilian Traction stock, such criticism was symptomatic of a pervasive concern among turn-of-the-century small investors that they were being divorced from control of their investments by the financiers who exercised increasing power over corporate policy. In the case of Brazilian Traction, many shareholders were justifiably perturbed by a course of events over which they felt they had had no influence. While the operational advantages made possible by the new corporate organization were probably in the long-range interest of the shareholders, the financial imperatives behind the exchange were of dubious benefit to the scattered small investors in the Rio and São Paulo companies. 'If I may give a personal expression of opinion,' one English investor informed Toronto, 'it is, to my mind, a great pity that a company carrying on so solid a business should be so lacking in prudent and conservative management of its finances. To my knowledge this has created a great absence of confidence in the company by the investment world.'[54]

The operating agreements were also subjected to a measure of criticism. The publication of the first annual report of Brazilian Traction, covering the period up to the end of 1913, gave rise to many queries as to the exact nature of the agreements under which $7,626,921 was reported as having been 'advanced' to the subsidiary companies. 'I should be pleased to be acquainted with its nature,' inquired one shareholder, 'so that the extent to which it is a real asset may be estimated.' After reviewing the company's financial statement, the prestigious London *Economist* commented that 'the whole position is an impenetrable maze at present.'[55] Although the company did not welcome such adverse comments, the complexity for which it was criticized was exactly what the board had intended. The operating agreements were designed to be enigmatic and to be understood by only a select few at the Toronto head office. This was amply confirmed when in 1917 one of the company's London accountants, Thomas Porter, protested that the corporate balance sheet was largely unintelligible. 'I have been through these accounts and compared them with the accounts for 1915,' Porter protested, 'and I can only say they appear to me to be drawn up in such a way as it is almost impossible for any ordinary person to have any idea as to what they mean.'[56]

A somewhat tarnished public image was not the only adverse effect of the merger. The most damaging outcome was the resignation of Alexander Mackenzie, the resident vice-president of both the Rio and São Paulo companies. The circumstances surrounding Mackenzie's sudden resignation in September 1912 and his subsequent refusal to occupy a seat on the board remain shrouded in mystery. In February 1911 (a full year before plans for formation of the holding company were drawn up), Mackenzie asked J.M. Smith, the company secretary in Toronto, to inform the board of his wish 'to be relieved of the place I hold as representative of the Company in Brazil.' Although he was prepared to continue his duties as late as July of the same year, Mackenzie urged the board to appoint Fred Huntress, the general manager, to replace him.[57] The intended departure of the leading and most respected representative of Canadian capital in Brazil portended serious consequences for the two companies in Rio and São Paulo. With his fluency in Portuguese, his mastery of Brazilian law, and his well-rooted network of political connections, Mackenzie was the indispensable link between the seat of operations in Brazil and head office in Toronto. While Huntress was a competent general manager, he could in no way hope to duplicate Mackenzie's *savoir faire* in anticipating and coping with the intricacies of Brazilian politics. Shocked at the prospect of losing so valuable an ally, Fred Pearson applied considerable pressure to Mackenzie and succeeded in convincing him to postpone his decision. This Mackenzie did until 13 September 1912 when, just two weeks after the share exchange had been declared effective, he resubmitted his resignation and was relieved of his duties. Less than a month later, on 2 October 1912, he withdrew his name as a candidate for the board. Brazilian Traction had lost its most valuable employee in Brazil.

The reasons for Mackenzie's departure are difficult to discern. The resignation was probably initially prompted by the cumulative effects of overwork and fatigue. As early as 1907, Mackenzie had complained that he had not been 'home' in five years and consequently was 'extremely anxious to leave' Brazil.[58] In 1908, Mackenzie married Mabel (May) Blake, sister of his good friend, W.H. Blake, the Toronto lawyer. When the heat and humidity of Rio's summer began to exact too heavy a toll on his new wife's health, Mackenzie sent her to England, where she established residence. This change of climate did not check the deterioration of May's health, and in March or April of 1911 she underwent what Mackenzie described as a 'rather serious operation.' It was the emotional strain of separation from his wife and concern for her health that probably explained Mackenzie's first attempts at resignation in February 1911.

It has been suggested that Mackenzie's departure in 1912 was the result of his personal dissatisfaction with the financial arrangements underlying the stock exchange.[59] This is not a very plausible explanation, especially when one considers that Mackenzie continued to hold a large number (8,869 as of 23 May 1913) of Brazilian Traction shares and that he continued to assist the company in its affairs on a periodic basis from his 'retirement' home in England. In June 1913, for instance, he was communicating with Bernardino de Campos and his son Carlos concerning several legal cases in Brazil. A more likely explanation of Mackenzie's break with the investors he had served for more than a decade lies in the fact that his resignation coincided to the day – 2 October 1912 – with the signing of the operating agreements. Mackenzie may have taken umbrage at the implicit shift in authority contained in the agreements. The key to Mackenzie's success in Brazil had been that he had operated free of interference from distant Toronto. Although the operating agreements promised to leave the subsidiary companies free to exercise their 'uncontrolled judgment and discretion,' Mackenzie may well have feared that in future all policy decisions were to flow from Toronto. This, Mackenzie had always maintained, was tantamount to corporate suicide. Significantly, Percival Farquhar, the other would-be Brazilian Traction director with business experience in the Brazilian environment, also withdrew from the new company on 2 October 1912.

Whatever the causes of Mackenzie's departure, his decision was not irrevocable. Realizing the crucial part Mackenzie could play in assuring a secure future for the company in Brazil, Pearson persisted in badgering the former vice-president in hopes of forcing a reversal of his decision. In February 1914, he succeeded in convincing Mackenzie to undertake 'a short trip' to Brazil so as to lend his assistance in the settlement of 'several important questions regarding our concessions.'[60] Exposure to the company's varied problems in Brazil must have aroused dormant instincts in Mackenzie, because in January 1915 Pearson gleefully announced that Mackenzie had agreed to assume full-time duties as general counsel and legal adviser. 'Personally,' Pearson wrote to E.R. Wood in Toronto, 'I am delighted to have him again with me as it relieves me of a great deal of responsibility, although Mackenzie during the past year had been kind enough to always devote his time to any questions which I referred to him when he was in this country.'[61] As Pearson himself sensed, Alexander Mackenzie supplied the one crucial ingredient necessary for the success of the venture in Brazil: leadership. Neither Pearson, whose talents were now expended on a global basis, nor Sir William Mackenzie, whose Canadian railway projects now almost completely monopolized his attention, had the time to provide the day-to-day, on-the-spot direction of company affairs that would ensure a profitable future in Brazil. 'It cannot be impressed too forcibly, however,' an American observer of foreign enterprise remarked a few years later, 'that the foreigner or the foreign firm, be the line that of engineering, railroading, making dock works or digging mines, looking toward Brazil as a field for action, must ever have in mind a high qualitative leadership, if any permanent success is anticipated.'[62]

By 1913, the Brazilian Traction, Light and Power Company Limited was, by any standard, a large, successful, binational utility corporation, well financed and with good prospects for continued growth in South

America's largest and fastest-growing urban market. The acquisition of the Rio and São Paulo subsidiaries, while adding another layer to the structure of corporate control, had simplified the capital structure of the Canadian investments in Rio and São Paulo. Despite the questionable increase in the capital stock in the course of the acquisition, Brazilian Traction emerged from the share exchange with a simple capital structure. With its total reliance on common and preferred stock, the company was unencumbered by a funded debt, except for the outstanding bonds of its subsidiaries. The promises of continued profits and dividends made by its promoters were fulfilled within a year, much to the delight of the shareholders of the new company. At the end of 1913, Brazilian Traction reported revenues from its subsidiaries of $11,266,138, plus an additional $256,698 in interest on the advances made to the subsidiaries under its operating agreements. Of these revenues, the sum of $8,185,495 was paid out in dividends to the holders of Brazilian Traction common and preferred shares and the amount of $3,012,998 was carried forward as a surplus. It was with little exaggeration that the company's annual report noted that 'the results of this Company's operations since its incorporation have proved very satisfactory.'

Whereas in the early years of both the São Paulo and Rio companies, dividends had been restricted to a relatively small pool of investors, most of whom were aligned with William Mackenzie, Brazilian Traction dividends enjoyed a wider dissemination. Although precise information on the breakdown of ownership is scanty, evidence indicates that the majority of Brazilian Traction common and preferred stock was held in England and on the Continent. Whenever requests were made for statistics on the disposition of shareholders, the company secretary, J.M. Smith, curtly replied that 'our Company has never given such information out.' Once, however, Smith's resolve weakened and he informed Greenshields and Co. in Montreal that of the 1,043,765 shares issued in 1914, 65.5 per cent were held in England and on the Continent and the balance of 34.5 per cent were in the hands of Canadian and American investors.[63] Over the next five years there was a shift towards North American ownership, so that by August 1919, Smith could report that ownership was evenly split, at 41 per cent each, between North American and European investors. A modest 2.5 per cent of Traction shares were in Brazilian hands, and 15.5 per cent were in the form of share warrants, which were predominantly held on the Continent.[64] The use of bearer share warrants was favoured by many European investors because they afforded their owners (whose identity was not indicated on the security) a degree of anonymity that enabled them to avoid taxation in countries like Belgium. From the company's point of view, the share-warrant system quickly became a nuisance, because the Toronto head office, like the Belgian government, had no idea in whose hands the shares reposed.

Despite some initial criticism, Brazilian Traction shares soon won a high repute in the eyes of most investors. Partially because the old São Paulo and Rio companies had created a reputation for solid profits and also because the new market for Brazilian Traction was so zealously cultivated by brokers like Dunn and Pellatt, Traction stock – or 'Traccies' as they were soon dubbed on the London market – were avidly purchased and held by investors. Large institutional investors and influential brokerage firms possessed large blocks of Brazilian stock. These shareholders varied from the Canadian Bank of Commerce, which Sir William Mackenzie described in 1916 as 'probably [the] largest individual shareholder,' to small Toronto brokers who maintained blocks of a few hundred shares each. In recognition of the Canadian Bank of Commerce's services to the company, Sir John Aird, the bank's general manager, was elected to the Brazilian Traction board in 1916.

Beyond the large holders, ownership of Brazilian Traction became increasingly scattered. In Canada, for instance, Traction shares won wide acceptance from all types of Canadian investors. Lawyers, clerics, academics, bankers, and politicians all prized the company's securities. The names of prominent or soon-to-be prominent Canadians filled the list of shareholders: Sir Frederick Williams-Taylor of the Bank of Montreal; Vincent Massey, scion of the wealthy family of farm-machinery manufacturers; W.L. Mackenzie King, a future prime minister of Canada and adviser to the Rockefeller family; B.K. Sandwell, a rising Canadian journalist, and Maurice Hutton, a distinguished philosopher at the University of Toronto. In the parlours of many of Canada's more affluent homes, discussion must have turned on occasion to the prospect of profits from tramway operations in the cities of distant Brazil.

The spreading ownership of Brazilian Traction shares over three continents necessitated changes in the ancillary services supporting what was now Canada's largest overseas investment. Up to 1912, the functions of registrar and transfer agent for English investors had been provided by

Horne-Payne and the British Empire Trust Company. As the financial business generated by the various Mackenzie and Pearson enterprises increased, the Toronto managers realized that a more permanent arrangement was necessary. In view of Horne-Payne's cantankerousness, it seemed advisable to remove the company's all-important financial relations with its English investors from the sway of the English financier. Accordingly, in February 1912, a federal charter was obtained for the Canadian and General Finance Company Limited. Despite its rather pedestrian name, the company was designed to serve as an agent for Brazilian Traction, and also for the Mexico Tramways, Mexico North Western Railway, Mexican Light and Power, Barcelona Traction, and San Antonio Land and Irrigation companies, all of which were part of the so-called Pearson group. To manage the London office, H. Malcolm Hubbard, an English lawyer with years of experience at Horne-Payne's British Empire Trust, was hired.

Hubbard's office in the city became a mandatory stopping place for the senior directors of the Traction company. Pearson had, by 1912, established a country residence outside London, and it was to Hubbard's office that he daily went when in England. Across Hubbard's desk passed an incredible volume of transfer certificates, telegrams, purchase orders, and press releases, all relating to Brazilian Traction. In this sense the London office usurped the role of the Toronto office as the focal point of the company's affairs outside Brazil. Although London's financial hegemony was coming under challenge from Wall Street, the City was still the financial mecca of the world. In deference to New York's rising power, Clarence Dillon of the influential New York firm of William A. Read and Co. was invited to join the board in 1916. To cater to the large body of continental European shareholders, a small office was opened, in conjunction with the interests of Percival Farquhar, at 9 rue Louis le Grand in Paris. Although representation on the board had been promised in 1912 to Belgian and French investors, no actual provision for this was made, although the Brussels brokerage firm of Stallaerts and Loewenstein continued to represent the company's interests on an *ad hoc* basis. The exclusion of European investors from the Brazilian Traction board was to become an irritant that would in time have serious consequences.

The opening of European offices and the widening board membership were symptomatic of the growing maturity of William Mackenzie's Brazilian enterprises. The focus of the Canadian promoters of the traction enterprise was shifting from pioneering entrepreneurship to routine management. The initial stages of the two Brazilian ventures had placed a strong emphasis on innovative engineering and financial dexterity. While the incredible growth of the urban and industrial power market in south-eastern Brazil would continue to exert strong pressures, many aspects of the company's activities began to assume a predictable nature and were best left in the hands of experienced managers like Alexander Mackenzie, Fred Huntress, and Malcolm Hubbard. Pearson's attention was more and more focused on the challenge of building the Barcelona power complex and the defence of his extensive utility interests in revolution-torn Mexico. Sir William Mackenzie's energies were becoming fixed on the task of seeing the Canadian Northern Railway through to its completion. Amidst these varied demands, Pearson and Mackenzie could look upon Brazilian Traction as their one relatively stable enterprise, which, although never entirely free from the problems of exchange, political unrest, and nationalism, could be left in the hands of competent managers.

Throughout this important transition, Sir William Mackenzie none the less remained firmly in control. Although share ownership became increasingly dispersed, Mackenzie and the original promoters of the Rio and São Paulo syndicates always made sure that they could muster sufficient shares to exert a controlling interest in company affairs. Thus, when a special general meeting of the Traction company was convened in May 1913, the Mackenzie interests were able to command 681,587 proxies. William Mackenzie himself was registered with 29,078 shares, which were joined by 1,917 shares in the possession of Mackenzie, Mann and Co. Close financial friends of the chairman registered substantial holdings, such as 2,401 shares in the hands of Z.A. Lash, 3,918 with Herbert Holt, 3,200 with James Ross, and 8,869 with Alexander Mackenzie. Dunn, Fischer and Co. in London had an astonishing 70,386 shares. William Mackenzie's overwhelming superiority on the list of shareholders afforded him unchallenged power over corporate decision making. As time passed, and as the financial needs of the Canadian Northern grew, however, Mackenzie gradually sold some of his Brazilian Traction stock. By the time of the second annual meeting in May 1915, he had reduced his holdings to only 12,406 shares.

Mackenzie's ability to pare his Brazilian Traction holdings at great personal profit reflected the overall operational and financial success of the enterprise. By 1915, the corporation was an established, well-organized, and smoothly operating public utility. This fact was not only clear to North American and European investors but was experienced daily by Brazilians in Rio and São Paulo. Despite his at times questionable financial practices, Sir William had helped to build a remarkable public-utility operation in a foreign land that had known neither Canadian capital nor modern electric services before his company's establishment. In both the scope and efficiency of its services and its ability to generate a healthy return on investment, Brazilian Traction excelled.

The most obvious reflection of the company's operations in Brazil by 1915 was its tramway service. The appetite of *cariocas* for electric traction had rapidly outstripped that of *paulistanos*. In 1913, the Rio de Janeiro Tramway, Light and Power Company carried 195,783,634 passengers over 378 kilometres of routes. The trams of the São Paulo company hauled 56,776,702 passengers over a 226-kilometre network. In the two cities, a combined fleet of 810 tramcars annually travelled more than 56 million kilometres. So great was the pressure for use of the tram system that the Rio company alone had rush orders placed for an additional one hundred cars.

The impact of the tram on urban life in Rio and São Paulo cannot be conveyed in terms of statistics alone. While totals of passengers carried or changing patterns of population density provide an impression of how trams affected the structure of the city,[65] they do not create an understanding of the tremendous qualitative changes wrought by mass transport on Brazilian urban society. In fact, few foreign visitors to Brazil's two leading cities failed to remark on the central part the trams had come to play in the daily work and play of *cariocas* and *paulistanos*. In Rio, for instance, the trams, in conjunction with the commuter trains of the Central and Leopoldina railways, carried thousands of blue- and white-collar workers to their work every day. With the inauguration of the 'trailer' service in 1909, blue-collar workers could ride to work at reduced fares. There were few regulations governing 'trailer' passengers, but passengers riding in the first-class cars were required, as befitted their status, to wear a tie and shoes. When *cariocas* turned to pleasure-seeking, the trams offered a ready escape from the congested inner core of the city. One could take a tram, for instance, from the Quinze de Novembro square in central Rio and travel along the shore of Botafogo Bay, through the tunnel to Copacabana on the Atlantic shoreline and on to the magnificent, unspoilt beach at Ipanema. Travellers visiting Rio frequently remarked upon 'Rio's beautiful tramway rides.'[66] 'It is through such matchless scenery,' an American noted,

that the Rio de Janeiro tramways carry more than half a million passengers daily. No one wonders that the enterprise which stands in Portuguese to the Cariocans as 'A Light' has brought forth admiration and appreciation. As far as it would seem possible during the last decade, it has brought to the inhabitants of the fair city by the sea both men and methods to match her mountains.[67]

The mobility offered by the tramways, whether used for pleasure or work, was part of the much greater process of modernization in Brazilian urban society. Access to safe urban transportation, for instance, helped to speed the emancipation of middle- and upper-class Brazilian women from the cloistered existence they had endured in the nineteenth century. Broad, clean avenues, such as those created by the reforms of Pereira Passos, well-lit parks, and regular tramway services allowed women to escape the confines of home and stroll unmolested in crowds that would, a decade earlier, have treated the sight of unattached women in public with amazement. 'Of the Carioca lady,' one Englishman flatteringly observed,

it is equally difficult to speak in general terms. She is getting nearer to Europe every day, and seemingly at an increasing speed since the opening of Rio's great avenues, the electricalization of the trams and the advent of the motor car. Previously she was, or elected to be, almost orientally immured, and did not care for travel.[68]

Once aboard a tram, however, the 'Carioca lady' often found herself taking an unwilling part in what Fred Huntress described as 'a favourite pastime in Rio.' The peculiar shape of the seat backs on Rio trams (designed to be flipped over when the car reversed direction) permitted men 'so disposed, to rub their knees against the lady sitting in front, on that part of her anatomy which would naturally protrude thru the space between the seat back and the seat, especially if she was the usual well-fed kind.'[69]

Electricity had been the handmaiden of progress, if not licentiousness, in other aspects of Brazilian urban life. By 1913, the Rio company supplied sufficient power to enable 26,927 lighting customers to burn 683,937 incandescent lamps, while its sister company in São Paulo furnished power to 12,148 customers with 175,395 lamps. City dwellers became dependent upon electricity, the marvellous 'white coal,' while continuing and increasing their reliance on gas. Gas had traditionally found a market in the lighting needs of the city, but now the Rio and São Paulo Gas companies had considerable success in introducing gas for cooking purposes. Convincing Brazilians to adopt gas in their homes required subtle persuasion. Gas company managers in São Paulo were fond in later years of telling the story of a prominent São Paulo public official who installed one of the first gas stoves in São Paulo. When asked some time after how the stove was working, the official replied 'Splendidly! it hasn't gone out since the cook lighted it.'

Success in placing gas and electricity services at the disposal of *paulistanos* and *cariocas* was echoed in a minor way by the company's efforts to introduce telephone service. As of 1913, only the Rio company offered telephone services to its customers, having acquired the concessions and primitive equipment of the German-owned Brasilianische Elektricitäts Gesellschaft soon after it established itself in Rio. By the end of 1913, the Rio Telephone Company had connected only 11,379 telephones, 73 per cent of which were used for business purposes. Service was poor and expensive, with the result that the public looked on the telephone as a luxury that could easily be replaced by a fleet-footed courier. None the less the company sensed a great potential for telephone service in Brazil. For their part, Brazilians showed signs of adopting the telephone with the same alacrity with which they had adopted electricity. The favourite samba at the 1917 Rio Carnival was entitled 'Pelo Telefone' – by phone. Later, this same popular song became the first samba to be recorded in Brazil. As early as December 1913, Fred Huntress was urging Pearson to begin planning for a long-distance telephone line between Rio and São Paulo, claiming that it would be 'an exceptionally important adjunct to our telephone business.'[7] To this end, the Rio company acquired the Interurban Telephone Company, a Brazilian firm that held concessions for the operation of toll lines throughout Rio State, parts of the state of São Paulo, and the cities of Niterói and Petrópolis.

As with gas and electricity, Pearson was reluctant to pour large sums of capital into a telephone system until he was assured of viable concessions and a reasonable chance of dominating the telephone market. The main obstacle confronting the company in this respect was that the Rio telephone concession, first negotiated by the German firm in 1898, expired in 1928. It was to renegotiate and lengthen this concession that Alexander Mackenzie had come out of 'retirement' and returned to Brazil in 1915. 'Whatever time it may take,' he reported to Toronto, 'the new franchise will be worth waiting for, as I feel confident that in this case, as in former negotiations with the [City] Council, we can wear them out.'[71] In the meantime, Pearson executed the take-over of the 'Companhia de Rede Telephonica Bragantina.'

Acquisition of this company, serving the small city of Bragantina, offered the Canadian company a foothold in the state of São Paulo. When a consultant had earlier reported that the Bragantina firm was not 'well managed' and might constitute 'the backbone of what may easily become a very much larger affair,' Pearson moved through his London financial friends, principally James Dunn, to buy up control from the English capitalists who controlled it.[72] Until this collection of scattered and mismatched telephone companies could be sewn together into one unified organization, the company's telephone services would remain embryonic and the target of considerable criticism. 'It would be extraordinary,' one English visitor noted,

if such a Colossus entering into the intimate domestic and municipal life of Rio had no critics; it is annoying if a telephone girl says, 'No reply' when you feel sure the person you seek is neither dumb nor out; but you cannot live in Rio many days before you appreciate the gigantic services rendered by the corporation to the city, the courage and foresight that have put nineteen millions into the job and loyal effective character of the administration.[73]

If the telephone service was the weak link in the system, the hydro-power plants were its crowning glory. The Parnaíba plant outside São Paulo and the Lajes plant in the hills behind Rio represented the backbone of the Canadian public-utilities system in south-eastern Brazil. Designed with ample capacity for an expanding market, the plants furnished the base load that had permitted the unimpeded expansion of tramway, lighting, and power services in both cities. With the completion in late 1913 of the nine-kilometre-long tunnel diverting water from the Piraí River into the Lajes reservoir, two additional generating units were added to the powerhouse, bringing its total capacity up to 62,650 kilowatts. By that year, the Rio company was supplying bulk power to 1,865 industrial consumers in the city with a total motor capacity of 47,400 kilowatts. After a visit to the Lajes plant, an American journalist declared that the facility was 'more than a big hydraulic plant; it is a constant object lesson to all Brazil of wide visioned engineering and sustained and ever expanding utility.'[74] In São Paulo, too, the byword was expansion. The Parnaíba plant was supplemented by the acquisition in 1914 of a small plant on the Sorocaba River. The absorption of this small power company serving the city of Sorocaba was the brainchild of Pearson. It was not the 2,980-kilowatt capacity of the plant that attracted Pearson, but the prospect of serving the power needs of Sorocaba city and of constructing a modern power plant on the river.[75] By early 1915, construction was completed on a new Sorocaba plant with three 7,460-kilowatt Westinghouse generating units. Half of this output was used to provide tramway and power services to Sorocaba, and the other half was delivered under contract to the São Paulo company.

The ability of North American engineers to harness the power of Brazil's rivers was perhaps Brazilian Traction's greatest advantage. Expansion of services and generation of profits both directly hinged on the availability of hydro power. A good measure of the Rio and São Paulo companies' initial success was attributable to their ability to stay ahead of power demand and thereby build up the market and avoid the protests that would inevitably have arisen in reaction to any power shortage. From an early date, company officials were acutely aware that the prosperity of the enterprise would depend on the steady expansion of power-generating capacity. 'The possession of a large water-power with immense storage reservoirs is the first consideration,' Alexander Mackenzie was to note in 1916. 'Large water-powers within reasonable distance of Rio de Janeiro are not numerous. Their developments and the transmission to Rio de Janeiro will involve the expenditure of an immense sum.' Already, by 1915, engineers were scouring the Brazilian countryside for exploitable locations for hydro-power production. Suitable sites were bought up by the company lawyers, partly to be held in reserve and partly to deny their use to would-be competitors. When promising waterfalls could not be found in the vicinity of Rio or São Paulo, survey teams were sent further afield. In 1911, for instance, Alexander Mackenzie dispatched a team to inspect the Paulo Afonso Falls on the borders of Bahia and Alagôas states in north-eastern Brazil. Although the falls showed tremendous potential for power generation, they were far too removed from Brazil's urban power market to warrant development.[76] The Paulo

Afonso expedition was indicative of the company's determination to build upon previous achievements, to fortify its competitive position, and to explore the possibilities open to foreign enterprise in the unfamiliar Brazilian environment. As a visitor to the company's installations concluded in 1917:

The Light and Power Company of Rio de Janeiro may impress the casual observer simply as a great and successful business enterprise. To one who gets behind the scenes, this Company appears more like a large, well-articulated band of congenial workers, a big business family, whose members enjoy working together toward a large and worth-while end. That this end is truly the ever enlarging serviceableness to vast populations, quite as much as money making, is abundantly clear.[77]

CHAPTER SIX

The Survival of the Fittest: Brazilian Traction and the First World War

The first decade of the twentieth century is often portrayed as a period of heroic enterprise, an era when great men did great things. Railways were built, vast industrial mergers executed, and countless new goods placed before a public rapidly becoming what is today called the 'consuming society.' The architects of this tremendous economic transformation were the 'captains of industry': the bold promoters who, the public believed, were the chief instigators of economic advance. Thorstein Veblen once said of the 'captain of industry' that he 'was a person of insight – perhaps chiefly industrial insight – and of initiative and energy who was able to see something of the industrial reach and drive of that new mechanical technology that was finding its way into the industries, and who went about to contrive ways and means of turning these technological resources to new uses and a larger efficiency, always with a view of his own gain from turning out a more serviceable product with greater expedition.'[1]

One such 'serviceable product' was, of course, electricity. Fred Pearson's global reputation as a 'captain' of electricity, along with William Mackenzie's repute as a builder of railways and tramways, attested to North America's prowess in the public-utility field in the years before the First World War. While the presence of trams clanging about the streets of Toronto, Winnipeg, Rio, and São Paulo testified to the success of the Pearson-Mackenzie formula, their success was more ostentatiously displayed by the sumptuousness of their palatial private homes. The captain of industry lived in the splendour to which he believed his entrepreneurship entitled him. 'Benvenuto,' William Mackenzie's baronial home on

Toronto's Avenue Road, and Fred Pearson's country estate at Great Barrington, Massachusetts, were monuments to the self-esteem of the electric-utilities promoter. Even less subdued architecturally were the homes of the financiers who had exploited the speculative possibilities of the street-railway and power ventures thrown up by Pearson and Mackenzie. The flamboyance of Sir Henry Pellatt's 'Casa Loma' was perhaps the best illustration of the turn-of-the-century financier's penchant for garish self-advertisement. In those years before the First World War when it seemed Toronto led the world in the building of utilities, the triumphs of the captains of industry were discussed in the salons and dining-rooms of mammoth homes, largely financed from the proceeds of Latin American tramway fare boxes and prairie rail receipts.[2]

The social philosophy publicly espoused by Mackenzie and Pearson was that of unbridled competition. While Mackenzie did not hesitate to seek government assistance or squeeze out competitors – like the Guinles – if it bettered his position, he attributed his success to the operation of the free-enterprise system. Like Andrew Carnegie, Mackenzie and Pearson both paid homage to the law of competition. It was, Carnegie had earlier declared, 'to this law that we owe our wonderful material development, which brings improved conditions in its train.' As a principle of economic life, competition was impossible to avoid; 'no substitutes for it have been found and while the law may be sometimes hard for the individual, it is best for the race, because it insures the survival of the fittest in every department.'[3] The devotion of Pearson and Mackenzie to this creed brought handsome rewards. Railways and utilities had been profitably established in the expanding and largely unregulated Canadian economy, and the same formula for utilities promotion had been applied to the even less regulated and potentially more profitable business milieux of Latin America and the Iberian Peninsula.

By contrast, in the second decade of the new century, Pearson and Mackenzie were to learn that the concept of survival of the fittest did not invariably work in their favour. Revolution in Mexico, commercial depression in Canada, self-inflicted financial ruin in Spain, the trauma of world war, and the rise of interventionist governments all combined to undermine the spectacular early success of the 'Pearson group.' By the end of the decade, the Mexican and Spanish utility ventures were in a shambles and had been removed from the control of their original promoters. The Canadian Northern Railway and Ontario electric enterprises of William Mackenzie had also succumbed to financial pressures and were well on their way to passing into state control. Even Brazilian Traction, so successful in 1913, suffered a measure of these misfortunes, yet it alone of the 'Pearson group' was to survive to fight again.

The first indication that the halcyon days of utilities promotion in Latin America were coming to an end came in May 1911 when eighty-one-year-old Porfirio Díaz, Mexico's long-time president, abandoned office and fled the country in the face of popular agitation for suffrage reform and land redistribution. Under Díaz's lax regime, Canadian-incorporated companies had been established to supply the power, lighting, and traction needs of Mexico City. Both the Mexico Tramway and the Mexican Light and Power companies operated under liberally framed concessions, as did the Mexican North Western Railway, a rail line designed to export the timber of northern Chihuahua state. All three Mexican enterprises relied on the technical expertise of F.S. Pearson and the promotional talents of William Mackenzie. With Díaz's departure, Mexico slid into constitutional chaos and civil war. Caught in the ebb and flow of civil war, Canadian utility companies in Mexico valiantly tried to maintain operations but, amid the turmoil of shifting battle lines and precarious provisional governments, soon gave up any pretence of orderly service. A succession of embattled governments under Francisco Madero, Victoriano Huerta, and Venustiano Carranza victimized, commandeered, and, at times, nationalized the Canadian power and tramway operations in Mexico City. In the north-west, roving gangs of guerillas under leaders such as Pancho Villa waylaid the trains of the Mexican North Western, robbed their passengers, and pilfered their freight.[4]

No amount of journalistic finesse on the part of Toronto managers or London financiers could keep investors from the knowledge that their Mexican investment was going to rack and ruin. 'For the past two years a state of revolution has existed in the territory in which the [railway] Company operates,' a distraught James Dunn complained to the British Foreign Office in 1912, 'and it has been a constant sufferer both from the destruction of its property and its inability to operate except at a heavy loss. This condition of things has continued so long and has resulted in such considerable loss to the Company that its credit is seriously damaged and great difficulty exists in raising further money to continue the operation of the properties.'[5] To the extreme annoyance of Dunn and the Toronto head offices of the enterprises, both the British and American governments refused to intervene in the Mexican situation, citing the fact that the companies in question were all of Canadian incorporation and therefore the responsibility of Ottawa. Since Canada had neither the diplomatic channels nor the political inclination to intervene in Mexico, the Mexican companies found themselves in a vacuum. While the Mexican hostilities persisted (as they did until the early 1920s), the Canadian railway, power, and tramway companies all continued their decline into insolvency and eventually succumbed to receivership and control by bondholders' committees. The ignominious demise of the Mexican companies had repercussions for the other members of the 'Pearson group.' 'There has been a good deal of selling of [Brazilian Traction] stock in the last two or three weeks,' Dunn reported from London in early 1913, 'partly owing to the depressed state of the general markets and somewhat to the especially disturbed state of Mexican securities with which through a somewhat common directorate the public consider it related.'[6]

Whereas a force largely beyond the control of foreign businessmen – the ravages of civil war – was responsible for the foundering of the Mexican companies, self-inflicted financial recklessness hobbled Barcelona Traction in Spain. Pearson's plan for developing the hydro-power potential of the Ebro River entailed the development of three separate power sites. Once construction began in 1912 on the Lérida dam and Seros powerhouse, Pearson proceeded at breakneck speed. By mid-1913, it became evident that Pearson's construction program on the Ebro was fast outstripping the ability of its promoters to finance it. When Alfred Loewenstein in Brussels voiced his 'profound feeling of dissatisfaction' over Pearson's mounting expenditures, Dunn in London admitted that 'the money at Barcelona has been spent very rapidly,' but that Pearson had assured him that he was 'quite positive he is right in his estimate of what the whole undertaking will cost.'[7] Pearson's reassurances proved illusory, and within a year French and Belgian bankers had little choice but to make sizeable cash advances to buoy up Pearson's latest project. These advances, totalling £2 million by July 1915, were secured by additional preference shares and bonds. Soon recriminations began. 'How many times,' Loewenstein fumed to Dunn, 'have I not also given to Dr. Pearson advices [sic] to be prudent in regard to this loan policy and his method of making "greater" than the capital of which he is disposed. In reality, all the worries which we now have result from this policy.'[8]

The outbreak of the First World War exacerbated an already precarious situation. In December 1914, lack of capital plus the hostilities in Europe forced a halt in construction of the power plants. Although Pearson continued his frantic search for capital in Europe and the United States, the financial moratorium imposed by the war compelled Barcelona Traction to default on its bonds, thereby forcing receivership. Subsequent consultants' reports urged that the power project be completed, but by early 1915 it was clear that the original management of Barcelona Traction, especially Pearson, its president, would have to be dislodged. Eventually a bondholders' committee was established to direct the corporation and it in turn appointed E.R. Peacock, another expatriate Canadian financier in London, as Barcelona Traction president. Whereas Pearson had come to represent financial irresponsibility in the investors' eyes, Peacock had a reputation for financial sobriety and conservatism. This by no means straightened the twisted affairs of the troubled corporation and, although its power-generating system was eventually placed in operation, European and North American courtrooms were to echo to the sounds of squabbling Barcelona Traction investors until 1970, when the International Court in The Hague finally delivered control of the company into Spanish hands.[9]

While revolution and financial recklessness gnawed at the Pearson enterprises in Mexico and Spain, the supposed perfidiousness of local politicians in north-eastern Brazil brought the downfall of the Bahia Tramway, Light and Power Company Limited. Organized in 1905 under the auspices of William Mackenzie, Percival Farquhar, and Fred Pearson, the Bahia company had a Maine charter and built its services around concessions bought from Belgian and German interests. As in Rio, the Bahia company had to fight against the powerful Guinle family to establish itself. After what Alexander Mackenzie described as 'the bitterest kind of warfare' with the Guinles, Brazilian courts upheld the primacy of the American company's concession in the city of Bahia.[10] Despite this, relations with local politicians were never good and, after a long period of friction, punctuated by anti-company riots in the streets of Bahia, the municipality offered to purchase the company in 1913. Realizing that they had no reliable mechanism of political self-defence, Pearson and Farquhar accepted the offer, taking £1.2 million in municipal bonds in payment for their assets. To the consternation of all foreign investors in Brazil, the city of Bahia promptly defaulted on its bonds. 'It has deliberately avoided its obligations, disregarded its admitted liability,' lectured *The Times*, 'and behaved in a manner which is a disgrace to any civilized community.'[11] For years to come the Bahia default was to remain a *cause célèbre*, as jilted bondholders sought redress for the city's arbitrary treatment. The case dragged on for years, with bondholders, Brazilian lawyers, and American and British diplomats all wrangling over the intricacies of the situation. In essence, Bahia Tramway failed because it had neglected to build a strong line of local defence. Unlike the Rio and São Paulo companies, it lacked a man of the calibre of Alexander Mackenzie to forge political and legal alliances in the local community and thereby prevent the company's isolation and possible ostracism.

The melancholy and unexpected events in Mexico, Spain, and Bahia provided an object lesson in the inherent dangers of 'utilities imperialism.' In the years immediately preceding the First World War, Fred Pearson's promotional genius was increasingly being diverted from promotion to the harrowing task of pressuring the Foreign Office in London and the State Department in Washington for diplomatic assistance, while at the same time placating irate financiers and investors. Pearson's problems were compounded by his involvement in innumerable other schemes, ranging from nickel refining in Canada to land irrigation in Texas; all of which were encountering political and financial problems brought on by the slump of 1913 and the outbreak of European war. Pearson's life by late 1914 was thus reduced to a routine of frantic transatlantic missions to confer with politicians, lawyers, financiers, and engineers about the perilous condition of many of his enterprises.

Sir William Mackenzie was faring little better in Canada. The apogee of Mackenzie's fame as a railway builder had come in 1911 when he received a knighthood in recognition of his services as the promoter of the Canadian Northern Railway. By 1914, however, the main line of the Canadian Northern was still incomplete, and financial problems had begun to overtake the promoters. In the first place, the economic downswing of 1913 had eroded the Canadian Northern's traffic in immigrants and freight. Diminishing receipts from this once-lucrative business were accompanied by the soaring costs of fuel and labour brought on by the war. By early 1914 the Canadian Northern was in serious financial trouble. Facing an imminent default on the interest payments of its securities, the Canadian Northern looked in desperation to Ottawa for assistance. Fearing the repercussions of the collapse of a major Canadian railway, the Conservative government of Robert Borden reluctantly supplied Mackenzie's bankers with guarantees for the Canadian Northern's bank loans, taking in return $40 million of the railway's $100 million common stock. Even with this help the railway's deficit continued to mount, with the result that Mackenzie soon renewed his visits to the nation's capital. In June 1916, Prime Minister Borden, in a moment of annoyance, noted in his diary that Mackenzie had again 'pestered me for more help for his infernal railway.'[12]

Mackenzie's adversity was temporarily interrupted in January 1915 when the main line of the Canadian Northern was triumphantly completed. In a ceremony at Basque, British Columbia, Sir William himself pounded in the last spike. Meanwhile in Ottawa, the Borden government reached the conclusion that it could not continue to prop up the wobbly finances of Mackenzie's railway. After a royal commission report in 1917 urged the government to take over the Canadian Northern and consolidate it with several other lines into a state-owned rail network, Borden decided to act. When the prime minister called the railway president to his office to inform him of his decision to nationalize, Mackenzie dissolved in tears. In subsequent negotiations, largely conducted by Z.A. Lash, Mackenzie and Mann were awarded $10.8 million in compensation for the Canadian Northern stock remaining in their hands. Sir William thus retired from the railway business. Mackenzie's loss of the Canadian Northern, coupled with the sale of his Toronto utility enterprise in 1921, constitute one of the most dramatic reversals of fortune in Canadian business history. When Mackenzie died in December 1923, the value of his estate revealed the extent of his lessened circumstances. After all claims were settled and his splendid home and cars sold, Mackenzie's heirs received approximately $800,000 plus the furniture from 'Benvenuto.' Among the few items of real marketable value in the estate was a large block of Brazilian Traction common stock.[13]

The durability of Brazilian Traction in the struggle for the survival of the fittest was partly the product of accident and partially that of careful stewardship. Whereas Mexico had disintegrated into civil war in the 1910s, Brazil enjoyed a remarkable political stability, largely attributable to the *café com leite* politics of the Old Republic. Although Brazil did participate in the First World War (the only South American state to do so), it did not enter the hostilities until 1917. In 1919, it took its place at the Versailles peace conference and signed the treaty as one of the victorious allies. While the war caused temporary dislocations and a re-sorting of economic priorities, it did not disrupt the Brazilian economy catastrophically. The ability of Brazilian industry to weather the war and expand production during the crisis greatly enhanced Brazilian Traction's prospects of survival. Unlike Barcelona Traction and the Canadian Northern, Brazilian Traction was not caught by the war and the ensuing international financial stringency at a time when it was engaged in costly construction projects. By 1914, the Rio and São Paulo companies were faced only with the relatively inexpensive process of expanding their generating and distribution facilities to keep pace with the growth of their markets. All these factors placed Brazilian Traction in a more enviable position than many of its sister companies in the 'Pearson group.' None the less, the company's overall fortunes during the war were dictated by the ability of its managers to respond to the very real challenges thrown up by the conflict in Europe.

Not the least of these was the steadily declining rate of foreign exchange on the Brazilian milréis. Since the subsidiaries had first begun generating revenue in Brazil, the exchange rate of the milréis had affected their ability to make remittances in dollars or pounds to their foreign creditors and shareholders. Fortunately, the period from 1899 to 1913 had seen a steady appreciation in the foreign value of the milréis, meaning that fewer milréis bought more dollars or pounds. By 1913, the company's remittances were leaving Brazil at an average exchange rate of 16d. per milréis. The slump of 1913 and the outbreak of war abruptly altered this situation. By March 1914, James Dunn warned Sir William Mackenzie that English investors in Brazilian Traction stock were becoming unnerved by 'the fear of a fall in Brazilian exchange,' knowing that such a fall would eventually be reflected in their dividends.[14] These premonitions were seen to be amply justified when war broke out and the exchange rate of the milréis, so dependent upon European trade (especially in coffee), slipped steadily downwards. In September, the company reluctantly reported to its shareholders that 'for several months it was practically impossible to remit money from Brazil for the purpose of the payment of coupons and dividends.' For the next three years, Brazil's foreign investors contended with an exchange rate that refused to return to pre-war levels. With exchange averaging between 12d. and 13d. throughout the 1915–17 period, Brazilian Traction's net revenue was diminished by the equivalent of $9.8 million when compared with revenues translated at the average rate prevailing in the five years before the war. Not until 1919 would the rate again rise above 14d. In the interim, the depressed rate of exchange placed enormous strain on the financial health of the company.[15]

Necessity being the mother of invention, the company proved ingenious in finding ways to ameliorate the vulnerability of its remittances. When exchange drafts became virtually unobtainable in late 1914, company managers in Rio took the cash from operations and invested it in coffee beans, which were subsequently shipped to the United States aboard the same ships the company chartered to deliver coal for its gas works. Brazilian Traction, an electric utility company, suddenly found itself speculating in the strange world of commodities. 'We cannot tell yet what the result of the coffee purchases will be,' Pearson excitedly informed Sir William, 'but unless there is a fall in the price here [New York] we shall make a very good profit on this transaction.'[16] By December 1914, 278,400 bags of coffee had been sold by the company on the New York market at an average exchange of $13\frac{54}{84}$d., a rate well in excess of the official rate.

Company accountants also learned to offset the effects of low exchange by developing the art of remitting to a fine state. Since large sums of money had to be remitted from Rio and São Paulo not only to London, but also to New York and Toronto, remittances had to be precisely timed to take advantage of the best available rate and at the same time ensure that sufficient 'hard' currency was produced to satisfy head-office needs. It was an art that required a delicate sense of timing, since funds could be remitted 'on sight' or as far in advance as ninety days. 'In the case of large remittances,' a company accountant in Rio warned Toronto head office, 'we should have at least thirty days advice, as with exchange in its present condition a few thousand pounds bought is apt to bring the rate down a point or two which is, of course, something we do not wish to do.'[17] The company's mastery of remittance explains in large part its ability to weather the war. If the flow of remittances had dried up, then Brazilian Traction would have run the risk of defaulting on its subsidiaries' bond payments or failing to honour its creditors' claims, either of which would have driven the enterprise into receivership, where it would undoubtedly have met the same unenviable fate as its Mexican and Spanish sisters. More importantly, without a favourable reputation in the eyes of foreign investors, Brazilian Traction would be unable in future to attract foreign capital to invest in the expansion of its services.

The company's ability to turn a bad exchange situation to its best advantage, however, did not mean that the shareholders escaped unscathed. Throughout 1913 and 1914, sufficient funds were remitted to enable the payment of dividends to both preferred and common shareholders at a rate of 6 per cent per annum. Wartime conditions forced the common share dividends to 4 per cent in 1915, and by 1917 caused the directors to consider whether any common dividends could be paid at all. After an agonizing board meeting, the directors decided to pay a quarterly dividend of 1 per cent 'hoping that conditions would improve in the near future, or before consideration of the next dividend.'[18] The company's financial situation was exacerbated by its inability to issue new securities on the frozen securities markets of Europe. The result of this constriction was that most of the company's remittances had to be applied to its essential imports and to its inescapable obligations to preferred shareholders and bondholders. This impasse forced cessation of all common share dividends in the last three quarters of 1917, a policy that was reluctantly followed until 1922. Shareholders were told that Brazilian Traction had 'no alternative but to continue to apply the surplus revenue in meeting the capital expenditure necessitated by the growth of the business of the companies.'

The non-payment of dividends did not meet with shareholder approval. At the annual general meeting in September 1919, a lawyer representing a group of English shareholders presented a motion protesting the failure to pay dividends. English shareholders, it was alleged, 'were not of large means' and 'the non-payment of dividends was a very serious matter to them.'[19] When William Mackenzie explained that the cost of obtaining outside capital was so prohibitive that no dividends could be considered, the lawyer dropped his protest. Mackenzie completed his pacification of the shareholders with an assurance that peace would soon bring a return of dividends. None the less, the dividend policy still attracted criticism. The Toronto *Mail and Empire* pointed out in 1920 that since 1917 Brazilian Traction had applied $33 million worth of earnings to its capital account.[20] 'The desire of shareholders, however, to see some return on their money is, of course, natural,' complained London's *Financial Times*, 'the feeling being that too much can be done for posterity, unless some of us are destined to attain the age of Methuselah.'[21]

For those who took the trouble to read beyond the dividend statement in the annual report, there was ample evidence that wartime problems went beyond the immediate difficulties of exchange and remittance. The most persistent and debilitating problem was the complete disruption of the coal supply for the Rio and São Paulo gas companies. The gas companies' traditional reliance upon imported English coal was broken by the outbreak of war. Not only did the increased consumption of coal by British industry drive the price upward, but the availability of vessels to deliver the coal to Rio and Santos was abruptly curtailed. Even when the company was able to charter ships, it stood a good chance of having them commandeered by the British Admiralty. If the colliers escaped the clutches of the Admiralty, they frequently fell prey to German u-boats. By 1918, the cost of ocean freight had risen by over 500 per cent when compared to rates prevailing in 1914. In 1918, the two companies carbonized 118,880 tons of coal, for which they paid $3,920,000, which was $2,851,200 in excess of the cost of the same coal at pre-war prices.[22] By mid-1918, the coal situation was perilous. The ninety-day reserve that the gas companies usually maintained had dwindled to a mere thirteen days' supply, and the Brazilian government, Fred Huntress reported to Toronto, was becoming 'frightened.' When the company suggested that coal could be saved by curtailing lighting in Rio's port area, the government objected, 'fearing disturbances and strikes among the stevedores and the handlers of coffee.'[23] None the less, the government acquiesced, and in September and October 1918 gas rationing was introduced and more than 12,000 Rio street lamps were temporarily 'suppressed.'

The coal situation became so acute that the company abandoned its traditional English suppliers and turned to suppliers on the American east coast. Here also shipping was scarce, and in desperation the company began chartering 'tramp' sailing vessels. When German submarines sank the first two of these slow-moving ships, the company retained the services of a former American diplomat to lobby the Shipping Board, an agency of Washington's wartime bureaucracy, to secure charter steamers. After a little gentle pressure from the Brazilian ambassador in Washington, the American government relented, and by the end of 1918 a reasonable amount of coal was arriving in Rio.[24] By 1919, the average price for a ton of coal landed in Brazil had fallen to $29.59 from $31.02 the previous year. As with many other adaptations forced by the war, the switch to Virginia coal would long outlast the war. Not surprisingly, the net earnings of the two gas companies declined steadily throughout the war, although the financial impact of these losses was blunted by the fact that customers' gas accounts were partially receivable in gold.

War in Europe had implications far beyond the disruption of the coal supply. Since their inception, the Rio and São Paulo companies had relied upon European electrical apparatus. War had the immediate effect of cutting the companies off from German and Austrian suppliers of turbines, telephone equipment, cable, and a host of similar equipment all necessary for the operation of utility services in Brazil. Severed from some European suppliers, the Canadian companies were left to join in the feverish competition for equipment manufactured by suppliers remaining within the Allied pale or in the still non-belligerent United States. As a result, by 1915 the general managers in Rio and São Paulo found themselves confronted by escalating prices and severe shortages of the parts they needed to keep their turbines in action and their trams on the street. At the annual meeting in 1918, Alexander Mackenzie informed the shareholders of the 'extraordinary increase in the price of all materials, all metals such as iron, steel, copper, cement and in fact everything that enters into the item of operating expenses.' With spare parts and new equipment failing to arrive, the companies could neither maintain a reasonable standard of service nor expand services. Any failure to honour the conditions of service stipulated in concessions might easily expose the whole Canadian enterprise in Brazil to criticism from those interested in stripping the company of its dominant position in the Rio–São Paulo market.

The Rio and São Paulo companies responded to material shortages by imposing what the annual reports called 'rigid economies' and by using their own machine shops to supplant foreign suppliers. Improvisation became the byword. Tramcar motors were, for instance, painstakingly rewound to avoid importing costly new armatures. In 1917, the machine shops and foundry facilities of Rio Tramway were enlarged, allowing the production of many parts that had previously been imported. By the end of the war, the Rio shops were building thirteen- and fifteen-bench passenger trams, ten-bench trailer cars, and freight trams, using an assortment of locally produced components, parts scavenged from 'worn-out' trams, and a few, much-prized imported items. Only in the field of telephone equipment, where manufacture required much precision and a high degree of labour skill, did the company continue to suffer from chronic wartime shortages of material.

Many benefits flowed from the company's mastery of improvisation. Production of equipment ranging from tramcars to copper wire immediately alleviated supply shortages and also saved the company precious dollars at a time of low milréis exchange. From the Brazilian perspective, the assumption of certain previously untried manufacturing activities by the company maximized the Canadian enterprise's contribution to the local economy. This benefit did not stop with the consumption of local raw materials but extended to the training and employment of local labour in the production of goods that in many cases had previously been beyond the skill of the average Brazilian worker. For years to come, the shops, car barns, and various other ancillary services surrounding the Light in Rio and São Paulo were to become a seed bed for Brazilian labour, from which would emerge an army of trained electricians, metal workers, and skilled craftsmen. A job with the Light was therefore a prized job.

The company's experience with wartime deprivation and improvisation provided a reflection, in microcosm, of the fortunes of Brazil as a whole during the conflict. 'Brazil has been in the war as an ally since October, 1917,' Alexander Mackenzie told the shareholders in 1918, 'and has not profited by the war. She has on the contrary suffered very much in consequence of war. She has suffered because she is five thousand miles away from her principal trading partner and she has lost several of her principal markets, such as Germany and Austria, Germany being a very important one, and for want of shipping, Brazil has not been able to send her products even to the markets which were open to her.' But, like the company, Brazil learned to adapt to the wartime situation and eventually to profit from it. The commercial slump of 1913, followed by the outbreak of war, completely disrupted the import-export nexus upon which the Brazilian economy depended. After more than a decade of steadily improving exchange, the milréis entered a period of depressed value. A further blow was the slackening of the price of coffee, which remained throughout the war at about 30 per cent below the price levels enjoyed in 1911–12.[25] The resulting contraction of export earnings greatly impeded Brazil's ability to import the manufactured goods of Europe and America.

Brazil's response to this crisis has been a subject of heated debate among historians of economic growth. The cardinal issue has been the degree to which the wartime economic crisis promoted industrialization in Brazil. Some scholars have advocated what has come to be called the 'shock' theory of Brazilian industrial development, a theory that credits abrupt changes in Brazil's terms of trade (especially those brought on by the two world wars and the Depression) with imposing forced industrialization on Brazil. Hence, the adverse terms of trade prevailing during the First World War created 'a great opportunity for Brazilian infant industries,' with the result that tremendous strides were taken by industries such as the textile industry. Such growth, the 'shock' theorists claim, helped Brazil diversify its economy away from staple exports.[26] In opposition to this, other economic historians have stressed the gradual evolution of Brazilian industry and dismissed the war as an economic aberration. The coffee trade, they argue, had had important economic 'spin-offs' since its inception and had in a gradual fashion fostered industrial growth by promoting industrial practices ancillary to the business of shipping coffee. Brazil's lack of 'hard' currency during the war sharply restricted the ability of would-be industrialists to expand their facilities because they could not procure the foreign-made machinery and capital necessary to expand production. Instead, they maximized their output in areas in which they already had capacity, such as textiles. 'In summary,' a leading gradualist has concluded,

World War I increased considerably the demand for domestic manufactured goods but made it almost impossible to enlarge the productive plant to meet that demand. The fortunes that were made during the war grew out of new lines of exports, twenty-four hour-a-day production, or out of mergers and reorganization. New plants and new lines of manufacture were not significant. It might be asked if the industrialization of São Paulo would not have proceeded faster had there been no war.[27]

The operational record of the Rio and São Paulo companies throughout the war supports the 'gradualist' theory of Brazil's economic development. Undeniably, the war brought an initial 'shock' to the Brazilian economy. For instance, tramway ridership in Rio and São Paulo fell marginally between 1914 and 1915 from 245,835,927 to 243,130,447. Financial results published in the 1915 annual report echoed this downswing. Revenue from the Brazilian subsidiaries dropped from $8,058,813 in 1914 to $5,612,876 in 1915, while the parent corporation's net income slipped from $7,600,000 in 1914 to $5,400,000 in 1915. These fluctuations were indicative of temporary economic dislocations, which soon disappeared as established patterns of tramway ridership and power consumption reasserted themselves.

The record of the São Paulo Tramway, Rio Tramway, and São Paulo Electric companies after 1915 was one of steadily increasing revenues from all sectors except gas, where the critical coal situation resulted in losses well into the 1920s. The power business in Rio and São Paulo grew in every year of the wartime economy with power connections expanding from 78,300 kilowatts in 1914 to 117,475 kilowatts by 1918. Growth in power sales came in steady and equal increments. Similarly, the total installed capacity of Brazil's electric industry grew steadily but not spectacularly throughout the war, from 303,438 kilowatts to 326,947 kilowatts between 1914 and 1918. Increasing sales were attributable to expansion in demand from traditional users, principally large textile mills, food-processing plants, and machine shops. Financial returns mirrored the smoothness of the market's wartime increase in size. After the slippage in revenues between 1914 and 1915, Brazilian Traction's net income steadily increased through the years 1916 to 1918 until $7.9 million was reported in 1919. As Alexander Mackenzie told the shareholders in 1918: 'our company has shown greater earnings than in any year of its history.' The rub, of course, lay in the fact that the shortage of exchange throughout the war hurt the company's ability to make remittances. The war was thus no godsend for Brazilian Traction. It neither restricted the steady growth of its services nor checked the advance of its milréis earnings; but it did create an awkward financial situation for the parent corporation in terms of its ability to convert milréis into dollars. From the Brazilian point of view, the availability of abundant electricity for industry and mass transport in the Rio and São Paulo markets continued, as it had before the war, to be a positive factor in propelling Brazil towards industrialization.

Brazilian Traction was able to satisfy the demands of industry for electricity only because the Rio–São Paulo system had sufficient surplus capacity to cope with the growth in demand stimulated by the war. With the completion of the Sorocaba plant outside São Paulo and the pre-war enlargement of facilities at the older Parnaíba and Lajes plants, the subsidiary companies had a combined hydro-power-generating capacity of approximately 134,000 kilowatts. Both the Rio and São Paulo systems had small reserve steam-generating plants that could be brought into service if circumstances demanded. At no time during the war years did the demand for power exceed, or indeed come close to, the generating capacity of either system. In São Paulo, for instance, the system had a rated capacity of 59,000 kilowatts in 1914 but was never called on to supply more than 23,250 kilowatts. By 1919, demand peaked at 32,800 kilowatts, still about half the available capacity. Only in the early 1920s would the coincidence of continued industrial growth and unprecedented droughts challenge the São Paulo system. Had there been a shortfall in generating capacity during the war years, the company would have been in a highly vulnerable position. While it was feasible to build trams in the company's Rio shops, any attempt to construct turbines and generators for power generation would have been doomed to early failure.

Although the power system escaped the daunting task of expanding capacity under wartime conditions, the Rio and São Paulo telephone systems faced it squarely. Since it had acquired its first concession in Rio in 1906, the company had sought to expand its telephone services to the point at which it could justifiably unify all telephone services in the Rio–São Paulo area. Unfortunately, this plan coincided awkwardly with the wartime shortage of capital and equipment needed to place telephone service on a solid operational basis. By 1913, the telephone service offered by the Canadian company was still restricted to the Rio concession obtained from the Brazilianische Elektricitäts Gesellschaft in 1906. Only 11,379 lines were in service, plus a handful in Petrópolis and Niterói controlled by the Interurban Telephone Company. This situation rapidly changed with the acquisition of the Companhia de Rede Telefônica Bragantina and the Companhia Telefônica do Estado de São Paulo, both of which gave the Canadians a foothold in the São Paulo market. Also in 1913, a beachhead was established in the state of Minas Gerais with the creation of the Companhia de Telefones Interestadoaes. By 1915 the whole telephone situation revolved around the problem of finding the best means of consolidating these varied holdings. 'We have no hesitation in saying that quite apart from the position shown by the present and prospective earnings of these companies,' Alexander Mackenzie reported in 1916, 'their material position will be greatly improved by a consolidation ... We remove powerful possible competitors in the territory of the Brazilianische and Interurban Companies and by connecting their various systems and improving them we create a large volume of new business.'[28]

The desired consolidation of the telephone companies was achieved in 1916 with the creation, under a Canadian federal charter, of the Rio de Janeiro and São Paulo Telephone Company. The entire share capital of the new company was issued, as fully paid stock, to the Rio company in consideration of the transfer of the shares it owned in the companies exploiting the telephone services in the city and state of Rio. Under working agreements made between the new telephone company and its five subsidiary companies, the Rio de Janeiro and São Paulo Telephone Company was entitled to all the subsidiaries' earnings; at the same time, it had the responsibility to provide for their capital and other requirements. While reorganizing the telephone companies presented no difficulties, securing sufficient capital to permit unification and expansion of services proved extremely trying. Cut off from the London bond market by the war, the company looked for the first time to New York as a possible source of funded debt capital. After protracted negotiations, which were personally directed by Alexander Mackenzie, the company was able to place an issue of $7.5 million worth of three-year 6 per cent notes on the New York market.

The success of the company's wartime sally onto the tight international financial market did not ensure the operational success of the consolidated telephone company. Chronic shortages of imported equipment impeded the important work of building up the telephone company's infrastructure. By 1919, only 57,216 'instruments' had been connected, and there was incessant pressure from potential customers for more telephones. The telephone situation was further complicated by the company's inability to renegotiate its telephone concessions. The linchpin was the Rio concession, slated to expire in 1928. Despite Mackenzie's attempts to secure an extension, the municipal *câmara* in Rio (under whose jurisdiction all local telephone services fell) refused to budge, and by 1919 Mackenzie was complaining that without a solid concession the company could not hope to finance properly the capital needs that were 'increasing by leaps and bounds owing to the demand for telephone service which we cannot begin to meet.'[29] From the beginning, Brazilian Traction's investment in the Brazilian telephone industry was thus plagued with problems that would not abate. The penalty for attempting to consolidate and expand its telephone system during wartime was restricted access to capital and equipment. Unlike the electric system, the telephone system was condemned to a constant struggle to catch up to demand without the guarantee of a solid foundation of long-term concessions. This situation was exacerbated by what was to become a long-standing disagreement between municipal politicians and company managers as to what constituted a reasonable concession for both the local citizenry and its foreign promoters. Lacking capital, equipment, and long-term concessions, Brazil's first large-scale local and interurban telephone system got off to an inauspicious start. The more the telephone service deteriorated, the less willing local politicians were to entertain the company's request for a long-term concession.

The problems of the telephone system mirrored a broader upheaval experienced by Brazilian Traction during the war. The war jeopardized the integrity of an enterprise whose affairs straddled three continents. Since their inception, the Rio and São Paulo companies had been nourished on a mixture of North American promotion and technical expertise combined with large injections of capital from both sides of the Atlantic. The war challenged this delicate intercontinental dependence in many ways. Not only did the severance of international arteries of finance and commerce pose a threat, but changes wrought in North American, European, and Brazilian society and government by the war would ultimately exact their toll. In this sense, the First World War was not only a test of the company's ability to adapt, but also the first major watershed in its affairs.

On the financial plane, the war cut Brazilian Traction off from many of its most faithful investors. As the German army swept into the lowland countries and France in 1914, many of the Belgian and French investors who held Brazilian Traction stock found themselves behind enemy lines. Furthermore, certain German and Austrian citizens holding company securities actually found themselves at war with the country in which their investment was domiciled. The company therefore found itself with no legal means of communicating with a large body of its European shareholders. Acting on a request from the British government, the company immediately ceased payment of dividends to shareholders in enemy countries. All dividends receivable by European shareholders were accordingly paid into accredited banks in London and held there pending the end of the war. Far more awkward for company officials was the fact that two of their subsidiaries, the Société Anonyme du Gaz and the Brazilianische Electricitäts Gesellschaft, had head offices behind enemy lines. Although the offices maintained by the Belgian gas company in Brussels and the German telephone company in Berlin served purely nominal functions (since all their stock was held by holding companies in Toronto and Maine), their wartime status did present problems. In 1915, the secretary of the gas company in Brussels complained to the parent corporation that he could not secure a quorum for the SAG's annual meeting because the majority of directors could not travel behind enemy lines. The solution was to make the secretary a director and vest the other directors' proxies in his name.[30] The German telephone company proved a more embarrassing problem. One of the reasons prompting the creation of the amalgamated telephone company in 1916, under Canadian charter, was the need to extinguish the 'German character' of the BEG in Rio.

Isolation from the once sought-after European investor and the virtual cessation of international financing in London obliged Brazilian Traction to look to the New York market for capital support. The successful issue of the gold notes for the telephone company in 1916 on the New York market was significant not only for the company but also for Brazil, which throughout the war saw itself further drawn under the growing power of American commercial and financial influence in Latin America. Although British capital was to remain pre-eminent in Brazil until the mid-1920s, the war provided a tremendous fillip to American economic ambitions in Brazil.[31] When Alexander Mackenzie was negotiating the 1916 loan in New York, he was aware that he 'was making propaganda of utmost importance to Brazilian finances,' especially since 'our loan will be the first of an industrial character made by Americans' to Brazil.[32] One symptom of the company's aroused interest in New York as a potential lender was the induction of Clarence Dillon, of the prestigious American financial firm of William Read and Co., onto the Brazilian Traction board in 1916. Despite Dillon's presence, representation of English financial power on the board remained strong, with R.M. Horne-Payne, E.R. Peacock, and H. Malcolm Hubbard all retaining seats.

The waning ability of the City to satisfy Brazilian Traction's pent-up capital needs was underscored in the immediate post-war period. In August 1919, after the lean war years, it was estimated that Brazilian Traction would need at least $10 million over the next three years to expand its services and to retire the gold notes it had floated for the telephone system. The prospects for obtaining new money in England were not encouraging. 'There are serious disadvantages in having to finance anywhere in these times,' E.R. Peacock warned E.R. Wood in August 1919. 'Where-ever we do our financing it will not be cheap, but the main consideration seems to me that it should be done on sound lines, and that proper provision should be made for the necessary expansion of the Company. I have all along recognized that it might in the end prove best to renew in New York.'[33] On 1 November 1919, the gold notes were consequently renewed for another three years in New York, and the search for new outside capital was postponed. The wisdom of this decision was confirmed early in 1920 when the English banking firm of J. Henry Schroder and Co. provided Brazilian Traction with a gloomy analysis of the English capital market. 'At the present time when the economic conditions of the world are so uncertain and in consequence international exchanges are fluctuating widely and all money markets are so stringent,' their report concluded, 'it would be most unwise to have recourse to such markets except in case of absolute need, which in your case does not appear to exist.'[34] The return of peace therefore brought with it a realization that the halcyon days of easy access to the capital markets of England and Europe were not likely to return.

Wartime changes to the company's financial standing corresponded to important changes in its status as a Canadian business corporation. In the first place, the war created small, yet irksome problems for head office in Toronto. When, for instance, conscription was introduced in Canada in 1917, the company was faced with the possibility of having its already much-depleted office staff deprived of its last reserves of experienced clerks and accountants. Company Secretary J.M. Smith responded to the challenge by petitioning Ottawa for 'exempt' status for several key employees (including himself). 'The details of the companies' affairs are more than usually intricate,' he explained, 'owing to the businesses being carried on in a foreign country.'[35] The exemptions were granted. The most serious challenge faced by Brazilian Traction in Canada during the war was not in the realm of military conscription but in that of federal taxation. Up until the outbreak of the First World War, the company had enjoyed an exemption from all forms of taxation in its homeland. The payment of certain fees, local taxes, and withholding taxes in Brazil, together with certain nominal registration fees payable to the Ontario and federal governments constituted the only financial obligations of the Brazilian Traction group to the state. In the era in which the Rio and São Paulo companies were founded, corporate and income tax did not loom large in the minds of either businessmen or politicians. The First World War changed all this.

In 1914, even before the outbreak of war, British government officials

had begun to examine the company's financial transactions in London
with an eye to imposing Britain's Income Tax Act upon them. When it was
suggested that all monies loaned to Brazilian Traction through the
medium of the British Empire Trust Company be taxed at a rate of $\frac{1}{2}$d. on
the pound, company officials objected vehemently. 'We have each time
taken the position,' the London office reported, 'that your company being
a Canadian company is not liable for British Income Tax and the
Government officials have not, up to the present, made any formal
demand for payment, and appear, at all events for the present to have
dropped the matter.'[36] The reluctance of British tax officials to push their
case was not shared by their Canadian counterparts when Ottawa
legislated a tax on business profits in 1916. In 1914, the Ontario
government had imposed modest taxes on the 'paid-up' capital and
revenues of any corporation 'which transacts business in Ontario.'
Brazilian Traction clearly did not fall beneath this fiscal net. The entry of
the federal government into the field of corporate income tax did,
however, send Brazilian Traction officials again hurrying to their lawyers.
After carefully considering the new act, Miller Lash, Zebulon's son and a
junior partner at Blake, Lash, Anglin and Cassels, assured the company
that 'no action need be taken by the Company as to making the return
called for [in the act] as the Company is operating in a foreign country.'[37]
A difficulty arose when the federal inspector of taxation pointed out that
there was 'no specific statement' in the act confirming this opinion.[38]
When the business-profits tax was stiffened in 1917 and personal income
tax was introduced in the same year, it became imperative for the
company to confirm its special status in Ottawa. In a cleverly argued
letter, Blake, Lash, Anglin and Cassels explained to federal officials that
Brazilian Traction's profits were generated by investments in Brazil, not
Canada, and that under the operating agreements with its subsidiaries,
Brazilian Traction received most of its earnings through the Bank of
Commerce in New York, where it paid its suppliers and shareholders.
Only bookkeeping was carried on in Toronto – 'as a matter of convenience.'[39] Convinced by this argument, the federal government amend-
ed the Income War Tax Act in 1918 to exempt from taxation 'the income
of incorporated companies whose business and assets are carried on, and
situate entirely outside of Canada.'[40] The confirmation of Brazilian
Traction as a '4-к' corporation, so called because of the section and clause
in which the exemption was placed in the act, was to have long-lasting

implications. It left the company immune to Canadian taxation and gave its managers every reason to keep its head office in Toronto. The '4-к' status was quickly sought by other Canadian corporations operating in foreign lands and, until it was annulled in the early 1970s, offered significant advantages to promoters wishing to incorporate in Canada.[41]

The war also gave birth to pressures for increased taxation within Brazil. Since their inception, the Rio and São Paulo companies had been subjected to some Brazilian taxation, either that stipulated in their concessions or that which applied to all companies. In 1915 Alexander Mackenzie reported with alarm that the Brazilian government was on the verge of increasing the 2.5 per cent tax it had traditionally imposed on corporate dividends, both foreign and national, to 5 per cent and extending its terms to cover payment of interest on debentures and bonds. Although the company's annual reports continued to stress that it enjoyed relations of a 'most cordial character' with the Brazilian government, the prospect of heightened taxation considerably soured these relations. While the budget containing the tax measure was still before Congress, the company gained an amendment to the tax bill, limiting the tax to shares and bonds issued *within* Brazil. This exemption held fast throughout the war, but in 1919 an attempt was made in Congress to quash the exemption. 'Important to have London financial papers criticise policy taxing income non-residents in case of dividends,' Mackenzie frantically cabled to Toronto, 'as through tax paid by Company it reduces income available for distribution ... Could draw attention different position Argentine where free from all taxation.'[42] In Rio, Fred Huntress (now a company vice-president) enlisted the support of the British ambassador, Sir Ralph Paget, and his fellow ambassadors from the United States, France and Italy to protest the 5 per cent tax. The ambassadors in turn lobbied the minister of foreign affairs and the president, Epitácio Pessoa, assuring both politicians that any tax on foreign capital invested in Brazil would 'create a bad impression in the United States, where capital was now looking toward Brazil.'[43] Despite these pressures, a *comissão de finanças* established to consider the case decided that continuation of the exemption would erode government revenues too seriously, and the 5 per cent dividend tax became law.

The war unleashed other social and economic forces in Brazil. Not the least of these was the growing mood of labour militancy in the Rio–São Paulo industrial heartland. Under the unrelenting pressure of wartime production, Brazilian workers, especially those in such skilled trades as metallurgy, sought to protect their rights through unionization. Employers opposed the union movement, especially after it became tinged with anarchistic and communistic elements.[44] The Rio and São Paulo tramway companies unavoidably found themselves involved in the ensuing struggle. As leading non-governmental employers whose workers were generally in jobs demanding a relatively high level of technical competence, the companies found themselves at the centre of the unionization fracas.

Traditionally, the conductors, drivers, labourers, and linemen of the Canadian companies had displayed a high degree of loyalty to their employers. For its part, the company had treated its workers in a benevolently paternalistic fashion, deliberately paying wages in excess of Brazilian norms. All tramway drivers and conductors were, for instance, issued ornate uniforms that indicated their rank and years of service with the company. Each braided gold ring around a conductor's cap was symbolic of five years' service. Company-sponsored medical and social facilities reinforced this sense of loyalty. Light workers therefore enjoyed a high status in the labouring community. The company not only offered an opportunity for a worker to acquire a technology-oriented skill (in short supply in Brazil), but also, since it was careful to pay its workers slightly in excess of prevailing wage rates, offered Brazilians a chance for a better-paid, long-lasting career. The Light also administered a 'Benefit Society' to which both it and its workers contributed to provide certain health and recreational benefits. As a result, a high degree of *esprit de corps* prevailed among Light workers. Previous attempts by outsiders to unionize Light employees had been rebuffed, much to the delight of the company's Toronto managers, who were well aware that their Brazilian tramways had much lower labour costs than their Toronto tramways.

In 1917, the storm broke. Hard pressed by the high wartime cost of living, large numbers of São Paulo textile workers went on strike; they were joined by small numbers of São Paulo tramway employees. When the tramway managers determined that the large majority of their employees wished to continue working, police protection was arranged so that these workers could maintain tramway and utilities services. Not surprisingly, the strikers' wrath turned on the cars and, even though the strike was against the Crespi and Matarazzo textile firms, several trams were burned and two people were killed in the ensuing strife. The textile workers eventually exacted a 20 per cent wage hike from their employers, and peace returned to the city. Similar scenes were enacted in both Rio and São Paulo in May 1919, when workers demanded an eight-hour day from employers. 'Since the 1st May there have been a series of strikes here and in São Paulo,' Alexander Mackenzie reported to Toronto. 'They hardly affected our men but this is only because we gave our men to understand that we would fall into line with the new [ILO] international programme affecting labour.' Subsequently the Light conceded the eight-hour day to its workers (thereby reducing the work day by one hour) and raised wages. Mackenzie was philosophical about these concessions, pointing out that they came 'at a time when earnings are climbing up in the most extraordinary way with exchange approaching 15d. Had we waited for a strike, we should have inevitably been obliged to concede at least what we have given.'[45]

The generally harmonious relations of the company and its employees thus survived the war more or less intact. Light employees continued in many ways to be the vanguard of skilled Brazilian labour. None the less, the war had created friction and mutual suspicion between management and labour, and from it there emerged a gradual recognition that the rights of Brazilian labour would have to be entrenched by the state. In 1923, the first step in this direction was taken with the imposition of a mandatory contribution of 1 per cent of net revenues to a workers' pension fund.[46]

In contrast to the labour situation, there were some wartime phenomena in Brazil that were completely beyond the company's ability to control or influence. In October 1918, the dreaded Spanish influenza appeared in Rio. As it had in Europe and North America, the flu exacted a gruesome toll in the densely populated cities of Rio and São Paulo. 'There has been, and is, hell to pay in this City,' Fred Huntress reported from Rio in late 1918:

The Grip [i.e., the flu] appeared and has paralyzed all business so the Government declared a three days holiday. Four thousand of our employees are ill, and practically all services stopped except supply of electric light and power.

The deaths of over four thousand [have occurred] in the city, and the cemeteries are full of dead with no one to bury them. Each night we have been carrying them in our large baggage cars piled in like dead cattle, no coffins and many stark naked. On arriving at the cemetery they are dumped upon the ground and left there sometimes for two days.

Many of our employees have died, one being Allen (Elmer Barton's assistant).
[Elmer Barton was the manager of the Rio tramway shops.] Antônio and Jorge Logi
both died and buried the same day ...

The Gas Company was badly hit, and with the shortage of coal there was every
likelihood of our going out of business any moment. Harrop, Carder, and others
have been working all day and night in the works trying to keep matters going.

It has been rather a trying time and is not yet over by any means. Out of a force of
650 telephone girls, we had only about 36 fit for service so the telephone service
evaporated into thin air. Today the epidemic is lessening without doubt, and some of
our people are commencing to return altho in a mighty weakened condition ...

Well, as I feel rather shaky and guess the Quinine and [word indistinguishable]
Powders are now getting in their fine work on me, I will start for Palmeiras and a
good sweat. Quinine may be all right, but 'enough is enough.'[47]

To combat the contagion, the company opened a dispensary at its Vila
Isabel office and dispatched its twelve staff doctors in company cars to
distribute drugs and minister to the sick throughout Rio. By the time the
epidemic abated, Alexander Mackenzie estimated that the flu had taken
25,000 lives in Rio and had cost the company $300,000 in lost revenues
and extra expenses.[48] There could, of course, be no price placed upon the
trauma and suffering endured by company employees and the Brazilian
population in general.

Cumulatively, then, the war subjected the company to an extended
period of uncertainty and challenge. It marked a sharp departure from
the profitable tranquillity that had characterized the first decade and a
half of its operations in São Paulo and Rio. Following immediately after
the slump of 1913, the war created an environment in which the problems
of exchange, supply, capital, and labour could mingle and fuse with
potentially devastating results. Coping with these challenges placed an
incredible strain upon company managers and called forth a unique
brand of managerial dexterity in Light managers. In an era of slow
oceanic travel and as-yet-imperfect global communications, the ability of
head office managers of multinational businesses to formulate appropriate policies for the varied economic circumstances in which their
enterprises operated was greatly impeded. The outbreak of war in
Europe only worsened an already difficult situation, especially because it
made transatlantic travel (an essential aspect of the routine of many
Brazilian Traction executives) both awkward and hazardous. It also

denied businesses the pre-war privilege of communicating in code. For those associated with the 'Pearson group,' the war thus represented a manifold increase in the difficulties of doing business in foreign lands. The débâcle of the Mexican companies involved investors on two continents and politicians in Mexico, Ottawa, Washington, and London. Similarly, the financial problems of Barcelona Traction were equally complex, involving lawyers, politicians, and financiers on both sides of the Atlantic. In both Mexico and Spain, the war abruptly severed the lines of communication between the Canadian-based companies and thousands of their European investors. European financiers like Alfred Loewenstein all abandoned their offices and fled across the Channel to wartime refuge in England.

Even where the war did not directly impinge upon the operations of its member companies, the 'Pearson group' experienced problems. Overambitious and ill-planned land development and irrigation projects in Texas, designed and promoted by Pearson, collapsed when would-be settlers balked at the prospect of buying parched stretches of land in the San Antônio district. In Canada, Pearson had joined forces with James Dunn and E.R. Wood to promote a new nickel company, the British American Nickel Corporation, which hoped to break into the tightly monopolized Canadian nickel industry. The implacable resistance of INCO and the reluctance of both the Canadian and the Imperial government to provide bounties for nickel smelted in Canada fatally diminished the prospects of the project. As a result of these trials and tribulations, Fred Pearson and his associates found themselves in a state of almost perpetual motion during the war.

By 1915, Pearson, Dunn, Wood, William Mackenzie, and Zebulon Lash were obliged to undertake financial, legal, and quasi-political missions that took them from their Toronto boardrooms to Ottawa, New York, London, Spain, and, occasionally, Central and South America. Pearson's trail through bankers' offices and politicians' waiting rooms on two continents was but the most prominent aspect of his frantic attempt to create makeshift financial and political expedients to prop up his sagging fortunes. Unfortunately, neither the politicians nor the bankers had much sympathy for Pearson's plight. Aware that the Mexican and Spanish power companies were already mired in financial problems, many must have suspected that the war would exact a fatal toll on the Pearson enterprises. Only the subsidiaries of Brazilian Traction with their steady, albeit reduced, wartime profits gave evidence that Pearson's star had not yet set. Yet even the São Paulo and Rio enterprises created worries. Concern over poor exchange, material shortages, and dividend policy were all reflected in the telegrams that Pearson hurriedly dispatched from some liner heading across the Atlantic or from his private railway car *en route* to San Antônio. 'Don't let anyone run away with the idea we are lying on a bed of roses here,' Fred Huntress later cautioned the Toronto office, 'with public, press and government departments howling their heads against our increased prices for lighting, power and gas due principally to the low exchange.'[49]

On 1 May 1915, Pearson completed another feverish round of business consultations in Toronto and New York and set sail from New York for England. As was his custom, he used the time afforded him by the sea voyage to study his business affairs and to plot his future course. On this trip, Pearson's attention was occupied by the plight of his Canadian nickel venture, an up-coming meeting with the bondholders of Barcelona Traction, and his obligation as president of Brazilian Traction to prepare that company's annual report. Pearson's work on these projects was tragically interrupted when his ship, the *Lusitania*, was torpedoed off the Irish coast by a German submarine on the afternoon of 7 May 1915. Fred Stark Pearson and his wife, Mabel, were both drowned. Pearson was only fifty-four years old. Two days later, when his body was hauled from the Irish Sea, a sodden, handwritten draft of Brazilian Traction's second annual report was found in his pocket. The president's report in the annual report that was subsequently published for 1914 was accredited to F.S. Pearson 'en route *S.S. Lusitania*, May, 1915.'

Pearson's death dealt a stunning blow to all those associated with the utility enterprises founded under the influence of his genius for electrical engineering. Pearson had overseen the construction of dams and tramway systems in São Paulo, Rio, Mexico City, and Barcelona and, no matter how serious the financial predicament they found themselves in by 1915, it was universally expected that Pearson's promotional talents would eventually restore every one of the 'group' to post-war prosperity. His loss on the *Lusitania* dashed this hope and threw many into despair. In the wake of the tragedy, Pearson's work was, of course, widely eulogized. 'His friends have to mourn this loss of a striking personality,' a prominent London stockbroker noted, 'and the world of hydro-electric activities is infinitely the poorer for his loss.'[50] The *General Electric Review* published a tribute to Pearson under the title 'The Paths of Progress,' honouring him as a 'great American engineer who has left behind him monuments which will testify for long years to come of his usefulness to mankind.'[51] Others paid homage in a more personal fashion. James Dunn took charge of the arrangements for return of the bodies of Mr and Mrs Pearson to the United States. Later, Alfred Loewenstein purchased the huge oak doors from Pearson's Great Barrington estate in Massachusetts and re-erected them after the war at his mansion in Brussels.

Tributes in the press and the desire of close friends to obtain mementoes of their association with the great engineer hardly disguised the fact that Pearson's death triggered widespread concern about the future of his Mexican, Brazilian, and Spanish enterprises. While the plight of the Mexican and Barcelona enterprises was common knowledge among the investing public, few could have suspected that Pearson himself was in desperate financial straits. On the eve of his untimely death, Pearson's salary from Brazilian Traction and its associated companies was $100,000, a princely sum, especially when one considers that there was no income tax levied in 1915.[52] Besides this huge cash income, Pearson was also in possession of a substantial amount of stock in the companies he had fostered. Incredibly, this immense wealth was until 1915 nothing more than a paper fortune. The reckless overspending on the Barcelona project and ruined state of the Mexican enterprises had forced Pearson to divert the bulk of his personal resources to a desperate attempt to resuscitate his failing ventures. By 1915, he had not only exceeded his own resources but was also indebted to the Canadian Bank of Commerce, the Bank of Scotland, and the Swiss Bank Corporation. Pearson was also in debt to brokerage firms, among them Dunn, Fischer and Co., and even to some of the investment firms, such as the Guarantee Insurance and Investment Company, that he himself had helped to create.

In the following months, the true extent of the financial shambles he had bequeathed to his executors became clear. Two months after his death, Pearson's son, Ward, desperately suggested that all creditors be asked to delay their claims for two years, an arrangement he felt would give sufficient time to allow a settlement 'satisfactory [to] all creditors.'[53] A year later, Alexander Mackenzie, to whom Pearson also owed money, bemoaned the fact that 'the estate is not only insolvent but there is absolutely nothing out of which my claim could be satisfied.'[54] As late as

1923, the Pearson estate was still judged to be 'insolvent.' Finally, in 1925, the executors of the estate took advantage of a provision in the Treaty of Versailles to sue the German government for reparation. Although the Mixed Claims Commission did award Pearson's heirs a total of $106,000, they dismissed any claim for a larger payment. 'The loss of Dr. Pearson's fortune did not result from his death,' the tribunal concluded. 'It was lost prior to his death due to revolution in Mexico, followed by the highly abnormal conditions throughout the world of finance, industry and commerce resulting from the World War. These conditions continued for at least three and one-half years after his death.'[55]

Despite their deep sorrow, Brazilian Traction's directors, headed by their chairman, Sir William Mackenzie, were faced with the pressing task of finding a new president. 'Just what effect his death will have upon the future of Brazilian and Barcelona remains to be seen,' commented the *Canadian Courier*, giving voice to the widespread concern that Pearson's death had occasioned in the financial community. 'Temporarily both companies will be affected, so far as the market price of their stock is concerned. Their future, however, will depend upon the finding of a successor who can command the confidence of the investing public.'[56] From the outset, any notion of maintaining unified control of the Brazilian, Spanish, and Mexican enterprises under a joint presidency was abandoned. Even though James Dunn in London characteristically urged the formation of yet another holding company to encompass the three principal members of the 'Pearson group,' the directors of Brazilian Traction were quick to realize that the Mexican and Spanish companies were too blemished to be put forward as suitable candidates for a union with their relatively prosperous Brazilian sister company. Any such amalgamation would have made Brazilian Traction vulnerable to a default or receivership in either of the other two companies, a possibility that seemed very real in 1915.

Accordingly, on 15 May 1915, a quorum of Brazilian Traction directors assembled in Toronto to select a new president. Before making their selection, William Mackenzie, Z.A. Lash, E.R. Wood, D.B. Hanna, and F.H. Phippen (chief legal counsel of the Canadian Northern and a newly elected director) expressed their sorrow at 'the irreparable loss suffered by the Company' when Pearson had drowned. The subsequent election of a new president provoked no debate and was unanimously approved.[57] In the minds of all those intimately associated with the affairs of Brazilian

Traction, there was absolutely no doubt that Alexander Mackenzie was the only man for the job. Although Mackenzie had resigned from the company in late 1912, he had gradually reassumed his duties in the intervening years and was, at the time of the late president's death, busy negotiating a telephone concession in Rio. Even before Mackenzie's name was placed before the board, the chairman, William Mackenzie, was applying considerable pressure on the man he wanted for the presidency. 'Under present position and conditions,' he cabled Alexander Mackenzie in Rio the day before the vote, 'Board consider your appointment [as] President would help everything to greater extent than any other person. It will not interfere with your staying there [Rio] so long as you consider [it] necessary. Wood, Lash and myself will do everything assist you every way ... We are satisfied your appointment will be in interest everybody concerned.'[58] Presented with such terms, Alexander Mackenzie had little option but to accept the offer of the company presidency. It was a post that he would not relinquish until 1928. Under Mackenzie's competent control, Brazilian Traction emerged as the fittest of the 'Pearson group.'

Alexander Mackenzie's greatest recommendation as a candidate for the Brazilian Traction presidency was his ability to work effectively within the Brazilian milieu. While Pearson had possessed a general understanding of Brazilian mores, Mackenzie was finely attuned to the temperament and intricacies of the country's social and political system. He knew exactly what the company could do in Brazil and precisely what it could not do. Mackenzie understood which constituents of the Brazilian body politic the company, as a foreign enterprise, could rely upon for support and which it would have to fend off because of their antipathy to foreign investment. Mackenzie's talents in this respect ensured that the operations of Brazilian Traction's subsidiaries were always supported, in the period of the Old Republic, by a solid popular consensus, thereby shielding the company's extensive investment in Brazil. Mackenzie was particularly adept at building a strong and lasting accommodation with Brazil's predominant political élites, especially those politicians from the hegemonic states of São Paulo and Minas Gerais who dominated the politics of the Old Republic. In this vital sense, Alexander Mackenzie was Brazilian Traction's greatest president.

During the years of his presidency, Mackenzie excelled in maintaining bonds of trust and co-operation between the company and those groups that relied upon and supported its existence in Brazil, principally

Brazilian liberal politicians, the company's own shareholders, the foreign diplomatic community, and the Brazilian commercial community. Mackenzie's positive relationship with many of Brazil's leading federal politicians was attributable to his ability to satisfy their desire to 'modernize' their nation. As the president of a large public-utility enterprise that had brought demonstrable advances to urban Brazil with its rapid and efficient tramway systems, Mackenzie had acquired a considerable reputation as a foreign technocrat. In the eyes of Brazilian statesmen like the Baron of Rio Branco and Rui Barbosa, Mackenzie's stature and the company's overall contribution since the turn of the century symbolized the route Brazil had to take to achieve economic maturity. The strong affinity of foreign business and members of the Brazilian national élite notwithstanding, one cannot overlook Mackenzie's position as one of Brazil's most affluent employers. Generous legal stipends, judiciously timed tokens of appreciation, and a special attentiveness to the importance of kinship in Brazilian business and politics all served to cement the relations of the foreign utility and the community it served.

In this fashion, the company tapped an important vein of Brazilian nationalism – the desire of the Brazilian upper class to emulate foreign models of economic development even at the cost of allowing foreign entrepreneurs to take a dominant role in controlling the course of this progression. In due course, this 'internationalist' approach to Brazil's economic development would breed reaction in more xenophobic circles.[59] The Light, in the meantime, provided an outstanding example of the ability of foreign investment to accelerate and diversify economic growth in Brazil. Mackenzie sensed this friendly disposition and deliberately cultivated it. When, for instance, in 1916 Lauro Müller, the Brazilian minister of foreign affairs, announced his intention of visiting Washington, Mackenzie prevailed on him to continue his journey northward to Canada. Mackenzie not only wished to expose the Brazilian politician to Canada's own industrial heartland but also hoped to provide a gentle nudge in the direction of the Allied cause to the still-neutral Brazilian government. While in Toronto, Müller toured the Canadian National Exhibition and made several speeches in which he declared that Brazil would willingly accept further Canadian capital. As a remembrance of the minister's visit, Mackenzie presented Müller's son with a McLaughlin Buick runabout, which was duly shipped all the way to Rio.[60]

Mackenzie's *persona grata* status with leading Brazilian politicians was also evident in his effort to induce Brazil to forsake neutrality and take up arms against Germany. Obviously, the company (and innumerable other foreign investors) stood to lose everything if Brazil, with its sizeable German ethnic minority, chose to fight against the Allies. Mackenzie, however, was always optimistic that Brazil would take a role that would benefit the Allied cause. 'The attitude of Brazil towards the Allies, from a sentimental point of view is exceedingly satisfactory,' he reported in April 1917, 'and I have a feeling that in the long run it will be of great benefit to Brazil, especially as regards its dealings with Great Britain and the United States. It is [in] marked contrast to the attitude of some of the other Latin American countries.'[61] Mackenzie's precise role in influencing the Brazilian declaration of war on Germany in October 1917 remains shrouded in mystery. It is clear that he did much to chivvy Brazilian politicians into abandoning their neutrality, especially after German submarines began attacking Brazilian shipping in mid-1917. In 1919, Mackenzie was knighted in recognition of these services.[62] Even before the war, Mackenzie had been remarkably close to the British, American, and French diplomats in Rio, and British diplomatic dispatches frequently indicated that His Majesty's ambassador or consul had deferred to the advice of 'Mr. Mackenzie, the local manager of the Light and Power Company.'[63] As the representative of a Canadian company, Mackenzie had by 1917 become one of the most influential members of the British community in Rio.

Mackenzie's success as a representative of foreign capital in Brazil was also rooted in his ability to relate the problems of investing in the Brazilian economy to the thousands of Canadians, Americans, Englishmen, Belgians, and other shareholders who had staked their savings on a distant and unfamiliar land. The Toronto offices of Brazilian Traction received constant inquiries from shareholders who were perplexed and anxious over the status of their investment. 'I do not of course expect you to inform me of any private details,' one English shareholder wrote in 1914, 'but one can gather so little of the *real* state of Brazil in our press that I am forced to venture to write you for your advice.'[64] During his presidency, Alexander Mackenzie worked to diminish the anxieties of shareholders by providing them with forthright explanations of their company's fortunes, thereby familiarizing them with the problems of Brazilian exchange, concession negotiations, and dividend policy without compromising the position of the company's managers in Brazil. In 1918, for instance, Company Secretary J.M. Smith wrote to inform Mackenzie in

Rio that the board members in Toronto were 'all of one mind that no person here could fill your place or have the effect upon the gathering [annual meeting] that your presence would have, especially as questions may be put to the chair which could be easily answered by yourself but might be awkward for others to answer.'[65]

It was significant that Mackenzie chose to conduct his administration of the company from Rio and not from Toronto. The secret of his adroit handling of the problems confronting the Rio and São Paulo companies lay in the fact that he was completely attuned to the environment in which they operated and was so situated that he could react immediately to any problem without the cumbersome procedure of communicating its nature to Toronto and awaiting instructions. Mackenzie's prowess in this respect meant that, in addition to his Brazilian Traction duties, he undertook to act as the local representative of other foreign enterprises as varied as the Brazil Central Railway, the Bahia Tramway, Light and Power, the Port of Pará Company, and the Madeira Mamore Railway, all of which were progeny of the syndicates of Percival Farquhar and William Mackenzie.

Mackenzie's acceptance in Brazilian circles extended beyond the immediate sphere of North American investment. In 1916, for instance, a group of 'influential Brazilian merchants' sought Mackenzie's assistance to represent their interests before the British Foreign Office in a commercial dispute with an English importing firm.[66] More importantly, Mackenzie assisted the Brazilian federal government in its attempts to float a large post-war loan on the New York market. Throughout 1920–1, he worked in conjunction with William A. Read and Co. in New York to establish Brazil as a trustworthy borrower in the eyes of American lenders.[67] While Mackenzie may have undertaken these causes out of a sense of altruism, there can be no doubt that his participation in issues that did not directly affect the company ultimately redounded to its credit. Either as the representative of the foreign community in Brazil or as the president of Brazilian Traction, Sir Alexander acquired towering stature in Rio and São Paulo. This stature – backed, undeniably, by the company's financial resources – provided the company with its greatest safeguard as a foreign enterprise in Brazil. No other Canadian, it can be claimed without exaggeration, has ever occupied so prominent a place in the minds and, to a great degree, in the hearts of Brazilians. Today, streets, schools, and apartment buildings in Rio and São Paulo bear his name and testify to an age in which the marriage of foreign capital and Brazilian business opportunities attracted little criticism and much encouragement.

When Sir Alexander resigned the Brazilian Traction presidency and departed from Brazil for the last time in 1928, the Brazilian press paid tribute to this record of mutually beneficial co-operation. In an editorial entitled 'Alexander Mackenzie: His Collaboration towards the Progress of Our Country,' the Rio paper *O país* saluted the Canadian businessman. 'This foreigner,' the editor emphasized fulsomely, 'having brought to us millions of dollars which he has invested in the work of organizing, in a progressive manner, some of the industries which have a greater influence in the aspect of modern life, has adopted the highest and noblest form of naturalization – a spiritual naturalization.'[68] *A noite* similarly concluded that Mackenzie's work in Brazil provided a testament to 'what a strong, calm man can accomplish in a few years.'[69] It was left to Assis Chateaubriand, Brazil's greatest newspaper publisher and a close personal friend of Mackenzie, to pay the highest tribute to the departing Canadian. Mackenzie and his Canadian friends, Chateaubriand wrote in *O jornal,* had supplied the 'organizing and technical capacity' that had served to transform Rio from 'a colonial village' into 'a great capital,' the population of which 'has a mentality capable of understanding the great lines of modern industrial life.' 'Others may love Brazil more effusively,' Chateaubriand generously concluded of Mackenzie, 'but no one strived for and served this land more profoundly and with more constant dedication.'[70] In later years, especially after the fall of the Old Republic in 1930, others would portray the contribution of Brazilian Traction to Brazil in less flattering terms; but in the first three decades of the century, it was evident that the company had found the right formula to ensure its survival.

CHAPTER SEVEN

Drought, Expansion, and the End of the Old Republic: The 1920s

Peace stirred great hopefulness in Brazil, as it did in all the victorious Allies. Brazil emerged from war with a buoyant economy – characterized by improved exchange, a healthy balance of trade, and signs that local industry had grown as a result of the wartime constriction of imports. The presence of Brazilian diplomats at Versailles reinforced the belief that Brazil was poised on the verge of great things, both economic and political. As if to symbolize this expectation, Brazilians elected Rodrigues Alves as their president. Many must have harked back to the days of prosperity that coincided with Alves's previous term as federal president (1902–6) and would in 1919 have looked to Alves to open the door to a new future for Brazil. For both Alves and Brazil, this was not to be.

In January 1919, Rodrigues Alves died at his home in Rio before he could take the presidential oath of office. He was succeeded by Epitácio Pessoa, a seasoned politician from the northern state of Paraíba. Pessoa's presidency and that of Artur Bernardes, his successor from 1922 to 1926, were marked by the friction that precipitated the disintegration of the Old Republic in 1930. In economic terms, peace ushered in an extended period of uncertainty, as the favourable exchange rates and trade balance of 1919 evaporated almost overnight and were replaced by a steadily declining exchange rate and serious balance-of-payment problems. Instead of blossoming into economic self-sufficiency, Brazil was confronted with what Celso Furtado has described as its 'propensity to external disequilibrium,' that is, the vulnerability of its economy to the fluctuating fortunes of its import and export sectors. The old monocultural coffee-based economy reasserted its dominance, so much so that by the end of

the decade Brazil's entire economic prosperity would again be precarious-
ly balanced on the fortunes of coffee.[1] Despite coffee's resurgence, the
Brazilian economy did make progress in building its industrial capacity
during the 1920s.

Throughout all this, Brazilian Traction contended with the mixed
consequences of Brazil's economic woes. On the one hand, the depressed
value of the milréis deflated the dollar value of its earnings, fed inflation,
and forced up the cost of living. On the other hand, low exchange
encouraged local industries to expand production through import
substitution, thereby stimulating demand for electric power. The situation thus had the paradoxical effect of pressuring Brazilian Traction to
embark on a wholesale expansion of its power facilities at a time when
the conditions of capital procurement and remittance were far from
auspicious. 'It is strange indeed,' a Canadian trade commissioner in Rio
later remarked, 'that a country may be internally prosperous and
externally poor, but on the face of it, this would appear to be the case in
Brazil.'[2] These were nervous years for Brazil's foreign investors and
politicians alike.

In January 1920, the milréis enjoyed a high exchange value of $17\frac{1}{16}$d.
This was its apogee for the decade. By 1921, it had slipped to an average
of $8\frac{3}{8}$d. and it subsequently sank as low as 5d. by the middle of the
decade.[3] Similarly, the country's trade surplus of £52 million in 1919
became a deficit of £17.4 million by the following year.[4] The price of
coffee, Brazil's primary earner of hard currency, declined in the early
1920s but recovered steadily through the rest of the decade. Despite a
mid-1920s slump, the Brazilian economy in general began to recuperate
and during the remaining years of the decade grew steadily but not
spectacularly.

From 1922 onwards, however, the federal government was confronted
with perennial budget deficits and a growing burden of foreign debts.
The Bernardes government (1922–6) exacerbated this situation by
pursuing policies of easy credit and by borrowing heavily abroad to
finance coffee 'valorization' (that is, the withdrawal of surplus coffee from
the market in order to maintain a higher international price for the
commodity). By 1923, foreign bankers began to reflect alarm at the
perilousness of Brazil's national finances. In early 1924, a commission of
English bankers submitted a report to the Brazilian president prescribing
a strong dose of fiscal conservatism based on balanced budgets, drastic

reductions in expenditure, prompt payment of foreign debts, and the institution of a more professional civil service. 'In conclusion,' they urged President Bernardes, 'we have to point out that our great anxiety with regard to the future of Brazil lies in the lack of continuity between Government and Government.'[5] The efforts of Bernardes's finance minister, Anibal Freire, to implement such policies were largely negated by the onset of a depression in the years 1924–6.

During the presidency of Washington Luís (1926–30), another attempt was made to impose order upon Brazil's contorted monetary system. Although Luís embarked upon a vigorous program of road building, he also sought to balance the federal budget and to stabilize the milréis. At the same time, the Luís government abrogated the federal government's role in the coffee 'valorization' process, thereby allowing São Paulo state to continue to indulge its coffee-growing economy to the hilt. Between 1925 and 1929, São Paulo coffee production grew almost 100 per cent, but only about two-thirds of the crop ever found its way onto the world market in any one year. Such saturation of the world coffee supply made Brazil ever more dependent upon coffee and, as Celso Furtado has noted, was simply 'a process of postponing the solution to a problem which tended to become more and more serious.'[6] The instability of the Brazilian economy did not go unnoticed by foreign observers, including the Canadian trade commissioner. 'The period from January to August,' he wrote of 1927, 'was probably one of the most depressing in Brazilian history. This depression was really the continuance of the reaction which followed the overproduction, overtrading and extended credit which ruled in 1923 and 1924.'[7] Brazil was rapidly acquiring a reputation for a 'boom-and-bust' economy.

The persistence of a weak milréis plagued Brazilian Traction throughout the decade. In November 1920, Alexander Mackenzie reported that the disastrous drop in exchange was the 'one black spot, apart from the Gas Companies' on the company's horizon. 'The condition of exchange and its uncertainties obviously removes from our minds any immediate concern about a dividend and I assume that our policy will be to sit as tight as possible, spending as little as possible and conserving as much as possible any surplus earnings.'[8] The primary effect of falling exchange was to increase costs and therefore reduce the amount of remittances. Poor exchange also meant that the milréis was to a large degree a non-convertible currency. Management therefore had the unenviable task of explaining to shareholders that although business in Brazil was generating handsome milréis earnings, the benefit of these earnings could not be fully passed on to investors in the form of dividends.

At the 1921 annual meeting, Vice-president Miller Lash told the shareholders that while business in Brazil was 'excellent,' the company's earnings when converted into dollars 'were little more than sufficient to meet the bond interest, sinking funds and preference dividend.'[9] The financial squeeze on the company was exacerbated by its inability to obtain outside capital on account of the high cost of borrowing. The idea of placing a Brazilian Traction bond issue on the New York market was abandoned in early 1922 when E.R. Wood advised that the bonds would add $500,000 annually to fixed charges.[10] Brazilian Traction was thus left with little alternative but to wait out the period of poor exchange and hope for the return of a stronger milréis. Although sufficient remittances were obtained in 1922 to permit the resumption of dividends, exchange remained low throughout the rest of the decade and, contrary to the allegations of its critics in Brazil, Brazilian Traction faced lean dollar profits throughout these years.

Sir Alexander Mackenzie seldom missed an opportunity to urge Brazilian politicians to pursue policies that would lead to higher exchange. The implications of low exchange extended beyond the simple matter of remittance. In 1926, the company comptroller calculated that Brazilian Traction had invested about $200 million in Brazil at an average exchange of $13\frac{9}{64}$d.[11] If exchange prevailed permanently at its mid-1920s level of about 6d., the whole Canadian investment in Brazil would be threatened by a gross deflation. It is easy to understand why Mackenzie fulminated against the low-exchange policies of the Washington Luís government. 'Monetary reform,' he complained to Toronto in 1926, 'that is what it is called. It ought to be sabotage or hara-kiri.'[12]

Low exchange also pushed up the costs of operations in Brazil and fuelled inflation. As costs climbed and the value of the milréis shrank, rates that were awarded under the terms of turn-of-the-century concessions bore increasingly little relation to the real cost of operating utility services. 'The President recognized that we are hurt pretty badly,' Mackenzie reported after a meeting with Washington Luís, 'but says he must concern himself with the good of the greatest number! He promises, however, that we shall receive some compensation and that he will help us in our fight to get better rates on the tramways and other things.'[13]

Mackenzie candidly added that he was not hopeful that action would be forthcoming in the near future from the politicians. The rate problem, like exchange, thus had an important political dimension and soon established itself as an ongoing problem for Brazilian Traction. As the years wore on, Alexander Mackenzie came to display a certain fatalism about the whole exchange problem. 'It might be safer to remember Sir Alexander Mackenzie's famous remark relative to exchange conditions,' a manager in Rio once remarked, 'and assume that as everything points to disaster, we can expect real prosperity in the near future.'[14]

The exchange situation was a two-edged sword. While low exchange severely eroded 'hard' currency earnings, it did much to stimulate industry within Brazil and thereby intensified demand for tramway and power services. 'The commercial position is really better than would appear from the low rate of exchange,' the 1922 annual report informed shareholders. 'Local industries which have been stimulated by low exchange and the consequent reduction in imports are generally prospering. This applies especially to the cotton mills, many of which are without stocks and are working overtime to fill orders.' Despite a temporary easing in the demand for power in 1924–5, the decade was marked by a steady advance in power sales. From 379,156,343 kilowatt hours sold in 1921, total power sales in Rio and São Paulo more than doubled to 816,557,897 kilowatt hours in 1929.[15]

Throughout the 1920s, then, Brazilian Traction was caught in the pincer movement of poor exchange and expanding power consumption. It was an unenviable predicament: not to expand the company's ability to meet demand would have thrown its concessions into political jeopardy and provided an opening for prospective competitors. Conversely, wholesale expansion of Rio and São Paulo power facilities would cost dearly at a time when external capital was scarce. In fact, Brazilian Traction had little choice but to expand. At all costs, the hold that the Rio and São Paulo companies had established over their markets could not be jeopardized, especially at a time when new customers were beginning to appear. Among the most promising of these potential consumers were Brazil's railways, notably the Central and the Paulista, which were electrifying their lines.[16] To fail to satisfy these users would have been tantamount to an open invitation to rival power companies (perhaps the Guinles) to penetrate the Light concession area.

The necessity of expanding generating capacity was given added impetus by a severe drought in the São Paulo region that began in 1923 and worsened throughout 1923–4. The São Paulo drought greatly reduced the flow of the Tietê River, thereby bringing about a disastrous depletion of the São Paulo company's reservoirs at Santo Amaro and Parnaíba. By March 1925, Miller Lash reported that 'this drought with all its consequences is the most serious thing that has happened to us in Brazil for a good many years.'[17] The drought was unprecedented in São Paulo's history. Not until it had all but emptied the reservoirs and brought about a 50 per cent reduction in power output did the company reluctantly introduce power rationing in the São Paulo region for the first time. In desperation, a steam-generating plant was disassembled and moved from Rio to São Paulo, where it was hurriedly re-erected to alleviate the acute power shortage.

The combined impact of drought and the relentless growth of the Rio–São Paulo power market pushed the Light to the verge of a massive expansion of its generating capacity, an expansion that would increase capacity from 125,400 kilowatts in 1921 to 318,452 kilowatts by 1929. It would also result in the construction of one of the world's largest and most innovative power-stations. While the problem confronting the company was easily defined by 1923–4, the response was not. Since the first decade of the century, neither the Rio nor the São Paulo company had undertaken a major expansion of its generating facilities. They had consequently lost the ability to plan and execute large-scale hydro-construction projects. Hugh Cooper and C.H. Kearny, the American engineers who had supervised the construction at Parnaíba and Lajes, had long since left the company's employ. For years, the Light had drawn upon the stellar talents of F.S. Pearson, who, although not a hydro engineer by training, possessed a unique ability to envisage daring power-generating schemes. Pearson's loss on the *Lusitania* had deprived Brazilian Traction of its guiding star. By the early 1920s, it was evident that a second Pearson would have to be found.

There was certainly no departure from tradition when Asa White Kenney Billings, an American hydroelectric engineer, was hired in 1922 to plan and supervise the first major expansion of the power system. Born in Omaha, Nebraska, in 1876, Billings was destined to perpetuate the pattern, initiated by Cooper and Pearson, of American engineers' laying the foundations of Brazil's hydroelectric industry. Billings's career as an engineer began at the age of eleven when, working part-time after school, he wiped grease from the dynamos of the local utility company in Omaha. Later, after graduating from Harvard in 1897, Billings acquired experience with the Pittsburgh Consolidated Traction Company and the Havana Electric Railway Company. From an early date, he displayed a special talent for the efficient supervision of electrical services and for the innovative use of reinforced concrete in dam construction, talents that brought him to the attention of Pearson, who hired Billings in 1911 as an assistant. In the years preceding the First World War, Billings designed and built two precedent-setting hydro dams for the Pearson organization, one at Medina, Texas, and the other at Talarn, Spain. Both dams employed a new, high-density type of cement that Billings himself had perfected. After a wartime stint with the US Navy, during which he constructed airfields in France, Billings established himself as a consultant in New York. The highlight of this period in Billings's career was the completion of the huge 102-metre-high Camarasa dam in Spain. While Billings was working for the Mexican company in 1921, R.C. Brown, a vice-president with both the Mexican and the Brazilian companies, suggested that Billings be dispatched to investigate the power situation in Brazil.[18] The Brazilian Traction board accordingly commissioned Billings first to undertake 'a careful study' of the Lajes power plant with an eye to expanding its capacity and, secondly, to supervise construction of a new hydroelectric station on the Paraíba River, to the north of Rio near the town of Antônio Carlos.[19]

Billings's six-week inspection of the power situation in the Rio and São Paulo regions confirmed Toronto's worst fears. Brazilian Traction was dangerously near the limit of its generating capacity. 'The growth of load, however, is believed to be fundamentally sound,' Billings reported, and 'the additional production is required for a widely diversified load. The growth of the city is not abnormal and the business is not dependent on any one industry or class of business.' It was essential to expand capacity. If the company became unable to supply all of Rio and São Paulo's power needs, it would 'lose its present control of the market and prestige, and severe or perhaps ruinous competition will be brought in, with government encouragement.'[20] To meet the challenge, Billings proposed a two-fold program. In the first place, the power crisis could be temporarily averted by stopgap solutions, ranging from the installation of additional units at Lajes and Sorocaba to the judicious use of steam-generating plants to tide the system over its annual dry-season shortages. The key solution put forward by Billings was a proposal to proceed immediately with the construction of the plant on the Paraíba River outside Rio. The Paraíba plant would not only alleviate the pressure on the Rio power system, but would also allow the Light to block any potential competitors and to secure several railway-electrification contracts that, Billings stressed, were important 'politically' if not commercially. Secondly, Billings proposed that an intensive investigation of undeveloped water-power sites in the Rio-São Paulo area be immediately undertaken. This survey, Billings speculated, would open the way to the development of another plant 'to work in conjunction with the Parnaíba and Sorocaba' plants already serving São Paulo.

The stopgap measures outlined by Billings were eagerly ratified by the board, despite the obvious scarcity of capital. A fourth unit, generating 20,100 kw, was ordered for the Sorocaba plant, and engineering studies were initiated to assess the feasibility of heightening the Lajes dam so as to boost its reservoir. A decisive step was taken in March 1922, when the board approved Billings's scheme to develop the Paraíba site. The Antônio Carlos 'water power' or, as it soon became known, the Ilha dos Pombos (Pigeon Island) location, had long been known to Rio Company engineers. Described as 'one of the wildest torrents in South America,'[21] Ilha dos Pombos had earlier been dismissed as incapable of development because of its furious flow and its distance (about 150 kilometres) from the Rio market. Advances in the technology of power transmission and Billings's bold scheme for damming the river allowed the Light to revise its opinion. Given the fast and steady flow of the Paraíba, Billings concluded that the new power plant did not need a reservoir, but could sustain a 'head' of about thirty-five metres by use of concrete 'sector gates' that could be lowered across the river, thereby diverting the swift flow of the river into a power channel leading to the generating station. This economical arrangement would allow two 28,000-kw units to be installed in the shortest possible time at the relatively reasonable cost of $4,634,000.[22] Ilha dos Pombos was to be a classic example of a 'run-of-the-river' station. It was to be used to carry the base load of Rio's power needs during the rainy season, thereby allowing the Lajes complex to carry a reduced load and fully replenish its reservoirs before the return of the dry season.

The Ilha dos Pombos project was designed and implemented with astonishing rapidity. The concessions for its development were finalized and put under the control of the Brazilian Hydro-Electric Company, a new subsidiary incorporated under a federal Canadian charter in February 1922. Construction began in June 1922 and was complete by late 1924. In the course of construction, Billings oversaw the complex task of assembling generating equipment from Switzerland and the United States, cement from Sweden, and flood gates from England, all of which had to be hauled into a site that had hitherto been virtually inaccessible. The triumph of Ilha dos Pombos lay not in the brilliance of its engineering, although Billings's concrete 'sector gates' were the largest yet seen in the world, but in the speed of its execution.

Ilha brought immediate relief to the power situation in Rio, but it did nothing to alleviate the acute shortage in drought-plagued São Paulo. When Billings turned his attention to the São Paulo region, he was heartened by the discovery that for years Sir Alexander had been pursuing a policy of acquiring any promising sites within feasible power-transmission distance of the city. In surveying and securing these concessions, Mackenzie had been greatly aided by a free-lance American geologist, F.S. Hyde, who had painstakingly made his way on horseback through all the river valleys in São Paulo state in search of promising hydroelectric sites. After reviewing Hyde's surveys, Billings came to two quick decisions. Since the drought was now reducing power output to such a point that streetcar service had to be curtailed, Billings concluded that a cheap but efficient power plant should be brought into service as quickly as possible to augment the flagging output of the Parnaíba station. Secondly, Billings sensed that a bigger, more definitive solution was needed to alleviate São Paulo's shortage and to enable the Light to re-establish its traditional power surplus. What was needed, Billings urged the Toronto head office, was a thorough examination of all the water-power locations in the São Paulo region by a trained geologist, upon whose findings the company could base its long-range plans. Accordingly, the company once again secured the services of F.S. Hyde to undertake this all-important survey.

As he had in Rio, Billings attained his first objective in São Paulo with remarkable speed. A site on the Tietê River at Rasgão, sixteen kilometres downstream from the Parnaíba plant, was selected for another 'run-of-the-river' plant. The Rasgão scheme immediately appealed to Billings because of its simplicity, speed of construction, and overall cheapness. 'While hauling to Rasgão will be an obstacle,' he noted, 'particularly during the rainy season, we believe rapid construction is easier here than elsewhere.'[23] Construction of the Rasgão dam and powerhouse was begun in October 1924 and its progress was watched with considerable anxiety. By March 1925, Billings reported that with the Sorocaba reservoir empty and the Santo Amaro reservoir only an eighth full, the drought in São Paulo had reached 'acute' proportions. Responding to this, work at Rasgão proceeded at a breakneck pace, with the result that the first generator went into operation on 5 September 1925, less than eleven months after work had begun. So desperate was the need for power in São Paulo that the unit was pressed into service before the walls of the powerhouse had even been erected and at a time when the concrete facing on the power canal extended less than a metre above the level of the water. When the second unit at Rasgão became operational later in the year, the São Paulo company had an additional 23,800 kw with which to serve its market,[24] just in time to avert the severe consequences of a systemic collapse of power production. The return of a normal rainy season in late 1925 allowed nature to lend a helping hand, with the result that the Santo Amaro and Sorocaba reservoirs were soon nearing their normal reserves.

The completion of Rasgão and the end of the drought did little to diminish the importance of Hyde's assignment. The steady growth in São Paulo's appetite for electricity provided a strong indication that the Light would have to augment its power supply on a continuous basis if it was to protect its market. By 1924, it was apparent that relatively small plants like Parnaíba, Sorocaba, and Rasgão did not hold the key to an assured future. What the company needed was a large, 'high-head' power installation that would provide a steady supply of power, thereby ending dependence on 'low-head,' 'run-of-the-river' plants that had already revealed their susceptibility to drought conditions. The problem lay in Brazil's peculiar physiography. Practically all of the water-power concessions and power plants the company owned in Brazil were situated on rivers that flowed over a gradual gradient into the interior of Brazil, where they eventually became part of the enormous Paraná-Paraguay river-basin system. Brazil's interior region could be likened to an enormous, shallow basin, into the centre of which flowed an immense network of rivers that all eventually converged into massive river systems such as the Amazon, São Francisco, and Paraná. The rim of this gigantic basin was formed by the Serra do Mar, the rugged and unbroken mountain range that rose sharply from the coastal plain and tilted the whole land mass of Brazil inwards. Consequently, Brazil's southern rivers, such as the Tietê on which São Paulo stood, frequently flowed away from the coast. 'The slope of these rivers,' Billings once remarked, 'is almost imperceptible. The valleys are shallow and broad and the country resembles rolling prairie. The result is that the heavy rains which fall on this plateau, even a few miles from the precipitous slope of the Serra do Mar, flow in sluggish rivers southwest.'[25] The large waterfalls that did exist in this sloping nexus of rivers, such as the enormous Iguaçu falls near the Paraguayan border, were too far from Brazil's urban centres to be economically exploited with the technology of the late 1920s.

By concentrating on the sluggish rivers flowing into Brazil's interior, the engineers of the São Paulo company had overlooked the tremendous opportunity for hydro-power development that lay at the crest of the Serra do Mar. Immediately inland from Santos, São Paulo's port city, the Serra do Mar rose to an altitude of just over 700 metres. Between the bottom and the top of this steep escarpment there was a dramatic difference in rainfall. On the hot, coastal plain at the foot of the Serra, rainfall averaged between 1.8 and 2.4 metres annually, but as the hot, humid air was cooled on its ascent up the Serra, rainfall reached as much as 6.8 metres annually, before tapering off as the less laden clouds moved inland. This remarkable rainfall pattern meant that the narrow strip of land along the crest of the Serra received one of the highest rainfalls in the world. This constant inundation so close to São Paulo offered hydroelectric engineers an unparalleled amount of water with which to generate power. 'The combination of heavy average rainfall, high head, favorable topography, sparse settlement of reservoir sites, and proximity to a large and rapidly growing market and to the sea, in this part of Brazil,' Billings later commented, 'is rare.'[26]

Unfortunately, the topography of the Serra offered little means of accumulating this immense rainfall. Either the rain water poured back down the slope of the Serra in a network of flash streams, or it trickled inland as runoff, eventually percolating into the river systems of the inland basin. The key to tapping the hydroelectric potential of the Serra do Mar lay in devising some means of trapping its bountiful rainfall, storing it, and redirecting its flow over the lip of the escarpment. A logical extension of this scheme would entail supplementing the stored rain water with water diverted from the Tietê River. The combination of stored rain water and redirected river water could, by means of pumping, be used to heighten the reservoir to exactly the level of the crest of the coastal range. From that point, gravity would take over.

The notion of turning the Serra do Mar, a long-standing obstacle to São Paulo's commercial growth, to its industrial advantage was brilliantly simple and straightforward; yet for decades it had been overlooked by survey engineers, who remained mesmerized by the hope of harnessing the power of the rivers flowing inland throughout São Paulo. 'At any time during twenty years,' Billings later remarked with incredulity, 'this plan could have been easily determined from the topographical maps of this region of which thousands of copies were sold to the public.'[27] Not until 1923 did F.S. Hyde make the discovery that had been eluding his fellow hydrologists for so long. One of the few water concessions Alexander Mackenzie had not been able to secure for the Light was that for the Capivary River, which was reputed to be 'the only river that came over the top of the *Serra* and had any basin at all on the plateau.'[28] Before Hyde began his survey work, Walter Charnley, a São Paulo company geologist, conducted a preliminary study of the Capivary site and concluded that, while the river was a small one, it could be augmented with waters from the Rio Grande River to create 'an extremely large storage reservoir.'[29] In 1923, Hyde read Charnley's conclusions and confided to Billings that he believed it was 'possible to improve on his [Charnley's] plan,' especially 'after seeing the *Serra do Mar* country and the wet conditions prevailing there in this dry season.' Since the Capivary concession was ceded to the Sorocaba Railway, Hyde determined to find another suitable location somewhere in the vicinity of Santos. What was needed was a low gap on the rim of the Serra that could act as a natural spillway for whatever water could be stored behind it on the plateau adjacent to São Paulo. It was not to be an easy quest.

By the time Hyde began his search, it was generally understood that the São Paulo company was about to embark upon a new hydroelectric project. Since the site that Hyde would ultimately select was bound to be outside the company's existing concessions, great care had to be taken not to alert would-be competitors or outright speculators as to the Light's intentions. The activities of Hyde and his survey crew were therefore deliberately veiled in secrecy. Hyde and his men were equipped with a small fleet of Model-T trucks laden with butterfly nets, cases of sample bottles, and other botanical paraphernalia in order to convince curious onlookers that they were in fact an American botanical expedition rather than the Light's latest attempt to locate a promising concession. This ruse was almost compromised when one of the trucks accidentally ran over a local farmer. A quick out-of-court settlement arranged by Alexander Mackenzie averted newspaper coverage of the incident, which would otherwise have revealed the company's intentions. Hyde conscientiously maintained complete secrecy about his work, keeping only a single pencil sketch of his elevations and calculations, restricting all written communications to generalities, and never mentioning specific locations. Along with the need for secrecy, Hyde had also to contend with the dense, snake-infested vegetation of the Serra and the unceasing rain and humidity.

In May 1923, Hyde found what he had been looking for. About 1,000 metres west of the main Santos–São Paulo road, he discovered the Rio das Pedras, a small rivulet that tumbled over the edge of the Serra at the 728-metre contour. The notch cut into the Serra by the Rio das Pedras offered a location for a forebay from which water could be fed into penstocks that would carry it down the escarpment to a powerhouse far below. The plateau land behind the small river offered ample room for an extensive reservoir. Venturing a rough guess, Hyde estimated that the Pedras project might develop '196,000 continuous hp.'[30] In November, Hyde took the company treasurer, A.W. Adams, who was visiting São Paulo, to inspect the Pedras gap. Adams reported that Hyde was still not 'absolutely certain' about the site. 'The *mato* is very dense in the section, and considerable cutting is necessary when you get off the trails.'[31] By the end of 1924, Hyde had hacked his way through sufficient undergrowth to be able to present Billings with a definite plan of action.

The first phase of Hyde's plan centred on the creation of giant reservoirs that would all eventually feed into the Pedras gap. Water for this system would be obtained by using a series of dikes and dams to capture the run-off along the crest of the Serra. These waters would be directed by tunnels and canals into the Rio Grande reservoir (at an elevation of 746 metres), which in turn would empty into the smaller Pedras reservoir (at 728 metres). The Pedras reservoir, acting rather like a cork in a bottle, would feed water into penstocks leading to the power plant below (at sea level). Billings and Hyde carried the plan one ingenious step further by proposing to divert water from the inland-flowing Tietê River into the Santo Amaro reservoir outside São Paulo. Such diversion would entail 'rectifying' or straightening the meandering

Pinheiros River, which led off the Tietê, and then installing a pumping station to lift stored water from the Santo Amaro reservoir to the Rio Grande reservoir. Power for the pumping station could be obtained at 'off-peak' hours from the same power plant the elaborate reservoir system was intended to serve. The final phase of the project involved the construction of two penstocks down the face of the Serra to a powerhouse containing two 47,700-kw generators. It was the small village of Cubatão where the powerhouse was to be located that gave the whole project its name: the Serra do Cubatão development. On 9 April 1925, the Brazilian Traction board authorized Billings to begin letting contracts 'with the various suppliers for the necessary equipment for the new *Serra* development.' Two months later, Billings reported that the new plant would cost an estimated $8,169,080.[32]

Once the board had made its decision, it remained for Alexander Mackenzie to secure the appropriate concessionary rights to make the whole project legally tenable. Mackenzie had a strong case to put before the politicians. In the first place, the Cubatão scheme offered the obvious solution to the acute power shortage that had gripped São Paulo. Secondly, by drawing off flood water from the Tietê, the scheme offered the city protection against the periodic flooding that did immense damage to the city. Thirdly, the Rio Grande reservoir system was held out as a means of promoting inland navigation between Santos and São Paulo. (Although the idea was somewhat far-fetched, a cog railway was proposed by Billings to carry the barges up the side of the Serra.) Lastly, the Cubatão scheme had the practical advantage of being located near the port of Santos; therefore it was less prone to shipping delays and the high costs of transporting generating equipment deep inland.

In March 1925 the federal minister of transport and public works, Dr Francisco Sá, approved the commencement of construction. Mackenzie's case before the state government of São Paulo, which governed the riparian aspects of the project, was immensely aided by the fact that Carlos de Campos, once the São Paulo company's lawyer, had assumed the state presidency in 1924. 'The President of the State will do everything that he reasonably can to help us,' Mackenzie informed Toronto, 'and, while we shall have a good many fences to cross, I do not think that any of them will be insurmountable.'[33] Stubborn opposition to the Cubatão project came from an Italian syndicate, S.A. Brasital, which argued that the diversion of the Tietê waters would deprive its planned development of the Itu falls of sufficient water to generate power. In November, Mackenzie took a delegation of state politicians to the Cubatão site in an effort to impress upon them the project's obvious potential.[34] After a 'stiff fight' in the state congress, Mackenzie obtained approval for the new development in December 1925. In return for the right to expropriate, a thirty-year exemption from state taxes, and the right to acquire state lands at a set price, the Light was obliged to re-establish the normal flow of any rivers it disrupted and repair any roads it dissected in the course of its work.[35]

From its inception, the new power project on the Serra do Mar was viewed by *paulistas* as an enormous step forward in their drive for industrialization. From the Light's point of view, the Cubatão project offered enticing possibilities. 'This is an extremely valuable concession which, besides being perpetual and free from any onus,' Mackenzie proudly noted, 'put us in excellent position to conveniently meet any possible competition in São Paulo.'[36]

The results of Hyde's survey and Mackenzie's success in the corridors of power opened the way for actual construction. Although Billings had undertaken his duties only temporarily, the calibre of his work had persuaded Brazilian Traction to lure him away from the Spanish and Mexican companies. 'The more I see of him,' Mackenzie confided to R.C. Brown, 'the more convinced I am that he ought to be tied to our group by some permanent arrangement.'[37] Accordingly, in December 1924, Billings was appointed to the board and named vice-president in charge of engineering and construction. In accepting these posts, Billings donned the mantle of Hugh Cooper, C.H. Kearny, and F.S. Pearson. The Cubatão project was destined, however, to bring Billings far greater fame in Brazilian eyes than any of his predecessors had attained. By reversing the flow of the rivers and making their waters flow over the edge of the Serra, Billings had not only defied nature but had also won the lasting respect of Brazilians, who (in the words of journalist, Assis Chateaubriand) looked on him as the 'American Moses.'[38]

Construction on the Cubatão project began in July 1925, and within six months Billings had marshalled an army of 3,500 labourers at the site and divided them into four groups, one for the powerhouse, another for penstock work, and one each for the Rio Grande and Santo Amaro reservoirs. Recruiting and retaining so large a labour force proved no easy task. A multitude of problems, ranging from the provision of pure

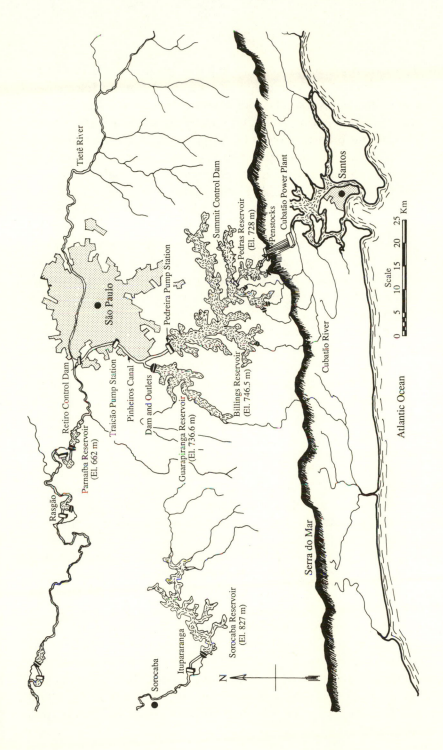

The Serra do Cubatão Hydroelectric Development, 1928

Tietê River

Rasgão

Retiro Control Dam

Parnaíba Reservoir
(El. 662 m)

Traicão Pump Station

São Paulo

Pinheiros Canal

Pedreira Pump Station

Dam and Outlets

Summit Control Dam

Pedras Reservoir
(El. 728 m)

Penstocks

Cubatão Power Plant

Santos

Guarapiranga Reservoir
(El. 736.6 m)

Billings Reservoir
(El. 746.5 m)

Cubatão River

Serra do Mar

Atlantic Ocean

Sorocaba

Itupararanga

Sorocaba Reservoir
(El. 827 m)

N

Scale

0   5   10 15 20 25 Km

drinking water to the suppression of malaria, plagued Billings and his construction manager, a young American named James McKim Bell. Most of these problems could be combated by such preventive measures as the erection of proper barracks and scrupulous medical vigilance, but there was nothing Billings could do to improve the far-from-salubrious climate. 'As you know,' he reported to Toronto, 'the crest of the *Serra* where our most important work is located has a very unusual climate; very chilly and foggy in the winter and with almost incessant fog and rain during the rest of the year ... The result is that the native workmen stay only a short time. Last month we lost two-thirds and this month so far three-quarters of the men sent to *Alto da Serra* have departed.'[39] In desperation, Billings unsuccessfully tried to bring in skilled Austrian labourers under the auspices of the International Labour Organization. Despite such bouts of anxiety, however, Billings's army of workers never fell behind schedule.

In some respects the Cubatão project was simply the application of conventional engineering knowledge on an enormous scale (although in other ways it created unique problems). The construction of the dams, dikes, and reservoirs on the plateau between São Paulo and the lip of the Serra was a relatively straightforward task for the hydraulic engineers. The gradient of the plateau was gentle and that of the river valleys broad and slow – ideal conditions for the formation of reservoirs. The powerhouse at the foot of the Serra likewise differed little from other contemporary powerhouses. Its two General Electric generators, developing 47,700 kw each, and its Pelton Wheel turbines were standard, 'off-the-shelf' pieces of electrical equipment. In general, the Cubatão power scheme was distinguished not by innovative technological advances but by the boldness of its overall design.

Only the penstocks, the steel tubes that carried water from the Pedras reservoir down the steep slope of the Serra to the powerhouse below, crossed new frontiers in hydro technology. Running down the Serra for more than a kilometre at an average angle of forty-two degrees, the penstocks were subjected to immense pressure. To achieve a velocity of 115 metres per second through the small nozzles that played onto the turbine in the powerhouse, the water drawn off the reservoir was fed into penstocks that diminished in diameter from 157 cm at the top to 137 cm at the powerhouse. To compensate for the pressure created by the resultant compression of the water, the thickness of the penstock walls more than doubled (to 4.1 cm) by the time the pipes entered the powerhouse. Huge concrete blocks were used to anchor the penstocks in place on the thin soil of the Serra, and the surrounding hillside was asphalted and planted with eucalyptus trees to prevent erosion from rainfall.[40] (Once, years later in 1939, a 'water hammer' [a sudden surge of water] broke open one of the penstocks. Before the powerhouse crew could turn off the flow, the jet of water from the broken pipe gouged a vast scar in the Serra, pushing before it rocks, debris, trees, and the cars of the inclined-plane railway that serviced the penstocks.) The most remarkable aspect of the penstock complex was that it was designed on the drawing-board by Billings and his engineers and then built to exact specifications by the Ferrum Company in Poland. When the thousands of tons of steel, rivets, and braces were finally assembled in Brazil, all the angles and joints had to marry perfectly – and they did! The penstocks and generators Billings installed at the Serra are still in service today.

On 12 October 1926, just fifteen months after construction had commenced, the first unit at the Serra plant came 'on line.' In the presence of 350 guests, State President Carlos de Campos pushed a button that set the first Cubatão turbine and generator in motion. 'For Billings,' Alexander Mackenzie noted, 'the day was rightly a real apotheosis, and his credit in this country can be considered definitely established.'[41] The inauguration meant far more than the completion of a new generating station. It signified the beginning of a new era in the availability of electricity in São Paulo. On account of the size of its reservoir system, Cubatão had been designed to expand whenever additional power was needed. 'To avoid the past error of planning on too small a scale and for too short a period,' Billings noted in 1926, 'the *Serra* project is planned to permit the development in successive steps of ample blocks of additional power at favorable prices. Therefore, another power shortage can never again recur unless there is plain neglect to carry out easy subsequent steps already provided for in the initial program.'[42] Accordingly, the second generating unit was brought into service in April 1927, and orders were placed for a third.

The Cubatão plant soon became the most prominent of the Light's installations in Brazil. The contrast between the silver penstocks descending the Serra with the vivid green backdrop of the *mato* unavoidably caught the attention of thousands of *paulistas* every weekend as they escaped the city for the magnificent beaches at Santos. On the plateau above the Serra plant, the huge Rio Grande reservoir became a favourite location for picnickers and fishermen. Perhaps the most eloquent praise of Billings's work at Cubatão came from Rudyard Kipling, England's great writer, who toured the installation in 1927. Kipling was treated to a ride up the side of the Serra in an open-sided car of the inclined-plane railway that serviced the penstocks. The trip left Kipling speechless; but not wordless, for he included a poem, 'Song of the Dynamo,' and a whole chapter, entitled 'The Father of Lightnings,' in his book *Brazilian Sketches*. Kipling predicted that the future belonged to electricity, which would in time completely displace oil and coal as energy sources. 'At that epoch (which will be heralded by the hara-kiri of the Oil Barons) Brazil,' Kipling's roseate prediction concluded, 'sitting with her back to illimitable electric power, will sell it between Twenty-five north and Sixty south on both sides of her continent – westerly to the 180th meridian, and easterly to somewhere on the far side of dry Africa.'[43]

As Kipling had sensed, the Light's newest generating station provided São Paulo industry with abundant power for future expansion. The intimate association of electricity and regional economic growth was symbolized at the inauguration ceremonies in October 1926 by the presence of such prominent São Paulo businessmen as Count Francisco Matarazzo, Brazil's leading food processer and textile maker, José Maria Whitaker, a leading banker, and Dr Roberto Simonsen, president of the Santos Construction Company. Matarazzo, Simonsen, and Whitaker all sensed that Cubatão could perpetuate the role begun by the Parnaíba station in 1900 and at the same time preclude any return to the power shortages of the early 1920s.[44] 'Our problem is now no longer one of producing ample power but of *selling* it,' Billings told E.R. Peacock. 'It is impossible to apply too much attention and effort to this commercial end of the business and the success of the São Paulo hydro-electric work will depend principally on the activity and judgment devoted to this for the next decade.'[45]

To capitalize on its new-found power surplus, the São Paulo Light embarked on a policy of 'broadening out,' whereby it bought up small utility companies operating in areas adjacent to its main concessions. In early 1927, a light and power company in the small city of Jundiaí, east of São Paulo, was purchased and became the first fruit of a policy that Sir Alexander believed would protect the company's overall competitive position and 'utilize some of our large surplus power.' Over the next few years, additional companies were acquired in São José dos Campos and Floriano, placing large areas of potential growth within the Light's concessionary area. The largest and most promising of these purchases was the City of Santos Improvements Company, which was obtained from its English owners by means of a share exchange in January 1929. The Santos company offered a ready-made *entrée*, just twelve kilometres from Cubatão, into the traction, light, and power services of Brazil's largest port.[46] The 'broadening out' of the late 1920s culminated the process by which Brazilian Traction established its concessionary presence in Brazil. The addition of these small utility companies to its established operations in Rio and São Paulo gave the Canadian company a firm grip on the electricity, gas, and telephone services of the most densely populated and prosperous area of Brazil. In time, population and industry would spill into the small provincial towns and cities of Rio and São Paulo states, and the Light would be waiting to supply their electrical needs. The maximization of concessionary rights did, of course, create certain dangers. As Toronto Vice-president Miller Lash was quick to sense, such expansion of the company's sphere of influence was apt to reinforce the impression that it was 'an octopus.'[47] For the time being, however, such criticism was neutralized by the success of the Cubatão plant.

The combination of surplus power and 'broadening out' stimulated power consumption in the late 1920s. From 1925 to 1929, population in the Light's concession area grew from approximately 2.7 million to 3.5 million, and its electricity consumers leaped from 185,853 to 301,196. Electricity sales reflected this expansion, increasing from 479,540,843 kilowatt hours in 1925 to 816,557,897 kilowatt hours in 1929.[48] This advance was pronounced in the São Paulo region. By the 1920s, the state of São Paulo had clearly established itself as the economic powerhouse of Brazil. In 1914, it had been responsible for 30.7 per cent of national industrial production. By 1929, this share had grown to 37.5 per cent and would continue to expand to 41.7 per cent by 1938.[49] Led by its strong export staple, coffee, São Paulo diversified into a wide variety of manufacturing activities, best typified by its booming textile industry. A solid infrastructure, notably São Paulo's extensive railway network, also accounted for this economic advance. Electricity was undeniably a central facet of São Paulo's economic predominance. It both stimulated industrial growth and fed off the result. From the electrification of state railways to the provision of power for cotton looms and coffee-bean huskers, electricity was an essential element in the drive to industrial self-sufficiency. For his part in this development, Billings received just recognition. 'The good fortune of the people of São Paulo rests in the hands of this maker of electricity,' *O jornal* noted in 1928. 'The exploits of Moses are child's play compared with the deeds of his disciple of this age of iron and aluminium.'[50] Unfortunately for Billings, the Light, and São Paulo, the dramatic economic reversal of 1929–30 was to prove that, just as industry and electricity could prosper in good times, they could also suffer in bad times.

Brazilian Traction took advantage of the brief glory days of the late 1920s to make the first increase in capital since its formation in 1912. At a special general meeting in January 1928, Vice-president E.R. Wood explained that the expansion of facilities, especially with the completion of the Cubatão plant, had placed a severe strain on capital resources. To meet this demand, as well as to finance 'broadening out' and to place the company in 'a strong liquid position,' Brazilian Traction's authorized capital would be increased from $120 million to $200 million. This was to be accomplished by the creation of 800,000 additional ordinary shares of $100 each. Existing shareholders were then to be offered one additional share at par for each five held as of 31 January 1928. If fully taken up, this offer would generate $24 million. The ordinary shares would subsequently be converted into no-par-value shares on a basis of four no-par-value shares for each old $100 share. The shareholders accepted Wood's proposal with alacrity, and some $23 million of the new shares were taken up. The share split and sale of new shares caused complete pandemonium in Belgium as shareholders besieged Brussels banks designated as places of exchange and subscription. As the deadline for exchange drew near, there were wild scenes as desperate shareholders, fearful that they would miss their opportunity, hurled wads of Brazilian Traction shares for exchange and bundles of francs for new purchases over tellers' wickets. In Toronto, the reports of Belgian bank managers ankle-deep in shares provided a gleeful diversion for Brazilian Traction executives otherwise preoccupied with the complexities of administering a large public utility in distant Brazil.

The post-war decade also brought problems that gave every indication of eroding the company's position in Rio and São Paulo. These problems were the result of both the Light's own success in Brazil and the coming of urban-industrial society to the south-eastern part of the country. The outstanding example of this was the tramway system in Rio and São Paulo. Although the tramways had acted as one of the prime facilitators of urban growth in Brazil's two largest cities during the first two decades of the century, the Light began to discover in the third decade that some of the urban changes its power and tramway system had unleashed now threatened to strangle the system. It was not that *cariocas* and *paulistas* no longer wished to ride the *bondes*. On the contrary, the system was strained to capacity. By 1925, the Rio and São Paulo trams were carrying in excess of half a billion Brazilians every year, and by 1929 this had climbed to 719,864,725 passengers, who travelled over 832 kilometres of routes on a fleet of almost 2,000 tramcars.[51] In the late 1920s, however, the efficiency of this system was severely tested by the growing and virtually unchecked urban congestion plaguing Rio and São Paulo. Especially in Rio, where the population was nearly a million and a half by mid-decade, the streets were becoming saturated with traffic, as heavily laden trams vied with pedestrians, motorized 'jitneys,' cars, and buses on the city's narrow streets.

In essence, the problem confronting the tramway system was that the concessions under which it operated had not kept pace with the changing nature of the cities it served. The clearest example of these changed circumstances was the appearance of gasoline-powered vehicles on Brazilian streets. 'The motor problem,' as company engineers quaintly labelled it, challenged the trams in many ways. Buses could move more freely through traffic, collecting and dropping off passengers with ease, often at the expense of trams, which were restricted to routes and stops fixed by their concessions and, needless to say, by their tracks. As the volume of downtown traffic increased, trams were reduced to a crawl, and accidents climbed dramatically. Beyond the confines of the densely populated inner city, trams were fighting a losing battle with buses and suburban trains for the residents of the sprawling Rio and São Paulo suburbs. Although the Rio company inaugurated limited bus service in 1926 under the auspices of a new subsidiary, Viação Excelsior,[52] Light managers remained convinced that the cheap, bulk transportation offered by trams still held the key to the efficient movement of Brazil's urban masses. The rub lay in the fact the company could not undertake the necessary expansion to achieve this without guarantees from Brazilian politicians of reformed concessions and fares that would provide a fair return on investment. The plea for reform became a familiar refrain in

Brazilian Traction annual reports throughout the decade. 'The existing tramway facilities both in Rio de Janeiro and São Paulo require extending, reinforcing, and a general bringing up to a standard more in keeping with the dignity of such great and growing cities,' the 1926 annual report bluntly stated. 'The carrying out of such work involves the expenditure of large sums and cannot be undertaken until the Company can be assured of a reasonable return on its investment.'

In 1925–6, Brazilian Traction made a bold attempt to effect reform of the urban transportation system in Rio and São Paulo. It commissioned Norman D. Wilson,[53] a Canadian consulting engineer, to investigate the transit problems of the two Brazilian cities and to prescribe a plan for reform. Wilson took little time to identify the problem. The transport systems of both cities had so deteriorated that a gallimaufry of trams, buses, 'jitneys,' and suburban trains were all vying pell-mell to carry *cariocas* and *paulistanos*. Wilson's principal recommendation was that unified control be imposed upon their public-transport systems. 'Competent direction and unified control is the first essential for good transportation,' he reported to the São Paulo *câmara* in May 1927. Without such control, 'a gross excess of transportation facilities' in central areas and 'an almost total absence of all transportation in the [sub]urban areas' would persist. In Rio, Wilson diagnosed a special need for a co-ordinated attempt at reform. One of the 'fundamental characteristics' of the Rio tramway system was that its routes had become so truncated that 'the great bulk of its business is short-haul local riding, and the assembly and distribution of the steam-railway and ferry traffic.'[54]

Having outlined his guiding principle of unification, Wilson proceeded to make detailed proposals for reform. In both cities, he advocated a vigorous rationalization of transport services in the inner-city areas. New routes, double-tracking, the elimination of head-to-head competition of buses and trams, and the adoption of modernized equipment took prominence in Wilson's plan. The *pièce de résistance* of his plan for each city was the introduction of a rapid-transit system that, in the crowded downtown areas, would go underground and become a subway system. Although a costly innovation, the rapid-transit proposal offered an effective means of relieving downtown congestion and of expeditiously moving large numbers of people in and out of the city. The proposal for a subway system was truly innovative. It acknowledged that the age of the *bonde* as the backbone of the transit systems had waned and that a new integrated approach to the problems of Brazilian urban transit was needed. 'The construction of such a high speed line,' Wilson predicted for Rio, 'would permit the long major routes of the [1907] Unified System from the outlying areas to down-town to be connected into short feeder routes, free these lines from the congested down-town, and materially relieve the congestion; would very materially reduce the number of cars on the streets down-town, and would permit an entirely new routing to fit present conditions.'[55] It was a revolutionary proposal, which, if implemented, would place Brazil's two leading cities in the forefront of world urban-transit development.

Wilson placed two conditions on the acceptance of his plan by the Light. In the first place, 'the offer of the Company to extend and recondition its transport service' was 'conditional upon the complete co-ordination under its management of all means of local common carrier transportation, both as the prime essential for a good transportation service ... and as the only basis of security for the great amount of capital that the providing of such services involves.' Secondly, it was imperative that Brazilian municipal politicians 'make new rules' for their public-transit concessions. The post-war rise in costs and the high cost of building a modernized system made it imperative that local government undertake part of the cost of the new system. To this end, Wilson proposed increased fares, a special surcharge on normal fares to defray the cost of the subway system, and an undertaking by the municipal governments to assume the cost of certain portions of the subway. On these two conditions, the whole project foundered. Even in large American cities like Boston and New York, the problem of reforming public-transit services held by private interests had often proved insurmountable, and the construction of modern subway systems had been undertaken by municipal authorities alone. The desire for an upward adjustment of fares in a period of post-war inflation had often been blocked by politicians' unwillingness to break the five-cent-fare barrier. These tensions were present in Brazil throughout the 1920s and were intensified for Brazilian Traction by the fact that it was a foreign corporation. 'With all due respect to contrary opinion,' Wilson himself gloomily concluded, 'I am convinced that a foreign company operating under a foreign name, will receive no favours.'[56]

The chances of effecting a wholesale transformation of urban transit in either Rio or São Paulo were further diminished by the fact that the age of heroic urban reform was over in Brazil. The post-war decade offered little opportunity for the emergence of another Pereira Passos or Antônio Prado. When, in 1920, Carlos Sampaio, an engineer, was elected as prefect of Rio, Fred Huntress had suggested that he might be a 'second Frontin,' a reference to the builder of Avenida Central. Although Sampaio tackled some of the city's problems, most notably the demolition of Morro do Castelo (a hill covering what is today a large portion of downtown Rio), the problems of modern urban Brazil had by the 1920s become too complex for one-man crusades. Relations with Sampaio's successor, Alaor Prata, were soured by an ongoing dispute over telephone rates, a situation that greatly lessened the chances of a constructive tramway policy.

Municipal intransigence coincided throughout most of the 1920s with a pervasive mood of suspicion towards foreign business in Brazil. As early as 1923, Alexander Mackenzie had complained that the uncooperative attitude of the Brazilian federal government and the Rio government was designed to 'enable the Prefect to say that the Government had forced the company to its knees and obliged us to deliver back some of the "stolen goods." '[57] Such hostility ensured that Norman Wilson's unique and innovative subway proposal became bogged down in endless discussion in the *câmaras* of Rio and São Paulo. Finally the Depression intervened, depriving both politicians and the Light of the capital necessary for so ambitious a project. In the meantime, the tramway situation continued to deteriorate. Norman Wilson became a frequent visitor to Brazil as a consultant throughout the 1930s and 1940s and on each visit he would detect a further decline into chaos and insolvency by the Rio and São Paulo tram systems.

The Light fared little better in seeking an upward adjustment of its rates. The lustre of the concessions negotiated and unified by Alexander Mackenzie and Fred Pearson in the first decade of the century had by the 1920s become tarnished. While the company's monopoly was still very much intact, the rates under which it provided its services had remained frozen at turn-of-the-century levels. The standard 200 réis tramway fare in São Paulo was the same in 1921 as it had been on the first day the company sent its cars through the city's streets in 1900. By the early 1920s, the erosion of tramway, telephone, and gas tariffs by Brazil's inexorable inflation and the shrinking external value of the milréis was threatening to push several Light services into insolvency. In 1921, E.R. Wood confided to Alexander Mackenzie that it was of 'utmost importance we should get revision of our concession in order to get more revenue.' If not, Wood surmised, the company's existence was 'in peril.'[58] 'Better results,' the 1922 annual report concluded, 'can only come from more remunerative rates for the various services or from a decided improvement in the exchange value of the milréis.' Since the company had little sway over exchange, it devoted its efforts in the 1920s to obtaining improved rates.

The first step in this process was shaped by Sir Alexander's belief that the public must be educated to the justice of the company's request. 'Our campaign,' Mackenzie determined, 'must be made before Municipal Council and in the newspapers and will be prolonged.'[59] Accordingly, an American utility-rates specialist, H.J. Hagenah of the Chicago firm of Hagenah and Erickson, was hired to report on the whole gamut of services offered by the Brazilian Traction group. After spending much of 1922 examining the Rio and São Paulo operations, Hagenah submitted a multi-volume confidential report. For the overall management of the Canadian enterprise, Hagenah had strong praise. The São Paulo company was 'well managed and the properties well maintained,' and its operating results, 'considering the adverse exchange conditions,' were 'commendable.' The Rio operating results 'as a whole' were 'excellent.' 'There are but few public utilities in the large cities in the United States,' Hagenah admitted, 'which possess a record of earnings more favorable than those herein discussed' for the period up to 1920. None the less, by the 1920s falling exchange and the 'extremely low fare' of the system threatened the system's financial future.[60]

If the tramways received a reasonably clean bill of health from Hagenah, the gas and telephone services emerged looking like financial invalids. Despite the fact that some rates were fixed to the price of gold, the gas and telephone services in general were chronically unprofitable. The Rio de Janeiro and São Paulo Telephone Company was in particularly dire straits. 'The business has not been profitable,' Hagenah concluded,

first because the service has never been fully developed, and secondly because of the great increase in labor and material prices and decline in Brazilian exchange. Obsolete and restrictive concessions have made proper financing impossible and the rates which were never reasonable have failed by a substantial margin to meet the recently increased costs of service. The unfavorable showing is not due to improper construction of plant or to mismanagement ... were the same measures of relief now granted to this company as have almost universally been granted in similar instances in other countries, its income statement would soon become entirely satisfactory.[61]

Alexander Mackenzie had been bargaining unsuccessfully for several years for a revised Rio telephone contract, but it was not until September 1922 that he reached agreement with the municipal government for a new concession that extended the exclusive monopoly over telephone service until 1950 and gave it the right to serve the market until 1990. The crucial breakthrough in the new contract was the guarantee that all telephone rates would vary according to fluctuations in exchange and were subject to revision every five years.

The telephone concession of September 1922 was unexpectedly transformed from breakthrough to débâcle. Although duly signed into law by Rio prefect Carlos Sampaio, Alaor Prata claimed that the concession was both unconstitutional and 'not a good thing for the public.'[62] The company's immediate response was to challenge this in the courts, but the attempt to salvage the telephone concession quickly slipped into a political quagmire from which it did not emerge for years. Through lawyers, among them Carlos de Campos, pressure was brought to bear not only on Alaor Prata but also on the federal president, Artur Bernardes, who appointed the Rio prefect. Bernardes proved to be long on promises and short on action. 'I believe that all the steps taken, both here and in London,' Vice-president Sylvester of the Rio company reported, 'have brought the President to realize that it would be a mistake to have the annulment proceedings continue, but at the same time he wants something to justify the *Prefeitura* desisting from their suit.'[63] When a basis for a compromise failed to materialize, the telephone case went to the courts and stayed there until January 1929, when the Supreme Federal Tribunal finally decided in the Light's favour.

The fracas over the telephone concession set the tone for other rate cases. Throughout the 1920s, the whole question of adjusting rates rested in limbo as politicians and company managers alike awaited the outcome of the Rio telephone case. This impasse had serious implications for both Brazilians and the company. Without new rates, the Light was reluctant to invest large sums in modernizing and expanding its telephone and tramway services. 'The open hostility which has been shown us since the inauguration of the present [Bernardes] Government continues,' Mackenzie complained in mid-1923, 'and this not only makes difficult the carrying out of our daily business but also makes impossible the interesting of anybody in any new projects we might have for bettering our conditions.'[64] Predictably, the calibre of telephone service declined appreciably throughout the decade. Given the high cost of cable, switchboard equipment, and telephones, the company felt little compulsion to improve its service as long as its rates remained unremunerative and its Rio concession was scheduled to lapse in 1930. 'There is absolutely no organization and the plant had not been engineered at all – simply thrown together,' a Rio company engineer admitted in 1927; 'I am not exaggerating – you can't talk from one end of Rio to the other – you can't talk to Santos or to Petrópolis, in fact you can't talk at all.'[65] Whenever it rained in Rio, aged and cracked cables admitted the moisture, thereby reducing the city's telephone service to a mass of short circuits and line static. Such service understandably served to heighten public discontent and to increase the problems of negotiating with the politicians. Brazilian Traction's tramway and power systems were saved from a similar fate not because they were able to resolve their rate problems, but because they were sufficiently well developed and possessed a surplus of capacity to weather the storm.

The Light's inability to rectify these difficulties was symptomatic of a larger breakdown in the life of Brazil during the twenties. The Old Republic was built upon the system of élite consensus, which allowed the economically powerful states of São Paulo and Minas Gerais to exercise an unchallenged sway over Brazilian federal politics. By the 1920s, the solidity of this base was beginning to show cracks that would eventually widen into large fissures and culminate in the Revolution of 1930. Several forces conspired to undermine the Old Republic. The long-standing dominance of São Paulo and Minas Gerais had generated strong regional and class tensions within the republic. The monopoly of *paulistas* and *mineiros* over the federal presidency bred a sense of alienation in other Brazilian states, among them Rio de Janeiro and the southern state of Rio Grande do Sul, both of which were now chafing at their subordinate role. At the same time, social tensions bred by the pressure of Brazil's increasingly urbanized and industrializing society began to gnaw at the social fabric of the nation and to challenge the hitherto closed and paternalistic nature of Brazilian democracy.[66] Pervading these regional and social tensions was an awakening sense of Brazilian nationalism, which, unlike the nationalism of Rui Barbosa and the Baron of Rio

Branco, with its tolerance for outside ideas, stressed Brazilian self-sufficiency. Although still very embryonic in the 1920s, this new stream of Brazilian nationalism was critical both of the internationalist outlook of many of the leaders of the Old Republic and of Brazil's dangerous reliance on the coffee staple. The nationalists also challenged the looseness of the 1891 constitution and berated its inability to support a strong central government. 'Understanding more fully both their strengths and weaknesses,' a historian of Brazilian nationalism has noted, 'the nationalists were eager to take the steps necessary to modernize their country. They advocated various reforms to effect such a modernization. That eagerness to remake the nation caused unrest and, on more than one occasion, rebellion. A coffee crisis in 1929, followed by a revolution in 1930, helped the nationalists to implement at least a part of their program.'[67]

It is conceivable that the São Paulo–Minas Gerais power bloc might have held the forces of regionalism, discontent, and nationalism in check throughout the decade; but this would have required a large degree of cohesion within the ruling élite and the continued prosperity of the coffee-based economy. Unfortunately, the system of *coronelismo* or clientage upon which the *café com leite* system was based began to collapse under its own weight. The politics of the Old Republic became increasingly prone to manipulation and internal squabbling. By the end of the decade, the *coroneis*, or political bosses, of São Paulo and Minas Gerais were unable to agree upon the presidential succession, the linchpin of the whole system. They therefore found themselves unable to perpetuate the political system that had served them so well for nearly forty years.

From the perspective of Brazilian Traction the gradual disintegration of the political system under which the company had established itself and expanded was a cause for growing anxiety. The rising hostility toward the old political order not only created an atmosphere of uncertainty that frightened foreign investors but also unleashed forces in Brazilian society that the company was unaccustomed to combating. Yet, just as Brazil groped for a new *modus operandi* throughout the 1920s, so too did Brazilian Traction hesitantly seek out new means of defending and expanding its place within Brazilian society.

The first evidence of unrest came in 1922, when a small group of disgruntled young army officers staged an abortive uprising in Rio de Janeiro. The incident was triggered when the 'official' candidate in the

1922 presidential election, *mineiro* Artur Bernardes, was openly opposed by Rio de Janeiro, led by Nilo Peçanha, and Rio Grande do Sul, led by Borges de Medeiros. This affront to the power of São Paulo and Minas Gerais was heightened by the active interest of the army in the presidential campaign. Although the army had played a quiescent role in politics since the 1890s, its interest in the national scene was now aroused by the reappearance of former federal president Marshal Hermes da Fonseca and by the disclosure of certain letters (later proved to be forgeries) in which President-elect Bernardes besmirched the army's honour. When President Epitácio Pessoa moved to suppress the army's outspoken criticism by arresting Fonseca and ordering the Clube Militar closed, the military revolted. With little preparation and no clear idea of their ultimate purpose, a small group of officers and men defied Pessoa's orders and seized the Igrejinha fortress on Copacabana beach in Rio on 5 July. After sporadic artillery exchanges with government forces, most of the insurgents surrendered. Later, when a handful of 'diehards' fought their way out of the fort onto the beach, they were shot or bayoneted by loyal troops. The 'Copacabana 18' not only became instant martyrs but provided a symbol for the emerging doctrine of *tenentismo*, an incoherent set of beliefs that emphasized Brazilian nationalism and a strong, authoritarian government as a cure for the nation's ills. If the revolt was a military disaster, it at least shook the nation's conscience. To ensure his successor's ascension to power, President Pessoa imposed martial law.

'We have just had the experience of a full dress revolution which, fortunately, completely failed,' Mackenzie reported from Rio, 'and we are once more carrying on as if nothing had happened or almost so because under the regime of martial law the newspapers are nearly as interesting as a parish magazine which means something to us after the blood and thunder utterings of the past year.' Mackenzie described how, in the middle of the night, he had been roused in his Rio apartment by the report of artillery fire coming from the direction of Fort Copacabana. 'I knew it had come at last.' The next day Mackenzie watched in fascination as the 'Copacabana 18,' with tattered pieces of the Brazilian flag pinned to their chests, left their sanctuary. The rebels 'marched out armed with rifles and a machine gun and met no opposition until they got about opposite my house, when they let go. There were several thousand men against them but they kept up the fight, taking cover behind the new sea wall under construction until they were all shot or bayoneted, and that was the end of that.'[68] Throughout the whole uprising, the company remained unscathed, although several errant artillery shells had landed dangerously close to its offices.

Mackenzie's reaction to the events of July 1922 was one of mixed horror and concern. He vehemently decried the intervention of the military in the realm of politics and praised the swift action of President Pessoa in quashing the insurrection. The country, Mackenzie correctly sensed, still had much to fear from certain elements in the army, notably the 'old sergeants' and the Clube Militar. 'My hope rests in the [junior] men who in due course will return to their civil occupations and who can hardly have [been] imbued in their two years training [with] the dangerous spirit of the old professionals.' In this respect, Mackenzie was to be disappointed, since the spirit of *tenentismo* continued to grow in the junior ranks throughout the 1920s and to act as an abrasive on the old political order.

The presidency of Artur da Silva Bernardes (1922–6) brought no respite from the 'nightmare of political agitation' that preceded it.[69] While the army remained in barracks during Bernardes's tenure, outspoken Brazilian nationalists came to the fore. Bernardes's years in office therefore constituted a period of acute anxiety for the Light. In the first place, the *estado de sítio*, or state of siege, remained in place. This introduced an element of political arbitrariness into dealings with Brazilian politicians. Under the fully constitutional rule of the Old Republic, the company always found a degree of flexibility in federal politicians in matters of rates and concessions. Under Bernardes the company was increasingly confronted by fiats and an unwillingness to negotiate. 'There may be some rude shocks in store for us,' Mackenzie prophesied in mid-1923, 'as nobody can tell what the President may or may not do, and he is not always guided by the counsel of his ministers.'[70]

The first 'rude shock' was Bernardes's reluctance to reverse the annulment of the Rio telephone concession. Whereas Sir Alexander had looked to the federal government for application of a little pressure whenever he encountered difficulties with an uncooperative local politician, he now found it impossible to obtain even an interview with the president. When Mackenzie eventually did succeed in gaining an audience, the British ambassador reported, he was confronted with a man who was quite 'abnormal' – 'a man with one fixed idea that he had a mission to govern, and, as his Excellency put it himself, "moralisar" [to uplift] Brazil.'[71] Given this attitude, Bernardes not unexpectedly focused his reforming zeal on large foreign corporations operating within his country. Alaor Prata's overturning of the Rio telephone concession was calculated to serve much the same end. 'I am credibly informed,' the British ambassador noted, 'that the prefect on assuming office, said, and I see nothing unlikely in the story, that he knew the best way to make himself popular was to attack the "Light." '[72]

Bernardes had other 'rude shocks' in store for the company. In 1924, for instance, the federal government announced its intention of removing the 75 per cent exemption from import duties that the company had traditionally enjoyed on all the electric equipment it had purchased abroad to build up and maintain its generating system. Mackenzie vigorously opposed this move, arguing that it betrayed the intent of the company's original concessions. 'We must hold on like grim death,' he declared.[73] After attempting to block the removal of the exemption in the federal congress, Mackenzie managed to offset its potential impact by negotiating with the São Paulo government a generous exemption of customs duties on all equipment imported for the Cubatão plant.

The Rio telephone battle and the tariff fight were far more than passing legal squabbles. They were indicative of a slow but portentous change in Brazilian attitudes. It was a change that Sir Alexander shrewdly detected. 'Our troubles with the authorities,' he confided to London financier E.R. Peacock as early as 1926,

arise from other causes, and the principal one, I regret to say, is, that being a foreign company we are considered fair game. I even think that a foreign concern exploiting a public utility in Brazil has had its day and is becoming an anachronism. There is always a fairly strong nationalist feeling – usually dormant but easy to rouse – and our late President Bernardes did everything he could during his first two years of office to excite public opinion against us. He was an extremist and there never has been anybody quite like him in public life. He alone was responsible for bringing the action to set aside our Rio Telephone contract.[74]

Mackenzie's success in establishing the São Paulo and Rio companies in Brazil had been rooted in his ability to secure the co-operation of leading local politicians. Sir Alexander was in this respect a past master in the art of understanding the politics of the Old Republic. He possessed a thorough knowledge of the mores of the élite that had guided Brazil since the 1890s. With his grasp of Portuguese, Mackenzie had adapted himself to Brazilian ways as few other North Americans ever had. He was at ease with prominent Brazilians ranging from Rui Barbosa, Brazil's great liberal intellectual, to such leaders of national politics and journalism as Nilo Peçanha and Assis Chateaubriand. Although they occasionally had their differences with Brazilian Traction, these men trusted Mackenzie and were prepared to work constructively with him. As the political underpinnings of the Old Republic came under pressure in the twenties, so too did the relations of Mackenzie and the rulers of Brazil. Bernardes's presidency provided Mackenzie with the first forceful evidence of this trend. As Mackenzie told Peacock, there had never before 'been anybody quite like him in public life' in Brazil. Just how the company was to defend itself against such new 'super-men,' as Mackenzie called them, and their ideas, was a subject that increasingly occupied his attention as the decade progressed. There were to be no easy solutions.

One line of defence was 'Brazilianization.' The more the company's interests in Brazil could be represented by Brazilians, Mackenzie reasoned, the more it would be able to deflect the assaults on it by anti-foreign elements. This had always been the Light's policy with regard to its legal affairs in Brazil. By the 1920s, the legal departments of the Rio and São Paulo Light had acquired a considerable expertise in defending the intricate operations of a large public-utility corporation. The legal departments, especially in the Rio Light, served as the nerve centre of the company's activities in Brazil. Ultimate control of corporate legal policy remained in Mackenzie's hands; and when Mackenzie was away, his nephew, Kenneth McCrimmon, a young Toronto lawyer who had come to Brazil in 1920, took charge. None the less it was on Carlos de Campos and his Brazilian colleagues that the company really depended for its legal defence. When Campos left the company's employ in 1924 to become president of São Paulo, his place was taken by Dr Prudente de Morais, the lawyer son of former Brazilian president, Prudente de Morais.

Another important step in giving Brazilians a more prominent role in the day-to-day operations of the Rio and São Paulo companies was taken with the promotion of local engineers. Once again, ultimate authority remained in the hands of North American engineers, but to an increasing degree they learned to delegate control to Brazilian-born subordinates. Billings guided the company's overall hydroelectric construction program and, in 1924, an English electrical engineer, Herbert Couzens,[75] was hired to replace the ailing Fred Huntress as vice-president of operations.

With considerable experience with English electric companies and the Toronto Transit Commission, Couzens's expertise supplemented Billings's skill as a hydraulic engineer. Both men quickly learned the wisdom of bringing talented young Brazilian engineers into the Light. A crucial step in this direction was taken in 1924, when Edgard de Souza was appointed general manager of the São Paulo company. In 1928, Souza became a director and vice-president of the São Paulo company. Although educated in Belgium, Souza was the first Brazilian to take a major role in operational affairs since Alípio de Borba had briefly served as traffic manager of the São Paulo company in 1900–1. The policy of promoting Brazilians to senior positions in the operational hierarchy was expanded in succeeding years to a point by the late 1940s at which the foreign managers represented a very small fraction of staff in Brazil.

'Brazilianization' of the Light was but the first tentative response to the changing social and political environment in Brazil. Mackenzie trusted that other appropriate responses would evolve as circumstances changed. In July 1924, the Light received a frightening illustration of what could happen when political change took an abrupt and violent turn. The policies pursued by Artur Bernardes incurred the displeasure not only of foreign businessmen but also of many of his countrymen. As a *mineiro* president, Bernardes was naturally closely scrutinized by *paulistas*, who by the mid-1920s saw themselves as the economic leaders of the nation and therefore entitled to the largest voice in deciding national policies. Bernardes's erratic administration soon aroused a feeling in São Paulo that the state's interests were being ignored. São Paulo's discontent took on a dangerous aspect when it began to fuse with elements of *tenente* opposition, which also had cause to call for the reformation of the republic.

The explosion came on 5 July 1924, when about 5,000 rebels, including disaffected federal troops and large elements of the Fôrça Pública (the state security force) seized control of São Paulo. State president Carlos de Campos fled his palace and went into hiding. By 9 July the rebels had gained sufficient ground to establish a provisional government. In the process of doing so, there was heavy fighting, and considerable damage was inflicted on the company's power lines, trams, and gas holders. To minimize the damage, Edgard de Souza suspended tram service and cut power to many of the city's substations. Since the telephone service constituted the most efficient means of communication both within and outside the city, it became a much-prized objective of both federal and rebel troops. Eventually the rebels succeeded in winning control of phone facilities within the city, and the federal troops managed to sever all long-distance lines, thus denying the rebels a means of spreading the revolt to neighbouring states. Inside the city, the rebels fortified their position by erecting barricades and digging trenches, often ripping up tram tracks in the process. With open fighting in the city's streets, many of the São Paulo Light employees failed to report for work and, it was rumoured, joined the general exodus from the city. Those who bravely continued to report ran a high risk of becoming involved in the strife. The rebel military commander, for instance, warned linemen not to attempt to repair damaged phone lines. Nervous troops, he warned, might mistake them for federal spies watching rebel troop movements and shoot them. Nevertheless two courageous engineers climbed up the side of gas holders to plug bullet holes with corks. 'Thousands and thousands of people have left their homes,' Daniel Mulqueen, a Canadian accountant in São Paulo, reported to Toronto, 'only taking with them what they could carry. When the trouble is over and they go back to their homes it is more than probable they will not find a thing left and perhaps not the house, surely War is Hell.'[76]

The revolt placed the Light in an extremely vulnerable position. On the one hand, it had little option but to co-operate with the São Paulo rebels. Not to have done so would have risked reprisals on property and perhaps even on employees. On the other hand, the Light could not afford to alienate the federal government by openly aligning itself with the dissidents. Since the federal side had the preponderance of military power and still controlled such vitally important matters as exchange rates, the Light would have been foolhardy to advertise its grievances against the Bernardes government by backing the revolt. Under these circumstances, the company opted for the only sensible policy – that of passive neutrality. Direction of the response to the revolt fell to Asa Billings who had the misfortune to be caught behind rebel lines. Deprived of communication with head office by federal censorship, Billings wisely chose a policy of acquiescence. 'He has all through been very careful,' Couzens reported from Rio, 'not to do or say anything which, if discovered, could be misinterpreted by any hostile critic.'[77] Although Billings correctly sensed that the revolt was essentially a regional protest, it was clear that if the company was perceived to have played an active role on either side of the conflict, nationalistic passions might easily be aroused.

If the managers in Brazil seemed to adjust to the crisis as best they could, the Toronto head office was in near panic. The revolt triggered an immediate exchange crisis. When news reached the English and Canadian press about the violent outbreak and the consequent plunge in exchange, investors' inquiries inundated the Toronto office, which, because of censorship of all outgoing communications by the Brazilian government, knew little more about the true state of affairs in São Paulo than the readers of the Toronto *Globe*. 'The whole thing is very upsetting and naturally worries us a good deal,' Miller Lash reported. 'We have floods of enquiries from bondholders and stockholders and families of employees who are in Brazil and we unfortunately are unable to give them much information.'[78]

The revolt ended as abruptly as it had begun. With the approach of federal troop reinforcements, the rebel forces slipped out of the city under the cover of night on 27 July and headed inland towards the state of Paraná. Although the military balance had swung in President Bernardes's favour, the rebels' ardour had not cooled and, in the epic 'Long March' that followed, the opponents of the Old Republic found another symbol of resistance to the old political order. For its part, the Light was left to assess the damage. The lifting of censorship enabled Billings, who had spent a harrowing three weeks in the besieged city, to communicate his impressions of the revolt and its consequences. 'Considering the amount of random shelling all over the city,' he reported to Toronto, 'it is remarkable that the damage to important parts of the apparatus and equipment was not greater. In nearly every case the shells which struck in or near our stations missed the important apparatus.'[79] None the less, damage from the revolt was considerable. Throughout the city power and telephone lines had been machine-gunned and lay in a tangled mess. Tramway tracks had been lifted from their beds and twisted beyond repair. The hostilities also caused heavy losses of revenue and inflicted damage on several principal power customers. The new Crespi cotton factory had, for instance, been destroyed by fire. A further expense was incurred as a result of the fact that the Light continued to pay all its employees throughout the revolt and made 'gratification' payments to those who actually stayed at their positions. On 9 August Billings tentatively estimated that the revolt had cost the company a total of $1,223,300, of which $1,052,600 was in lost revenues.[80]

The São Paulo revolt of 1924 left a profound impression on Brazilian Traction. It was the first time serious physical damage had been inflicted on the company as a result of political strife in Brazil. While the company could repair damage to its facilities, it was powerless to arrest the disintegration of the Old Republic. The danger now was that the company would find itself in an alien and possibly hostile political environment. Even before the uprising of July 1924, Sir Alexander had perceptively sensed the implications of Brazil's discontents. 'Politics are seething,' he noted. 'There has been somewhat of a break up in the state of São Paulo, and while our principal friends will remain in control it will be, I fear, much more difficult to push through contentious business such as ours in that state without getting into the limelight which a factious opposition may use for its own purely political purposes.'[81]

Until 1930 when Getúlio Vargas, an ambitious *político* from Rio Grande do Sul, dealt the final blow, the fate of the Old Republic was by no means clear. In the interim, Brazil was governed by Washington Luís, a former president of São Paulo, whose presidency (1926–30) was marked by a decline of political factiousness. Washington Luís at least eased tensions by ending the state of siege imposed by Bernardes and by unmuzzling the press. His goal of political pacification was made more attainable by the return of economic prosperity, which enabled the president to stabilize the currency, secure foreign loans, and embark upon a vigorous program of road building. After what Mackenzie had called the 'pure dictatorship' of Bernardes, the presidency of Washington Luís gave the company a respite from the virulent nationalism of the first half of the decade. Mackenzie openly applauded Luís's attempts to stabilize Brazilian exchange and to balance the federal budget, reforms he felt would restore Brazil's prestige in the eyes of foreign bankers and investors. In November 1928, the president, accompanied by the prefect of Rio and the federal minister of transport and public works, visited the Light's power plants outside Rio and announced that he was 'keenly interested' in the public services of the nation's capital.

Despite the many seemingly propitious aspects of the Washington Luís administration, strong tensions continued to strain the fabric of Brazil's political system. The reappearance of economic depression, especially in São Paulo's important textile industry, and a slump in the world price of coffee in the last years of the decade served to undercut the livelihood of Brazil's most prosperous state. By the time the final dénouement of the Old Republic took place in the early months of 1930, its vitality had been completely drained. As historian Peter Flynn has noted, the Old Republic 'was mined from within,' and the disastrous coincidence of the collapse of the world economy and yet another Brazilian political crisis, foolishly provoked by outgoing President Luís, was all that was needed to bring the whole edifice down.

It was somehow appropriate that in the lull before the final storm that carried away the Old Republic, Sir Alexander Mackenzie should have retired from Brazilian Traction. Mackenzie, the Canadian who had adapted so magnificently to the intricacies of Brazilian politics, took his leave just before the curtain fell on the final act of a political system that refused to adjust to the realities of modern Brazilian society. Mackenzie's decision to step down from the presidency was, however, moulded by personal considerations and not by a prescient vision of Brazil's political future. Mackenzie's wife, Mabel, had never enjoyed good health and had remained at Mackenzie's English country home in Berkshire throughout her husband's tenure as president. Sir Alexander seemed able to bear long separations from his wife, but, when his own health began to deteriorate in early 1928, the prospect of continuing to oversee a large corporation in a foreign land began to pall. 'I must confess,' Vice-president Miller Lash sympathetically noted in April 1928, 'that it worries me a good deal to think of the poor old chap stuck down in Brazil with miserable health himself and with his wife again very ill.' Not surprisingly, therefore, Mackenzie reached the decision in August 1928 that 'owing to the condition of his health and upon the advice of his physicians' he would resign, although he would continue to tender advice on policy matters.

By the time of his resignation, Mackenzie had amassed a comfortable fortune, mainly in Brazilian Traction stock, and throughout the 1930s he used it to finance a rather nomadic retirement. In 1930, he sold his English home and bought a villa on the outskirts of Florence, Italy. Every summer he returned to a summer home in his native Kincardine, Ontario. Throughout these perambulations, Mackenzie remained a member of the Brazilian Traction board. In 1938, Ken McCrimmon, Mackenzie's nephew, reported that he had visited the former president in Italy and found him 'to be very interested in the major questions of policy, taxation, etc.,' but 'not concerned at all about details.'

Mackenzie's departure left a huge gap in management. In choosing Miller Lash,[82] the lawyer son of Zebulon Lash and a company vice-president since 1913, to succeed Mackenzie, the board made a remarkable reversal of a long-standing policy. The key to Mackenzie's success as president lay in his insistence that decisions affecting both routine and policy matters be taken by officials 'on the spot' in Brazil. Proximity to the site of operations afforded managers optimum flexibility in responding to the exigencies of doing business in Brazil. The Toronto head office had always played only a nominal role in the operations of the Rio and São Paulo companies. Despite the fact that he served on innumerable 'Pearson-group' boards, William Mackenzie never played an active role in the daily operations of Brazilian Traction, or its subsidiaries, apart from the initial underwriting of their securities. Decisions affecting the management of the system in Brazil were always taken by men with a comprehensive personal knowledge of Brazil. Alexander Mackenzie had carried on this tradition. Miller Lash, on the other hand, was a product of the Toronto business 'establishment.' He spoke no Portuguese and had little grasp of Brazilian mores. Although he resolved to pay an annual visit to Brazil, Lash entertained no thought of establishing a permanent residence there as Mackenzie had done. Instead, Herbert Couzens would serve as resident executive vice-president in Brazil and, together with Billings and young McCrimmon, would be responsible for keeping Lash abreast of affairs in Brazil by means of coded telegrams and confidential letters. The divorce of the seat of effective decision making from the site of operations introduced a fundamental weakness into the company's situation. Lash was in many respects a capable businessman. He had considerable experience in the legal intricacies of the Spanish, Mexican, and Brazilian companies of the 'Pearson group,' but by remaining in his Bay Street office he was deprived of the opportunity of accustoming himself to the vicissitudes of business in Brazil. At a time when Brazilian society and politics and the Brazilian economy were clearly entering a period of flux, Lash's decision to remain in Toronto placed the company at a considerable disadvantage.

When Miller Lash made a short inaugural visit to Rio de Janeiro in late 1928 (the Brazilian summer), he was confronted with ample evidence of the extent of the 'corporate empire' he had inherited from Sir Alexander Mackenzie. Brazilian Traction's subsidiary companies in Rio and São Paulo employed more than 30,000 Brazilians. At a special dinner, Lash met with over 600 employees who had served for more than twenty years. Throughout the Rio and São Paulo areas, the Light provided an array of tramway, bus, power, lighting, telephone, and gas services that were unrivalled in their scope and efficiency throughout the continent. Despite the persistence of problems relating to rates and fluctuating exchange, Brazilian Traction had remained a solid financial performer throughout the twenties. Since the resumption of dividends in 1922, sufficient income had been received from the subsidiaries in Brazil to give shareholders modest, though not spectacular, dividends of between 4 and 6 per cent. Even after the onset of the Depression, Lash reported that he could see 'no reason for pessimism' regarding the company's earning capacity, especially in view of the 'diversity' of its services and the fact that many of the same were 'necessities' of life. 'I have myself been surprised,' he concluded, 'at the manner in which our earnings hold up under adverse conditions and consider it is a remarkable illustration of the stability of the enterprise.'[83]

That Brazil, despite its political and economic problems, remained an attractive market for electricity producers was vividly illustrated by the appearance of a new competitor in the Brazilian hydroelectric industry during the last years of the decade. Whereas up to the 1920s British and Canadian capital had dominated public-utilities investment in Latin America, the post-war decade witnessed the arrival of American 'utilities imperialism' in South America with a vengeance.[84] In 1927, the Electric Bond and Share Company, a wholly owned subsidiary of the General Electric Corporation, purchased the properties of the Emprêsas Elétricas Brasileiras, the electricity company of the Guinle family, and then in dramatic fashion acquired a further seventeen small Brazilian utilities companies in Recife, Bahia, Vitória, Petrópolis, Niterói, Curitiba, Pôrto Alegre, and areas of the state of São Paulo. Suddenly, Brazilian Traction had a large, well-financed, and aggressive competitor. Although the holdings of the Electric Bond and Share were not neatly concentrated in one compact area like those of Brazilian Traction, the rapidity of the Electric Bond and Share's arrival on the Brazilian scene caused considerable alarm. This alarm was heightened by the fact that the American corporation was busily acquiring other holdings in Ecuador, Cuba, Chile, Colombia, Venezuela, Mexico, Costa Rica, India, and even China. 'I see outside of Brazil,' Herbert Couzens noted, 'they are continuing to buy electrical properties very fast and should soon control the public utilities of the world.'[85] It was also feared that the very overt manner in which Electric Bond and Share had acquired its Brazilian properties (in marked contrast to the subtle way in which Brazilian Traction had secured its original concessions) might well excite 'a very strong public feeling' against *all* foreign power corporations in Brazil.

Although Light lawyers assured management that there was little ground on which the Americans could challenge their Rio and São Paulo concessions, Miller Lash was much relieved to receive a personal reassurance that the Americans had no intention of even attempting such an ouster. After an interview with the president of the Electric Bond and Share Company, Lash reported that the American was 'very friendly and apparently desirous that we should be on the best of terms in every respect.'[86] The Brazilian electricity market, it seemed, was large enough for two large competitors. Given the rapid growth of the Rio-São Paulo market for power and the Light's immense surplus of Cubatão power, Lash himself entertained no ambition of expanding the Light beyond the bounds of its lucrative, established market. Brazilian Traction's earnings, he predicted in 1930, would continue to show a 'very gratifying increase' and, despite exchange fluctuations, this would be matched by solid dollar earnings. Such confidence was firmly rooted in the Toronto management's faith in Brazil's future. In September 1928, when Miller Lash paid his first official visit to President Washington Luís, he stressed to his Brazilian host that he continued to be 'a firm optimist on Brazil's future.'[87] On the threshold of the momentous decade of the thirties, Lash could have little idea of what the next ten years really held in store for Brazilian Traction.

CHAPTER EIGHT

The Belgian Croesus

The challenges met by Brazilian Traction in the 1920s were not confined to the steep slopes of the Serra do Mar and the offices of Brazilian politicians. The most dramatic crisis faced by the company during the 1920s – perhaps since its inception – was, paradoxically, never mentioned in the annual reports. The name of Alfred Loewenstein, the flamboyant Belgian financier who between 1926 and 1928 made two well-publicized and aggressive attempts to wrest control of the corporation from its Toronto managers, never once appeared in the company's annual communication to its shareholders. None the less, the events leading up to Loewenstein's sudden and mysterious reversal of fortune in 1928 constitute one of the most fascinating episodes in the history of financial capitalism.

By the 1920s, Brazilian Traction had achieved a considerable degree of maturity as a business organization. Its structure had remained essentially unchanged since 1912, and the problems it faced had to a large degree assumed a routine nature.[1] The 'old guard' of promoters who had staked out concessions in Brazil and guided the company's early financial fortunes now found themselves playing a less prominent role in its affairs. This was especially true of the early São Paulo and Rio syndicates. The *Lusitania* had taken F.S. Pearson to his death in 1915. In December 1923, Sir William Mackenzie died. Mackenzie's death had been preceded in 1921 by that of Zebulon Lash, the legal genius who had masterminded the incorporation of all the Brazilian Traction subsidiaries. In 1924, Monty Horne-Payne, the domineering English financier who had so dextrously placed Rio and São Paulo securities throughout the British Isles, resigned from the board. A year later, Sir Henry Pellatt, Toronto's best-known financial wizard, departed the boardroom. Pellatt's exit removed the last stalwart of the speculative element that had predominated through the early years of the São Paulo and Rio companies. Only D.B. Hanna, Sir William Mackenzie's lieutenant at the Canadian Northern, and F.H. Phippen, the railway's solicitor, remained on the board as a reminder of the breed of promoters who had established Brazilian Traction.

If the 'plungers' seemed absent from the ranks of Brazilian Traction by the mid-twenties, it was not because they had lost interest in the company. Brazilian Traction common stock enjoyed a reputation in the minds of investors on both sides of the Atlantic as one of the most reputable and stable utility securities in the world. Although dividends had suffered in the immediate post-war period, investors had held onto their 'Traccies' and valued them highly, especially after dividend payments were resumed. Brokers watched the Brazilian Traction market with keen interest in hopes of turning a quick profit on a rising market from the stock. Some with grander ambitions saw inviting possibilities for the creation of enormous 'electricity trusts' that would gather scattered utility companies into one vast company encompassing continents. In this respect, Brazilian Traction, with its established reputation and solid earnings, offered a perfect target for any would-be promoter intent upon using the company as a nucleus for an embryonic trust. Nothing created more fear in the minds of Brazilian Traction directors than the thought of losing control of their enterprise to interests who might use its good name as a short-cut to quick profits. Accordingly, E.R. Wood, Malcolm Hubbard, E.R. Peacock, and other friends of the company well-connected in the world of finance spent much of their time keeping watch for incipient speculative activity. Even before the decade began, the company was receiving distinct signals from the financial district of Brussels that something was afoot. No one was especially surprised to discover that the source of the emanations was Alfred Loewenstein.

Alfred Loewenstein was by 1920 no newcomer to the Brazilian Traction scene. He had acted as a loyal link in the chain of financiers who had underwritten issue after issue of São Paulo, Rio, and Brazilian Traction securities and had skilfully built up a market for these securities among the small investors of the British Isles and the Continent. On one occasion in particular, Loewenstein had performed yeoman service for the Rio de Janeiro Tramway, Light and Power Company. In the late months of 1907, the financial markets of New York were hit by an unprecedented financial 'panic.' The ensuing period of financial stringency caught the Rio company at a very awkward juncture. Having finally secured its 'unified' tramway concession from the city, it was faced with an imperative need for capital, which had suddenly become all but unobtainable. In this moment of desperation, Alfred Loewenstein had stepped into the breach with a daring proposal to go to the European money market with a second issue of Rio Tramway bonds with a nominal value of £3.5 million.

Under Loewenstein's guidance, the details of the bond issue were hurriedly finalized during the early months of 1908. In order to maximize the bonds' appeal to both European and English investors, it was decided to make the issue in two denominations; one in French currency, at 500 francs, and the other in English currency, at £100. The two issues would rank *pari passu* and would pay interest semi-annually in the local currency of each country at a rate of 5 per cent. The bonds were officially described as 'Fifty Year, 5% Gold Second Mortgage Bonds.' From the very beginning the word 'gold' was of crucial importance, and from the beginning there was confusion. The English bonds were stamped as 'Five Percent, Fifty Year Second Mortgage Bonds,' whereas the French issue was franked as being 'obligation de cinq cents francs 5% *or*.' At the time nobody remarked upon the rather indefinite status of the word 'gold.' It was a careless and fatal error that was eventually to cost both the company and the bondholders dearly.

Oblivious of the ultimate consequences of the bonds' status *vis-à-vis* gold, Alfred Loewenstein orchestrated the flotation of the second-mortgage bonds with gratifying success. By the time selling ceased, 113,220 bonds of the French series had been placed on the Continent and 30,160 bonds of the English series were in the hands of English investors. With the capital generated by these sales, the Rio company's construction program proceeded unimpeded. In later years, Alfred Loewenstein made frequent reference to his activities as a seller of Rio bonds in 1908. From 'the moral point of view,' he emphasized, the company owed him a considerable debt. 'I am not in the habit of putting feathers in my cap when I am not entitled to them, but there is no doubt that it was my action at this time which saved the Rio Company.'[2] Under Loewenstein's careful vigilance, the Rio second-mortgage bonds remained a stable and popular investment until the eve of the First World War. The depression of 1913 and the instability induced by the deteriorating political situation in

Europe hit the Belgian securities market hard. In response to the worsening financial situation, the Belgian government imposed exchange restrictions that had the immediate effect of diminishing the trading value of the French series of the Rio bonds. Once again Loewenstein came to the rescue. To counteract the falling value of the bonds in Belgium, Loewenstein, aided by James Dunn in London, bought up a large number of the bonds and sold them to friendly English investors. As a quid pro quo for their efforts, Dunn and Loewenstein demanded that the coupons on the French bonds be made payable at a fixed rate of 9s. 11d. sterling for every 12.50 fr. coupon tendered in London. To satisfy this stipulation the Brazilian Traction board duly passed a resolution authorizing the 9s. 11d. rate of exchange and extending a guarantee to Dunn, Fischer and Co., Dunn's London investment firm, that all such coupons would be honoured at that rate.[3]

The ease with which the company granted a fixed rate of exchange for some of the French series bonds indicated that little thought had been given to the serious implications of the move. The 1914 resolution undermined any pretence that the French and English series were equal by discriminating against European bonds that were unable to traverse the Channel. By 1919, Belgian exchange had declined so severely that the company found itself paying over 60 per cent more than face value on the 12.50 fr. coupons redeemed in England. Not surprisingly, Sir Alexander Mackenzie admitted that this was highly discriminatory and 'unfair' to the bondholders residing in Belgium. Recognizing the error of its ways, the board rescinded the 1914 resolution in December 1919 and instructed London banks to redeem the 12.50 fr. coupons 'at the current rate of exchange.' When the London office reported that Loewenstein had taken a 'very firm attitude' against the board's reversal of policy on the coupon payments, it was clear that relations between Brazilian Traction and its principal European ally had taken an abrupt turn for the worse.

However, the deterioration of friendly relations began before the board's volte-face on the French bond coupons. At least two years earlier, the Belgian financier had begun to display openly his displeasure at Brazilian Traction's persistent refusal to grant him a seat on the board. Since the formation of Brazilian Traction, Loewenstein had tirelessly put his name forward as a candidate for the board. Belgian investors, he argued, deserved to be represented in the affairs of a company in which they had so large a stake. Sir Alexander Mackenzie's persistent refusal of this request was founded in the desire not to jeopardize the tightly knit solidarity of the company's Toronto promoters. It was also, one can surmise, a reflection of the subtle, yet pervasive anti-Semitism that flavoured Canadian business in these years. By 1918, Loewenstein's annoyance at Mackenzie's intransigence mounted to the point where he threatened to 'take extremely stong measures even to the point of breaking off the relations between my firm and the Company.'[4]

Excluded from the Brazilian Traction board and denied payment of his Belgian bond coupons at a fixed rate, Loewenstein was by the early 1920s in an angry mood and looking for a cudgel to take up against Brazilian Traction. He found the perfect weapon in the issue of whether the Rio second-mortgage bonds were in fact 'gold' bonds. Loewenstein fired his first salvo against Brazilian Traction in May 1920 when, after conferring with a Belgian lawyer, he informed the company that, in view of the prominent use of the world 'gold' on the bonds, 'there is no doubt that the payment in sterling of coupons of the Belgian and French bondholders cannot be refused by the company.'[5] Loewenstein's insistence that the 'gold' status of the bonds be openly acknowledged at once struck a sympathetic chord in the hearts of European bondholders. The company's case against Loewenstein's contention that the bonds were in fact gold-based was taken up by Walter Gow, a Blake partner who had experience in the legal affairs of the 'Pearson group' dating back to the turn of the century. After closely inspecting the trust deed and prospectus of the Rio second-mortgage bonds, Gow presented the opinion that 'the prospectus imposes no obligation on the company to pay otherwise than in the legal tender of the place where payment is made.' Gow was forced to admit, however, that the whole issue was clouded by legal ambiguities that might put the outcome of any court case in doubt. 'It is idle, however,' Gow warned, 'to shut one's eyes to the fact that the court might easily convince itself that the prominent use of the word "or" was an invitation to a prospective purchaser to treat the bonds as payment in gold or on a gold basis.'[6]

Gow's legal brief did little to steel the resolve of the Brazilian Traction board to continue its opposition to Loewenstein's demands. To commit the company to a long and fractious legal battle seemed to invite ominous consequences. 'In the last analysis,' Gow himself had taken pains to stress, 'the question seems to me to be one where expediency must largely govern.' Brazilian Traction's managers instinctively turned toward a compromise. This course of action with Loewenstein was first tentatively broached in October 1920 by Walter Gow himself, who suggested that a crisis might be averted by a 'restricted resumption' of payments on the bond coupons at the rate conceded by the 1914 arrangement with Dunn, Fischer and Co. Coupon payments at a fixed rate based on sterling would be resumed and applied to only those bonds of the French series that had crossed the Channel in 1914. The obvious flaw in the proposal was the virtual impossibility of identifying which bonds did and did not qualify. None the less, the proposal had the distinct pragmatic advantage of minimizing the danger of a head-on legal battle. In Sir Alexander's words, Gow's proposal for pacifying Loewenstein was clearly 'the less evil.' Predictably, Loewenstein snatched at the offer placed before him and agreed to act as the intermediary in a scheme designed to neutralize the approximately 15,000 bonds that (Loewenstein claimed) had been affected by the 1914 fixed-exchange agreement. Although the company endeavoured to protect itself by stipulating that the agreement 'in no wise' affected or prejudiced its rights *vis-à-vis* its other bondholders, it was painfully evident that Loewenstein had scored a major victory.

There was nevertheless cause in the 1921 agreement with Loewenstein for considerable relief in the offices of Brazilian Traction. The company had adopted a policy of expediency that had seemed, at least in the short run, to have succeeded. The ultimate consequences of many years of confused policies and tactical errors had yet to be realized. Alfred Loewenstein remained a dangerous menace. The schism between Brazilian Traction and Loewenstein was rooted in the fact that the company had developed a pathological distrust of the Belgian financier. Although Loewenstein might well have been pacified by naming him to the board, there was a strong feeling in the company that, once on the inside, Loewenstein would have wrecked the company with financial methods for which they had nothing but disdain. That Loewenstein had earlier employed similar talents to help establish the Rio and São Paulo companies mattered to a degree from 'the moral point of view,' but by the 1920s the dictates of sound, conservative corporate management took priority over any consideration of short-term financial gain. In essence, Alfred Loewenstein, as seen through the eyes of Brazilian Traction's Toronto managers, symbolized financial capitalism at its most flamboyant: the antithesis of the managerial capitalism they now strove to practise.

By 1921, the directors of Brazilian Traction had ample reason to fear Alfred Loewenstein. His reputation as the 'Belgian Croesus,' 'the Brussels Santa Claus,' and 'the mystery man of European finance' was founded on a hard-won ascendancy in the world of international finance that seemed almost heroic in proportion. Born in Brussels in 1877, the son of a German *emigré*, Loewenstein had begun his financial career soon after his twentieth birthday by entering into a partnership with Edouard Stallaerts for stock issues and financial placements.[7] In later years, Alfred Loewenstein boasted that he had built his fortune, said to be the third largest in the world, upon 'sound business "hunches," on industrial trends, and on an original capital of a few thousand francs plus unlimited energy.'[8] Realizing that Belgium's myriad small investors were hungry for the shares of the new utility companies that were appearing throughout Europe, North America, and Latin America, Loewenstein devoted his energies to cultivating this promising trade. The 'Pearson group' of Mexican, Brazilian, and Spanish utilities offered the Belgian financier his most profitable opportunity to lure Belgians with the prospect of a steady return on investment in distant lands. Stallaerts and Loewenstein's Brussels office thus became the farthest outreach of the flourishing group of Toronto-based public utilities into the European investment world.

The outbreak of the First World War completely fractured the securities network upon which Loewenstein had depended for his livelihood. As the German army swept across Belgium, Loewenstein abandoned both home and brokerage business and fled across the Channel to London. Only with the return of peace was Captain – a rank granted him by the Belgian army for his work as a quartermaster – Loewenstein able to return to his Brussels brokerage firm to try to recreate the pattern of his pre-war prosperity. In the post-war years, Loewenstein and many others in the financial fraternity learned with remarkable acuity to redirect their energies into new areas of investment. If new traction companies could not be created, then old ones could be amalgamated into enormous trusts or 'rings' under the auspices of holding companies. The utilities trust was not a new phenomenon. One of the world's largest electric trusts, the Belgian-based Société Financière de Transports et d'Entreprises Industrielles (SOFINA) had been active in Europe since the early years of the century. It was not until the twenties, however, that the creation of electricity trusts assumed the proportions of a boom.[9] While the promoters of the trusts justified their creations on grounds of economic efficiency and technology transfer, their real motivation more often than not was a desire to indulge in clever financial manipulation.

The investment trust was ideally suited to Alfred Loewenstein's character and ambitions. It opened to him a whole new field of speculative possibilities in electrical and 'artificial silk' companies. Few securities glittered in the eyes of investors more than those of the booming artificial-fibres industry (an industry that had received a tremendous fillip from the technological advances of the First World War) and the ever-profitable utilities industry. Loewenstein's actions in the early years of the post-war decade deliberately capitalized on the desire of small investors to profit from these two industries. As the *Economist* later remarked, 'Captain Loewenstein was not content merely to hold investments. He wanted control. He aimed at big amalgamations. Whether he had in view merely the making of stock market profits in the placing of the securities of his companies, or whether he had the more constructive view of helping these industries by forming international cartels, remains unanswerable.'[10] What the *Economist* found 'unanswerable,' others found immediately explicable. Alfred Loewenstein did not create holding companies for 'constructive' purposes. His interest was defined solely by his desire to feed upon investors' credulity and to reap quick and spectacular profits.

Alfred Loewenstein's initial sortie into the world of trusts came with the creation of the International Holding and Investment Company, under English laws, in May 1922. Intended as a vehicle for the amalgamation of various European 'artificial-silk' companies, International Holding encountered troubles from the beginning. Loewenstein quickly became embroiled in an acrimonious dispute with two Swiss chemists, Henry and Camille Dreyfus, over the disposition of royalties from the patents for the new 'wonder' fabrics, nylon and rayon. Eventually, the Dreyfus brothers triumphed in court, winning control of a company that was later to become British Celanese. Undeterred, Loewenstein launched his second major holding company in 1923. The Société Internationale d'Energie Hydro-Electrique (SIDRO) was brought into existence to expand the influence of SOFINA by giving the Belgian company an interest in the companies of the 'Pearson group.' In this Loewenstein acted with the blessing of Dannie N. Heineman,[11] the American-born managing director of SOFINA. Heineman's backing lent immense prestige to the Belgian's scheme. Loewenstein was soon boasting that he already had 'practical control' of Mexico Tramways and Barcelona Traction. Only Brazilian Traction remained beyond his reach. As *The Times* of London remarked, the creation of International Holdings and SIDRO 'crystalized the financial ambition of Loewenstein, which was to be a king in the world of hydro-electric and artificial silk enterprise.'[12]

From an early date, Loewenstein had learned to clothe his regal ambitions in a flamboyant style. In his personal life, Loewenstein appeared the ultimate embodiment of financial success. He lived in baronial splendour in a large, castle-like home in Brussels. When not in Brussels, Loewenstein frequented the French resort town of Biarritz, a favoured haunt of Europe's rich, where he maintained no less than eight villas. A country home in Leicestershire provided the Belgian millionaire with sufficient acreage to indulge his passion for horses. Absence from any one of his many homes imposed no hardship upon Loewenstein. He always travelled on the fastest liners and stayed in the best hotels. To expedite his movements around Europe, he purchased a Fokker trimotor passenger airplane and used it to ferry from his private airfield in Leicestershire to Biarritz or Brussels. After surveying the Belgian financier's lavish domestic arrangements, the *New York Times* estimated in 1928 that Loewenstein's household budget totalled $100,000 a week.[13]

Assessments of Alfred Loewenstein's character left little room for vague description; he was a man of pronounced characteristics. His only topics of conversation were horses and business, of which he talked authoritatively and incessantly. He possessed a violent and brutish temper and an absolute intolerance of opposition, especially when it impeded his enormous will to personal and financial power. Business colleagues who dared differ with the Belgian's opinions were usually treated to an abusive tirade. What perturbed Loewenstein's financial associates more than his explosive temper and verbal abuse was the fact that, as the decade progressed, he increasingly refused to play the financial game by the established rules. 'When Loewenstein is operating,' Miller Lash once complained to Montreal financier and fellow Brazilian Traction director J.W. McConnell, 'he is surrounded by such a mass of rumours that it is exceedingly difficult to sort out the facts. Many of these rumours are started by himself and it is characteristic of him that he makes statements constantly as to who is with him and supporting him and frequently these statements have no basis of fact.'[14] Whenever Brazilian Traction stock began to fluctuate on the market, Sir Alexander instinctively suspected 'Mr. Puffstein.'

By 1925, Sir Alexander had ample reason to suspect that the Belgian Croesus was trying to rouse the public's interest in Brazilian Traction. Still bitter over the company's refusal to grant him a boardroom seat, Loewenstein had decided to force the issue of the 'gold' status of the Rio bonds. The agreement he had exacted from the company in April 1921 had reaffirmed the precedent originally set in 1914 when the board had agreed to buy *some* of the French bond coupons at a fixed rate. Eager to force the issue back into the courts, Loewenstein induced a Belgian national by the name of Derwa to present some of the contentious Rio bond coupons for payment at a Toronto bank branch in October 1924. When the bank refused to make payment in anything but Belgian or French francs at the prevailing rate of exchange, the lawyers instantly converged on the case. Although the Derwa claim was not to be resolved for four years, it enabled Loewenstein to adopt the mantle of a bondholders' champion and to draw the company into the legal fight it had unceasingly sought to avoid. Loewenstein's resort to the courts was soon followed by other threatening signs.

The first indication that Loewenstein was readying an assault on the share capital of Brazilian Traction came in the late months of 1925 when Sir James Dunn reported from London that his erstwhile Belgian friend was putting together a 'new company' that would, by means of a share exchange, fuse various Canadian-based enterprises and SIDRO into one enormous company.[15] The surest indication that Loewenstein was on the march was provided by the steady rise in the market value of Brazilian Traction common, which from a low of 52 in mid-1925 climbed to reach a peak of 115 by August 1926.[16] Furthermore, the company learned to its consternation of rumours that the prominent Montreal financial and utilities tycoon, Sir Herbert Holt, was willing to vest his own holdings of Brazilian Traction in Loewenstein's proposed company.[17] With such Canadian allies, Loewenstein's 'fusion' plan took on very sinister proportions.

Early in September 1926, Loewenstein unveiled his latest creation, the Hydro-Electric Securities Corporation, a Quebec-incorporated holding company 'formed for the purpose of acquiring interests in public utility enterprises.' The board of Hydro-Electric Securities was headed by Loewenstein and included prominent members of the transatlantic banking and utilities fraternity. On the New York stock exchange, brokers joked that Loewenstein's latest creation was 90 per cent 'water' and 10 per cent electricity.[18] It was widely rumoured that the Belgian had set his sights on control of 35 per cent of Brazilian Traction's shares. The press described Loewenstein's latest holding company as a 'new and gigantic melting pot' designed by the 'greatest mixer of modern times.'[19] The company's response to Loewenstein's sudden moves was guided by E.R. Peacock, who, better than any other member of the board, understood the mores of European finance. Peacock's first move was to determine the extent of Montreal support for the Belgian's plans. 'As you know,' he wrote directly to Sir Herbert Holt, 'our friend Loewenstein had been causing all of us a good deal of anxiety and trouble. He ran a high-class circus at Biarritz accompanied by a campaign in the press which took such forms that I began to doubt his sanity.'[20] The import of Peacock's letter was reiterated to Holt in person by E.R. Wood, who reported that both J.W. McConnell and Holt were 'in accord' and would not openly back the Belgian's fusion scheme.

By late October 1926, the tide began to turn against Loewenstein. Dannie Heineman, who had no interest in seeing SIDRO become a full-fledged rival of SOFINA, began to voice his opposition to any scheme that would affect the influence of SOFINA. At the same time, Alexander Mackenzie warned that any fusion of Brazilian Traction with the Mexican or Spanish utilities would lead to a violent outburst of Brazilian nationalism, because Brazilians would conclude that they were being 'bled' to prop up the financially ailing Spanish and Mexican companies. As the Toronto *Evening Telegram* reported on 23 November: 'The feeling was that the Loewenstein proposal was based on using Brazilian, with its great future possibilities and its high earning power, to provide a background on which to hang a carcass composed of other enterprises not so favorably situated, to say the least of it.'

The climax of the fusion scheme came in December 1926, when Loewenstein announced his intention of placing his exchange proposal before a SIDRO and Brazilian Traction shareholders' meeting in Brussels, called for the evening of 22 December. As the decisive meeting approached, it was Dannie Heineman of SOFINA, not Brazilian Traction, who declared his willingness to fight Loewenstein in the open field. 'A compromise with our group is impossible,' Heineman told Peacock on 17 December. 'I definitely wish to put an end to this most unpleasant situation. We wish to do constructive work, and to do it calmly. There are so many other things to attend to ... and we have no time to waste in endless discussion of the fantastic schemes of a boxing financier.'[21]

On the evening of 22 December, nearly a thousand Belgian investors, principally holders of Brazilian Traction and SIDRO shares, crowded into a theatre in downtown Brussels. Loewenstein, surrounded by many of the European directors of his newly created Hydro-Electric Securities, sat on the platform at the front of the hall. At the other end of the stage, Dannie Heineman sat placidly.

To Loewenstein's annoyance, the chairman of the meeting arbitrarily ruled that there was an insufficient quorum to allow a vote on the fusion proposal. None the less, Loewenstein took the floor and launched into a long and vigorous defence of his proposal. The Belgian defended the central principle of his whole fusion scheme, 'the amalgamation of small concerns with powerful enterprises.' When Loewenstein concluded his remarks, the audience responded with applause. Heineman then rose and addressed the audience. In contrast to Loewenstein's 'tone and anger,' one spectator reported, Heineman 'started very coolly and collectively to expose all Mr. Loewenstein's plans, describing him as a man of crazy ideas and his scheme as a dream and all for self-power.' Heineman left little doubt that he considered that Hydro-Electric Securities represented an unwarranted increase in the capital stock of the companies it was swallowing and that Loewenstein had provided no credible explanation for this inflation. Heineman then turned his attention to *ad hominem* criticism of his adversary. 'Mr. Loewenstein has had fights with everybody,' he charged. 'This is due to his mentality, to his need of coming out, to his wish of exposing his ideas; sometimes he takes his desires for reality.'[22]

The dénouement of the evening's proceedings came with a vote, not on the share-exchange proposal, but on a motion to increase the number of SIDRO directors. When Loewenstein rose to address the motion, he was 'hissed and booed' and, realizing that he had lost the audience's sympathy, he promptly announced that he would abstain from voting his shares and proxies. Loewenstein's motion to add directors to the SIDRO board was subsequently defeated 218,992 to nil.

Although the battle had been won, the war was not yet over. Loewenstein had been checked, but he still enjoyed certain strategic advantages that could provide the basis of another assault on Brazilian

Traction. The case of the Rio second-mortgage bondholders was still before the Ontario Supreme Court and, if the Derwa claims were upheld, would give the Belgian a tremendous victory over the board of the Toronto corporation. Furthermore, Loewenstein continued to hold a large number of Traction shares, which could readily be employed in a renewed take-over attempt. From the company's point of view, the position of Sir Herbert Holt in Montreal remained a source of worry. Throughout the fracas, Holt had maintained a non-committal stance. No one could be sure that Holt would not suddenly align himself with Loewenstein and go for control of Brazilian Traction. Finally, there was also the question of Loewenstein's character. Most suspected that the humiliation of the Brussels meeting had served to harden his resolve and deepen his resentment of the forces of 'established' finance. Loewenstein did not disappoint their suspicions.

Loewenstein's first overtly hostile move came in August 1927, when yet another one of his holding companies emerged in Montreal. Incorporated under Quebec law, the International Holding and Investment Co. Ltd was simply a Canadian reincarnation of Loewenstein's 1922 English holding company of the same name. This time it had a distinctly Montreal flavour, with several executives of Holt's Light, Heat and Power on its board. Rumours that the Belgian was hatching a new Canadian fusion plan coincided with reports from E.R. Peacock that Loewenstein was again in a 'very strong financial position and very active' and had managed to buy up at least sixty thousand Brazilian Traction shares. 'I am told that he is breathing fire and slaughter against Heineman and all his associates,' Peacock warned Lash.[23]

On 19 April 1928, Loewenstein sailed for New York on the *Ile de France*. By the time the liner had docked on 26 April, it had become clear that Loewenstein was about to launch a two-pronged assault on Brazilian Traction. On the one hand, he would demand 'justice' for the holders of the Rio second-mortgage bonds, and on the other, he would demand a seat on the Brazilian Traction board by virtue of his allegedly large holdings of Brazilian stock. As soon as Loewenstein set foot in New York, he informed Lash that it was his intention to continue his journey to Toronto, where he hoped to meet with the board of Brazilian Traction and to work out a final solution to the bond dispute. On 2 May, Loewenstein and his Fokker, with its cargo of secretaries, valets, and hangers-on, arrived in Toronto. The Toronto press flocked to Leaside airport to inspect the trimotor, the first private business aircraft ever to visit the city. On Bay Street, the directors of Brazilian Traction nervously awaited the Belgian's appearance. As soon as he had been ushered into the boardroom, Loewenstein began to denounce Heineman in a 'most violent manner, using names that were absolutely inexcusable.' Loewenstein then turned his wrath on Alexander Mackenzie, whose underhanded methods, he charged, had been responsible for the reversal of his 1926 fusion plan. When the Belgian's tirade had subsided, Walter Gow calmly explained that, since the question of the 'gold' bonds was before the courts, the company did not feel it was appropriate to make further comment on its position. After once again abusing the reputations of Heineman and the management of the Barcelona, Mexican, and Brazilian companies, Loewenstein abruptly departed.

Loewenstein returned to his temporary base in New York, and the company was left to try to penetrate the thick fog of rumours he had left behind. One fact that company executives were able to winnow from the confusion was that the Belgian was essentially operating on his own. Both E.R. Peacock and J.W. McConnell reported that the influence of Holt and his financial allies, principally Toronto financier J.H. Gundy, would not be used to further Loewenstein's cause. Reassured in this respect, Brazilian Traction awaited the Belgian's next move. On 14 May, Loewenstein made his second appearance in Toronto. This time he came in even grander style. After landing at Leaside airport in his Fokker, the Belgian and his staff of nine secretaries, all heavily laden with file cases, motored to the King Edward Hotel and installed themselves in the hotel's most lavish suite.

Loewenstein's first business call in Toronto was at the board meeting of the Mexican Light and Power Company. Here, once again, he was confronted by his nemesis, Dannie Heineman, who, as a director of Mexico Tramways, had hurried to Toronto to reinforce his colleagues in their hour of need. When Heineman sought the board's permission to read a prepared statement refuting Loewenstein's insinuations of mismanagement, the Belgian reacted violently and, rather than listen to the charges, stormed out of the meeting. After a brief retreat to his hotel suite, Loewenstein again sallied forth in the early afternoon. This time his destination was the directors' meeting of Brazilian Traction at 357 Bay Street. Awaiting him there were Brazilian Traction directors Lash, Wood, Brown, White, McConnell, Phippen, and Hanna. To everybody's surprise

Loewenstein did not renew the intemperate behaviour of previous meetings but instead quietly requested that the board acknowledge the substantial amount of company stock held in Belgium by granting him a seat on the board and, secondly, that the 'gold'-bond dispute be settled forthwith in favour of the Belgian bondholders. In response, E.R. Wood reiterated the position that the courts would settle the bond case and that, because the Toronto head office had little idea of who held the bearer share warrants in Belgium, no attempt would be made to accommodate their wishes until their proxies were presented at the company's annual meeting on 16 July. Upon hearing this, Loewenstein withdrew from the meeting and within forty-five minutes was again heading for New York in his Fokker.

When Loewenstein sailed out of New York for Europe on 19 May, there was every indication that a bitter battle between the Belgian and Heineman was once again to ensue in the meeting halls of Belgium. If Heineman could be vanquished, Loewenstein could then return with sufficient proxies to work his will upon the Brazilian Traction board at the July annual meeting. Throughout June, Loewenstein shuttled between Brussels, Paris, and London, endeavouring to hold his numerous creditors at bay and to gather as many proxies as he could for the forthcoming fray in Toronto. By late June, Miller Lash in Toronto confided to his colleagues that in all probability the Belgian's efforts were doomed to failure. Realizing that they could 'take no chances,' the senior executives of Brazilian Traction had wasted little time after Loewenstein's departure in gathering sufficient proxies, including those 'from almost all large holders in Montreal and Toronto,' to outvote the Belgian bearer-warrant proxies at the upcoming annual meeting. From Montreal came the reassuring news that the Holt-Gundy 'influence will not be used in favour of any attack on the existing Brazilian Traction control.' Fortified by the knowledge of his tactical supremacy, Miller Lash confidently bided his time in Toronto, waiting for the battle.

The battle never took place. On 4 July, Loewenstein flew from Brussels to London for a day of consultation with his financial allies. Just after six o,clock that evening, he reboarded the Fokker at Croydon airport for the return flight to Brussels. By the time the trimotor had attained its cruising altitude of four thousand feet, Loewenstein had quietly settled to reading a book. There were six other passengers aboard, all employees of the Belgian financier. As the Fokker neared the French coast, Loewenstein rose from his seat and headed toward the rear compartment of the aircraft. As he did so, he motioned (for the cabin was full of noise from the engines) to his private secretary, Hodgson, that he was retiring to the toilet in the rear of the aircraft. When, fifteen minutes later, Loewenstein had not reappeared, Hodgson left his own seat and went aft to investigate. To his horror, he discovered that Loewenstein was neither in the toilet nor in the corridor space beside it. On the floor lay Loewenstein's collar and tie, and on the right-hand side of the corridor the aircraft's outer door rattled ajar. The wooden frame beside the door's lock was splintered. Numb with shock, Hodgson stumbled to the front of the aircraft and slipped a hastily scribbled note to the pilot: 'Captain Loewenstein has fallen out of the aeroplane.'[24]

With one accord, the stock markets of Europe and North America reacted dramatically to the news. 'The perplexity of the scared pilot landing the aeroplane on the sands of Dunkirk without the millionaire owner who stepped into it at Croydon,' the *Economist* noted in its next issue, 'is almost equalled by the perplexity of the "jobbers" in the Stock Exchange who have to deal in a "one-man" market with the one man dead.' In New York, the stock of International Holding and Investment tumbled from $215 to $100 within hours of the opening of trading and only recovered to $145 by the close of the day. Brazilian Traction officials reacted with shock and relief at the news of the Belgian's mysterious disappearance. 'Mr. Loewenstein's death came as a great shock to everyone,' one of them wrote, 'and I am sure that we all sympathize with his family in his sudden and tragic disappearance. On the other hand, one cannot avoid realizing that his death removes a great deal of trouble which would have arisen in the future not only to our group of companies but to others, and also, I feel sure, in the long run to himself.'[25] Miller Lash was quick to endorse this sentiment: 'of course present and future nuisance is eliminated.' It was not until 17 July that Alfred Loewenstein's battered body was pulled from the Channel by a fishing smack. Coroners, friends, and journalists were unable to provide a conclusive explanation of the Belgian's death.

On the day following the discovery of Loewenstein's broken body, the fifteenth annual meeting of Brazilian Traction took place in Toronto. It was a short, simple affair during which the dead Belgian's name was not once mentioned. When the time came for voting on resolutions in the annual meeting, the management of Brazilian Traction revealed the extent of the confidence invested in it by its shareholders. Miller Lash quietly tabled proxies in his name to a total of 1,916,623 new shares (out of a possible 7,600,000) as well as proxies for 104,861 old $100 shares that had yet to be exchanged under the terms of the January 1928 share split. The bearer share-warrant holders, Loewenstein's potential source of support, were represented by only 79,457 certificates of deposit. After the perfunctory election of a new board of directors and a shareholders' resolution proffering some 'very appreciative remarks regarding the administration,' the meeting adjourned.

The dénouement of the Loewenstein affair came a week later on 24 July, when the Supreme Court of Ontario ruled in the company's favour on the question of the Rio second-mortgage bonds. In his lengthy judgment, Mr Justice Rose ruled that '[no]where, either in the coupons, the bonds, the deed of trust and mortgage, or in any other document that has been produced, is there to be found any direct promise or expression of obligation to pay anything other than francs.'[26] The verdict was firm and definitive. In the wake of the Derwa decision, the company wisely decided to reach a settlement with the holders of the French bond series. Realizing the futility of further legal action, the bondholders proved amenable to the company's proposal that each 500-franc bond be endorsed by the company to represent a principal amount of £14.5.0 and that all future coupons on the bonds be calculated on the basis of 5 per cent interest on this amount.

It was easy for almost everybody concerned to forget all about 'King Loewenstein.' In the wake of his disappearance, the public learned something of the tangled finances of the man who had reputedly been the third-richest man in the world. The *New York Times* reported that an estate of $55 million had been deeply eroded by the claims of creditors and revenue men. In an editorial entitled 'Picturesque Rich Men,' the paper congratulated Americans on the fact that their 'great fortunes' were based 'not on manipulation but on productive effort.'[27] In Toronto, Brazilian Traction executives were little concerned with writing epitaphs for their late foe. 'Where is he?' J.W. McConnell asked rhetorically in a letter from Montreal. 'Perhaps he is saying somewhere,' he suggested, '"What meeting is this we are in now?"'[28]

CHAPTER NINE

Nationalism and Depression: Brazilian Traction in the 1930s

After Getúlio Vargas, Brazil's legendary *gaúcho* president, nothing was ever the same again, both for Brazil and for Brazilian Traction. (*Gaúcho* – literally cowboy – is the term used to describe someone from Brazil's southernmost state of Rio Grande do Sul.) Vargas's impact was great partly because he directed his nation's affairs for so long, from 1930 to 1954, with the exception of the years 1946–50. More importantly, under his various regimes as revolutionary leader, dictator, and finally elected president, Brazil acquired many of the attributes of modern nationhood. Under Vargas, Brazil became a society aspiring to greater political and economic self-determination governed by a strong, interventionist government. Without doubt, Vargas became the most influential figure in modern Brazilian history: he unleashed powerful forces in Brazilian society and by means of delicate compromise, adroit manipulation, and skilful procrastination, used them to further what he conceived of as his own and Brazil's best interests, interests that eventually became synonymous in his own mind. Unlike the Old Republic, which derived its support from the economically powerful interests of São Paulo and Minas Gerais, the political base that supported Vargas was fashioned from a broad, amorphous collection of forces, encompassing regional, class, and political differences.

Vargas's magic lay in his ability to juggle interest groups as varied as the quasi-fascist Integralists, with their emphasis on authoritarian government, and the idealistic young *tenentes* of the army, with their emphasis on the radical restructuring of society. As Vargas juggled, the managers of foreign enterprises in Brazil stood by and watched with feelings of fear and anxiety as the comfortable predictability of the Old Republic disappeared and was replaced by mild hostility to foreign capital and chronic instability. While Vargas pragmatically moved to remake the social and economic fabric of Brazil, Brazilian Traction strove to defend and adapt itself. Vargas's attempts to reform the basis on which public utilities operated in Brazil were by no means transitory challenges, but represented a permanent alteration. That this shift coincided with a severe economic depression made the thirties a doubly portentous decade. By the time Brazil entered the Second World War in 1942, the continued existence of the largest producer of electricity in Brazil provided ample proof of the ability of the Canadian enterprise to adapt to Vargas's Brazil.[1]

The Great Depression did not come to Brazil as an economic cataclysm in late 1929. As early as 1926, the managers of the São Paulo company had reported with some alarm that production in the large textile industry had begun to slacken, thereby curtailing the demand for power. Between 1926 and 1928, textile production slumped by 20 per cent in the state of São Paulo.[2] Although tramway earnings held up, industrial demand continued to decline throughout the last years of the decade. 'It is very difficult, if not impossible, to give any accurate prediction as to the future of this industry, as there is a great variation of local opinion relative to details,' a company engineer reported in 1930, '... not only is the present situation most serious but the future outlook is very gloomy.'[3] The same years, paradoxically, marked tremendous prosperity for Brazilian coffee, which remained the leading or 'dynamic' sector of the national economy. Despite the precariousness of their reliance upon coffee, Brazilians eagerly applied the proceeds of its export to the purchase of costly imports that they were unable to produce themselves. The managers of the Light decried this export-import syndrome as the prime contributor to the underdevelopment of the Brazilian economy. 'Undoubtedly the future hope for Brazil lies in increasing its exports,' Vice-president Herbert Couzens noted as early as 1927, 'and this should be one direction in which something can be done. If only the people of this country could also be persuaded to supply their own needs in certain directions, such as the matter of wheat, it would be also a very great advantage.'[4] The promotion of local industry would not only have left Brazil less at the mercy of international economic conditions, but, by creating industrial employment, would have helped to solve another problem that Couzens felt contributed to Brazil's imbalanced economy, namely 'the low purchasing power of the masses.'[5] Local industry and a more stable national economy would also create a larger demand for electricity and alleviate Brazil's perennial problems with exchange.

The onset of world-wide depression accelerated the deterioration in Brazil's economic situation. Coffee suffered a disastrous loss in value on international markets. By 1931, the price of Brazil's key export had fallen to one-third of its 1926–9 average. Brazil's plight was vividly symbolized by the burning of millions of bags of surplus coffee in a desperate attempt to prop up its price by restricting the supply. The subsequent constriction of 'hard'-currency earnings crippled Brazil's balance of payments and seriously impeded its ability to service its foreign debt and buy imports. Early in 1930, J.M. Bell, a São Paulo company vice-president, reported that the 'general trade depression, somewhat accentuated by the exchange weakness, but already desperate in view of the drop in coffee prices, has reduced everyone to the verge of panic.' Bell concluded that the outlook for power sales to manufacturers was not promising, especially since the country had large stocks of manufactured goods on hand. In the near future, Bell warned, manufacturing in Brazil would be a 'very hazardous and speculative proposition.'[6]

The early 1930s indeed witnessed all-round stagnation in Brazilian industry, particularly in the Rio and São Paulo areas served by the Light. Between 1928 and 1932, the São Paulo economy declined steadily at a rate of 1.3 per cent of GNP annually, with the result that many of the state's leading industries, especially the beleaguered textile industry, were 'clearly battered.' In January 1930, for instance, the consumption of power by general consumers was 11.06 per cent below the level of the corresponding month in the previous year. In Rio, the situation was equally forlorn. Between 1927 and 1929, power consumption dropped 27.5 per cent at the seventeen largest textile factories serviced by the Light.[7]

While the Depression brought hardship for Brazilian Traction and the Brazilian industrial economy, it did not bring ruin. The Light was protected from the worst effects of the downturn by the diversity of its services and by the fact that the gold clause (which ensured that some of its utility accounts were linked to gold) protected it from the worst effects of plummeting exchange. Secondly, and more importantly, Brazilian industry staged a remarkable recovery in the years after 1933. With the continued depression of the coffee market and the consequent shortage of exchange, Brazilians were forced to forgo the luxury of imported goods and turned instead to goods produced locally. The thirties therefore 'witnessed the first real industrialization thrust in Brazil.'[8] The ensuing diversification saw accelerated growth in such areas as the chemical, paper, furniture, and metallurgical industries. Once the grim early thirties were past, established Brazilian industries, especially textiles, flourished under the shelter of heightened protection and government-imposed prohibitions on the importation of new machinery. The south-eastern industrial 'pocket' of Brazil, which was almost exclusively supplied by the power plants of the Light, benefited handsomely from this industrial growth.

For the first time in Brazilian economic history, the dynamic centre of the national economy lay in the industrial sector, not in agriculture. During 1933–9, Brazilian agricultural output expanded only 1.6 per cent per annum, and agricultural exports, principally coffee, expanded by only a meagre 1.1 per cent per annum, whereas industrial production grew by 11.2 per cent annually.[9] 'Probably no country in the world,' the Canadian trade commissioner enviously noted in 1934, 'has been in a more favourable position than Brazil through the depression in regard to industry, maintaining high production at high price levels.' In 1934, for instance, consumption of electrical energy by industry in Rio and São Paulo increased 12.23 per cent over the previous year.[10] Brazil's burgeoning industrial economy favoured the state of São Paulo, which exceeded the national rate of industrial growth during 1933–9 by nearly 3 per cent per annum. Such growth was accompanied by a pronounced diversification of São Paulo industry, as local manufacturers responded to the scarcity of imported goods. This transformation was facilitated by the availability of plentiful energy, almost exclusively supplied by the Light. Between 1933 and 1939, the power load of São Paulo factories more than doubled from 158,232 kilowatts to 322,756 kilowatts. By 1939, 97 per cent of installed power capacity in the state was supplied from hydroelectric plants. São Paulo by the end of the decade led Brazil in almost every category of industrial production: 28.8 per cent of all industrial plants, 34.9 per cent of industrial workers, and 37.4 per cent of installed electrical capacity.[11]

Responding to this stimulus, both the Rio Light and the São Paulo Light registered steady advances in sales throughout the middle and late years of the decade. Sales of electrical energy increased from 797,832,000 kilowatt hours in 1931 to 1,550,000,000 kilowatt hours in 1939. Gas sales displayed similar growth with sales of 144,480,000 cubic metres in 1939. The number of connected telephones doubled between 1931 and 1939, although supply still lagged sadly behind demand. The best indicator of the resuscitation of the industrial economy of south-eastern Brazil was tramway ridership. *Cariocas* and *paulistanos* rode the Light's trams in direct proportion to the prosperity of the local economy. In the early years of the decade tramway ridership remained steady at about 725 million passengers a year, but after 1933 growth resumed and by 1940 the *bondes* of Rio and São Paulo carried more than a billion passengers annually. In all its activities except telephone service, the Light was thus able to respond to the enlarged demand for its services by employing the large margin of excess capacity it had built up in the 1920s. The Cubatão plant outside São Paulo provided this cushion of surplus power. The greatest attribute of Billings's plan for the Cubatão station was the ease with which capacity could be increased in a step-by-step fashion. Accordingly, in 1936, a third penstock, turbine, and generator were added, providing an additional 64,454 kilowatts for the São Paulo market. Similarly, two new units were added to the Ilha dos Pombos plant, thereby furnishing Rio Light with an extra 73,800 kilowatts.

Only towards the end of the decade did Light engineers again turn their attention to large-scale extension of their power network. As early as 1933, Billings had predicted that a 6 per cent annual rate of growth in power demand would lead inevitably to some prohibition on the connection of new customers. By 1935, Billings was warning Toronto that it was 'essential' to modernize the Lajes plant outside Rio by increasing the size of its reservoir and upgrading its six aging generators. After some hesitation, the Brazilian Traction board undertook a $1.32 million modernization of the Lajes plant. In São Paulo, however, the power situation became dire by 1939, and Billings urged Miller Lash to authorize new units for the Serra plant, or perhaps even a second Serra station, 'in the immediate future.' The unexpectedly strong growth in the demand for power throughout the late 1930s and the fear that the outbreak of hostilities in Europe would make electric-generating equipment unobtainable made it imperative to start the expansion of the Serra plant. If new units were not ready for operation by 1944, Billings emphasized, the São Paulo Light would face a crisis situation.

Lash's hesitant response to Billings's plea for expansion was at first glance peculiar. In normal circumstances, a power company faced with a steady growth in demand would have reacted with alacrity, but the climate for enterprise in Brazil during the thirties was anything but normal. Such considerations led the board to react coolly to the request for additional facilities, despite the fact that Billings was the Light's senior hydraulic engineer. Billings himself was forced to admit that, while expansion was warranted from the engineer's point of view, it appeared questionable, even foolhardy, when considered from the political and financial perspective. In short, the decade was marked by a pervasive fear of 'committing ourselves to unknown dangers in the future.'[12] This fear was occasioned by a double apprehension, first because the financial return on new hydro investment might never be reaped because of the chronic weakness of Brazilian exchange, and secondly because 'restrictive legislation' enacted by Brazil's 'revolutionary' politicians challenged the very existence of foreign utilities in Brazil.

Depressed exchange was not, of course, a new problem for Brazilian Traction. Unstable economic conditions during the First World War and in the early 1920s had impeded the company's ability to remit funds from Brazil, but the complete collapse of Brazil's export economy during the 1930s introduced a prolonged exchange crisis that troubled the company's managers to the point of desperation. The persistently low value of the milréis again placed the Light in a paradoxical position. While the prosperous condition of industry enabled the company to capitalize on the demand of its consumers *within* Brazil, its inability to convert its milréis into 'hard' currency condemned it to slow financial strangulation. Consequently, the Light provided a paradigm of the whole Brazilian economy during the Depression; it was internally prosperous but externally poor. Initially, the company did not react with alarm. On a visit to Rio in mid-1930, President Lash reported that on account of the gold clause in many of the concessions, 'dollar earnings' were keeping up 'well.'[13] Within a year, smugness turned to near panic as the milréis slipped as low as $3\frac{13}{16}$d. Vice-president Herbert Couzens in Rio began to have visions of a complete monetary collapse. 'In other words,' he warned, 'they would do as Germany did with their old mark, and the *milréis* value would drop to nothing.' 'Without foreign capital coming in and in substantial quantities,' Couzens gloomily predicted, 'Brazil is from the standpoint of foreign borrowings financially sunk.'[14] So, too, would be Brazilian Traction.

As the exchange rate continued its decline, two fears preoccupied the minds of Brazilian Traction's managers. Any major default by the Brazilian government would unavoidably damage the company's reputation in the eyes of its own shareholders, thereby making any future offering of securities a virtual impossibility. A more immediate danger was the concern that as Brazil's 'hard'-currency income became depleted, the ability of foreign companies to remit funds would be eroded to a point at which all remittances might be 'blocked' entirely. These fears began to assume a degree of reality in 1931 when the Brazilian federal government partially suspended payments into the sinking fund of its foreign debt. A complete default was averted in September 1931 by the successful negotiation of an £18 million sterling refunding loan in London with Rothschilds. The price paid by Brazil for assistance from European bankers was an undertaking to put its financial house in order. A financial 'mission' headed by English banker Sir Otto Niemeyer left little doubt that it expected reform in the administration of Brazil's monetary and fiscal affairs.[15]

In the wake of Niemeyer's call for government austerity and a stable currency, the Brazilian federal government attempted to shore up sagging exchange by giving the Banco do Brasil (its semi-official central bank) a monopoly on all exchange transactions. The Banco do Brasil immediately instituted a priorities system under which 'hard'-currency funds were primarily to be utilized for servicing the national debt and for buying essential imports. The Banco do Brasil monopoly had dire implications for foreign investors. 'You may not and possibly will not agree with me,' Couzens warned Lash, 'but it seems to me that our Company and all other foreign companies are now more or less living in a fool's paradise, due to the accumulation of funds here, which of necessity have been and are being considered on a gold basis and which are daily increasing in volume. The more funds accumulate, the greater the problem will be.'[16]

Given the mounting accumulation of milréis, the Light was increasingly tempted to resort to the black market as a means of obtaining hard currency. While such clandestine operations offered a ready solution to the company's financial woes, the dangers involved made them unconscionable. 'Knowing, as we do, the requirements both at Head Office and at London,' Couzens frankly admitted in May 1932, 'it is hard to let sizeable amounts of exchange slip by, but we have always taken the long view, realizing that any other would lead to complications and possibly heavy fines ... I have reason to know that the Companies' refusal to do exchange business on anything but a clean straight contract with the Banco do Brazil, is known by that institution, and has been marked up in our favour.'[17] None the less, the shortage of 'hard' currency forced the company to squeeze as much exchange value out of its milréis balances as possible. This meant maximizing purchases from local producers and adopting such practices as paying for external travel in Brazilian currency. In later years, J.M. Bell referred to these frantic efforts to exploit every chink in the wall of Brazilian exchange regulations as 'our horse trading methods of '32 and '33.'[18]

From the perspective of stark financial reality, the exchange situation remained 'the most difficult problem' of the Depression, as the 1932 annual report stressed. This view was shared by foreign diplomats. In September 1932, the commercial secretary at the British Embassy in Rio reported that 'the problem of currency accumulations awaiting remittance' had reached crisis proportions and that, he estimated, as much as £15 million in milréis earnings of foreign companies had been 'blocked.'[19] Similarly, the Canadian trade commissioner in Rio reluctantly warned Canadian exporters to exercise 'great caution before accepting new business in Brazil' on account of the unpredictability of Brazilian exchange.[20] In June 1933, some relief for the holders of 'blocked' currency was afforded by an agreement between the Brazilian government and N.M. Rothschild and Sons of London, Brazil's perennial financial saviour. The agreement provided for conversion of milréis into sterling at a guaranteed rate, 5 per cent below the official rate, for a period of six years. Despite this, the remittance situation continued to be grim. The combination of poor exchange and lack of convertibility in the early 1930s thus resulted in a steady deterioration in the net revenue accruing to Brazilian Traction in Toronto. From record profits of $16,861,096 in 1929, net revenue slipped inexorably to $3,428,955 by 1933 and remained well below the level of the late 1920s until the early forties.

Brazilian Traction's inability to secure sufficient exchange had severe implications for both its shareholders and its managers. The first casualty was the payment of dividends on common stock. In December 1929 the board reluctantly replaced the usual 1½ per cent quarterly dividend on the common stock with a stock dividend. A stock dividend had the advantage of allowing the company to conserve what little cash it had been able to remit from Brazil for other purposes. Six stock dividends were paid down to September 1932. Not until July 1937 was a small cash dividend of fifty cents per share again paid. In late 1938, dividends were again reluctantly suspended. Meagre and sporadic dividends throughout the decade naturally created displeasure among shareholders. No matter how frequently the Toronto management explained that it needed all re-mittances to cover fixed charges, administrative expenses, and essential purchases, letters of inquiry flooded into the Bay Street head office. Many shareholders found it difficult to grasp the fact that the Brazilian currency was to a large degree non-convertible. Others wrote to pass on 'helpful' suggestions. One shareholder, a Quebec country doctor, wrote to tell Lash that he had suffered such heavy financial losses in the Depression that he could not 'afford even to buy good coffee for my breakfast.' The doctor then placed a unique proposal before the president:

I know that the government forbids the export of milréis, *and prevents you from distributing the profits made by the company. I know also that the same government burns some million sacks of coffee every month to prevent the depreciation of the price of this precious beverage which is so plentiful in Brazil and so dear in our country.*

Therefore, may I ask you if it would not be possible for your company to buy some coffee and offer it to your shareholders as a part of the dividends they should receive, were the profits of the company distributed. For my part, I would be very glad to accept a good many hundred pounds if the thing was feasible. [21]

Lash politely replied that the scheme was not feasible and pointed out that not all shareholders were coffee lovers.

The uncertain cash flow out of Brazil also jeopardized attempts to modernize, renew, and expand services in Brazil. Although the machine shops of the Rio and São Paulo Light performed wonders of improvisa-tion, the company could not avoid importing certain items, such as turbines and electric motors, which simply could not be produced in Brazil. Since it could never be sure that the Banco do Brasil would furnish sufficient exchange to cover the cost of imported machinery, the company was left to agonize over every foreign purchase. Only after 1934 did Brazil again liberalize its exchange policy. The return to free ex-change was temporarily interrupted in 1937 when a deteriorating trade balance forced the Brazilian government to reimpose the exchange monopoly and to introduce a 3 per cent tax on all exchange transactions. This changing array of exchange regulations caused constant worry and, at times, considerable bitterness. 'As far as I can make out,' Herbert Couzens complained in 1935, 'the Bank of Brazil is so much disorganized internally that they hardly know where they are.' Only when the economic effects of the Second World War served to reverse Brazil's terms of trade did this sense of bafflement and anxiety subside.

If Brazilian Traction executives were baffled and embittered by Brazilian exchange in the 1930s, they could at least attribute their woes to certain traditional weaknesses in the economy. Unfortunately, the same could not be said of the tortuous course of Brazilian politics in the same decade. Just as industrial diversification allowed Brazil to move gradually away from its precarious reliance on staple exports, so too did political experimentation in the 1930s allow Brazil to construct a tentative new political structure out of the rubble of the Old Republic. The political ferment of the thirties brought Brazilian Traction an unwelcome sense of insecurity that it was largely unable to allay. In place of the Old Republic, with its liberal constitution, tolerance of local autonomy, and élitist politics, a new Brazil emerged. The new polity was characterized by a strong central government unafraid to intervene in the economy, to invest itself with sufficient constitutional rights, and to impose its will on the mighty state governments. Although by no means a perfect evolution, nor a complete break from the past, the new Brazilian state was consistently shaped by several influential forces. The most powerful of these were economic nationalism and an implicit trust in the efficacy of promoting social and economic change through bureaucratization. These 'new ideas' were accompanied by 'new men,' ranging from the members of Brazil's nascent Communist party, who favoured radical and deep-rooted change, to the fascist, authoritarian Integralists, who favoured social change along more conservative, corporatist lines. In the centre of this varied panorama stood political pragmatists like Getúlio Vargas, who drew eclectically upon the programs of these groups to build what eventually became the Estado Novo, or 'new state.' Amid this welter of new men and new ideas, Brazilian Traction groped to find its political bearings. In doing so, it abandoned the tried-and-true ways it had so diligently followed during the Old Republic and adopted flexible new tactics better suited to the exigencies of Vargas's Brazil. The Light's success in creating a new formula for survival amid the political chaos of the thirties ultimately explains why it was able to maintain its place in the Brazilian economy until the late 1970s.

Like most Brazilian political upheavals, the revolution of 1930 was a non-violent affair. When Getúlio Vargas made his triumphal entry into the national capital, it was aboard a train, not a tank. The formation of the provisional government was accompanied by the cheers of *cariocas* and not by bloody street fighting. Vargas did not 'make' the Brazilian revolution of 1930; he simply capitalized upon certain disintegrative tendencies that had long been present in the Old Republic. The canker of regional discontent had slowly been destroying the Old Republic's constitution for decades. Those outside the pale of the powerful São Paulo–Minas Gerais 'machine' looked on jealously as the self-perpetuating dynasty of *paulista* and *mineiro* presidents monopolized federal power. In the end, however, internal jealousies *within* the axis caused the old republican system to collapse. Washington Luís, the federal president from 1926 to 1930, broke the 'golden rule' of the political alliance by failing to groom a successor who was acceptable to *both* senior partners in the federal political arena. As a *paulista*, Washington Luís ought to have given his blessing to a prominent *mineiro* when the time came for succession. The obvious choice in this respect was Antônio Carlos de Andrada, the ambitious state president and protégé of former federal president Artur Bernardes, who was also a *mineiro*. By late 1928, it was becoming distressingly apparent that Washington Luís favoured Júlio Prestes de Albuquerque, the state president of São Paulo. The prospect the São Paulo, which by the late 1920s was clearly outstripping the rest of the nation economically, would install its politicians on a permanent basis in the federal presidency was sufficient to fracture the old central-Brazilian political axis beyond repair.

No longer able to rely upon the automatic support of their erstwhile political allies, disaffected *mineiro* politicians led by Antônio Carlos de Andrada began to look for new allies. They did not have far to look. In June 1929, Antônio Carlos formed an alliance with two leading lights in the political life of Brazil's southern state, Rio Grande do Sul. Borges de Medeiros, the crusty, authoritarian *éminence grise* of *gaúcho* politics, joined Getúlio Vargas, his current understudy in the Rio Grande do Sul presidency, in promising to combine forces in the upcoming 1930 federal election. The 'Liberal Alliance,' as the pact was dubbed, was little more than a loose amalgam of political malcontents lacking any semblance of a political credo. As events developed, the absence of a distinct platform allowed the Liberal Alliance to serve as an organization point for a wide variety of disaffected regional and sectional interests, held together by nothing more than disgust at the political corruption of the Old Republic.

The presidential election of 1930 provided a last opportunity for the *coronelismo*, or vigorous political string pulling, of the old regime to exercise its influence. Júlio Prestes de Albuquerque, the 'official' candidate, faced the challenge of the Liberal Alliance candidate Getúlio Vargas and his running mate, João Pessoa, the president of north-eastern Paraíba, and in an election that was 'polluted by the usual corruption'[22] captured 950,000 of the 1,500,000 ballots cast. In the wake of the election, discontent continued to simmer. Ardent members of the Liberal Alliance decried the election and argued that Prestes must be prevented from assuming the federal presidency. Rumours of a 'revolution' or a *golpe* (*coup d'état*) became widespread. In many ways, the Liberal Alliance was too anaemic to pose any real threat. Only the onset of the Depression and the active intervention of the army tipped the balance. Disgusted by the flagrant abuses of the old *políticos*, young idealists in the army, including *tenentes* like Juarez Távora and João Alberto, gravitated into the rebel camp. They were joined by young politicians, such as Osvaldo Aranha, an ambitious lawyer from Rio Grande do Sul, who shared the military's impatience with the old order. Finally, the Liberal Alliance won support from influential elements of the old political order itself, men like former president Artur Bernardes, who resented Washington Luís's high-handed behaviour. In the face of this mounting opposition, neither Washington Luís nor his would-be successor, Prestes, showed the least sign of seeking a compromise.

Smouldering discontent turned to active plotting when, in July 1930, defeated vice-presidential candidate João Pessoa was assassinated in an ice-cream parlour in Recife. Although the incident was unrelated to national politics, it stiffened the opposition's resolve to prevent the accession of Júlio Prestes. The name most frequently mentioned as the 'revolutionary' successor to Prestes was that of Getúlio Vargas. Finally, on 3 October 1930, rebel army units in Rio Grande do Sul, Paraíba, and Minas Gerais moved against the government. Resistance to the rebel forces never materialized, and the Old Republic disintegrated ignominiously. Washington Luís was arrested and imprisoned in Fort Copacabana.

The bloodless *coup* allowed a military *junta* to seize power and, three weeks later, to deliver power to Vargas, whose responsibility it would be to arrange new presidential elections. Nobody could have guessed that Brazilian voters would not be called to the polls again to elect a federal president for fifteen years. Almost everyone underestimated the *gaúcho* provisional president's will to power.

The key to understanding the political longevity of Getúlio Vargas lies in the fierce environment in which the political battles of his native Rio Grande do Sul were fought. Vargas was born in 1883 at São Borja just across the Uruguay River from Argentina. Like his cattle-ranching father, Vargas was imbued with the fierce sense of frontier independence and partisanship that typified life in Rio Grande do Sul. Developing in isolation from the more northern Brazilian states, political life in this most southern state exhibited a penchant for *caudilhismo* or 'boss'-oriented leadership. This in turn bred an instinct for adroit political management in *gaúcho* politicians, a skill that they complemented with a talent for ruthless political discipline.

Vargas had not initially planned a political career. After a brief stint as an army sergeant, he enrolled in 1903 at the law school of his state capital, Pôrto Alegre. While at law school, Vargas was first drawn into state politics. Elected a state assemblyman in the year he graduated, Vargas immediately aligned himself with Borges de Medeiros, the leader of the state Republican Party and Rio Grande do Sul's most powerful *caudilho*. Vargas's star rose quickly under Borges de Medeiros. He proved an apt student of 'machine' politics, rising to become leader of the state assembly, a federal deputy, and, from 1926 to 1928, federal minister of finance in the Washington Luís administration. Finally, in 1928, he became state president. In essence, Vargas was a superb manager of men. If he lacked the stellar qualities of a statesman, he possessed 'poise, discretion and self-control'[23] in abundance. As Peter Flynn has so colourfully put it, Vargas was 'a phlegmatic figure of opaque inscrutability, a cold, calculating manipulator strangely lacking in what are perceived to be the more typically Brazilian qualities of spontaneity and fiery enthusiasm.'[24]

As the events of 1930 unfolded, executives of Brazilian Traction looked on with fascination. Their immediate concern was for the safety of their extensive facilities in Rio, Minas Gerais, and São Paulo. Since electric-generating equipment and telephone-switching gear were very susceptible to physical abuse, the Light adopted a policy of passivity in the face of the revolt. As Vice-president Billings informed Lash, 'we have taken steps to put armed guards of our own at some of our plants, particularly at the Serra, but I do not think any such measures are very effective.' When the federal government requested that the telephone company restrict interstate telephone calls at the height of the crisis, the Light obliged. Similarly, employees made no attempt to oppose rebel troops when they appeared at the Lajes power plant on 6 October. Only at the Ilha dos Pombos generating station was there any violence. When rebel and loyal federal troops engaged in a bout of 'wild shooting' outside the plant, employees fled in terror. Thanks to two brave workers who refused to desert their posts, the plant was safely shut down and damage to the turbines avoided. Power in Rio and São Paulo was not once disrupted during the 'hostilities.'

Once the fear of outright violence had passed, the Light was left to contemplate the changed political circumstances in which it operated. Amid the intrigues and uncertainty, executives on the spot were inclined to draw pessimistic conclusions. 'I am thoroughly disgusted with this situation,' Billings reported to head office,

as there is no clear principle for which they are fighting. To me it seems merely the attempt of unsuccessful candidates to seize office in entire disregard of the true interests of the country. I am not by any means an admirer of the present Brazilian political system, but I think the Government class is honest although grossly extravagant in many directions. We certainly would not get any better and very probably would fare worse if the rebels were successful ... I do not see how this struggle can end quickly nor how it can fail to depress Brazilian economic conditions for a long time to come. The effect on our Company is therefore evident even though so far we have had no damage whatever.[25]

Billings, an American, was most perturbed by the spectre of 'communistic' attempts to undermine Brazilian society, but this was in large measure a transference of a North American 'red-scare' phobia, rather than an accurate assessment of Brazil. Herbert Couzens, an Englishman, produced a less alarmist analysis. 'Our Company,' he wrote in early 1930, 'has a real background in Brazil, extending over many years and has good straight and honest friends – new and old – and no authority in their right mind wants to recklessly interfere with something, which, throughout this recent affair was about the only one factor which went steadily about its business and kept going on peacefully – externally anyway.'[26] It was important, Couzens stressed, to distinguish between rhetoric and reality. 'All sorts of horrifying things have been suggested as likely to happen at once, but somehow they don't materialize.'

Couzens was able to winnow a few grains of prescience out of the revolutionary chaff. There would be, he surmised, a spate of new legislation affecting Brazilian society. The lot of the Brazilian worker would be the focus of much of this legislation. 'There is a good chance of capitalizing on the situation,' he suggested, 'by gracefully doing certain things *before* there is any question of coercion.' More worrisome, in Couzens's mind, was the sudden infusion of unknown faces into Brazilian federal politics. For years, the Light, especially under Sir Alexander, had worked within the politics of the Old Republic. 'The whole of the old people have been cleared out lock, stock and barrel,' Couzens noted. The familiar faces of *mineiro* and *paulista* politicians had been replaced by unfamiliar Rio Grande do Sul politicians. A few names in the new provisional government gave Couzens cause for satisfaction. José Maria Whitaker, the new finance minister, was a São Paulo banker and 'the finest thing about the new government.' Those who most worried Couzens were men like Juarez Távora, the new transport minister, who had ties to idealistic revolutionaries. Here was a seedbed of unpredictable ideas. Sir Alexander, observing the events of 1930 from his Italian villa, failed to see this crucial aspect of the revolution. 'I believe,' he cabled Lash, 'we have nothing to fear from new regime. Rio Grande do Sul element apparently preponderate now but we will have many friends including Minister of Foreign Affairs, Finance Minister, President of Banco do Brasil all of the highest standing.' The promised election would, Mackenzie predicted, see the return of Antônio Carlos de Andrada, and everything would return to pre-revolutionary normality. Vargas, Mackenzie later noted, 'has little experience of public life' and was 'not a strong man.'[27] Nothing could have been farther from the truth.

During the first years of the revolution, Brazilian Traction existed in a limbo of indecision as Brazil experimented with its future. Instead of facilitating a new election, the provisional government solidified its grasp on the central government. In November 1930, the federal Congress was dissolved, as were the legislative bodies of the states and municipalities. This draconian reduction of political freedom was followed by the installation of federally appointed *interventores* (literally interveners) in all

Brazilian states. Social, political, and economic reform was initiated in a pragmatic fashion. For the first time, for instance, Brazil acquired ministries of labour, education, and public health. Despite these advances, Brazil, with its economy in the doldrums, found difficulty in setting a new course. 'To sum matters up,' Couzens complained in late 1931, 'the only thing that seems clear is that everything is in a muddle.'[28] The muddle was in large part due to growing ideological polarization. The demise of the Old Republic had unleashed a broad array of conflicting opinions as to the role of government in shaping what was to be a better Brazil. It was inevitable that the Light, as the largest business enterprise in the country, should have been drawn into the contentious process of defining exactly what constituted a 'better' Brazil.

The most insistent pressure for reform came from the *tenentes*, the young army officers who had taken a leading role in toppling the Old Republic. Intolerant of the easy ways of liberal democracy, the *tenentes* were impatient to modernize, or *renovar*, Brazilian society. To achieve this, they urged the application of state power to those sectors that had traditionally lagged behind in the Brazilian economy. The reliance of the Old Republic on the import-export nexus was portrayed as an impediment to progress. The key to a self-sufficient future lay in fostering such indigenous industries as petroleum and steel.[29] 'There are among the revolutionists some young army officers,' Sir Alexander informed Sir Otto Niemeyer, 'who are idealists and propose to create a new heaven and a new earth through the "Second Republic" which they have helped to bring about. They are well meaning but quite without experience of affairs and in their zeal are apt to make a sad mess of the "New Republic."'[30] Despite their zealous rhetoric, the *tenentes* were in essence *bourgeois* reformists who respected the capitalist order and favoured state intervention only to promote national economic self-sufficiency. None the less, the 'October Third Club' acted as a 'ginger' group on the provisional government. For Asa Billings, they were like Roosevelt's 'brain trusters': idealistic bureaucrats meddling in the established economic order. Typical of their number was the aforementioned Juarez Távora, who had led rebel forces in Recife and subsequently been given the transport portfolio in Vargas's government. However, by no means all of the progressive reformists around Vargas were drawn from army ranks. Osvaldo Aranha, a young lawyer from Rio Grande do Sul who had led the rebel occupation of Rio de Janeiro, was appointed justice minister.

Pressure from the *tenentes* was not sufficient to force Vargas's hand. The provisional government was besieged by other influential bodies of opinion, ranging from the embryonic Communist party to a residue of old *políticos*. Vargas's first finance minister, José Maria Whitaker, the São Paulo banker, insisted on tackling the Depression with such timeworn orthodox remedies as a balanced budget. Only when the economy failed to respond to such policies did Whitaker resign, allowing Aranha to take his place. It became apparent that Vargas possessed a singular talent for preserving his flimsy political alliance on the slimmest margin of consensus. Such political prestidigitation may have held Brazil back from further political chaos, but from Brazilian Traction's perspective it created very unsatisfactory uncertainty. Early in 1931, Miller Lash confided to Alexander Mackenzie that these various groups in the provisional government were 'finding it difficult to unite in one settled government or policy.' 'This is not an unnatural phase,' Lash observed, 'as I have noticed it a number of times before when revolutions have taken place in different countries, but it has an unsettling effect.'[31]

By 1931, company managers began to distinguish several disturbing tendencies emerging from the political fog. Nurtured by the economic nationalism of the *tenentes*, a strident hostility towards foreign capital began to permeate Brazilian politics and journalism. No more inviting target for such antagonism existed than the Light. 'There is a wave of nationalism to be noted since the revolution,' Sir Alexander noted with dismay. 'The tramway, electric, telephone, gas, etc., companies ... are being charged with enjoying extraordinary privileges, with collecting extortionate rates, making extravagant profits and disregarding the rights of Brazilians by employing foreigners, etc.'[32] No amount of careful explanation of the accounting realities of the Light's financial position, especially of the squeeze imposed by low exchange, served to stem this flood tide of suspicion. In the popular mind, the Canadian traction company was 'rolling in money' and had to be brought under tight control, if not nationalized, in order to curb its supposedly immense profits.

The reasons for what Herbert Couzens called 'this wave of Jacobinism' were complex and diverse. Fundamentally, hostility towards foreign enterprise was rooted in the legitimate desire of Brazilians to be masters in their own economic house. In many minds, the Old Republic had become synonymous with Brazil's perilous reliance upon fickle foreign markets.

The Depression had provided another painful lesson in the economic and social costs of this reliance and had strengthened the resolve to insulate Brazil against further depressions. Economic diversification and control over the import-export economy were the two most obvious courses open to Brazilians. The Revolution of 1930, in this sense, represented an assault on the long-incumbent coffee oligarchy of São Paulo by the forces of economic nationalism. Unfortunately, the new political regime discovered that while it had been easy to identify economic shortcomings, it was far more difficult to plot an economic course for the new republic.

Not surprisingly, the debate over Brazil's economic future contained certain confusions and contradictions. The advocates of more self-sufficiency all too often succumbed to the temptation of condemning without distinction all foreign enterprise in Brazil. There was a failure to distinguish between predatory foreign business and contributory foreign enterprise. There was considerable justification for Brazilian suspicion of such foreign-financed schemes as the plans of American entrepreneur Percival Farquhar to exploit Brazil's iron-ore wealth or Henry Ford's ambitious scheme to create rubber plantations in the Amazon, because these projects represented a real alienation of Brazilian natural resources and did little to promote economic diversification.[33] On the other hand, utility companies such as the Light had helped for almost three decades to build the economic infrastructure of Brazil by providing plentiful electricity and public transportation. While it had imported large amounts of foreign-built electrical equipment, the Light had also encouraged local substitution of imported machinery and had fostered a tremendous diffusion of work skills relating to the hydroelectric, telephone, and tramway industries. The price paid by Brazil for this was the drain on its balance of payments created by the remittances made to Brazilian Traction in Toronto. Over the years, the parent corporation had prospered from its Brazilian investment, although war and poor exchange had not infrequently produced lean years. Under the Old Republic, the trade-off between technical and economic progress for Brazil and profits for foreign shareholders had been acceptable to both parties, but in the 1930s this equilibrium was threatened.

Brazilian Traction's very success attracted the scrutiny of Brazilian nationalists. It was the largest and most prominent foreign corporation in Brazil. Its streetcar, telephone, and power services touched the daily lives of every Rio and São Paulo citizen. Public-utility operations the world over offered natural targets for those disgruntled with the economic and social status quo. This resentment was given an added edge in Brazil by the fact that some of the Light's rates were fixed to a gold rate of exchange. The 'gold clause' provided some insurance against the vicissitudes in the rate of milréis exchange. It had, however, the unfortunate effect of making utility bills increase at times of poor Brazilian exchange and gave many *paulistanos* and *cariocas* understandable grounds for resentment of the Canadian 'octopus.' None the less, the largest factor motivating national-istic attacks on the Light was political opportunism. 'Every politician desirous of winning popularity,' the newspaper *A nação* noted, 'does what every journalist lacking a subject practices, namely he attacks the Companies providing public services.'[34] A confidential British diplomatic report of 1934 was equally blunt:

The wide-spread increase in this form of Xenophobia is undoubtedly due to the realisation that foreign interests are particuarly vulnerable, since probably their government would never go to the length of armed intervention in their defence. No further urge is needed than that which moves a hungry dog. The needy Brazilian politician, lawyer, or journalist, etc. sees in these flourishing foreign enterprises an obvious opportunity for plunder, promotion, or blackmail, according to his bent. A pretext for raising public feeling against a stranger is never difficult to find in a country like Brazil: indeed baiting the foreigner is not only profitable but actually becomes a virtue if conducted as a patriotic act of devotion.[35]

In response, Brazilian Traction pointed out that the Light was not a shareholders' Eldorado. Dividends had on average been low and had been completely suspended between 1917 and 1922. By the late 1920s the company was remitting an average of £3,350,000 annually to cover its financial commitments abroad. 'All the rest of our earnings together with the new capital subscribed [in 1928] had been employed in new works,' Alexander Mackenzie pointed out. 'This is the short history of the octopus which in the language of a section of the press is sucking the life blood of the nation and remitting abroad to the detriment of the trade balance what ought to remain within the four walls of Brazil.'[36]

Another factor contributing to antagonism towards the Light was the fear that it had a monopolistic grasp on Brazil's hydroelectric industry. This was accentuated by the realization that hydroelectric companies, whether they were under domestic or foreign control, were not governed by any national code but were instead regulated by a jumble of municipal, state, and federal concessions that lacked any central principles. Similarly, other utility services operated by Light subsidiaries were governed by a hodge-podge of tramway, gas, and telephone concessions. The need for legislative reform and the fear of monopoly motivated much anti-Light criticism. Politicians increasingly pressed for the rescinding of the 'gold clause,' the investigation of the Light's concessions, and a national codification of all laws relating to the hydroelectric industry. At first, company officials tended to discount such demands as post-revolutionary rhetoric. 'I think the chief men in the Government,' Miller Lash observed in 1931, 'are thoroughly alive to the foolishness of frightening foreign capital by attacks on concessions, etc., and that the difficulty comes from some of the radical and hot-headed officials and others who are hard to control.'[37] Lash underestimated the tenacity of the 'hot-headed officials.' By 1934, the Light faced the very real possibility that Brazil's new constitution would contain 'advanced views ... in connection with Water Rights, Mineral Rights, etc., the Regulation of Public Services by Commission.'[38]

The success of nationalist 'radicals' in proselytizing for their views was the result of their access to the restricted circle of advisers around Getúlio Vargas. Out of necessity, Light executives learned that in 'revolutionary' Brazil this was also their formula for survival. Under the Old Republic, the company had been able to protect its interests by availing itself of the protection of all three levels of Brazilian government. The imposition of a virtual dictatorship under the provisional government deprived Brazilians and foreigners alike of any constitutional free play. All political power in Brazil flowed from the office of the federal president. No group could afford to find itself without access to the sole arbiter of political decision making in Brazil. 'The revolution in a sense has put an end to all constitutional safeguards,' Sir Alexander perceptively noted. 'There is no longer any legislative body, federal, state or municipal. The President of the Republic is a dictator and makes by decree the laws he pleases. He appoints in the States "Interventores" to whom he attributes like powers within their spheres, and they in turn appoint Municipal officers with similar authority.'[39] This represented a dramatic departure from the Light's situation under the Old Republic, when Sir Alexander had mastered the art of playing one level of government against another. After 1930, everything depended upon the whims of the provisional president. After one particularly annoying reversal of policy at Vargas's hands, Mackenzie bitterly complained: 'Protests in suitable terms of course must be made but they get one nowhere. A dictator can do what he likes and converted into a decree his orders, however unjust, have the force of law.'[40]

Brazilian Traction was not alone in its distaste for the authoritarian bent of the new Brazilian government. The politically powerful state of São Paulo did not enjoy being bridled by Brazil's *gaúcho* president. When Vargas appointed João Alberto, a young *tenente*, as *interventor* in São Paulo, regional discontent swelled. Vargas's dilatoriness in bringing forward a new constitution further enraged the *paulistas*. By June 1931, Asa Billings reported that the people of the state had become 'completely "fed up."' Vargas greatly underestimated the strength of this regional alienation and was clearly caught off guard in early July 1932 when an open revolt broke out in São Paulo. Backed by the well-armed Fôrça Pública, the revolt lasted three months and represented the most serious threat yet encountered by the Revolution. Unlike most outbreaks of civil strife in Brazil, the São Paulo revolt was marked by violence. Because the rebel forces squandered their initial advantage of surprise and superior numbers, the conflict soon became a war of attrition that lasted until federal forces under General Goés Monteiro marched up the Paraíba Valley and took possession of the city of São Paulo in October.

Despite some sympathy for São Paulo's cause, Brazilian Traction was appalled by the rebellion. In the first place it divided the Light's concession area neatly in two. With the Rio Light under federal control and the São Paulo Light under the rebels, the company was placed in a very vulnerable and awkward position. 'From our Company's point of view the main danger, as I see it,' Herbert Couzens warned, 'is that in the event of São Paulo winning, there would very likely be a period of grave disorder here, in Rio, during the time of transfer from one side to the other, because all the disorderly and disappointed elements would be let loose and take full advantage of the situation.'[41] Consequently, the Light adopted a policy of strictest neutrality. Sitting on the fence proved to be a delicate and nerve-wracking task. The provisional government set up in São Paulo began, for instance, to issue its own scrip, which the company was obliged to accept as legal tender on its trams, although for exchange purposes it was worth absolutely nothing. Furthermore, the rebels declared a moratorium on the payment of the state's foreign debt, bearing out the claims of some foreign bankers that the revolt would ultimately jeopardize all foreign investment in Brazil. Throughout this chaos, the São Paulo Light clung to its policy of neutrality.

The Light's hope for an uneventful return to normalcy received an abrupt setback on the morning of 28 July when a float plane of the Brazilian navy appeared over Cubatão and dropped several bombs on the power station and its penstocks. Fortunately, most of the bombs missed their mark and exploded harmlessly, leaving small craters in the soft ground beside the penstocks. One direct hit was scored on the main powerhouse when a bomb pierced the concrete roof and exploded inside the plant beside the main control room. Nobody was injured, although a Canadian engineer named Bracken was blown out of his chair in the control room and hurled against a wall. Miraculously, Bracken suffered no injury other than a temporary loss of hearing. The only damage sustained by the plant was the shattering of all its windows and a gaping hole in its roof. More significant was the way in which the bombing finally destroyed the long-standing belief, first shaken by the 1924 revolt, that Brazilian Traction's facilities were immune to the occasional violent aspects of Brazil's political conflicts. This realization was reinforced when the aircraft reappeared on the following morning and staged another exhibition of inaccurate bombing. On this occasion not one of the bombs found its target. Company engineers subsequently estimated that the two raids had inflicted only $2,470 of damage.

In the wake of the bombing, Light officials busied themselves repairing the physical damage and applying diplomatic pressure to ensure that there was no repetition of the incident. Ken McCrimmon, the Canadian lawyer heading the Light's legal department in Rio, immediately lodged an unofficial protest with the Brazilian finance minister, Osvaldo Aranha, who 'expressed great surprise and indignation at the occurrence.'[42] McCrimmon made it abundantly clear to Aranha that if such bombings became a regular feature of business life in Brazil, foreign investors would take flight. At the same time, the British chargé d'affaires, Edward Keeling, made vigorous representations at the foreign office in Rio. Federal officials were obviously caught off guard by both the bombing and the vehemence of the company's reaction. Not until 5 August did Keeling receive any response to his protest. The minister of foreign affairs, Afrânio de Melo Franco, explained that the naval aircraft was on a routine patrol when it had developed engine trouble and, in preparing for a forced landing, had accidentally jettisoned its bomb load directly above the Serra plant. This struck Keeling as a 'fatuous excuse.' 'I observed,' he reported to London, 'that it was a somewhat curious coincidence that the machine should have developed engine trouble and dropped its bombs on precisely the same spot on two consecutive days. His Excellency, who had evidently forgotten that there had been two occasions, was painfully embarrassed.'[43]

Melo Franco's embarrassment became all the more palpable on 13 August when three federal aircraft bombed the Bocaina power plant, a small installation on the outskirts of São Paulo. Once again the aviators displayed a singular talent for inaccuracy, and no damage was sustained. None the less, the foreign office in London deemed the incident 'a very serious matter.' 'I think that Mr. Keeling is right in assuming that the military authorities propose to embark on a campaign of systematic bombardment of the Light and Power Company's stations, and that nothing but the very strongest representations will bring them to their senses.'[44] Company managers and British diplomats speculated that the commander of the federal forces, General Goés Monteiro, had ordered the plants bombed in order to sever the power supply to munitions plants operating in São Paulo. On 20 August, Keeling therefore informed Melo Franco that London had instructed him to 'protest most strongly against these apparently systematic attempts to destroy the property of this important British Company, which has at all times rendered valuable services to Brazil.' It was one of the very few occasions when the Light sought direct diplomatic intervention on its behalf. The protest brought an expression of 'the regret of the Federal Government for this occurrence' from Foreign Minister Melo Franco: 'It is not, nor could it be, the policy of the Federal Government,' the minister stated, 'to attack, in the defence of public order, foreign property not involved in the civil conflict.'[45] Strict instructions were issued to federal military pilots to avoid all Light installations on future flights.

The bombing of the Serra and Bocaina plants was in all probability the work of 'some hotheads,' in Couzens's words, who were trying to neutralize São Paulo industry by crippling its chief power supply. Some months later Finance Minister Aranha confided to Ken McCrimmon at a luncheon that the raids had been the result of 'an act of indiscipline committed by an *attaché* of the Minister of Marine' and some of the 'more fiery-spirited' junior officers.[46] Even with the Light operating, federal troops were able to quell the São Paulo rebellion in mid-October, and the most serious challenge to the Revolution was surmounted. Miller Lash was elated by the news that São Paulo had been brought back into the federal fold and that 'we haven't been compromised.'[47] Lash's relief was short-lived. If aerial bombardment had failed to score a direct hit on the company, the announcement during 1934 of a series of 'codes' governing Brazilian natural resources landed squarely on target.

Despite its dramatic impact, the São Paulo revolt did little to accelerate constitutional change in Brazil. Vargas continued to contend with an increasing number of pressure groups, from which he desperately endeavoured to construct a power base. While he proved a skilful master of the art of preserving political consensus, it had become apparent by late 1932 that he was an innately conservative politician averse to 'root-and-branch' change. Vargas began to display the attributes of a superb pragmatist. The maintenance of personal power, not the remaking of Brazil, became his guiding star. None the less, Vargas could not completely overlook the expectations to which the 'October Revolution' had given rise. In particular, the *tenentes*, who had helped to clinch military victory for the revolution, could not be disappointed in their hopes for a greater degree of national control over the economy. Several of the more ardent *tenentes*, notably Juarez Távora, held cabinet positions in the provisional government and insisted that Vargas honour his debt to them. It was becoming apparent that Vargas did not share the *tenentes*, strident views about the necessity of exorcising foreign capital from the Brazilian economy. When Brazilian Traction's president paid his first courtesy call on the president in September 1931, Vargas assured him that he could tell his shareholders 'that contracts will be respected and they need have no fear for any capital they invest here.'[48] Despite such assurances, however, Vargas's instinct for political survival told him that something had to be done to appease the *tenentes*. Vargas's primary goal throughout 1933 and early 1934 was to ensure that his presidency was confirmed by the Constituent Assembly. Until the assembly elected him and ratified a new constitution, Vargas was not in a position to embark upon any precipitous political initiatives or to alienate any substantial bloc of his support. In the interim, the Light was left to contend with a plethora of rumours, which for the most part hinted at imminent legislation in the field of natural-resources regulation. These were the 'advanced views' of which Herbert Couzens had warned. 'The general situation, at any rate outwardly, is quite calm,' Couzens reiterated, 'although there is undoubtedly a great deal of intrigue on foot, and my opinion, such as it is, still inclines to the view that Dr. Getúlio Vargas will be elected President, after which anything may happen.'[49]

A foretaste of the future was provided in November 1933 when the federal minister of transport and public works, José Américo de Almeida, issued a decree arbitrarily abolishing the gold clause in public-utility contracts.[50] It was the first concrete sign that Vargas was prepared to allow the *tenentes* some concessions. The cancellation of the gold clause most severely affected the Rio Light. On 29 December 1933, the prefect of the federal district decreed that the gold clause no longer applied to the company's electricity rates. The company had freely admitted that a 'considerable' part of its earnings in Brazil during times of depression were generated by the gold clause.[51] Such earnings served to alleviate the financial strain imposed by the necessity of purchasing supplies, such as electrical equipment, abroad. At the same time the gold clause excited much resentment among customers, whose utility bills rose when they could least afford to pay. In this sense, the abolition of the gold clause by fiat was a shrewd political move. 'The matter,' a Brazilian lawyer working for the Light noted, 'has been taken out of the judicial field and into the sentimental. Our opponents seem to think that it is damaging to Brazilian patriotism and nativism to establish in a contract for public utilities, payments based on the value of a foreign gold currency.' In reality, the gold clause was a simple guarantee, 'a criterion of value,' that protected the company against falls in the value of the national currency.[52]

The loss of the gold clause had the effect of immediately reducing the income of several Light operations by 25 per cent. When the minister imposed new rates on the Rio Gas Company, for example,[53] the company contended that they were only 'temporary.' In a bid to have the government reverse its decision, Vice-president Couzens lobbied the British ambassador in Rio, and Sir Thomas White (a director of Brazilian Traction and a Toronto banker) applied pressure on the Canadian government for diplomatic intervention. The Foreign Office, reluctant to intrude in Brazil's domestic affairs, concluded that the Light would be best advised 'to negotiate an equitable settlement by itself,' and Sir Thomas White reported that it was 'not probable' that Ottawa would see fit to act either.[54] There was little point in protesting further. Any attempt to reduce service or refuse the 'temporary' rates would simply have fed the fires of nationalism. 'The Minister is getting the popularity he sought,' Alexander Mackenzie commented. 'I have no doubt that among those who are active in the Constituent Assembly are some who confidently look to the gradual absorption of our property by the State by judicious admixture of taxes, pensions, low rates and abrogation of rights of ownership and I firmly believe that the process is well on the way.'[55]

Mackenzie's prophecy was partially fulfilled within a year. The Constituent Assembly finally ratified the new Brazilian constitution in July 1934. The decentralized nature of the 1891 constitution disappeared as the federal government assumed a host of new powers, especially in the social and economic realm. The document, for instance, contained clauses guaranteeing minimum wages to Brazilian workers and establishing labour courts to arbitrate disputes with employers. The constitution was clearly an attempt to lay the foundations of a 'new' Brazil. In many ways, however, it was not workable. As historian José Bello has commented, 'it reflected the confusion of the times and the political inexperience of most of its authors ... The constitution of 1934 was, in short, a set of compromises between various ideological currents, such as the Catholics and the Socialists, the Communists and the Integralistas.'[56] One of these compromises was the inclusion of a measure of economic nationalism in deference to *tenentes* like Juarez Távora. The constitution directed the state's attention to the need for Brazilians to control their economic patrimony.

Mines and other riches of the sub-soil [the constitution proclaimed], and also waterfalls constitute distinct property of the state. Their industrial development depends upon authorization, or federal concession, in the form of the law. The concessions will be conferred exclusively on Brazilians or on companies organized in Brazil. The law will regulate progressive nationalization of the waterfalls, or other sources of hydroelectric energy.

'This decree is, I think, the most violent in its effects on the Companies' business,' Couzens noted with alarm, 'and is in my opinion well nigh disastrous.'[57] All regulatory powers pertaining to the hydroelectric industry were to be placed under federal control. No longer would the Light's services be regulated by a motley collection of concessions negotiated with all three levels of Brazilian government. The designation of hydroelectricity as a 'national' industry under federal control came as no shock to the Light. 'One cannot question the right of the Government and people of Brazil to adopt a new law in relation to waterpowers,' Couzens acknowledged, 'for the previous legislation has been incomplete and defective.'[58] As Vargas himself admitted two years later on a visit to Lajes, the government's new policy regarding the nation's water powers was 'the consequence of administrative necessity.'[59] What deeply worried Brazilian Traction executives was not this administrative reform but the tone of xenophobic nationalism that underlay it. Although the constitution did contain guarantees of 'economic liberty' and 'the right of property,' it also contained vague but threatening terms like 'progressive nationalization' that both perplexed and frightened Brazilian Traction. 'It is true there may be some loopholes found,' Couzens remarked, 'but how can any foreign enterprise continue to operate on such a basis, which at best would be a gamble with the dice loaded against the foreigner.'[60]

The odds against the foreigner were made all the steeper by the publication on 10 July 1934 of the Código de Águas, or Water Code (see Appendix). Whereas the constitution had set out general principles, the Water Code was intended to provide for the specific management of Brazil's water-power resources.[61] The code reiterated the constitution's assertion that all hydroelectric sites in Brazil were part of the public patrimony and fell under federal jurisdiction, which would be administered by a 'Federal Commission on Waterpowers.' The commission was empowered to limit the length of all water-power concessions to thirty years, after which time they would revert to the state. All utility rates would be adjudicated by the commission on a basis of providing a fair return to investors as measured by the 'historical cost' of the investment; that is, on its value as calculated in milréis fixed at the time of investment and not in milréis adjusted to take account of the decline in the external value of the currency. 'Historical cost' was therefore the antithesis of any accounting practice that allowed for inflation and thereby ensured investors a realistic return on their capital. What made the concept of 'historical cost' doubly injurious was the stipulation in the Water Code that it be applied retroactively. In addition, the Water Code was quickly followed by another decree creating a special tax on all electrical capacity, in terms of kilowatts, possessed by power companies in Brazil. The so-called kilowatt tax was to be levied to provide revenue for the development of Brazil's national water resources.[62]

'Historical cost' was a deadly prescription. If it were applied to determine return on investment, foreign investors would see the capital base upon which they took their profits wither to the point of oblivion as the milréis continued its inexorable external loss of value. In this sense, 'historical cost' was a confiscatory principle and could only be accepted as legitimate practice by utilities accountants in countries that possessed extremely stable currencies. As Asa Billings acutely noted: 'every Brazilian shuts his eyes to the continued and intentional depreciation of the currency.'[63] If measured in terms of 'historical cost,' the $350 million investment made by Brazilian Traction since 1899 would have evaporated almost in the twinkling of an accountant's eye.

After recovering from the initial shock of the Water Code, Light executives were able to take some consolation from the fact that it had yet to be implemented. Despite the fact that the decree bore the signature of Getúlio Vargas, its potential impact remained ambiguous. Brazilian law relied heavily on broad codes to establish general principles from which specific regulations, such as the application of 'historical cost,' could be perfected. The 'regulamentation' period (a phrase coined from the Portuguese verb *regulamentar*, to regulate) afforded the company a hiatus in which it could attempt to come to terms with the Water Code. In particular, the Brazilian government would have to revise all the Light's pre-1934 concessions and determine a mutually acceptable rate base for all future services. Light lawyers employed two primary arguments in the face of these initiatives. In the first place, the code was portrayed as an 'unworkable' document, the product of zealots who had little grasp of the technical and financial realities of the hydroelectric industry. In this respect, Brazilian Traction's management reflected the general scepticism of the North American power industry to the whole notion of regulation. Just as private power producers in the United States railed against the Tennessee Valley Authority scheme, so Brazilian Traction's managers opposed the spectre of regulation in Brazil. Secondly, it was alleged that the code posed a dire threat to foreign investment in Brazil, because it might be interpreted to deny a fair return on investment.

In the meantime, the Water Code had the very negative effect of freezing all the Light's rates at 1934 levels, as well as prohibiting any expansion or modification of its hydroelectric network. The company would be obliged to face this deadlock until it could reconcile its interpretation of the Water Code with that of its political sponsors. Given the rather imprecise impact of the code, the Light had no option but to bide its time until the contentious aspects of the code, particularly the question of historical cost, could be satisfactorily defined and implemented. Few could have guessed in 1934 that this process would take four decades.

The Water Code was the product of *tenentes* like Juarez Távora and José Américo, who had an abundance of patriotic fervour and a complete lack of knowledge of the practicalities of generating electricity. For Asa Billings, there was only one response to this challenge: 'This tendency of these theorists, without practical experience, to experiment with their ideas at the expense of the enterprise, will have to be combatted by those in charge of the companies.'[64] Company officials tended to believe that certain 'radicals' and the 'yellow press' had cajoled the majority of 'apathetic' politicians into supporting the Water Code. Once its serious implications were clearly understood by 'reasonable' politicians, the code would be reformed. Modification would come when Brazilian leaders were made to realize that its clauses were injurious not only to the company but also to the general economic well-being of Brazil. 'Undoubtedly, it is extremely objectionable in principle,' Herbert Couzens said of the code, 'but I think you will agree not as fundamentally vicious, from our Company's point of view, as some of the other things that have been done, and will be likely to cause more trouble to the country's credit abroad than to our Company's interests in Brazil.'[65]

Couzens's view was shared by many Brazilians. Dr Roberto Simonsen, a prominent São Paulo industrialist and scholar of Brazil's economic history, vigorously defended the role of foreign capital. Simonsen's views were echoed by *O estado de São Paulo*, which editorialized on the necessity of maintaining the international flow of goods and capital. 'Try as we may to defend the virtues of economic nationalism, no one can deny that with a nation like ours where everything is underdeveloped and to be achieved, it is impossible to do without foreign assistance in the way of capital. Unhappily we are losing the opportunity of attracting such capital because we are doing away with all the chances of any return.'[66] From his retirement in Italy, Sir Alexander formed a very dogmatic response to the same situation. 'I know,' he wrote to Miller Lash, 'that you and Couzens do not favour such propaganda or consider it dangerous. My answer to that is that you have to form public opinion and if you let the demagogues do all the talking you need not be surprised if they get away with it.'[67]

Those who had lived through the confused evolution of Brazilian politics since 1930 were not inclined to follow Sir Alexander's advice. Political life in Brazil since the revolution had been characterized by turmoil, as Getúlio Vargas strove to build a power base and to parry the varying forces of reform. In this changeable climate, Light executives realized that precipitous action might well occasion a nationalistic outburst and thereby provide the provisional president or one of his 'radically' minded associates a sterling opportunity to solidify the provisional government's fragile political base. Acting on this belief, the company adopted what Lash dubbed 'a policy of silence' in response to the Water Code challenge and opted for more conciliatory tactics. Cooler minds in Rio and Toronto realized that the best means of handling the Water Code was a large measure of patience and a well-prepared legal defence. 'We are rather in the position of the unfortunate gentleman in the parable of the good Samaritan, though our plight is I hope not quite as serious,' Couzens noted, 'because the prospect is that we shall only be subjected to the treatment given by the Pharisees, however much we hope and look for the good Samaritan.'[68]

It was a wise strategy. The Water Code soon became stranded on the shifting shoals of Brazilian politics and, despite innumerable attempts to make it a workable piece of legislation, remained unimplemented, particularly with respect to the Light's unrevised concessions and frozen rates. The code quickly became a rhetorical fancy of Brazilian politicians, a convenient touchstone for those who periodically wished to arouse nationalistic fervour. A small core of politicians and bureaucrats clung to the ideals of the original Water Code, but most public figures adopted a more pragmatic attitude to the idea of greater national control over Brazil's hydroelectric industry. Even Getúlio Vargas was capable of delivering a scathing assault on the Canadian 'octopus' as a predatory foreign utility and then, within days, calmly reassuring foreign businessmen that they had nothing to fear. In December 1936, for instance, Vargas frankly admitted to a group of Light workers that 'The Government has never done the Light any favours and has only imposed upon it onus and sacrifices. I must do this justice, and I take the opportunity to testify that this Company has always obeyed Brazilian laws and has never approached the Government to plead for any illicit favours.' He concluded 'by affirming that he would never try to fight foreign capital, because he understands that we require it seeing that we are a country poor in capital and rich in possibilities.'[69] Four months later, the same man told a military audience in Petrópolis that foreign companies were feeding money to his political foes and that they would be 'repaid' for their ill doing.

Although the Water Code fell prey to political opportunism, it remained part of a broad movement towards national control of Brazil's natural resources that, while frequently superseded by more immediate concerns, was ultimately destined to triumph. The Revolution of 1930 did not produce any sudden, spectacular changes in the social and economic fabric of Brazilian society, but it did set in motion, or accelerate, certain inexorable tendencies, one of which was the necessity of controlling the national patrimony. As historian John Wirth has concluded: 'Brazilian policy makers developed a future orientation and a confidence in national purpose that in the broadest sense can be called developmental nationalism.'[70] In developing the Brazilian steel and petroleum industries, the state was to assert its role relatively quickly – by the 1940s and 1950s – but in the hydroelectric industry, where there was an established and efficient foreign presence, the process would take longer.

The first step in the Water Code's long journey to implementation came in early 1935 when the Brazilian Congress appointed a special committee to investigate it on a clause-by-clause basis. The Light resisted the temptation to rush to the congressional committee to present its case. Instead, the legal department of the Light quietly prepared a case against what it considered to be the 'illegal' aspects of the code, especially its apparent contradiction of the federal constitution's article 113, which stated that no law 'shall prejudice acquired rights.' At the same time, evidence was assembled to counter the widespread public notion that the Light's concessions were fabulously remunerative. Particular attention was paid to the fact that many of the company's utility rates were chronically out of date and in need of renegotiation. By April 1935 the committee had made little progress. This was in large part due to the broader political unrest that plagued Brazil. Besieged by the demands and violent methods of Communists and the fascist Integralistas, Vargas concentrated his energies on the tricky business of maintaining political order rather than upon expediting legislative codes. In the midst of this confusion, the minister of agriculture, Odilon Braga, paid a visit to the Lajes power plant, where he assured Billings that the Water Code would have to be 'modified.'[71] Such statements were indicative of the history of the Water Code down to the Second World War. A long succession of politicians learned to colour the Water Code to suit their own ideological (and sometimes base, political) instincts. Accordingly, the Light's reaction to the threat of the code tended to wax and wane. Unfortunately for the company, the Water Code never waned to the point of extinction. It was always a haunting presence in the minds of Brazilian Traction executives.

Faced with little progress in regulating the Water Code, Vargas was forced to extend the deadline for its implementation. Throughout 1935–6, the *commissão especial* continued its hearings, but seemed incapable of definitively modifying the code. In August 1935 the first major crack in the Water Code appeared, when Vargas allowed the state of São Paulo, which violently objected to the federal government's centralization of power, to reclaim its control over state water power. This dangerous precedent seriously jeopardized the would-be national code. To an increasing degree, the fate of the Water Code came to rest on the outcome of a deep-rooted struggle between a clique of 'hard-core' advocates of the 1934 code and pragmatists who were prepared to modify it. In the interim, many of the problems confronting the Light, including the renegotiation of rates and concessions, were left unattended.

The likelihood of ongoing deadlock was suddenly diminished by a *coup d'état*, in November 1937, which ushered in the Estado Novo, or 'new state,' with its strong corporatist, authoritarian tendencies. After 1935, Vargas had found it increasingly difficult to control the social and political tensions within Brazil. On the left, the Aliança Nacional Libertadora, a popular-front workers' movement, made impressive gains; gains that were vigorously opposed by the right-wing Integralist movement, with its anti-democratic, authoritarian bias. The outbreak of a short-lived but violent rebellion in the federal army in late 1935 confirmed right-wing suspicions that the Communists were infiltrating the Brazilian government. Although the institution of a 'state of siege' and censorship effectively crushed the Aliança, preparations for the elections to select a successor to Vargas in 1938 gave every indication of reigniting the strife. The 1934 constitution expressly prohibited the re-election of the incumbent president. The appearance of a *tenente* or 'radical' candidate, in the person of José Américo de Almeida, and a São Paulo candidate, Armando Sales de Oliveira, augured a rancorous campaign. This fear was heightened when Luís Carlos Prestes, the Communist leader, announced his candidacy. Fearful of political turmoil and no doubt with an eye to the preservation of his own political power, Vargas gravitated into the camp of the *Integralistas* and certain elements of the army that favoured a strong central government. Francisco Campos, a lawyer from Minas Gerais and Vargas's justice minister, quietly readied a new corporatist-style constitution, which concentrated all state power in the president's hands and destroyed virtually all regional and congressional checks. All that was needed to inaugurate the Estado Novo was the specious threat of another Communist uprising. On 10 November 1937, the federal congress was summarily dismissed and the presidential election abruptly abandoned. Getúlio Vargas thus became a virtual dictator.

The initial reaction of Light officials to the bloodless *coup* was one of relief and mild optimism. At least, they reasoned, the *coup* had removed several of the extremist groups that had mired the political process. 'I personally feel,' Ken McCrimmon predicted, 'that our tasks here will be greatly simplified and that we will in future have a more direct and intimate contact with the Executive power whose tendency will be benevolent rather than the contrary.'[72] Although the new constitution reiterated many of the claims to the 'progressive nationalization' of water powers, McCrimmon was 'firmly convinced' that under the new regime 'we have every reason to feel the greatest encouragement' that the Water Code problem would be promptly and favourably resolved. As early as January 1938, J.M. Bell in São Paulo alerted Lash in Toronto that a new draft of the water-power legislation was about to be tabled. 'It is by no means an ideal document, but I believe is a workable project and relatively favourable to us.' The revised code exempted previous concessions from its terms, moderated the kilowatt tax, and left the question of 'progressive nationalization' to future legislation.

Unfortunately, both McCrimmon and Bell had underestimated the resilience of 'developmental nationalism.' The seemingly 'favourable' draft legislation of 1938 met an early death in the federal bureaucracy and, in its place, 'a very hostile code similar to but worse than the Juarez Távora one of July 1934' appeared. As Billings explained to Lash, the hostile 'brain trusters' had taken inspiration from a recent federal decree that required exploitation of oil in Brazil to be undertaken by Brazilians alone. Once again stringent nationalistic provisos appeared in the code and, as Billings dejectedly admitted, the Light once again had 'a terrible mess' on its hands. The bureaucrats were checked only when McCrimmon made overtures to Francisco Campos, Osvaldo Aranha, and Goés Monteiro, all of whom served as political confidants to the president.

Aranha and Monteiro in turn lobbied Vargas, who agreed to 'hold action' on the Water Code in deference to the sensibilities of foreign investors. Two weeks later, Vargas gave McCrimmon a personal audience and reaffirmed his desire for 'collaboration' with foreign capital.[73] Another crisis was thus averted, and the Water Code returned to its previous unregulated state.

The Light's response to the threat of the Water Code was indicative of a new style of political defence. The old method of making political representations died with the Old Republic. Alexander Mackenzie had acted as the company's leading representative in Brazil in an ambassadorial style. In almost regal manner, he paid official visits to the leaders of municipal, state, and federal governments. His presence was universally welcomed in an era when Brazilians were prepared to accommodate foreign capital on an equitable basis. Since the Light was always careful to surround itself with competent Brazilian lawyers, the possibility of head-on conflict with the state was minimized by the flexibility of the Brazilian constitutional system and the fact that Mackenzie was perceived as *persona grata* by Brazilian authorities. The Revolution of 1930 wrecked this felicitous and productive relationship. It deprived Brazilian politics of its constitutional flexibility by greatly strengthening the federal government's powers and, by 1937, delivering all political power into one man's hands. It also intensified Brazilian nationalism to the point that foreign businessmen were generally viewed with suspicion. In this new milieu, Sir Alexander's political methods were no longer practicable or advisable. Foreign capitalists in the 1930s encountered a combative mood whenever they moved. A new *modus operandi* was needed if Brazilian Traction's huge investment was to survive the tumultuous thirties intact. Just as its style during the Old Republic was embodied in Sir Alexander, so the Light's response to the thirties came to be embodied by Major Kenneth Howard McCrimmon.

McCrimmon was the product of the same Scottish Presbyterian community in Ontario that produced his uncle, Sir Alexander. Born in Kincardine in 1890, McCrimmon had won a Distinguished Service Order in the First World War before returning to law school in Canada. In 1920 he accepted an offer from his uncle to come to Brazil and soon after was appointed legal secretary of the Light in Rio. Like Sir Alexander, McCrimmon mastered the Portuguese language and Brazilian legal system with alacrity and from an early date showed a remarkable talent for representing the companies' affairs in the corridors of Brazilian power. Unlike his uncle, a man of sober and upright bearing and a pillar of Presbyterian rectitude, McCrimmon displayed a taste for the 'good life' that Rio had to offer. He brought to his social obligations the same zest and unfettered enthusiasm with which he tackled the company's business. He exuberantly indulged in Rio's ample night life, joined the crowds on the city's renowned beaches, danced in the streets at Carnival, and kept a stable of fine horses for his weekend amusement. In social and business circles, McCrimmon excelled in making Brazilian friends and establishing contacts. During the 1920s, he had taken a leading role in planning the Light's defence of its interests when President Bernardes arbitrarily cancelled the Rio telephone contract. None the less, he remained in his uncle's shadow, using the latter's extensive network of contacts and conforming to Sir Alexander's style of operations. McCrimmon's first decade in Brazil was thus a rather pleasurable experience, so pleasurable that he even had time to act as the Brazilian correspondent for *The Times* of London.

Only after Sir Alexander left Brazil in 1928 and the events of 1930 had completely disrupted the Light's political standing did 'the Major' rise to prominence. It was McCrimmon's unique talent to be able to build new bridges of communication with the 'new faces' of Brazilian politics. While Sir Alexander had relied upon friendships with established politicians of the Old Republic, McCrimmon faced the more difficult task of establishing the company's credentials before a group of political unknowns from states such as Rio Grande do Sul that had previously been excluded from federal politics. Whereas presidential elections under the Old Republic usually yielded a predictable new incumbent, the revolution produced men like Getúlio Vargas and Osvaldo Aranha, who were strangers to federal politics. It was a tribute to McCrimmon's skills as a representative of Canadian capital that by the end of the decade he was accorded the privilege of personal interviews with President Vargas and enjoyed the personal friendship of Osvaldo Aranha and Goés Monteiro, the two politicians who exercised the most influence in the presidential palace. As Vice-president J.M. Bell frankly admitted in 1938, McCrimmon had made himself 'indispensable' to the Light. This was undoubtedly due to the Major's 'intimate personal contacts' and 'the absolute gall to tick off the powers that be at times in the manner which Ken seems to be able to do successfully and still retain everyone's friendship and admiration.'[74]

McCrimmon's ability to establish 'intimate contacts' was, in the first place, built upon his knack for conviviality. He possessed an easy-going, winning way that charmed and won the friendship of all who were exposed to it. Secondly, and more importantly, he was able to convince many of the 'revolutionary' politicians that their country could not do without foreign capital. If McCrimmon was able to 'tick off' Brazilian politicians, it was because he had detected, behind all the nationalistic rhetoric, a realization on the part of 'moderate' Brazilian politicians that foreign capital might take flight from Brazil if companies like Brazilian Traction were harshly treated or 'progressively nationalized.' While McCrimmon never hoped nor attempted to win the sympathy of extremists like Juarez Távora, he knew that a large and influential body of public opinion could be won over from the strident nationalism that the Revolution had triggered.

No other aspect of the Light's history has produced so many anecdotes as Major Ken McCrimmon's abilities as a social convener. It would be a gross understatement to say that McCrimmon was simply a 'good host.' To be invited to his home in Rio or to his country farm at Teresópolis was to be introduced into a convivial society that was frequented by the leaders of business and politics in Brazil. Some years later in 1945, a Canadian diplomat, F.H. Soward, had occasion to visit Rio on official business and witnessed McCrimmon in action. 'The Company,' he reported back to Ottawa,

has been most active in maintaining its private contacts with politicians and key personalities. One official remarked to me that they had five different 'diplomatic agents' for contact with the President, rival political leaders, and officials of the Ministry of Finance. When I was invited to luncheon by Major McCrimmon, the guest of honour was the first Brazilian Minister to Canada [João Alberto], who is now the Chief of Police in the Federal District and one of the President's most trusted advisers. The Chief of Police is a school mate of a Communist leader in Brazil and Major McCrimmon took part in a private conversation for over two hours between these two men without either one expressing any surprise at his doing so. It was generally agreed that Major McCrimmon's bluff manner, skill as a host, and command of Portuguese, made him an admirable contact man with Brazilians of all sorts. He told a friend of mine that he spent an hour a day in one of the less respectable bars in Rio since it was essential for contact purposes.[75]

Despite his success as a 'contact man,' McCrimmon did not lack detractors. The 'radical' press delighted in portraying the Major as the subverter of Brazil's moral fibre. *A democracia*, an extremist newspaper, viciously assailed him in 1938 for his part in opposing the Water Code, alleging that he had had 'to resort to larger and larger doses of whisky in order to loosen the resolve of his opponents.'[76] Such attacks overlooked the fact that McCrimmon stood on solid legal ground when he challenged such nationalistic legislation. Nor did he ever disguise his intentions. In 1944, for instance, he boldly took his case against the Water Code to Vargas himself.

I asked the President to forgive me for my frankness and stated that I did not wish to be rude but that I was sure he would expect me to call a spade a spade. I told him that as matters now stood the foreign investor did not feel that he had any guarantees for his capital and that capital must be defined whether for purposes of 'encampação' [take-over] or for the fixation of rates and tariffs.[77]

McCrimmon's activities can only be judged by the political and ethical standards of contemporary Brazilians. Any political system functions most smoothly when it is bound together by a network of 'friends.' Kinship and political cronyism had been at the heart of politics in the Old Republic, and they survived as a central facet of Brazilian politics after the revolution. The cultivation of influence was central to the Brazilian way of life. To have scrupulously avoided the influence game would have jeopardized if not destroyed the Light's chances of survival. A precise definition of 'influence' is, of course, impossible. It covered everything from having access to the minister of finance to obtaining a sympathetic hearing in the office of a petty municipal bureaucrat. The notion of influence is perhaps best conveyed by the peculiar Brazilian term '*jeito*,' meaning the 'knack' or having 'what it takes.' Every Brazilian talks of *jeito* – the possession of which is indispensable to success in everyday life. Along with every other element of Brazilian society, the Light strove for its own share of *jeito*.[78]

Sufficent 'influence' was not the only protective measure practised by the Light in the thirties. The policy of 'Brazilianizing' its management was accelerated. Head office in Toronto fully realized that the larger the number of Brazilians occupying senior-management positions, the better the company was insulated against the currents of nationalism. Brazilian-born engineers began to rise to prominence in the organization, and by the end of the decade certain aspects of operations were entirely under Brazilian control. Edgard de Souza was promoted to a vice-presidency of the São Paulo Light, while his brother, Odilon, became general manager in 1935. Four years later, Dr J.G. de Aragão became general manager of the Rio Light.

It was in the Light's legal department that the process of inducting Brazilians went the furthest. Under McCrimmon's direction, the legal department was staffed with clever young Brazilian lawyers who were better trained than any North American to tackle the legal intricacies of the codes that appeared during the Vargas years. To implement the labour legislation introduced by Vargas, McCrimmon hired Charles Julius Dunlop, a young lawyer who had specialized in the new labour legislation. Perhaps the most promising of McCrimmon's legal acquisitions was Antônio Gallotti, a young lawyer from the southern state of Santa Catarina who joined the staff in 1933. Gallotti arrived with the highest recommendation of Francisco Campos, his former law professor and the architect of the 1937 Estado Novo constitution. Despite his lack of knowledge of English, Gallotti learned to work closely with management and, by the outbreak of the war, had acquired a considerable reputation. McCrimmon's carefully planned mixture of 'influence' and legal talent thus provided an effective antidote to the nationalism that had swept through Brazilian society in the thirties. 'I think a fairly good atmosphere has been created in the Palace,' McCrimmon confidently reported to Lash in May 1938, 'through the intervention, principally, of Osvaldo Aranha and General Goés Monteiro.'

On 11 November 1938, McCrimmon's confidence abruptly turned to dismay when Vargas issued a decree reaffirming the 1934 Water Code in its unadulterated form. Once again, the bureaucrats had scored a tactical victory, despite all the Light's efforts to erect a sturdy legal defence. The 1938 interpretation of the Water Code reiterated all the earlier claims for 'progressive nationalization' of the hydroelectric industry, but it stripped the states of São Paulo and Minas Gerais of any sway over water-power rights within their own borders. The decree reaffirmed the 'kilowatt tax' and even specified that the Light convert all its power to a fifty-cycle current.[79] The decree left the managers of the Light in shock. 'This decree-law obviously tears up all our contracts and destroys the entire basis of our hydroelectric developments in this country,' Billings bitterly remarked, 'leaving any further operation of these and any further development entirely to the whims of the Water Service Department. It also stops effectively any further investment of our capital in hydroelectric enterprises in Brazil.'[80] Most dismaying was the fact that the whole cycle of 'regulamentation' was once again initiated. After four years of contending with the old Juarez Távora code, all that the Light had achieved was a stay of execution. When, in May 1939, the National Council of Water and Electric Energy was created to put the code into workable form, the Light had no option but to regroup and prepare to re-enter the fray.

The thirties thus ended as they had begun, on a note of uncertainty. By 1939, the undeniable conclusion reached by all Brazilian Traction managers was that the new style of Brazilian nationalism, with its strong bias towards economic nationalism and bureaucratic regulation, was a fact of life in Brazil. Among executives there remained little agreement on how the company should face such pressures. Couzens, Bell, and Billings all doubted the efficacy of McCrimmon's avowal of building a strong defence of influence and legal expertise. It seemed that this merely bought time and did little to alter the complexion of the problem. Couzens in particular did not like McCrimmon's style of operation and complained to Toronto that his colleague was 'apt to overestimate what he can do.' Billings was inclined to join Couzens, believing that a 'slow campaign of education' would erase false notions of 'historical cost' from the minds of bureaucrats and politicians. Once this was achieved, a 'fair' and 'reasonable' version of the Water Code could be worked out through consultation. James McKim Bell, the hard-driving general manager of the Rio Light, sensed that tactics based upon reasonableness alone would not succeed. 'In the present case, however,' he wrote in McCrimmon's defence, 'the battle has been too long drawn out, and so much mud has been slung by both sides that there is a firm conviction in the minds of those in power that neither side is telling the truth, and, I believe, we are credited with the greatest of exaggerations, to such an extent that while we would be courteously received I do not believe we would obtain any appreciable advantage.'[81] By 1939, Light executives knew that they could expect Vargas to be all things to all men; full of praise and reassurance for the company one week and full of damnation for the Canadian 'octopus' the next. From McCrimmon's point of view it was therefore imperative to establish links with the president's closest advisers and, by mid-1939, the Major was again a frequent visitor to the Rio offices of bureaucrats and politicians, most notably Osvaldo Aranha. It was, as McKim Bell shrewdly noted, a very 'Brazilian response' to a Brazilian problem.

The political manoeuvring that enveloped the Light during the thirties had the effect of deflecting attention from the creeping crisis that was overtaking it. With the Water Code hanging over it, management recoiled at the thought of any major expansion of the Light's power system. Similar problems faced the Light's transportation services. As early as 1931, Lash had complained that the Light's tramway fares, established in the first decade of the century and left untouched since then, were 'ridiculously low.' The persistent refusal of municipal governments in Rio and São Paulo to increase fares and rationalize their cities' transportation systems forced the companies to curtail any expansion of their services. Both Rio and São Paulo began to suffer increasingly from the problems of uncoordinated and overcrowded transport systems. The rate problem was exacerbated by the fact that several of the Light's concessions were nearing expiry. The original São Paulo tramway concession, for instance, was due to expire in 1941 and, without a revision of its terms, the Light was reluctant to undertake any expansion or modernization of the system.

The paralysis of the Brazilian utilities industry also brought about a near-complete halt to expansion of the power-generating sector. Uncertainty about the Water Code militated against any plans to embark upon a capital-intensive power project. Fortunately, the combined effect of the depressed Brazilian economy up to the mid-decade and the Light's generous margin of surplus power held the problem at bay throughout most of the 1930s. By 1939, however, Billings was issuing stern warnings that the Rio power situation was becoming 'urgent' and that its solution 'involves practically all the major points under the Code.' Without new generating capacity, the Rio Light would face an acute power shortage by 1944–5.

President Lash in Toronto showed no inclination to initiate another costly power project. The president wondered 'whether we would not be making a major mistake if we were to go ahead with large matters of this kind in the present uncertain conditions ... we would be practically announcing to the authorities that we are pretty well satisfied after all with the present legislation.'[82] Billings was fully aware that any power shortage would simply incite foes to further attacks and probably accelerate the ratification of the Water Code. In desperation, he suggested to Lash that 'if and when it could be clearly established that our Companies cannot increase their generating capacity, I would suggest ... that the situation be explored from the standpoint of building a plant in partnership with the Government, provided that some way can be found to safeguard the Company's investment.'[83] It was a radical proposal, although it contained a large measure of prescience. Lash rejected the idea out of hand. Above all else, the thirties had created an attitude of mutual suspicion between the Light and elements of Brazilian politics. Any notion of resuming the harmonious relations that had prevailed in the first decades of the century would have to be postponed until the contentious issue of the Water Code had been resolved.

If the climate for enterprise in Brazil had deteriorated during the Depression, so too had the mood of Brazilian Traction's management in Toronto. From his office in Toronto, Miller Lash must at times have felt that he was presiding over the final dissolution of the Pearson 'empire.' On all sides, the utility enterprises that Fred Pearson and William Mackenzie had established in Spain, Brazil, and Mexico seemed to be besieged by the forces of rampant nationalism. As a vice-president of Barcelona Traction, Lash was forced to watch helplessly as the Spanish Civil War raged around Barcelona. In 1936, after reading press reports of anarchist activity in the city, he wrote disconsolately to fellow Barcelona director Walter Gow that 'the outlook for Barcelona is very gloomy indeed, as it seems to me that whoever wins we are for it in any case.' Shortly thereafter, a workers' committee, acting with the blessing of Spain's Republican government, seized the Barcelona company's plants and 'froze' its bank accounts. Although Franco's victory in Spain eventually restored the company to its Canadian owners, Barcelona Traction never regained the level of profits it had enjoyed in the 1920s and early 1930s. After the Second World War, Barcelona Traction fell prey to the Spanish financial adventurer Juan March, who dragged the company's Toronto management into an involved and ultimately successful legal battle for control of its assets. The Mexican companies, of which Lash was also president, were also plagued by the problems of aroused nationalism in the thirties, especially after 1938 when the government nationalized the holdings of all foreign oil companies. With European financiers eager to increase their share in the Mexican companies and Mexican politicians intent upon adding electricity to their collection of nationalized industries, the directors of Mexican Light and Power and Mexico Tramways lived in a state of constant anxiety. 'It is very difficult to maintain even a decent pretence of directing the Mexican Companies from Toronto,' Gow complained in 1937. In 1946, Mexico Tramways was taken over by the government, followed a few years later by Mexican Light and Power.

The view from the corporate boardroom was, to say the least, not very encouraging. The declining fortunes of the 'Pearson group' in Mexico and Spain were in no way offset by the relentless flow of bad news from Brazil. In a moment of exasperation, Walter Gow, the Blake legal firm's lawyer who had become a Brazilian Traction vice-president in 1932, confided to Lash that he would sell his job for a 'plugged nickel.' At times, Lash must have shared this sentiment. Not only did the decade bring an unending succession of business woes to Lash, but it was also marked by personal tragedy. He had suffered heavy financial losses in the 'crash' and, in 1935, suffered a terrible emotional blow when his only son died. Throughout the decade, Lash laboured under a burden of personal debt. Not surprisingly, the strain of professional and personal worries combined to break Lash's health by 1940. Although he held the presidency for another year, Lash was a 'broken' man, and Herbert Couzens had to be called out of retirement in England to assume many of the ailing president's duties. In October 1941 Lash died, and Couzens became the fourth president of Brazilian Traction.

At times during the thirties it must have seemed that the corporate obituary of Brazilian Traction was being written. Vargas's reaffirmation of the 1934 Water Code in 1938 and the reluctant decision of the board to suspend dividends once again in late 1938 seemed to be the *coup de grâce*. But Brazilian Traction refused to die. Its resilience in the face of adversity and its eventual recovery were the result of two persistent features of its existence in Brazil. It was, in the first place, a virtually immovable fixture in the urban and industrial life of south-eastern Brazil. It had a solid record of performance in supplying Brazilians with the electricity upon which their daily lives and employment depended. If it was an 'octopus,' it was a necessary 'octopus.' While Brazilians may have felt the urge to assume the role of supplying their own electricity, there was still little doubt that they lacked the technical and managerial skills to operate so extensive a utilities network by themselves. By encouraging the entry of Brazilians into every aspect of its operations, the Light was gradually preparing the way for the complete 'Brazilianization' of the company. The second reason for the Light's continued existence in Brazil was its ability to acclimatize itself to a changing political climate. Just as Sir Alexander had tailored the Light to the political exigencies of the Old Republic, Ken McCrimmon had striven to establish a *modus operandi* better suited to the political currents of the thirties. It was by no means a perfect formula. Its development had been attended by much friction and disappointment. But by 1940, even though the Water Code was far from settled, there was little concern among Light executives that their enterprise might be on the same course as the Mexican and Spanish companies. They were in fact fond of citing a saying that had become popular with Brazilians: 'Governments come and go but the Light goes on forever.'

CHAPTER TEN

The Second World War and the Changing of the Guard

The implications of Brazil's declaration of war on the Axis were major and long lasting. The political and economic consequences of war were out of all proportion to the actual sacrifice of blood exacted from Brazil. Although the country's late entry into the conflict in 1942 and its military unpreparedness limited its contribution, Brazilians have always proudly seen their role in the war as a coming of age. Some years after the war, an impressive war memorial was erected on the shores of Rio's Guanabara Bay to express Brazilians' esteem for the achievement of the Fôrça Expedicionária Brasileira in Italy.[1] Brazilians attach similar significance to the fact that their nation was a charter member of the United Nations in 1945. The war thus acted as an incubator in which many of the social, economic, and political tendencies of pre-war Brazil underwent forced growth from which they emerged transformed and attuned to the realities of modern Brazilian society. These were years of maturation and compromise.

One of the first to suffer the effects of this transformation was President Vargas himself, who by 1945 found himself unable to stem the tide of democracy that the war in defence of European democracy had unleashed. The war proved conducive to democratic ferment in Brazil, thereby promoting political and economic compromise on a broad range of contentious issues that had emerged throughout the Depression. The strident economic nationalism of the pre-war years, so evident in the Water Code of 1934, mellowed in the face of demands imposed by a wartime economy and adjusted itself to accommodate foreign participation in Brazil's industrialization. At the same time, however, economic nationalism scored victories. The steel works at Volta Redonda (midway between Rio and São Paulo) and the iron mines of the Rio Doce Valley Company, both state-owned enterprises initiated during the war, provided evidence that Brazil had not completely discarded nationalized enterprise as a means of fostering a balanced economy. Projects such as Volta Redonda, one historian has noted, gave Brazilians 'a most visible monument, a status symbol of the kind developing nations have been eager to obtain' and thus represented 'a great step beyond the regulatory legislation of the early 1930s.'[2] As Vargas himself declared in 1943, Brazil was forging 'the basic elements for the transformation of a vast and scattered agrarian community into a nation capable of providing its fundamental necessities.'[3] It was indicative of this pragmatic response to wartime problems that large foreign-owned enterprises, such as Brazilian Traction, continued to find a place in Brazilian society both during and after the war.

'Undoubtedly the atmosphere down here so far as we are concerned has improved all along the line to a degree which at the moment seems extraordinary,' Miller Lash, the president of Brazilian Traction, wrote from São Paulo less than a week after hostilities commenced in 1939. 'This,' he continued, 'is very marked in connection with the important piece of legislation with which we have been so much preoccupied [the Water Code]. There is a realization from the bottom to the top of the fact that there will be a considerable shortage very soon if we are not permitted to carry on in a reasonable way with our new work, and it is probably this realization which has caused the change of attitude.'[4]

Miller Lash's optimism was not immediately borne out by events in Brazil. On the diplomatic front, it was feared that Brazil would remain neutral or, worse still, align itself with the Axis. Not only were there certain similarities between European fascism and the corporatist ideology of Vargas's Estado Novo, but since 1933 Hitler's Germany had deliberately cultivated better commercial relations with Brazil. By 1939, Germany was one of Brazil's largest trading partners (accounting for 25 per cent of its imports and 19 per cent of its exports) and had established itself as the leading force in Brazilian commercial aviation. The *Graf Zeppelin* was a familiar sight in the skies over Rio.[5] As late as March 1940, Ken McCrimmon reported that German interests were 'heavily subsidizing' certain Rio newspapers and that German sympathizers were present in the ranks of 'the military class.' While none of these pro-Nazi elements had made 'the slightest allusion to our Companies,' McCrimmon did not need to point out the consequences of a triumph of the Nazi will in Brazil.[6] Political concerns were paralleled by lingering economic problems. By 1940, the Light was encountering increased demand, *matériel* shortages, and the as-yet-unsettled Water Code question. The early war years therefore brought little relief from the tensions of the previous decade. None the less, war in Europe had created a situation that Brazil, and Vargas in particular, could not avoid indefinitely.

The combination of adept diplomatic and economic pressure by the Allies and German diplomatic blunders was by 1942 sufficient to shunt Brazil into the war on the Allied side. Once this fateful step was taken, there was no restraining the forces of political and economic change. As historian Peter Flynn has remarked, 'the war brought rapid changes, acting as an important political catalyst. Once Brazil had decided to support the Allied cause and had defined, at least in the short term, the direction of its foreign interests, there was no longer room for such painful fence-sitting.'[7]

The end to fence sitting came none too soon for Brazilian Traction. After the country's strong economic growth in the 1933–9 period, the war in Europe initially threatened to disrupt Brazilian trade by cutting off the country from many of the traditional purchasers of its commodity exports and by denying it access to the producers of the machinery needed to build up Brazil's industrial base. The war did slow Brazilian economic growth. After steady growth at the rate of 5 per cent per annum from 1933 to 1939, annual growth in the Brazilian GNP declined to an average 3.6 per cent per annum during the years 1940–5.[8] Furthermore, exports of some of Brazil's leading staples continued a fall begun in the previous decade. Coffee exports continued their decline from the record levels of the booming mid-1920s. In 1935, for instance, cotton and coffee had accounted for 68.4 per cent of all Brazilian exports, but by 1941 their share had slipped to 44.9 per cent. The loss of the German market, the largest pre-war destination of Brazilian cotton, largely accounted for this slippage. The European war, especially after the Americans joined it, also crimped the Brazilian economy by restricting imports of fuels and machinery essential to the maintenance and expansion of Brazil's industrial base, notably the hydroelectric-power sector.

Despite these debilitating pressures, the Brazilian economy did show remarkable resilience. 'It might be said that the greater part of the year

1940 represented a period of adjustment to wartime conditions,' the Canadian trade commissioner in Rio reported, 'and 1941 might be considered as more indicative of the true effects of war on the Brazilian economy. The results have been less calamitous than was feared. In fact, it could be said that, in some respects, Brazil was a benefitor [sic] rather than a loser. Despite the loss of European markets there was a steady growth in exports throughout the year, both as regards physical volume and value.'9 The relative strength of Brazil's economy was attributable to trade opportunities created by the war economies of Europe and North America. Either Brazilian raw materials such as rubber and iron ore found a ready market in Britain, Canada, and the United States, or Brazilian manufactured goods, especially textiles, found new markets in the vacuum left by the withdrawal of German suppliers. At the same time, the inability of Brazilians to buy in European and American marketplaces forced them to rely more upon internal industrial production. The combination of buoyant exports and curtailed imports brought about a remarkable reversal in the terms of Brazilian trade. From a modestly favourable trade balance of £5,497,184 in 1938, Brazil's trade surplus burgeoned to £10,050,388 in 1939. This positive trade balance greatly eased Brazil's perpetually precarious exchange situation and led, by late 1939, to the adoption of a policy of virtually free exchange. Although the milréis (and after November 1942 the cruzeiro)[10] did not stage a spectacular recovery *vis-à-vis* the stable currencies of Brazil's trading partners, the availability of hard currency for remittance at least ensured that foreign companies, including Brazilian Traction, would not encounter the problem of 'blocked' earnings as they had during the Depression.

The impact of war on the economy was accentuated in the industrial heartland of São Paulo and Rio. In the period between 1939 and 1943, for instance, the state of São Paulo experienced industrial growth averaging 7.8 per cent annually. This was based upon strong growth in demand in the textile and metallurgical industries. 'The acceleration in the rhythm of Brazil's industrial development during 1941,' the Canadian trade commissioner noted, 'was perhaps the most outstanding feature of the year and the one most likely to project its effects on the Brazilian economy in future years. Not only did existing industries increase their production and their capacity by the installation of additional equipment and erection of new plants, but a number of entirely new industries made their appearance.'[11] A year later, the trade commissioner reported that the consumption of electrical energy in the Rio and São Paulo regions had grown 38.5 per cent between 1939 and 1943.

Continued Brazilian industrialization both pleased and worried the management of Brazilian Traction. On the one hand, they were gratified that the war had not isolated Brazil economically, thereby bringing a relapse into depression. Growth in demand for electricity and improved exchange did not, on the other hand, ease concern over the rapid depletion of the company's surplus capacity. Neither the Rio nor the São Paulo Light had undertaken a major expansion since the 1920s. The inevitable exhaustion of what was once a generous surplus from plants such as Cubatão outside São Paulo had been delayed by the Depression. Company engineers had sensed by the late 1930s that this stay of execution was about to expire, especially in view of the strong industrial resurgence in São Paulo since 1933. Any attempt to plan new generating facilities was impossible, not only because the Water Code of 1934 had expressly prohibited such expansion but also because the code and other state encroachments on private business created an atmosphere of uncertainty not conducive to large-scale capital investment. When, in May 1940, the Brazilian minister of war, General Eurico Dutra, visited the Lajes plant, the general manager of the Rio Light, J.G. de Aragão, took pains to inform his visitor of the impending power crisis. 'I pointed out that we were approaching a crucial moment,' he reported, 'when unless we added to our existing installations, we would be compelled to refuse fresh demands for power supply, as in fact we had already been forced to do recently in one or two cases.'[12]

During the next three years the situation continued to deteriorate. By October 1943, Brazilian Traction's chief hydraulic engineer, A.W.K. Billings, bitterly complained that the peak load of the Rio Light system had grown by 13 per cent a year since the beginning of the war and that the saturation point had been reached. What alarmed Billings most was the prospect of impending demands for electricity from the new government steel works at Volta Redonda, from a number of railway-electrification schemes, and from a large automobile factory outside Rio.

Billings's anxiety was heightened by the realization that war had made it virtually impossible to obtain new generating equipment abroad. The completion of the Lajes 'A' generating unit, one of the few expansions of generating capacity actually undertaken in the 1930s, was greatly hampered by the outbreak of war. The new generator, which was intended to supply Rio with an additional 42,500 kilowatts, was built by Siemens Electric of Germany and, when hostilities began in Europe, many of the parts of the generator were still sitting in German warehouses. Since Brazil was not yet a belligerent, Brazilian Traction officials in London managed to skirt the embargo placed upon all British companies trading with the enemy by arranging to ship the remaining components to Rio via Switzerland and the Italian port of Genoa. This desperate move might easily have brought severe diplomatic repercussions from the British or the German government. None the less, it worked, and the Lajes 'A' unit came 'on line' in 1940. There was, however, no question of further purchases of German electrical equipment and, with the extreme pressure being exerted upon British and American power producers by wartime industry, there seemed little likelihood that equipment could be secured elsewhere. Despite this grim prospect, it was imperative that the Light join the long queue for future deliveries of generating equipment. This it was reluctant to do until the Brazilian government gave some clear indication of its intentions with regard to the long-unregulated Water Code. As the war crisis deepened, Light officials reluctantly adopted a wait-and-see attitude, acknowledging what Herbert Couzens described as 'the inescapable necessity to keep our needs down to the irreducible minimum to enable the companies to exist.'

Slowly the government's attitude to Brazil's power problem began to change. First came acknowledgment of the problem's existence, followed by an attempt at a constructive solution that would both respect the role of foreign capital in Brazil's hydroelectric industry and at the same time satisfy the aspirations of the ardent economic nationalists who had promoted the regulatory legislation of the 1930s. In essence, the wartime power crisis transformed the dogmatic, highly theoretical economic nationalism of the 1930s into a more pragmatic philosophy characterized by a willingness to create workable solutions. It was destined to be a process of gradual compromise and redefinition. The basic tension between foreign and national control of Brazilian electricity would continue, but the old spirit of outright antagonism began to be superseded by a mood of accommodation. As early as 1939 Osvaldo Aranha, Brazil's minister of finance, confidentially informed a company official that 'the policy of super-nationalization was all wrong' and that he was 'violently opposed to it.'[13] As Getúlio Vargas himself told an audience at the Volta Redonda steel works in 1943: 'I am not an "exclusivist," nor would I commit the error of advising the repudiation of foreign capital for employment in the development of Brazilian industry;' but, he insisted, 'the utilization of water powers should be kept the right of Brazilians.'[14]

The first acknowledgment by the government of the impending power shortage came in June 1939 when the ministry of agriculture, which had authority over the hydroelectric industry, established procedures relating to inter-company power connection between private companies. In July 1940, for instance, the São Paulo Light was ordered to interconnect its power supply with that of the Companhia Campineira de Tração, Luz e Fôrça in order to alleviate power shortages in the city of Campinas. Further evidence of the need to promote growth of the power sector came in March 1940, when a federal decree opened the way for companies holding concessions that predated the Water Code to expand their facilities.[15] The federal government's willingness to regulate the power industry on a day-to-day basis was again revealed by a decree of October 1942 that authorized rationing of electric power. Although this measure was not strictly enforced during the war, both the Rio and São Paulo tramway operations were obliged to implement *ad hoc* rationing. The acute wartime shortage of gasoline produced a boom in tramway ridership in both cities. To conserve energy, the number of stopping places for trams was reduced. Electricity rationing was followed by gas rationing, which was instituted in Rio, Santos, and São Paulo.

The growing intervention of government was felt in another aspect of the São Paulo tramway operations. In 1941, the tramway concession originally negotiated by Gualco and Souza at the turn of the century expired. In view of the Light's inability to negotiate what it considered a fair adjustment of its tramway rates and the municipal government's refusal to rationalize the city's transportation system, the São Paulo Light was reluctant to renew the concession. None the less, in June 1942 the federal government issued a decree obliging the company to continue operating the São Paulo tramway service under the conditions of the expired concession until the end of the war.

The imposition by government fiat of interconnection rationing and service without concessions represented one side of the new, more pragmatic mood of Brazilian economic nationalism. If the government was, on the one hand, prepared to intervene in the operational life of Brazil's private hydroelectric companies, it also began to show signs of yielding ground on some of the contentious issues that had blocked the expansion of those same utility companies for a decade. Fearful that the incipient power crisis might paralyse the nation's drive towards industrial self-sufficiency, Brazilian politicians were obliged to adopt a more flexible attitude to the needs of Brazil's public utilities. While the desire to establish a national presence in the industry remained strong, there was an acknowledgment that this would have to be an evolutionary rather than a revolutionary process and that in the interim some form of co-operative understanding would have to be reached with the private utilities operating in Brazil.

For the next three decades the approach of the Brazilian government to the problem of building up hydroelectric capacity was to be governed by this pragmatic ideology. Rates and concessions would be revised and renegotiated as long as this strategy ensured an improvement in service. There was to be no return to the regulatory vacuum that had prevailed before the Revolution of 1930. Instead, public utilities were to remain under the watchful eye of the government, which would govern performance and profits on a strict basis of quid pro quo. At the same time, Brazilian politicians would strive to establish a state presence in the power industry. It was destined to be a delicate coexistence, especially since the xenophobia of the 1930s continued to hold sway over certain elements of the political spectrum in Brazil. The process of accommodation had begun in 1939 with the creation of the Conselho Nacional de Águas e Energia Elétrica (CNAEE) to oversee the electric industry in Brazil. As Herbert Couzens correctly sensed, with its powerful mandate over the whole industry, from the generation to the distribution of power, this council held the power to make or break the Light. None the less, Couzens concluded, as long as the council members were 'fair minded,' they might serve as 'a useful buffer for the public utilities' industry.[16]

Fair-mindedness was elsewhere evident when in 1940 the authorities conceded certain increases in gas and telephone rates. The rates prevailing for gas service in Rio de Janeiro had not, for instance, been adjusted for years and, with the war-created shortage of coal driving costs up, were reduced to unremunerative levels. Between 1939 and 1942 the cost of coal for gas production climbed 86 per cent. In an effort to alleviate such increases, the Rio municipal government agreed to a rate structure that would vary with the cost of coal, on condition that the Rio Gas Company expanded and modernized its services. Similar rate adjustments were afforded the Rio and São Paulo telephone company in 1940–1. Once again, the new rates were conditional upon the company's expanding and updating its services.

The cost of providing all services had risen steeply under the pressure of the wartime economy. In 1940, the federal government had, for instance, instituted a minimum wage for all workers to enable every Brazilian worker to afford 'his normal needs of food, housing, clothing, hygiene and transportation.' By the end of 1943, the British Chamber of Commerce in São Paulo reported that the cost of living had grown by just under 80 per cent since 1939. The impact of increased costs had to be absorbed with, for example, no compensating hike in the archaic 100 réis fare that tramway passengers continued to pay on Rio and São Paulo trams. In December 1942, the general manager of Rio Tramway, José de Aragão, outlined the financial predicament of his enterprise to President Vargas. 'He gave,' it was reported, 'the usual story of extreme onus placed on the Company, our great difficulty in operating under present conditions, and the increasing difficulty – in fact impossibility – of recruiting new staff under present wage scales, which were already too high for the economy of the trams but inadequate for the men under present living conditions.' When Aragão emphasized 'the inadequacy of the 100 *réis* fare,' Vargas 'expressed great surprise, saying that he was not aware that the 100 *réis* fare still existed and that he thought the matter had already been cleared up.'[17]

Vargas's 'great surprise' led within weeks to a major breakthrough on the question of revising the tramway rates. On the last day of 1942, a federal decree authorized the prefect of the Federal District to enter into negotiations with the Rio company for the revision of its existing contracts 'on certain defined bases including a fair return on the capital employed in the service.' The *modus vivendi* underlying this new arrangement was the government's willingness to peg tramway fare increases to mandatory wage increases imposed by the federal government. On 1 May 1943, for instance, Light workers received wage increases of from ten to twenty centavos an hour. On the following day, tramway fares were increased proportionately.

Another federal decree of May 1945 applied a 10 per cent surcharge on the rates for all electric, gas, water, and telephone services. The decree expressly stated that the proceeds from the increases were to be used to offset the impact of mandatory wage increases. Such surcharges in no way added to profits: they simply offset the impact of increased costs on operations. The surcharges did nothing to alter the basic rate structure, which, in the case of the electric service, had been frozen since the appearance of the Water Code. They did, however, introduce a measure of relief into the companies' financial situation, in that they helped to keep gross operating revenues abreast of operating expenses. From the government's perspective, the adoption of rate surcharges tied to wage increases conveniently served to defuse the politically explosive problem of utility rates.[18]

The tinkering with gas, telephone, and tramway rates and the allowing of surcharges on electric rates were accompanied by concessions in principle. For the first time since the Water Code legislation had frozen the Light's rates in 1934, the government opened the *possibility* of rate revision. Under Decree Law 5764 of August 1943, existing state and municipal concessions governing the production, transmission, and distribution of electricity (other than street lighting) were all brought under the jurisdiction of the federal government. The same decree also instituted a provisional rate system whereby the then-prevailing contractual rates would be maintained until the contracts were revised, subject to such modifications as might be determined unilaterally by the government. Although the 1943 decree ended the long period of uncertainty that had prevailed since 1934, no actual rate increases (as opposed to surcharges on rates) were in fact to materalize until 1955.

Two years before the 1943 decree, the federal government had finally instituted guidelines for the implementation of the concept of 'historical cost' first prescribed in the Water Code of 1934. This too represented a positive, if somewhat tentative, step towards the resolution of the Water Code tangle. The federal government established a procedure for taking an inventory, or *tombamento*, of the fixed assets of electric companies in order to determine the remunerable investment, expressed in terms of 'historical cost,' on which a 10 per cent return to the investor would be allowed.

This scheme of asset inventory on the basis of historical cost in milréis by the *tombamento* method did not, of course, meet with the entire approval of Brazilian Traction executives. The notion of strict historical cost – that is, the evaluation of assets on the basis of acquisition cost in national currency with no allowance for the subsequent devaluation of local currency – had aroused vehement objections from company management from its first appearance in the 1934 code. 'It is profoundly unjust, it is even confiscatory,' one of the company's Brazilian lawyers later noted, 'that the conversion of such amounts of the country's currency be made without taking into account exchange variations which might have occurred or which may occur in the future, creating to the investor a tremendous sacrifice and discouraging him irremediably from attempting new initiatives.'[19] Nevertheless, the *tombamento* decree represented the first small step towards resolving the confused regulatory situation that had prevailed in the electric industry since the appearance of the Water Code. It was also an unhurried step. Despite the *tombamento* decree, the process of correcting the Light's basic rate structure was to remain stalled for another twenty-five years.[20]

The prospect of 'historical cost in *milréis*' was offset by some softening in the government's attitude on the Water Code and by the partial easing of government restrictions on hydroelectric expansion. Since the prohibition on expansion placed on the electric companies in the early 1930s, the Light had made no major additions to generating capacity. The Water Code legislation had been prompted by a belief that all future hydroelectric development in Brazil would be undertaken by Brazilians or by the Brazilian government. The realization that neither the capital nor the entrepreneurial expertise existed in Brazil to undertake the hydroelectric challenge was disguised throughout the 1930s by the fact that growth in demand for power in south-eastern Brazil was accommodated within the Light's available capacity. The war-induced prosperity of the Brazilian economy had abruptly ended this deceptive situation and introduced the prospect of severe power crises by the mid-1940s. It had also become evident that, despite nationalistic rhetoric and mooted legislation, Brazil was little closer to undertaking a leading role in the hydroelectric industry than it had been in 1934. Consequently the Brazilian government found itself in the awkward situation of having to weigh the respective merits of pursuing a rigidly nationalistic policy or of loosening the restrictions on foreign producers of electricity.

The critical importance of supplying sufficient electricity to ensure steady industrial growth had already been made manifest in May 1940 by the federal decree that allowed power companies to amplify or modify their plants at the discretion of the CNAEE. As soon as the government had indicated its willingness to adjust rates upwards in 1943, both the Rio Light and the São Paulo Light sought permission to enlarge their respective power-generating facilities at Lajes and Cubatão. The decrees authorizing such expansion represented the first hesitant steps in what was to become the Light's next major electrical-construction program, a program that would stretch well into the 1950s and would allow the Light a manifold increase in its generating capacity. In a very important sense, the Light had been given a new lease on life.

Wartime expansion of power facilities was undertaken in a rather piecemeal fashion. This reflected the still uncertain political atmosphere and the fact that war made importing electrical equipment almost impossible. Consequently, wartime efforts to alleviate the impending power crisis centred upon improving the efficiency of existing plants rather than augmenting their maximum generating capacity. By increasing the volume of the reservoirs serving the Lajes and Cubatão power stations, the Light was able to reduce its vulnerability to droughts and to maximize the utilization of its existing turbines and generators. The Lajes dam was, for instance, heightened by twenty-eight metres to allow a 250 per cent expansion of its adjacent reservoir, thereby producing an increase in the firm power capacity of the Rio system from 152,000 kw to 194,800 kw.[21] The old reservoir, built in 1905, had proved susceptible to extended drought and to the unavoidable drop in water flow occasioned by the annual dry season. The new reservoir enabled Lajes to function at peak capacity throughout the year. Similarly, engineers of the São Paulo Light continued expanding the Rio Grande, Guarapiranga, and Pinheiros canals that channelled water into the Rio Grande reservoir above Cubatão. The Pedreira pumping station was also completed, thereby enabling more water to be diverted from the Tietê River to the lip of the Serra do Mar. Measures such as these permitted the generating capacity of the Rio and São Paulo power systems to be increased from 524,484 kw in 1939 to 662,570 kw by the end of the war.

The ultimate insufficiency of simply optimizing the potential of existing plants was soon revealed by the wartime growth in power demand. The total connected load of the Rio and São Paulo Light system grew from 1,121,011 kw in 1939 to 1,725,853 kw six years later, while the total number of power consumers, both domestic and industrial, multiplied from 523,003 to 662,570. Expansion of such magnitude could not be satisfied indefinitely by a policy of amplifying existing facilities. Instead, new hydroelectric projects had to be planned. As early as 1939, Asa Billings had schemed about building a second Cubatão-style plant to serve São Paulo. Once again, the unique river-diversion principles first elaborated in the 1920s were to be employed to generate an additional 730,000 kilowatts. A model of the proposed development was displayed at the 1939 New York World's Fair. Similarly, a new plant for the Rio power system was planned for a location on the Lajes River, downstream from the original Lajes plant, near the town of Ponte Coberta. The Ponte Coberta plant was envisaged as a run-of-the-river operation that would utilize the same water flow as the main Lajes station. Hence the downstream plant would reuse the water of the main plant, thereby enabling conservation of the stored capacity of the Lajes reservoir.

Two obstacles barred the way to the construction of large, new hydroelectric plants in the early 1940s. In the first place, they were capital-intensive projects and, in the midst of a war, Brazilian Traction had no means of obtaining sufficient capital to embark upon such costly additions. Billings estimated that the 'new' Serra plant would cost $4.3 million dollars, and there was no way that a project of that magnitude could be undertaken using retained earnings. Furthermore, even if outside capital were obtained, there was little likelihood that the Light would have been able to purchase sufficient equipment from foreign suppliers to undertake a major expansion. The second impediment to construction was political. While Brazilian politicians had softened their stance on the expansion of *existing* power concessions held by foreign interests, nothing had been done to allow them to undertake *new* concessions. This was circumvented in the case of the proposed Ponte Coberta plant by the argument that a new station just five kilometres downstream from an established plant was in fact simply an amplification of the existing Lajes concession. The government accepted this argument and in March 1944 issued a decree authorizing the construction of the Ponte Coberta plant. This proved an isolated victory.

By 1944, the combined effect of capital scarcity and political uncertainty brought consideration of further major power projects to a virtual standstill. This did not, however, produce unbroken gloom at the Brazilian Traction head office. The knowledge that the war was going in the Allies' favour gave hope that the company would soon have access to European and American capital. Furthermore, Light officials were sufficiently encouraged by the Brazilian government's willingness to compromise on the issue of rates to hope that an agreement for large, new power projects could ultimately be negotiated, especially in view of the deteriorating power situation in Rio and São Paulo.

The willingness of the Brazilian government to accommodate the interests of foreign power producers did not necessarily mean that the nationalistic goals enunciated in the 1934 Water Code had been abandoned. Victories had also been won. The federal government had in 1943 effectively asserted its jurisdiction over all hydroelectric concessions in the country and had the unquestioned right to set public-utility rates. It had therefore made substantial progress in replacing the pre-1934 regulatory vacuum with a federal hegemony. It had not displaced the foreign element in Brazilian electricity with indigenous enterprise, nor had it successfully promoted the development of an exclusive state presence in hydroelectricity. Instead, the idealistic legislation of the 1930s had given way to peaceful coexistence by which the strong foreign presence in Brazilian electricity was tolerated beside the weak but growing national share in the same industry. Realizing that it possessed neither the capital nor the technical expertise to undertake electricity production on its own, Brazil chose to continue its reliance upon foreign capital and engineering skill in this most important energy-producing sector of the national economy. Hence, to allow the Light to perish would jeopardize the national economy. Where nationalism and dogma had once ruled, nationalism and expediency now prevailed.

Much the same was true of the creation of Brazil's national steel industry. The inauguration of construction on the Volta Redonda steel works in 1943 was the product not only of Brazil's determination to be master in its own economic house, but also of a large dose of American capital assistance and technical advice. As historian John Wirth has concluded, 'the government's approach to policy-making with regard to steel was flexible and contingent in line with the usual style of the Estado Novo. After years of debate, Brazilians agreed on the need for a modern steelworks: they disagreed on the means.'²² Much the same was true with electricity. In 1934, the Water Code had seemingly allowed little scope for the continued existence of private electricity producers in Brazil; by 1943 the Light was once again considered a 'means' to a national goal. In December 1943, the Federal Council on Foreign Trade put forward the idea of a National Electrification Plan by which the Brazilian government would foster the establishment of its own hydroelectric plants, not in the industrial heartland of Brazil, but in underdeveloped areas. At the first meeting of the newly created Commission of Economic Planning in January 1945, the commission's president, General Freire, stressed that 'the development of water power becomes imperative as an immediate solution to the power problem. It is the condition suitable for an intensive industrial development, linking the improvement of the standard of living of the rural population with the amelioration and cheapening of railway and urban transportation.'[23] The first evidence of the state's desire to complement the private sector in hydroelectric development in Brazil came in 1945 with the creation of the Companhia Hidro Elétrica do São Francisco (CHESF), a state corporation dedicated to the development of the hydro potential of the São Francisco River in northern Bahia state.[24] CHESF represented the first tangible step in the direction of a national presence in the Brazilian electric industry.

The development of peaceful coexistence between the Light and its political hosts paralleled the development of diplomatic relations between Canada and Brazil during the war. Since the establishment of the São Paulo Light in 1899, Canadians had done business in Brazil without the aid of Canadian diplomatic representation. This was hardly surprising, given the meagre flow of trade between the two countries and the paucity of shared international interests. In 1939, the whole of South America accounted for 1.8 per cent of all Canadian exports and supplied 2.8 per cent of all Canadian imports.[25] Throughout the 1930s, Brazil had become the object of courtship by the German and American governments, both of whom had sought to draw the non-aligned Brazilians into their respective spheres of influence. While Hitler's Germany made progress in establishing technical and commercial ties, the United States found a friend in the person of Osvaldo Aranha, Vargas's revolutionary colleague and close adviser. As Brazilian ambassador in Washington after 1934, Aranha had been in a position to observe and admire the New Deal reforms of President Roosevelt. Like the Baron of Rio Branco and Rui Barbosa, Aranha was deeply impressed by North American liberalism and believed that Brazil's future lay not in the emulation of European fascism but in Pan-Americanism. In 1939, Aranha negotiated a credit agreement in Washington designed to stimulate Brazilian trade with the United States and to ease Brazil's exchange problems. By 1940, it was clear that the American government placed a high priority on drawing Brazil into what it considered its zone of 'hemispheric defence.'[26]

Osvaldo Aranha, as foreign minister since 1938, delicately guided

Brazil into the Allied camp by 1942. Pockets of overtly pro-German sentiment in Brazil and Vargas's determination to drive a hard bargain with the Allies made Aranha's task doubly difficult. One small step in this process of alignment with the Allied cause was taken with the establishment of diplomatic relations between Canada and Brazil in 1941. In the last years of the previous decade, the Brazilian government had made soundings through the British ambassador in Rio to see whether Ottawa was willing to establish a mission in Rio. Prime Minister Mackenzie King characteristically vacillated. The opening of an embassy in Rio represented a major step for Canadian diplomacy, in 1939 still very much in its infancy. The fact that Brazil seemed unwilling to reciprocate with an embassy in Ottawa and King's indecision as to which of the 'ABC' countries (Argentina, Brazil, and Chile) should first be graced with a Canadian embassy doomed Brazil's initiative to failure. Realizing the futility of dealing with the Canadians through the agency of the British ambassador, Foreign Minister Aranha determined by 1940 to establish a direct dialogue with Ottawa. There was one obvious means to this end.

Major Ken McCrimmon, a resident vice-president of both the Rio and São Paulo Light, was by 1940 the most prominent Canadian in Brazil. Repeated conferences during the 1930s with Osvaldo Aranha over the unending problem of the Water Code had allowed the relationship of government minister and company executive to develop into a friendship. Aranha turned to McCrimmon in June 1940 in hope of rekindling interest in the idea of an exchange of ministers between Canada and Brazil. On the eve of McCrimmon's departure for Toronto, Aranha confided his desires to his North American friend. Aranha, McCrimmon reported, was 'of the opinion that a more intimate association of Canada and Latin American affairs would be of political value not only to Canada itself but also to the United States in its endeavour to hold the South American countries more or less in line with democratic institutions.'[27] McCrimmon realized that the use of a private businessman to convey a diplomatic overture 'offends normal diplomatic procedure,' but because his association with Aranha was 'somewhat intimate,' he had little choice in the matter. Once in Canada, McCrimmon contacted Hugh Keenleyside of External Affairs and conveyed the Brazilian message. Despite further delay occasioned by Mackenzie King's fear that Latin America was a 'trouble zone,' a diplomatic accord by which Canada and Brazil were to exchange ministers was finally reached in the dying days of 1940. 'It has been a source of satisfaction to me,' McCrimmon informed Under-Secretary of State for External Affairs O.D. Skelton, 'to learn that the plunge has now been taken with regard to the exchange of diplomatic missions between Canada and Brazil ... I need hardly reiterate that I shall be most happy to place my own personal services at the disposal of our new Canadian Minister.'[28]

Not until June 1941 was a Canadian ambassador appointed. Jean Désy, Canada's former ambassador in Belgium, was named to head the Canadian mission in Rio, and João Alberto Lins de Barros, an adviser to the president and former *tenente* whose views had considerably moderated since the Revolution of 1930, was named to the Brazilian ambassadorship in Ottawa. Both appointments were much to the company's liking. João Alberto had taken part in the drawn-out work of trying to implement the Water Code and, although McCrimmon described his departure from this work as 'a great loss,' his appointment to Ottawa was welcomed as a sign of political moderation. Désy was soon on intimate terms with McCrimmon, upon whom he relied for candid assessments of Brazilian politics. McCrimmon's role in promoting Canadian-Brazilian diplomacy was indicative of the prominent part he had come to assume both within and outside the company in Brazil. As *O congresso* observed some years later, 'he is so much a part of our life that not even the name of McCrimmon, despite its foreign origins, suggests a foreigner to us. Major McCrimmon, owing to the affection he bears to this land – a fact confirmed by all those who know him intimately, ... [is] not an honorary Brazilian but a real one.'[29]

McCrimmon was not without his detractors in Brazil. Extreme-nationalist newspapers portrayed him as a subverter of national politics. Many cited McCrimmon's admittedly flamboyant style of entertaining friends as a questionable practice for a foreign businessman in Brazil. Under a system of government that was essentially authoritarian, as was the Estado Novo, no social or economic interest group could have afforded not to have 'friends' in high places.

Ken McCrimmon's forthright and vigorous approach to corporate affairs in Brazil was not matched by the corporation's senior management in Toronto. To a remarkable and worrisome degree, Brazilian Traction management in Toronto had remained unchanged since the First World War. The closely knit circle of promoters and financiers who had established the São Paulo and Rio companies had retained firm control of the enterprises for the next four decades. There had been some attrition, such as the tragic loss of Fred Pearson in 1915, and there had been challenges, such as that mounted by Loewenstein, but the character of the Brazilian Traction board remained strikingly unchanged throughout the 1920s and 1930s. The board remained bound by the closest family and corporate ties. Miller Lash, who assumed the presidency from Sir Alexander Mackenzie in 1928, was the son of Zebulon Lash, the brilliant lawyer who had masterminded the creation of Brazilian Traction in 1912. Other faces in the hierarchy did not change at all. E.R. Wood, Canada's most respected financial manager, continued to hold a seat on the board through the whole post-First World War period. Prominent Toronto bankers and financiers, such as Sir Thomas White, Sir John Aird, and D.B. Hanna, were perennially reappointed. The intimate connection with the Blake legal firm in Toronto was perpetuated by the presence of Walter Gow, who by the late 1930s was both a Brazilian Traction vice-president and a senior partner with the legal firm. Even Sir Alexander Mackenzie, despite his retirement, remained on the board throughout the 1930s. The board was thus best described as an 'old guard,' drawn from the core of the Toronto business establishment. In many respects, it had acquitted itself admirably. Toronto had provided sufficient capital to allow the hydro-generating and -distribution network to be expanded; it had fended off Loewenstein's take-over attempt and had given shareholders a reasonable, albeit at times broken, record of dividends.

Unfortunately, by 1940 the 'old guard' was beginning to show its age. And by 1945 it was showing signs of being overwhelmed by the magnitude of the post-war challenges. Because corporate by-laws made no provision for the mandatory retirement of directors, the average age of the board had risen steadily. By the late 1930s, death began to exact its inevitable toll. Sir John Aird and D.B. Hanna both died in 1938. The venerable *éminence grise* of the Toronto financial community, E.R. Wood, died in 1941. The hardest blow fell in 1943 with the death of Sir Alexander Mackenzie at his summer home in Kincardine, Ontario. Driven from his Italian villa by war, Mackenzie had passed his wartime winters in South Carolina and California, returning each summer to his native Kincardine. As his health deteriorated through the summer of 1943, he expressed the wish that he be allowed to gaze upon Kincardine's magnificent sunset once again before he died. On the morning of 13 July, shortly after sunrise, Sir Alexander passed away. Distinguished careers such as Mackenzie's, the *Globe and Mail* editorialized, 'shed lustre upon their native land' and gave Canada proof 'that brains and character are one of its best exports.'[30]

As death took its toll, little effort was devoted to recruiting new talent. When new faces did appear in the boardroom they contributed little. In 1939, for instance, former Ontario premier Howard Ferguson was elected, not because he possessed any special business acumen but because, as one of Ontario's greatest political orators, his stentorian voice was considered a great asset at the annual meeting. In another instance, fate intervened to deprive the board of a promising new director. Gordon W. Scott, a talented Montreal accountant who had joined the board in June 1939, was drowned when the ship on which he and Minister of Munitions and Supply C.D. Howe were travelling was torpedoed in mid-Atlantic in late 1940. Such losses contributed further to the board's atrophy. By 1945, the board was distinctly geriatric. Sir Thomas White, finance minister in the Borden government of 1911–20, had, for instance, been a director since 1920 and was approaching eighty. Amidst the growing senescence, Walter Gow rose to prominence. Gow's connection with the company dated from the turn of the century when he had overseen much of the legal work for the São Paulo and Rio companies; but by the 1940s Gow was a septuagenarian with a distinctly conservative cast of mind.

The growing senility of Toronto management was symptomatic of problems besetting the Brazilian Traction presidency during the war. When Miller Lash's health collapsed under the weight of personal and business pressures in 1940, a frantic search for a replacement began. This was made exceedingly difficult by the fact that the war effort was monopolizing the talents of Canadian business executives. In desperation, the board invited Sir Herbert Couzens, who in 1936 had retired from his duties as a Brazilian Traction vice-president, to come out of retirement in England to serve as interim president while Lash regained his health. Couzens was an extremely capable electrical engineer and a superb manager, talents he combined with impeccable English manners. Couzens was not only fondly remembered for his outstanding contribution to operations in Rio and São Paulo but also warmly praised by Torontonians for his work in establishing the Toronto Transportation Commission. 'He took over an old, worn-out system and converted it into one of the finest on the continent,' the *Evening Telegram* noted in 1937, 'changing a miserable service into one of the best to be found anywhere.'[31] In 1937, Couzens had received a knighthood for his contribution to the establishment of reliable electrical service in England, Canada, and Brazil. In every respect, he was an exceptionally well-qualified candidate for the company's most senior office. 'In this appointment,' the *Toronto Star* noted, 'Brazilian Traction has done itself honour. Sir Herbert Couzens is one of the outstanding engineers of the present day, with organizing and managerial abilities which round out his qualifications for his new office.'[32] As outstanding an engineer as Couzens was, he was still a man who had come out of retirement at the age of sixty-four. The necessity of seconding Couzens from retirement in England was indicative of the failure of senior management to introduce new managerial talent into the Brazilian Traction organization during the 1920s and 1930s.

One of the few new faces to appear in Brazilian Traction's head office during Lash's long presidency was that of Frank A. Schulman, the young lawyer who had been sent by the London office to shadow Alfred Loewenstein's movements in Europe during the ill-fated take-over attempt of 1926–8. Unlike most of the head-office staff, Schulman possessed a knowledge of Brazil (the place of his birth), English finance, and Toronto business. One of Couzens's first acts upon returning to Toronto in 1941 was to promote Schulman to assistant to the president. The only other new face to appear at head office before the end of the war was that of George Troop, who became treasurer in 1943. Born in Halifax, Troop had attended the University of Toronto, and, like many of those who were later to serve in financial positions at Brazilian Traction, had acquired a solid grounding in accountancy at the offices of Clarkson, Gordon, Dilworth and Nash in Toronto. Troop had a brilliant and retentive mind and soon mastered the intricacies of the company's intercontinental accounting procedures.

In October 1941, Miller Lash died in Toronto, and the board confirmed Couzens in the position of president. Couzens's addiction to work had assumed the proportions of a legend even before his retirement in 1936, but his efforts after his return in 1941 assumed Herculean dimensions. Whether in Rio or Toronto, Couzens was in his office by 7:00 a.m. every morning and worked into the early evening. Since he seldom emerged from his office, he was a virtual stranger to most of the head-office staff. It was rumoured that he had a simple lunch of milk, bread, cheese, and fruit delivered to his desk every day at noon. A Saturday or Sunday seldom passed without his making an appearance at the office.

Couzens faced daunting problems as Brazilian Traction's senior executive. All the tensions resulting from the difficulties over rates, concessions, and regulatory legislation surfaced on his desk. He had responsibility for over forty-two thousand employees in Brazil and was answerable to more than twenty-five thousand shareholders in North America and Europe. Ministering to these duties in wartime proved especially arduous. The war had, for instance, completely disrupted travel between Canada and Brazil, with the result that every time Couzens undertook to visit Brazil he had to obtain clearances and travel permits from Ottawa and Washington. On his first trip to Rio in August 1942, Couzens reported that the war was having a beneficial effect on both the company and Brazil. 'Generally,' he wrote from Rio, 'conditions in Brazil are good, in fact abnormally so, though there are some indications of slowing up. For example, our output of electrical energy ... has been increasing at an abnormally rapid rate.'[33] Despite these encouraging signs, Couzens was quick to recognize major problems on the horizon. The war, he realized, was creating inflationary pressures that would push wages and salaries steadily upwards. Couzens's worries were intensified a few days later when Brazil finally entered the war on 22 August 1942. Brazil's decision to join the Allies was provoked by a spate of German submarine attacks off the Brazilian coast. The same attacks prompted Couzens to ponder the now very real danger that the war might result in actual physical damage to the company's plants. The memory of the 1932 aerial bombardment of the Cubatão plant could not have been far from his mind.

The cumulative effect of enduring the rigours of wartime travel and fretting over the Light's seemingly congenital problems destroyed Couzens's health. In the summer of 1943, he visited Rio, where he conducted friendly discussions with Vargas and the new Canadian ambassador. Despite several encouraging developments in the realm of the Water Code and the company's rates, Couzens returned to Toronto weighed down with worry about what he perceived as an unavoidable post-war power crisis in Brazil. A return visit to Rio in July 1944 did little to ease his worries. Within days of his arrival, Sir Herbert collapsed and was taken to hospital. A diagnosis of stomach cancer led almost immediately to surgery, from which Couzens emerged greatly weakened and in need of a lengthy recuperation. His days as Brazilian Traction president were over. Couzens's only wish was that he be allowed to return to his Devonshire home to live out his last days. Eager to comply, the company arranged for him to be flown by private aircraft to New York and thence to England. Although chartering an aircraft for an oceanic flight in wartime proved exceedingly difficult, Sir Herbert was brought to New York in mid-October and then carried to England by steamer. On 9 November, with his condition now precarious, Couzens resigned the presidency. Eight days later he died after a second operation for cancer in London. 'We all feel that one of the "household words" of the dictionary of Public Utilities had been torn from the book,' one of Couzens's Toronto friends sadly noted.[34]

Couzens's death left the company facing a now-familiar dilemma: where to find a new president. Experience had amply shown that the most successful Brazilian Traction presidents had been able to function effectively in both Canada and Brazil. Given the supreme importance of upholding the company's rights in the stormy Brazilian political milieu, the president of Brazilian Traction had above all else to be able to move adroitly in the Brazilian environment. At the same time, he needed a grasp of the financial and legal imperatives that governed the company's standing in the eyes of its shareholders in the North. Sir Alexander Mackenzie's singular success as president was attributable to these talents. By 1944, there seemed to be nobody in the pool of existing executive talent at Brazilian Traction capable of perpetuating this tradition. The best candidate, and the man who eventually did replace Sir Herbert, was A.W.K. Billings, the company's top hydraulic engineer in Brazil.

Since joining Brazilian Traction in the early 1920s, Asa Billings had established a reputation as one of the world's leading hydraulic engineers. The Cubatão station had become the focus of international engineering curiosity and had solidified the foundation of the Light's generating system in the 1920s. Unfortunately, Billings was too much the engineer. While he mastered Portuguese and was by no means blind to the complexities of Brazilian politics, he lacked the subtle touch of a Sir Alexander or a Sir Herbert. He was always the engineer: direct, goal-oriented, and impatient with obstacles that stood in his way. He had not been recruited for his administrative capabilities and had never been eager to shoulder overall responsibility for managing the Light. As a vice-president, he had been content to oversee the operation and expansion of 'his' power-generating system and to leave consideration of financial and political factors to others. An indication of Billings's forthright preoccupation with engineering concerns was provided by a bizarre mishap at Cubatão in the early 1930s. During a routine inspection of one of the penstocks, a Light employee had climbed through an inspection hatch at the top of the penstock to examine the inner surface of the pipe for metal fatigue. Although the water flow had been disconnected, the worker slipped on the still-wet surface and, losing his balance, shot down the steep pipe like a bullet. Given the angle of the penstock and the fact that the pipe was more than a kilometre long, nobody expected to find the worker alive at the end of his involuntary journey. Yet, when another inspection hatch was pried open just in front of the valve chamber in the powerhouse at the foot of the Serra, the bewildered worker climbed out with only a few bruises as a souvenir of his rapid descent. When this miracle was duly reported by telephone to Billings in São Paulo, the vice-president's first reaction was to inquire whether 'his' turbine had been damaged.

Billings's selection as the new president was, none the less, greeted with wide acclaim. The National Council of Water and Electric Energy in Rio hailed Billings 'as an engineer of universal renown.'[35] Above all else, Billings commanded the respect and trust of Brazilians. Furthermore, he enjoyed 'very cordial and satisfactory' relations with President Getúlio Vargas. Despite these encouraging factors, ominous signs accompanied Billings's ascendancy to Brazilian Traction's senior executive post. In the first place, he was sixty-eight years old and was in failing health. (Like Couzens, Billings was addicted to work and in twenty-two years of service had taken only a single month of vacation leave.) In April 1944, he had visited the Mayo Clinic and had been warned to retire as soon as possible or risk irreparable damage to his health. Consequently, he had arranged in May 1944 to retire. The subsequent collapse of Couzens's health forced Billings to alter his plans and ultimately to assume the president's mantle. Within a year, these new responsibilities precipitated the decline of Billings's own health. As he himself admitted in September 1945, 'the tremendously involved and chaotic political and economic situation has swamped me completely.' Once again, the failure to develop new talent at the senior-executive level during the 1930s was having serious repercussions as Brazilian Traction braced itself to face the post-war world.

As an experienced hydraulic engineer, Asa Billings had no delusions about the post-war power situation in south-eastern Brazil. Within a month of taking the presidency, he had obtained an interview with President Vargas and frankly told him that, while the Light had 'succeeded in carrying the load' throughout the war, 'this could not be guaranteed in the future as it depended upon rainfall, load growth, delivery of material, labour market and other conditions.'[36] The 'other' conditions, most notably the still-unsolved political problem of rates and regulation and the prospective scarcity of post-war capital, were to bedevil Billings's presidency, break his health, and eventually provoke a major crisis in the company's management. After more than four decades of competent, cohesive senior management, Brazilian Traction encountered its first serious boardroom strife. Even though many of the 'old guard,' including Billings himself, would not weather the storm, Brazilian Traction emerged from the crisis intact and, equally importantly, with a reunified and reinvigorated senior management.

The incipient post-war shortage of electrical energy was the most ominous problem facing Billings. Few expected that with the conclusion of the war Brazil would slip into economic depression, as it had after the First World War. Instead, there was widespread recognition that the end of the war would trigger a surge of consumer spending and industrial growth. The war had starved Brazilians of many goods they had traditionally imported, thereby promoting the growth of indigenous industry through import substitution. As well, exports of raw materials had boomed during the war and had given Brazil a tremendous reservoir of foreign currency. Canada's trade commissioner in Rio, Maurice Bélanger, was quick to sense the coming boom in his 1945 report on the Brazilian economy. 'The high level of industrial and commercial activity has caused a substantial rise in earning power and greatly increased the number of potential customers of imported goods,' he reported to Ottawa. 'There is also a tremendous backlog of demand for capital goods of all kinds; transportation equipment, building materials and equipment, roadmaking machinery and materials, plant equipment.'[37]

In keeping with the historical pattern of Brazil's economic growth, Brazil's post-war industrial growth would be concentrated in the Rio–São Paulo heartland and would threaten to overload the Light's already overstrained power system. The inadequate supply of energy gave every indication of being the major bottle-neck in south-eastern Brazil's post-war economy. From 1935 to 1945, installed hydroelectric capacity in the whole of Brazil increased by 26 per cent, but consumption of electricity per capita rose by 70 per cent.[38] Such growth completely soaked up surplus generating capacity and forced the introduction of wartime rationing. Although rationing was abandoned in 1945, the general post-war power situation was, as Billings reiterated to Vargas in July 1945, 'not too secure.'[39]

By 1944, Billings was arguing that piecemeal additions to the system would not avert the coming crisis and that a 'general construction program' would have to be adopted 'as fast as we can obtain the equipment and the labour to install it.'[40] Billings advocated the addition of 'successive units' of 67,000 kw each to the Cubatão plant. Billings then recommended a similar expansion of the Rio system. The installation of an additional six generating units at Lajes would boost capacity by 210,000 kw, and the construction of the Lajes 'auxiliary' or Ponte Coberta plant would furnish a further 45,000 kw. The water necessary to operate these new units would be provided by an ambitious river-diversion scheme that would take water from the Paraíba River and pump it through tunnels and overland canals into the Lajes reservoir. The Ilha dos Pombos plant, also serving Rio, would receive an extra generator. Billings's blueprint for the post-war expansion of the Light power system was both bold from the engineering point of view and realistic from the market point of view.

The magnitude of the proposed expansion was further increased by the necessity of matching every increase in generating capacity with a comparable increase in the Light's distribution grid. The most innovative feature of the Billings construction plan was the proposal to interconnect the Rio and São Paulo systems. Since their creation, the two systems had functioned as distinct entities. This separation was initially due to the fact that existing technology did not permit the efficient transmission of power over the 335 kilometres that separated the Lajes, Parnaíba, and (after 1926) Cubatão plants. As transmission technology improved, Light engineers continued to advise against interconnection on grounds that Rio's reliance on fifty cycles and São Paulo's on sixty cycles made the two systems incompatible. Conversion of one of the systems to the other's frequency was deemed prohibitively expensive. Hence there was no opportunity for one subsidiary of Brazilian Traction to transfer power to its sister company in times of drought or peak load. By the end of the war,

Billings was convinced that the time had come to rationalize the whole Light system, regardless of cost. A transmission link between the Lajes and Cubatão stations offered 'the only feasible and rapid solution' to the post-war power situation. 'The Cubatão plant,' he argued, 'possesses the necessary water reserves to permit continuing the supply of power to the São Paulo system, in addition to relieving the power crisis of the Rio system.' A frequency converter mid-way along the transmission link would marry the two systems.

There were few critics of Billings's prescription for the future development of the Light's generating system. Criticism arose only when attention shifted to the financial and political implications of so extensive a program. In March 1945, Toronto head office estimated that the total cost of the proposed Lajes-Cubatão upgrading would be $11,445,000, of which $3,303,000 was needed for the transmission link alone.[41] By November 1945, Treasurer George Troop reported that this total had been revised and advised the board that, if all the implications of Billings's construction scheme were followed and a reasonable expansion of the distribution and telephone systems was included, the Light would be committed to an expenditure of more than $87,000,000 by 1948. Troop admitted that there was 'a considerable measure of uncertainty' attached to the estimate in view of the difficulty of predicting accurately the availability of materials, exchange fluctuations, and the cost of labour.[42]

The suggestion that the company faced capital expenditures in the neighbourhood of $90 million in the next three years had a shattering effect on the board. Billings had framed his recommendations with a mind to the operational imperatives that governed the Light's successful operation. Many of the directors in Toronto viewed the proposals from the perspective of prevailing financial conditions in the North and, in 1945, that perspective was far from auspicious. Expenditure on the scale envisaged by Billings could not be met by ploughing back profits, a practice that the company had adhered to throughout the 1930s. Instead, resort would have to be made to outside capital. The majority of the board, led by Chairman Gow, were not only reluctant to do this but were also quick to point out that there would be a tremendous post-war scramble for capital and that the company would be obliged to pay dearly for any bond issue placed on the European and North American markets. This infuriated Billings and led to a dangerous divergence of opinion between Light management in Brazil and the head office in Toronto.

Faced with what he considered the absolute necessity of raising a large amount of capital to underwrite his expansion plans, Billings became highly critical of the cautious financial policies pursued during the preceding two presidencies. 'Its finance,' he wrote of his own corporation, 'has been ultra-conservative; in fact, this leads (in the writer's opinion, which is shared, I believe, by all our officials in Brazil) to unnecessary increase of danger to the enterprise as a whole. The proportion of preferred stock, debentures and bonds to the common stock is extremely low and the fixed charges are consequently almost negligible.' Billings also found fault with the policy, pursued through the Depression and war years, of ploughing back profits at the expense of dividends. Over the last thirteen years, he estimated, 55 per cent of Brazilian Traction's earnings had been ploughed back. 'The attitude of the shareholders has been assumed in these discussions to continue as entirely passive,' he warned. 'We do not believe that this will be the case as soon as the war-time restrictions are released or removed. All shareholders will desire to receive as large a proportion of the earnings as is reasonable and in addition the shareholders of our company are entitled to receive a considerable amount of the cash and securities on hand in compensation for the period of suspension of dividends.' The company needed to adopt an entirely new attitude to its financing if it were to survive in Brazil and remain in the good graces of its shareholders. Billings chose to describe this as a policy of 'orderly finance.' The first step in this direction was for the board to recognize 'the urgency of proceeding at once with the legal and financial studies which are essential before proper financing can be determined and commenced.'[43]

There was much truth in these criticisms. Dividend policy throughout the Depression and early war years had been far from generous. In 1939 and 1940, no dividend had been paid, and it was only in 1944 that holders of common shares found themselves in receipt of a reasonable dividend of $2 a year. It seemed unconscionable to expect shareholders to bear the brunt of capitalizing post-war expansion. Even though Treasurer George Troop estimated that continued reliance upon ploughed-back profits would still result in a shortfall of $27 million in meeting the costs of expansion, the board in Toronto was reluctant to depart from established practices. There was a pervasive belief among the majority of the board that no change in financial procedures would be needed in the post-war world.

The board's intransigence on the issue of 'orderly finance' was not the only problem. Billings's ambitious program of post-war expansion was impeded by the prevailing political instability in Brazil, the product of another old guard. Although the war had witnessed a gradual moderation in the attitude of most Brazilian politicians on the contentious issue of regulating the hydroelectric industry, the Water Code remained unsettled, with the Light's rates still effectively frozen at 1934 levels. Furthermore, there was the lingering fear that the question of 'progressive nationalization' might again become contentious. No foreign investor would willingly invest millions in Brazil's post-war electric expansion if it were likely to be unfairly regulated or expropriated by a rampantly nationalistic government. It was this concern that Ken McCrimmon had bluntly voiced to President Vargas in March 1944. 'I told him that as matters now stood the foreign investor did not feel that he had any guarantees for his capital and that capital must be defined whether for purposes of *encampação* [take-over] or for the fixation of rates and tariffs.'[44] The same sense of unease was reflected by the British ambassador in Rio, when in 1946 he reminded the Brazilian government that 'a liberal treatment of foreign enterprise should be regarded as essential to the organization of the world economy.'[45]

Concern over Brazil's post-war course was heightened by the political crisis of 1945. The war had acted as a potent 'political catalyst'[46] and had released new forces in Brazilian society that would eventually act as a solvent on the totalitarianism of the Estado Novo. Participation in the great fight against fascism had kindled hope that the narrow political base of Vargas's Estado Novo could be overturned and a broader, more democratic system put in its place. Political mobilization took place in many segments of Brazilian society. The army returned from Europe with a sense of democratic mission. While Brazilian soldiers fought for democracy abroad, Brazilian workers at home became imbued with a new sense of solidarity, *trabalhismo*. New political movements, including a reinvigorated Communist party, began to coalesce. The only bond uniting these disparate groups was a common resentment of the political monopoly of Getúlio Vargas. Sensing this ferment, Vargas announced in February 1945 that a free, democratic election for the national presidency would be held later in the year. Almost immediately, two leading candidates appeared. Eurico Gaspar Dutra, an army general from Mato Grosso, led the forces of the Social Democratic Party (PSD), a party that had the blessing of the existing government. The forces of opposition combined behind the National Democratic Union (UDN) and its candidate, Brigadier Eduardo Gomes. Not content simply to lend his support to the PSD alone, Vargas also actively encouraged the Brazilian Labour Party (PTB) as a vehicle of working-class interests.

The prospect of a free presidential election became clouded as 1945 progressed. There were ominous signs that Vargas might deviously try to engineer his own return to power. Demands for a constituent assembly to elect the new president became mixed with cries of '*Queremos* Getúlio' ('We Want Getúlio'). Instinctively, Vargas began to display his populist side. Aware that mass public support was daily increasing the possibility that deposed Argentine leader Juan Peron would be brought back to power, Vargas tried to evoke the same wave of popular support by exciting nationalistic resentment of foreign participation in the Brazilian economy. The Light was an inviting target. Although only a year earlier he had assured McCrimmon that he was a 'firm believer in the exploitation of public services under private enterprise,' Vargas unhesitatingly picked up the theme of 'hidden' alien forces within the Brazilian economy. The president's behaviour caused Light executives several months of great anxiety. 'While no one can say for sure what is Getúlio's actual intention regarding the presidency,' Norman Wilson reported from Rio, '... there is a pronounced anticipation that he will risk some "double cross" to continue in office.'[47]

The expected political crisis came in October 1945 when Vargas moved to appoint his brother, Benjamin, police chief of Rio. When the president refused to undo this nepotism, his old *tenente* friend General Goés Monteiro resigned as minister of war and mobilized the armed forces according to a prearranged plan that met with the approval of both presidential candidates. In the absence of widespread popular support, Vargas bowed to the army's wish and resigned. On 31 October 1945 he quietly slipped out of Rio and retired to a cattle ranch in his native Rio Grande do Sul. In his stead, Brazil's chief justice, José Linhares, was appointed as *pro tem* president, and the nation resumed its preparations for the election of a new president. In December 1945, General Eurico Gaspar Dutra captured 56 per cent of the popular vote and became president-elect.

In fifteen years as the linchpin of national politics, Getúlio Vargas had irreversibly changed the character and direction of Brazilian life. His rule was marked by 'important precedents,' as historian Thomas Skidmore has noted, that were to outlast their creator. Under the Estado Novo, Vargas had strongly centralized the Brazilian state. The autonomy enjoyed by Brazilian states under the Old Republic had been displaced by the fortified power of Rio. The central government had used this power to redefine and redirect Brazil's energies. Motivated by an undercurrent of economic nationalism, the state had intervened in Brazilian society and in its economy. Whether to ensure a minimum wage or to foster the growth of a steel industry or, as in the case of the Water Code, to impose a measure of regulation on the hydroelectric industry, Vargas used the state as a vehicle for national ambitions. As Vargas himself proclaimed in May 1944, 'the country has entered into a new era of realizations. The Government is pledged for important initiatives and will certainly sustain the rhythm of our economic development and will increase the turn-over of our business, assuring to all, capitalists and workers, a plentiful remuneration for their efforts.'[48]

In Vargas's hands, economic nationalism took on varying hues: sometimes positive, sometimes negative. The steel works at Volta Redonda gave evidence that a 'new era of realizations' had indeed dawned. The initiation of the state-sponsored São Francisco hydroelectric project in north-eastern Brazil served notice that the Light might soon have national partners. Billings's willingness to counsel the formulators of the National Electricity Plan was indicative of the Light's willingness to coexist with the emerging state presence in the hydroelectric industry, a recognition that the Light alone could not handle all of south-eastern Brazil's electricity needs. It was only when Brazilian economic nationalism assumed a negative character that Brazilian Traction's willingness to co-operate turned to panicky anxiety. It was characteristic of the political enigma of Getúlio Vargas that both Brazil's desire for economic self-determination and its acknowledgment of the need for foreign capital found voice in his legacy.

In the dying months of 1945, it was not at all clear to Light executives what direction the new political guard would take in Brazil. 'There is a tendency in all quarters,' Billings reported to Toronto, 'for the Government to adopt a waiting attitude, at least until after the election is over. It will depend upon who is elected and how soon the choices are definitely known before we can count on very much constructive action.'[49] The December elections did little to clarify the situation. By April 1946 Billings was complaining that the 'present political situation is very unsettled and the company's own situation depends primarily on this. The new President [Dutra] is not showing the firmness that was expected of him, in fact, people ask "when is he going to take office."'[50] At the same time, Billings noted with alarm that the well-organized Communist party was filling the newspapers under its influence with tales of the company's 'fabulous' profits and urging its followers to nationalize the Light.

Amid these distressing currents, Asa Billings came to the very realistic conclusion that the best means of countering the 'strong tendency toward nationalization' was to accelerate the company's efforts to 'Brazilianize' itself. While Brazilian Traction had made tremendous progress toward giving Brazilians opportunities in the operational and executive activities of the Rio and São Paulo Light, virtually nothing had been done to allow Brazilians to invest in the Light. 'The natural desire of Brazilians,' Billings shrewdly suggested,

to participate in our enterprise has always been difficult, and in practice impossible, to satisfy, because of the set-up of the companies and the opposition of the directors to such participation. It is nevertheless extremely important that such participation be facilitated. It should be emphasized, however, that this opportunity to participate does not mean that there will be any important subscription by Brazilian investors ... The opportunity *for Brazilians to subscribe is of the greatest importance to our company. Failure to provide such opportunity will increase the chance of unfair treatment at such time.*[51]

The offering of shares to the Brazilian public would provide a measure – however much a token – of political insurance, thereby in a small way diminishing the company's large post-war capital requirements. The alternative was not only the loss of possible new capital but also the possible loss of the company itself if the Dutra government should adopt a vigorously nationalistic tack. As the debate developed over the merits of 'Brazilianization,' Billings frequently directed the board's attention to the events unfolding in Argentina, where Juan Peron was nationalizing the country's predominantly British-owned railways, gas works, and telephone systems.

Billings's bold assessment of Brazilian Traction's prospects in post-war Brazil was not greeted with enthusiasm in Toronto. His repeated emphasis on the need for a vigorous hydroelectric expansion and greater

Brazilian participation was met with indifference and, eventually, complete hostility. Although Billings occupied the president's chair, it soon became apparent that he did not control the board. The president's inability to work his will on the board was the direct result of the strong strategic advantage that its chairman, Walter Gow, enjoyed. Like Alexander Mackenzie, Billings held the firm belief that the Light was best managed from Rio, not Toronto. In recognition of this, the board had reactivated the position of chairman of the board in 1944 and had elected Gow to occupy it. It was hoped that Gow would carry the burden of routine executive matters in Toronto, thereby allowing Billings to devote his own energies to operational affairs in Brazil. Unfortunately, what had seemed an admirable arrangement in theory soon deteriorated into a state of open dissension in practice. The root cause of the ensuing schism was Billings's rather bullish way of advocating reform and Gow's intransigent opposition to it. Unlike Vargas, Gow and Billings did not go gracefully.

Walter Gow was the epitome of old-style Brazilian Traction management. In his day, he had lent his legal talents to the company's affairs with great effect. He had, for instance, personally handled the intricate details of the purchase of the Société Anonyme du Gaz from its Belgian owners in 1904–5. By 1945, however, Gow was well past his prime. He had been born in 1872 and had put in long service as a partner at the Blake legal firm, as a vice-president of Brazilian Traction, and as a director of several other companies. A confirmed bachelor, Gow had developed into somewhat of a curmudgeon with a distinct trace of parsimony in his character. Having seen Brazilian Traction prosper for four decades as a result of a proven set of corporate policies, Gow saw little reason even to contemplate a departure from the beaten path. He was not an ideal candidate for the chairmanship in times of change. He shared with many of the old board members the belief that post-war capital needs could be met out of earnings and that any talk of outside financing was heresy. Gow based his perception of post-war needs on the flimsiest understanding of actual conditions in Brazil. He was above all else a head-office man. Furthermore, he shared the scepticism of many at head office about the wisdom of allowing Brazilians a more responsible role in the company. Brazilians, it was reasoned, even as shareholders, could never be made privy to the company's executive affairs. When confronted with Billings's call for 'orderly financing' and a greater degree of 'Brazilianization,' Gow responded with a flat 'no.'

Billings had few allies in Toronto. Most directors succumbed to the pressure exerted by Gow for a status quo response to the president's proposals. Conspicuous among the dissenters to Gow's attitude were the the treasurer, George Troop, and a director, Norman Wilson, both of whom had joined the board in 1944. Troop was one of the few at head office who fully comprehended the company's post-war capital requirements. He appreciated the folly of attempting to meet these out of earnings and the necessity of inducing Brazilian investment in the company. 'The psychological importance of financing in Brazil,' he stressed, 'even though the amount that might be realized would go only a very short way toward meeting our needs, is emphasized by all our senior executives in Brazil.'[52] Norman Wilson, the only other member of the board who shared Asa Billings's assessment, had maintained a watching brief on the tramway operations since the mid-1920s and was fully aware of the immensity of the effort needed to keep abreast of the coming post-war boom in Brazil. Wilson was also conscious of the repercussions of failure to meet the challenge of expansion. Like Billings, he understood the negative aspects of Brazilian nationalism. 'It is like fire damp in a coal mine,' he later commented, 'always present in greater or lesser degree, and a tiny opportune spark may have devastating results.'[53]

Despite these two sympathetic colleagues in Toronto, Billings faced other exasperating obstacles. He was by no means backed by a solid phalanx of Light executives in Brazil. To his dismay, Billings discovered that the local management of the Rio and São Paulo Light had become severely factionalized. The principal combatants in this fray were Ken McCrimmon and J.M. Bell, the two senior managers in Brazil. To be blunt, the two men heartily disliked each other and viewed each other's every move with the deepest suspicion. Unfortunately for Billings, each man was indispensable. McCrimmon, with his intimate ties to the Brazilian legal and political world, and McKim Bell, with his engineering expertise, had both served the company since the 1920s and jealously guarded their prerogatives. In an attempt to resolve this impasse, Billings recruited an experienced English electrical engineer, Humphrey Style, to come to Brazil to provide a non-partisan focus for a reunified Light management. It would, however, take several years for Style to master the rudiments of managing an organization as large as the Light. In the interim, Billings was left to contend with the squabbling of McCrimmon and McKim Bell.

Billings had not only to contend with this clash of personalities; he had also to cope with his own declining health. He had accepted the presidency out of a sense of duty in 1944, against his doctor's orders. The battle with Gow exhausted both his loyalty and his health. In September 1945, he confided to a friend that he was 'very anxious to be released from all my work except clearing up the long-range planning and corresponding discussions with the authorities.' Soon afterwards, he confided to Gow that the potentially explosive problems both within and outside the company had broken his health. On 3 September 1945, Billings 'insisted' that the board accept his resignation.

While Billings's resignation may have brought Gow the momentary satisfaction of knowing that the president would now desist in his demands for a renovation of company policies, it also created an awkward dilemma. Who would replace the retiring president? With the death of Couzens and the departure of Billings, the implications of the failure to promote a new echelon of management in the 1930s became glaringly apparent. Gow reached the obvious and sensible decision that he himself was too old. Similarly, it would have been folly to deliver control of the company into the hands of either Ken McCrimmon or J. McKim Bell. To have done so would have sparked intense internecine strife. Humphrey Style, despite much experience in Latin American utilities, was still too new and untried to be trusted with the presidency. To all concerned, it was obvious that Brazilian Traction had exhausted its store of fresh executive talent.

Throughout the last months of 1945 Gow acted like a man motivated by deep desperation. He persuaded Billings to postpone his formal resignation until an appropriate successor could be found. He realized that Brazilian Traction must obtain the services of a new and, preferably, much younger senior executive officer. Ideally, an acceptable candidate would have to possess a record of business achievement in Canada and at the same time be versatile enough to adapt to the unique demands created by operations in Brazil. Gow's search for the appropriate outsider was aided by the fact that the war economy in Canada had allowed many businessmen to show their mettle, either as 'dollar-a-year' men in the federal bureaucracy or in industry. Unfortunately, competition for the post-war services of these men was intense. Gow's first candidate for the presidency was Donald Gordon, a young Toronto banker who had performed stalwart service for the nation during the war as the head of the Wartime Prices and Trade Board. Gow approached Gordon with an offer and was delighted to learn that Gordon was attracted by the challenge. Before committing himself to the position, however, Gordon contacted C.D. Howe. As minister of munitions and supply, Howe had directed civil servants and seconded businessmen in harnessing the national economy for war. Howe was enthusiastic about the job – Brazilian Traction was, after all, one of Canada's leading corporations – but it was not the job that he had in mind for Donald Gordon. The former head of the WPTB should reserve his energies for a challenge that would build a better Canada, not a better Brazil. Gordon obediently took the minister's advice and turned down Gow's offer. (Donald Gordon subsequently in the early 1950s became head of the Canadian National Railway system.) Disheartened, Gow began his search anew.

Early in 1946 Gow found the man he had been searching for. His attention was drawn (probably by Norman Wilson, who had also served in the wartime Ottawa bureaucracy) to the presence of a successful young corporate lawyer in Toronto. Henry Borden was at first sight an unlikely candidate for the presidency of Brazilian Traction. He had little previous experience in public utilities, and his dealings with the business community had been limited to those of a lawyer advising corporate clients. None the less, Gow was quick to recognize tremendous potential in Borden. A Haligonian, born in 1901, Borden was the nephew of Sir Robert Borden, Conservative prime minister from 1911 to 1920. He had excelled as a student at McGill and Dalhousie and had crowned his academic career with a Rhodes scholarship in 1924. Although he had served a brief stint with the Royal Bank in the 1920s, Borden had determined on a career in law and in 1927 was called to the bar in Nova Scotia, Ontario, and England. In 1936, he became the senior partner in the Toronto legal firm of Borden, Elliot, Kelley, Palmer and Sankey, and in 1938 he became a King's Counsel.

The outbreak of war in 1939 completely changed the complexion of Borden's career. Like many others in the private sector, he hearkened to Ottawa's call for executive talent to administer Canada's wartime bureaucracy and economy. Working under the dynamic leadership of C.D. Howe, Borden served as the general counsel to the Department of Munitions and Supply from September 1939 to October 1943. It was a position of crucial importance in the wartime bureaucracy. Every contract let by the department was vetted by Borden's staff to ensure that it was legally acceptable and did not violate profiteering guidelines. Given the scope of the department's wartime responsibilities, Borden found himself shouldering an immense burden. At the height of the wartime crisis, Borden worked eighteen-hour days to keep abreast of the flow of contracts. Late in 1942, he assumed the chairmanship of the Wartime Industries Control Board, the central regulating agency of the 'controlled' wartime industries. A year later, his health suffering from the strain of overwork, Borden resigned his duties in Ottawa and returned to his legal practice in Toronto. At the end of the war, C.D. Howe praised Borden's contribution to Canada's wartime efforts by noting that 'no man ever left the service of Canada with a better record of public service.'[54]

It was Borden's ability to work under trying and unfamiliar conditions that convinced Gow that he had found a candidate capable of meeting the challenge of the Brazilian Traction presidency. After conducting preliminary negotiations in late January 1946, Gow reported to Billings that Borden's background was 'excellent in every respect and he had a sound training in corporation law, which I regard as a very desirable qualification for whoever fills this post.' Furthermore, Gow added, Borden had 'a very pleasant personality.'[55] In light of the rancours of the past year, it was imperative that the new president should be able to work harmoniously with both the board in Toronto and senior executives in Brazil. It was also important that the prospective new president have good health and relative youth. Both these Henry Borden possessed.

The rancour had not, however, ended. Even in the selection of a new chief executive, Gow and Billings found cause for disagreement. Gow believed that Borden was best suited to fill the position of chairman and that another candidate should be found to serve as president. 'I still think, however, that we really need two men at this end (Toronto),' Gow suggested, 'a Chairman (in this case Mr. Borden) plus a President who should be a public utility man and one able to spend a considerable part of his time in Brazil ... I do not think that any lawyer, no matter how eminent he may be in his profession, can do the two jobs satisfactorily.' Billings took violent exception to this. In the first place, the chief operating officer would never be able to fulfil his duties from a desk in Toronto, no matter how frequently he visited Brazil. Secondly the 'divided responsibility' between the president and chairman would 'surely cause indecision and trouble.' If the chief of operations in Brazil was resident in Toronto, an additional echelon of authority would be interposed between the operational personnel and the board. This would inevitably lead to 'a lack of initiative in the local staff and a confusion of responsibility.' Billings was joined in this opinion by Humphrey Style, his understudy in Brazil. Any shift of operating responsibility from Brazil to Toronto, Style warned Gow, 'would be fatal to the future of the Companies.' In a bid to calm the situation, Billings suggested to Gow that Style eventually be appointed president after a 'further period of trial and improved acquaintance with local conditions' in Brazil. The company would thus have a chief operating officer in Rio and a chief executive officer in Toronto. Gow's only response to this proposal was to ask Billings to remain as president until the annual meeting in June 1946. Billings replied that he would oblige Gow in this request only if the financial and legal planning studies he had long advocated were immediately initiated.

While Gow and Billings bickered, Henry Borden pondered his future. Gow's offer had come as a 'complete surprise.'[56] A return to his legal practice would have brought continued success in the Toronto legal community. There was also the possibility of a career in politics, which, given Borden's strong Conservative sympathies, had a definite attraction. Finally, Brazilian Traction offered the opportunity of a new career in the business world. It was this last possibility that gave him the most anxiety. Not only did he lack experience in public-utilities management, but he had little knowledge of Brazil or international business. Borden sought the advice of the Honourable Howard Ferguson, who as a Brazilian Traction director was able to provide some insight into the challenge. In late February 1946, Henry Borden accepted Walter Gow's offer. With that decision Borden signified his willingness to postpone his ambition of pursuing a legal or political career.

Borden's decision was followed by yet another skirmish between Gow and Billings. As soon as Borden joined the board, Billings handed over all his executive duties in Brazil to Humphrey Style. Freed of these responsibilities, he devoted his energies to the preparation of technical memoranda on the Water Code and to continued efforts to persuade the board to undertake the much-debated legal and financial studies. 'I, and all the responsible officials in Brazil,' he bluntly informed the board, 'concur in believing that delay in dealing with this financial problem is highly inadvisable and dangerous.'[57] Despite such prompting, Billings made little progress against Gow's implacable will. In a gesture of complete desperation, Billings announced in early May that he would sever all ties with the company as soon as the annual meeting was concluded in June. The complete 'passiveness' of the board in the face of the obvious need for policies of 'financial order' and 'Brazilianization' had ruined his health and forced him to give 'it all up in disgust.' On 1 May Billings resigned all his remaining positions and went into retirement. Shocked by this action, Gow concluded that the now former president was a 'very sick man' who was 'not himself at all.' When Norman Wilson pointed out that the loss of Billings as a technical consultant would be 'colossal,' Gow finally decided to act. He immediately proposed that Frank Schulman, the assistant to the president, be dispatched to Rio to conduct a thorough investigation of the Light's prospects. Satisfied that he had finally achieved something, Billings withdrew his resignation and agreed to remain as president until June. To ensure that he had not simply been given a placebo, Billings contacted Borden by telephone from Rio and secured from him an understanding that the new president would 'undertake actively and with an open mind' to consider the results of Schulman's report. Borden also gave Billings some assurance that he would act to ensure greater Brazilian participation in the company and to cease the practice of financing expansion solely out of earnings. Billings was elated by the willingness of his successor to address himself to the major problems confronting the Light. Accordingly, he agreed to continue serving as a consulting engineer after Borden took over.

On 27 June 1946, the shareholders at Brazilian Traction's annual meeting were informed that Billings had resigned and that Henry Borden, a director since February, had been elected to succeed him. At the same time, it was announced that Gow had presented his resignation as chairman. On the surface, it was a smooth and courteous transition of power without a hint of the frictions that had preceded it. Not only had the company gained a new president; it had also managed to retain the services and loyalty of two of its most valued senior executives. Gow had agreed to remain on as a director, and Billings would continue to serve as a vice-president without executive duties. A major obstacle to the process of effective decision making had been removed and the way opened for a constructive new approach to post-war problems. The old order had passed.

Two weeks before his official retirement, Billings was awarded the Order of the Southern Cross, Brazil's highest decoration. At a banquet on 12 June 1946, the foreign minister in the new Dutra government, Dr João Neves da Fontoura, officially bestowed the decoration on the retiring president of Latin America's largest utility company. 'The Brazilian

Government is today rendering homage to a great engineer and an exceptional man of action,' noted Dr Euvaldi Lodi, the president of the National Federation of Industries. 'Mr. Billings did not by any means come to Brazil as an adventurer ... He did not come to South America as an occasional visitor looking after his business and interests. He came here and stayed here, like many others who are cooperating with us in the progress of our country, developing our natural resources and making them available to our people.' 'No individual, no matter how great his efforts,' Billings modestly replied, 'can accomplish great works by himself, even if he is one of the heads of an important organization.' The credit, he insisted must be shared by 'hundreds of engineers and specialists, the majority of whom are Brazilians.'[58] Billings's self-effacement by no means deterred the Light, in response to public demand, from renaming the Rio Grande reservoir the Billings Reservoir in May 1949. Five months later, Billings died in California.

The accolades bestowed on Billings as past president were in stark contrast to the feelings of the new president of Canada's largest overseas investment. Henry Borden had inherited a corporation that, despite its tremendous prestige in investors' eyes, faced an uncertain future. Unlike all his predecessors, Borden came to Brazilian Traction as a complete outsider. One of his first impressions of the corporation he had taken charge of was 'the more or less family compact manner in which the company had been run over the years.' The board of directors with which he would have to map out the company's post-war policies was distinguished principally by the advanced age of its members. 'It was management on the pre-and-mid-Victorian scale,' he candidly admitted, 'and I soon discovered the mess I had inherited.' Almost immediately, Borden grasped that there had been ample reason for Billings's repeated demands for a thorough investigation of the company's financial prospects and for some attempt to introduce greater Brazilian participation in its affairs. 'It seems obvious,' he later recalled, 'that at least one hundred million dollars had to be secured to catch up on the back-log created by the war years and the rapidly expanding industry in the Rio and São Paulo regions.' Judged from even the most optimistic perspective, the problems confronting the new president appeared daunting and, by Borden's own admission, 'of impossible resolution.' At times, Borden must have pondered the idea of returning to his lucrative Toronto law practice and forsaking the challenge of Brazilian Traction. It was a temptation that he did not entertain for long. 'I decided not to look back and never did.'[59]

Epilogue:
'Run Like the Light'

The American economist Ray Vernon has likened the multinational corporation operating in the developing world to an 'obsolescing bargain.' Such bargains are initially struck when the foreign investor's superiority in terms of capital, technology, and managerial *savoir faire* is most evident. Eager to emulate the material progress of the developed world, the host country compliantly provides a salubrious climate for foreign investment. Out of fear that the capital and technology may wander elsewhere, the underdeveloped nation exacts few 'economic rents' from its would-be benefactor and rests quiescent in the knowledge that powers – technological, financial, and managerial – otherwise beyond its ability have been brought within its reach. Such is the satisfaction derived from this foreign-financed advancement that considerations of sovereignty and economic self-determination are placed in abeyance. Sanctioned and guided by the national élites, foreign capital, Vernon points out, is broadly perceived in the developing country as 'benign and unthreatening.' Thus the multinational establishes itself.[1]

The terms of the bargain eventually turn. As the developing economy matures, diversifies, and attains a measure of self-sufficiency, the bargaining power of the foreign investor is eroded. In prospering, the multinational brings on its own eclipse. As technology and skills are absorbed by the host and as competitors, both local and foreign, materialize, the multinational encounters pressure to enhance the bargain it brings to the local economy. 'As long as a foreign-owned goose can still lay golden eggs, however,' Vernon has picturesquely observed, 'the policy of most developing countries has been to squeeze the goose, not to destroy it or to have it fly away.'[2] Such gentle pressures are coloured by the nature of the business. Those exploiting natural resources face demands for secondary processing within the host country's borders; foreign utility corporations encounter agitation for the regulation of hitherto unregulated and monopolistically held services. Xenophobic antagonism to foreign enterprise will increasingly gravitate from the periphery of public consciousness towards its centre. Sensing this shift, national élites will prove less stalwart in their defence of foreign capital's legitimacy within their borders. Eventually, 'the basic asymmetry,' as Vernon puts it, of host country and multinational becomes starkly apparent. Demands for secondary processing and regulation turn to pressure for expropriation or nationalization. The multinational may respond – by rejuvenating its technology, for instance, or by accommodating local participation in equity and management – all to preserve what Vernon calls its 'unique function,' within the host economy. There is no denying the ultimate logic of obsolescence. The cycle thus completes itself.

The story of the Light in the years 1899–1945 is in some ways the chronicle of such an obsolescing bargain, but a bargain with remarkable endurance. Fred Stark Pearson's appearance in São Paulo in mid-1899 as a messiah of foreign technology and capital coincided perfectly with the ambitions of *paulistano* liberal reformers. From the kernel of the Gualco concession, the São Paulo company took to the field of Latin American utilities with the incomparable advantages of American technology, European capital, and Canadian entrepreneurship. There was little to check its progress, or that of the Rio company after 1904. The skill with which power stations were erected, transmission lines strung, tracks laid, and schedules maintained testified to the initial superiority of northern utilities imperialism. It was both a beneficial and a profitable imperialism. The efficiency and relative cheapness of the electricity provided by the Light was of prime importance in the industrial genesis of south-eastern Brazil. Nothing symbolized the sudden urban and industrial expansion of Rio and São Paulo better than a tram jostling its way through a crowded *carioca* street or the black penstocks of the Cubatão power plant climbing precipitously up the green slopes of the Serra. If Brazilians got their part of the bargain in terms of efficient utility services and unimpeded industrial growth, so too did the promoters and shareholders of the Light in profits.

Born in the age of financial capitalism, Brazilian Traction was the

product of consummate capitalists, adept at negotiating airtight concessions and decimating would-be competitors. Brazilian Traction arrived
and stayed in Brazil for profits. What was remarkable was that for more
than four decades it succeeded brilliantly in keeping the 'asymmetry' of its
bargain – the natural tension of remitted profit and national economic
self-suffiency – largely out of sight and out of the Brazilian mind. It did so
by combining efficient service with an astute sensitivity to evolving local
sensibilities. The Light never limned the caricature of a rapacious foreign
corporation. As an enterprise, it seemed instinctively to know that survival
in Brazil could not be ensured through the methods of a Percival
Farquhar, an Alfred Loewenstein, or, in his declining years, even of its
first chairman, Sir William Mackenzie. Instead, the Light set and
maintained its course in Brazil by the temperament and intuitions of Sir
Alexander Mackenzie, who from 1915 to 1928 served as its second and
greatest president.

If there was a 'basic asymmetry' between the Light and the nation it
served, Mackenzie sought to ease its tensions. He learned to manage the
company in harmony with Brazilian social, commercial, and political
mores, not in spite of them. Never 'the ugly Canadian,' Sir Alexander
urbanely strove to place the Light in the mainstream of Brazilian life.
Through his close personal liaison with Brazil's urban, liberal élite, he
realized that the Light's longevity as a foreign enterprise – its ability to
perpetuate its 'unique function' – in a land subject to pronounced swings
of political opinion and commercial fortune depended on the preservation of a sense of trust and satisfaction in the minds of its customers and
those who directed Brazil's political life. From his home on the cool,
forested slope of Corcovado, Mackenzie was both figuratively and literally
able to take the broad view of the Canadian company's place in Brazil; it
was a view that from an early date encompassed the necessity of efficient
service, reasonable rates, and a steady evolution of Brazilian participation
in corporate management. Despite problems resulting from the intervention of drought, periodic political upheavals, and the burgeoning growth
of their cities, Brazilians recognized the quality of the Light's service. The
proverb 'Run like the Light' quickly found its way into Brazilian Portuguese as a means of saluting prompt and efficient service in any endeavour.
To this day, *cariocas* and *paulistanos* refer to electricity as 'light,' a calque
derived directly from their close association with the Canadian corporation that served their utility needs for almost seventy years.

Sir Alexander, for all his prescience, was under no illusions that the Light could maintain its 'bargain' in Brazil *ad infinitum*. 'Our troubles with the authorities arise from other causes,' he gloomily reported to London financier Edward Peacock in 1926 in the midst of one of the company's increasingly prevalent contretemps with the federal government, 'and the principal one, I regret to say, is, that being a foreign company we are considered fair game. I even think that a foreign concern exploiting a public utility in Brazil has had its day and is becoming an anachronism.'[3]

However accurate Mackenzie's prediction ultimately was, it was remarkably premature. For another half century, the Light was to serve south-eastern Brazil. It did so in the face of a steady evolution of the political and commercial circumstances under which it conducted its business and over which it had little control. The Light was challenged on two fronts. As a foreign corporation, it had to contend with Brazilians' determination to capture greater economic benefit from the presence of foreign capital within their borders. As a private enterprise providing utility services that nations around the world were coming to regard as part of the public domain – to be exploited and regulated for the public good, not for profit, on a basis of 'service at cost' – the Light was obliged to respond to legitimate shifts in Brazilian public opinion. These pressures coalesced and became legally and politically persistent in the Water Code of 1934. The arbitrary nature of the Estado Novo and Getúlio Vargas's erratic statesmanship obliged the company to change its methods, but not its goals. Ken McCrimmon's crafty and at times unsavoury defence of corporate interests in the 1930s and early 1940s perpetuated the Light's abiding desire to preserve its *jeito* – its niche, its respect – in Brazilian society. McCrimmon conformed to, not broke, the political norms of the Estado Novo. Like his uncle Alexander before him, McCrimmon confirmed the wisdom of placing the company's destiny in the hands of the 'man on the spot.' 'It is not improbable that the "Light" may pass through difficult times in the present period of Brazilian economic and political difficulties,' Canadian diplomat F.H. Soward reported from Rio in 1945, 'but judging from its reputation and the type of personality they have in Brazil, it should be as successful as any foreign company can be in Latin America in facing the future.'[4]

If the Light survived, it did so because it shifted with its future. Vargas's ouster and the return of democracy in 1945 diminished McCrimmon's ability as the company's chief agent in Brazil. In the free play of democratic forces that was to characterize the Dutra administration, the Light instinctively returned to its policy of 'Brazilianization.' For this, McCrimmon had prepared the way. The appointment of Brazilian professionals to staff positions in the Light had been accelerated throughout the late 1930s. In particular, the hiring of a young lawyer, Antônio Gallotti, in 1933 was ultimately to prove McCrimmon's greatest legacy to his company. In Gallotti, Brazilian Traction was to find a Brazilian national capable of assuming complete executive authority for its operations in Brazil. What Mackenzie and McCrimmon had initially recognized – the necessity of reducing non-Brazilian management of the Light to an absolute minimum – Henry Borden endorsed and perpetuated in the 1950s.

When Borden arrived on his first visit to Brazil in September 1946, he was immediately confronted by the scale of the challenge he had accepted. Brazilian Traction was Canada's largest overseas investment, with assets in 1946 of US $477,000,000. The Light supplied 60 per cent of the total power produced in Brazil; it supplied approximately 75 per cent of the nation's telephones. Its concessions in the states of Rio, Minas Gerais, and São Paulo, as well as in the Federal District, covered 342,000 square miles. Its trams and buses moved more than 1.1 billion *cariocas* and *paulistanos* annually. Power sales of 2,825,522,186 kilowatts touched the daily lives of 731,751 customers. The combined receipts of power, telephone, gas, transit, and water operations totalled US $79,060,881, from which US $23,101,481 in net revenues was derived. Probably the most telling statistical evidence of the Light's impact on south-eastern Brazil was the fact that it was Brazil's largest private employer, with nearly 50,000 people on its payroll.[5] A career in the Light was a career with a future. 'There is said to be a proverb in Brazil,' diplomat Soward reported from Rio, 'that it is the ambition of every family to have one son a priest and another in the employ of the Light.' To serve the Light was to be an employee of Latin America's most efficient public utility. 'It has been able to provide its facilities at very low prices,' Soward observed, 'lower than the TVA [Tennessee Valley Authority] – average fare for the street cars is one cent – telephones in Rio are $4 a month for a business phone and $1.75 for a private phone.'[6] Such were the fruits of the bargain struck by Fred Pearson, Alexander Mackenzie, and Antônio Gualco and the city of São Paulo in September 1899.

Despite the statistical grandeur of the enterprise over which he now presided, Borden pondered the Light's future with foreboding. Could he, in essence, prevent Canada's huge investment in Brazilian utilities from becoming not just an obsolescing, but an obsolete and therefore unworkable bargain? Three daunting tasks faced the Light in 1946 – expanding the system, financing the expansion, and establishing a regulatory regime remunerative to the foreign investor and acceptable to Brazilian politicians.

The necessity of a massive expansion in power capacity was, by 1946, undeniable. Power sales climbed 3.8 per cent between 1945 and 1946; consumption in some sectors, such as tire production and metallurgy, was expanding at a rate of 15 per cent annually. 'Brazil is now, at this moment, at the parting of the ways,' Borden concluded. 'Either she goes ahead on the basis that her power needs will be met (i.e., those for the next few but important years) or she stands still with a terrible power shortage.'[7] For the Light, the price of standstill was systemic collapse, public discontent, and eventual *encampação*, or take-over. Expansion carried the risk of a slow descent into bankruptcy as the inadequacy of the company's rates – rates still enmeshed in the controversy over the Water Code and 'historical cost' – were quickly overtaken by the burden of financing expansion. After his inaugural visit to Rio, Borden decided that expansion was to be the Light's byword. 'My philosophy,' he later recalled, 'was that we had to take chances and move ahead and tidy up afterwards.'[8]

Over the next decade, Borden guided the Light with verve and imagination of an order it had not seen since its formative decades. To meet the power shortage in Rio, the company embarked upon a massive expansion of its generating facilities around the old Lajes power station. By means of an imaginative scheme that diverted water from the Piraí and Paraíba rivers, pumped it uphill into the Lajes reservoir, and then fed it through a mountainside to a cavernous underground generating station, an additional 330,000 kilowatts of capacity was added to the Rio Light system. In São Paulo, the Light constructed its first thermal-electric generating plant to relieve the peak load strain on that system. The Piraí-Paraíba Diversion (PPD) project and the Piratininga steam plant, together with other smaller projects, underlay a 150 per cent expansion of the Light's generating system from 662,000 kilowatts to 1,422,000 kilowatts. Every kilowatt of new capacity necessitated costly additions to transmission and distribution grids.

Despite this increase, the Light found itself pushed to the limits of its capacity in the early 1950s. 'Brown-outs,' occasional rationing, and long waits for connection became endemic, as Brazil's two leading cities experienced unprecedented growth. The Light found itself in a post-war footrace with its markets; failure to keep pace would have, as the New York *Herald Tribune* colourfully suggested, left the company 'to feel the warm breath of Brazilian nationalism' on its neck.[9]

Once committed to expansion, Borden had to pay for it. Between 1946 and 1955, the Light's capital expenditures totalled nearly US $500 million. There was, as Billings had suspected, no hope of furnishing this entirely through retained earnings, especially while the unresolved Water Code kept the Light's rates frozen at 1934 levels. The sluggish capital markets of the United States and Europe precluded any resort to Brazilian Traction's traditional investors. Borden deftly removed the company from this financial impasse by negotiating three loans from the International Bank for Reconstruction and Development – the World Bank. Guaranteed by the Brazilian government, the loans – one for US $75 million in 1949, a second for US $15 million in 1951, and a third in 1954 for US $18.8 million – were the first made by the bank to a private corporation. Despite their precedent-setting nature, the loans perfectly fit the World Bank's mandate to 'make loans to any member or any political sub-division thereof and any business, industrial, and agricultural enterprise in the territories of a member.'[10] Brazilian Traction's three loans inaugurated a long and productive tradition of World Bank support for hydroelectric projects in the developing world. 'The Company that got the loan is no ordinary one,' *Time* magazine reported. 'In Washington, an unidentified spokesman for the World Bank cautiously explained last week that the Bank considered the Light a good risk. Then, in a burst of unbankerish enthusiasm, he added that the Light's management was perfectly wonderful.'[11] Elsewhere in Washington, the World Bank's president, Eugene Black, confided in Canadian Ambassador Hume Wrong 'that the loan to your company was the best loan on the Bank's books.'[12]

Borden's bold initiatives on the power-generating and financial fronts were not matched by advances on the long-stalled regulatory front. The Water Code of 1934 remained unimplemented, thereby freezing the Light's rates at levels long since eroded by Brazil's chronic inflation. Light executives lived in fear that the code would be arbitrarily promulgated with the result that power rates would be fixed on a basis of service at cost calculated on the 'historical cost' of the Light's physical plant. Without correction of the gross devaluation of these assets at the hand of Brazilian inflation, a service-at-cost rate system would have had catastrophic fiscal consequences for the Light. The prospects of reconciling corporate and public interests in this contentious issue were dealt an ironic blow when Getúlio Vargas won democratic re-election to Brazil's presidency in late 1950.

Vargas's return bedevilled the Light's relations with its political hosts. The old spirit of assertive economic nationalism tinged with xenophobia began to re-emerge, artfully fanned by the president. In an era when Peron was nationalizing British railways in Argentina and Mexico was creating a state oil monopoly, there was ample evidence in other Latin American countries that governments were closing out their bargains with foreign entrepreneurs. When visiting the PPD project in early 1951, Vargas told a group of Brazilian construction workers that 'they should be proud to be associated with such a great undertaking and should realize that when they were working for the Companhia Light they were really working for their country.'[13] This superb *double-entendre* was later followed by frequent unsubstantiated allegations of 'criminal plots' on the part of foreign businessmen designed to undermine Brazil's autonomy. On other occasions, Vargas gave private and public assurances that he had 'no intention of nationalizing the Light.'[14] In this paradoxical environment, the Water Code remained in limbo.

Vargas's last term became a tragi-comedy. The administration became mired in cronyism and ineptitude, culminating in the sensational, bungled attempt to murder one of the president's most outspoken critics, a Rio newspaper editor named Carlos Lacerda. Rather than bow to army pressure for his resignation, Vargas shot himself in his bedroom on 24 August 1954. In a dramatic suicide note, he once again indicted 'international economic and financial groups.'[15]

Brazilian Traction reacted to these inauspicious events by redoubling its commitment to 'Brazilianization.' One lasting legacy left to Brazil by Vargas was Eletrobrás, the state-owned power company first proposed in 1954, although not ultimately created until 1962.[16] In the early 1950s, state-owned power companies such as Centrais Elétricas de Minas Gerais (CEMIG) in Minas Gerais began appearing, finally investing the rhetoric of public power with a reality of concrete and turbines. In 1955, the state governments of São Paulo and Minas Gerais launched plans for Brazil's first state power development, the 1.1 million kilowatt Furnas generating plant on the Rio Grande River. Knowing that the Light had neither the rate base nor the capital reserves to support similar development, Henry Borden welcomed Furnas and what it represented. The Light, he reasoned, must look and act like a partner, not a competitor, in Brazil's national drive for electricity.

'Continuing attention is being given to informing the public on the development of the various services provided by the operating companies,' the 1955 annual report rather meekly noted, 'and also of the difficulties encountered by the companies in recent years.' 'Brazilianization' offered Brazilian Traction a means of emphasizing its contribution to Brazil's economy and society while at the same time insulating it from occasional flare-ups of economic nationalism. The end result, Borden earnestly hoped, would be some bending in the government's reluctance to act on the rate issue. While there was widespread acknowledgment of the company's formative role in the emergence of south-eastern Brazil's industrial economy, there was little political or bureaucratic will to confront the rate issue head on, particularly when the principal beneficiary of such reform, however rightfully, was 'the Canadian octopus.' 'There is, moreover, the basic problem of having to deal with a public opinion that is inherently hostile to foreign capital,' Canadian Ambassador J.S. Macdonald noted in 1950. 'Public opinion in Canada is, of course, much more reasonable but we need only imagine a comparable situation in which, let us say, the power, electric light, gas, telephone and tramway services of Montreal, Toronto and Ottawa were in the hands of a Company directed from Lisbon or Brussels and whose dividends, almost entirely, went to foreigners, to understand the magnitude of the public relations problem.'[7]

Throughout the 1950s the Light countered its 'problem' with vigour. Late in 1956 the São Paulo Light and the Companhia Telefônica Brasileira transferred their head offices to Brazil from Toronto. The following year legislative approval was obtained in Ottawa to permit the remaining three Canadian subsidiary companies – Rio de Janeiro Tramway, Light and Power, Brazilian Hydro Electric, and São Paulo Electric – to be domiciled in Brazil. Brazilian charters for the subsidiaries created the option of cruzeiro financing – either as loans or as equity – in Brazil, thereby partially obviating future reliance on offshore dollar financing. Brazilian incorporation and prospective financing afforded the Light a measure of political accommodation while, of course, in reality not jeopardizing Brazilian Traction's ultimate control of the enterprise. In 1957, the São Paulo Light established an administrative council, composed of prominent Brazilian businessmen and professionals, to advise the Toronto parent on major policy and financial issues in Brazil.

In 1947, Borden had presaged these shifts of the 1950s by creating a management company – the Companhia Brasileira Administradora de Serviços Técnicos (COBAST) – designed to centralize all decision making affecting the Light's subsidiaries in Brazil. COBAST thus precluded any reoccurrence of the McCrimmon–McKim Bell frictions of the 1940s and thereby ensured Borden's suzerainty over the entire enterprise. Since Borden as president chose to remain resident in Toronto, it was imperative that the executive vice-president of COBAST act as the president's man on the spot in Rio. Initially, Borden believed that a North American could keep the Light, through COBAST, closely aligned to Brazilian sensibilities. Given the temper of the Brazilian times, this proved unworkable. Humphrey Style, the English engineer brought in by Billings, departed in 1950 after a conflict with Borden over the adoption of thermal generation in São Paulo. Neither McKim Bell nor McCrimmon (now reincarnated as COBAST's vice-president, public relations) had the youth or modern management skills to oversee a corporation of nearly fifty thousand employees in the face of severe nationalistic and economic pressures. In one last attempt to find another Sir Alexander Mackenzie, Borden brought John R. Nicholson, another of C.D. Howe's dollar-a-year men, to Rio as executive vice-president of COBAST. Nicholson's stellar credentials in Canadian business did not translate into effective management in Brazil. There were to be no more Mackenzies – the social, economic, and managerial complexities of the Light had moved beyond the grasp of any North American. Unlike the American and Foreign Power Company (AMFORP), Brazil's other large utilities multinational, which clung to a tradition of management by Americans supported by diplomatic intervention, Brazilian Traction now placed the Light's future in Brazilian managers' hands.

In the dying days of 1955, Borden flew to Rio and offered Antônio Gallotti, a forty-seven-year-old Light lawyer who had risen to corporate prominence in the World Bank negotiations of the late 1940s, the post of executive vice-president of COBAST. Gallotti accepted and was for the next two decades the prime mover in the defence of the Light's interests in a country increasingly bent on following the logic of a nationalized hydroelectric industry. The son of Italian immigrants, Gallotti possessed an amazing talent for hard work, unique prescience, and great ambition. Brazilian Traction had never had, and would never again witness, as close and as trusting a relationship in its management as the team of Gallotti and Borden. While Gallotti guided the Light's fortunes in Brazil, Borden managed Brazilian Traction in Toronto. Through Gallotti, the Light was able to nationalize its affairs in Brazil to the fullest extent possible without in any way jeopardizing ultimate control of the enterprise.

The mid-1950s brought not only a full acknowledgment of the necessity of Brazilianizing the Light but also a measure of relief on the regulatory front. Since 1934, the Light's rates had not been adjusted once, except through 'additionals' designed to compensate for wage increases. Finally, in mid-1955, the Rio Light was allowed, on an *ad hoc* basis, to increase its power rates; this was followed in March 1956 by a reformed tariff structure for the São Paulo Light. In the wake of these rate hikes, the federal government introduced a bill in Congress providing for the upward adjustment of rates on a periodic basis to compensate for the devaluation of the cruzeiro. Despite this hopeful sign, detailed regulations were enacted to implement the original Water Code – the basic law governing electric utilities in Brazil. These reaffirmed the concept of historical cost in national currency and limited earnings to a fixed return on a rate base so computed. Given the steady march of Brazilian inflation, the Light reiterated its belief that the historical-cost principle was 'altogether unrealistic and results in grave injustice to the light and power utilities operating in Brazil.'[18] After this brief flurry of activity, the rate question again succumbed to political lassitude.

The implications of the Light's dilemma of being squeezed by fixed rates and rampant demand became starkly apparent in the late 1950s. Under the dynamic leadership of Juscelino Kubitschek, Brazil's president from 1956 to 1961, the Brazilian economy began a spurt of growth that would eventually culminate in the 'economic miracle' of the late 1960s. Promising 'fifty years of progress in five,' Kubitschek perfected a style of forced growth that combined strong central economic direction with free enterprise and foreign investment. Overall industrial production under Kubitschek grew by 80 per cent, steel output by 100 per cent, mechanical industries by 125 per cent, and transportation-equipment production by 600 per cent. Hothouse economic growth created, as the president had promised, *um novo país*, 'a new country,' but it also induced serious inflation – 40 per cent in the Rio–São Paulo area in 1959 – and pushed the external value of the cruzeiro down. Inflation gnawed further at the Light's frozen rates, and the devalued cruzeiro pushed up the costs of a utility reliant on much imported equipment. In the Congress, there were by 1959 disquieting signs that the historical-cost concept would be pushed through to fruition. At the Canadian embassy in Rio, Ambassador Jean Chapdelaine opined that the Light was now left with two alternatives: selling out or 'eventual strangulation.' 'The days of highly profitable investment in public utilities abroad are gone,' he concluded. 'To a firm like Brazilian Traction, the problem is one of survival: survival as a corporate entity against the attacks of the nationalists, survival as a going concern against the difficulties attendant upon a public utilities concern in a developing, but inflationary economy.'[19]

The early 1960s saw the Light's anxieties turn to nightmare. Under the presidencies of Jânio Quadros and João Goulart, Brazilian society became politically fragmented and economically unstable. By early 1964, inflation was running at an annual rate of 140 per cent. The value of the cruzeiro abroad plummeted. National economic growth skidded from 10.3 per cent in 1961 to 1.5 per cent in 1963. In the face of these pressures, Brazilian Traction reported a net loss of US $1.2 million in 1963. The corporate roof seemed to be caving in. A year earlier, as if in anticipation of this reversal, the directors sought the shareholders' permission 'to carry out negotiations for the sale of the company's interest in its subsidiary utility companies.'[20]

On 31 March 1964, both Brazil and the Light received a reprieve. Affronted by President Goulart's populist promises of 'basic reforms' affecting land tenure and free enterprise, the Brazilian army staged a bloodless *coup* and took power. Undemocratic and often heedless of individual liberty, Brazil's government after the 'Revolution' was pledged to economic development guided by central, technocratic planning and driven by a hybrid mixture of free enterprise and state companies. 'Brazil,' President Castello Branco announced in May 1964, 'will favour foreign capital which desires to cooperate in the process of development, without giving it privileges or subjecting it to discrimination.'[21] As if to exemplify this spirit, a series of decrees issued by the Ministry of Mines and Energy in November 1964 finally established a realistic base upon which the Light's rates could be calculated on a basis of 'service at cost.'

Although a definitive inventory (or *tombamento*) of the companies' remunerable investment would be carried out, the Light had finally been accorded – after a thirty-year wait – a rate base that reflected the ravages of Brazilian inflation.

The Light could now face its future with some equanimity. The huge costs of expanding its distribution system could be planned with some assurance of a reasonable return on investment. Where rates were insufficient or problems insurmountable, there was the prospect of negotiating a withdrawal from the market with a government conscious of its reputation in the eyes of foreign investors. In October 1964, the Brazilian government purchased the American and Foreign Power Company's ten subsidiaries for US $135 million, leaving the Light as the sole foreign utility in Brazil. The Light was not itself blind to the inevitability of nationalization. Where concessions had lapsed or services were no longer tenable in private hands, the company surrendered its rights without a fight. In 1947, the São Paulo trams, the original seed of the whole enterprise, were sold to the municipal government.[22] The Rio trams followed in 1963. In 1965, the impossibility of maintaining telephone service in five burgeoning Brazilian states could no longer be denied. With a backlog of nearly 800,000 telephone orders, the Companhia Telefônica Brasileira estimated that US $450 million would be needed to rectify the situation. In March 1966, the telephone system was thus sold to Embratel, the Brazilian state telecommunications company, for US $96 million. In 1967, the São Paulo Gas Company was likewise sold. Increasingly, the Light therefore relegated itself to the role of a power distributor. Just as it could not afford to modernize its telephone or gas network, neither could it consider the huge cost of expanding its power-generating system. In future, increased demand would be met by purchases from state companies.

Back in Toronto, Brazilian Traction reacted galvanically to the changes in Brazil. In 1963, Henry Borden retired, to be succeeded by the executive vice-president, J. Grant Glassco, a seasoned accountant with a mind for managerial systems. Under Glassco, the company – now simply Brazilian Light and Power – began a fundamental shift. With the repatriated monies from the telephone sale, the company invested US $21 million in shares of John Labatt Limited. Over the next decade, other North American investments would perpetuate this diversification. In 1969, the Canadian government rescinded the '4-K' taxation status that had historically protected Brazilian Traction's offshore earnings from Canadian taxation. To symbolize this corporate metamorphosis, the company changed its name that same year to Brascan Limited.

For the next ten years, the Light rode the Brazilian economic roller-coaster. Under the technocratic guidance of its military leaders, Brazil found itself in the vanguard of the so-called newly industrializing nations. In the years of the 'economic miracle,' Brazil's real gross domestic product grew at an annual average of nearly 10 per cent, growth concentrated and accentuated in the Rio–São Paulo axis. Electricity was at the heart of Brazil's phenomenal economic spurt. From 1970 to 1980, consumption of hydraulically generated electricity grew from 39.8 million kilowatts to 128.9 million kilowatts. Moreover, as Brazil painfully adjusted to the impact of two 'oil shocks,' electricity's share of national energy production increased from 23.4 per cent to 40.7 per cent over the same years.[23] Nothing better illustrated Brazil's inveterate reliance on electricity than the enormous Itaipu power project on the Paraná River. Begun in the 1970s, Itaipu – the largest hydroelectric development in the world – will generate 12,600 megawatts when complete in 1991. Other projects, such as the Tucuruí project in the Amazon Basin, will help Brazil tap the 150,000 megawatt potential of its national rivers. Throughout the developing world, but particularly in Brazil, hydroelectricity has served as a powerful symbol of the will to economic self-determination. What began for Brazil in a Canadian investment on the Parnaíba River outside São Paulo in 1899 has become a central driving force in Brazil's push to join the ranks of the developed world. Today, Brazilian hydraulic and electricity engineers – many of them initially trained by the Light – purvey their skills to other developing nations in Africa and the Middle East.

On 12 January 1979, Canada severed its link with the Light. For US $380 million, Brascan sold all its share in Light Serviços de Eletricidade SA – the Light – to Centrais Elétricas Brasileiras SA, or Eletrobrás, the national power company owned by the Brazilian federal government. The sale was an amicable transaction that ended a period of growing friction between the government and the private utility. Underlying the friction was Brazil's insatiable appetite for electricity in the 1970s. Although the Light had forsaken any thought of expanding its generating system, it was left with the financially onerous task of expanding its distribution grid to supply the power needs of more than twenty million people in the Rio–São Paulo area. During the five-year period 1974–8, the Light's capital expenditures totalled US $1.3 billion. The Light faced the challenges not only of outright expansion but also of acquiring costly new electric technologies for the distribution of power. The Light's ability to pay for such expansion hinged directly on the overall economic health of Brazil at a time of frenzied growth, mounting foreign debt, and spiralling inflation. None of these, especially when translated into federal regulatory policies, augured well for the Light.

The regulatory system of service at cost, established in the mid-1960s, acted as the financial life-blood of the Light. Service at cost shielded the company from inflation's erosion. Up to 1971, earnings were in fact excellent. The Light was able to maintain a low debt-equity ratio and face the prospect of a 10 per cent annual increase in demand in the knowledge that expansion could be financed through internal generation of funds. Unlike the state power companies, the Light as a foreign-owned company was precluded from borrowing from several state funds earmarked for national electrification. Even though the Light collected taxes for these funds, most notably the Global Reversion Fund, it was denied access to these ready pools of domestic financing.

In 1972 and 1973, the Light earned the maximum allowable remuneration of 12 per cent on its rate base. More than 65 per cent of the US $222 million in capital funds spent in these two years was thus from internal sources; the rest was provided by loans and equity subscription. The 'oil shock' of 1973 and the subsequent deterioration of the Brazilian economy in the years down to 1978 quickly destroyed the Light's ability to finance expansion through internal earnings. In 1974, changes in wholesale power rates charged by the state-owned generating companies resulted in the Light's paying 30 to 60 per cent more than state-owned distributors for much of its power. The next year, regulatory authorities reduced the allowable return on the rate base from 12 to 10 per cent. This was followed by other alterations in the way in which the Light's rate was calculated. Many of these adjustments were driven, as Brascan's annual report politely put it, by the emergence of 'other national priorities' in Brazil, principally the need to cool the overheated rate of inflation and to generate capital through consumption taxes on power users for future power development. By 1978, for instance, the Light was collecting almost US $500 million from its customers in taxes and similar charges, money that was then paid over to the Brazilian government for subsequent lending to other companies in the electric sector.

With the continual reduction in internally generated funds, the Light became almost completely dependent on external sources of capital. Since the company did not qualify for capital available from the state electricity-development funds and because local equity markets could not support the Light's huge needs, the only option was borrowing on external capital markets. Herein lay the squeeze that would force Brascan's retreat from the Brazilian electrical sector; herein lay the final obsolescence of the 'bargain' that had served Brazil and Brazilian Traction for almost seven decades.

Although the Brazilian government undertook to quarantee such loans, the Light was obliged to turn to syndicated bank loans, arranged by international banks, and bond issues in the Eurobond markets. By 1978, the interest rates on these foreign borrowings were averaging approximately 4 per cent more than the 10 per cent return allowed by the Brazilian government on the company's rate base. Furthermore, the average life of such borrowings was approximately five years, a period inconsistent with the expected twenty-five- to thirty-year life of the Light's plant. Consequently, the Light faced an ever-increasing volume of refunding obligations, a relentlessly expanding demand for its services, and a steady erosion of its rate base. In short, the Light owed more and earned less by the day. Return on investment fell from 19.7 per cent on US $608 million in 1974 to 13.5 per cent on US $850 million in 1978. Given the persistence of Brazil's sky-rocketing inflation and burgeoning economy, not even the most roseate optimist would have predicted a reversal of this downward spiral.

The sale of the Light was not the product of corporate fiat in Toronto or government decree in Brasília. Instead, it was the outcome of a smooth negotiation built on a recognition by Brascan of the inevitability of the transaction and the Brazilian government's determination to be seen to treat a foreign investor fairly. At the annual shareholders' meeting in May 1978, John H. Moore, Brascan's president since 1969, reviewed the Light's deteriorating ability to meet its financial and servicing commitments and then issued the following momentous statement: 'If the Government of Brazil wishes to acquire Light, we will co-operate.' Moore did not have long to wait. Rumours soon began to surface that negotiations were under way in Rio between the redoubtable Toni Gallotti and Shigeaki Ueki, the minister of mines and energy in the military government of Ernesto Geisel.

Just after lunch on 28 December 1978, Jake Moore revealed to the

Brascan staff that he had just received word that the Geisel government had given final approval to the sale of the Light to Eletrobrás. Moore disclosed that the Brascan board had 'considered and accepted' an offer to purchase Brascan's entire investment in the Light for US $380 million. The transaction would close in fifteen days. Payment of US $210 million was to be made in New York on closing, and the Brazilian government guaranteed payment of the balance ninety days later.[24] The outstanding feature of the agreement was the fact that the sale was made on what amounted to a cash basis. Unlike the AMFORP sale of 1965 and the sale of its own telephone system in 1966, the Light deal allowed the proceeds to leave Brazil with no requirement that any portion be reinvested in the country. 'If I rejected the offer,' Moore told the *Financial Post* a few days later, 'I'd be a bloody fool.'[25] Backed by Gallotti, Moore had defied the predictions of many Brazil watchers and had sold the Light before it either succumbed to a slow financial death or was nationalized outright.

The purchase of the Light was the culmination of Brazil's long quest for a nationally controlled electrical industry. In paying only US $380 million – about half of the Light's book value – for the entire Light system, Eletrobrás had acquired a first-class electrical system at a bargain price. In February 1979, the minister of mines and energy in Brasília confirmed this by acknowledging that the purchase had given Eletrobrás one of the 'largest and best run utilities in the world.'[26] *Jornal do Brasil* echoed this belief in commenting that Rio and São Paulo were 'much indebted to the Light for their development.'[27] In the press release announcing the sale, Brascan itself noted that 'an era comes to an end for Brascan with the government acquiring the last major foreign-controlled utility in Brazil.' It was a theme that the *Financial Post* picked up in an editorial.

In a great burst of creative energy at the beginning of this century, when Canada itself was barely settled, our engineers and entrepreneurs brought power, telephones and mass transit to many of the cities of Latin America. Space does not permit an assessment of how this achievement came to be denounced as neo-colonialism abroad, and totally forgotten at home. But neither the jealous protectionism now prevalent in the Third World, nor the government aid which is the only form of foreign investment considered respectable, has yet produced comparable economic growth. Brascan's Brazilian investment was so burdened that the company is being applauded for escaping with about half its book value. Private capital will not lightly undertake such enterprises again. And everyone will be the poorer.[28]

The Canadian tourist in Rio or São Paulo does not have far to look for evidence of the Light, once Canada's largest overseas investment. Although Eletrobrás broke up the Light, apportioning it to the state power companies of Rio and São Paulo, the Light's logo, a double stylized L formed into a lightning bolt, is still much in evidence – on utility trucks, power substations, hydro poles, and manhole covers. In the hills behind Rio and on the outskirts of São Paulo, Canadian-built generating stations quietly continue to supply electricity to *cariocas* and *paulistanos*. Every day thousands of tourists ride up the precipitous side of Rio's Corcovado mountain in a cog railway conceived by the great Brazilian engineer Pereira Passos but perfected and operated for decades by a Canadian company.

The Canadian tourist in search of a truly nostalgic journey is, however, best advised to make his way to the Largo da Carioca, a bustling square in central Rio. There, every fifteen minutes, narrow-gauged tramcars – somewhat grubby and battered – leave a nondescript station, set off over the picturesque Arcos da Lapa viaduct, and then clamber through the hillside district of Santa Teresa. The fare is cheap, the seats are hard, and the view is spectacular. These little trams, or *bondinhos* as Brazilians call them, are a last quaint, anachronistic reminder that in their heyday Canadian streetcars annually carried more than a billion Brazilians about their daily affairs in two cities under the Southern Cross.

Summary Interpretation of the Water Code and Related Legislation in Brazil

The rights and duties of the various electric companies composing the Light organization were laid down in long-term contracts (some had no stated termination date) signed early in the century with the states and municipalities within whose borders the companies operated. The Water Code embodied in Decree No. 24.643 of 10 July 1934 provided that within one year of its publication (effected on 20 July 1934) all such contracts then in force were to be revised in order to adapt them to the requirements of the code. Pending such revision, electric companies were forbidden to expand or modify their plant, to increase rates or to sign any new supply contracts (Para. 3 of Article 202).

The proclamation of Decree No. 24.643 (signed by the chief of the provisional government and by the nine ministers of state) subsequent to the date of promulgation of the 1934 Constitution gave rise to a controversy as to its constitutionality, but this was confirmed in due course by the federal Supreme Court. The Water Code was thus legally in force as from 20 July 1934, though the application of many of its provisions was delayed for years and some, such as the required revision of the concession contracts, were never implemented. The provisions of the code were later confirmed, supplemented, and modified by numerous decree-laws under the 1937 Constitution, as well as by further laws and decrees under subsequent constitutional regimes.

The prohibition on plant expansion and modification and on the signature of new supply contracts, imposed by the Water Code, was lifted in 1940, by Decree-law No. 2.059. The freeze on electric rates decreed by the code remained legally in effect until 1943. The rates thus frozen were the rates prevailing in 1933 under the original concession contracts, less the reductions effected as a result of the elimination of the gold clause from the contracts, further to Decree No. 23.501 of November of that year. Decree-law No. 5.764 of 19 August 1943 federalized existing state and municipal concession contracts relating to the production, transmission, and distribution of electricity (other than street-lighting contracts), and instituted a provisional rate system whereby the then prevailing contractual rates would be maintained until the contracts were revised, subject to such modifications as may be determined unilaterally by the government. Though this permitted rates to be increased, the freeze effectively continued for the Light until 1955 (Rio system) and 1956 (São Paulo system), when the only rate increases granted to the companies between 1934 and 1965 were authorized under Decree-law No. 5.764. (Numerous surcharges or supplementary charges were added to the rates during the late 1940s and the 1950s, but these – which were formalized in the detailed regulations set out in Decree No. 41.019 of February 1957 – were earmarked to cover inflation-induced increases in wages, costs of fuel oil, and purchased-power and debt-service costs. They were not rate increases.)

Rate fixing on the basis of service at cost – the principal financial provision of the Water Code – was not implemented until 1965. Article 180 of the code called for the establishment of reasonable rates (to be revised triennially) that would cover all operating expenses, depreciation, and fair remuneration on invested capital, fixed assets being valued (for purposes of determining invested capital) at historic cost less depreciation. Remuneration presupposed an approved rate base. In 1941, seven years after the Water Code, the procedures to be followed by the regulatory authorities in establishing the value of invested capital were set out in Decree-law No. 3.128, which also fixed the allowable rate of return thereon at 10 per cent. In 1957, detailed regulations governing electric energy services were published in Decree No. 41.019. These regulations contained provisions designed to facilitate implementation of service at cost, but failed to provide for the adaptation to the regime of the Water Code of companies operating under concession contracts that pre-dated the code. They still retained the concept of valuing plant at historic cost and, for the first time, specified the various components, in addition to plant, of remunerable investment. They also spelled out, in a clearer manner than the Water Code itself, the right of the concession holder to amortize his invested capital by the recovery thereof, directly or indirectly, through rates. In all this time, however, no steps were taken by the authorities to determine the historic cost of the capital invested in plant (and depreciation thereof), and the companies continued to operate under the transitional rate regime established by Decree-law No. 5.764 in 1943.

Historic cost presupposed that the internal and, particularly for foreign-owned companies, the external value of the national currency would remain stable. Otherwise, historic cost in the strict sense, involving the valuation of fixed assets permanently at their acquisition cost in national currency regardless of changes in the value of the latter, would result in erosion of the investment, completely nullifying one of the basic principles of the Water Code itself and of the Brazilian constitution – viz, the guarantee of the financial stability of electric utilities. What happened to the internal value of the currency is indicated by the fact that the cost-of-living index for Rio de Janeiro increased fifteen times between 1934 and 1958. Externally its value fell from 6.6 cents US in 1934 to less than 1 cent US in 1958. The only true and economically tenable interpretation of the principle of historic cost was first legally recognized in November 1958, when Law No. 3.470 institutionalized the annual monetary correction or revaluation of the fixed assets of corporate bodies in order to up-date the original acquisition cost of such assets by expressing it in cruzeiros of current value. Another six years were to pass, however, before the monetary correction of fixed assets and related depreciation were recognized for electric utility rate-making purposes. Such recognition coincided with the implementation of service at cost in 1965, more than thirty years after the Water Code, both measures resulting from three acts of the Executive power on 4 November 1964 (Decrees No. 54.936, No. 54.937, and No. 54.938). The first of these provided for the application of monetary correction to the original historic cost of the fixed-asset component of the rate base (and related depreciation), as determined by the regulatory authorities. The second set out the procedures to be followed by the *tombamento* commissions already appointed or to be appointed to determine the value of invested capital (i.e., the historic cost of plant less depreciation), and further provided that pending determination of the rate base by those commissions, provisional rates could be set under the service-at-cost regime, the remuneration and depreciation components of such rates being based on the companies' calculations (including monetary correction of net plant). The third decree revised the detailed regulations set out in Decree No. 41.019 to bring these into line with the concept of up-dating historic cost by monetary correction.

Further to the foregoing developments, realistic rates were established for the companies of the Light group by increases approved early in 1965. These rates were based on service at cost – i.e., they were designed to produce revenues sufficient to cover operating expenses, depreciation and remuneration on, and amortization of, invested capital. Depreciation was computed for this purpose on the monetarily corrected value of plant, and invested capital included (as its principal component) the monetarily corrected value of depreciated plant. Only at this point was the Water Code fully implemented, and only then did the companies cease to operate under the transitory regime established by the 1943 Decree-law No. 5.764, which had prolonged, with some modifications, the original concession contracts. Law No. 5.655 of May 1971 consolidated the foregoing legislative developments under a system capable of achieving the declared objectives of the Water Code of adequate service, reasonable rates, and financial stability for the utilities. Over the period 1970–4, the *tombamento* commissions substantially confirmed the companies' calculations of the rate base, with minor differences.

Operating Statistics of the Principal Subsidiary Companies of the Brazilian Traction, Light and Power Company, 1912-1978

There is a natural tendency to accompany descriptions of hydroelectric and public-utility systems with legions of statistics describing the growth and scope of services. After a point, such statistics have the effect of numbing the reader's sensibilities. For most laymen, kilowatts, megawatts, load factors, and reservoir capabilities are terms that remain shrouded in mystery. This book has attempted to introduce statistics and technological terminology only where appropriate and only by way of substantiating what has already been made clear in the text.

Some resort to statistics is none the less necessary. The accompanying table offers the reader a statistical encapsulation of the growth of the Light's principal activities in the public-utilities industry of south-eastern Brazil. The statistics cover the tramway, light, power, gas, and telephone services operated by Brazilian Traction's main subsidiaries. They are drawn from the statistical synopses provided for shareholders in the Brazilian Traction annual reports. They furnish an understanding of the primary areas of the Light's operations, but leave undisclosed innumerable other areas of the company's operations in Brazil. The operational results of the Rio and São Paulo Light before 1912 have been excluded, but have been cited where relevant in the early chapters of the book.

Public utilities are immensely complex enterprises and may be measured in many ways. Electric services could, for instance, be measured by the growth in kilometres of the network of transmission and distribution lines. Such statistics are available to the interested reader in the annual reports. What follows is the essential statistical picture.

Two words of explanation are necessary. In the first place, the growth

	Tramway passengers	Available generating capacity – São Paulo (in kw)	Available generating capacity – Rio (in kw)	Total kilowatt hours sold (in 000s)	Total light and power customers	Telephones in service	Total gas sales (in 000s cu m)
1912	231,385,668	20,000	32,000	230,983	28,750	9,020[a]	45,656
1915	243,130,447	59,000	61,000	299,469	66,927	13,786[b]	49,300
1918	283,466,433	59,000	61,000	378,303	109,384	47,642[c]	57,973
1921	377,082,951	59,000	61,000	458,061	140,344	67,862	65,358
1924	498,242,281	59,000	105,000	479,527	175,397	77,977	65,043
1927	584,055,133[d]	159,000	105,000	629,558	230,721	86,053	91,590
1930	743,795,671	179,724	134,000	791,519	317,494	105,828	114,368
1933	753,786,219	179,724	134,000	903,467	366,094	122,253	102,044
1936	882,882,798	232,000	134,000	1,235,689	442,057	165,852	120,328
1939	978,561,798	364,739	178,000	1,555,197	532,003	208,633	144,480
1942	1,160,506,565	370,304	248,000	1,984,507	622,051	261,549	144,082
1945	1,289,612,655	370,304	248,000	2,606,418	694,957	305,889	152,175
1946	1,162,589,794	374,804	248,000	2,825,522	731,751	325,893	166,081
1947	908,513,656[e]	460,204	283,000	3,092,006	768,014	349,492	176,426
1948	735,455,108	538,497	283,000	3,482,345	811,338	380,260	194,935
1949	748,281,956	538,647	328,000	3,874,529	858,981	398,396	211,469
1950	735,489,253	604,788	353,000	4,051,703	909,661	427,889	223,648
1951	704,370,302	604,788	353,000	4,302,538	979,696	467,237	245,983
1952	620,726,645[f]	604,685	353,000	4,472,511	1,056,871	510,430	254,765
1953	580,875,027	738,937	423,000	4,601,389	1,137,005	546,871	267,566
1954	541,620,660	738,937	683,000	5,173,345	1,220,284	599,235	292,214
1955	539,460,900	738,937	683,000	5,701,104	1,299,573	646,733	314,641
1956	485,309,111	990,771	683,000	6,584,980	1,377,651	677,316	330,041
1957	465,242,064	990,771	683,000	6,949,373	1,474,692	698,974	325,774
1958	451,861,507	989,676	683,000	7,812,890	1,571,367	729,857	326,410
1959	396,655,579[g]	990,426	683,000	8,422,799	1,671,069	756,694	323,374
1960	328,791,341	1,305,426	683,000	9,362,503	1,766,362	787,198	335,383
1961	243,468,443	1,370,426	683,000	10,216,568	1,868,632	812,037	330,132
1962	211,688,379	1,370,426	729,750	11,093,116	1,975,331	832,047	342,509
1963	192,813,783[h]	1,370,426	776,500	11,182,880	2,076,710	844,725	328,260
1964		1,369,699	777,124	11,241,000	2,182,275	862,648	340,771
1965		1,369,699	777,124	11,641,000	2,285,025	877,525[i]	329,800
1966		1,369,699	777,124	12,797,000	2,403,078		319,914
1967		1,369,699	778,114	13,645,000	2,536,389		308,114[j]
1968		1,368,243	753,114	15,329,000	2,662,376		261,542[k]
1969		1,368,243	753,114	16,880,000	2,847,602		
1970		1,368,243	754,000	17,919,000	3,056,593		
1971		1,368,243	754,000	20,310,000	3,273,943		
1972		1,368,243	754,000	22,402,000	3,485,000		
1973		1,368,243	754,000	24,957,000	3,699,000		
1974		1,368,243	754,000	27,376,000	3,862,000		
1975		1,368,243	754,000	29,081,000	3,973,000		
1976		1,368,243	754,000	32,334,000	4,173,031		
1977		1,368,243	754,000	35,500,000	4,365,470		
1978		1,368,243	754,000	38,500,000	3,561,847		

a Rio de Janeiro only
b Includes Rio, Niterói, Petrópolis, and Barra do Piraí
c Includes São Paulo state telephones
d Now includes tramways, funicular railway, electric buses, and gas buses
e On 1 July 1947 the São Paulo tramway system passed to municipal ownership.
f Santos tramway system was transferred to municipal ownership.
g In January 1959 tramway zones in Rio were reduced, and the basis of calculating ridership was revised.
h On 30 December 1963 all tramway services were transferred to the state of Guanabara.
i Brazilian Telephone Company was sold to the Brazilian federal government.
j In 1967, gas service was discontinued in Santos and taken over by the municipality in São Paulo.
k Gas service in Rio was transferred to the state of Guanabara.

of services was the product not only of expanding capacity but also of expanding concession areas. Whereas the tramway concessions in Rio and São Paulo were firmly established by 1912, the company's telephone concessions were augmented right up to the sale of the telephone company in 1965. Secondly, operational results were also affected by changes in technology. In the 1920s, for instance, tramway operations were augmented by the introduction of bus service. Bus ridership, albeit small, has been added to tramway ridership. Where necessary, such changes have been noted in explanatory notes.

Notes

Abbreviations Used in Notes

BA   Brascan archives, Toronto
RL   Rio Light archives, Rio de Janeiro
SPL   São Paulo Light archives, São Paulo
PAC   Public Archives of Canada, Ottawa
RG   Record group, used to designate government records at the PAC
DEA   Department of External Affairs archives, Ottawa
PRO   Public Record Office, London
FO   Foreign Office records at the PRO

Introduction

1 Charles Wilson, *The History of Unilever: A Study in Economic Growth and Social Change* vol. 1 (London 1954) v

Chapter 1 North America in South America

1 T.W. Bevan to A.W.K. Billings, 15 May 1934, BA file 0-7-1-41
2 D. Mulqueen to A.W.K. Billings, 5 Mar. 1934, BA file 0-7-1-41; *Correio paulistano* 8 May 1900, and Waldemar Corrêa Stiel, *História dos transportes coletivos em São Paulo* (São Paulo 1978) ch. 7. For Prado's concern about competition in local public utilities see: *Relatório do anno de 1899 apresentato ;a câmara municipal de São Paulo pelo prefeito dr. Antônio da Silva Prado, em 31 de março de 1900* (São Paulo 1900).
3 *O estado de São Paulo* and *Correio paulistano* 8 May 1900
4 Rev. J.C. Fletcher and Rev. D.P. Kidder, *Brazil and the Brazilians* (Boston 1866) preface. See J.C.M. Ogelsby, 'Mission Diplomacy: The Flight of the Snowbirds, 1866–1968,' in *Gringos from the Far North: Essays in*

the History of Canadian–Latin American Relations 1866–1968 (Toronto 1976) 9–39.

5 O. Mary Hill, *Canada's Salesman to the World: The Department of Trade and Commerce, 1892–1939* (Montreal 1977) 8

6 *Report of the Commissioners from British North America Appointed to Inquire into the Trade of the West Indies, Mexico and Brazil* (Ottawa 1866)

7 *Debates of the House of Commons* 8 May 1879, 1853

8 W. Darley Bentley, *Direct Trade between the Dominion of Canada and the Empire of Brazil* (London 1880) 8

9 Ibid. i

10 Ibid. 16

11 Instituto Brasileiro de Geografia e Economia (IBGE), *Anuário estatístico do Brasil* (Rio de Janeiro 1939–40) 1367. For an early attempt at educating Canadians to the economic potential of Brazil, see Grey, Secretary of State for Foreign Affairs, 23 June 1916, microfilm reel c-341, Borden Papers, PAC. See also 'Brazil: consular reports 1899, 1913–1937,' file 10374, Governor-General's Office, RG 7, PAC. In 1912, George Foster, Canada's minister of trade and commerce, instructed one of his trade officials, H.R. Poussette, who was temporarily stationed in Rio, that the 'object aimed at in all this is to secure an active and business-like canvass for markets for Canada in South America.' Foster to Poussette, 25 Apr. 1912, file 285, vol. 1414, RG 20, PAC

14 'Report of Trade Commissioner A.S. Bleakney,' Rio de Janeiro 1927, PAC, RG 20, vol. 1482. A regular steamer service to Brazil from Canada was finally initiated in 1929.

15 Celso Furtado, *The Economic Growth of Brazil: A Survey from Colonial to Modern Times* (Berkeley and Los Angeles, Calif. 1963) 102. Furtado's thesis has been challenged and expanded in the following works: Warren Dean, *The Industrialization of São Paulo, 1880–1945* (Austin, Tex. 1969); Wilson Cano, *Raizes de concentração industrial em São Paulo* (São Paulo 1977); Sérgio Silva, *Expansão cafeeira e origem da indústria ão Brasil* (São Paulo 1976); and Mircea Buescu, *Evolução econômica do Brasil* (Rio de Janeiro 1974).

16 E. Bradford Burns, *A History of Brazil* (New York 1970) 226

17 Furtado, *Economic Growth of Brazil* 119. See also Werner Baer, *Industrialization and Economic Development in Brazil* (Homewood, Ill. 1965); Dean, *Industrialization of São Paulo*; and Simon Kuznets, W. Moore, and J. Spengler, eds, *Economic Growth: Brazil, India and Japan* (Durham, NC 1954).

18 See Stanley J. Stein, *The Brazilian Cotton Manufacture: Textile Enterprise in an Underdeveloped Area, 1850–1950* (Cambridge, Mass. 1957) esp. ch. 8.

19 *A energia elétrica no Brasil: Da primeira lampâda a Eletrobrás* (Rio de Janeiro 1977) 54. See also *Energia elétrica: Pioneirismo e desenvolvimento na regiao Rio-São Paulo* (Rio de Janeiro 1966).

20 *A energia elétrica no Brasil* 56; *Energia elétrica: Pioneirismo* 73–5; and Roberto C. Simonsen, *Evolução industrial do Brasil e outros estudos* (Sáo Paulo 1973) 18

21 Dean, *Industrialization of São Paulo* 8
22 See, for instance; Harold C. Passer, *The Electrical Manufacturers 1875–1900: A Study of Competition, Entrepreneurship, Technical Change and Economic Growth* (Cambridge, Mass. 1953).
23 H.R. Poussette to Hon. George Foster, 28 May 1912, PAC, RG 20, vol. 1414, file 285
24 Albert Lauterbach, *Enterprise in Latin America: Business Attitudes in a Developing Economy* (Ithaca, NY 1966) 5, 10
25 Ibid. 77. Richard Graham, a historian of the 'modernization' process in Brazil, has also noted: 'Attitudes regarding "risk-taking" and "profit-making" are evidently of key importance to development. We have noted how the willingness to risk money for the sake of possible profits lay at the root of the dynamic and creative aspects of the Victorian age. This spirit stood in direct opposition to the static agrarian life of Brazil, where profits were still considered akin to usury.' *Britain and the Onset of Modernization in Brazil, 1850–1914* (Berkeley, Calif. 1968) 207. For exceptions, see Warren Dean, 'São Paulo's Industrial Elite, 1890–1960' (PHD diss., University of Florida 1964).
26 None of the foregoing is meant to imply that Brazilian entrepreneurship, however different it may initially seem to the foreigner, is inferior to the business culture of more northern economies. Brazilians are wily, well-educated professionals in business. While the 'economic miracle' of the 1970s may have been stimulated by technocratic state control, it was given velocity and diversity by Brazil's business class. 'Brazilians,' the *Economist* of 17 January 1987 noted, 'have a taste unusual in their part of the world: they like business and do well at it ... Brazil has drive, the way Tokyo and Silicon Valley have it. From shoeshine boys upwards, people want your business and they hustle to get it ... The focus of this dynamism is in the country's south, especially São Paulo ... They created a century-long, labour-intensive boom on the backs of, first, coffee, and then cheap electricity ... The city is an ant-hill of small-business activity.'
27 Alan K. Manchester, *British Preëminence in Brazil: Its Rise and Decline – A Study of European Expansion* (Chapel Hill, NC 1933) ix. See also Ana Célia Castro, *As emprêsas estrangeiras no Brasil, 1860–1913* (Rio de Janeiro 1979); Roberto de Oliviera Campos, *Economia, planejamento e nacionalismo* (Rio de Janeiro 1963); Carlos Geraldo Langoni, *A economia da transformação* (Rio de Janeiro 1975); and Oliver Onody, 'Quelques aspects historiques des capitaux étrangers au Brésil,' in *L'Histoire quantitative du Brésil de 1800 à 1930* (Paris 1973).
28 J. Fred Rippy, *British Investments in Latin America 1822–1949: A Case Study in the Operations of Private Enterprise in Retarded Regions* (Minneapolis, Minn. 1959) 150–3
29 Unable to master the awkward pronunciation of the 'til' accent in words such as São, Anglophones substituted San for São when referring to the city and state of São Paulo.

30 Rippy, *British Investments* 153–5. See also Graham, *Britain* chs 2–5.

31 Manchester, *British Preëminence* 326–7

32 Irineu Evangelista de Souza (1813–1889), created Baron Mauá, was in many ways an atypical Brazilian entrepreneur. See Anyda Marchant, *Viscount Mauá and the Empire of Brazil: A Biography of Irineu Evangelista de Souza 1813–1889* (Berkeley and Los Angeles, Calif. 1965); Visconde de Mauá, *Autobiografia* (Rio de Janeiro 1942); and Heitor Ferreira Lima, *Três industrialistas brasileiros: Mauá, Rui Barbosa, Roberto Simonsen* (São Paulo 1976).

33 Robert H. Mattoon, Jr, 'Railroads, Coffee and the Growth of Big Business in São Paulo, Brazil,' *Hispanic American Historical Review* 57:2 (May 1977) 278. See also D.C.M. Platt, ed., *Business Imperialism 1840–1930: An Inquiry Based on British Experience in Latin America* (London 1977).

35 Mattoon, 'Railroads, Coffee,' 273. In 1852, the government had passed a law guaranteeing 5 per cent interest on railway investments made in Brazil. In 1884, this was increased to 6 per cent. See Law 1,030 of 7 Aug. 1862 and Law 9,248 of 19 July 1884.

35 Graham, *Britain* 276

36 Gilberto Freyre, *Order and Progress: Brazil from Monarchy to Republic* (New York 1976) xvii. See Graham, *Britain* ch. 7. For a revisionist interpretation of Barbosa's career see R. Magalhães, Jr, *Rui Barbosa, o homen e o mito* (Rio de Janeiro 1965). See also E. Bradford Burns, *Nationalism in Brazil: A Historical Survey* (New York 1968) 39.

37 Graham, *Britain* 1967, and Raymundo Austregésilo de Athaydee, *Pereira Passos, o reformador do Rio de Janeiro: Biografia e história* (Rio de Janeiro 1944). Not all economic thinkers in Brazil shared the belief that progress was only possible through co-operation with foreigners. Alberto Torres (1865–1917) staunchly opposed the notion that Brazil could march forward only in company with foreign investors. In his *O problema nacional brasileiro* (1914), Torres insisted that 'the independence of a people is founded on their economy and their finances ... In order for a nation to remain independent it is imperative to preserve the vital organs of nationality: the principal sources of wealth, the industries of primary sources of wealth, the industries of primary products, the instrumentalities and agents of economic circulation, transportation, and internal commerce.' Burns, *Nationalism in Brazil* 78

38 See, for instance Norma Evenson, *Two Brazilian Cities: Architecture and Urbanism in Rio de Janeiro and Brasilia* (New Haven, Conn. 1973). For the problems of Rio and the work of Passos, see Afonso Arinos de Melo Franco, *Rodrigues Alves: apogeu e declínio do presidencialismo* (Rio de Janeiro 1973) vol. 1, 307–60.

39 Richard M. Morse, *From Community to Metropolis: A Biography of São Paulo, Brazil* (Gainesville, Fla. 1958) 172–8. See also Ernani da Silva Bruno, *História e tradições da cidade de São Paulo* (Rio de Janeiro 1954); Mircea Buescu, *Brasil: Disparidades de renda no passado* (Rio de Janeiro 1979);

and Paul Singer, *Desenvolvimento econômico e evolução urbana* (São Paulo 1968).

40 Morse, *From Community to Metropolis* 184. Much the same point is made by Joseph Love in *São Paulo in the Brazilian Federation, 1889–1937* (Stanford, Calif. 1980) 81.

41 James R. Scobie, *Buenos Aires: Plaza to Suburb, 1870–1910* (New York 1974) 108–10, 232–4

42 Graham, *Britain* 123

43 John P. McKay, *Tramways and Trolleys: The Rise of Urban Mass Transport in Europe* (Princeton, NJ 1976), and Sam Bass Warner, Jr, *Streetcar Suburbs: The Process of Growth in Boston, 1870–1900* (Cambridge, Mass. 1962)

44 Harold C. Passer, *Electrical Manufacturers* 341

45 Sam Bass Warner, Jr, *The Private City* (Philadelphia, Pa. 1968) 4

46 Toronto Transit Commission, *Wheels of Progress: A Story of the Development of Toronto and Its Public Transportation* (Toronto, 5th ed. 1953); and Richard M. Binns, *Montreal's Electric Streetcars: An Illustrated History of the Tramway Era 1892–1959* (Montreal 1973)

47 See Christopher Armstrong and H.V. Nelles, *The Revenge of the Methodist Bicycle Company: Sunday Streetcars and Municipal Reform in Toronto, 1888–1897* (Toronto 1977) esp. ch. 11.

48 *Toronto Illustrated: Its Growth, Resources, Commerce, Manufacturing Interests, etc.* (Toronto 1893) 38. For a broad treatment of the coming of electric utilities to Canada, see Christopher Armstrong and H.V. Nelles, *Monopoly's Moment: The Organization and Regulation of Canadian Utilities, 1830–1930* (Philadelphia, Pa. 1986).

49 Charles J. Dunlop, *Os meios de transporte do Rio Antigo* (Rio de Janeiro 1973) 36–7

50 Stiel, *História dos transportes* 65–72

51 Bevan to Billings, 15 May 1934, BA file 0-7-1-41; and Stiel, ibid. 69–70

52 Little is known of Antônio Gualco (1840–99), except that he had been born in Italy and had served in the Italian navy. In 1888, he had married Josephine Wojhoska, the widow of a Polish engineer who had worked in Trois-Rivières, Quebec. Josephine Gualco's ties with the São Paulo enterprise were to last long after her second husband's death.

53 *Globe* (Toronto) 11 Sept. 1896; and *Debates of the House of Commons* 10 Sept. 1896, 958

54 *Debates of the House of Commons* 21 June 1897; 4861

55 See Peter Flynn, *Brazil: A Political Analysis* (London 1978) ch. 3: '1889–1930: The Coffee Oligarchy and the Old Republic.' See also José Maria dos Santos, *A política geral do Brasil* (São Paulo 1930); Edgard Carone, *A república velha* (São Paulo 1970); Sertorio de Castro, *A república que a revolução destruiu* (Rio de Janeiro 1932); and Leonico Basbaum, *História sincera da república de 1889 à 1930* (Rio de Janeiro 1958).

56 See Riordan Roett, *Brazil: Politics in a Patrimonial Society* (New York, rev. ed. 1978) ch. 2; and Love *São Paulo* 152–8.

57 For the relationship of national élites and foreign business, see Raymond Vernon, *Sovereignty at Bay: The Multinational Spread of U.S. Enterprise* (New York 1971) ch. 6.

58 Stiel, *História dos Transportes* 66

59 Board of Directors, São Paulo Tramway, Light and Power Co. Ltd, 'Documents Relating to the Organization, Concessions, Franchises, etc. of the São Paulo Tramway, Light and Power Co. Ltd' (Toronto, Mar. 1902) 29–30

60 Rippy, *British Investments in Latin America* 152. See also Linda and Charles Jones and Robert Greenhill, 'Public Utilities Companies,' in Platt, *Business Imperialism* 81–2.

61 Mira Wilkins, *The Emergence of Multinational Enterprise: American Business Abroad from the Colonial Era to 1914* (Cambridge, Mass. 1970) chs 3, 8

62 Asa Briggs, *History of Birmingham* vol. 2, 1865–1938 (London 1952)

63 'Report of R.C. Brown on the São Paulo Railway, Light and Power Company,' 1 Mar. 1899, BA file B 24

64 See, for instance, Charles A. Gauld, *The Last Titan: Percival Farquhar 1864–1953 – American Entrepreneur in Latin America* (Stanford, Calif. 1964) chs. 2, 3; and Walter Vaughan, *The Life and Work of Sir William Van Horne* (New York 1920) esp. 274–5 and ch. 22.

65 See T.D. Regehr, *The Canadian Northern Railway: Pioneer Road of the Northern Prairies, 1895–1918* (Toronto 1976).

66 Board of Directors, São Paulo, 'Documents Relating' 19–21

67 'Minute Book of the Board of Directors of the São Paulo Railway, Light and Power Co. Ltd,' meetings of 19 May, 26 May, and 30 May 1899, BA

68 An Agreement made between William Mackenzie and the São Paulo Railway, Light and Power Co. Ltd, 26 May 1899, BA document file

69 Power of Attorney for F.A. Pearson and A. Mackenzie, 29 May 1899, BA document 5-P-6

70 Board of Director, São Paulo, 'Documents Relating' 37–48

71 Ibid. 51–6

72 'Petition to Federal Government for authority to operate in Brazil,' 17 July 1899 and Decree no. 3349 of 17 July 1899, ibid. 25–7

73 J.C. Alves de Lima, 'A Talk about the Light and Power Company,' nd, BA file 0-7-1-41

74 Morse, *Community to Metropolis* 180. Not content simply to explore São Paulo's potential for power, Pearson also used his time in São Paulo to investigate the possibility of providing financial and technical backing for schemes for caustic-soda production, railway construction, and jute processing. None of these promotions ever materialized. See: Pearson to R.C. Brown, 28 Feb. 1900, Pearson letterbook, SPL.

75 E.E. Barton to A.W.K. Billings, 21 Mar. 1934, BA file 0-7-1-41

76 The old Brazilian money system was based upon the real (pl. réis). One thousand réis equalled one milréis, and one thousand milréis equalled one conto. Foreign exchange was expressed in terms of dollars or pounds sterling per milréis.

77 'Deed of cession and transference of privileges and concessions,' 28 Sept. 1899, signed by José Cândido da Silveira, notary public, BA document 1-L-20

78 Mrs Josephine Gualco, file B 16, B.A. and F.S. Pearson to A. Mackenzie, 9 June 1904, Pearson letterbook, SPL

79 The directors of the São Paulo company voted in February 1900 to pay all the medical costs incurred by Gualco during his fatal illness. 'Minute Book ... São Paulo,' 1 Feb. 1900

80 F.S. Pearson to R.C. Brown, 19 Dec. 1899, Pearson letterbook, SPL. Pearson added that Gualco's death was 'not unexpected.'

81 *North America in South America* (Toronto 1901) preface

Chapter 2 In Pursuit of a 'Rich Return'

1 W.H. Blake, 'Two Cities under the Southern Cross,' nd (*c.* 1908–9) BA file B 69. William Hume Blake was a partner in the Blake, Lash, Anglin and Cassels legal firm. He is best remembered for his 1921 English translation of Louis Hémon's novel *Maria Chapdelaine*. Blake's sister, Mabel, married Alexander Mackenzie in 1908. The word 'socialism' had a much wider meaning at the turn of the century. It was employed in Canada to describe a broad range of doctrines and ideas that were perceived as threatening to the status quo. In Brazil, it had as yet little meaning. See Everardo Dias, *História das lutas sociais no Brasil* (São Paulo 1962); and Edgar Rodrigues, *Socialismo e sindicalismo no Brasil* (Rio de Janeiro 1969).

2 The population of the Federal District of Rio de Janeiro in 1900 was 691,563. Richard Morse, in his study of São Paulo's rise to commercial dominance in Brazil, enumerates six ingredients that were of crucial importance in propelling the city's economy forward: an extensive road and rail network, accessibility to a relatively prosperous market, raw materials, capital generated by the coffee trade, an influx of immigrant labour, and, lastly and most importantly, readily available hydro power. Morse, *Community to Metropolis* 225–8. See also Bruno, *História e tradiçoes*; and Singer, *Desenvolvimento econômico*.

3 See Regehr, *Canadian Northern Railway*. See also D.B. Hanna, *Trains of Recollection: Fifty Years of Railway Service* (Toronto 1924) ch. 11.

4 Vincent P. Carosso, *Investment Banking in America: A History* (Cambridge, Mass. 1970) 29. For the evolution of merchant banking in England, see Richard Kellett, *The Merchant Banking Arena* (London 1967); and E.V. Morgan and W.A. Thomas, *The Stock Exchange: Its History and Functions* (London 1962).

5 See Carosso, *Investment Banking* ch. 3.

6 See Ian M. Drummond, 'Canadian Life Insurance Companies and the Capital Market, 1890–1914,' *Canadian Journal of Economics and Political Science* 28:2 (May 1962) 204–22.

7 Hanna, *Trains of Recollection* 244

8 Ibid.
9 J.W. Flavelle to Z.A. Lash, 19 Dec. 1906, B.E. Walker Papers, University of Toronto Archives
10 See Regehr, *Canadian Northern Railway* 28–40. See also T.D. Regehr, 'A Backwoodsman and an Engineer in Canadian Business: An Examination of a Divergence of Entrepreneurial Practices in Canada at the Turn of the Century,' in Canadian Historical Association, *Historical Papers* 1977.
11 Regehr, 'A Backwoodsman' 160
12 Regehr, *Canadian Northern Railway* 28
13 *Saturday Night* 31 Jan. 1920
14 Hanna, *Trains of Recollection* 172. Also cited in Regehr, *Canadian Northern Railway* 45
15 See Patricia E. Roy, 'The British Columbia Electric Railway Company, 1897–1928: A British Company in British Columbia' (PHD diss., University of British Columbia 1970) 35–59; *The Times* (London) 31 Jan. 1929; and G.R. Stevens, *History of the Canadian National Railways* (Toronto 1973) 183.
16 Horne-Payne's clumsy, wobbling signature on company correspondence and documents suggests that he suffered from some form of nervous condition.
17 For an account of a visit to 'Merry Mead,' see Pelham Edgar, *Across My Path*, ed. Northrop Frye (Toronto 1952) 39.
18 Hanna, *Trains of Recollection* 243. A small railway town in northern Ontario bears Horne-Payne's name.
19 *General Electric Review* 18:9 (Sept. 1915) 929
20 Ibid. 931
21 Ibid. 930
22 Since F.S. Pearson left behind no substantial collection of personal papers, the only source of information for his biography lies in an unpublished biography of the engineer written in the late 1940s by Professor Stearns Morse of Dartmouth College. Entitled 'The Yankee Spirit,' the book is a study of New England entrepreneurship, in which Pearson figures as one of several prominent New England success stories. A typescript was kindly made available by Mrs H.F. Stearns Morse.
23 See Passer, *Electrical Manufacturers*.
24 *General Electric Review* 18:9 (Sept. 1915) 931; and Bevan to A.W.K. Billings, 15 May 1934, BA file 0-7-1-41
25 Warner, *Streetcar Suburbs* 25–6
26 Stearns Morse, 'The Yankee Spirit,' 209
27 See F.S. Pearson, 'The Latest Developments in Electric Conduit Railways,' *Cassier's Magazine* 16 (Aug. 1899).
28 Passer, *Electrical Manufacturers* 339
29 BA file 100.3
30 *Globe* (Toronto), 1 Mar. 1902
31 The Hon. George Albertus Cox (1840–1914). See Michael Bliss, 'Getting on

in Life: The Saga of George Cox,' *Canadian Journal of Life Insurance* 1:5 (May 1979) 17–20; and Bliss, *A Canadian Millionaire: The Life and Business Times of Sir Joseph Flavelle, Bart., 1858–1939* (Toronto 1978) ch. 3.

32 Sir William Cornelius Van Horne (1843–1915). See Vaughan, *Sir William Van Horne.*

33 See H.V. Nelles, *The Politics of Development: Forests, Mines and Hydro-electric Power in Ontario, 1849–1941* (Toronto 1974) ch. 6.

34 Frederic Nicholls (1856–1921). See Nelles, *Politics of Development* 230–3.

35 'Minute Book ... São Paulo,' meetings of 26 May, 6 July, and 6 Dec. 1899. Pat Burns (1857–1937), 'The Cattle King of the Prairies,' was born in Oshawa, Ontario, but spent most of his childhood in Kirkfield, where he first met William Mackenzie. See Grant MacEwan, *Pat Burns, Cattle King* (Calgary 1980).

36 'Minute Book ... São Paulo,' 1 Feb. 1900

37 At the 2 Jan. 1900 meeting, the newly incumbent directors voted payments of $50, and $100 in one case, to the departing directors.

38 A.W. Mackenzie (1877–1907) had a largely passive role in the São Paulo company's affairs. Mackenzie's eldest son, Roderick, played an active part in his father's railroad-building activities in Canada and eventually became a partner in Mackenzie, Mann and Co.

39 See E.P. Neufeld, *The Financial System of Canada: Its Growth and Development* (Toronto 1972) esp. chs 7, 8, 9, and 14.

40 Bliss, *Canadian Millionaire*

41 Neufeld, *Financial System of Canada* 489. Edward Rogers Wood (1866–1941)

42 Drummond, 'Canadian Life Insurance Companies,' 221

43 'Minute Book ... São Paulo,' meetings of 27 June 1899 and 1 Feb. 1900

44 'Minute book of the Board of Directors of the National Trust Company Ltd,' meetings of 22 Aug. and 14 Sept. 1898 and 4 Apr. 1900

45 William Thomas White (1866–1955) was born in Halton County, Ontario, and educated at the University of Toronto. After being called to the bar in 1899, he worked for the City of Toronto and then as general manager of the National Trust. A life-long Conservative, he served as finance minister in the government of Robert Borden from 1911 to 1919. He served as a Brazilian Traction director from 1920 until 1946.

46 Henry Mill Pellatt (1858–1939). See Carlie Oreskovich, *Sir Henry Pellatt: The King of Casa Loma* (Toronto 1982).

47 Loan agreement, 28 Nov. 1900, BA document 4-A-5

48 'Minute Book ... São Paulo,' meeting of 30 Nov. 1900

49 Loan agreement, 22 Apr. 1901, BA document 4-A-6 and 'Minute Book ... São Paulo,' 29 Apr. 1901

50 See J.H. Plummer, Asst Gen. Mgr, CBC, to Frederic Nicholls, 22 Apr. 1901, BA document 4-A-6.

51 J.H. Plummer to J.M. Smith, 23 Sept. 1901, BA file B 3 and 'Minute Book ... São Paulo,' 29 Nov. 1901

52 Nelles, *Politics of Development* 229

53 *Globe* (Toronto) 1 Mar. 1902
54 Pearson to Brown, 1 Mar. 1900, Pearson letterbook, SPL. The lack of
technical education was often cited by Brazilian 'modernizers' at the turn
of the century. Dr Paulo Souza, who founded the São Paulo Polytechnic
School in 1894, once told his students: 'Yes, Gentlemen, if technical
knowledge were taught to our people, we would have ... a diversified,
prosperous, and well-managed industry ... In our own land we would
easily have what we must now import with great expense from foreigners.'
(Quoted in N.H. Leff, *The Brazilian Capital Goods Industry, 1929—1964*
[Cambridge, Mass. 1968] 18.) Those Brazilians who did obtain proper engineering training concentrated their energies on railroad, port, and public-
works projects, not on the new electricity industry. It is a general characteristic that the developing nations are all perpetually condemned to emulate
the technical advances of the developed world. Brazilian engineers, for
instance, were dedicating themselves to learning railroad engineering at the
same time that North America's leading engineers (like Pearson) were
pioneering electrical technology. See also Graham, *Britain* 47; and Roberto
C. Simonsen, *Evolução industrial do Brasil* 349—50.
55 T.W. Bevan to A.W.K. Billings, 15 May 1934, BA file 0-7-1-41
56 Pearson to Brown, nd (*c.* Nov. 1899), Pearson letterbook, SPL
57 Pearson to Mulqueen, 21 June 1901, ibid. The period 1898—1902 was one
of rising exchange value for the milréis. From $7\frac{3}{16}$d. in 1898 it rose to
$9\frac{1}{2}$d. in 1900 and then to $11\frac{31}{32}$d. by 1902. See J.F. Normano, *Evolução
econômica do Brasil* (São Paulo, 2nd ed. 1975).
58 See Duncan McDowall, 'A Streetcar Few Desired: The Bermuda Trolley
Company, 1910—11,' *Business History* 27:1 (Mar. 1985); and Christopher
Armstrong and H.V. Nelles, 'A Curious Capital Flow: Canadian Investment
in Mexico, 1902—1910,' *Business History Review* 58 (Summer 1984).
59 'Domino' (pseudonym of Augustus Bridle), *The Masques of Ottawa* (Toronto
1921) 254
60 Ibid. 256
61 Brazilian Traction annual report, 1923
62 'Domino,' *Masques of Ottawa* 255. W.H. Moore, a Canadian author and
friend of Mackenzie, noted on the railway-builder's death that 'Mackenzie was never greedy for money. Laurier knew that, all of Mackenzie's
friends knew that; he did have a deep-rooted desire to succeed in
whatever he had undertaken. It might be a tramway in Brazil, or a game of
bridge, whist — whatever it was, he played his hands bent on success.'
Saturday Night 15 Dec. 1923

Chapter 3 The São Paulo Company

1 A. Mackenzie to Lash, 19 July 1901, BA file B 29
2 Mulqueen to Smith, 28 Feb. 1901, BA file B 70, and A. Mackenzie to Smith,
30 Apr. 1903, SPL Mackenzie letterbook

3 Parnaíba was originally spelled Parnahyba but since the turn of the century Brazil has had several orthographic reforms, the principal one occurring in 1943. Unless otherwise indicated, the most modern spelling has been employed.

4 Hugh Lincoln Cooper (1865–1937). See *New York Times*, 26 June 1937.

5 The 'head' at any proposed power development is the fall from 'pond' or reservoir level to the level of the powerhouse turbines.

6 Construction reports by H.L. Cooper, 2 and 15 Dec. 1899 and 1 Jan. and 14 Feb. 1900, BA file B 23. By 1900, there were 963,486 immigrants in the state of São Paulo or 42.2 per cent of the population. Italians constituted 66 per cent of this immigrant group and Portuguese only 10 per cent. See Annibal Villanova Villela and Wilson Suzigan, *Política do govêrno e crescimento da economia brasileira 1889–1945*, 2nd ed. (Rio de Janeiro 1975) 252.

7 Brown to B.F. Pearson, 5 Feb. 1900, BA file B 24

8 Pearson to Brown, 13 Jan. 1900, SPL, Pearson letterbook

9 Pearson to Nicholls, 7 June 1901, BA file A 38

10 Pearson to James Mitchell, 23 Nov. 1901, SPL, Pearson letterbook

11 Board of Directors, São Paulo, 'Documents Relating,' 27

12 Brown to William Mackenzie, 23 May 1900, BA file B 21½

13 See Bevan to Billings, 6 May 1934, BA file 0-7-4-41.

14 Pearson to Brown, 19 Dec. 1899, SPL, Pearson letterbook

15 Pearson to Nicholls, 7 Apr. 1900, BA file B 24

16 A. Mackenzie to Pearson, 26 Dec. 1900, BA file B 70

17 A. Mackenzie to Smith, 13 Jan. 1906, BA file B 30, and Walker to Plummer, 22 Apr. 1903, Walker Papers, Fisher Rare Book Room, University of Toronto

18 Board of Directors, São Paulo, 'Documents Relating,' 75–80

19 A. Mackenzie to Lash, 15 July 1901, BA file B 29. See Acto No. 135 (of the São Paulo municipal council) de 26 de Agôsto de 1902.

20 Board of Directors, São Paulo, 'Documents Relating,' 106. See Stiel, *História dos transportes* 107–22.

21 Morse, *Community to Metropolis* 184–5

22 Brown to Smith, 14 Dec. 1900, BA file B 21½

23 Brown to William Mackenzie, 23 May 1900, ibid.

24 It is difficult to provide an indication of the purchasing power of 200 réis for a Brazilian city-dweller in 1901. For a worker to transit the entire city, across the company's three zones, the fare would have been 600 réis or, over a twenty-day working month, 24 milréis. Mircea Buescu, a Brazilian economic historian, has estimated that the monthly wage of a dockworker in 1901 was 70 milréis. Tramway travel was therefore a factor in the lives of only the most prosperous of the working class. The introduction of trailers for *operários* at 100 réis a zone soon offset this tendency. Another measure of the cost of a 200 réis journey is provided by the fact that in 1901 a kilogram of rice cost 394 réis and a kilogram of beans, a staple of the Brazilian diet, 227 réis. See Mircea Buescu, 'Evolução vencimentos publicos

federais no inicio da República, 1889–1902,' *Verbum* 22:2 (July 1976) 101–3.

25 Pearson to James Mitchell, 26 Sept. 1901, SPL, Pearson letterbook
26 A. Mackenzie to Smith, 30 Apr. 1903, SPL, Mackenzie letterbook
27 F.S. Pearson, 'Report on São Paulo Tramway, Light and Power Co.,' 20 Dec. 1905, BA file B 85
28 Brown to Smith, 14 Dec. 1900, BA file B 21½
29 A. Mackenzie to Smith, 31 Mar. 1903, SPL, Mackenzie letterbook
30 Pearson to James Mitchell, 26 Sept. 1901, SPL, Pearson letterbook
31 Ibid., 25 Apr. 1902
32 See Stiel, *História dos transportes* 136–7 and the annual report of the São Paulo Tramway, Light and Power Co. Ltd, 1909, and 'Minute Book ... São Paulo,' 6 Aug. 1909.
33 A. Mackenzie to Toronto office, 24 May 1900, BA file B 24
34 Annual reports 1904 and 1908. There is some confusion in the early annual reports, since the term 'railway department' was sometimes inadvertently used to describe the financial return of the *whole* company's operations.
35 Comparative costs of operation in Toronto and São Paulo calculated from statistics in BA file B 19. Toronto track mileage of 105 miles is based on 1905 figures. The figures used were originally cited in miles and have been left as such.
36 'Synopsis of Report Rendered by F.S.P. to Board upon his return from Brazil in October, 1906,' dated 29 Nov. 1906, BA file B 39
37 Imperial Decree No. 5071 of 28 Aug. 1872. For the evolution of gas services in São Paulo, see N. Biddell's 'History of the San Paulo Gas Company, Ltd,' dated 13 Mar. 1934, BA file 0-7-1-41; and Gerald Michael Greenfield, 'Lighting the City: A Case Study of Public Service Problems in São Paulo, 1885–1913,' in D. Alden and W. Dean, eds, *Essays Concerning the Socio-economic History of Brazil and Portuguese India* (Gainesville, Fla. 1977) 118–49.
38 Secretária da Agricultura, Comméricio e Obras Públicas do Estado de São Paulo, *Actos officiaes, relativos à Companhia de Gaz* (São Paulo 1916) 3–49, and Greenfield, 'Lighting the City,' 136–7
39 São Paulo Municipal Law No. 407, 8 July 1899
40 'Contract with Municipality declaring concessionaires, rights and responsibilities under concessions for making electric installations in the streets of the city,' 28 Sept. 1899; in Board of Directors, São Paulo, 'Documents Relating,' 45–8
41 Pearson to Brown, 19 Dec. 1899, SPL, Pearson letterbook. Despite its name, the Água e Luz had never provided water service in São Paulo.
42 'Minute Book ... São Paulo,' 1 Feb. and 11 June 1900; Pearson to Nicholls, 7 Apr. 1900, BA file B 24
43 Pearson to Brown, 13 Jan. 1899 and 19 Mar. 1900, SPL, Pearson letterbook
44 For excellent discussions of the whole public-illumination imbroglio see

Greenfield, 'Lighting the City,' 140–9, and Edgar de Souza, *Esboço sobre a história da São Paulo Light* (privately published, São Paulo 1949) 275 ff

45 Walmsley to Smith, 24 Jan. and 26 Aug. 1907, BA file B 83

46 Souza, and Maria de Lourdes P. Souza Radesca, 'O problema da energia elétrica,' in Aroldo de Azevedo, ed., *A cidade de São Paulo* (São Paulo 1958) vol. 3, 102

47 Pearson to Walmsley, 5 Dec. 1907, SPL, Pearson letterbook

48 Greenfield, 'Lighting the City,' 146

49 Annual reports, São Paulo Tramway, Light and Power Co. Ltd, 1901–8

50 Pearson to William Mackenzie, 1 June 1906, BA file B 85

51 'Power Customers: São Paulo,' 31 July 1904, BA file B 62. Francisco Matarazzo (1854–1937) was the pre-eminent member of the Italian business community in São Paulo. He began his career as an immigrant dealing in lard, but eventually diversified into flour milling, opening a large, modern mill in São Paulo in 1899. Rodolfo Crespi was another successful Italian entrepreneur whose cotton mills formed an important part of the growing Brazilian textile industry.

52 Pearson to Wood, 11 May 1908, BA document 11

53 All statistics from IBGE, *Annuário estatístico* 1295, 1297, and 1318.

54 Freyre, *Order and Progress* xv

55 Morse, *Community to Metropolis* 227–8

56 Stein, *Brazilian Cotton Manufacture* 99

57 Dean, *Industrialization of São Paulo* 8, and Baer, *Industrialization and Economic Development* 16

58 A. Mackenzie to Wood, 30 Dec. 1902, SPL, Mackenzie letterbook

59 Pearson to A. Mackenzie, 5 June 1903, SPL, Pearson letterbook

60 Annual reports 1901–10

61 Walker to Plummer, 22 Apr. 1903, Walker Papers, University of Toronto Archives

62 A. Mackenzie to Blake, 30 Nov. 1903, SPL, Mackenzie letterbook

63 Pearson, 'Report' 15 Dec. 1905, BA file B 85. Net income as a per cent of total capital invested ranged between 9.16 per cent in 1904 and 17.7 per cent in 1911.

64 Pearson to Smith, 5 May 1906, BA file B 85

65 Pearson to Walmsley, 13 Dec. 1907, SPL, Pearson letterbook. Alexander Mackenzie felt that the blame lay with Toronto during the 1907 squeeze on capital, especially since the Toronto office had been 'caught napping when the big smash took place.' Mackenzie to W.H. Blake, 4 Jan. 1908, RL, Mackenzie letters

66 'Minute Book ... São Paulo,' 30 Apr. 1902. Disposition of the new stock remained entirely in the control of the directors. In July 1902, for instance, Mackenzie, Nicholls, and E.R. Wood were appointed by the board to arrange underwriting for nine thousand shares with a commission of up to 5 per cent. Ibid. 16 July 1902

67 See Wood, vice-president, Dominion Securities, to Smith, 22 Oct. 1904, BA file B 47.
68 W.T. White, manager of the National Trust Co., to Smith, 20 Dec. 1901, BA file B 54. Mackenzie's friends acquired their bonds at generous discount prices. Mackenzie acquired his large holding at prices ranging between eighty and ninety cents on the dollar.
69 'Minute Book ... São Paulo,' 1 Feb. 1900. See Carl Hall, 'Electrical Utilities in Ontario under Private Ownership, 1890–1914' (PHD diss. University of Toronto, 1968) 155–9.
70 'Minute Book ... São Paulo,' 15 Mar. 1906, and H.M. Hubbard, manager of British Empire Trust, to Smith, 17 Mar. 1906, BA file B 9
71 Pearson to William Mackenzie, 24 Nov. 1906, BA file B 103
72 Pearson to Wood, 11 May 1908, BA file B 11
73 Pearson to William Mackenzie, 10 Mar. 1908, ibid.
74 'Minute Book ... São Paulo,' 30 Apr. 1902
75 A. Mackenzie to Wood, 31 Oct. 1902, BA file B 17
76 See Graham, *Britain* 98–9. The company quoted its exchange rates in British currency because practically all of its financial transactions were done through British banks operating in Brazil. The best dollar-exchange rate was available from the New York coffee market. See: A. Mackenzie to Wood, 31 Oct. 1902, SPL, Mackenzie letterbook.
77 William Mackenzie to Wood, 12 Mar. 1908, BA file B 12
78 Smith to Horne-Payne, 17 Sept. 1907, BA file B 10
79 A. Mackenzie to Smith, 1 Feb. 1905, BA file B 29
80 See A. Mackenzie to William Mackenzie, 6 Feb. 1907, ibid. In 1907, the state government of São Paulo held eight million sacks of coffee off the market. Ironically, the 'valorization' program was financed using foreign loans. See Villela and Suzigan, *Política do govêrno* 20–1. See also Mircea Buescu, 'O sopre inflacionário durante a Belle Epoque,' *Verbum* 32:1 (Mar. 1977).
81 T. Aitken, Bank of Scotland, to Walker, 25 July 1900, BA file B 24
82 See Flynn, *Brazil* ch. 3.
83 'Alexander Mackenzie's Report for 1906,' 1 Feb. 1906, BA file B 31
84 Ibid. Richard Morse has attacked the prefecture of Antônio Prado (1899–1910) because his 'government did not guide but could only timidly and unimaginatively embellish São Paulo's growth' (*Community to Metropolis* 239–40). While this may be an accurate assessment of some of Prado's policies, it certainly does not apply to the way in which he encouraged the growth of electrical services in the city.
85 A. Mackenzie to Smith, 31 Mar. 1903, BA file B 29
86 Pearson, 'Report'
87 Walmsley to Pearson, 29 June 1906, BA file B 83
88 A. Mackenzie to William Mackenzie, 11 May 1915, BA file B 115
89 Blake, 'Two Cities under the Southern Cross,' BA file B 69
90 See *A energia elétrica no Brasil* 60, 234.

91 Mulqueen to Smith, 12 Mar. 1901, BA file B 70
92 Pearson to Brown, 13 Oct. 1900, SPL, Pearson letterbook
93 Pearson, 'Report'
94 Ibid.
95 'Minute Book ... São Paulo,' 16 Apr. 1902; A. Mackenzie to Pearson, 1 Sept. 1903, SPL, Mackenzie letterbook; and A. Mackenzie to Smith, 21 July 1910, BA file B 35
96 Pearson to Mitchell, 31 Dec. 1901, SPL, Pearson letterbook
97 Pearson to Mitchell, 30 Apr. 1902, SPL, Pearson letterbook. Joseph Love's *São Paulo in the Brazilian Federation* substantiates this point. Love argues that the successful foreign companies in São Paulo were those that 'cut in' prominent local leaders (269). In this respect, Love suggests that, by his estimation, Antônio Prado had 'the largest number of intra-elite business and family linkages' in his sample group of the São Paulo élite. Prado had, for instance, close ties with the leading foreign coffee-exporting houses (206).
98 Pearson to A. Mackenzie, 3 Oct. 1907, RL, Mackenzie letters
99 A. Mackenzie to Pearson, 31 Jan. 1908, RL, Mackenzie letters
100 Pearson developed a genuine friendship with Antônio Prado and took pains to cultivate a wide circle of acquaintances in São Paulo. In 1906, for instance, he instructed General Manager Walmsley to distribute Christmas cards to São Paulo politicians, etc. 'The Brazilian appreciates a little courtesy of this sort very much and it pays to take considerable trouble in matters of this sort which in this country would be a waste of time.' Pearson to Walmsley, 3 Dec. 1906, SPL, Pearson letterbook
101 Walker to Plummer, 22 Apr. 1903, Walker Papers, University of Toronto
102 See P.G. Garland, *Doing Business in and with Brazil* (Rio de Janeiro 1971). 'Brazil,' Garland warns, 'is a challenging, tiring and rewarding jurisdiction for attorneys, accountants, auditors and their clients, in whose lives legislative modifications play a major role' (75).
103 A. Mackenzie to Lash, 19 July 1901, BA file B 29
104 A. Mackenzie to Blake, 3 Jan. 1906, RL, Mackenzie letters
105 A. Mackenzie to Blake, 4 Jan. 1908
106 Blake, 'Two Cities under the Southern Cross'
107 W. Haggard to Sir Edward Grey, 12 July 1907, PRO, FO 368, file 26094

Chapter 4 The Rio de Janeiro Company

1 Charles Darwin, *A Naturalist's Voyage Round the World* (London 1913) 30
2 Fletcher and Kidder, *Brazil and the Brazilians* 15
3 Norman D. Wilson, 'Report on Rio Tramways,' July 1925, RL. Wilson should have placed Rio at the 'eastern' not 'western' end of the Federal District.
4 See reports from British Embassy, Rio, in PRO, FO 13.
5 Melo Franco, *Rodrigues Alves* vol. 1, 310. Rio's history has been amply

documented in: Herculano Gomes Mathias, *Rio de Janeiro* (Rio de Janeiro 1976); Eulalia Maria Lahmeyer Lobo, *História do Rio de Janeiro: Do capital comercial ão capital industrial e financeiro* (Rio de Janeiro 1978); and Francisco de Paula e Azevedo Pondé, *O gas na iluminação e calefação da cidade do Rio de Janeiro* (Rio de Janeiro 1971).

6 Rodrigues Alves (1848–1918) served as president of the state of São Paulo from 1900 to 1902 and again from 1912 to 1916. His federal presidency covered the years 1902 to 1906. He was re-elected Brazilian president in 1918 but died before taking office. See Melo Franco, *Rodrignes Alves.*

7 Melo Franco, *Rodrignes Alves* vol. 1, 328

8 Quoted in Evenson, *Two Brazilian Cities* 38

9 Melo Franco, *Rodrignes Alves* vol. 1, 316–19

10 See Raymundo Austregésilo de Athayde, *Paulo de Frontin, sua vida e sua obra* (Rio de Janeiro 1961).

11 Alured Gray Bell, *The Beautiful Rio de Janeiro* (London 1917) 19. One contemporary Rio newspaper editor likened Passos's work to a 'stroke of magic.' For more Brazilian reaction to the transformation of Rio, see Melo Franco, *Rodrigues Alves* vol. 1, 326–7.

12 Burns, *History of Brazil* 227. See Nancy Stepan, *Beginnings of Brazilian Science: Oswaldo Cruz, Medical Research and Policy, 1890–1920* (New York 1976).

13 See Graham, *Britain* ch. 4.

14 Melo Franco, *Rodrigues Alves* vol. 1, 330

15 Ibid. 337. It has been estimated that between 1898 and 1913 Brazil obtained foreign loans for the purpose of building up its infrastructure – roads, railways, ports, etc. – totalling £59 million and 300 million gold francs. See Normano, *Evoluçao econômica* 152–3.

16 Bell, *Beautiful Rio* 19

17 A. Mackenzie to Dr Alcindo Guanabara, editor of *O país*, 15 May 1906, RL, Mackenzie letters

18 Dunlop, *Os meios de transporte* 43

19 Marchant, *Viscount Mauá* 58–9

20 Josef Barat, *Estrutura metropolitana e sistema de transportes: Estudo do caso do Rio de Janeiro* (Rio de Janeiro 1975) 99–105

21 Wilson, 'Report on Rio Tramways,' 6

22 Fletcher and Kidder, *Brazil and the Brazilians* 41

23 Decreto no. 3,329 de 1 de julho de 1899, *Documentos referentes à organização, às concessoes, aos privilégios etc. da Rio de Janeiro Tramway, Light and Power Co. Ltd* (Rio de Janeiro 1908) 172–91

24 Report of Alexander Mackenzie, nd, BA files A 130 and 140

25 Decreto no. 734 de 4 de dezembro de 1899, in *Documentos* 65–7. Reid's actual contract with the municipality was signed in June 1900. Under Brazilian law, an initial decree was required simply to enable the various parties involved to enter a specific contract. See also C.J. Dunlop, *Apontamentos para a história dos bondes no Rio de Janeiro* (Rio de Janeiro 1953) 249–51

26 Pearson to A. Mackenzie, 9 Apr. 1903, RL, Mackenzie letters
27 Ibid. 1 May 1903
28 Pearson to A. Mackenzie, 4 Aug. 1904, ibid.
29 See Hélio Lobo, *Docas de Santos* (Rio de Janeiro 1936).
30 John B. Orr to Pearson, 11 Apr. 1904, RL, Mackenzie letters. Orr was a contractor, probably American, working in Rio.
31 Pearson to A. Mackenzie, 9 Mar. 1904, ibid.
32 Orr to Pearson, 11 Apr. 1904, RL, Mackenzie letters
33 Farquhar's life of reckless business adventure is sympathetically told in Gauld's *Last Titan*. Gauld mistakenly attributes the initiation of the Rio company to Farquhar, who did not arrive in Rio until 'early in 1904,' long after Pearson had begun pursuing the Reid concession. See Gauld, ch. 5. There is a persistent belief that Farquhar was *the* initiator of the Rio company. No documentary proof for this notion exists in the Brascan archives. As in most of his endeavours, Farquhar's interest in the Rio Company was speculative, not abiding.
34 A. Mackenzie to Lash, 6 July 1906, RL, Mackenzie letters and Gauld, *Last Titan* 66
35 Orr to Pearson, 11 Apr. 1904, RL, Mackenzie letters
36 *Documentos* 7–14
37 'Minute Book of the Board of Directors of the Rio de Janeiro Tramway, Light and Power Co. Ltd,' 13 June 1904. The first board meeting was held in the Blake legal offices.
38 'Minute Book of the Brazilian Securities Co. Ltd,' 24 June 1904. Brazilian Securities had a capitalization of $19,000, of which $6,000 was owned by William Mackenzie, $3,000 each owned by Pearson, Van Horne, and W.L. Bull, $1,500 owned by Hon. G.A. Cox, and $1,000 owned by Z.A. Lash. Ibid. 18 Nov. 1904
39 'Agreement with Brazilian Securities Co. Ltd,' signed 10 Aug. 1904, in 'Minute Book ... Rio,' 13 June 1904
40 'Minute Book ... Brazilian Securities,' 18 Nov. 1904
41 Pearson to A. Mackenzie, 30 Nov. 1906, RL, Mackenzie letters
42 'Minute Book ... Brazilian Securities,' 10 Dec. 1904
43 Smith to J.B. Kenny, 13 Dec. 1905, BA file A 34
44 'Agreements of 15 May and 20 July, 1905, between Percival Farquhar, J.H. Dunn and Dunn and R.A. Demmé, re: purchase of securities,' BA file A 138
45 BA file A 166
46 C.W. Patrick to Smith, 18 Jan. 1910, BA, pre-1923 file 69
47 Pearson to A. Mackenzie, 31 July 1907, RL, Mackenzie letters
48 See *Jornal do comércio* 25 and 26 March 1907, reprinted in Edgard Carone, ed. *A primeira república* (São Paulo 1973) 179–94.
49 A. Mackenzie to Pearson, 17 Nov. 1906, RL, Mackenzie letters
50 A. Mackenzie to Smith, 1 Apr. and 25 Sept. 1905, BA file A 60, and Decreto n. 5,539 de 30 Maio de 1905, in *Documentos* 5

51 A. Mackenzie to Smith, 6 Nov. 1906, BA file A 60
52 W. Haggard to Sir Edward Grey, 13 May 1910, PRO, FO 368, file 20099. For the evolution of Brazilian economic nationalism, see Heitor Ferreira Lima, *História do pensamento econômico no Brasil* (São Paulo 1978); and Nicia Vilela Luz, *A luta pela industrialização do Brasil* (São Paulo 1975).
53 Pearson to A. Mackenzie, 2 May 1906, RL, Mackenzie letters. Pearson had little tolerance for Brazilian politics and was always expressing a hope that the next minister would 'be more of a business man.'
54 Pearson to A. Mackenzie, 5 Mar. 1906, RL, Mackenzie letters
55 Milne Cheetman to Sir Edward Grey, 18 Jan. 1909, PRO, FO 368, file 5149
56 A. Mackenzie to Lash, 5 Dec. 1906, RL, Mackenzie letters
57 Pearson to A. Mackenzie, 30 Nov. 1906, ibid.
58 Arthur Peel to Sir Maurice de Burser, 10 May 1916, PRO, FO 368, file 2536
59 G.M. Greenfield has noted the highly influential position of men like Alexander Mackenzie in his essay 'Lighting the City,' 147–8: 'As representatives of developed nations, these corporations enjoyed a special position and wielded far more power and influence than domestic impresarios. Thus, Alexander Mackenzie, president of Light, became "one of the most influential personages in the country." Conscious of their inferior developmental status and anxious to replicate the achievements of "progressive" nations, paulista officials were predisposed to find wisdom in the suggestions of foreign administrators.'
60 Pearson to A. Mackenzie, 3 Oct. 1907, RL, Mackenzie letters
61 A. Mackenzie to Pearson, 13 Nov. 1907, ibid.
62 Ibid. 29 Apr. 1908
63 A. Mackenzie to Rui Barbosa, 15 Dec. 1905, ibid.
64 A. Mackenzie to Pearson, 3 Apr. 1907, RL, Mackenzie letters
65 W. Haggard to Sir Edward Grey, 13 May 1910, PRO, FO 371, file 20099
66 A. Mackenzie to Pearson, 1 Aug. 1907, RL, Mackenzie letters
67 Decreto No. 7668, de 18 de Novembro de 1909 and Contracto – de 27 Novembro de 1909, in *Eletricidade e gaz: Legislação – contratos* (Rio de Janeiro 1940) 490–514
68 James Mitchell, 'Estimate of Cost of Construction, Earnings and Operations of the Rio de Janeiro Tramway, Light and Power Co. Ltd,' *c.* 1903, BA file A 39
69 The experience of constructing the Parnaíba station had shown Pearson that ample allowance had to be made for the effects of the dry season on any reservoir. 'Report of J.D. Schulyer,' 22 Nov. 1905, BA file A 79
70 Kearny to Smith, 5 Mar. 1906, BA file A 77
71 A. Mackenzie to Pearson, 5 Aug. 1905, RL, Mackenzie letters
72 Dr Abel Vargas, 'The Malaria Epidemic of São João Marcos,' nd, BA file 0-7-1-41. The company's critics accused it of creating a 'lake of death' (i.e., the Lajes reservoir) in which the mosquitoes had bred. A government inquiry disproved such allegations. It was likely that by bringing together its construction workers from all over Brazil, the company had contributed

to the epidemic by introducing to the area men who were already afflicted with the disease.

73 'Report of General Manager for 1909,' 10, RL

74 'Report of J.D. Schulyer,' 22 Nov. 1905, BA file A 79

75 Pearson to A. Mackenzie, 14 May 1907, RL, Mackenzie letters

76 Ibid. 3 Oct. 1907

77 Pearson to Huntress, 19 Apr. 1907, ibid.

78 Huntress to J.M. Smith, 3 Oct. 1905, BA file A 44

79 'Report of General Manager for 1910,' RL. Huntress's opinion was anticipated by the British ambassador who, as early as 1907, had admitted that Rio was on its way to becoming 'one of the best lighted cities in the world.' W. Haggard to Sir Edward Grey, 12 July 1907, PRO, FO 368, file 26074

80 'Report of the General Manager,' 1908–10; annual report of the Rio de Janeiro Tramway, Light and Power Co. Ltd, 1907–10. See Stein, *Brazilian Cotton Manufacture* 238.

81 E.M.L. Lobo, *História do Rio* vol. 2, 599. In 1907, Rio contributed 29.9 per cent of Brazil's industrial production and São Paulo contributed 16.1 per cent. See Carone, *A república velha* 75.

82 Annual reports, 1907–10. The electric trams almost always pulled 'trailers.'

83 See Graphic No. N-2 in Barat, *Estrutura metropolitana* 98.

84 Wilson, 'Report on Rio Tramways,' 2, and E.M.L. Lobo, *História do Rio* vol. 2, 828. Santa Teresa is in fact a district in central Rio, but its situation on a steep hillside had previously made it inaccessible to *cariocas*.

85 Mitchell, 'Estimate of Cost ... Rio Tramway'

86 Pearson to William Mackenzie, 1 Sept. 1905, BA file A 39

87 Pearson, 'Report to the Board,' 31 Dec. 1906

88 Smith to A. Mackenzie, 30 June 1905, BA file A 60

89 Manager, Toronto branch, Canadian Bank of Commerce, to Smith, 22 Apr. 1907, BA file A 31

90 This episode is treated in greater detail in chapter 8.

91 A. Mackenzie to W.H. Blake, 4 Jan. 1908, ibid.

92 List of Rio bond underwriters, 16 Dec. 1905, BA file A 88, and 'Rio Common Stock issued up to and including October 18, 1905,' BA file A 88

93 J.H. Dunn to Smith, 9 Nov. 1905, BA file A 53

94 Quoted in Stevens, *History of the Canadian National Railways* 183.

95 25 Apr. 1907

96 30 Apr. 1907

97 Horne-Payne to Smith, 31 Jan. 1906, BA file A 68

98 Arthur Chapman to Foreign Office, 5 June 1907, PRO, FO 368, file 20902

99 See Roy, 'British Columbia Electric Railway Company.' Roy observes that Horne-Payne was 'carefully tuned to the state of the money markets' in England at all times (48) and that his guiding principle was ensuring 'the security of the investment.'

100 Horne-Payne to Pearson, 23 June 1906, BA file A 27

101 Lash to A. Mackenzie, 27 Mar. 1906, RL, Mackenzie letters
102 Smith to Horne-Payne, 8 Feb. 1906, BA file A 80
103 Horne-Payne to William Mackenzie, 6 Aug. 1907, RL, Mackenzie letters
104 Pearson to A. Mackenzie, 29 Aug. 1907, ibid.
105 Ibid. 2 Oct. 1907
106 'Minute Book ... Rio de Janeiro,' 28 Mar., 14 Apr., 29 Apr., and 23 June 1908. All these meetings were held in London. The three European directors were Jean Javal and Edouard Quellenac of Paris and Thomas Verstraeten of Brussels.
107 Smith to A. Mackenzie, 30 June 1905, BA file A 60
108 Pearson to William Mackenzie, 9 Feb. 1907, BA file A 73
109 Lash to A. Mackenzie, 27 Mar. 1906, RL, Mackenzie letters
110 Pearson to A. Mackenzie, 21 Nov. 1907, RL, Mackenzie letters
111 J.H. Dunn to Martin Schiff, 28 Feb. 1907, PAC, Sir James Dunn Papers, vol. 252
112 Stearns Morse, 'The Yankee Spirit,' 290. (See present book, Notes, ch. 2, n. 22.)
113 Wilkins, *Emergence of Multinational Enterprise* 65. For a more analytical framework for the spread of electrical systems in England, the United States, and Germany, see Thomas P. Hughes, *Networks of Power: Electrification in Western Society, 1880–1930* (Baltimore, Md 1983).
114 Sir W. Haggard to Sir Edward Grey, 13 Jan. 1913, PRO, FO 368, file 1738

Chapter 5 The Creation of Brazilian Traction

1 Mackenzie to Ralph Peto, 21 Jan. 1909, RL, Mackenzie letters and Milne Cheetman to Foreign Office, nd (1907), PRO, FO 368
2 Pearson to Walmsley, 29 Apr. 1908, SPL, Pearson letters
3 Patrick to Smith, 18 Jan. 1910, BA pre-1923 file 69
4 Circular by Playfair, Martens and Co., 23 Sept. 1910
5 See Greenfield, 'Lighting the City.'
6 'Minute Book of the San Paulo Gas Co. Ltd,' 19 and 23 May 1911
7 Pearson to Smith, 7 Aug. 1911, BA pre-1923 file 90
8 Smith to Pearson, 7 Nov. 1913, BA pre-1923 file 38
9 Memorandum by A. Mackenzie to Foreign Office, 6 May 1910, PRO, FO 368, file 15833
10 Memorandum by A. Mackenzie to W.E. O'Reilly, 2 Oct. 1911, PRO FO 371, file 41688
11 Pearson to A. Mackenzie, 1 June 1905, RL, Mackenzie letters
12 Decreto No. 1033, de Abril de 1907 and Contracto de 24 Abril de 1907, both signed under authority of the president of the state of Rio de Janeiro
13 A. Mackenzie to Pearson, 29 Sept. 1911, RL, Mackenzie letters, and 'Memorandum Regarding the Pirai Concession from the State of Rio de Janeiro,' 18 Nov. 1911, PRO, FO 371, file 45991
14 W.E. O'Reilly to Foreign Office, 3 Oct. 1911, PRO, FO 371, file 41668

15 W. Haggard to Foreign Office, 13 May 1910, PRO, FO 368, file 20099
16 A. Mackenzie to Sir William Mackenzie, 11 May 1915, BA pre-1923 file 166
17 A. Mackenzie to Pearson, 1 Aug. 1911, BA document file 1-J-2
18 A. Mackenzie to Pearson, 27 Mar. 1912, PAC, Dunn Papers, vol. 37. Some evidence of the inability of the Companhia Brasileira de Energia Elétrica to meet the demand for electricity is provided by the fact that in the state of Rio de Janeiro (which was largely under CBEE concessions), industrial power consumption grew only 29 per cent, from 4,498 to 5,836 kilowatts between 1906 and 1915; whereas in the Federal District, where the Rio company operated, a growth of 207 per cent (to 22,313 kilowatts from all types of energy) was recorded (E.M.L. Lobo, *História do Rio* vol. 2, 599).
19 A. Mackenzie to Walter Gow, 10 June 1908, RL, Mackenzie letters
20 A. Mackenzie to Pearson, 29 Apr. 1908, ibid.
21 Dunn to Loewenstein, 15 July 1914, PAC, Dunn Papers, vol. 269
22 W. Haggard to Sir Edward Grey, 13 May 1910, PRO, FO 369, file 20099
23 Milne Cheetman to Foreign Office, 18 Jan. 1909, PRO, FO 368, file 5149. For the early history of labour in São Paulo, see A. Piccarolo, 'Tentatives de socialismo e de lutas operários no Brasil,' in Carone, ed. *A primeira república* 239–43.
24 Cable, Rio office to A. Mackenzie, 10 Sept. 1912, BA pre-1923 file 105
25 Huntress to Sir William Mackenzie, 23 June 1915, BA pre-1923 file 113
26 A. Mackenzie, 'Report on the Concessions of the Companies in Brazil controlled by Brazilian Traction, Light and Power Co. Ltd,' 15 Aug. 1916, BA pre-1923 file 93
27 A. Mackenzie to Brown, 25 Jan. 1921, BA pre-1923 file 90
28 See Nelles, *Politics of Development*.
29 See Toronto Transit Commission, *Wheels of Progress*.
30 Flavelle to Lash, 19 Dec. 1906, Walker Papers, University of Toronto Archives
31 See Hall, 'Electrical Utilities in Ontario,' 76–87.
32 A. Mackenzie to Brown, 25 Jan. 1921, BA pre-1923 file 90
33 Pearson to A. Mackenzie, 20 Oct. 1908, RL, Mackenzie letters
34 Dunn to Henry Borden, 15 Jan. 1947, BA file 0-7-1-41
35 See Arthur Chapman to Foreign Office, 5 June 1907, PRO, FO 368, file 20902.
36 See annual report for 1942.
37 'Letters Patent Incorporating the Brazilian Traction, Light and Power Co. Ltd,' 12 July 1912, BA file 3-C-1; 'Minutes of Meeting of the Provisional Board of Directors of Brazilian Traction, Light and Power Co. Ltd,' 15 July 1912; and interviews with Frank Schulman 1978–9
38 'Letter to Shareholders,' 15 July 1912, copy in BA file 139A
39 Smith to Pearson, 21 Aug. 1912, BA file 139A
40 Dunn to Sir William Mackenzie, 8 July 1912, PAC, Dunn Papers, vol. 263. For Dunn's financial methods and career, see Duncan McDowall, *Steel at*

the Sault: Francis H. Clergue, Sir James Dunn and the Algoma Steel Corporation, 1901–1956 (Toronto 1984) ch. 5.

41 Cable, Dunn to Loewenstein, 9 July 1912, PAC, Dunn Papers, vol. 263
42 Cable, Dunn to Loewenstein, 12 July 1912, ibid.
43 Smith to Moody Manual Company, 20 Mar. 1913, BA file 20
44 Cable, Dunn to Pearson, 4 Mar. 1913, PAC, Dunn Papers, vol. 264
45 Dunn to Dyment, 31 Mar. 1913, ibid.
46 Ibid. 31 Apr. 1913
47 Cable, Dunn to Loewenstein, c. 29 May 1913 and 3 June 1914, and Dunn to Frick, 4 June 1914, ibid. vol. 269
48 Dunn to Pearson, 4 Mar. 1913, ibid. Dunn Papers, vol. 264
49 Cable, Dunn, Fischer and Co. to Pellatt, 7 May 1913, ibid. vol. 265
50 Agreement dated 2 Oct. 1912 between the São Paulo Tramway, Light and Power Co. Ltd, and the Brazilian Traction, Light and Power Co. Ltd, BA file 7-A-5
51 Smith to President, American and Foreign Securities Corporation, 4 Dec. 1916, BA pre-1923 file 20
52 G.W.G. Townley, London, England, to Brazilian Traction, 8 July 1913, ibid.
53 Le comptant 15 Apr. 1914. An unsigned telegram, probably from Pearson, warned the Toronto head office that 'Le Comptant lives on blackmail, publishing articles with hope we would pay large amounts to prevent further attacks. Similar articles published Brussels at same time by same people. Loewenstein expects to put Brussels editor in jail but useless and dangerous us to answer.' Cable dated 13 May 1914, BA pre-1923 file 166
54 Walter Holmes to Brazilian Traction, 26 Aug. 1915, BA pre-1923 file 20
55 As quoted in George Davidson to Brazilian Traction, 17 June 1914, ibid.
56 Smith to A. Mackenzie, 21 Aug. 1917, BA pre-1923 file 90
57 A. Mackenzie to Smith, 3 Feb. 1911, BA pre-1923 file 35
58 A. Mackenzie to Farquhar, 21 Aug. 1907, RL, Mackenzie letters
59 Gauld, Last Titan 82. Gauld provides no evidence for his assertion.
60 Pearson to Miller Lash, 20 Feb. 1914, RL, Mackenzie letters. Mackenzie was paid a fee of $25,000 to undertake this mission.
61 Pearson to Wood, 26 Jan. 1915, BA pre-1923 file 136
62 Clayton Sedgwick Cooper, The Brazilians and Their Country (New York 1917) 142
63 Smith to Greenshields and Co., 19 and 28 Oct. 1921, BA pre-1923 file 20
64 Smith to Wood, 11 Dec. 1919, BA pre-1923 file 41
65 See Barat, Estrutura metropolitana chs 2–4.
66 Bell, Beautiful Rio 49
67 Cooper, Brazilians 160
68 Bell, Beautiful Rio 188
69 Huntress to Brown, 9 Apr. 1921, RL, Administration letterbook No. 1
70 Huntress to Pearson, 2 Dec. 1913, BA pre-1923 file 75
71 A. Mackenzie to Miller Lash, 16 Nov. 1915, BA pre-1923 file 70

72 'Report on the Bragantina Telephone Company's System,' Gill and Cook, London, 14 Mar. 1914, and cable, Dunn to William Mackenzie, 9 June 1915, ibid.

73 Bell, *Beautiful Rio* 188

74 Cooper, *Brazilians* 177. Obviously, the opinions of foreign travellers reporting their impressions of Brazil, especially 'progress-minded' North Americans, must be taken as being somewhat superficial. None the less, the frequency with which visitors to Brazil commented upon the large place of the 'Light' in Rio and São Paulo is worth noting.

75 Pearson, 'Memorandum Regarding the São Paulo Electric Company,' nd BA file 534

76 'Report of the Paulo Afonso Water Falls,' na, Aug. 1911. The Paulo Afonso falls were eventually developed by the state agency, Companhia Hidro Elétrica do São Francisco (CHESF), four decades later.

77 Cooper, *Brazilians* 177

Chapter 6 The Survival of the Fittest

1 Thorstein Veblen, 'The Captain of Industry,' in Max Lerner, ed., *The Portable Veblen* (New York 1948) 378–9

2 See William Dendy, *Lost Toronto* (Toronto 1978).

3 Andrew Carnegie, 'Wealth,' *North American Review* (June 1889)

4 See J.C.M. Ogelsby, 'Canadians and the Mexican Revolution, 1910–28,' in J.C.M. Ogelsby, *Gringos from the Far North* 154–81.

5 J.H. Dunn to Rt Hon. Sir Arthur Nicolson, Permanent Under-Secretary of State for Foreign Affairs, 1 Oct. 1912, PAC, Dunn Papers, vol. 263

6 Dunn to A.E. Dyment, 24 Feb. 1913, PAC, Dunn Papers, vol. 264

7 Loewenstein to Dunn, 15 July 1913, and Dunn to Loewenstein, 24 July 1913, ibid. vol. 265

8 Loewenstein to Dunn, 6 July 1914, ibid. vol. 57

9 See John Brooks, 'Annals of Finance, Privateer, Part II,' in the *New Yorker* 28 May 1979.

10 A. Mackenzie to Farquhar, 30 Aug. 1907, RL, Mackenzie letters

11 *The Times* 19 Oct. 1916. See also the *Economist* 21 Oct. 1916. A similar fate befell Farquhar's Port of Pará venture.

12 As quoted in Regehr, *Canadian Northern Railway* 409.

13 E.R. Peacock to Lash, 11 Feb. 1924, BA file 100.45

14 Dunn to Sir William Mackenzie, 24 Mar. 1914, PAC, Dunn Papers, vol. 268

15 All exchange rates are taken from Brazilian Traction annual reports, 1914–19. For a synopsis of wartime exchange conditions, see Normano, *Evolução econômica* 183.

16 Pearson to A. Mackenzie, 7 Oct. 1914, BA pre-1923 file 38

17 Ryan to Smith, 4 Nov. 1916, BA pre-1923 file 49

18 Smith to A. Mackenzie, 18 Jan. 1917, BA pre-1923 file 90

19 'Extract from Minutes of Annual General Meeting,' 25 Sept. 1919, BA pre-1923 file 39
20 29 July 1920
21 23 Aug. 1923
22 'Alexander Mackenzie's Address at Annual Meeting,' 5 Sept. 1918, BA pre-1923 file 39, and Brazilian Traction annual report 1918. Between 1911 and 1914, Brazil annually imported an average of 1,900,000 tons of coal. Between 1915 and 1918, the total fell to an average of 911,000 tons, or a decline of 52.3 per cent from the previous period. See *A economia brasileira e suas perspectivas* (Rio de Janeiro 1980) 372.
23 Huntress to A. Mackenzie, 10 Aug. 1918, BA pre-1923 file 90
24 A. Mackenzie to the Brazilian ambassador, Washington, 20 Sept. 1918, BA pre-1923 file 90, and 'U.L. Havens, Representative in Washington, 1917–18,' BA pre-1923 file 135
25 Villela and Suzigan, *Política do govêrno* 22–4. See also Flavio and Maria Tereza Versiani, 'A industrialização brasileira antes de 1930,' in *Estudos econômicas* (São Paulo 1975) 5:1.
26 Baer, *Industrialization and Economic Development* 16–18
27 Dean, *Industrialization of São Paulo* 104
28 A. Mackenzie to W.E. Rundle, Gen. Mgr, National Trust Company, Toronto, 20 Oct. 1916, BA pre-1923 file 73
29 A. Mackenzie to H.M. Hubbard, 20 Feb. 1919, BA pre-1923 file 12
30 E. Hauman to Hubbard, 13 Nov. 1915, BA pre-1923 file 89
31 See Manchester, *British Preëminence in Brazil*, and Mira Wilkins, *The Maturing of Multinational Enterprise: American Business Abroad from 1914 to 1970* (Cambridge, Mass. 1974) ch. 1.
32 Cable, A. Mackenzie to F.A. Huntress, 9 Nov. 1916, BA pre-1923 file 12
33 Peacock to Wood, 12 and 14 Aug. 1919, BA pre-1923 file 149
34 J. Henry Schroder and Co. to A. Mackenzie, 6 May 1920, BA pre-1923 file 90. In passing, the Schroder report praised Brazilian Traction as 'a sound and well-managed business which shows every promise of a satisfactory expansion.'
35 Standard conscription exemption form, BA pre-1923 file 182. Smith was referring to the Brazilian, Mexican, and Spanish companies.
36 British Empire Trust Co. to J.M. Smith, 15 Apr. 1914, BA pre-1923 file 106
37 'Memo: Business Profits Tax,' 29 June 1917, BA pre-1923 file 117. The lawyers also cited the fact that the company's profits had not exceeded 7 per cent during the war years and were therefore not liable to the tax. See Sir Thomas White, *The Story of Canada's War Finance* (Toronto 1921) 32–3.
38 J.W. Muir to J.M. Smith, 13 Mar. 1918, BA pre-1923 file 117
39 Blake, Lash, Anglin and Cassels to R.W. Breadner, 3 Jan. 1919, ibid.
40 BA file 0-2-16-1
41 Sir Thomas White, the federal minister of finance under whose guidance the wartime tax acts were introduced, later became a long-standing Brazilian

Traction director. White had pre-war experience with the National Trust, the company's trustee. Izaak Walton Killam's Montreal-based International Power Company was another example of a Canadian '4-K' corporation providing public-utility services in Latin America.

42 Cable, A. Mackenzie to Toronto office, 11 Dec. 1919, BA pre-1923 file 90

43 Huntress to New York office, 1 Jan. 1920, ibid. For the exemption of taxes and duties on foreign companies, see Jorge Street, 'Defesa da indústria,' first published in *Jornal do comércio*, 11 Dec. 1912, reprinted in Carone, ed. *A primeira república* 167.

44 See J.W.F. Dulles, *Anarchists and Communists in Brazil, 1900–35* (Austin, Tex. 1973), and Boris Fausto, *Trabalho urbano e conflito social* (São Paulo 1976) 192–245.

45 A. Mackenzie to Smith, 24 May 1919, BA pre-1923 file 90

46 A. Mackenzie to Lash, 19 Sept. 1923, BA pre-1923 file 8

47 Huntress to Brown, 23 Oct. 1918, BA pre-1923 file 96

48 J.C. Herlyck to Billings, 27 Mar. 1934, BA file 0-7-1-41, and A. Mackenzie to J.M. Smith, 4 Apr. 1919, BA pre-1923 file 90

49 Huntress to Brown, 9 Apr. 1921, RL, Administration letterbook No. 1

50 C. Stocken to Dunn, 11 May 1915, PAC, Dunn Papers, vol. 63

51 *General Electric Review* (Sept. 1915) and *New York Times* 9 May 1915

52 Smith to Gow, 6 Dec. 1922, BA pre-1923 series

53 Cable, Ward Pearson to J.H. Dunn, 19 July 1915, PAC, Dunn Papers, vol. 64

54 A. Mackenzie to W. Pearson, 1 Nov. 1916, BA pre-1923 file 90A

55 *Consolidated Edition of Decisions and Opinions of Mixed Claims Commission: United States and Germany, 1925–6* USA on behalf of W.E. Pearson, F.A. Pearson, etc., *vs.* Germany, 5 Jan. 1925, copy in BA file 0-7-1-41

56 'Money and Magnates: Death of Dr. F.S. Pearson,' *Canadian Courier* (May 1915)

57 'Minutes of the Brazilian Traction, Light and Power Co. Ltd Board of Directors,' 14 May 1915

58 Cable, Sir William Mackenzie to A. Mackenzie, 13 May 1915, BA pre-1923 file 41

59 See Burns, *Nationalism in Brazil* 70–1, 80–1.

60 Smith to Huntress, 18 Sept. 1916, BA pre-1923 file 193, and cable, A. Mackenzie to Huntress, 6 Sept. 1916, BA pre-1923 file 12. Müller, who had been accused of pro-German sympathies, resigned his post when Brazil entered the war on the Allied side.

61 A. Mackenzie to Brown, 25 Apr. 1917, BA pre-1923 file 90

62 See *Globe and Mail* 13 July 1943, and *The Times* (London) 9 Jan. 1919.

63 See, for instance, Sir Arthur Peel to Sir Maurice de Burser, 10 May 1916, PRO, FO 368, file 2536.

64 G.W. Robins to Brazilian Traction, 13 Mar. 1914, BA pre-1923 file 20

65 Smith to A. Mackenzie, 18 July 1918, BA pre-1923 file 39

66 H. Malcolm Hubbard to Under-Secretary of State for Foreign Affairs, 13 Jan. 1916, PRO, FO 382, file 9133

67 A. Mackenzie to B.E. Walker, 22 Feb. 1921, Walker Papers, box 24, University of Toronto Archives. Clarence Dillon of W.A. Read and Co. was a member of the Brazilian Traction board.

68 *O país* 9 Aug. 1928

69 *A noite* 9 Aug. 1928

70 *O jornal* 4 Aug. 1928. Francisco Assis Chateaubriand Bandeira de Mello (1891–1968) was a young lawyer from Paraíba who in the 1920s came south to Rio where he began a journalistic career. He soon began his own newspaper, *O jornal*, which he used as the kernel of what eventually became a newspaper empire. When Chateaubriand, or 'Chatô' as he was called by Brazilians, died in 1968, the Diários Associados controlled thirty-two newspapers, eighteen television stations, twenty-four radio stations, and four magazines. Chateaubriand was also politically active in Rio in the Revolution of 1930, as well as having a stake in commercial aviation. He donated much of the art contained in the São Paulo Museum of Art. Although no documentary proof exists, it has been said that Mackenzie lent Chateaubriand the money with which he initiated *O jornal*. Certainly, Mackenzie and 'Chatô' were always close friends.

Chapter 7 The 1920s

1 See Furtado, *Economic Growth of Brazil* chs 27, 30. See also: Antônio Delfim Neto, *O problema do café no Brasil* (São Paulo 1950), and Mircea Buescu, *A moderna história econômica* (Rio de Janeiro 1976).

2 'Report of Trade Commissioner L.S. Glass for 1935,' PAC, RG 20, vol. 1482

3 All exchange figures are taken from the Brazilian Traction annual reports for 1920–30.

4 José Maria Bello, *A History of Modern Brazil 1889–1964* (Stanford, Calif. 1966) 235–51. See also Villela and Suzigan, *Política do govêrno* ch. 5.

5 *Report Submitted to His Excellency the President of the United States of Brazil* (Rio de Janeiro 1924)

6 Furtado, *Economic Growth of Brazil* 197–8

7 'Report of Trade Commissioner A.S. Bleakney for 1927,' PAC, RG 20, vol. 1482

8 Wood, 23 Nov. 1920, BA pre-1923 file 90

9 'Summary of Chairman's Address at Annual Meeting,' 20 July 1921, BA pre-1923 file 23

10 Wood to A. Mackenzie, 31 Mar. 1922, BA, Brazilian Hydro Electric file 3

11 A. Mackenzie to Peacock, 29 Dec. 1926, BA file 306

12 A. Mackenzie to Miller Lash, 12 Dec. 1926, ibid.

13 Ibid.

14 Huntress to A. Mackenzie, 24 May 1921, BA pre-1923 file 90

15 All power statistics are taken from Brazilian Traction annual reports 1920–9.

16 Power contracts with the Central and Paulista Railways, 1919–21, BA document files 9-A-12 and 9-A-4

17 Lash to Wood, 24 Mar. 1925, BA file 100.46

18 See Adolph J. Ackerman, *Billings and Water Power in Brazil* (Madison, Wis. 1953).

19 Cable, Brown to A. Mackenzie, 13 June 1921, and Lash to A. Mackenzie, 30 Jan. 1922, BA file 189. Billings was to be paid £45,000 annually to act as 'construction manager' for the Spanish, Brazilian, and Mexican companies.

20 'Report on the Power Situation in Rio de Janeiro and São Paulo for the Brazilian Traction, Light and Power Co. Ltd,' Apr. 1922, BA document file 1-R-17

21 'The Paraíba Development,' *Brazilian American* 10 Feb. 1923, and Ackerman, *Billings and Water Power* ch. 4

22 'Minutes ... Brazilian Traction,' 22 Nov. 1922

23 Billings to Toronto office, 20 Sept. 1924, BA file 536

24 Billings to Lash, 27 Oct. 1925, ibid. The biggest problem at Rasgão was the delivery of machinery from Santos. Imported equipment that took an average of 6½ weeks to reach Santos from its port of origin took 9½ weeks to reach the site from Santos.

25 A.W.K. Billings, 'Water Power in Brazil,' *Engineering Journal* (Aug. 1930)

26 A.W.K. Billings, 'Water Power in Brazil,' *Civil Engineering* (Aug. 1938)

27 Billings, 'Water Power,' *Engineering Journal*

28 W.G. McConnel to Lash, 15 Jan. 1923, BA file 540.23

29 'Preliminary Report on Capivary Site by Walter Charnley,' 17 Jan. 1922, ibid.

30 F.S. Hyde to Billings, 17 May and 9 June 1923, BA file 540.21–3

31 Adams to Billings, 26 Nov. 1923, BA file 540.14

32 'Minutes ... Brazilian Traction,' 9 Apr. and 11 June 1925

33 A. Mackenzie to Lash, 31 July 1925, BA file 537

34 See *O estado de São Paulo* 30 Dec. 1925.

35 São Paulo State Decree No. 2109, 29 Dec. 1925

36 A. Mackenzie to H.M. Hubbard, 12 Jan. 1926, BA file 537

37 A. Mackenzie to Brown, 2 Sept. 1924, BA file 100.Z

38 *O jornal* (Rio) 19 Dec. 1928

39 Billings to Lash, 27 Oct. 1925, BA file 537

40 See A.V. DeBeech, 'The *Serra* Hydro-Electric Development,' paper presented to Edison Electric Institute, Chicago, 6 May 1941.

41 A. Mackenzie to Brown, 25 Oct. 1926, BA file 537

42 Billings to Lash and Brown, 2 Mar. 1926, BA file 537

43 Rudyard Kipling, *Brazilian Sketches* (New York 1940) 45

44 Warren Dean, the leading historian of São Paulo's emergence as an industrial centre, has described the Cubatão plant as 'the most important addition to [economic] overhead' of the 1920s in São Paulo. Dean, *Industrialization of São Paulo* 110

45 Billings to Peacock, 23 Feb. 1926, BA file 537

46 See BA file 213. A full list of the small utility companies acquired between 1927 and 1929 is given in the Brazilian Traction annual reports for 1928 and 1929.
47 Lash to Couzens, 18 Jan. 1928, BA file 211.010
48 All statistics are from the Brazilian Traction annual report for 1929.
49 IBGE, *Anuário estatístico do Brasil* 1318
50 *O jornal* 19 Dec. 1928
51 All statistics are from the Brazilian Traction annual report for 1929.
52 For an account of the coming of the automobile and bus to Rio streets, see Dunlop, *Os meios de transporte* ch. 6.
53 Norman D. Wilson (1884–1967). See the *Globe and Mail* 3 Mar. 1967.
54 'Memorial presented to the President and Members of the Municipal Council of São Paulo,' 25 May 1927, BA file 511.02
55 Wilson, 'Report on Rio Tramways,' July 1925, RL
56 Ibid. 32–42. For São Paulo, see Stiel, *História dos transportes* 187–9.
57 A. Mackenzie to M. Lash, 8 Aug. 1923, BA, BHE file 8
58 Wood to A. Mackenzie, 25 Aug. 1921, BA pre-1923 file 189
59 A. Mackenzie to Toronto office, 7 Sept. 1921, BA file 187
60 H.J. Hagenah, 'Investigation of the Property Values, Earnings and Operations of the Rio de Janeiro and São Paulo Tramway, Light and Power Companies,' Oct. 1922. For the intricate process of adjudicating public-utility rates, see D.F. Wilcox, *Analysis of the Electric Railway Problem* (New York 1921).
61 Hagenah, 'Investigation'
62 Sylvester to A. Mackenzie, 4 Apr. 1923, BA, BHE file 8
63 Sylvester to Lash, 10 July 1923, ibid.
64 A. Mackenzie to Lash, 8 Aug. 1923, ibid.
65 Norman Lash to Lash, 23 Mar. 1927, BA, loose files. See G.J. Boggiss, 'History of the Introduction and Development of the Telephone in the Federal District and Southern Central Brazil 1877–1935,' 1935 typescript in BA.
66 See Flynn, *Brazil* 34–58.
67 Burns, *Nationalism in Brazil* 71
68 A. Mackenzie to Lash, 9 July 1922, BA file 90
69 Artur da Silva Bernardes (1875–1955). See Bruno de Almeida Magalhães, *Artur Bernardes: Estadista da república* (Rio de Janeiro 1973).
70 A. Mackenzie to Lash, 31 Aug. 1923, BA, BHE file 8
71 John Tilley to Austen Chamberlain, 25 Mar. 1925, PRO, FO 371, file 10607. The British ambassador likened Bernardes's behaviour to that of George III.
72 John Tilley to Foreign Office, nd, ibid. file 9516
73 A. Mackenzie to Couzens, 9 Mar. 1925, BA file 010.5
74 A. Mackenzie to Peacock, 29 Dec. 1926, BA file 306
75 Henry Herbert Couzens (1877–1943) was born in Devonshire, England. He began his engineering career as an apprentice in an electrical-supply

firm and then rose to prominence as a city engineer in Bristol and Hampstead. In 1913, he was appointed general manager of the Toronto Hydro-Electric System. When the City of Toronto 'municipalized' the Toronto Street Railway in 1921, Couzens was appointed general manager of the Toronto Transportation Commission.

76 D. Mulqueen to F.J. Mulqueen, 9 July 1924, BA file 011–21. For the politics of the 1920s, see: Hélio Silva, *O ciclo de Vargas* 2 vols (Rio de Janeiro 1954); Boris Fausto, *A revolução de 1930* (São Paulo 1976); and Santos, *A política geral.*

77 Couzens to Lash, 22 July 1924, BA file 011–21

78 Lash to A. Mackenzie, 16 July 1924, ibid.

79 Billings to Lash, 5 Aug. 1924, ibid.

80 H.H. Couzens, 'Estimate of Damage,' 9 Aug. 1924, ibid. The company instigated proceedings against the federal government for indemnification of its losses. After a long legal battle, it succeeded in obtaining partial payment for its damages in 1937.

81 A. Mackenzie to Lash, 5 Feb. 1924, BA file 100.1

82 Miller Lash (1873–1941), son of Z.A. Lash, was born in Toronto. He attended Upper Canada College and the University of Toronto. After reading law with Blake, Lash and Cassels, he was called to the bar in 1897 and was eventually created a KC in 1921. Besides holding executive positions with the Mexican, Barcelona, and Brazilian Traction Companies, Lash was a director of the Bank of Commerce, the National Trust, the British American Trust, and Western Assurance.

83 Cable, Lash to Toronto office, 9 Aug. 1930, BA file 306

84 See Wilkins, *The Maturing of Multinational Enterprise* chs. 1 and 4.

85 Couzens to Lash, 21 Apr. 1929, BA file 013.7

86 Cable, Lash to Couzens, 29 Jan. 1929, BA file 013.7

87 'Notes on Miller Lash's interview with President Luís,' 24 Sept. 1928, BA, loose file

Chapter 8 The Belgian Croesus

1 See Alfred D. Chandler, Jr, *The Visible Hand: The Managerial Revolution in American Business* (Cambridge, Mass. 1977).

2 Loewenstein to A. Mackenzie, 3 Aug. 1926, BA file 316.2

3 Pearson to Dunn, Fischer and Co., 30 Mar. 1914, BA file A 5F

4 Loewenstein to A. Mackenzie, 26 Nov. 1918, BA pre-1923 file 41

5 Loewenstein to Brazilian Traction, 26 May 1920, BA pre-1923 Rio file 6

6 Gow to Brazilian Traction, 9 June 1920, BA pre-1923 file 5F

7 The best synopsis of Loewenstein's career is available in Fernand Baudhuin, *Histoire economique de la Belgique 1914–1939* tome 2 (Bruxelles 1944) 277–83. See also: *The Times* (London) 6 July 1928.

8 *New York Times* 5 July 1928

9 British Electrical and Allied Manufacturers Association, *Combines and Trusts in the Electrical Industry: The Position in Europe in 1927* (London 1927) 19

10 *Economist* 14 July 1928

11 *Finance et production* 8 Jan. 1927. The holding company has always occupied a place of prominence in Belgian business. See Peter Readman, with Jonathan Davies, Michael Hoare, and David Poole, *The Europe Money Puzzle* (London 1973) 96–7. Dannie N. Heineman (1873–1962) was born in Charlotte, North Carolina, and educated in electrical engineering at the Hanover Technical College. His first job was with the Union-Elektricitäts-Gesellschaft (a General Electric affiliate). Before joining SOFINA, he worked extensively on electrification projects for numerous European streetcar systems. Despite his low profile in the business world, Heineman was active and generous in many charities. In 1914, he helped to organize the Belgian Relief Commission and was a strong advocate of a 'united' Europe throughout his life. See *New York Times* 2 Feb. 1962.

12 *The Times* (London) 6 July 1928, and Dunn to Robert Hayward, Dillon, Read and Co., New York, 18 Jan. 1923, PAC, Dunn Papers, vol. 286

13 *New York Times* 6 July 1928

14 Lash to McConnell, 4 Apr. 1928, BA file 310.10

15 Dunn to C. Cambie, manager of London branch of the Canadian Bank of Commerce, 6 Nov. 1925, PAC, Dunn Papers, vol. 295

16 See *The Times* (London) 10 Aug. 1926.

17 Peacock to Hubbard, 24 Aug. 1926, ibid.

18 Baudhuin, *Histoire economique de la Belgique* 280

19 *L'Argus financier* 14 Sept. 1926

20 Peacock to Holt, 24 Sept. 1926, BA file 310.11

21 Heineman to Peacock, 17 Dec. 1926, ibid.

22 F.A. Schulman to Hubbard, 24 Dec. 1926, ibid.

23 Peacock to Lash, 21 Mar. 1928, BA file 310.11

24 Consideration of the circumstances surrounding the demise of Alfred Loewenstein lies beyond the scope of this book. A recent study by American journalist William Norris (*The Man Who Fell from the Sky* [New York 1987]) has concluded that the Belgian was probably murdered. After being incapacitated in the cabin of the aircraft (possibly by drugs), Loewenstein was ejected from the aircraft's rear door, which had been removed to facilitate the deed. The Fokker subsequently landed on a deserted stretch of French beach where a replacement door (hidden on board) was fitted before French authorities arrived. Norris concludes that Loewenstein's wife, Madeleine, had most to gain from his death. The evidence is not conclusive and other theories persist.

25 Cable, Hubbard to Lash, 6 July 1928, BA file 310.11

26 Judgment: Derwa *vs* Rio de Janeiro Tramway, Light and Power Co. Ltd, Ontario Supreme Court, 24 July 1928

27 *New York Times* 8 July 1928

28 McConnell to Lash, 9 July 1928, BA file 100.47

Chapter 9 The 1930s

1 See John W.F. Dulles, *Vargas of Brazil: A Political Biography* (Austin, Tex. and London 1967), and Richard Bourne, *Getúlio Vargas of Brazil, 1883–1954* (London and Tonbridge 1974). For the political history of Brazil in the 1930s, see Flynn, *Brazil*, and Thomas Skidmore, *Politics in Brazil 1930–1964: An Experiment in Democracy* (London 1967).
2 See Villela and Suzigan, *Política do govêrno* 296, and Stein, *Brazilian Cotton Manufacture*.
3 Bell to Lash, 5 Feb. 1930, BA file 011.1
4 Couzens to Lash, 3 Jan. 1927, ibid.
5 Ibid. 16 Dec. 1929
6 Bell to Lash, 5 Feb. 1930, ibid.
7 Bell to Lash, 5 and 12 Feb. 1930, ibid., and Villela and Suzigan, *Política do govêrno* 296–9
8 Villela and Suzigan, *Política do govêrno* 170. This view is shared by Celso Furtado and Werner Baer. Furtado sees the shift from agriculture to industry in the 1930s as a 'shift in the dynamic centre' of the economy. Dean, in *Industrialization of São Paulo*, argues unconvincingly that there was 'no very pronounced transformation' in the structure of the Paulista economy between the wars.
9 Villela and Suzigan, *Política do govêrno* 138
10 'Report of Trade Commissioner A.S. Bleakney for the year 1932,' PAC, RG 20, vol. 1482
11 Villela and Suzigan, *Política do govêrno* 302–4
12 Billings to Bell, 28 Oct. 1937, BA file 531.5
13 Cable, Lash to Toronto office, 9 Aug. 1930, BA file 306
14 Couzens to Lash, 1 Apr. 1931, ibid.
15 *Report Submitted to the Brazilian Government by Sir Otto E. Neimeyer* July 1931. See Marcelo de Paiva Abreu, 'A missão Niemeyer,' *Revista de administração de empresas* 14:4 (Julho-Agôsto 1974).
16 Couzens to Lash, 24 Mar. 1932, BA file 306
17 Ibid. 20 May 1932. In 1935, an American utility company, a subsidiary of AMFORP operating in Chile, was fined more than $7 million for violating exchange regulations. Toronto *Evening Telegram* 11 Dec. 1935
18 Bell to Lash, 3 Jan. 1938, BA file 306
19 J. Garnett Lomax to London, 21 Sept. 1932, PRO, FO 371
20 *Trade and Commerce* 12 Jan. 1935, and Lester Glass to L.D. Wilgress, 7 Dec. 1934, PAC, RG 20, vol. 286
21 Dr J.H. Fortin to Lash, 29 Jan. 1940, BA file 310.51
22 Bello, *History of Modern Brazil* 270
23 Ibid. 281
24 Flynn, *Brazil* 97
25 Billings to Lash, 21 Oct. 1930, BA, loose files
26 Couzens to Adams, 8 Nov. 1930, BA, loose files

27 Cable, Mackenzie to Lash, 5 Nov. 1930, and Mackenzie to Niemeyer, 28 Jan. 1931, BA file 011

28 Couzens to Lash, 20 Nov. 1931, BA file 011.4

29 See Burns, *Nationalism in Brazil* ch. 5, and Robert J. Alexander, 'Brazilian *Tenentismo*,' *Hispanic American Historical Review* 36 (May 1956).

30 Mackenzie to Niemeyer, 28 Jan. 1931, BA file 011

31 Lash to A. Mackenzie, 19 Jan. 1931, BA file 100.1

32 A. Mackenzie to Niemeyer, 28 Jan. 1931, BA file 011. For an example of such anti-foreign sentiment see: 'Against the Monopolies of Avidity,' *O globo* 26 Oct. 1934.

33 See Gauld, *Last Titan* esp. ch. 17, and John D. Wirth, *The Politics of Brazilian Development, 1930–1954* (Stanford, Calif. 1970) 6–8.

34 *A nação* 27 Oct. 1934

35 Report on the 'Economic Structure and Development of Brazil,' 26 Dec. 1934, PRO, FO 371, file A404

36 A. Mackenzie to Niemeyer, 28 Jan. 1931, BA file 011

37 Lash to Hubbard, 22 Apr. 1931, BA file 601.2

38 Couzens to Lash, 4 May 1934, BA file 011.4

39 A. Mackenzie to Niemeyer, 28 Jan. 1931, BA file 011

40 A. Mackenzie to Lash, 8 Jan. 1934, BA file 601.21

41 Couzens to Lash, 29 July 1932, BA file 011.23

42 Couzens to Lash, 30 July 1932, BA file 011.23

43 Keeling to Foreign Office, 4 Aug. 1932, PRO, FO 371, file A4828

44 Foreign Office minute by P. Mason, 18 Aug. 1932, ibid. file A5157

45 A. de Melo Franco to Keeling, 29 Aug. 1932, ibid.

46 'Notes on an informal luncheon with Oswaldo Aranha,' by K.H. McCrimmon, 20 Oct. 1932, BA, loose file

47 Lash to Adams, 21 Oct. 1932, BA file 011.23

48 Notes on meeting with President Vargas, 11 Sept. 1931, BA, loose file

49 Couzens to Lash, 11 May 1934, BA file 011.4

50 Decree No. 23,501, 27 Nov. 1933. José Américo was a writer from Paraíba. He had been the personal secretary of João Pessoa and was closely aligned with 'radical' *tenentes* like Távora. José Bello has remarked that 'José Américo appeared to symbolize the purest revolutionary spirit.' Bello, *History of Modern Brazil* 295

51 Lash to Sun Life Assurance Co., 7 Jan. 1930, BA file 302

52 Eurico Sodré to Billings, 8 Nov. 1933, BA file 601.23

53 Decree No. 23,703, 5 Jan. 1934

54 Sir W. Seeds to Foreign Office, 6 Dec. 1933, plus departmental marginalia, PRO, FO 371, file A8866, and cable, Adams to Lash, 18 Nov. 1933, BA file 501.21

55 A. Mackenzie to Hubbard, 8 Jan. 1934, BA file 501.21

56 Bello, *History of Modern Brazil* 292–3

57 Couzens to Lash, 14 June 1934, BA file 011.4

58 Couzens to Lash, 18 Aug. 1934, BA file 011.54

59 Speech by Vargas, given at Lajes, Dec. 1936, BA file 011.4
60 Couzens to Lash, 8 June 1934, ibid.
61 Decree No. 24,643, 10 July 1934. See Departamento Nacional de Águas e Energia Elétrica, *Código de águas legislação subsequente e correlata* (Rio de Janeiro 1974). The nascent Brazilian petroleum industry was subjected to similar scrutiny from the *tenentes*. See Peter S. Smith, *Oil and Politics in Modern Brazil* (Toronto 1976) ch. 2, esp. 27–8.
62 Decree No. 24,673, 11 July 1934, and Decree Law No. 2281, 5 June 1940
63 Billings to Lash, 18 Feb. 1937, BA file 601.21
64 Ibid.
65 Couzens to Lash, 31 May 1934, BA file 0.11
66 *O estado de São Paulo* 16 Oct. 1935. Among Simonsen's books are *A indústria em face da econômica national* (São Paulo 1937) and *História econômica do Brasil, 1500–1820* (São Paulo 1937).
67 Mackenzie to Lash, 24 Nov. 1934, BA file 011.54
68 Couzens to Lash, 14 June 1935, BA file 011.54
69 Speech by Vargas at Lajes, Dec. 1936, BA file 011.4
70 Wirth, *Politics of Brazilian Development* 217
71 Billings to Couzens, 30 Apr. 1935, BA file 011.54
72 McCrimmon to Lash, 13 Nov. 1937, ibid.
73 McCrimmon to Lash, 18 May 1938, ibid.
74 Bell to Lash, 3 Mar. 1938, ibid.
75 'Some Notes on the Position of the Brazilian Traction, Light and Power Co. Ltd.,' by F.H. Soward, 4 Oct. 1945, Department of External Affairs file 5683–40
76 10 May 1938
77 McCrimmon to Couzens, 7 Mar. 1944, BA 'Presidential Interviews' file
78 North Americans have always had difficulty understanding the role of influence in Brazilian life. In 1952, Canadian Trade Commissioner C.R. Gallow tried to convey some sense of the place of influence in Brazilian business life. 'It also seems to be an accepted fact in business circles here that it is not what you know, but whom you know that enables a person to secure either public contracts or import licenses. It is an unfortunate state of affairs and of course where public officials place personal interest before that of their country you always find plenty of private citizens willing and able to encourage them provided it is to their material advantage to do so. It makes it very difficult therefore to be able to forecast trends or interpolate regulations accurately because you sometimes find individuals who have succeeded in circumventing them. Contributing directly to the growth of such conditions is the attitude of businessmen towards regulations in general – the feeling that they are for suckers only – as a result you have trafficking in import licences; fake declarations on imports and exports to permit accumulation of dollar exchange abroad ... all of which benefits the few at the expense of the vast majority and is a measure of the unhealthy state of business. Such activities are not peculiar

to Brazil alone; all countries experience these difficulties in varying degrees but in Brazil, unfortunately, they are common enough to be readily noticeable.' Report by Trade Commissioner C.R. Gallow for 1952, PAC, RG 20, vol. 1484

79 Since their inception, the Rio and São Paulo Light companies had operated on different current frequencies. São Paulo used sixty cycles and Rio fifty cycles. This difference was due to the fact that the early electric companies in each city had adopted differing North American and European electric standards.

80 Billings to Lash, 16 Nov. 1938, BA file 011.54

81 Bell to Couzens, 16 Feb. 1939, ibid.

82 Lash to Billings, 28 Mar. 1939, ibid.

83 Billings to Lash, 2 Feb. 1939, BA file 011.54

Chapter 10 The Changing of the Guard

1 Brazil sent 25,000 troops to fight in Italy. Of these, 451 never lived to see their homeland again.

2 Wirth, *Politics of Brazilian Development* 129

3 Quoted in Skidmore, *Politics in Brazil* 45

4 Lash to Gow, 14 Sept. 1939, BA, loose files

5 During periods of state of siege when the Estado Novo prohibited coded commercial messages, Brazilian Traction entrusted much of its correspondence to passengers on the German airship.

6 McCrimmon to Lash, 29 Mar. 1940, BA file 112.7

7 Flynn, *Brazil*, 109

8 Villela and Suzigan, *Política do govêrno* 201

9 'Report of Trade Commissioner Lester S. Glass for the year 1941,' PAC, RG 20, vol. 1486

10 In November 1942, Brazil converted its monetary system from the milréis to the cruzeiro on the basis of one milréis equalling one cruzeiro. This reform was prompted by the fact that inflation had made milréis sums long and ungainly and also because the milréis, with its monarchical connotations (*rei* = king), was deemed inappropriate for the republican Estado Novo. Thus Cr. $1 = 1$000 (milréis).

11 'Report of Trade ... 1941,' ibid. In 1944, a new Canadian trade commissioner reached a different conclusion. 'Unplanned and wide-scale industrialization, in many instances, justified only by a continued scarcity of imported consumer goods and the lure of immediate profits,' he reported, had given Brazil 'a surface appearance of increased economic activity and greater national income but may, in the long run, result in a net loss in Brazil's permanent assets and production capacity.' 'Report of Trade Commissioner Maurice Bélanger,' 1944, PAC, RG 20, vol. 1486

12 J.G. de Aragão to Lash, 15 May 1940, BA file 011.54

13 C.A. Sylvester to Lash, 25 May 1939, BA file 011.54

14 *Jornal do comércio* 8 May 1943
15 Federal Decree Laws 1345 and 2059, 14 June and 4 Mar. 1940
16 Couzens to Lash, 3 June 1939, BA file 011.54
17 J.M. Bell to Couzens, 8 Dec. 1942, BA, loose files
18 Judith Tendler, *Electric Power in Brazil: Entrepreneurship in the Public Sector* (Harvard 1968). The rate increments fixed to external factors such as wage rates were known as 'the additionals.' Tendler is quite mistaken, however, when she states (64) that 'the study of the additionals starts in 1945, even before the basic rate had become a problem.' The Light had faced a severe 'basic-rate' problem since 1934, when its rates had been frozen at existing levels (or where the gold clause had been cancelled at lower than existing levels) by the introduction of the Water Code. As earlier chapters of this study have illustrated, the rate problem had been with the company in varying forms from as early as the 1920s. On page 50, Tendler does acknowledge that the Light received no hike in its basic rate from 1934 to 1955–6. While her analysis of the accommodation between government and company, to which the additionals contributed, illustrates one aspect of the problem, she fails to realize that the additionals did nothing to better the company's return on investment. The additionals did not 'solve' the Light's basic-rate problem in any sense. They only prolonged a painful financial situation.
19 Notes on Water Code regulations by Antônio Gallotti, 11 June 1951, BA file 011.54
20 The timing and nature of Water Code regulations and decrees in the late 1930s and early 1940s was predominantly governed by a process of bureaucratic in-fighting. Jurisdiction over the hydroelectric industry had been divided since 1939 between the Waters Division of the ministry of agriculture, which had traditionally represented the concession-granting power, and the National Council of Water and Electric Energy (CNAEE), which had been created in 1939 as a collective body with limited authority, largely consultative, to act as a court of administrative appeal in relations between concession holders and the concession granter. Inevitably, jurisdictional disputes arose between the two bodies. These tensions were exacerbated by the fact that each body had a distinct ideological bias. The Waters Division tended to be a bastion of 'hard-line' nationalists, who were intent upon applying the Water Code along the lines on which it had been drafted by the *tenentes* in the mid-1930s. The CNAEE was staffed by more pragmatic nationalists who had realized by the early 1940s that the interests of foreign-owned utility companies had to be accommodated to some degree. Light executives therefore always showed a greater willingness to deal with the CNAEE than with the Waters Division. In the early 1940s, the company enjoyed good relations with the head of the CNAEE, Col. Peixoto da Cunha.
21 Brazilian Traction annual report for 1942, and 'Heightening the Lajes Dam, Rio de Janeiro,' *Engineering* 1 and 8 July 1949

22 Wirth, *Politics of Brazilian Development* 128
23 *O estado de São Paulo* 11 Jan. 1945
24 See *A energia elétrica no Brasil* section 3.7.
25 See D.R. Murray, 'Canada's First Diplomatic Missions in Latin America,' *Journal of Interamerican Studies and World Affairs* 16:2 (May 1974) 154.
26 In November 1940, the American military attaché in Ottawa made a request, through the Canadian Department of Defence, to Brazilian Traction in Toronto that the company provide a list of its power facilities 'for the purposes of strategic area study essential to proper hemisphere defence.' The company had little option but to comply. See H. Des Rosiers, Dep. Min. of Defence, to W. Gow, 14 Nov. 1940, BA file 007.01.
27 'Confidential Memo re: Request of Brazilian Foreign Minister for exchange of diplomatic representatives with Canada,' by K.H. McCrimmon, 18 June 1940, BA file 112.7
28 McCrimmon to Skelton, 31 Dec. 1940, BA file 112.7
29 *O congresso* June 1948
30 16 July 1943
31 27 May 1937
32 28 Oct. 1941. See also *Financial Post* 8 Nov. 1941.
33 Couzens to H.M. Hubbard, 11 Nov. 1942, BA file 100.5
34 George Nightingale to D.H. Cromar, 20 Nov. 1944, ibid. For other tributes to Sir Herbert Couzens, see *Saturday Night* 2 Dec. 1944, and *O jornal* 5 Dec. 1944.
35 Ackerman, *Billings and Water Power* chs. 10 and 11
36 Billings to Gow, 1 Jan. 1945, BA, 'Presidential Interviews' file
37 'Trade Report for 1945,' by M. Bélanger, PAC, RG 20, vol. 1484
38 Villela and Suzigan, *Política do govêrno* 368
39 Notes on interview with President Vargas, 31 July 1945, BA, 'Presidential Interviews' file
40 A.W.K. Billings, 'General Construction Program,' 25 Sept. 1944, BA file 537
41 Memo by G.R.F. Troop, 26 Mar. 1945, BA file 5399
42 Memo by G.R.F. Troop, 20 Nov. 1945, ibid., and 'Construction Programme,' by G.R.F. Troop, 20 Nov. 1945, BA file 309. Troop estimated the cost of hydroelectric construction at $36,614,000, additional distribution capacity at $16,400,000, and telephone-system expansion at $24,000,000.
43 Billings to Gow, 14 Feb. 1946, BA file 309
44 McCrimmon to Couzens, 24 Mar. 1944, BA, 'Presidential Interviews' file
45 See cable, Acting Secretary of State for External Affairs to Jean Désy, Rio, 11 June 1946, PAC, RG 20, vol. 716
46 See Flynn, *Brazil* 108.
47 Wilson to Gow, 1 May 1945, BA file 011.4
48 Quoted in Odilon de Souza to Couzens, 2 May 1944, BA file 011.54
49 Billings to Gow, 27 Nov. 1945, BA file 011.4
50 'Mr. Billings' remarks to the Board,' 11 Apr. 1946, BA file 100.2

51 Billings to Gow, 14 Feb. 1946, ibid.
52 Memo for Col. Gow, 'Construction Estimates,' 21 Nov. 1945, BA file 309
53 Wilson to H. Borden, 23 Oct. 1945, ibid.
54 See John de N. Kennedy. *History of the Department of Munitions and Supply: Canada in the Second World War* 2 vols (Ottawa 1950).
55 Gow to Billings, 4 Feb. 1946, BA, Borden files. All subsequent quotations are from the same file.
56 Henry Borden, unpublished memoirs
57 Billings to Gow and Brazilian Traction Board, 23 Apr. 1946, BA file 100.2
58 Quoted in Ackerman, *Billings and Water Power* 93
59 Borden memoirs

Epilogue

1 Vernon, *Sovereignty at Bay* 195, 284. See also Raymond Vernon, *Storm over the Multinationals: The Real Issues* (Cambridge, Mass. 1977).
2 Vernon, *Storm over the Multinationals* 171
3 Mackenzie to Peacock, 29 Dec. 1926, BA file 306
4 Memorandum by F.H. Soward, 4 Oct. 1945, DEA file 5683-40
5 All operational and financial statistics in this epilogue are from Brazilian Traction / Brascan annual reports, 1945–79.
6 Soward memorandum
7 H. Borden to H. Style, 6 Nov. 1947, BA file 309
8 Ibid.
9 1 Oct. 1953
10 International Bank for Reconstruction and Development, Articles of Agreement. See Edward S. Mason and Robert E. Asher, *The World Bank Since Bretton Woods* (Washington 1973).
11 *Time* 22 Nov. 1948
12 Hume Wrong to Borden, 30 Jan. 1951, BA file 309
13 Cable, J.R. Nicholson to Borden, 26 Jan. 1951, BA file 531.01
14 Ibid. 8 Feb. 1954, BA, Borden private files
15 Dulles, *Vargas of Brazil* 334
16 *A energia elétrica no Brasil*
17 'Memo by J.S. Macdonald on the senior personnel of the Brazilian Traction, Light & Power Co. Ltd. in Brazil,' 16 Oct. 1950, DEA file 5683-40
18 1957 annual report.
19 Despatch by Jean Chapdelaine, 16 Dec. 1959, DEA file 5683-40
20 1962 annual report.
21 Cable, Gallotti to Glassco, 27 Apr. 1964, BA file 0-7-1-14
22 The state quickly discovered that the private sector had no monopoly on the problems of running a public utility. Shortly after acquiring the São Paulo tramway system, the municipal government attempted to rectify the financial ills of the tram operation by boosting fares by 150 per cent. 'We were yesterday the witnesses of a popular demonstration of the so-called

"will of the people,"' the Canadian trade commissioner reported from São Paulo. A 'mob ... went mad' protesting the new fares and destroyed fifty-nine trams and fifteen buses. Long pampered by artificially low fares, *paulistanos* proved no more forgiving of their city fathers on the issue of transit fares than they had been of the 'Canadian octopus' (J.C. Depocas, Trade Commissioner, to Ottawa, 2 Aug. 1947, PAC, RG 20, vol. 716). São Paulo abandoned tramway service in 1961 when it became impossible to maintain an increasingly decrepit service in the face of an onslaught of automobiles. *Paulistanos'* mass transit needs are now served by a chaotic mixture of state and private companies offering bus and subway service.

23 Ministério das Minas e Energia, *Balanço energético nacional* (Brasília 1986)
24 Circular to the shareholders, 20 Feb. 1979
25 6 Jan. 1979
26 See João Martins, 'Light: What Brazil Bought,' *Manchete* 3 Feb. 1979.
27 30 Dec. 1978
28 7 Jan. 1979

Glossary

agua Water.

AMFORP The American and Foreign Power Co. Ltd.

bonde Tram, a term unique to Brazilian Portuguese. In Portugal, a tram-car is an *elétrico*. The origin of the use of *bonde* is somewhat uncertain. It is said to have developed either from the 'bonds' that foreign companies used to underwrite their Brazilian utilities ventures or from the coupon-like tickets sold to tramway riders.

Cachoeira do Inferno 'The rapids of hell,' the location of the São Paulo company's first hydroelectric station outside the city of São Paulo. Later the plant became known as the Parnaíba station.

café com leite Literally, coffee with milk. A term used to denote the political axis of São Paulo, with its coffee wealth, and Minas Gerais, with its cattle wealth, which dominated the Old Republic up to 1930.

câmara Chamber, or, when capitalized, municipal council.

cambista An exchange banker.

canadense Canadian.

carioca A resident of the city of Rio de Janeiro.

caudilho A leader or political boss; hence *caudilhismo*.

CEMIG The state power company of Minas Gerais (Centrais Elétricas de Minas Gerais).

CESP The state power company of São Paulo (Centrais Elétricas de São Paulo).

clientelismo A political system that binds leader and led through a system of patronage and kinship.

Clube Militar A club for army officers, founded in 1877, which played a crucial role in promoting revolutionary agitation in the 1920s.

COBAST Companhia Brasileira Administradora de Serviços Técnicos, the management company established by Brazilian Traction in 1947 to manage its affairs in Brazil.

comissão A commission; hence a *comissão de finanças* is a financial commission.

companhia A company.

conselheiro A councillor.

conselho A council.

conto A thousand milréis.

coronel (*pl.* coroneis) A colonel, often used in the sense of a political boss.

coronelismo The clientelistic style of politics that generally prevailed in Brazil up to the Revolution of 1930. It was a system by which political bosses dominated vast segments of Brazilian political life, especially in rural areas. Vestiges of *coronelismo* survived past 1930.

cruzeiro The basic unit of Brazilian currency from 1942 to 1986.

CTB Companhia Telefônica Brasileira. Brazilian Traction's principal telephone subsidiary in Brazil. The CTB provided telephone services in five Brazilian states.

Diário oficial The official gazette of the Brazilian federal government, used to promulgate laws.

Eletrobrás The federal, state-owned electricity company, created in 1961.

emprêsa A company or enterprise.

Encilhamento A sensational financial boom and crash in the early 1890s brought on by the policies of Finance Minister Rui Barbosa.

entreguistas A term applied by extreme Brazilian nationalists to those other Brazilians who willingly co-operate with foreign capitalists.

estado de sítio A state of siege.

Estado Novo Literally, the New State. Used to describe the corporatist state that prevailed under Getúlio Vargas between 1937 and 1945.

fazenda A farm.

Fôrça Pública The state security police force in the state of São Paulo.

gaúcho Literally, a cowboy or cattle breeder. A term applied to the citizens of the state of Rio Grande do Sul.

getulismo The pragmatic, reformist political philosophy of Getúlio Vargas.

getulista A follower of Getúlio Vargas and *getulismo*.

IBRD The International Bank for Reconstruction and Development, also known as the World Bank.

Integralista An adherent of *integralismo*, the Brazilian fascist movement of the 1930s.

interventores Officials arbitrarily appointed by Getúlio Vargas in the early 1930s to head the Brazilian state governments.

largo A square.

latifúndio A large rural landholding.

luz Light.

mato Dense underbrush.

milréis The basic unit of Brazilian currency up to 1942. Literally, a thousand réis.

mineiro A citizen of the state of Minas Gerais.

morro A hill, or hillock, used to describe the barren volcanic plugs that dominate the terrain around Rio de Janeiro.

novo New.

operário A worker.

país A country or nation.

parecer An opinion or judgment, usually used in the legal sense.

paulista A resident of the state of São Paulo.

paulistano A resident of the city of São Paulo.

Petrobrás The federally owned state oil company in Brazil, founded in 1953.

prefeito A municipal prefect or mayor.

PSB Brazilian Socialist Party.

PTB Brazilian Labour Party.

SA An abbreviation for *sociedade anônima*, a joint stock company.

secretário A secretary.

Serra do Mar The steep coastal escarpment that parallels the coast in southeastern Brazil.

tenente Literally, a lieutenant. In the context of the Revolution of 1930, *tenente* is used to denote a member of the political opposition during the 1920s and one who provided much of the revolutionary fervour after 1930.

tombamento An inventory or the taking of inventory.

Triângulo Literally, a triangle. Used to describe the urban core of the city of São Paulo.

tunel A tunnel

viação Transport or means of conveyance.

Index

Adams, A.W. 254
Aemilius Jarvis and Company 189, 360
Aguiar, Gen. Souza 146, 149
Aird, Sir John 199
Aitken, W.M. 157
Alberto, João 311, 320, 335, 359
Alcan Ltd 5
Alfonso XIII 181
Almeida, José Américo de 324, 328, 331, 440n
Alvear, Torcuato de 28
Alves, Rodrigues 12, 32, 110, 114–15, 125, 127–9, 146, 148, 242, 424n
American and Foreign Power Company (AMFORP) 391, 394, 398
Ames, A.E. 70–1, 104
Andrada, Antônio Carlos de 310, 314
Aragão, J.G. de 337, 347, 351
Aranha, Osvaldo 315–16, 321–2, 332–4, 337, 339, 348, 357–8

Backer, Alfredo 151–2, 171
Baer, Werner 101, 439n
Bahia Tramway, Light and Power Company Ltd 212, 240
Banco do Brasil 306–9, 314
Banco Nacional Brasileiro 137, 142, 168

Bank of Scotland 235
Banque Internationale de Bruxelles 140
Barbosa, Rui 24, 28, 116, 129, 143, 147, 155, 176, 238, 269, 274, 357
Barcelona Traction, Light and Power Company 181, 186, 200, 211–12, 215, 233–5, 291, 296, 340
Beck, Adam 178, 180
Bélanger, Maurice 366
Bell, James McKim 258, 302, 307, 332, 334, 338–9, 375–6
Bello, José 325
Bermuda 418n
Bernardes, Artur 242–4, 268, 271–5, 277–8, 310–11, 334
Berton, Pierre 4
Bevan, T.W. 12, 64, 76
Billings, A.W.K.
– and 1924 São Paulo Revolt 276–8
– as president 364–5, 391
– as vice-president 262, 274, 280, 313
– dispute with head office 373–80
– early career 247–8
– joins Brazilian Traction, early projects 247–51, 435n
– oversees Cubatão project 251–60, 304
– reaction to politics of 1930s 313,

315, 320, 330, 337–9
- reaction to politics of 1940s 372–3
- retirement and death 380–1
- views on power development in early 1940s 347, 354–5, 364–70, 372, 388
Birmingham Tramway Co. 35, 38, 49, 55
Black, Eugene 388
Blake, Edward 57, 118
Blake, Mabel (Lady Mackenzie) 118, 196, 279, 415n
Blake, Samuel 57, 118
Blake, W.H. 48–9, 103, 112, 118, 120–1, 157, 196, 415n
Blake, Lash and Cassels 39, 74, 117, 141, 185, 228, 360, 374
Borba, Alípio de 32–3, 86, 90, 106, 275
Borden, Henry 377–81, 386–8, 390–2, 394
Borden, Sir Robert 314, 377
Borden, Elliot, Kelley, Palmer and Sankey 377
Boston and Lowell Railway 61
Botanical Gardens Railway Company 130–1, 133, 140, 142, 149, 167–8
Botelho, Oliveira 172
Braga, Odilon 330
Branco, Castello 393
Brascan Ltd 4, 8–9, 395–7
Brazilian Electro Steel and Smelting Co. Ltd 169
Brazilian Hydro-Electric Company 250
Brazilian Labour Party 371
Brazilian Securities Co. Ltd 138, 140–1, 157, 425n
Brazilianische Elektricitäts Gesellschaft 130, 141, 204, 223, 225
Bridle, Augustus 78
British American Nickel Corporation 233
British Celanese 290
British Columbia Electric Railway 58, 159

British Empire Trust Co. 75, 105, 200, 228
Brown, Robert Calthrop 11–13, 36–7, 38–9, 42, 46, 61, 64, 66–7, 76, 77, 80–1, 83, 86, 88–92, 96, 99, 113, 117, 118, 120, 248, 256, 296
Buenos Aires 28, 111, 125
Bull, William L. 137–8
Burns, Pat 67, 417n

Campos, Américo de 31
Campos, Bernardino de 31–2, 114, 116, 196
Campos, Carlos de 32–3, 42–5, 88, 106, 119, 176, 196, 255, 259, 268, 274–5
Campos, Francisco 332, 337
Canada Life 69
Canadian and General Finance Company Limited 200
Canadian Bank of Commerce 58, 69–71, 74, 96, 103, 104, 109, 135, 156–7, 169–70, 199, 235
Canadian General Electric 69
Canadian Northern Railway 40, 50, 53, 55–6, 58–60, 73, 75, 78–9, 105, 138, 186, 201, 209, 213, 215, 236, 284
Canadian Pacific Ltd 31, 35, 38, 50, 51, 54–5
Carioca Company 142, 149
Carnegie, Andrew 209
Carranza, Venustiano 210
Cassels, Walter 118
CEMIG 389
Central Canada Loan and Savings Co. 69–70, 71, 157
Central London Railway 87
Chandler, Alfred D. 8
Chapdelaine, Jean 10, 393
Charnley, Walter 253
Chateaubriand, Assis 4, 7, 241, 256, 274, 434n
CHESF 357
Chile 54

City of Santos Improvements Company 261

Clark, Robert J. 156

Clarkson, Gordon, Dilworth and Nash 362

Clouston, E.S. 135, 157

Clube Militar 271–2

COBAST 391

Commission of Economic Planning 357

Communist Party 370, 373

Companhia Água e Luz 96, 111

Companhia Brasileira de Energia Elétrica 145, 167, 170, 173–4, 176, 429n

Companhia Carris de Ferro de São Paulo e Santo Amaro 88

Companhia de Carris Urbanos 131, 142, 149

Companhia de Rede Telephonica Bragantina 205, 223

Companhia de Telefones Interestados 223

Companhia Ferro-Carril da Vila Isabel 130, 134, 140–1, 149

Companhia Industrial de São Paulo 100

Companhia Nacional de Eletricidade 133

Companhia São Cristovão 130, 142, 149

Companhia Telefônica Brasileira 390, 394

Companhia Telefônica do Estado de São Paulo 223

Comptoir d'Escompte 87

Constituent Assembly 323, 325

Convention of Taubaté 109

Cooper, Hugh L. 42–3, 46, 65, 81–5, 117, 247, 256

Corcovado Railway 25, 142, 154

Couzens, Herbert
– and Brazilian politics 281–2, 301, 306, 313–14, 320, 322–5, 328, 338
– as president 341, 350, 361–5

– as vice-president 276, 280–1, 305–6, 309, 313–14, 338
– early career 361–2, 436–7n
– joins company 274

Cox, George A. 66–7, 68, 69–70, 71, 72, 74, 86, 103, 105, 163

Credit Valley Railway 53

Cruz, Oswaldo 127

Cubatão 255

Darwin, Charles 123–4

Dean, Warren 19, 101, 435n

Demerara Electric Company 71

Demmé, Rod A. 140

Derwa Case 292, 295, 299

Deutsche Bank 141

Díaz, Porfirio 164, 210

Dillon, Clarence 226

Dominion Coal Company 66

Dominion Iron and Steel Company 66, 69

Dominion Securities 69, 70–1

Dreyfus, Henry and Camille 290

Drumond, Baron 130

Dunlop, Charles J. 337

Dunn, James H. 141, 158, 162, 165–6, 175, 182, 185, 189–92, 199, 204, 210–11, 215, 233, 235–6, 286, 292

Dunn, Fischer and Co. 105, 161, 192, 201, 235, 286, 288

Duprat, Raimundo da Silva 173

Dutra, Eurico 347, 370–1, 373, 386

Dyment, A.E. 191

Ebro Irrigation and Power Company 181

Edgar, E. Mackay 135, 158, 183

Electric Bond and Share Company 177, 281–2

Electrical Development Company 66, 79, 163, 180, 183

Eletrobrás 389, 395, 398–9

EMBRATEL 394

Emprêsas Elétricas Brasileiras 281

Emprêsa Ferro-Carril Vila Guarani
130
Encilhamento 24, 107
Escher-Wyss Company 83
Estado Novo 309, 331–2, 337, 344,
356, 359, 370, 372, 385
Estrada de Ferro Central do Brasil
132, 151, 154–5, 240, 246
Estrada de Ferro Dom Pedro II 25
Estrada de Ferro Paulista 25, 111

Farquhar Percival 137, 161, 163, 187,
197, 200, 212, 240, 317, 384, 425n
Ferguson, Hon. Howard 361, 379
Ferraz, A.J. Pinto 42, 116
Flavelle, Joseph 53, 69, 71–2, 179
Flynn, Peter 279, 312, 345
Fonseca, Marshal Hermes da 271
Fontoura, João Neves da 380
Fôrca Expedicionària Brasileira 343
Ford, Henry 317
'4-K' corporation 228–9, 394, 433n
Franco, Afrânio de Melo 321–2
Franco, General 340
Freire, Anibal 244
Freire, General 357
Freyre, Gilberto 24
Frick, Henry C. 191
Frontin, Paulo de 127, 266
FURNAS 390
Furtado, Celso 18, 242, 439n

Gafrée, Cândido 135, 146
Gallotti, Antônio 337, 391–2, 397–8
Geisel, Ernesto 397–8
General Electric 11, 34, 84, 87, 96,
136, 144, 171, 174, 258, 281
General Gas Securities and Trust Co.
Ltd 169–70
Germany 21–2, 220
Glassco, J. Grant 394
Global Reversion Fund 396
Gomes, Eduardo 371
Gordon, Donald 376
Goulart, João 393

Gow, Walter 141, 160, 287–8, 341,
360–1, 368, 374, 376, 380
Graham, Richard 24
Grand Trunk Railway 52
Greenshields and Company 198
Grey, Sir Edward 16, 121
Gualco, Francisco Antônio 31–7,
40–3, 66–7, 81, 86, 100, 135, 349,
383, 386, 413n
Gualco, Josephine 32
Gualco e de Souza, Incorporadores
33, 40–3
Guarantee Insurance and Investment
Company 169, 235
Guinle and Co. 100, 111, 112, 135–6,
143–4, 145–9, 152, 154, 165, 167–8,
171–4, 176–7, 209, 212, 246, 281
Gundy, J.H. 296–7
Gunn, James 40–1, 68

Hagenah, H.J. 267
Haggard, William 121, 145
Halifax Electric Company 65, 164
Halifax Tramway Co. 36, 66
Hanna, D.B. 53, 58–9, 157, 187, 236,
284, 296, 360
Hartwell, Harry 88–9
Haussman, Baron 28, 126
Havana 38, 55
Havana Electric Railway Company
248
Heineman, Dannie N. 290, 293–4,
296–7, 438n
Hirt, Louis J. 64
Holt, Herbert 53–4, 158, 201, 292–3,
295, 297
Horne-Payne, R.M.
– conflict with company 159–62, 183,
226
– early career 58–9, 159
– financial activities in London 58–9,
66, 73, 75, 103, 105, 108, 138,
158–60, 165–6, 168, 174, 183, 187,
190, 200
– resignation from board 283

Howe, C.D. 361, 377–8, 391
Hubbard, H. Malcolm 187, 200–1, 226, 284
Huerta, Victoriano 210
Huntress, F.A. 64, 66, 151, 153, 166–7, 177, 195–6, 201, 203–4, 218, 229, 234, 266, 274
Hutton, Maurice 199
Hyde, F.S. 250, 253
Hydro-Electric Power Commission of Ontario 179–80
Hydro-Electric Securities Ltd 294

INCO 233
Income War Tax Act, 1918 228
Integralists 300, 309, 331
International Bank for Reconstruction and Development 388
International Holding and Investment Company 290, 295, 298
Interurban Telephone Company 204, 223
Itaipu 395

J. Henry Schroder and Co. 227, 432n
Jacarepagua Railway 170
Jamaica 36, 38, 55, 60
John Labatt Limited 394

Kearny, C.H. 150–2, 247, 256
Keeling, Edward 321–2
Keenleyside, Hugh 358
Kincardine 117–18, 279, 333, 360
King, W.L.M. 199, 358
Kipling, Rudyard 260
Kitcat and Aitken 105

Lacerda, Carlos 389
Lake Manitoba Railway and Canal Co. 55
Lash, Miller
– as president 279–82, 304–5, 313, 319, 323, 328–9, 332, 337, 344, 360–2
– as vice-president 245, 261, 277

– battles Alfred Loewenstein 291, 295–9
– early ties with company 187, 228, 437n
– private life 308, 341
– retirement 341, 361–2
Lash, Zebulon A.
– as company director and executive 74, 77, 80, 88, 103, 115, 119, 137, 141, 162, 185, 187, 193, 233, 236–7, 280
– as investor in Brazilian companies 72, 157, 201
– as William Mackenzie's lawyer 39–41, 59, 66, 70–1, 72, 118, 180, 182–3, 214
– death 283
Laurier, Sir Wilfrid 31
Le Corbusier 126
Leopoldina Railway 155
Liberal Alliance 310–11
Light Serviços de Eletricidade SA 395
Linhares, José 371
Lodi, Euvaldi 381
Loewenstein, Alfred 106, 140, 156, 161, 183, 189–91, 211, 233, 235, 283–99, 362, 384, 438n
London and Brazil Bank 42, 116
Luís, Washington 244–5, 278–9, 281, 310–12
Lynch, Charles 4

McConnell, J.W. 291, 293, 296, 299
McCrimmon, Kenneth 274, 279–80, 321–2, 333, 335–8, 342, 344–5, 358–9, 370–71, 375–6, 385–6
Macdonald, Sir John A. 57
Macdonald, J.S. 390
McDougall and Cowans 189
Mackenzie, Alexander (Liberal prime minister) 57
Mackenzie, Sir Alexander
– adaptation to Brazilian conditions 119, 161–2, 165–7, 237–41, 259–60, 266–8, 333, 342, 364, 374, 384–6, 391, 426n

- becomes president 235–41
- corporate expansion in Rio 128–9, 132–4, 137–40, 142–53, 156–7, 161–2, 176–8, 204–5
- corporate expansion in São Paulo 96, 98, 101, 103, 111–12, 115–21, 170–4
- early life and career 117–19, 196, 415n
- early years in Brazil 12, 42–4, 77, 80, 85, 88, 91, 93
- policies during First World War 219–20, 224, 229
- policies in 1920s 244–7, 250, 253–6, 259–60, 266–8, 318
- politics in Brazil 110–12, 129, 147–8, 237–41, 245, 271, 314, 316, 328
- problems of Brazilian exchange 107
- relations with A. Loewenstein 286, 292–3, 296
- retirement years 325, 360
Mackenzie, A.W. 68, 103, 417n
Mackenzie, Sir William
- activities in Mexico and Spain 164, 209–15, 233, 340
- death 214, 283
- developing Rio concession 135, 138–9, 158, 160–1, 164
- developing São Paulo concession 36, 41–6, 108, 116, 167
- early career and methods 35–6, 50, 53–60, 66, 73, 75, 77–9, 105, 110, 116, 197, 384
- problems in First World War 209–17, 233–7
- reputation and skills 7, 77, 110, 121, 138, 163–4, 166, 208, 240, 340
- role in creation of Brazilian Traction 166–7, 169, 177, 179–80, 183, 184–6, 188, 190, 192, 197–9, 201–2
Mackenzie, Mann and Co. 56, 69, 157, 201, 214, 417n
Madeiros, Borges de 271, 310, 312
Madero, Francisco 210

Maia, Alfredo 106
Mangue Canal 124
Mann, Donald 50, 53–5, 79
March, Juan 340
Mascarenhas, Bernardo 19
Massachusetts Pipe Line Company 66
Massey, Vincent 199
Matarazzo, Francisco 84, 99, 230, 260, 421n
Mauá, Baron 22–3, 24, 130, 132
Metropolitan Railway Company 65
Metropolitan Street Railway 62
Mexican Light and Power Company 164, 181, 200, 210, 296, 340
Mexican North Western Railway Company 164, 200, 210
Mexico 14, 60, 77–8, 170, 209, 213–14, 281, 340, 389, 418n
Mexico Tramways 164, 200, 210, 291, 296, 340–1
Miranda, Luis Rocha 137
Mitchell, James 34, 92–3, 150, 155
Mixed Claims Commission 236
Monteiro, Goés 320, 322, 332–4, 337, 371
Monterrey Tramway Light and Power Company 164
Montreal, Bank of 135, 157, 199
Moore, John H. 397–8
Morais, Domingos de 12
Morais, Prudente de 12, 32, 110, 274
Morse, Richard 101
Müller, Lauro 127, 129, 144, 238, 433n
Mulock, Sir William 158
Mulqueen, Daniel 76, 80, 113

National Council of Water and Electric Energy 338, 350, 353, 365, 443n
National Democratic Union 371
National Electrification Plan 356, 372
National Trust Company 53, 69, 70–1, 72, 74, 105, 190
New England Gas and Coke Company 66

Nicholls, Frederic 67, 68, 72, 74, 77, 87, 103, 137–8
Nicholson, John R. 391
Niemeyer, Sir Otto 306, 315
Niterói 167, 174, 204, 223, 281
Noranda Ltd 5
Nordheimer, Samuel 158

Old Republic 32, 214, 237, 242, 269–70, 273–4, 276, 278–9, 300–1, 309–11, 314–17, 319, 333–4, 336
Oliveira, Armando Sales de 331
Ontario Hydro 110
Ottawa Electric Company 71
Owen, Beverley 6

Paget, Sir Ralph 229
Pan American Union 17
Passos, Francisco Pereira 24, 28, 61, 125–9, 145–6, 203, 266, 399
Paulista Railway 246
Peacock, E.R. 212, 226, 260, 273–4, 284, 293, 295–6, 385
Pearson, B.F. 36, 60, 65, 67–8, 72, 83
Pearson, Frederick Stark
– activities in Spain and Mexico 181–2, 209–11, 233–4, 340–1
– death and estate 234–6, 283, 360
– developing Rio concession 128–9, 133–6, 138–40, 143–7, 150, 156–7, 159, 162–3, 174
– developing São Paulo concession 41–6, 71, 74–5, 81–2, 84–92, 94, 96–100, 102–4, 111, 114–17, 119, 414n, 423n
– early career 38, 60–6, 77, 416n
– early contacts with Brazil 36, 61
– problems in First World War 232–6
– reputation and skills 6, 77, 145, 162–3, 200, 208–9, 234–5, 247, 256, 266, 383, 386
– role in creation of Brazilian Traction 166–7, 182, 185–90, 192, 196, 200–1
Pearson, Mabel 234

Pearson, Ward 235
Peçanha, Nilo 128, 151–2, 171, 271, 274
Pedro II, Dom (Brazilian emperor) 17, 25, 132
Peel, Arthur 16
Pellatt, Henry Mill 70–1, 103–5, 157, 180, 187, 189, 190–2, 199, 209, 284
Pena, Afonso 146
Peron, Juan 371, 373, 389
Pessoa, Epitácio 229, 242, 271–2
Pessoa, João 311
Petrópolis 125, 167, 204, 223, 281
Phippen, F.H. 236, 284, 296
Piraí–Paraíba Diversion 387
Pittsburgh Consolidated Traction Company 248
Plummer, W.P. 64, 70, 167
Port of Para Company 240, 431n
Portugal 17, 21
Positivism 23
Prado, Antônio 12–13, 24–5, 28, 44, 46, 88, 92–3, 95–6, 98, 111–13, 116, 128, 173, 266, 423n
Prata, Alaor 266, 268, 273
Prestes, Júlio 310
Prestes, Luís Carlos 331
'privatism' 29
Pujo Committee 52

Quadros, Jânio 393

Reid, William 133–4, 137–9, 143–4, 149, 152, 173, 176
Rice, E.W. 64
Rio Branco, Baron of 17, 116, 136, 148, 172, 238, 269–70, 357
Rio de Janeiro and São Paulo Telephone Company 223
Rio de Janeiro City Improvements Co. Ltd 27
Rio de Janeiro Flour Mills and Granaries Co. Ltd 22, 154
Rio de Janeiro Gas Company 141

Rio de Janeiro Street Railway Company 130
Rio Doce Valley Company 344
Rio Telephone Company 204
Robert Fleming and Co. 161, 183
Rock Island Railway 163
Rodolfo Crespi Cia 100, 230, 277, 421n
Root, Elihu 153
Ross, James 35–6, 38–9, 50, 53, 66, 87, 201
Rothschild and Sons 108, 128, 306–7
Royal Bank 377

Sá, Francisco 255
Sales, Manuel Ferraz de Campos 32, 44, 110
Sampaio, Carlos 266, 268
San Paulo Gas Co. 22, 95, 97–8, 109, 111, 120, 167–70, 394
San Paulo Railway 22–3, 85, 126
Sandwell, B.K. 199
Santos 22, 46–7, 84, 136, 218
Santos Docks Company 136, 176
São Paulo Electric Company 169–70, 186, 193, 222, 390
Schiff, Martin 162
Schulman, Frank A. 362
Schulman, Henry 106, 169–70
Scott, Gordon, W. 351
Seabra, J.J. 127
Serra do Mar 22, 49, 62, 123, 250–4, 256, 258, 354, 383
Setúbal, Olavo Egydio 3
SIDRO 290, 293–4
Siemens Electric 348
Simonsen, Roberto 260, 328
Skelton, O.D. 359
Skidmore, Thomas 372
Smith, Adam 25
Smith, J.M. 40–1, 74–5, 76–7, 104, 108, 139, 144, 156, 158–61, 167, 188, 190, 193, 195, 198, 227, 239
Social Democratic Party 370

Société Anonyme du Gaz de Rio de Janeiro 132–3, 134, 140, 143–4, 149, 155, 158, 225–6, 244, 324, 350, 374
SOFINA 289–90, 293
Sorocaba Railway 253
Southern Securities Limited 169
Souza, Antônio de 33–7, 40–3, 67, 349
Souza, Edgard de 275, 337
Souza, Odilon de 337
Soward, F.H. 335, 385–6
Spain 14, 60, 77, 170, 181, 209, 213, 248, 340
Spanish influenza, 1918 231–2
Spencer, Herbert 25
Sperling and Co. 58–9, 105, 157
Stallaerts, Edouard 289
Stallaerts and Loewenstein 106, 161, 200, 289
Stein, Stanley 101
Style, Humphrey 375–6, 379, 391
Sun Life Assurance Company 157
Swiss Bank Corporation 235

Távora, Juarez 311, 314–15, 323, 325, 328, 332, 335, 337
Tennessee Valley Authority 327, 386
Thompson, David E. 136
Thomson, Elihu 64
Thomson-Houston Electric 34, 63
Toronto Street Railway 7, 29, 35, 38, 40, 54–5, 68, 73, 76, 79, 90, 93, 179–81, 182
Toronto Transit Commission 275, 361, 437n
Torres, Alberto 145, 412n
Trade and Commerce, Department of 16
Troop, George 362, 368–9, 375
Trudeau, Pierre E. 5, 7

Ueki, Shigeaki 397
Unilever 9

United States 21–2, 346

Van Horne, Sir William 38, 59, 66, 137–9, 157, 187
Vargas, Benjamin 371
Vargas, Getúlio
– and Second World War 343–4, 351
– background 300, 314
– builds Estado Novo 309–12, 320, 323, 334, 337–8, 372
– company's reaction to 315, 319, 323–4, 329–33
– introduces Water Code 327, 329–33, 341, 348–9, 363, 365–6, 370, 385
– ouster in 1945 371–2
– return to power and death 389
Vasconcellos, Senator 149
Veblen, Thorstein 208
Venezuela 7
Vernon, Ray 382–3
Viacão Excelsior 263
Viacão Paulista 30, 34, 86–7, 88–9, 93, 104, 111
Victoria Electric Railway and Lighting Company 58
Villa, Pancho 210

Walker, B.E. 70–1, 103, 109, 117, 135, 157
Walmsley, W.N. 112, 117, 120, 166–7

Wartime Industries Control Board 378
Wartime Prices and Trade Board 376
Water Code 327–33, 336–42, 344–5, 347–9, 352–3, 356, 358–9, 363, 370, 372, 379, 385, 387–9, 401–4, 443n
West End Railway 62
West Indies 14–15
Westinghouse Electric 150
Whitaker, José Maria 260, 314–16
White, W.T. 71, 296, 324, 360–1, 417n, 432–3n
Whitney, Henry Melville 62, 65–6
Whitney, James 179
William A. Read and Company 200, 226, 240
Williams-Taylor, Sir Frederick 199
Wilson, Charles 9
Wilson, Norman 264–6, 371, 375, 377
Winnipeg and Great North Railway and Steamship Company 55
Winnipeg Electric Railway Company 163
Wirth, John 330, 356
Woburn and Somerville Electric Light 62
Wood, E.R. 68–9, 71, 74, 100, 103, 105, 107, 137, 141, 156–7, 187, 189, 197, 226, 233, 236–7, 262, 266, 284, 293, 296–7, 360
World Bank 388, 391
Wrong, Hume 388